DATE DUE			

A SOCIAL AND RELIGIOUS HISTORY OF THE JEWS

High Middle Ages, 500–1200: Volumes III–VIII

VOLUME VIII

PHILOSOPHY AND SCIENCE

A SOCIAL AND RELIGIOUS HISTORY OF THE JEWS

By SALO WITTMAYER BARON

Second Edition, Revised and Enlarged

High Middle Ages, 500–1200: Volumes III–VIII

VOLUME VIII

PHILOSOPHY AND SCIENCE

Columbia University Press
New York and London
The Jewish Publication Society of America
Philadelphia

LIBRARY OF CONGRESS CATALOG CARD NUMBER: 52-404

First printing 1958
Second printing 1965

MANUFACTURED IN THE UNITED STATES OF AMERICA

CONTENTS

A SOCIAL AND RELIGIOUS HISTORY OF THE JEWS

Ancient Times

High Middle Ages

PHILOSOPHY AND SCIENCE

XXXIII

MAGIC AND MYSTICISM

Incompatibility of devotional prayers and songs with much of the existing secular poetry had long been recognized by the leaders and public alike. But it was a sign of the new appreciation of deeper philosophic quests that contemplation as such was placed on a par with devotional immersion in the Infinite. Halevi sounded the new keynote when his Jewish spokesman assured the king of Khazaria that "he who seeks purity of thought in philosophic studies, or purity of soul in prayer, feels uncomfortable [after an excess of food and drink as well as] in the association with women and scoffers or during the recitation of jocular and love songs." In an extensive epistle attributed to Maimonides and reputedly addressed to his beloved pupil Joseph ibn 'Aqnin, the conduct of the true worshiper was thus described: "He who prays shall turn to the Lord standing on his feet, with a joyous heart, hands outspread, and his speaking organs uttering words, while his other limbs are trembling. He shall not cease singing pleasant tunes . . . until he shall find his soul immersed in the world of Intelligences . . . and it will make him immune from all matters accessible to the senses." [1]

Immersion in the celestial world was, indeed, not merely the pursuit of knowledge for its own sake or for the satisfaction of intellectual curiosity—as such by no means denounced as idle curiosity—but the fulfillment of a major religious duty. Even those who were inclined to doubt man's ability really to know God, tried to approach some solution of the mysteries of existence through understanding the widely assumed intermediary forces which, at least in the popular mind, were identified with the traditional world of angels and demons. To mystically minded worshipers, in particular, the daily prayers, if recited with due concentration and complete immersion in the hidden meaning of the traditional formulas, could serve as a means of direct communion with God or these secondary celestial powers. This conviction was facilitated by the aforementioned parallelism between Israel's worship on earth and the praises sung by angels to God on high. Nor was man's eternal quest to control the dark forces of nature around him ever absent from the Jewish scene during the high Middle Ages. In their vast majority living in either a Graeco-Roman or a Persian environment, where magical papyri, gemmas, doorpost inscriptions, and household utensils had long been standard equipment in most homes, Jews, too, tried to utilize these techniques to conjure the assistance of the benevolent and ward off the interference of the inimical supernatural forces which, their vast majority felt, were in permanent contact with the human world.

Such perennial interplay of mystical beliefs with magical practices seems to have aroused very little opposition in the early post-talmudic centuries. It was, in fact, strongly, if unconsciously, promoted by some talmudic sages themselves, and doubtless gained ground particularly in those difficult years before and after the rise of Islam, when the Jewish people and its neighbors lived through an endless series of violent crises, both natural and manmade. The decline of the Jewish academies from the sixth to the eighth centuries, and the ensuing weakening of all central controls, reduced whatever restraints were exercised by these spokesmen of "normative Judaism" and led to the untrammeled upsurge of those ancient folkloristic beliefs and practices which had previously found but inadequate reflection in the official Hellenistic and talmudic letters.

HOMILETICAL-MYSTIC HERITAGE

Jewish thinkers, mystic as well as rationalist, during the Renaissance of Islam likewise did not begin *ab ovo*. Theirs was not only the old heritage of Hellenistic-Jewish thought, particularly Philo's —we need but recall that translations of the Alexandrine philosopher's works still circulated in the ninth century—but also the vast body of cosmological, anthropological, and ethical speculations accumulated in the talmudic and posttalmudic Aggadah. While essentially appealing to the masses and often preached by philosophically untrained minds, these ancient homilies contained an enormous reservoir of both rational and mystic thoughts which lent themselves to easy elaboration and modification. They certainly offered many quotable sayings which could be cited in support of several points of view, investing each with the halo of antiquity. Remnants of the ancient apocalyptic and eschatological speculations, the debris of which are still extant in our apocryphal and pseudepigraphic literature, here entered into new combinations with the popular philosophies then current throughout the Near East. They also absorbed many ingredients from the ever swelling stream of the Hellenistic, Parsee, and Judeo-Christian gnosis. The Bible itself with its story of creation, the visions of prophets (particularly Ezekiel's imagery of the divine Chariot), the searching questions of Job and Ecclesiastes, and the often obscure mythological allusions in the book of Psalms, stimulated and also lent sanction to such speculations by inquiring minds. Unavoidably, the outlook on the world of the average Jew, reacting to such diverse environments, revealed great divergences in detail, even though there was basic agreement in fundamentals.

Jewish leadership in Palestine and Babylonia could not dream of imposing a single consistent *weltanschauung* on the far-flung dispersion, with its thousands of communities subjected to different environmental pressures and striving to meet the great variety of social and cultural needs of their members. It had to be satisfied with securing a more or less uniform mode of Jewish living. Even here, as we have seen, many compromises with local customs had become unavoidable. Threatening total heterogeneity was prevented only by the failure, studied or accidental, of the rabbinic authorities to record sermons and interpretations offered by any but the leading scholars of each generation, and to incorporate them in the living oral tradition of their respective academies. But the manifold energies generated by the lesser lights were not completely lost. In many local communities traditions must have been kept alive for generations which substantially amplified, if they were not altogether at variance with, the official doctrine.

Certainly, not all persons who by native endowment and temperament, or by mere outside challenge, were predisposed toward philosophic speculation could be silenced by the Mishnah's warning, "He who meditates about four matters, what is above and what is below, what was before and what will be thereafter, such an one would be better off unborn." The talmudic rabbis themselves had often disregarded the implied advice. The very first generation of Amoraim, most members of which had come from Judah the Patriarch's academy, which had been responsible for the compilation of the Mishnah, included mystics like R. Hoshaiah, who speculated, for example, on the distinction between the upper and the lower waters in the story of creation (Gen. 1:6–10)—an eminently "gnostic" preoccupation previously indulged in also by such a great master of Jewish mysticism as R. Ishmael. R. Hoshaiah's colleague, R. Joshua ben Levi, one of the greatest talmudic homilists, likewise left behind many mystic sayings. He meditated, for instance, about the reception given to Moses in heaven during the Sinaitic revelation. Supposedly the angels, often depicted in the Aggadah as jealous of man's and Israel's prerogatives, had argued against giving Moses the Torah, "a precious treasure hidden for nine hundred and seventy-four generations before the creation of the world." Thereupon God allegedly instructed the lawgiver, "Hold on to the throne of My Glory, and give them an answer." We have here the remarkable combination of the doctrine of the Torah's preexistence with those of Moses' ascension to heaven and his inspiration through the contemplation of the Throne or Chariot—all basic ingredients of later Jewish mysticism. Had not the tannaitic historian R. Jose the Galilean figured out that, with the twenty-six generations from Adam to Moses, there had elapsed a total of a thousand generations from the Torah's original composition to its ultimate revelation to man? This allegedly was the meaning of the psalmist's description, "A word which He commanded to a thousand generations" (105:8). About R. Johanan we are told that he even tried to force instruction in the mysteries of the Chariot on a reluctant pupil, Eleazar ben Pedat, a recent arrival from Babylonia.[2]

On the other hand, Rab, upon his return to Babylonia, is recorded to have transplanted there many of the Palestinian teachings on both the Chariot and the works of Creation. Among his numerous pertinent sayings none became more influential than his enumeration of the ten elements created on the first day (heaven and earth, *tohu* and *bohu,* light and darkness, wind and water, and the categories of day and night), and of the ten instrumentalities in the process of creation (wisdom, understanding, knowledge, power, voice, might, righteousness, justice, grace, and mercy). He also intimated that the great talent of Bezalel, the builder of the desert Tabernacle, whose name meant that he was living "in God's shadow," had consisted in the ability to combine letters of the alphabet with which heaven and earth had been created.[3]

So long as the Palestinian and Babylonian academies retained their supreme control over world Jewry, such teachings remained largely esoteric, inasmuch as, like most other sayings of the great leaders, they were handed down orally within the limited confines of the schools. We recall that even the two Talmudim were long transmitted in this fashion, thus remaining the proud possession of but small groups of elect academicians. During the dark half-millennium (400–900 C.E.) in the Holy Land, however, and during the somewhat shorter eclipse of the Babylonian leadership, new and uncontrolled forces, both orthodox and heretical, came to the fore.

Among the very academic leaders of the posttalmudic period there again appeared mystically inclined individuals to whom the mysterious, even magical, elements of their tradition appealed no less than those affecting law and ritual. A leading Babylonian teacher, Moses ha-Kohen, we are told, made use of talismans and magical adjurations on a par with some of his talmudic predecessors. Another, Joseph ben Yehudah, prided himself on having seen and spoken to Elijah. Countless local leaders or simple members, too, endeavored to fathom the mysteries of existence and to exert some control over those hidden forces through the use of magical words and implements. The very large number of Aramaic incantation texts extant from that period still bears mute witness to the strong hold these practices exerted on popular imagination. In so far as they were of Jewish provenance, these incantations revealed approximately the same affinities to the more formal mystic literature of that time as had those between the magic gemmas of the Graeco-Roman period and the ancient apocalyptic and semignostic letters, or as those, at a later date, between the "practical" and the "theoretical" Kabbalah.[4]

Like their ancient and modern confreres, the writers of these texts were, for the most part, medicine men interested in the practical results of their incantations rather than in theoretical implications or logical consistency. They and their clients believed that most of the ills afflicting humanity were the effects of undesirable interventions by evil spirits. For this reason the best remedy for physical ailments, mental maladjustments, and even social ills like poverty was to be sought in the appeasement or, still better, in the silencing and banishment of these spirits. Sometimes these effects could be secured by imploration of the antagonistic forces themselves. More frequently and efficaciously, however, they were obtained by direct divine counteraction, or that of the divinely ordained "messengers." Convinced of the autonomous power of the word, magicians placed extreme reliance in the invocation of the various names of God, the angels, or the demons, often repeated several times for greater emphasis. They were confident that, by using the proper name at the proper time and in a proper context, they could influence the supernatural world to do their bidding. At times, it appears, magicians prepared over-all formulas which required merely the filling in of the names desired by clients to become immediately operative. A particularly efficacious method, it was assumed, consisted in inscribing these formulas on bowls placed upside down in the ground, because thus the evil spirits were best confined and "sealed" off, so that they could do no further harm. A typical incantation read:

> Upset, upset is the earth, Upset is the earth. RQY'WS [perhaps a corruption from Raqi'a, meaning that Heaven is likewise upset]. Upset are all the vows and curses and spells and sorceries and bad knocks that *are lodged against* those people (to wit) 'Apila, son of Maḥlapta, and his wife and his sons and all he has. In the name of Hapki'el the angel that upsets the curses and spells and bad sorceries that they have evoked against him. . . . In the name of Hapki'el, and Raḥmi'el, and *'Aqri'el* and *Yahzi'el* shall ye remove the enchantment and curse and knock from 'Apila son of Maḥlapta and Hindoy daughter of 'Ahata.

In the name of "Holy, holy, holy is the Lord of hosts; the whole earth is full of His glory" [Isa. 6:3]. Amen, Amen, selah, halleluiah. For Thy name I act.[5]

In this relatively simple incantation the names of only four angels are invoked, names clearly intended to betray their function. The relatively rare names Hapki'el and 'Aqri'el were obviously formed to indicate the main purpose of upsetting and uprooting the evil spirits, while Raḥmi'el, often considered the angel of mercy and love, was doubtless invoked as protector of 'Apila's family life. Yahzi'el alone seems to be a fairly meaningless combination with the Yah compound, reminiscent of the far more prominent angel Yehoel (Jaoel) of ancient and medieval angelology. The citation of the *sanctus* from Isaiah or the daily prayer book was not very widespread, but the phrases *amen, selah* (sometimes pronounced *salah*), and *halleluiah* were standard weapons of these magicians. They are, indeed, found in a talmudic formula. Talmudic and earlier antecedents going back to ancient Babylonia could also be invoked for the practice of naming the intended beneficiary not by his patronymic but by his mother's name. The magicians did not wish to take any chances in misnaming, to spirits presumed to be well informed, a person whose natural father may not have been identical with his socially recognized progenitor.[6]

Not all incantations containing Hebrew or Aramaic names of God and the angels were necessarily written by Jews or for Jewish clients. Just as in the ancient magical papyri the invocation of *Yao* or, more specifically, of "Iao, god sabaot, god Adonai, god Michael, god Suriel, god Gabriel, god Raphael, god Abrasax [Abraxas]" had merely betrayed the general pagan indebtedness to Jewish prototypes, so did inclusion of such formulas in medieval Aramaic texts often reveal merely the general preference of magicians for strange and mysterious borrowings from any foreign language or faith. Jews themselves were often attracted to Greek formulas, particularly in regions where Greek was *not* the common medium of communication (for instance, in a magic formula communicated by the Babylonian Abbaye). Under the influence of the vast body of Hermetic writings Jews did not hesitate to invoke the name of Hermes, whether or not they were familiar with the origin of that name in the Greek pantheon. Many, like Moses ibn Ezra, identified Hermes with the biblical Enoch. On the other hand, few, if any, seem to have been cognizant of the frequent Hellenistic identification of the magician Hermes Trismegistos with the equally reputed wonder-worker Moses.[7]

On the other hand, Jews, Christians, and later, under their influence, the Arabs were inclined to place dispossessed foreign idols among the evil spirits (the *jinns,* a term which, in the guise of "a *jinn* of Solomon," seems to occur already in a pre-Muslim Aramaic incantation). Especially the closely intermingling groups of Jews, Syriac Christians, and Mandaeans inhabiting the small town of Nippur before its Muslim conquest readily indulged in such mutual borrowings. Living in an area where the traditions of ancient Babylonian mythology were still much alive, the Nippur magicians even ventured to write, "Charmed are all Gods, and Temple-spirits, and Shrine-spirits, and Idol-spirits, and Ishtars ['Astartas]." The latter term was used as a synonym for female demons, without special reference to the proper name of the original goddess of love. Similarly forgotten was the original Babylonian designation of Lilith, who, as the alleged first wife of Adam, had become completely judaized and received in the process a countless number of parallel designations. Nor were the medieval Jews at all cognizant of the ancient Babylonian background of their eschatological monsters the *shor ha-bar* (the Steer) and the Leviathan, whose names they sometimes invoked in their incantations.[8]

An outstanding feature of these texts, as James A. Montgomery rightly observed, is their manifest eclecticism. "Babylonian, Jewish, Mandaic, Gnostic, Hellenistic, and indirectly Egyptian, elements are there, in various combinations. The Jew contributed a certain quality of monotheism and made it palatable by his angelology; his Divine Name, his Scriptures and apocrypha and liturgy, were storehouses of magical lore. All this was fused with like elements from parallel sources and the product was useful to any body of magicians, even as it was in demand on the part of every class of clients, pagans, Persians, Jews, Christians, every kind of sect." Professional magicians doubtless were but a small minority among those who dabbled in these secret rites. Many laymen, often barely literate (hence the numerous grammatical and orthographic errors in these texts as well as their general naïveté), endeavored for their own or their families' benefit to exorcise the hostile forces from their dwellings, particularly their bedchambers. But occasionally they also tried to pierce somewhat the veil of uncertainties shrouding their existence.[9]

Some of these views and practices clearly bore the imprint of their original Babylonian, Hellenistic, or Persian habitat; some were unmistakably tinged with heretical leanings toward dualism and antinomianism. In extreme cases, they undoubtedly helped form some of those sectarian movements which characterized the spiritual fermentation in the entire Near Eastern world shortly before Mohammed, as well as during the first two centuries of Islam. Many more individuals, however, must have made a studied effort to harmonize their views with the established system of talmudic Judaism which, itself extremely lenient toward purely theoretical deviations, was able to accommodate an enormous richness of divergent forms of piety so long as they did not infringe on the accepted orthodox ways of practical living.

WORKS OF CREATION AND OF THE CHARIOT

It was in those obscure but religiously highly creative centuries before and after the rise of the new "universal" faith that the first Hebrew mystic literature was born. The same period that saw the rise of a new Jewish sectarianism, brought forth those memorable biblical studies culminating in the comprehensive structure of the *Masorah,* produced most of our midrashic works, and gave rise to the *piyyuṭ,* also witnessed the compilation of such classics of Jewish mysticism as the *Sefer Yeṣirah* (Book of Creation) and the whole array of writings reflecting the mysticism of *Merkabah* (Chariot) and *Meṭaṭron.* Among these the so-called Great and Lesser *Hekhalot* (Books of Divine Palaces), the much-debated *She'ur qomah* (Measure of the Divine Stature), the *Otiot de-Rabbi 'Aqiba* (Alphabet of R. 'Aqiba), and *Sefer Reziel* (Book of Reziel), have long been recognized as outstanding creations of their genre. Some, like the "Sword of Moses" or the Hebrew "Enoch," have been published only in recent decades; others are still dormant in manuscript form in the world's leading libraries. Many of the latter were, of course, accessible to medieval readers. Still others are now totally lost. For example, Qirqisani's brief reference to certain books current among the Rabbanites of his day cannot be elucidated further than by what seems to be intimated in their eloquent titles: "Fear of Sin," "Book of Gehennah," and "Ahab's Repentance." With one exception the same holds true for the mystic books sharply condemned by Qumisi a century earlier. There doubtless existed in the ninth and tenth centuries many more such writings or fragments thereof, whose very titles are now irretrievably forgotten. Not surprisingly, those current in Hai's day appeared to him "endless and countless." [10]

Mention of both *piyyuṭ* and *Masorah* evokes no mere mental associations, however. There were, in fact, many direct links between the new liturgical movement and the mystical literature, particularly of the so-called *Yorede merkabah* (Descenders of the Chariot). It has long been recognized that, like the Midrash, the new mysticism greatly influenced poets like Qalir and his school, and continued to color much Italian and German sacred poetry in the following generations. But no attention has been paid to the liturgical factor as an independent propelling force in both these domains. The same cantor who, in improvising new prayers, detected some new interpretations and elaborations of the biblical texts and thus contributed greatly to the formation of new *aggadot,* doubtless also often injected into his hymns of divine praise mystical allusions generated by his own fertile imagination. The less standardized Jewish liturgy was, the more did the congregations expect their leaders to fill in the gaps by creations of their own, even if these were not always comprehensible to the public. The same audiences which tolerated, indeed encouraged, the Qalirian school's linguistic neologisms and new homiletic turns were the more ready to accept mystery-filled hymns and prayers, as they had long been inured to believing in the irresistible power of incomprehensible words. Biblical and rabbinic Judaism, as we recall, had long accepted the notion of the angelic hosts joining Israel in the adoration of the divine holiness. It was appropriate, therefore, to invest particularly the daily recitations of "Holy, holy, holy" with major supernatural portents. "From the praise and song of each day, from the rejoicing and chanting of each season, from the sound emanating from the mouths of the holy ones and from the tune which streams forth from the mouths of the servants, a fire is kindled and mountains of flame accumulate, and new paths are hidden away every day." [11]

Most characteristically the evidence for this statement is adduced by the author of the Great *Hekhalot* from Isaiah's *Trishagion,* whose recitation in unison by Jews and angels had become a major feature of the focal *qedushah* liturgies. The alphabetic hymn *Ha-Adderet ve-ha-emunah le-Ḥai 'olamim* (Excellence and Faithfulness are His who Lives Forever), still recited today on High Holidays, seems to be lifted bodily from the Great *Hekhalot.* It, and many other hymns like it, however, were more probably first composed by some ecstatic poet-cantors for private or public recitation, and only later incorporated in mystic collections. Equally telling is another excerpt from the same work:

> Like the sound of water in rushing streams, like the waves of the sea of Tarshish, when the southern wind smites them, so is the sound of the song about the throne of Glory, which chants and praises the exalted King. A host of voices, a tremendous noise, in which many mix their voices with the throne of Glory, to help it and to strengthen it, when they sing and praise the Mighty One of Jacob, as it is written, "Holy, holy, holy is the Lord of hosts." Blessed in heaven and earth are ye, Descenders of the Chariot, so that ye may tell and announce before Me [*le-panai* or better *le-banai* to My sons] what I do on every morning, afternoon or evening prayer, whenever Israel recites "Holy" before Me. Teach them and say to them: Lift your eyes to heaven in the sight of your house of worship, at the time when ye recite "Holy" before Me, for in the entire universe which I created I find no greater delight than during the hour when your eyes turn toward My eyes, and My eyes turn toward yours, during the hour when ye say "Holy" to Me. For the breath which emerges at that hour from your mouths winds its way upward toward Me like the pleasing smell of sacrifices.

During that hour, moreover, God is supposed to caress the image of Jacob, engraved on His throne. According to the *Alphabet of R. 'Aqiba,* the whole world, as well as Israel for whose sake the world was created, exists only "on account of the song and chant." It is small wonder, then, that liturgical poets, like the blind Naharwani, could allegedly open the gates of Baghdad by invoking the "name" of God, just as, conversely, later some leading

German pietists and Spanish kabbalists wrote some of the most moving and inward liturgical poems.[12]

We should not be astonished to find that much of this homiletic elaboration was essentially a verbal, rather than ideational, amplification of long-cherished concepts. Pleonasms are at the very root of mystic expression. To the mystic the heaping of synonyms, especially in his adoration of the Divine majesty, often appeared as the most eminent means for securing total immersion in his object. That is why he had to disregard the frequent objections to such polylogy by talmudic sages like R. Ḥanina, who believed that heaping of adjectives was comparable to the praise "of a human ruler possessing myriads of gold denars, for the possession of a silver denar" (Berakhot 33b). Incidentally, the story here told offers a striking illustration of the improvisation by a pietistic precentor at the pulpit of a pleonastic prayer of adoration. The objection of inadequacy, or even R. Johanan's sharper condemnation of that practice as bordering on blasphemy punishable by being "torn out of the world" (Megillah 18a), carried the less conviction with the genuine mystic, as he knew from repeated personal experience how greatly such multiplication of adjectives, or even outright reiteration of the same words, helped him psychologically to shut out the disturbing influences of the environment and to immerse himself fully in the contemplation of divine grandeur. In fact, rabbinic opposition itself was far from uniform or consistent, especially since the prayers composed by the leading talmudic sages themselves were full of pleonastic verbiage.

Less obvious, but intrinsically very strong, was the nexus between the intellectual pursuits of the masoretic schools and the letter mysticism of the Book of Creation. Belief in the power of the word and of each constituent letter had old and venerable antecedents in the ancient Near East. Manipulation of letters and of their numerical equivalents (*gemaṭrias*) had also been accepted practice, both magical and ordinary, throughout the Hellenistic and Roman worlds. Yet the preoccupation with each letter of the Bible, its form and pronunciation, was never so intensive and passionate as among those schools of biblical experts who dedicated their lives to the ascertainment of every minutia of the biblical text. However dry and technical their actual work undoubtedly was, the underlying theory and emotional compensation could only stress the cosmic significance of each letter. A false step, a misreading of but a single letter, it was agreed, would not only be a serious scholarly error, might not only lead to grave legal and ritualistic dissensions, but might also have adverse repercussions in the upper worlds. That is why the opening declaration of the author of the Book of Creation that God had created the world "with three principles (*sefarim*): book, number, and word," evoked such an eager response among the Masorites. Aaron ben Asher himself, despite his apparent leanings toward Karaite rationalism, was deeply impressed. Similarly, R. 'Aqiba was supposed to have construed his entire *Alphabet* in terms of letter symbolism by commenting on each letter. Here the whole Hebrew alphabet is presented in a picturesque contest as to which letter should be used in the work of creation, the *bet* of *bereshit* ultimately emerging victorious. More, in the light of a popular talmudic legend, R. 'Aqiba allegedly derived here mystic lessons from each of the decorative lines adorning the letters of the Torah.[13]

Nor must we overlook the mystic influences of the Gentile environment. The heritage of Graeco-Roman syncretism, Parsee angelology and demonology, and the ancient Christian as well as Jewish gnosis still was much alive, although principally in the fringe movements of the established religions. The factors responsible for the speedy flowering of the new Muslim mysticism, which soon was to celebrate its greatest victories in the works of the Brethren of Purity, the distinguished martyr Hallaj, the widely influential Ghazzali, and, later, of Ibn al-'Arabi and the Persian poet Ḥafiz, operated also within the "protected" communities. Certainly, a confirmed ecstatic in a state of religious frenzy did not stop to inquire as to whether a certain vision or concept had become familiar to him from outside sources. Such a state of frenzy was sometimes self-induced with the aid of gestures and other mechanical means. "Many scholars thought," Hai Gaon once informed his questioners, "that one distinguished by many qualities defined and explained [in tradition] and desirous of beholding the Chariot and of securing a glimpse of the chambers of angels on high must follow certain procedures. He must fast a number of days, place his head between his knees, and whisper to the earth many songs and hymns known from tradition. Then he perceives the interior and the chambers, as if he saw the seven palaces with his own eyes, and views them as though he entered one palace after the other and saw what is therein." Nor did the mystics hesitate to use appropriate Greek terms which had become familiar to them through their own or their confreres' usage, and to continue using them even at the time when Greek ceased to be the spoken language of their environment. In the latter case, the very strangeness of the term must have sounded alluring. Too many mystic currents charged the entire Near Eastern intellectual and emotional atmosphere and were too readily imbibed through conversations or readings whose contexts were speedily forgotten for the individual mystic to trace back such external influences, even were he inclined to do so.[14]

As a rule, such "alien" ingredients were of little concern to him, as long as they could be harmonized with the fundamentals of his own faith. But where Parsee dualism, for instance, or the Marcionite insistence on the distinction between the God of the New Testament and the mere Demiurge of the Old was in obvious conflict with Jewish monotheism, it was more or less uniformly eschewed. The doctrine of "two powers" was indeed regarded as a supreme evil by all talmudic sages. Later, however, when Zoroastrianism and Marcionism disappeared as a living menace, Jewish mystics of the Meṭaṭron school began tolerating a demiurge in their system. Trying to account for the eternally puzzling problem of evil and the world's imperfections, they saw in such a created mediator a "little Lord," that is an instrument of divine government, if not necessarily also of the original process of creation. They were no more clearly conscious of the intrinsically Zoroastrian origin of that doctrine than was the seventh-century Christian Syriac author who spoke of "the shameful error, the Israelite cult" believing in *Adonai qaṭan* (the "little Lord") as the "commander in chief" (*rab ḥela*) of the great Lord (*Adonai gadol*). Symptomatically, if unwittingly, this writer employed in this context the very designation applied by the Talmud to the Persian generalissimo.[15]

ATTITUDE TOWARD LAW AND HISTORY

Only antinomianism threatening the very core of Jewish survival could not be tolerated even by the mystic wings. Because of the great emphasis on ceremonial laws among both Byzantine-Syriac Christians and Muslims, opposition on principle to law and observance was a rather inconsequential issue and was largely limited to heretical fringes. Even here the debate was more concerned with disregard or modification of specific laws and rituals than with the repudiation of the entire body of laws as such. Nor did the popular anti-intellectual trends, occasionally to come to the fore, as we have seen, in some later Yemenite midrashim, reveal any directly antinomian bias.

Not surprisingly, therefore, the author of *Hekhalot rabbati* not only frequently extolled the Torah, which to an ordinary Jewish reader meant that he greatly stressed its commandments, but on one occasion he reported God as saying:

> I know what ye request, and My heart recognizes what ye desire. Ye request much Torah, a lot of Talmud, and a multitude of traditions. Ye look forward to asking questions of law, and ye covet a great many of My secrets, in order to heap mountains upon mountains [of laws]; to increase "sound wisdom" in hills upon hills [of detailed interpretation]; to extol the Talmud in the streets, and dialectics on the roads; to multiply *halakhot* like the sand of the sea, and My secrets like the dust of the world; to establish academies in the gates of tents, so as to explore what is forbidden and what is permitted; to declare impure what is impure and to purify the pure; to validate the valid and to disqualify the defective; and to examine the types of blood, in order to teach menstruating women what to do.

He also insisted that, in order to qualify for "descent to the Chariot" a man had to prove that "he had read the Torah, Prophets, and Hagiographa, and studied the Mishnah and the Midrash of *halakhot* and *aggadot* and the interpretation of the laws of the forbidden and permitted matters, and also that he had observed every prohibition written in the Torah and complied with every injunction of the laws, judgments, and teachings revealed to Moses on Sinai." While antinomianism, or at least treatment of all outward ceremonies as decidedly secondary, was too germane to any mystic ecstasy and ultimately was to emerge with a new rationalization as a powerful trend in the Shabbetian movement, law observance was so deeply ingrained in the entire Jewish tradition that few mystics dared seriously to deviate from it. They did not even rationalize it in the fashion of some of their Muslim confreres who believed, according to R. A. Nicholson, that "the true saint keeps the law, not because he is obliged to do so, but through feeling himself one with God." The representative medieval Jewish teachers of the secret lore seem never to have doubted their own subjection to that supreme religious obligation of every pious Jew. After all, the greatest ancient teachers to whom a credulous posterity attributed the main classics of Jewish mysticism—'Aqiba, Ishmael, Simon bar Yoḥai—had all been renowned halakhists. It would have been extremely difficult for a medieval writer to persuade his audience that any of these distinguished Tannaim had repudiated their own legal doctrines.[16]

Negatively, the impact of the Perso-Byzantine heritage also made itself strongly felt in the revival of the ancient prophetic emphasis upon the kingdom of God. If in ancient Israel this belief had served as a sharp challenge to the Near Eastern pagan concepts of the divine nature of the ruler, the mystics developed here in great and graphic detail the rabbinic concept of the sole divine cosmocrator, the "king of kings of kings." The absolute power of the Persian "king of kings," the splendor of his court and its bureaucratic hierarchy, and the corresponding apotheosis of the Byzantine caesaropapist emperor and his court etiquette partly developed along Persian models, unavoidably impressed all subjects, including Jews. In answer, Jewish leadership of all wings stressed the supreme power of God, and God alone. This was elaborated by homilists, and particularly by the mystics among them, with detailed descriptions of the divine government of the world along superlatively exaggerated but essentially familiar lines of the existing earthly autocracies. A most remarkable specimen of such a sustained parallel between the *civitas Dei* and the *civitas terrena* is offered by a brief mystical midrash bearing the characteristic title *Kisse ve-ippodromin shel Shelomoh ha-melekh* (King Solomon's Throne and Hippodromes). Here Solomon's throne is expressly designated as resembling "the shape of the throne of Glory in the upper world." The detailed description, however, follows the accepted pattern of a hippodrome in Constantinople. With an unmistakable allusion to the contemporary conditions, the midrash concludes on the optimistic note of a saying attributed to R. Johanan, stating that in the messianic age "the smallest man in Israel will be greater than Solomon in the days of his royal power." Occasionally, as in the early chapters of *Hekhalot rabbati,* the evil power of Rome was clearly recognized, particularly in connection with the suffering of the Four Martyrs (including the book's reputed author, R. Ishmael). Even here Samael, Rome's angelic "prince," acted only on God's order, however. In the *Merkabah* and, still more, in the *Meṭaṭron* mysticism, some Jews found an answer to the eternally disturbing phenomenon of Jewish powerlessness.[17]

Characteristically Jewish also was the equation of the demiurge, often called in the ancient gnosis the "prince of the world," with the "prince of Torah." *Sar torah* is the title of an independent mystic treatise, which may, however, originally have been but a chapter of *Hekhalot rabbati.* The special sanctity attached to this tract is evident from R. Ishmael's alleged report in the name of R. 'Aqiba that R. Eliezer the Great had recommended that anyone wishing to immerse himself in the Midrash *Sar Torah* should launder his garments and undergo strict personal ablutions, then spend twelve successive days in complete isolation, fasting during the days and consuming only bread and water in the evenings. During that period the student was to recite that midrash three times daily as a part of his prayers. After each recitation he was to invoke twelve times the names of the angelic princes and adjure each "with the seal." R. Eliezer was said to have followed this advice with the names of the angels and more detailed hints as to the best methods of conjuring these supernatural beings, concluding: "After completing these twelve days he [the student] may devote himself to any form of study he desires, that of the Bible, the Mishnah, or the viewing (*ṣefiyyat*) of the *Merkabah.*" Similarly, the entire letter *'ayin* in the *Alphabet of R. 'Aqiba* is given over to a paean of praise for the Torah "with which the upper and the lower worlds are maintained . . . and with which heaven and earth will be renewed in the world to come." The Torah's preexistence was generally taken for granted, as was the eternal validity of its commandments. Even speculation upon the latter's underlying reasons, which was to engage so much attention of the more rational philosophers, was discouraged and their ultimate revelation in the messianic era promised instead. In similar fashion was explained the absence of a logical order in Scripture. Rabbi Eleazar ben Pedat is quoted in *Midrash Tehillim* as saying that "had the Torah's parts been revealed in proper order, all those able to read them [in a mystical-magic way] could resuscitate the dead and perform miracles." [18]

Nor was there any serious doubt voiced with respect to the fundamental outlook on Jewish and world history inherited from the talmudic age. Like other mystics, the authors of the *Merkabah* and *Yeṣirah* literatures evinced little interest in daily historical developments—they shared this indifference with most masters of the more wordly Aggadah—but they unhesitatingly accepted the basic biblical chronology and high appreciation of the biblical luminaries, as well as the current doctrines of the messianic age. If Enoch and Noah continued to play their traditional roles as the original teachers of mysticism, Abraham now became the most venerated spokesman of the ancient secret lore, underscoring its specifically Jewish origins. The revered patriarch served as the alleged author not only of such rather obscure works of Jewish gnosticism as the Apocalypse of Abraham, but was generally considered also as the main author of the Book of Creation. Moses, too, retained his lofty eminence. Apart from such special treatises as the aforementioned "Sword of Moses," the *Merkabah* writings glorified Moses as the divine guardian over "all the treasures of Torah, all the treasures of wisdom, all the treasures of understanding," and so forth, called him "the father of all prophets and the father of all sages," and often dealt with the mystically significant symbols of Moses' death and the location of his grave.[19]

Ultimately, the mystics also construed for themselves a novel "chain of tradition." Just as the author of *She'ur qomah* did not hesitate to paraphrase the conclusion of the Babylonian Talmud and to enjoin the daily recitation of his own "Mishnah" in lieu of the *halakhot,* so did the author of the Hebrew Enoch report the spiritual genealogy from Meṭaṭron's revelation of the Torah to

Moses, which he describes with dramatic detail, to the people of his own day. Significantly altering the end of the traditional *isnad* of the beginning of the Sayings of the Fathers, he contended that after Moses had received the Torah he gave it "to Joshua, Joshua to the elders, the elders to the prophets, the prophets to the Men of the Great Synagogue, the Men of the Great Synagogue to Ezra the Scribe, Ezra the Scribe to Hillel the Elder, Hillel the Elder to R. Abbahu, R. Abbahu to R. Zera, R. Zera to the men of faith, and the men of faith to the men of beliefs, in order to preserve it carefully and to heal with it all the ailments which afflict the world." Apart from the perhaps accidental inversion of the sequence of Ezra and the Men of the Great Synagogue, the most noteworthy feature of this genealogy is its accent on magic. Not only is the conclusion directed at supernatural healing, but the two new names here introduced, those of R. Abbahu and R. Zera, are evidently those of famous mystics. The latter is frequently mentioned in the Talmud as a wonder worker, while R. Abbahu is either the well-known Amora of Caesarea (*ca.*300 C.E.) or, more probably, identical with R. Abba, the reputed disciple of Simon bar Yoḥai who is frequently cited in the *Zohar*. His name also appears in a quaint syncretistic context in one of the incantations of Nippur. Here the writer conjured the spirits "in the name of Gabriel and Michael and Raphael, and in the name of the angel 'Asiel and Ermes (Hermes) the great lord. 'Asiel, 'Asiel the angel, and Ermes the [great lord]; in the name of Yahu-in-Yahu and the great Abbahu . . . and the great Abrakas [Abraxas] guardian of good spirits and destroyer of evil spirits." [20]

Nor could this mystic literature escape entirely the brunt of Jewish ethics. Although at first seemingly averse to connecting ethics with cosmology and trying to relegate it, like the commandments, to the periphery of their outlook, these authors finally yielded to the irresistible pressure of Jewish tradition. They now correlated the gradual progression of the human soul in its ascent through the seven heavens with an equal number of stations in its attainment of moral perfection. The *Alphabet of R. 'Aqiba* extolled loving-kindness and the humility of a "broken heart" above all other virtues, largely because, in its eyes, Israel was the "poor" of this world. In return, it also assured its readers, "even

Meṭaṭron cannot stand between the Almighty and the man of flesh and blood." Nor were the spiritual and physical prerequisites, including even their chiromantic ingredients, completely devoid of ethical features. We need but recall the mortification of the flesh demanded in the student's preparation for the absorption of the mysteries of the Prince of the Torah. Moreover, the very fact that ethical behavior was here imbedded in the general vision of *Merkabah* gave it additional sanction, even if the individual acts differed but little from accepted Jewish morality.[21]

In contrast thereto relatively little stress was laid on the doctrine of emanation and the all-pervading principle of light, which were to dominate the thinking of the later mystics as they had that of many ancient gnostics. These teachings are mentioned occasionally, but they are not offered as a major explanation of the riddles of the universe. In fact, even *Sefer Yeṣirah,* which so greatly emphasized the doctrine of the ten *sefirot,* treated them primarily as "living numerical entities," rather than as successive stages of emanation, which they were to become in the later Kabbalah. Yehudah Halevi was not altogether wrong in his attempt at rational justification of that work which, in his dialogue, he made the most decisive factor in the conversion of the Khazar king. He contrasted the *sefirot* as the quantitative principle with the twenty-two letters of the Hebrew alphabet, which represented the qualitative principle in the entire divine work of creation. Rather than light, it was fire together with the two other elements of air and water (in the Book of Creation lumped together under the abbreviation *Emesh*) which constituted the basic cosmic elements. This concept also penetrated the Midrash. Apart from the aforementioned statement by Rab, one might quote the following telling passage from *Exodus rabbah:* "Three creations preceded that of the universe: water, air, and fire. Water became pregnant and gave birth to darkness; fire became pregnant and gave birth to light; air [*ruaḥ,* also meaning spirit] became pregnant and gave birth to wisdom. And with these six creations the world is governed: air [spirit] and wisdom, fire and light, darkness and water." Water was indeed a preeminent cosmic principle with these mystics, of course in a way totally different from that of Thales. A variation therefrom postulated the presence of snow under the chariot, which evoked in the minds of some of these ecstatics the picture of marble.[22]

While these and other cosmogonic teachings greatly concerned the disciples of the Book of Creation, the authors of the *Hekhalot* cycle laid their main stress on the extremely painful peregrinations of the individual soul in its difficult ascent through the seven heavens. Numerous dangers lurked in each of the manifold chambers, which were guarded by antagonistic angelic forces. Even here, however, the accent was not placed on the experiences and transformations of the individual soul, but on the might and "Glory" of God. The main theme is indeed the contemplation of that Glory, or rather, to use the biblical phrase which had become the fountainhead of all these speculations, the "throne of Glory." Hence also that climactic emphasis on those "numinous hymns," whereby humans as well as the angelic hosts immersed themselves in the adoration of the Lord and His works.[23]

One must not overdraw, however, this differentiation between the school of *Hekhalot* and that of *Yeṣirah.* Unavoidably, if incidentally, the former's contemplations, too, were drawn to the early phases of creation, especially in connection with the role played by Meṭaṭron, the demiurge. Conversely, *Yeṣirah*'s cosmogonic speculations often imperceptibly slid into cosmology and the explanation of the present divine government of the world. In describing the ten *sefirot,* for example, the author even came close to using the characteristic overtones of the other school. "The ten *sefirot* out of nothing," he reiterated, "have to the onlooker [*ṣefiyyatan*] the appearance of lightning, and their goal is without end. His word is in them when they move to and fro, and at His command they speed like the storm wind, and they bow down before His throne." Similarly, in describing the crucial polarity in the functions of the seven "double" letters as corresponding to the six dimensions (height, depth, east, west, north, and south), the writer added, "and the sacred palace (*hekhal ha-qodesh*) is placed exactly in the center and carries them all." Although Hai equated this palace with the Temple on earth, it is far more likely that the author used this term in the meaning of "heavenly palace." A clear link between these two lines of thought is found in a paragraph of the *Alphabet of R. 'Aqiba* which was clearly written under the influence of the Book of Creation. Discussing in particular the group of twelve letters and their impact upon Creation, "R. 'Aqiba" wrote, "All these letters are made of fire, and their appearance is like that of lightning and they are surrounded by a bright flame. Each has the height of 210,000,000 parasangs, and all are adorned by crowns of luminous sparks, for they have been engraved with a pen conducted by the finger of the hand of the Holy One, blessed be He." Truly a *Merkabah* mystic's reinterpretation of the *Yeṣirah* mystic's view of the story of Creation![24]

Most of these teachings are expounded not only with general poetic flourish and picturesque imagery, rather than with precise definition, but also with studied obscurity. The author of the Book of Creation interprets the difficult Jobian term *belimah* (nothing)—we recall his harping on the theme of *Sefirot* "out of nothing" (*belimah*)—by a pun, *Belom pikha* (Shut thy mouth). That is why so many controversies could arise among both medieval commentators and modern scholars as to the meaning of crucial passages. Of course, many of the medieval students of *Yeṣirah* were less concerned with pure exegesis than with the exposition of views which they themselves held, and which they wished to reinforce by the authority of a revered ancient text. Generally true of the medieval exegetical literature, this is doubly the case in the numerous commentaries on *Yeṣirah* from those by Saadiah, Dunash ibn Tamim, and Yehudah bar Barzillai to those attributed to Abraham ben David and Naḥmanides and another incorrectly ascribed to Saadiah. Almost anything could be read into this brief text of some 3,300 weighty words (more than half of which were doublets and copyists' insertions), which were evidently designed to conceal as much as they revealed. Under the circumstances it is rather surprising that the interpretations did not diverge even more widely.[25]

MIXED RECEPTION

Understandably, the attitude of Jewish leaders to these mystical writings was even more ambivalent than that to the Aggadah in general, of which they were considered integral parts. On the one

hand, mystics had a wide popular following. Although addressing themselves to the elect and hardly understood fully by even their own disciples, they readily acquired a reputation of sanctity and genuine piety in the community at large. Since they stressed beliefs and ecstatic self-forgetfulness more than the fulfillment of every iota of ceremonial law, without in any way preaching antinomianism, many appealed to popular circles to whom intensive study of the law was beyond personal reach and hence appeared arid and unproductive.

Mystics had on their side, moreover, the force of an ancient and powerful tradition going back to early biblical times—in fact, as we now know, even to prebiblical Babylonian astral computations, Canaanite-Ugaritic epic combats between gods, and Egyptian speculations. To the uncritical medieval mind, claims of ancient authorship for these writings were subject to little doubt. Saadiah was one of the few to state publicly, with reference to the *She'ur qomah,* that "it appears that many of these books are attributed to men who did not write them. They were composed by others who published them under the names of some great sages so as to enhance the reputation of their works." Even he, however, unhesitatingly accepted the Abrahamic foundations of the Book of Creation, only insisting that the Patriarch had originally formulated in oral form its basic teachings which, at a much later date, were confided to writing by some unknown Palestinian scholar. The names of the letters quoted in *Yeṣirah,* and particularly the double pronunciation of *resh* included in the seven "double" letters, clearly betrayed, in Saadiah's opinion, its Palestinian origin. Few of the gaon's contemporaries went that far. In fact, very few seem to have doubted even the authenticity of a responsum attributed to the geonim Naṭronai and Naḥshon, bearing the characteristic title *Sidre de-shimmusha rabba ve-sidre hekhalot* (Orders of [Magic] Usage and Orders of Palaces) and clearly intended for magical purposes.[26]

On the other hand, some of the views expressed in these works could not readily be reconciled with the official talmudic traditions, and still less with the more refined intellectual tastes of the Muslim age. The gross anthropomorphisms of a book like *She'ur qomah,* although to some extent but an expansion of a homily by

Rabban Johanan ben Zakkai on Nebukadrezzar's reputed boast (Isa. 14:13–14), seemed especially revolting to the tastes of the new generations and also became the source of serious embarrassment to their leaders. They were ready targets for attack by such opponents as Archbishop Agobard of Lyons in the days of Charlemagne and the Karaites, Daniel al-Qumisi in the ninth century, and Qirqisani or Salmon ben Yeruḥim a century later. After attacking the Christians for the use of icons, evidently a reflection of the iconoclastic controversy then raging in the entire Near East, Salmon pointed an accusing finger at "the evil speech of your masters, R. Ishmael and his friend R. 'Aqiba, who joined together to veil in mystery the word of the Almighty [*Shaddai*]. They both contended that they had gone up to view the splendor and shape of the Almighty, their Creator, Ishmael telling you His measures." [27]

These enemies readily overlooked not only the superstitious ingredients of their own faiths—it has always been easy to call irrational beliefs of others "superstitions" while regarding those of one's own religion as the effects of an inscrutable divine will—but also the reservations of these mystics themselves. The greatest culprit, the author of the *She'ur,* whether this was originally an independent work or merely a chapter in the Great *Hekhalot,* clearly indicated that his measurements were not to be taken literally. In describing the size of the divine limbs in terms of parasangs (Persian land measures), he insisted that "those parasangs are nothing like ours. God's parasang equals a million ells, each such ell equals four spans, and each such span extends from one end of the world to the other." In other words, these measurements were intended merely to illustrate to the reader the infinite extension of God's awe-inspiring appearance, and thus actually to discourage speculations about His essence. In this respect they may have resembled the apparently interrelated statements by ancient homilists that the Tree of Life of the biblical story of creation had a circumference of a five hundred years' journey and that the Tree of Knowledge had not been revealed to Adam nor would it ever be revealed to man. Maimonides, who sharply repudiated the *She'ur qomah,* nevertheless made good use of these homilies. Apparently accepting the current astronomic computa-

tion that the distance between the earth and the moon equaled a five hundred years' journey, he saw in these *aggadot* hints of man's ability, and duty, to acquire knowledge of the sublunary world, but not beyond it. What the author of the "Measure" lacked in speculative precision he, like other mystics, made up by the immediacy of his religious experience, as indeed the question of God's incorporeal and yet personal nature was to remain a permanent bone of contention between rationalists and mystics.[28]

Perhaps the most widely accepted resolution of these conflicting feelings was that offered by Hai Gaon. Himself a moderate rationalist, who in legal matters staunchly resisted the encroachments of aggadic views, the last distinguished gaon of Pumbedita conceded the presence of angels and demons, allowed the use of talismans and adjurations, and generally accepted the doctrines of talmudic sages concerning the supernatural world and its relations to man. When asked about some of the new mystic writings, he replied,

> It certainly is as you say. There are books and titles like the Great and Lesser Hekhalot, the Prince of Torah, and other *mishnayot,* which inspire fear in the onlooker, as they did in our forefathers. We, too, have the same feeling, and we never approach them except with fear and trepidation and in a state of purity. We have also heard insistent rumors that many persons who had become involved in them were speedily lost. All this on account of the holiness of the Name [of the Lord] and the holiness of the *shekhinot* [forms of the Divine Presence] and the angels around them, and the holiness of the Chariot.

With this intimation of warning against indiscriminate use Hai left the matter quite open. This was indeed the official attitude whenever inquiries appeared. The only astonishing fact is that there were so few inquiries, showing that even the local leaders were not seriously disturbed.[29]

Curiously, the practical aspects of the *Merkabah* and *Meṭaṭron* mysticism and its connection with magic arts were less emphasized by opponents. These connections were obvious not only in such hybrid works as the Book of Reziel, the *Raza rabba* (Great Mystery) and some mystical midrashim, but also in the *Hekhalot* and the *Alphabet of R. 'Aqiba.* The opening paragraph of *Hekhalot rabbati* underscored the ability of the "descender of the Chariot," upon reaching the seventh heaven called *'Arabot,* to "see all that is done before the throne of Glory and to know all that is going to happen in the world." Such precise knowledge of the ultimate fate of one's neighbors and their most secret acts, even in the intimate recesses of their homes, would naturally give the successful diviner immeasurable power over his fellow men. The *Alphabet* actually warned against indiscriminate use of divine names. "When a man uses them [for magic purposes], every heaven is filled with fire, and they [the angels] descend to consume the world with fire." They desist from destroying the earth only when they realize how strongly "the corners of the earth are knotted together with the corners of heaven and sealed with the ring of 'I am that I am.' " Even the Book of Creation, containing no direct magic ingredients, was associated in the minds of man with the weird talmudic tale of a calf having been created weekly by two rabbis with the aid of a "book of creation." [30]

Obviously, enlightened Karaites like Salmon or Qirqisani would have liked to view with disdain all magic practices and to consider them as running counter to clear biblical prohibitions, but the matter was not quite so simple. Apart from the deeply ingrained beliefs and daily usages among the populace, which at least a propagandist like Salmon did not dare lightheartedly to attack, the biblical tradition itself had reported "miracles" performed by Moses and other prophets, as well as magic counteraction by Egyptian "sorcerers" having similar effects. Since prophecy and its attestation played, as we shall see, a tremendous role in all medieval theological debates, it became extremely important to draw a line of demarcation between divinely inspired and magically induced changes in natural phenomena.

Qirqisani therefore devoted several chapters in his section on criminal law to those aspects of magic and divination which he considered prohibited, and to others which were not to be frowned upon. Among the former he enumerated incantations, amulets, divination with or without the aid of astrology, communication with the dead and demons—"all practices which one actually sees employed among the majority [Muslims] and the Rabbanites." He also objected to certain methods, which he graphically described, of securing visions in dreams by spending nights at temples or cemeteries. At the same time, this Karaite teacher had to exercise all his ingenuity in answering attacks by agnostics,

Jewish as well as Muslim, on the institution of prophecy as being but a variant of outlawed magic arts. It was this difficulty, indeed, which seems to have discouraged many enlightened Rabbanite leaders from taking a clear stand against any form of magic. On the occasions when Saadiah spoke of magic practices, he did it without heat and even without direct disapproval. Discussing, for example, the "crowns" adorning the letters of the Torah, he calmly reported that "the ancient makers of amulets (*qemi'ot*) have stated that, if written without their 'crowns,' these were perfectly useless." It stands to reason that most Jewish philosophers opposed magic on principle, but only Maimonides took a public stand against it. At least in his main philosophic work he wrote sharply about the misuse to which the various divine names had been put. "Such fictions," he added, "originally invented by foolish men, were in the course of time committed to writing, and came into the hands of good but weak-minded and ignorant persons who were unable to discriminate between truth and falsehood and made a secret of these *shemot* [names]. When after the death of such persons those writings were discovered among their papers, it was believed that they contained truths, for 'the simple believeth every word.' " Even the sage of Fusṭaṭ thus did not dare to accuse the manipulators of divine names, widely revered for their piety, of outright fraud.[31]

BOOK OF THE BRIGHT LIGHT

In his repudiation of the anthropomorphism of the mystical writings represented by *She'ur qomah,* Maimonides attributed them to some of the "Greek preachers," a class for which he generally evinced little respect. This was not merely the result of the feeling of provincial superiority which often characterized the sage's utterances concerning the Christian and particularly the Byzantine communities. Maimonides seems to have possessed a trustworthy tradition on this score, historically the more probable as Jews in Christian countries generally felt far less the brunt of hostile criticisms aimed at the biblical and talmudic passages describing God's corporeal characteristics. As we recall, that issue loomed much larger in Muslim-Jewish controversies than in those between Jews and Christians, whose beliefs in Trinity, Immaculate Conception, and Incarnation were clearly more anthropomorphic than anything found in Jewish letters.[32]

Modern scholars have been reluctant to accept the Byzantine provenance of much of that literature, mainly because of the absence of any reliable documentary evidence for the intellectual creativity of the Jewries in the Byzantine sphere of influence during the eighth to the tenth centuries when most of these works were written, rewritten, or compiled. But, weak as are all such *argumenta a silentio,* they are doubly weak in this case, for many independent hypotheses and observations converge on the point of showing that, though little of their intellectual creativity long maintained in oral form has come down to us, the "thousand" Jewish communities of the Byzantine Empire pursued a vigorous intellectual career of their own. It certainly is of importance that the earliest liturgical poems which reached us from any European country were those of the ninth-century *payyeṭan* Amittai ben Shefaṭiah, which were so deeply imbued with the spirit of the *Merkabah* literature. Similarly, the first Hebrew book written in Christian Europe was Shabbetai Donnolo's *Commentary on Yeṣirah.* Both authors lived under Byzantine domination in southern Italy. Nor is it purely accidental that later, too, the greatest Rabbanite author arising in Balkan Jewry was the homilist Tobiah ben Eliezer, who not only occasionally included mystical teachings in his biblical hermeneutics, but also publicly defended the mystical letters attributed to R. Ishmael and R. 'Aqiba as being "all correct to the man of understanding." This preoccupation with mystical and homiletical learning was so characteristic of Byzantine Jewry that even the greatest twelfth-century Karaite author, Yehudah Hadassi, defying the precedents set by his revered Palestinian predecessors from Qumisi to Yeshu'a ben Yehudah, included many "fabulous elements" in his encyclopedic work. Certainly, those great nineteenth-century scholars who looked for the origin of many homiletical collections in Italy intuitively felt that it was in that area that Jewish homiletical creativity was at its highest. They should, however, have limited this geographic designation primarily to those parts of the Appenine Peninsula and Sicily which were under Byzantine domination. Nor is there any valid reason for assuming that other provinces of the Byzantine Empire lagged so far behind. Even in the sphere of jurisprudence Byzantine contributions were not quite so arid as is generally assumed. In fact, we have quite a few indications of the composition of several important halakhic works of the late geonic period by one or another Byzantine Jew.[33]

A Byzantine background for much of the early mystical literature helps to explain some of its unusual features as well as its sudden impact on Western Jewry in the twelfth century and after. Gnostic and Manichaean teachings had always been a powerful ingredient of the sectarian struggles and theological controversies in the Eastern Roman Empire, that direct successor of the ancient Graeco-Roman civilization. However sharply suppressed by the Orthodox Church and state and often driven underground, this mystical heritage of the ancient mystery religions, Mithraism, Marcionism, and Christianized Manichaeism, played a powerful role in shaping the thinking not only of outright sectarians, but also of independently searching souls of all denominations. Jews could not remain unaffected; the less so, as their own historic continuity postulated the maintenance of many forms of Jewish living, long since suppressed in the better controlled Palestino-Babylonian areas. We recall the great role attributed to them by Byzantine churchmen in the protracted iconoclastic controversy. Exaggerated though these reports evidently are, they demonstrate some involvement of individual Jews in the raging sectarian clashes in the Empire. Social segregation being far less there than in the West, many a Jew doubtless also evinced some curiosity in the teachings of such sectarians as the Paulicians or Bogomils, whose effective mission as well as violent suppression by the authorities often kept his Christian neighbors in a state of turmoil.[34]

Italo-Byzantine influences on the upsurging communities of western Europe, always strong, increased greatly after the First Crusade. Highly instrumental in bringing together the eastern and western Christian countries in their joint struggle against the world of Islam, the Crusades also established more vigorous contacts between the Jewries of the various European lands. At the same time, the spiritual impact of the crusading movement and the tragedy of many western communities created a state of mind extremely favorable to the spread of mystical teachings. As has been pointed out, the returning veterans of the Crusades helped disseminate among their western compatriots the ramified doctrines of the Eastern heresies and thus added new stimuli to whatever questioning of the established doctrines of the Church had been rife in previous generations. The same factors which had led to the rise of the Western heresies of the Albigensians and Catharii, particularly in the Provence, that point of contact between Christendom and Islam, operated also to arouse more independent minds among Provençal Jewry to look for new answers to the perennial riddles of existence. Among both Christians and Jews, moreover, these new movements brought back to life long-dormant forces, such as had already come to the surface in the works of the eleventh-century homilist Moses ha-Darshan of Narbonne. Here was resuscitated not only the heritage of the ancient Alexandrian synthesis between Judaism and Hellenism, but also much of that obscure syncretistic tradition of the declining Roman world, whose original forms themselves are known to us only through a few chance survivals.[35]

In this frame of mind twelfth-century Provençal Jewry was prepared to receive and eagerly to study an eastern compilation called *Sefer ha-Bahir* (Book of the Bright Light). Despite its obvious crudities, this book marked a turning point in the history of Jewish mysticism. Although, according to a tradition reported by a thirteenth-century author, the book had reached Provence via the Jewish mystic circles of Germany, it had little to do directly with the development of the German brand of pietism, which will be analyzed later on in this chapter. But it made a strong impression on certain mystically oriented groups in southern France. It is essentially a combination of disjointed homilies, obviously stemming from different periods and different environments. One of its important sources is the book *Raza rabba* (Great Mystery), which had been listed among the objectionable mystic writings by the ninth-century Karaite Bible exegete, Daniel al-Qumisi. While most of the other books enumerated by this foe are totally lost, Gershom Scholem was able to recover at least some lenghty quotations from the "Great Mystery" in an anonymous commentary on *She'ur qomah,* probably written by a German mystic at the end of the thirteenth century. Although these passages do not quite bear out Qumisi's classification of that entire literature as "books of sorcery," it is possible that the commentator, interested in its theoretical more than its practical magic elements, selected only those portions which seemed particularly relevant to his interpretation of that much-maligned classic, the *She'ur qomah.* This is essentially true also of the compiler of *Bahir,* who in the same manner may have discarded also the magical indoctrination offered by the other tracts so sharply condemned by Qumisi.[36]

After its arrival in central Europe, and more especially in the Provence, the "Book of the Bright Light" seems to have absorbed some newer teachings, in the form of both additions to and reformulations of older sayings. Only in a few cases can we put our fingers on the sources of these accretions, as when entire passages seem to be lifted verbatim or paraphrastically from the works of the great scientist and ethical philosopher, Abraham bar Ḥiyya, written early in the twelfth century. Others show strong affinities with homiletical outpourings from the school of Moses the Preacher of Narbonne, of which only small segments have been preserved by Jewish copyists and such non-Jewish students as Raymond Martini. On the other hand, the users of that book unhesitatingly deleted passages which seemed to them incongruous or heretical. Such self-censorship, often quite unconscious, has led to the omission of many passages in all extant manuscripts, although their echoes have been preserved in later quotations and references by both friends and foes. Nor were the *illuminati* readers particularly interested in the sequence of the sayings, which from the very outset had almost never been arranged in any systematic or logical order. Hence came those extreme variations in the arrangement of sayings in the existing versions, both manuscript and printed, which have added greatly to the confusion of modern students.[37]

As in the case of many other collections of hermeneutic-homiletical content, the fact that the book opens with a statement attributed to the ancient sage R. Neḥuniah ben ha-Qanah sufficed to persuade most readers to believe that the whole work had been compiled by that second-century rabbi. It is, indeed, called the *Midrash R. Neḥuniah ben ha-Qanah* in much of the later mystical literature. The ancient problem, again raised in this statement, concerning the relation of light and darkness and the role of both in the creation of the world and its continued divine management, sounds one of the keynotes of the entire book. This question, which had so deeply agitated the minds of all dualists, especially among Zoroastrians and gnostics, never came to rest, particularly in areas with strong underground dualistic survivals.

Obviously, our author was not satisfied with Saadiah's aforementioned answer that darkness was not really an independent entity, but that it merely represented the absence of light. Varying a talmudic homily on the same subject, our author quotes Neḥuniah as preaching:

> One scriptural verse says: "And now men see not the light which is bright [*or bahir*] in the skies" [Job 37:31], while another verse states, "He made darkness His hiding place" [Ps. 18:12], and again, "Clouds and darkness are round about Him" [Ps. 97:2]. How is one to reconcile this? There comes a third verse and harmonizes them all. "Even the darkness is not too dark for Thee, But the night shineth as the day; The darkness is even as the light" [Ps. 139:12].

Obviously, the homilist wished to give here substantially the same answer as that given in the Talmud, namely that God is surrounded by light "in the interior chambers" and by darkness "in the exterior chambers." But he went further. He substituted the talmudic query from the verse in Daniel (2:22), "And the light dwelleth with Him," by the verse in Job, with its special emphasis on the "light which is bright," thereby intimating that the divine light is so bright that only God can view it; to the ordinary human it becomes invisible and hence the equivalent of darkness, whereas what to God is darkness may appear as ordinary light to the human eye. This reversal of the roles is indeed spelled out by Solomon Labi, an outstanding commentator of the *Zohar*. That intimation is reinforced by our compiler through another alleged citation of a saying of an ancient sage, this time R. Bun or Abun. Explaining the well-known Isaianic anti-dualist pronunciamento "I form the light and create darkness" (45:7), "R. Bun" declares that light having a substance of its own was "formed" by God, whereas darkness, devoid of independent substance, had to be "created." Perhaps to make doubly clear that he did not think that even earlier darkness had been the mere absence of light, the author adds the variant that darkness has no "existence" of its own because it had required mere "segregation and separation," just as the related Hebrew term *hibri* (recovered from an illness) merely indicates the cessation of a status of privation of health. Even here, however, our author by no means conceded Saadiah's point, because whatever its original status, darkness, once created by God, attained some substance of its own.[38]

From this discussion we may get an inkling of the studied obscurities with which our author tries to resolve some of the most disturbing cosmological problems. If the passages culled by him from various sources are not quite clear, often in their ultimate consequences contradictory, this was hardly considered by him and by most of his readers a serious weakness. Like most other authors of this genre, he was satisfied with raising questions and throwing out some general suggestions rather than offering complete and final answers. By their very nature, mystic categories of thinking are not systematic. They do not seek to propound well-rounded logical solutions, but rather to offer temporary, impulsive speculations on matters of deep concern, regardless of how these would ultimately measure up against other speculations formulated in other contexts.

For this reason even the order in which such speculations were arranged seemed immaterial. The sequence of the passages in the *Bahir* was probably from the beginning quite haphazard; its planlessness increased further as a result of constant accretions and deletions. The compiler evidently took a leaf out of the *Yeṣirah* literature by speculating on the symbolism of the Hebrew vowels, just as, along the lines of the *Alphabeta de-R. 'Aqiba,* he accentuated the meaning of the shape of Hebrew letters. In its present form at least, the book does not follow even the order of the alphabet, but interrupts elaborations of the symbolic meaning of letters with other homiletical observations. Nor did the compiler mind inserting a second query relating to *dalet* after the discussion of the meaning of *ḥet* (the fourth and eighth letters of the alphabet, respectively). In fact, when the first analysis of the meaning of *dalet* is followed by the logical query concerning the mystical implication of the fifth letter, *he,* our author makes the apocryphal teacher R. Amorai scold his disciples, saying "Have I not told you not to ask me about a later matter before one that precedes it?"

This scolding, so obviously running counter to the accepted alphabetical sequence, itself had hidden mystical implications, and caused later commentators considerable difficulty. But it enabled the homilist to expound here, apparently for the first time in kabbalistic literature, the doctrine of the two *he*'s in the Tetragrammaton, which were supposed to represent the higher and the lower divine "Presence" (*shekhinah*), a doctrine which became quite important in the mystical speculations of the thirteenth and fourteenth centuries.[39]

More suspect to some traditionalists was *Bahir*'s reiterated emphasis on the doctrine of transmigration of souls. In its briefest formulation our author, quoting ancient rabbinic homilies, inquires into the meaning of the psalmist's assertion that the "Lord will reign . . . from generation to generation" (*le-dor ve-dor;* Ps. 146:10). He quotes R. Papias as connecting this verse with that in Ecclesiastes, "One generation passeth away, and another generation cometh" (1:4), which, because of its reversal of the natural order of the generation first coming and then going, had intrigued many homilists and commentators. R. 'Aqiba had, therefore, explained that verse to mean that the passing generation had previously "come," that is, been in existence. Elaborating on this idea, our mystic illustrates this occurrence by the parable of a king who had clad his slaves in beautiful garments, but when they misbehaved he took the garments away from them and, after acquiring a new set of slaves, put those garments on his new retinue. The implication clearly was that God, whenever he is dissatisfied with man's behavior, takes his soul away from his body and invests it in a body subsequently born. Transmigration was also used to explain the ancient riddle of the theodicy. The righteous man who fares badly in this world, our author explains, is being punished for his transgressions during his previous earthly existence. While this moderate doctrine does not presuppose the transmigration of souls through a series of animals and even inanimate objects, it must have grated on the ears of more philosophically trained contemporaries who were familiar with the rejection of the whole doctrine by Saadiah and other Jewish philosophers. Nor did the particular parable seem acceptable. The long-accepted notion was that the human soul, essentially immaterial, is physically clothed by the body and does not, as in this parable, serve as the latter's garment.[40]

It is small wonder, then, that many rationalistic readers were shocked by the content of the book as well as its form. The mid-thirteenth-century Narbonnese scholar Meir ben Simon doubtless was not alone in denouncing the *Bahir,* in which, punning on its name, he declared, the readers "had seen no light." In his circular letter Meir not only denied the book's authorship by R. Neḥuniah ben ha-Qanah, but sweepingly declared, "The language of that book and all its subject matter prove that it was written by a man unfamiliar with literary style and beautiful phrasing and that it includes many heretical and atheistic statements." [41]

PROVENÇAL CONVENTICLES

Such criticisms were not entirely unanticipated. Upon its first appearance in western Europe, the *Bahir* had to make its way against the opposition of the newer rationalist circles as well as of the spokesmen of the Halakhah. The latter had long been inured to mystic teachings included in the Aggadah. They also had learned to get along with the students of *Yeṣirah,* especially as that work was presented to them through Saadiah Gaon's *Commentary*. But they were opposed to, or at least had an ambivalent attitude toward, the mysticism of the Chariot, particularly in its more anthropomorphic manifestations. Perhaps to disarm the opposition, the compiler of *Bahir* inserted the following statement:

> R. Reḥomai said: It is written, "And reproofs of instruction are the way of life" [Prov. 6:23]. This is to teach us that he who becomes a regular student of the works of Creation and the works of the Chariot cannot help but stumble [*yikkashel*], as it is written "And let this stumble [*ve-ha-makhshelah*] be under thy hand" [Isa. 3:6]. This refers to matters which a man cannot grasp unless he stumbles. And yet Scripture speaks of "reproofs of instruction," through which, in fact, he [the student] acquires the "way of life." That is why he who wishes to acquire the way of life must suffer the reproofs of instruction [fol. 66ab No. 150].

Such arguments undoubtedly appealed to mystically minded individuals who often learned from experience that their impulsive and emotional thinking was full of pitfalls and called for constant reconsideration. But it hardly removed the objections on the part of the more rationalistic elements in Jewish leadership.

A serious breach in the opposition was caused, however, by the appearance of Yehudah bar Barzillai's *Commentary on Yeṣirah.* Here was a tract written by an outstanding European halakhist whose other works served all Western students as an inexhaustible supply of geonic materials. In its lengthy and discursive way it elaborated some of the mystical teachings of that ancient classic in a philosophically far less rigorous way than the author's prototype, Saadiah. Much more than in Spain, however, where Yehudah's works had formed but a small part of a rich halakhic literature, his impact on Jewish learning in Narbonne and its environs was both instantaneous and profound. Whether he personally visited the southern French city, or whether one of the latter's outstanding leaders, Abraham ben Isaac, "Father of the Court," visited him in Barcelona, there is no question that Abraham was so deeply impressed by his learning and the sources he had accumulated that he paraphrased Yehudah's data and findings and incorporated them in his own major juridical work, the *Sefer ha-Eshkol.* Abraham was equally impressed by Yehudah's mystical comments on *Yeṣirah.* However, he was far more restrained in communicating to the public the Barcelona rabbi's or his own mystical thoughts than he was with respect to the law. Despite its old roots, probably going back in unbroken continuity to Roman times—the Visigothic and Muslim regimes marked here much less of a break than in Spain—Narbonnese Jewish learning was long transmitted only in oral form. Abraham and his colleague Moses ben Joseph were among the first to break the ice in the field of Halakhah, just as Moses the Preacher, a century before them, had pioneered in lending literary expression to the old local traditions in the field of Bible exegesis and homiletics.[42]

Moses ben Joseph is designated by a later author "one of the fountainheads of the Kabbalah in these parts"; this term may refer to the mystic lore or more generally to the "traditional lore" in all its manifestations. But there is no question that Abraham ben Isaac gave much thought to mystic speculation. Although in his literary works he merely communicated some "chapter headings," to quote the fourteenth-century mystic Shem Tob ben Abraham ibn Gaon, his oral teachings greatly impressed many of his disciples, including his distinguished son-in-law Abraham ben David of Posquières (who had also studied under Moses ben Joseph) and the latter's sons, Isaac and David. From that circle undoubtedly originated also the commentary on *Yeṣirah* "by the scholars of Narbonne," which is attested by Moses bar Ḥisdai Taku (of Tachau) in the thirteenth century, but of which no fragments seem to have survived. At the same time the impact of the *Bahir,* or of some of its sources, made itself strongly felt. Nor could these early mystics resist the influence of the rationalist philosophers whose writings were then in vogue throughout the Mediterranean world. Not only was Saadiah's *Commentary on Yeṣirah* quite influential directly, as well as through Yehudah bar Barzillai's mediation, but the Spanish Jewish philosophers exercised a tremendous fascination on all educated classes across the border. Not surprisingly, the pietistic and nationalistic brand of philosophy represented by the works of Baḥya ibn Paquda and Yehudah Halevi proved particularly attractive. It was partly under the influence of these mystic circles that one of their compatriots, Yehudah ibn Tibbon, undertook to translate Baḥya's and Halevi's Arabic works into Hebrew. Thus began, as G. Scholem observed in an early study, the second major phase in the development of medieval Jewish mysticism, "the transition of the Kabbalah from the world of Gnosis to that of Neoplatonism, an attempt to synthesize the old currents so strongly permeated with mythical elements with the entirely divergent teachings of scholastic philosophy. As a result there emerged the genuine mystical theology of Judaism." [43]

It was from these diverse, and intrinsically far from harmonious, sources that Provençal mysticism, doubtless in part continuing its own native traditions reaching back to Moses the Preacher and his spiritual ancestors, received its main nourishment. At the same time, its chief spokesmen realized that they were introducing many an innovation, for which they could find no support in any of the sources at their disposal. In a good mystic fashion they professed to have received their new insights through a direct inspiration from the Prophet Elijah. Self-assertive Abraham ben David, in particular, who even in his halakhic works liked to pursue an independent course, often appeared to his successors as a divinely inspired thinker who could allow himself even original deviations from tradition in the legal field. At least they thus interpreted his occasional expostulations for having recorded legal interpretations for which he had had no backing from his teachers. He facilitated that interpretation by the studied obscurity of some of his allusions and even the use of such terms as that his teachings were derived from a "mystery" (*sod*) in accordance with the psalmist's assurance that "the counsel [*sod*] of the Lord is with them that fear Him" (25:14).[44]

Like many of his fellow mystics, Abraham ben David drew a sharp line between the mystic lore which should be communicated only to initiates and the perfectly public halakhic debates. Of course, it was not always easy to keep the two domains strictly apart. Precisely because he felt himself to be in possession of secret teachings, Abraham often spoke with a tone of superiority even in juridical matters. While not altogether a stranger to rational philosophy and evincing interest at least in the more pietistic branches represented by Baḥya and Halevi, he had no patience for the pure Aristotelianism of Ibn Daud or Maimonides. Of course, at the time when he wrote his strictures on the Maimonidean Code he could not yet have been acquainted with the comprehensive formulation of the Maimonidean philosophy in the *Guide,* or even with the few pertinent sections of his adversary's *Commentary* on the Mishnah still unavailable in a Hebrew translation. He had to rely on the scanty intimations in the first section of the Code. Confident of his possession of superior mystic truth, he haughtily dismissed many of the codifier's juristic doctrines and attacked in particular the latter's cherished dogmatic assertions. The doctrine of divine corporeality was, as we recall, a thorn in the flesh of the Jewish philosophers and apologists under Islam. For this reason Maimonides actually counted among the heretics any believer in God's anthropomorphic essence. This assertion called forth Abraham ben David's well-known sharp rebuttal, "Greater and better men than he have followed that trend of thought because of what they had seen in the Bible and still more of what they read in certain *aggadot.*" Occasionally, Abraham revealed even more directly his mystical biases. In a passage suppressed by most copyists of the Maimonidean Code but preserved by some commentators, Abraham objected to the Maimonidean explanation of Moses' much-debated request of God, "Show me, I pray, Thy glory" (Exod. 33:18), as consisting in the quest for knowledge of the peculiar essence of the divine being in contrast to that of other beings. Harking back to aggadic sayings, Abraham objected that during the forty days of his sojourn on Sinai Moses had already seen what no other prophet had been allowed to view and that even "the angels had envied him and wished to cast him down to earth so that he had to hold fast to the Throne of Glory." But in offering his own explanation, Abraham drew short of elucidating the crucial difference between God's "face" and "back" in that great theophany (33:23). "This is a great mystery," Abraham declared, "and it is inappropriate to reveal it to all men. Hence the author of this statement [Maimonides] is perhaps unfamiliar with it." At times these differences of opinion carried over into the more strictly juridical domain, at least with respect to the dim and distant messianic future. Maimonides, in keeping with the prevailing rabbinic opinion, taught that the messianic era would restore the ancient sacrificial system at the Temple of Jerusalem, "for the *shekhinah* cannot be abrogated." In his stricture Ben David commented: "Ezra knew in advance that the Temple and Jerusalem were going to change and to become sanctified through another eternal form of sanctity in the Lord's Glory for evermore. This has been revealed to me by God's mysterious instruction to those who fear Him. That is why one who now enters there [into the former location of the Holy of Holies] is no longer subject to the usual penalty." [45]

Abraham ben David was more specific in his commentaries on various talmudic tractates and still more in his private communications to disciples which were often quoted in later generations. Of course, in these cases we are never quite sure whether the citation had not undergone some alteration in the course of transmission. Mystics were notoriously careless in reproducing statements by predecessors, which without any malice aforethought they often rephrased to suit their own deeply cherished convictions. But some have a fairly authentic ring. The distinction drawn by the sage of Posquières, for example, between the "cause of causes" which is completely invisible and the "demiurge" created by God who alone had manifested himself in human shape to Moses or Ezekiel, seems well attested by Abraham's grandson, Asher ben David. This distinction is doubly remarkable as Abraham acted without the compulsion of the Trinitarian dogma which often led Christian sectarians to postulate some such separation between God the Father and the other members of the Trinity. At the same time the Provençal rabbi's "demiurge" is, unlike his Marcionite or Catharist counterpart, a benign principle and hence not the antithesis to the "good God." Abraham's demiurge appears to be materially, but not morally, inferior. Perhaps to him rather than to the "cause of causes" would apply Abraham's comparison of the two divine attributes of Mercy and Justice with the two-faced creation of Adam and Eve, which, although recorded only in the fourteenth-century commentary on Naḥmanides by Meir ibn Sahula and some fairly late manuscripts, is, despite its unwonted wordiness, substantially derived from Abraham's teaching. However, these novel concepts of the early Provençal founders of the medieval Kabbalah can become clear only in connection with the more fully developed doctrines of the thirteenth-century authors, including Abraham's own sons, which will be analyzed in a later volume.[46]

GERMAN ḤASIDISM

Notwithstanding some basic similarities, the mystic currents which took shape among the German Jews about the same time differed substantially in both nature and origin. Reaching a climax in the schools of Yehudah bar Samuel he-Ḥasid (the Pious, *ca.*1140–1217) and his chief disciple, Eleazar bar Yehudah of Worms (*ca.*1160–1238), German pietism from the outset reached wider circles of the population and more permanently molded the outlook and behavior of Central and East European Jews than did its Provençal counterpart.

As in the Provence, Jewish pietism in western and southern Germany was nurtured from a variety of older and newer sources. We recall that in both its communal life and its ritualistic observances Franco-German Jewry seems to have carried down the ages traditions antedating the Carolingian and probably even the

Merovingian eras. Like its Christian neighbors, it had lived for centuries in nearly total isolation from the outside world and had felt the impact of the Eastern centers of Jewish learning only through some sporadic correspondence and infrequent personal exchanges through the few Eastern immigrants and the occasional Western pilgrims returning from Palestine. It developed, therefore, certain unique ways of life which later appeared strange even to its own members reared on talmudic and geonic law, such as Jacob Tam. On the other hand, these few contacts with the more advanced East and its cultivation of mores carried down from Roman times enabled it to pioneer among its Christian neighbors not only in the economic sphere, but also through the basically democratic patterns of its rich communal life. If it suddenly found its intellectual outlook revolutionized by the impact of Eastern learning vigorously espoused by the schools of Gershom and Rashi, this talmudic reformation, however successful, did not entirely displace the older traditions and modes of living, which continued to be respected under the guise of local customs.[47]

Rabbinic learning itself was, of course, not limited to the field of *halakhah*. Once the Western Jewries established their living rapport with the Palestino-Babylonian centers, they received from them also some fruits of their age-old homiletic, hermeneutic, and mystical learning. With amazing erudition Simon Qara was soon able to marshal an enormous number of aggadic sources for his famous *Yalquṭ Shime'oni*. This thirteenth-century Frankfort Jew, the most likely author of that compilation, had at his disposal as rich a collection of midrashic writings as any Mediterranean scholar; some of them are in fact, no longer available today. Folk tales, too, were a constant source of amusement and speculation among the northern Italian Jews and their German successors. Italy had not in vain become the mother country of those renowned folkloristic collections known as Yosephon, the Book of the Just, and the Chronicle of Yeraḥmeel. No less powerful was the influence of that vast mystic-magical popular "literature" which ever since ancient times had circulated in the Graeco-Roman communities and which remained much alive in the entire Byzantine sphere of influence. The closer German Jewry became linked with Italy and the Balkans, especially as a result of the rapprochement of the age of the Crusades, the stronger became the regenerative forces of that ancient heritage in its midst.

Into this fertile ground fell many new kernels of thought and practice communicated by Eastern arrivals and Eastern books. We recall the impact upon the southern Italian communities of the settlement among them of the Babylonian mystic, Aaron or Abu Aaron. This influence readily communicated itself also to the Jews across the Alps, Eleazar of Worms himself claiming that his ancestors and those of Yehudah the Pious had "received the correct order of prayers and other mysteries teacher from teacher all the way back to Abu Aaron son of R. Samuel the Prince." According to another tradition, R. Moses bar Kalonymus of Lucca, Abu Aaron's pupil, had brought with him to Mayence certain ritualistic customs which soon were generally accepted throughout Germany. Eastern influence was no less strong in the sphere of "superstitious" beliefs and practices, as is naively attested by the chronicler Aḥimaaz of Oria. That much of the *Merkabah* literature had also found its way into Germany is evident from the numerous *piyyuṭim* composed there entirely in the spirit of that mystic school. As we have just seen, the German mystics anticipated even their Provençal coreligionists in acquiring copies of that secret literature, such as the *Raza rabba* and the *Bahir*. Nor did the rise of mystic and pietistic trends among the German Christians remain without some reciprocal influence on Jews. Certainly, the intellectual barriers between the two groups of the population have frequently been overstated by historians who were easily misled by the tenor of their predominantly "isolationist" sources.[48]

All of this was resolved in the crucible of the great emergency of the Crusades. The spirit of religious enthusiasm and self-sacrificial devotion to one's ideal bred a state of mind wholly conducive to a new religious revaluation of the traditional sets of beliefs and standards of behavior. There was nothing consciously revolutionary in these doctrines. In fact, in theological fundamentals the German pietists merely borrowed many accepted doctrines of the Aggadah and unperturbedly mixed with them concepts peculiar to the *Merkabah* literature and others expounded by rationalist philosophers. Just as the Provençal mystics found much kinship with the philosophic teachings of Baḥya and Halevi, so did their

German compeers draw much illumination from Saadiah. Not only the gaon's *Commentary on Yeṣirah,* but also his main philosophic treatise was used to such advantage that the German pietists were prepared to count him among the great mystic teachers of the past. Ultimately, they even attributed to him another, purely mystic commentary on *Yeṣirah,* written by one of their own scholars, although this work was totally at variance with Saadiah's genuine book under this title. Not surprisingly, the spurious tract before long wholly displaced the authentic work, which had to be uncovered again by nineteenth-century scholars. Since it had never been translated into Hebrew, it was not immediately accessible to Western students. Not surprisingly, these German mystics blended with genuine Saadianic notions doctrines which would have been abhorrent to the gaon. They were particularly prone to employ lavishly demonological concepts which would have been utterly strange to a sharp antidualistic thinker like Saadiah. A characteristic passage, quoted by Moses of Tachau from Yehudah the Pious' lost *Sefer ha-Kabod* (Book of [Divine] Glory), well illustrates this naive mixture of heterogeneous teachings. Discussing prophecy and the peculiar ways of prophetic inspiration, Yehudah asserts:

> The Creator is infinite. Hence the prophet cannot know the Creator because He is not finite nor does He have any physical appearance. The prophet is in no position to know or to sense from where the speech comes or who the speaker is. For sometimes it is demons who speak and one cannot distinguish when the Holy One, blessed be He, speaks, the prophet being unable to tell whether [his message] comes from the Holy One blessed be He or from the spirit of impurity. For this reason there was a need for the [created] Glory and the heavenly hosts in various places to resemble man, and for all the mighty spirits [to stand] at His right and His left. This is the meaning of "He sits on the Throne," for no throne would fit the Creator whose greatness is without fathom. This is only to make the prophet know that He is the Lord over all the angels. When the prophet gazes at the sight of all these miraculous and glorious visions all around God, he realizes that the speech comes from the Holy One blessed be He, for the demons have none of that.[49]

Demonology was not a merely theological doctrine. Medieval man, Jew and Gentile, particularly in western and central Europe, lived in a world where benign and malevolent spirits and ghosts of deceased persons appeared to be part of daily reality. Removed by centuries and thousands of miles from the Zoroastrian civilization, he was not quite aware that he echoed the fundamentals of the dualistic doctrine. When Eleazar of Worms presented the picture of man being attached to a rope at which God and Satan tug from opposite ends, with God ultimately prevailing, he did not know that he was reproducing here the world picture of the former much-hated Magi of the talmudic age. He probably was familiar with the Manichaean survivals of ancient dualism mainly through the indirect channels of medieval Hebrew letters, Eastern or Provençal, although the Bogomil-Catharist agitation had reached the Rhinelands long before his birth. Certainly the burning of several "heretics" in front of the Jewish cemetery of Cologne in 1163 must have made a lasting impression on that community and its neighbors. In any case, man's daily communications with demons, even in the intimate sexual sphere, were simply taken for granted. So was the return to earth of the ghosts of deceased relatives or friends in their erstwhile human shape to expiate their previous sins or to warn the survivors against certain impending dangers. We recall how much credence the community of Mayence gave to the rumor of a congregation of ghosts praying aloud one night in the local synagogue. This was, at least in retrospect, viewed as a portent of the impending tragedy of the First Crusade.[50]

Of course, the presence of these innumerable spirits offered great temptations for man to try to enlist their aid for his private purposes. Folk mysticism frequently went hand in hand with magic arts. Out of this eternal craving for mastery over the forces of nature the German Jew, like many of his Eastern ancestors and Western Gentile contemporaries, sought to put these dark forces to his service. So widespread was this desire that even Yehudah the Pious felt the need to warn his readers that "he who practices invocation of angels, or of demons, or [other] magic imprecations, will not have a good end; all his life he will see misfortunes befall him and his children. For this reason man should stay away from all these practices, as well as from the interpretation of dreams. Neither must one allow others to perform such services for him." But so deeply ingrained in the popular mind was the belief in the existence of these occult forces, which Yehudah himself had stressed on many occasions, and in the ability of saintly individuals effectively to manipulate them that before long innumerable legends were told and retold in all the German Ḥasidic circles about the awsome miracles performed by this revered master in person with the assistance of these superhuman powers. Ultimately, his followers attributed to him the creation of a regular homunculus, generally considered the very acme of magic prowess, indeed, the goal unattainable to most practitioners of occult arts. Basically different from the somewhat related tale about Ibn Gabirol creating the figure of a woman servant, this story of Yehudah's alleged *Golem* greatly strengthened the faith of the numerous believers in its feasibility and perfectibility during the following generations.[51]

Equally remarkable is the dichotomy between Yehudah and his school in the field of eschatology. Though a firm believer in the doctrine of rewards and punishments after death, which the compiler of the "Book of the Pious" stresses in various connections, as well as in the ultimate coming of the Redeemer, he nevertheless tries to discourage messianic speculations of any kind and particularly all attempts at "computing the end." In the immediate continuation of the antimagical passage just quoted, the author sounds a sharp warning against all predictions of the coming of the Messiah, a practice which he places on a par with sorcery. He threatens that the angels or demons whose services were enlisted in securing that information will take revenge for their enforced futile exertions and cause the initiator to be exposed "to shame and ridicule before the whole world." Apart from his general hostility to unauthorized magic practices, one senses here the Ḥasid's painful apprehension lest the ensuing disappointments cause much despair among the masses and ultimately lead weaker souls to abandon their faith. It was this apprehension which had induced him, as we recall, to suppress a messianic computation in the travelogue of Petaḥiah of Ratisbon. Perhaps for this reason the preceding paragraphs deal extensively with renegades and the treatment of the voluntary returnees. The connection between apostasy and magic is stressed by Yehudah himself in the pithy apothegm: "If you see a Jew who converts himself not for the sake of fornication [intermarriage] nor because of terror, know that he, his ancestors, or his mother had engaged in the invocation of spirits and other works of sorcery, so that they [the demons] were given permission to lead him astray." [52]

In these and many other assertions in the "Book of the Pious" one perceives the deep concern of the Ḥasidic circles over the inroads of the Christian mission. Despite certain fundamental similarities in the general approaches of the Christian (both Catholic and heretical) and Jewish pietistic movements of the period (a fact realized by Yehudah and his associates and effectively illustrated in a searching essay by Y. Baer) the estrangement between the leading spokesmen of both camps was no less deep than that existing in the more rationalistic circles of the two denominations. While in their extraordinary emphasis upon ethical behavior the Jewish pietists wished to see the same superior morality permeating also the Jew's relations with his Christian neighbors, they were deeply convinced of the Church's implacable hostility toward Judaism and the Jewish people. They viewed the "protective" governments as merely bent upon exploiting their Jewish subjects, and believed that the ordinary Gentile was interested only in harming the Jew. For this reason unethical behavior toward Gentiles is to be doubly shunned, for apart from hurting the particular individuals, it might bring down severe retaliation upon the entire Jewish community. Concern for the welfare of the Jewish people as a whole is, indeed, one of the *leitmotifs* of the "Book of the Pious" and the other works emanating from the school of Yehudah the Pious. Dissatisfied though these pietists generally were with German Jewry's concentration on moneylending, and though, in a different way than Peter of Cluny, they wished to see more Jews deriving their livelihood from agriculture, they never condemned the honest acquisition of wealth through other means. In fact, they considered material well-being a blessing in itself, provided it was shared with one's neighbors. Punning on the two related Hebrew terms, the author of the "Book of the Pious" even contended that "he who is now poor [*rash*] is going to be a leader [*rosh*] in the future." There certainly was nothing in that Book which resembled the early Christian or Franciscan ideal of poverty. All that mattered was honesty in dealing with both Jews and Gentiles and charitableness in dispensing the fruits of one's labors. Untiringly the author reiterates his injunctions concerning business ethics and threatens the transgressors with ultimate business ruin. One characteristic passage reads:

He who lends all his money on interest [partial investments of this type could not be denounced under the existing circumstances], engages in coin clipping, and commits wrongs in weights, measures, the quality of merchandise, or other matters, will ultimately lose his fortune, his children will separate from one another in a strange land, and will require public support. . . . [A similar fate will befall] those who withhold the hired man's wages, purchase stolen objects, make a profit on Church utensils, candles, jewels, or vestments, or violate the ban imposed by the community to pay so and so much tax per pound.

However, business successes honestly arrived at could be regarded only as signs of divine grace and as incentives for charitable acts.[53]

Despite their insistence upon business morality also in dealings with non-Jews, an attitude sharply contrasting with the generally prevailing double standard of morals toward coreligionists and infidels, and their preachment of relative good-will toward Gentiles, these pietists advocated no relaxation in the general rabbinic efforts to segregate the Jews from the nations by rigorous ritualistic requirements. True, the occasional injunctions for the *ḥasid* to go beyond the laws of the "Torah" and to obey the laws of "heaven" could be utilized for antinomian preaching. But no more than the Provençal halakhist, Abraham ben David, did any of the German pietists dream of weakening in any way the hold of Jewish law on the entire population. On the contrary, their preachment aimed at more, rather than less, of the "yoke of Torah." Their generally ascetic world outlook and mode of living made them cherish acts of supererogation going far beyond any legal requirements. Legend had it that Yehudah himself was so inured to fasting that he could not enjoy even the food served on the Sabbath, although he agreed that this was to be a day of pure rejoicing. He was also supposed to have regularly fasted on two successive Days of Atonement. It was this extraordinary rigor in the application of Jewish law which attracted his followers most. Not by chance were Yehudah, Eleazar, and the other leading members of the group distinguished halakhists in their own right; some, like Eleazar, were authors of distinguished law books. At the same time their ethical preachment and, particularly, their new emphases and variations on the old rabbinic themes of social ethics, carried great appeal to the down-trodden masses. These vital aspects of German Jewish pietism will become clearer in the general context of the social evolution of German Jewry in the later Middle Ages.[54]

OCCULT BYWAYS

In Germany the mystic-folkloristic attitude toward life gained immediate widespread acceptance. Represented by men of great learning as well as piety, some of them like Yehudah claiming descent from the illustrious Kalonymid family, the historic transplanters of Jewish learning from Italy to the Rhinelands, it encountered little overt opposition. The "Book of the Pious," in particular, that collection of stories and epigrams stemming from the entire school rather than from a single author, seemed to uncritical readers to differ but slightly from the traditional midrashim. Even its fictional superstructure differed but little from what the populace had long been accustomed to hear from preachers and storytellers. Had not such a revered master of Halakhah as Nissim bar Jacob ibn Shahin himself compiled a large collection of stories for the amusement and edification of friends? Here all stories carried an even more directly ethical, indeed strongly hortatory, message. These pietists' occasional excursions into the realm of metaphysics, or rather theosophy, and their more intuitive than logically refined speculations on the nature of God and the intermediary powers could be supported by quotations from such mystic classics as the *Sefer Yeṣirah,* with its distinguished commentaries, and even from many midrashim, whether stemming from Eastern lands or from the school of Moses the Preacher closer home. True, a less mystically minded expert like Simon Qara may well have sensed the difference in the new approach and still more in certain new emphases and reinterpretation. Perhaps for this very reason he felt impelled to present to his coreligionists a comprehensive collection of authentic midrashic sayings arranged as a running commentary on the whole Bible. But apparently even he did not dare openly to contrast his sources with the new pietistic literature, which to most readers appeared as in direct line of tradition with the ancient Aggadah.

Nor did the leaders of German pietism require an apology for their uncomplicated outlook and methods before a rationalistically trained intelligentsia such as existed in Muslim countries or the Provençal borderland. Heinrich Graetz and David Neumark may have gone too far in trying to explain the rise of the medieval Kabbalah exclusively as a Spanish-Provençal reaction to the inroads of speculative philosophy. But even such southern French jurists as Abraham ben Isaac and Abraham ben David were aware of the challenges offered by the scholastic philosophy and felt the need of answering some of the fundamental questions which that philosophy had raised, even though in their opinion it had failed to answer them. Such searching questions forced these thinkers to delve more deeply into cosmogony and cosmology, and to speculate on the nature of Godhead and the relations between God and man. It was they, rather than their German confreres, who laid the foundations for the new theosophy of the *Zohar* and the ramified doctrines of medieval kabbalism which was increasingly to dominate Jewish life and learning in the later Middle Ages and early modern times. In the process they borrowed much from their Christian environment, both orthodox and sectarian, just as their predecessors in the East had been nurtured from the undying springs of the pre-Christian and Christian gnosis and, to a lesser extent, of Muslim *ṣufism*. But almost unconsciously they absorbed all these foreign ingredients, as their homiletical predecessors of all ages had done, and integrated them organically into the fabric of Jewish thought by constant reinterpretation and hermeneutic confirmation by the words of Scripture.

Such theosophic speculations in their wholly Judaized garb encountered little opposition either on the part of leaders or among the masses. Individual "enlightened" thinkers may have felt a certain *malaise* about these foreign importations and some of their clandestine heterodox implications. But, so long as they remained within the realm of pure speculation, they evoked no concerted reaction. Judaism had long learned to be lenient with respect to theoretical diversity so long as it did not affect adversely the actions of its adherents and their living in accordance with the requirements of the Halakhah. It was only when they deviated from the accepted legal norms and the traditional way of life that the orthodoxy of Jewish individuals or groups could seriously be impugned.

Here we notice the crucial difference between Jewish mysticism and the corresponding expressions of mystical involvement among Christians and, to a lesser extent, among Muslims. Gnostic Christianity, though filled with a ritualism of its own, always carried with it a basically antinomian message. Jewish mysticism, at least in all its medieval forms, was fundamentally nomistic. Certainly, no Rabbanite mystic would have seriously challenged the ancient homilist's equation of the Oral Law with the "mysteries of the Torah" which, according to God's design, were to serve as the main distinguishing mark between Israel and the nations. Rather than counseling its adherents to break the traditional commandments, Jewish mysticism, especially in its German pietistic forms, insisted upon their ever more rigid application. Even where modern scholars have rightly detected direct influences of the Christian environment as in the development by the German pietists of a "penitential tariff" with its regular schedule of self-imposed penalties in ratio to the purported severity of each particular sin, Jewish contemporaries saw only an intensification of their own traditional forms of law observance. Ironically, modern, especially Teutonic, Jew-baiters have often derided Jewish legalism and accused it of maintaining a sort of bookkeeping system between man's good deeds or sins on the one hand and their wages at the hand of God or man on the other hand. They did not realize that its extreme form, as expressed in the penitential scale of German Ḥasidism, was but a borrowing from the German system of penances adopted by the Churches themselves with some misgivings from the primitive Teuton legal system. However, this method of squaring one's conscience was so clearly in line with the Jewish nomistic tradition that hardly any of its medieval practitioners could sense its foreign origin. To them it appeared as merely a self-imposed intensification of the traditional legal requirements, for which ample precedents could be adduced from the recorded acts of supererogation of many revered talmudic sages.

The absence of any real compromises with the halakhic requirements may be seen particularly in the crucial domain of family and sex. From time immemorial asceticism often demanded sexual abstention. Celibacy not only of priests and monks but also of laymen became, indeed, a major postulate of the contemporary Christian ascetics. But in its far-reaching practical application such abstention would have undermined the very ethnic basis of Judaism and threatened its ultimate survival. In the extensive Judeo-Christian religious debates this divergence in sex ethics often came to the fore. We recall, for example, to what lengths Joseph Qimḥi went in that very period in defending the Jewish sex morals against the accusations of the celibatarian clergy. Jewish mystics did not dissent. Whatever antifeminist utterances appear in the contemporary literature, including the "Book of the Pious"—these can easily be balanced by equally numerous profeminist statements—they in no way affected the traditional Jewish outlook on the vital role of the family within the entire structure of Jewish law and life. None of the Jewish mystics endeavored to deny the *duty* of every individual to procreate and thus help to maintain the Jewish people in its progression towards its messianic goal.

For these reasons there really was no fundamental dichotomy between the accepted teachings and practices of traditional Judaism and those of its more radically mystical and ascetic wings. Even the latter's magical ingredients could not be sharply denounced in the light of the innumerable precedents mentioned with approval, even veneration, in the Talmud itself. Some rationalists like Maimonides may have frowned upon these "superstitious" practices, but even they were forced to make at least some concessions to these human "weaknesses." In general, the very imprecations of magic bowls, talismans, and exorcisms were shoved aside as private concerns of individuals which, even if not to be communally encouraged, were not to be formally suppressed. In this vast domain of occult practices, which as a rule did not deviate from the law but merely went outside and beyond it, the Jewish masses found an outlet for their individual cravings without running counter to the traditional norms and communal controls. Certainly, the practical efforts of magicians and their employers to convert stars into human beings, stones into animals or vice versa, must have appeared an innocuous game to most rationalist communal leaders and a perfectly legitimate exercise of human skills to their more credulous confreres. Nor did the magicians' attempts thus to master the forces of nature or even to go beyond reality in interpreting the occult recesses of the human mind and life appear objectionable so long as they did not depart too abruptly from the highway of orthodox lore. Just as in the whole domain of aggadic speculation and storytelling, so also in these practical manifestations of individual and group self-expression many "superstitious" or mystically-minded Jews found a large area for personal self-fulfillment, noninterference with which had long become a guiding principle of communal leadership.[55]

XXXIV

FAITH AND REASON

In the twelfth century, mysticism and magic still occupied only peripheral places in the totality of Jewish life. Notwithstanding the great role played by occult practices in the daily life of innumerable Jews, practitioners often felt a certain *malaise* concerning their permissibility from the standpoint of Jewish law. Except in Germany, they were, as a rule, given the "silent treatment" by the communal leaders. In Muslim lands, where the vast majority of Jewry and its economically and intellectually most advanced segments still resided, leading jurists occasionally questioned the very legitimacy of acts designed to conjure supernatural powers. Even the philosophically much more respectable speculations of the *Merkabah* mystics, the *Bahir,* or the Provençal scholars were still the patrimony of restricted circles of visionaries and dreamers, and they enjoyed but little communal influence or even visibility. The great days of the Kabbalah as a major historic force in the destinies of the Jewish people lay in the future.

In contrast thereto, Jewish scholastic philosophy achieved an importance far beyond the numerical strength of its devotees and those able to comprehend its teachings. In its heyday, from the tenth to the twelfth centuries, it reached not only qualitative heights unmatched by any earlier or later Jewish attainments, but it also dominated the thinking of many influential Jewish circles with unprecedented vigor and intensity. In some respects this quest for new answers and the philosophic justification of long-accepted religious verities was but a sign of the higher degree of Jewish integration in the vast, dynamic, and fairly "open" Islamic society of the Great Caliphate. In ways analogous to those of their Alexandrian forefathers, the Jews of Baghdad, Cairo, or Cordova sought to reconcile their inherited system of beliefs and observances with the postulates of human reason as represented by the works of the outstanding Greek thinkers, now increasingly available in Arabic translation to students of all denominations. Other cities may not have been quite so broad-minded as Baghdad in allowing that free meeting of minds in the philosophers' assemblies attended by Muslims of all sects, "agnostics, Parsees, materialists, atheists, Jews and Christians," about which Aḥmad ibn Sa'id was so dolefully to reminisce. But there probably were throughout the vast expanses of the Caliphate many meeting places for Jews and members of other denominations, where, by mutual agreement, the discussion was conducted not on a plane of rivaling dogmas but on that of the exclusive use of "arguments derived from human reason." In the liberal atmosphere of free exchange, as well as in that of the less tolerant religious disputations, many new vistas were opened to inquiring Jewish minds and many an intellect was sharpened through the new philosophic dialectics.[1]

Unlike the Alexandrian Jews, however, their successors in the Great Caliphate faced challenges of kindred monotheistic rather than of wholly alien pagan religions. There now existed among the leading intellectuals a basic similarity in approach: many matters previously under sharp debate appeared completely noncontroversial. Spokesmen of all three major religions, on the contrary, now jointly faced their common antagonist in the heritage of Graeco-Roman pagan science and thought, and all of them tried in essentially the same way to overcome the inherent difficulties of reconciling the latter's basically secular interpretations with their own traditional religious beliefs. Outside the narrow range of strictly religious polemics, therefore, members of all three denominations found it to their advantage to learn from one another and even freely to borrow from each other's concepts and interpretations. In such fundamentals as God's existence, His Oneness (whether or not modified by the Trinitarian dogma), His Creation of the world, a world of spheres and intelligences, and the broad realm of human ethics, the similarities in the outlook of the representative thinkers of the three faiths far exceeded their dissimilarities. The very existence of such common bonds served, on the one hand, as a constant invitation to emulation and, on the other hand, offered a constant challenge to look beyond the likenesses for the differentia which alone could provide the justification of the peculiarities of one's own faith.

GROWTH OF RATIONALISM

For this reason anthropomorphism became such an overriding Jewish issue, internally as well as in the debates with outsiders. There evidently existed a deep inner conflict between the religion of the ordinary people buttressed by the simple meaning of crucial passages in the authoritative sources of ancient Judaism and the new speculative conceptions of God, which began spreading among the Jews as among the Muslims and Christians. This dichotomy had had to be resolved, as we recall, already in ancient Alexandria. It must have continued in the Hellenistic Diaspora in the following centuries. Perhaps it was this inner conflict which, according to Suidas, caused the Jewish philosopher and mathematician Domninus to "pervert" many Platonic teachings. We know that even Proclus, who was said to have attempted to eliminate that perversion, unavoidably injected new elements into the traditional teachings of the Platonic schools. In the Muslim age, however, internal as well as external attacks multiplied in intensity, and the issue had to be faced more squarely. The constant growth of educated classes, the sharp sectarian controversies, and the increasing spread of and reverence for the works of the most representative Greek thinkers and scientists (now accessible in Arabic translations to educated readers of all faiths) in the Caliphate and the new interrelated forces of individualism and the quest for scientific discovery—all these factors made questioning of accepted beliefs and practices a common phenomenon among all religious groups. Because of basic similarities in the nature of the rationalist challenges and the ensuing affinities, despite many detailed variations, of the solutions offered, the medieval religious philosophies of Muslims, Christians, and Jews have much more in common than have most of the outstanding theological works of the three faiths in modern times.[2]

Understandably, the first to come to grips with these new problems were the heterodox members of each community. Prepared to repudiate, often from political and social motivations, accepted doctrines or rituals, and hence ready to reject the authority of their canonical sources, they had to suggest new answers to the problems of human existence. The independent intellectual stirrings among the Jewish population of the eastern provinces, which had given rise to the Karaite repudiation of talmudic traditions, also brought forth the first medieval Jewish religious philosopher, Benjamin of Nahawend. Not at all surprisingly, this ninth-century sectarian leader and jurist was primarily concerned with the problems of Creation and angelic intermediaries, since these problems had stood in the very focus of the debates among the adepts of *Yeṣirah* and *Merkabah* mysticism. He was followed by the enigmatic Ḥivi al-Balkhi, who, apparently without heterodox intent, asked a number of serious questions concerning the Bible itself, but whose own answers have unfortunately not been preserved. Even most of his questions, as we recall, can no longer be reconstructed from the replies, made by such opponents as Saadiah.[3]

Another enigmatic but significant contributor to the intellectual debate was David ibn Merwan al-Muqammiṣ of Raqqa. In his youth David became a convert to Christianity and studied at the famous Syriac academy of Nisibis, but early in the tenth century he reverted to Judaism. As a pupil of Syriac Bible scholars and Muslim thinkers, this tenth-century Uriel d'Acosta acquired new vistas on basic questions of Jewish theology as well, which, upon his return to Judaism, he began formulating in an Arabic work called "Twenty Tractates" and in a commentary on the Bible. Regrettably, the latter is totally lost, while the "Tractates" are known to us mainly through brief quotations occupying some ten pages in Yehudah bar Barzillai's Hebrew Commentary on *Yeṣirah*. These Hebrew renditions, though apparently quite accurate, may not be genuinely representative of all that Al-Muqammiṣ had stood for. This is doubly regrettable, since his overriding concern for the meaning and theological implications of divine attributes was undoubtedly owing to his intimate association with the Christian teachers of Nisibis. Further investigations of these links may prove very rewarding, for the Syriac Christians, in their capacity as both chief translators of ancient Greek texts and theologians in their own right, influenced greatly the rise of Muslim, and indirectly that of Jewish, philosophy.[4]

These pioneers were followed by other thinkers among both Karaites and Rabbanites, who, for the most part, wrote either outright Bible commentaries or monographs related to the airing, often apologetical or polemical, of problems raised by biblical passages. Most of these writings are extant, at best, in small fragments by unknown authors. Even Isaac ben Solomon Israeli's lengthy but incomplete philosophic commentary on Genesis is known to us only from a few subsequent quotations. His treatise on logic and some other philosophic tracts are merely mentioned in later Arabic handbooks. We possess, however, substantial fragments of his Book of Definitions and Book of Elements, the latter only in Hebrew and Latin translations. Perhaps even these segments have been preserved principally because of their author's distinction as a physician who, during his century-long life (*ca.*850–950), published a series of medical monographs which were to achieve great renown in the later Middle Ages. Israeli's work was continued by his pupil, Dunash ibn Tamim.[5]

All these writings were overshadowed by the superlative achievements of Saadiah Gaon. Like his contemporaries, the gaon expatiated on his theological doctrines in his comprehensive Bible commentaries and, to a lesser extent, in his polemical pamphlets, in part designed only for private circulation. There is also much theology in his poetry and in many asides included in his juridical works. However, he also elaborated many of his philosophic and theological views in his extensive *Commentary on Yeṣirah.* This commentary, which within a century was available to R. Yehudah bar Barzillai in Barcelona in a Hebrew version (curiously the Catalan rabbi, though cognizant of Arabic could not secure a copy of the original), exercised great influence on all subsequent mystic speculations on the doctrine of Creation. This influence is clearly noticeable in Dunash ibn Tamim's similar works. In addition, the gaon felt the need of composing monographs on a variety of philosophical and theological subjects. During the enforced leisure occasioned by his banishment from the academy of Sura, he revised these monographs into chapters of his comprehensive *Beliefs and Opinions,* the first classic of medieval Jewish philosophical literature, which was to be more or less fully preserved in both the Arabic original and the twelfth-century

Hebrew translation by Yehudah ibn Tibbon. In both languages the work soon became influential among philosophers and the educated public alike.[6]

Only Saadiah's younger contemporary, Shabbetai ben Abraham Donnolo, although familiar with Arabic through several years of captivity in Muslim lands, seems to have remained unaffected by either the gaon's *Commentary on Yeṣirah* or his philosophic work. Donnolo continued in this field, too, the Palestino-Byzantine tradition of his homeland in the south of Italy. True, we know very little about the development of theological thinking among the southern Italian Jews of that early period, and only a careful analysis of the mystic ideas expounded by the local Hebrew poets, especially Shefaṭiah and Amittai, can shed some light on the thought processes of the distinguished physician-philosopher as well. All these works reveal many traces of an independent tradition, mainly leading back to the Palestinian *Merkabah* mysticism and the mystically minded liturgical poetry of the school of Qalir as well as to some general Byzantine environmental influences. We certainly must never lose sight of the fact that in the Byzantine Empire continuity of ancient thought was never completely severed by the inroads of Christianity.[7]

Much more is now also known about the philosophic ideas of Qirqisani, Saadiah's outstanding Karaite contemporary, whose encyclopedic "Book of Lights," frequently referred to in these pages, was published more than a decade ago. Anyone desirous of familiarizing himself with the regnant world outlook of the early Karaite groups must, nevertheless, still painfully reconstruct it from their various Bible commentaries and polemical treatises, written by Jephet ben 'Ali in the tenth century, and by Joseph al-Baṣir (the Seer) and his pupil Yeshu'a ben Yehudah (Abu'l Faraj Furqan ibn Asad) in the eleventh century. We do not know whether any of these men, and particularly Yeshu'a, is truly representative of Karaite theological doctrine, since Karaism still prided itself on its unbounded individual quest for truth. Nevertheless, the mere presence of these influential Karaite Mu'tazilites enabled such opponents as Halevi or Maimonides to condemn the whole sect for its excessive, or at least excessively mechanistic, rationalism.[8]

Saadiah and his Rabbanite, as well as Karaite, successors thus were primarily concerned with the philosophic problems raised in the Muslim camp by that conglomerate of schools known by the name *Kalam,* and particularly its rationalist Mu'tazilite wing. When the center of gravity of Jewish intellectual endeavor had moved to the Iberian Peninsula, the impact of these schools paled into insignificance compared with the influence of Platonism, or, rather, a peripatetically attenuated Neoplatonism. Ibn Gabirol, especially, may be said to have resumed at the point where the *Yeṣirah* and *Merkabah* mystics had left off. Whether or not the author of the Book of Creation had consciously restated certain doctrines of Proclus in Jewish terms, the categories of thinking of these early Jewish mystics revealed many similarities with those cultivated at the Alexandrian Academy at the turn from ancient to medieval times. Now with Plato's *Republic* and *Laws* available in Arabic renditions and provided with extensive commentaries, especially by Farabi, a serious effort could be made to integrate these doctrines into the fabric of traditional Judaism. To be sure, neither Jews nor Muslims nor Christians were sufficiently well informed to read the ancient Greek classics in their true historic context. Even when they made a rare effort to understand an author out of his own premises, as did Farabi in his rendition of Plato's *Laws,* they could not help adjusting—even distorting—his views. Nevertheless, even in their opaque reproduction these works of the Greek philosopher exercised a tremendous fascination on the newly awakened speculative curiosity of the leading intellectuals of all three faiths.[9]

When Ibn Gabirol undertook in his "Fountain of Life" to reinterpret the Platonic doctrines, he did it so subtly and detachedly that the nexus between his teachings and those of Judaism was not immediately evident to the reader. He succeeded in avoiding even biblical citations, at that time customarily invoked in support of one's own arguments. When this work in its Latin translation, prepared by the later converted Jew, Johannes Hispanus Avendeath, in cooperation with Dominicus Gundissalinus, entered upon its remarkable career within Christian scholasticism, its readers remained uncertain as to whether its author, known as Avicebron (or Avicebrol), was a Muslim or a Christian. No one, until Salomon Munk's famous discovery of 1846, ventured to suggest its authorship by a Jew. On the other hand, Ibn Gabirol's other works were avowedly Jewish. Not only were his Hebrew poetic creations, including his "Royal Crown," filled with traditional Jewish concepts, but this was the case also with his major ethical treatise, "On the Improvement of Moral Qualities," written in Arabic in 1045.[10]

Clearly ethics, related to human conduct, which in turn depended greatly on particular folkways and mores, could not be treated with as little reference to one's denominational attachments as was the realm of pure metaphysics. Even Baḥya ibn Paquda, therefore, who about 1080 went out to prove that the "Duties of the Heart" were superior to all ceremonial laws, presented his entire argument in traditional Jewish terms. So did the unknown, but probably slightly younger, author of the "Investigation of the Soul," wrongly attributed to Baḥya.[11]

Even more ardently and outspokenly Jewish was Yehudah Halevi. His quasi-Platonic dialogue before the Khazar king (written about 1140) was devoted entirely to an apologia for Judaism and the presentation of a new comprehensive philosophy of Jewish and world history.[12]

Similarly strong Jewish accents were audible in the slightly earlier philosophic work written in the 1120's by the distinguished Jewish mathematician, Abraham bar Ḥiyya, known in the Christian Middle Ages as Savasorda. Not only his major ethical work, "Contemplation of the Soul," but also his "Scroll of Disclosure," dedicated less to the avowed aim of "disclosing" the date of the advent of the Messiah than to the formulation of what might be designated as an "astrological concept of history," are unmistakably works of a Jewish traditionalist. These two books, moreover, had the distinction of being the first philosophic treatises to be written in Hebrew by a medieval Jewish philosopher.[13]

Equally Jewish are the astrologically oriented works by Abraham ibn Ezra, written in Hebrew, or the more purely metaphysical treatise on man as the "Microcosm," originally composed in Arabic by Joseph ibn Ṣaddiq. The latter, a Hebrew poet of the Moses ibn Ezra and Halevi circle, also composed an Arabic treatise on logic, known only by title. On the other hand, Abraham ibn

Ezra included many philosophic observations in his far more widely read Bible commentaries.[14]

In some respects a new chapter in Jewish philosophy began with the ingress of Aristotelian doctrines about the middle of the twelfth century. Many works by Aristotle had long been known among Christians, Jews, and Muslims in the East. They were made doubly influential through the authority of the great Persian Aristotelian, Avicenna. Few indeed were the thinkers who ventured to defy their authority. Among the Jewish philosophers only Abu'l Barakat al-Baghdadi approached them critically, maintaining a position independent of both the Kalam and peripatetism. This independence, as well as his general brilliance and erudition, secured for him a great reputation among Muslim philosophers (he is counted among the five greatest Arab philosophers by a modern Turkish historian) but his influence among Jews (at least until Crescas) remained negligible, in part precisely because Aristotelianism now reigned supreme in the Jewish camp. Certainly his conversion to Islam in his old age (probably some time before 1135) discouraged Jewish authors from mentioning him.[15]

Aristotelianism's full impact made itself felt among Spanish Jews first in the work of the historian-philosopher, Abraham ibn Daud. Like his successors, Ibn Daud viewed the Stagirite's works through the deeply colored lenses of their Hellenistic and Arabic commentators. Nevertheless, in his "Exalted Faith Showing the Concordance of Philosophy and Religion," Ibn Daud opened the period of philosophic synthesis between Aristotelianism and Judaism which was to culminate in the legend, widely believed all over Europe, that in his old age the Stagirite had converted to Judaism.[16]

The greatest and most universally influential exponent of that synthesis was Moses Maimonides, whose concern with basic philosophical and theological problems permeated almost all of his works. This interest seems to have been cultivated from his early youth by a philosophically interested father, author of a brief but interesting ethical treatise. The family tradition was, in turn, maintained by the son of Maimonides' old age, Abraham, who wrote a comprehensive ethical work on the "High Ways of Perfection." It is small wonder, then, that even when writing a technical commentary on the Mishnah Moses ben Maimon converted his introduction to the Sayings of the Fathers into a lengthy monograph on the ethics of Judaism which came to be known under the separate title of "Eight Chapters." In his opening comments on the last chapter of Sanhedrin, too, he so succinctly summarized the basic thirteen tenets of the Jewish faith that, in an abridged form, they were incorporated in the prayer book for daily recitation. Similarly, he devoted the first of the fourteen sections of his great Code of Laws to a restatement of the "Principles of the Torah," that is, its theological fundamentals. Discussions of theological problems are scattered also through Maimonides' numerous "Epistles," particularly those on the messianic idea addressed to Yemen, and on the subjects of Resurrection and Conversion. These letters became widely read theological tracts in their own right. At an early age he also composed a small treatise on "Logical Terms." But his philosophic magnum opus was to remain his "Guide for the Perplexed," written some time between 1185 and 1190. This work, translated into Hebrew by Samuel ibn Tibbon (1204) in consultation with the author, and not much later rendered again by Yehudah al-Ḥarizi in a more elegant and fluent, but less precise, Hebrew style, soon became a subject of controversy. It nevertheless was speedily recognized by Muslims and Christians, as well as by Jews, as the greatest work of Jewish religious philosophy of all times.[17]

Apart from these original works in religious philosophy, the medieval Jewish thinkers contributed their share to the intellectual ferment by helping familiarize the Jewish and non-Jewish public with works of other authors, particularly from Hellenistic antiquity, through more or less adequate translations. Maimonides was not alone in feeling (in the well-known letter of 1199 to his translator, Samuel ibn Tibbon) that a translation was a sort of new composition, and, hence, "the translator serves as a copartner of the author." To be sure, we possess no records indicating that Jews were active, alongside the Syriac Christians, in the early translations of the Greek philosophic and scientific works into Arabic. The great period of Jewish translators was to come later in the western countries, where they were to become the leading exponents of Graeco-Arabic lore. This function seems to have begun as early as the tenth century, when the Jewish statesman Ḥisdai ibn Shapruṭ took a significant part in the translation of a text of Dioscorides, a copy of which had just been received at the court of Cordova as a gift of Emperor Romanos II. Two centuries later Abraham ibn Ezra translated several Muslim astrological treatises, while Yehudah ibn Tibbon, the "father of translators," is said to have reproduced one of Farabi's essays on logic. Many smaller writings by Rabbanite or Karaite thinkers may also have been but paraphrases of similar Arabic works since lost. That process of appropriation from one civilization to another certainly was not restricted to the field of romances and popular pearls of wisdom.[18]

Still another way of making an important contribution to learning, very popular throughout the Middle Ages, was to compose a commentary on some older, authoritative work. The commentator often used his exposition as an effective vehicle for the expression of his own thoughts, as much as for the explanation of the ideas presented by the original writer. Originality generally was not the forte of medieval writers; in fact it was not even considered a virtue by most of their contemporaries. An outright innovation (Arabic *bida'*) was seriously frowned upon by the conservative majority. Hence the difference between an independent work of scholarship and one appearing in the form of a commentary on an older work was not very great. The titles of the two known philosophic works by the Jewish pioneer, Isaac Israeli, indicate that they were intended principally as "collections of philosophers' dicta" and "a book compiled from dicta of ancient philosophers." In all cases there was an avowed dependence on earlier authorities, the exegete being only slightly more restricted than an original writer in the exposition of his views by the statements commented upon and their sequences. Even translators took considerable liberties with texts before them, especially in passages running counter to their own deep-rooted convictions. The works of the "philosopher" (Aristotle), especially, were subjected to such careful scrutiny via the exposition of commentators that, in the minds of even such distinguished contemporaries as Maimonides, the difference between the original work and that of the commentators was almost totally blurred. Here, too, the greatest flowering of Jewish commentaries on Aristotle and even of supercommentaries on Averroës' commentaries, was to come in the West from the thirteenth century on, in which context it will be more fully analyzed. In any case, to judge from the available, rather meager evidence, the earlier Jewish exegetical contributions to philosophic studies lagged behind the parallel efforts in the fields of science. However, some such expositions of great classics must have at all times circulated also among Jewish adepts of philosophy, albeit for the most part in oral form only.[19]

THREE-FRONT WAR

In all these writings the medieval Jewish thinkers, with whatever aura of detachment they may have intentionally surrounded themselves, were locked in a fateful combat for their embattled faith. This was a three-front war. In the first place, as members of a fighting minority, they had to justify their struggle for survival and their persistence against tremendous odds in the face of unceasing attacks by Muslim and Christian controversialists. This battle, as we recall, was further complicated by internal Jewish heresies, many of the heretics applying exactly the same weapons and using exactly the same arguments as the anti-Jewish apologists. To be sure, there was little of that internal dogmatic confusion which characterized the early partisan struggles among Muslims, and which gave rise to the main Mu'tazilite ("neutralist") brand of Arab rationalism. Judaism long had its established system of beliefs and rituals, and it could easily enough distinguish between a "sinner" and an "infidel." With its ethnic emphases, moreover, it could consider even an infidel a sort of suspended member of the community, to which he could easily return the moment he repented. The well-known rabbinic adage, "An Israelite, even if he sins, is still an Israelite," remained uncontested. Nevertheless the external and internal sociopolitical and ideological pressures on Jewish leaders, too, were strong enough to call for new and unprecedented rationalizations.[20]

A second front consisted of Jewish skeptics, whether of the intellectual or the vulgar type, who either speculatively denied some fundamentals of the Jewish faith or merely wished to rid themselves of the burden of Jewish laws and observances. Such "persons adhering to Judaism in name only and partaking of humanity in their body only," as Joseph ibn Ṣaddiq called them, abounded in certain periods and areas under early Islam, just as there existed similar exponents of theoretical or practical unbelief among the Muslims and Christians. Did not the unknown author of the aforementioned "Early Theologico-Polemical Work" fulminate with equal vehemence against the Jewish rationalists of the school of Al-Jubai, as against the Samaritans, Christians, Muslims, and Karaites? Even a remote community like Raqqa on the Euphrates produced in the tenth century, apart from Al-Muqammiṣ, three Jewish "philosophers" recorded in Arab writings. So convinced were these men of the universal validity of philosophic doctrines that one of them suggested that philosophy ought to become the common property of the masses without the study of ponderous treatises, just as languages are mastered without arduous work in philological textbooks. In so far as they formally belonged to the group calling itself "philosophers," many such persons could almost be classified as members of another faith. In the chequered sectarian fabric of the Caliphate one could not easily draw the line between a sect and a mere school of thought. That is why in his famous dialogue Halevi could present a "philosopher" as the spokesman of an independent outlook on life, even a "belief," at variance with that of the three faiths. About the same time, Abelard formulated his apologia of Christianity in terms of a tricornered debate between a Christian, a Jew, and a philosopher. Maimonides, too, readily stressed "the opinion which is taught by our religion, and which differs from the evil and wrong principles of the philosophers." [21]

Most painful, however, was the struggle on the third front: against the conservative leaders of the Jewish communities and their mass following. True, ancient sages themselves often indulged in semi-metaphysical speculations; some of them dared to question the very righteousness of certain ways of the Lord, although they usually ended up with some rationale or the admission of their inscrutability to human perception. But they shunned all purely logical, nonhermeneutic reasoning. There was a grain of truth in Al-Jaḥiẓ' assertion that in his day (ninth century) there was "lack of science among the Jews" because they considered "philosophic speculation to be unbelief." Some such suspicions continued to be harbored in conservative circles also in later generations, especially outside the world of Islam. Not that there was fear of outright religious persecution. Not until the thirteenth century and the raging anti-Maimonidean controversy, which was largely limited to the Provence and northern Spain, do we have the record of any organized effort to suppress liberal opinions. At that time, indeed, the Provençal Joseph Kaspi could legitimately accuse some local rabbis of outright obscurantism, just as he conversely derided the "philosophizing" students who "scoff at the words of the rabbis." The difficulty really was that the majority of conservatives were not obscurantists, but rather upholders of an age-old tradition, which considered philosophic speculations as part of that "brood of aliens" already repudiated by Isaiah. These conservatives had, indeed, express statements in the Talmud on their side, such as the oft-cited warning to all pious Jews to abstain from futile speculations about what is below and what is above. The enlightened gaon, Hai, could not help but interpret another talmudic injunction, "Keep your children away from *higgayon,*" as referring to "the science of logic and other sciences." In a responsum erroneously attributed to him, Hai also was supposed to have argued for the superiority of the study of Jewish lore over that of philosophy. "Do not follow those," he had allegedly urged his correspondents, "who assert that its [philosophy's] way is smooth and leads to the knowledge of the Creator blessed be He. Know ye, that these men in fact cheat you." Although not written by the great gaon of Pumbedita, this responsum nonetheless voiced an opinion widely held among the most influential and representative Jews who believed that "speculation leads to unbelief, and is conducive to heresy." [22]

Certainly, by immersing oneself in a religious philosophy basically common to all three faiths, one unconsciously built a bridge to the understanding of the other creeds. Not without reason were such Arab students of comparative religion as Shahrastani suspected of heresy. How much more dangerous must the scaling of interdenominational walls have appeared to members of an embattled minority in any case subjected to endless conversionist pressures! Saadiah's attempt to dismiss such opinions as held only by the uneducated masses was clearly a case of whistling in the dark. It had not been so very long since he himself, in commenting on Proverbs 30:4, had declared that it was futile to speculate on the creation *ex nihilo* and the nature of the four elements (*Oeuvres*, VI, 185 ff.).

Saadiah's case (and not only his) was aggravated by his holding an official position of leadership in the Jewish community. In all other matters, when approached by a local constituent or the leader of a distant community to resolve a question of law, the gaon applied his great gifts and erudition to marshaling the talmudic evidence in as objective a fashion as possible, in order to determine what was the regnant law. Here he had to run counter to the unmistakable wishes of the talmudic sages. The same dilemma faced Baḥya and Ibn Ṣaddiq, both reputed members of Jewish tribunals, or Bar Ḥiyya, whose high sounding title *nasi* was apparently derived from his having served as a synagogue functionary. Ibn Gabirol, though formally free, was on the payroll of communal dignitaries like Yequtiel and Samuel ha-Nagid. Even the financially independent physicians, Halevi and Maimonides, were students of the Halakhah and its ardent admirers. To be sure, the Jewish community, as a rule, prosecuted "heretics" and others who, through their actions, disturbed the public order established by the accepted law and observance, but it rarely interfered with the expression of mere opinions. Nor was there any censorship of writing before the invention of printing made possible direct communal interference with the production and circulation of undesirable publications. Nevertheless, public opinion in a closely-knit community sufficed to deter most of the responsible intellectual spokesmen from recklessly wounding the sensitivities of the majority.

Even an ascetic thinker like Baḥya, preaching a pietistic and unworldly way of life, could not entirely escape the combined impact of a sustained tradition and public opinion. He severely scolded "the majority of our contemporaries who take lightly the theory and practice of the duties of the limb, and even more so those of the duties of the heart." True, he also reprimanded the one or other among them "who volunteers to study the wisdom of the Torah, but who devotes himself only to matters through which he will be called a sage among the illiterate, and acquire the reputation of a knowledgeable man among the alleged great." Such clinging to the nonmetaphysical aspects of Jewish law was obviously more rewarding and less hazardous. But even Baḥya could not avoid trying to prove from the very same authoritative sources the equality, or even superiority, of the "duties of the heart" *within* the structure of Halakhah. In this respect he differed sharply from an otherwise kindred spirit, Al-Ghazzali, who considered all jurisprudence as a purely worldly pursuit of little concern to the theologian.[23]

It is not surprising, therefore, that even the intellectual minority was greatly confused by these diverse cross currents. Saadiah was prompted to write his work because he saw in his community many men "who were sunk, as it were, in seas of doubt and overwhelmed by waves of confusion," a state of mind which he graphically described in his introduction. Maimonides, too, avowedly addressed his *Guide* not to the uneducated or mere tyros, nor to the students of the "canonical law" alone; rather he intended it

> to enlighten a religious man who has been trained to believe in the truth of our holy Law, who conscientiously fulfills his moral and religious duties, and at the same time has been successful in his philosophical studies. Human reason has attracted him to abide within its sphere; and he finds it difficult to accept as correct the teaching based on the literal interpretation of the Law, and especially that which he himself or others derived from those homonymous, metaphorical, or hybrid expressions [the main theme of the first part of the *Guide*]. Hence he is lost in perplexity and anxiety.

Echoing another statement in the *Guide,* Abraham Maimonides likewise testified that his father had "intended to teach a single wise man who comprehends the subject in its true light, even if he was misunderstood by a thousand fools." This was not so much intellectual haughtiness, or the reflection of an "aristocratic" disdain for the masses, as the realistic observation of the great communal need to furnish guidance to the small but articulate and influential intellectual group which, essentially loyal to the Jewish tradition, was perplexed by the apparent conflict between the new truths discovered by reason and those embedded in their revealed and traditional sources.[24]

Of course, if these requirements were taken seriously, the vast majority of potential readers would have been automatically eliminated. Yet they were more than a mere figure of speech or even a safeguard against the anticipated outcries of conservatives—the title *Dalalat* was soon to be renamed by opponents *Salalat* (Misguidance of the Perplexed)—such as was offered also by Maimonides' contemporary Averroës. Books of this type were written for the use of a small class of readers; in contrast, for example, to the Maimonidean Code, which was addressed to the learned Jewish public at large. It is futile to discuss, as has frequently been done, which of his two great works Maimonides himself valued more highly, since they were addressed to different audiences. There certainly is no doubt that he considered his Code his "great work," whether we translate the term *ḥibbur* by *summa,* as Blau suggested, or by "compilation," as Strauss insists, because the work is essentially but a summary of the talmudic sources. It is applying modern standards of originality to the medieval quest for authoritative truths to consider an all-embracing summation, a real *summa* of the authoritative sources of Judaism, in any way inferior in the minds of either author or reader to an independent discussion of even the "great things," as the Talmud calls the mysteries of Creation and the Chariot.[25]

In this sense none of the philosophic literature was intended for popular consumption, with the possible exception of Baḥya's work, whose avowedly simple language and terminology appealed directly to the masses and ultimately lent itself even for recitation as a purely devotional exercise. Even Ibn Ṣaddiq and Ibn Daud, who wrote "for beginners," had in mind readers whose preoccupation with philosophic problems, on whatever level of competence, had undermined the naive faith they had inherited from their forefathers. Ibn Ṣaddiq could not suppress a sigh in contrasting the biblical period, when "on account of His [the Creator's] great predilection for this people it was worshiping Him innately," with his own far more complex age which required the aid of many specialized disciplines.[26]

How large, then, was the prospective readership of the *Guide,* for an extremely busy practitioner of medicine and communal leader like the sage of Fusṭaṭ (according to his own interesting description in the oft-quoted epistle to Samuel ibn Tibbon) to devote to it many years of arduous thinking and painstaking writing? It is difficult to say. Of course, this book, even more than any other of his works, was written by Maimonides for his own clarification. However, by making it public in Arabic and by encouraging its translation into Hebrew, he knew that he faced not only the dictates of his own conscience, but also an interterritorial public which had come to admire him greatly as a jurist and leader. The number of philosophically "perplexed" people may have been larger in his day than in those of Saadiah, although that of confirmed antireligious "philosophers" may well have diminished. The heyday of the Mu'tazila and the Dahriya had passed, and even the more venturesome spirits in the world of Islam felt the impact of the conservative theological reactions initiated in diverse fields of thought by Ash'ari, Hallaj, and Ghazzali. Doubtless that is also why none of the philosophers after Saadiah ever predicted with such optimistic abandon that his philosophic teachings would become the common property of the people. Even in Muslim Spain, where religious indifference was not inconsiderable, William of Auvergne's observation that among the Jews there "who concern themselves with philosophy there are but few true Jews" is a decided overstatement.[27]

There undoubtedly were more practically indifferent or theoretically "perplexed" people than outright atheists or even skeptics of Ḥivi's type. Yet both groups apparently were not negligible in numbers and quite important because of their intellectual and social influence. They must have been most strongly represented in the higher echelons of the leisure classes, which indulged in intellectual debates with coreligionists and even with members of other faiths. They thus constituted a problem which had to be met by thoughtful leaders. As usual, however, apologetic literature of this type was probably read mainly by persons predisposed to the authors' point of view, and served to fortify the faith of confirmed believers rather than to convert unbelievers or even serious doubters.

Under these circumstances the Jewish thinkers had to tread softly, and to write with extreme circumspection. Even Maimonides, sharp opponent of *Merkabah* mystics and in his earlier writings bent upon the popularization of the basic teachings of Judaism, took a leaf out of their book. Quoting a well-known talmudic statement, he declared that he was discussing essentially the problems covered by the ancient accounts of Creation and the Chariot. Following the talmudic injunction, he therefore communicated only some chapter headings of his doctrine. "Even these have not been methodically and systematically arranged in this work, but have been, on the contrary, scattered, and interspersed with other topics which we shall have occasion to explain." Anyone familiar with the Fusṭaṭ sage's great love of systematization, and real talent for it, will recognize that he must have adopted this style of presentation only with a heavy heart. At the same time he enjoined the reader to take seriously every word in his book, the "result of deep study and great application," and above all "not to add any explanation even to a single word; nor to explain to another any portion of it except such passages as have been fully treated by previous theological authorities." Strauss may go too far in developing his thesis that Maimonides consciously "reveals the truth to those learned men who are able to understand by themselves and at the same time he hides it from the vulgar. . . . [He] makes contradictory statements about all important subjects; he reveals the truth by stating it, and hides it by contradicting it." Yet there is no question that Maimonides and, to a lesser extent, the other medieval Jewish theologians frequently followed the supposed Hypocratic observation, already quoted with approval by Isaac Israeli, and wrote "according to the custom of philosophers . . . to put in their words an evident meaning which is the opposite of their hidden meaning." Contrary, therefore, to Baḥya, who specifically stated that he would not use difficult terminology, even Ibn Ṣaddiq professed not to wish to argue with the totally ignorant majority.[28]

No sharper contrast need be adduced than that which exists between Ibn Gabirol's philosophic work addressed to the intellectual élite and his ethical writings addressed to the broader public. He who had not hesitated to leave the lofty elevation, in both technique and content, of most of his religious and secular poems and to descend to the level of the traditional *piyyuṭ* when he wished his liturgical creations adopted for synagogue recitation by the masses, also employed an entirely different style and approach in his strictly speculative work and in works intended for the moral improvement of the ordinary citizens. The un-Jewish character of his "Fountain of Life" did not escape critics. Abraham ibn Daud, himself anything but an obscurantist, found fault with its style and argument. Ibn Gabirol, in his opinion, had "believed that many untrue proofs can take the place of a single true demonstration," and could have presented his teachings in a book one tenth its present size without any loss of substance. Nevertheless, Ibn Daud added, he "would not have attacked Ibn Gabirol's statements, had not the latter cast aspersion on the nation." This seems indeed to have been the typical reaction of Jewish students of philosophy. Despite their enormous admiration for Ibn Gabirol as a poet, none of them, not even the prolific Al-Ḥarizi, deigned to translate the "Fountain of Life" into Hebrew. Medieval Hebrew readers, unfamiliar with Arabic or Latin, had to get along with its brief epitome included later in Ibn Falaquera's encyclopedic work. Even the Hebrew-writing Abraham bar Ḥiyya wrote in a different style when addressing himself to the intelligentsia in his "Scroll of Disclosure," and in another when submitting to the broader public his "Contemplation of the Soul." The latter, more fully described by the author as the "Contemplation of the Saddened Soul When It Knocks at the Gates of Repentance," may indeed have been intended for private recitation during the Ten Days of Repentance (from the New Year to the Day of Atonement), as suggested by Bacher and others. The Scroll, on the other hand, was certainly written for intellectual enlightenment, not for edification.[29]

In general, most medieval students of philosophy had been students of the Talmud as well. In fact, the great majority of them must have received intensive training in talmudic lore long before they embarked on the study of philosophy, which was cultivated only in few publicly supported schools. There also were many more competent teachers of the rabbinic disciplines than there were trained expounders of any school of philosophic thought. That is why in addressing themselves to the educated Jews, in works usually written in Hebrew script even when in the Arabic language, the medieval writers could presuppose not only general familiarity with talmudic doctrines, but even unconscious thought processes along talmudic modes of thinking. Most of these philosophers themselves had undoubtedly studied Aristotle and his commentaries in the same way in which they tried to unravel the mysteries of the Talmud. That is why Harry A. Wolfson is undoubtedly right that one cannot fully comprehend the meaning of any medieval Jewish philosophic argument by merely applying to it the customary Aristotelian categories. We must rather try to pursue it step by step along the lines of the "hypothetico-deductive" method of talmudic logic.[30]

SEMANTICS, RATIONALES, AND HISTORY

The task of the medieval Jewish thinkers was long aggravated by their enforced use of a totally alien terminology. With the progressive rediscovery and translation of the writings of ancient Greek philosophers, the medieval scholastics, whether Muslim, Jewish, or Christian, attempted to express their old religious beliefs in a new idiom. Unconsciously, they thus had to bridge the gap between ideologies of entirely different cultures and to read new meanings into old words. In the case of Jews there was the additional complication that their own sources were written in Hebrew or Aramaic, while they themselves had long used almost exclusively the Arabic medium. When Tobiah ben Moses, the Tibbonides, and other translators, as well as the philosophers living in a Christian environment, began composing philosophic tracts in Hebrew, they had to superimpose upon an Arabic terminology, itself a derivative from the Greek via Syriac, a new Hebrew terminological structure. In retrospect, it appears surprising that their endeavor proved so eminently successful, and that their formulations met so well their new needs without doing violence to the old meanings. As we learn from the prefaces to their renditions, Moses ibn Chiquitilla, Yehudah ibn Tibbon, and Samuel ibn Tibbon were fully cognizant of their difficulties and worked hard and conscientiously to resolve them. In most cases they indeed succeeded in finding more or less adequate Hebrew equivalents for the Arabic terms, even though at times they could achieve this result only at the expense of the general readability of their text. With all these allowances, however, one cannot escape the feeling that the chains weighed heavily upon them all, authors and translators alike.[31]

Although the teachings of Philo had been almost entirely forgotten by the Jewish people, only rare references to his writings having come down from the early Muslim age, many of the new philosophies showed interesting similarities. Again the Jews, in their attempt to synthesize Greek thought, or what they imagined to be Greek thought, with the tenets of Judaism, had to do some violence to both. Even Neoplatonism and the reformulation of the teachings of Aristotle by Alexander of Aphrodisias and the later commentators, however deeply imbued with oriental wisdom and religiosity, did not suffice to make the task easy. The weapon of Greek logic, however, sharpened by the dialectics of the talmudic schools in Babylonia, the Christian sectarian polemics in Syria, and the juridical controversies throughout the Muslim world, was wielded with astounding ease to resolve the most evident contradictions. The medieval mind, bent upon inclusiveness rather than consistency, accepted without demur the dictates of opposing authorities. In the long run, this imposed an impossible burden. These ever-renewed efforts of the outstanding thinkers of the age, often men of the greatest acumen and erudition, were therefore much more significant in their inquisitive persistence and comprehensive analysis than in the fundamental solutions offered. The variations in the most representative systems were due not only to the inherent difficulties of the task, the differences in personal temper or education, and the constant adaptation of newly translated texts, but also to dynamic developments in Islamic and Jewish society.

Reinterpretation of Jewish tradition in the light of Greek thought was greatly facilitated by the assumption, now resuscitated, of the ancient Alexandrian Jewish schools that the Bible had served as a source of inspiration for the most prominent Hellenic thinkers as well. This assumption also served the incidental purpose of disarming the anti-philosophic conservatives.

It could be argued that through the Greek and Arabic works some of the lost wisdom of King Solomon and other Israelitic sages had been salvaged.

Jews as well as Muslims knew little, if anything, about civilizations preceding that of the ancient Hebrews. The fine achievements of Arabic historiography were centered on the past of the Muslim peoples and, to a far lesser extent, on that of their immediate predecessors and neighbors. The mist enshrouding the early days of mankind had obscured the works of Hellenistic thinkers, and it became in the course of time still more dense, particularly in Christian Europe, where history and myth were indistinguishably interwoven. Under these circumstances, Jewry naturally felt flattered when other peoples were ready to acknowledge that the origin of all human wisdom was to be found in ancient Israel. Even Yehudah Halevi, however critical he may have been of the achievement of science in general, could not refrain from taking pride in the fact that "the roots and principles of all sciences were handed down from us first to the Chaldaeans, then to the Persians and Medians, then to Greece, and finally to the Romans." Medieval Jewish folklore went further, and, as we recall, it eventually made of Aristotle a repentant convert to Judaism.[32]

In the new religious setting, to be sure, in which both Muslims and Christians acknowledged the original Old Testament revelation, such assertions lost much of their significance. Nevertheless, the representative Jews incessantly reiterated their belief that the first language known to mankind was Hebrew and the first book written the Torah; therefore, they must necessarily have served to guide the Greek philosophers as well. Conversely, for the same reason all the essentials of Greek philosophy must have been contained in the Bible. This conviction added momentum to allegorical interpretation as a method for determining the hidden meanings behind the apparent Hebrew terms. Not surprisingly Ibn Gabirol, whose own philosophy had been furthest removed from the ordinary meaning of Scripture, but whose general approach resembled more than that of any other medieval thinker the methods of the Alexandrian apologists, also indulged in most radical excursions into the realm of allegory, as we learn in part through quotations in Abraham ibn Ezra's Bible commentaries. This harmonistic attitude sometimes bore strange fruits; for instance, Ibn Daud's interpretation of Psalm 139 as reflecting the ten categories of Aristotle. In many cases, even more serious concessions to Greek thought had to be made. To quote Ibn Daud again, he may have attacked Ibn Gabirol's detached philosophy as un-Jewish, but he himself felt bound to admit that the various parts of the Torah are not fully equal in rank. This statement, with which he concluded his philosophical *magnum opus,* was not openly accepted by any other philosopher, although some sympathized deeply with this point of view.[33]

On showing the basic concordance of philosophy and religion, Ibn Daud pursued in his entire work the method of first presenting the philosophic findings and then supporting them by scriptural quotations. He repeatedly emphasized that "you will not find in Scripture explicit statements concerning the subjects elucidated by true philosophy, but you will find there hints which the alert will understand while the blind will take literally" (I.2, 5, pp. 12, 19). Since almost anything could be interpreted as a hint and hence almost any doctrine could be found to have scriptural support, it all depended on making sure that that doctrine belonged to "true philosophy." In drawing such a line of demarcation one could follow consciously only the dictates of one's own reason, although subconsciously, of course, the choice was greatly affected by many irrational motivations.

How reliable an instrument, however, is human reason? This question forced Jewish thinkers to enter the complicated realm of epistemology and to establish criteria to distinguish between the true and false findings of reason. Sharp debates on these problems were conducted in Saadiah's time among both the Jews and their neighbors. Discussing the various schools of thought concerning creation versus the eternity of the world, the gaon enumerated thirteen theories, the last four of which were based on certain assumptions concerning human cognition. One group argued in favor of eternity because it believed only "in what is subject to the perception of their senses." Next to these "materialists" were the "sophists," who considered everything both eternal and created because "the reality of things depends solely on [men's] opinions concerning them." A third school of "skeptics," or rather "ephectics," claimed that "human reason is full of uncertainties" and hence rejected the idea of any objective truth altogether. Even more extremely the school of "agnostics" feigned complete ignorance. Repudiating both the teachings of science and the perception of senses, they asserted "that nothing possesses any reality whatever." Some of these approaches had been inherited from the ancient schools of philosophy, but they were further refined through the speculations of Greek and Syriac theologians and Muslim scholars and applied with particular ardor to the problems of the relations between faith and reason.[34]

In their overriding quest for certainty the Jewish thinkers were prepared to adopt the regnant Aristotelian theories of cognition, only revising them so as to fit their religious needs. They all agreed on the importance of sensual perceptions as the basis of human experience and, hence, also of human knowledge, but they stressed both the fallibility of the senses and their own inability to reach beyond corporeal things. Man has, therefore, been endowed also with both "the knowledge of the intellect" (a term apparently used by Saadiah as a substitute for Aristotle's primary premises), which increases vastly the range of his immediate knowledge, and the "knowledge of necessary things," that is, derivative knowledge secured by cogent demonstration, or what Aristotle had called scientific knowledge. Many medieval writers, beginning with Israeli, sometimes saw in these parallel or postsensationary faculties the operation of special "internal" or "spiritual" senses with which the human being was equipped. As a physician Israeli was interested in Galen's, Ḥunayn's, and Razi's speculations on the location of these senses in various chambers of the brain, but he proceeded to an independent examination of their epistemological features. Among these internal senses "imagination" was only one step removed from "common sense," which Aristotle had postulated as the main coordinator of the five corporeal senses, but which Israeli placed in the intermediary position between the two sets of senses. More important were "cogitation," which alone made man into an intelligent being, and, finally, "memory," for which Israeli supplied four distinct definitions. In this latter category one could, by easy extension, include not only the individual memory of man, but also the collective memory of the human race or of each group, that is, "tradition." [35]

It was primarily in this relation between cogitation and collective memory that the conflict between faith and reason unveiled itself. Faith was not only religious faith. Some men believed strongly in what they achieved through their own meditation. Others, like many of the persons whom Saadiah observed in his immediate environment, were either uncertain about the truths they had detected or were constantly changing their beliefs. Even Saadiah admitted that doubt per se was not unjustified, provided it led to intensive cogitation which resolved that doubt in favor of firm truth. There was even in his thought an anticipation of the Cartesian doubt, and of its resolution through the observation of the necessary existence of the cogitating individual. Young Maimonides observed that of the four propositions which are generally accepted "to be true and require no proof for their truthfulness" only the first two, namely "perceptions" (of what, for instance, is black or white) and "first ideas" (such as that the whole is greater than the part) are universally recognized. However, the other two, "conventions" and "traditions," are often known among one people and not among others.[36]

Some of the Jewish philosophers, beginning with Saadiah, resolved the difficulty by a "double faith" theory—quite different from the "double truth" theory of the European Avveroists (not Averroës himself) and of the Renaissance age—according to which they believed that the teachings of Scripture are truths both self-evident and demonstrable. For this purpose the gaon assumed that there are really three independent sources of knowledge (sensation, intuition, and logical necessity). But to these he and the other "monotheists" added "the validity of authentic tradition, by reason of the fact that it is based upon the knowledge of the senses as well as that of reason." In many ways Saadiah was an epistemological dogmatist, for he believed that everything in religion could be demonstrated by reason, except the profounder mysteries of the divine essence, hence also the details of the work of Creation as well as the specific aspects of life after death. To ask that man understand these would, in his opinion, be tantamount to asking that man become God. Otherwise, if there is any conflict between sound reason and an expression in Scripture or of "one of us monotheists" relating to God, "there can be no doubt about it, that that expression was meant to be taken in a figurative sense which the diligent students will find if they seek it." At the same time Saadiah was not a sworn champion of reason as the exclusive guide of man's behavior. Although he often insisted that the quest to know God is a commendable, indeed obligatory pursuit—we recall that he agreed in this point with both the Karaites and Baḥya but was controverted by Halevi—he nevertheless felt that naive adherence to the commandments of the Torah on the part of the uneducated masses is by no means reprehensible. In fact, "women and young people and those who have no aptitude for speculation can thus [through adherence to revelation] also have a perfect faith" within their reach. In the ultimate sense, even for the confirmed rationalist Saadiah, philosophy was decidedly but a handmaiden, albeit an extremely important one, of theology, or rather, of the religious way of life.[37]

Maimonides went further than Saadiah in his insistence on the absolute concordance between faith and reason. Where reason is sure of its own findings, he taught, as in regard to God's incorporeality, all contrary-sounding assertions of Scripture must be interpreted figuratively. Only when an argument is not fully proved, as in the case of the eternity of the Universe, it "is not sufficient reason for rejecting the literal meaning of a biblical text and explaining it figuratively"—a task which Maimonides found less difficult, if it were really needed, than the reinterpretation of the "corporeal" phrases. Not unjustifiedly, indeed, he was called an adherent of "the single faith theory of the rationalist type." Even Maimonides, however, recognized Reason's basic limitations. Not only are there fundamental differences, he contended, between different individuals, but also "a boundary is undoubtedly set to the human mind which it cannot pass." To resolve this conflict he drew a line between the sublunary and the superlunary worlds. Taking, as was customary then, "the philosopher" (Aristotle) as the representative of human reason at its highest, he declared,

I hold that the theory of Aristotle is undoubtedly correct as far as the things are concerned which exist between the sphere of the moon and the center of the earth. Only an ignorant person rejects it, or a person with preconceived opinions of his own, which he desires to maintain and to defend, and which lead him to ignore clear facts. But what Aristotle says concerning things above the sphere of the moon is, with few exceptions, mere imagination and opinion; to a still greater extent this applies to his system of Intelligences, and to some of his metaphysical views; they include great improbabilities, . . . [promote] ideas which all nations consider as evidently corrupt, and cause views to spread which cannot be proved.

It is only in that realm closed to human reason, however, that we may accept the teachings of tradition unquestioningly. Elsewhere we are in duty bound to prove by reasoning the truth of everything asserted by tradition. Where no such proof is possible, the fault is evidently not with reason as such, but rather with our personal faulty understanding of the sources of our tradition. Evidently, revelation is not to be taken literally in these cases, but rather subjected to a close, if allegorical, interpretation which would harmonize it with reason. That is why "homonyms" play such a great role in the whole Maimonidean system; in his opinion, the same words have an altogether different meaning when applied to God than they have in the ordinary world of man.[38]

Ibn Gabirol's position is still more complicated. One of his main contentions, permeating both his philosophic and his poetic writings, is man's total inability to grasp God's divine majesty. It has been pointed out that for this reason he used several hundred different designations for God—a confession, as it were, of his utter helplessness before God's unfathomable grandeur. In his "Royal Crown" he chanted: "By the side of Thy wisdom, all human knowledge turneth to folly." Combining the heritage of *Merkabah* mysticism with the Neoplatonic doctrine of emanation, he believed that the Throne of Glory is high above the sphere of Intelligence, which emanated from it, and that human imagination can reach only up to that sphere. On the other hand, the intelligible soul of man, though but slightly above the senses, is in direct line of the descending emanations, and hence at least potentially shares the knowledge of ultimate things. In it were imbedded from the outset the knowledge of the secondary substances and the secondary accidents, which it grasps through the operation of the senses, although only the primary substances and accidents are directly accessible to the latter. It is, says our poet-philosopher, like the reading of the book. Only after we note the letters through the sense of vision "is the soul reminded of the reading of these letters and their true meaning." The entire process of cognition is, indeed, such a series of reminders of what the intelligible soul had potentially known from its origin in the world of the Intellect, since "the form of the Intellect embraces all forms, for all forms exist in it." In short, human reason, starting with the cognition of corporeal things, communicated to it by the senses, may through total immersion in the realm of the Intellect secure an understanding of the highest forms up to the very sphere of the Intellect, just below the Throne of Glory. Even in such ecstatic immersion, however, man cannot look forward to a real "union" with God, but at best only to a "communion" with Him.[39]

Mysticism of this type, though stressing the limitations of reason and insisting upon ecstasy's superiority over pure speculation as a source of knowledge of ultimate things, was nevertheless far from antirationalist. There was nothing in Ibn Gabirol's teachings that even faintly resembled the attitude of such Muslim opponents of the rational faith as Maulana Jalalu'ddin Rumi, the influential thirteenth-century founder of a Persian order of dervishes, who declared "From Satan logic, and from Adam love," a statement which was to find its counterpart in Luther's even sharper rejection of reason—"the devil's whore,"—in matters of faith. For Ibn Gabirol, logic was an integral part of wisdom, which was not only divinely ordained but the most direct emanation from the Deity. Hence true logic could not possibly controvert the revealed word of God. On the contrary, the attainment of true knowledge was, in Ibn Gabirol's opinion, the very goal of human existence. From knowledge springs action, and together "knowledge and action liberate the soul from the captivity of nature, and cleanse it from its obscurity and darkness. Then the soul returns to its upper world." Since the knowledge of the First Being, however, is unattainable, because His essence "is above everything and infinite," one must try to contemplate His creatures and through His works secure an inkling of Him.[40]

In his other works, Ibn Gabirol added the Bible as a source of knowledge. On proper reading of Scripture, he believed, if need be with the aid of allegory, one may find there some of those hidden insights open to the intelligible soul in a state of ecstasy. Although we know nothing of Ibn Gabirol's direct Bible commentaries and in his "Fountain of Life" no biblical passages are cited, we possess through Abraham ibn Ezra's mediation a fair sampling of his allegorical method, as in the aforementioned example of Jacob's ladder (Gen. 28:12), which, in the poet's interpretation, represented the higher soul, while the angels marching up and down on it reflected the process of the acquisition of wisdom. At least as a poet, however, Ibn Gabirol felt that in such return to the upper world from which it had come the human soul requires divine aid and direction. In one of his most moving religious poems, *Sesoni rab bekha,* he sang,

My joy in Thee is great, O Dweller of my abode!
  I remember Thee, and all my sorrows pass away.
To Thee belongs the grace, and I can only thank Thee,
  But I have naught to do it, except the words I pray.
If the beings on high cannot comprehend Thy might,
  How could my thought dare it, being so much weaker still?
Prepare and guide me with grace along the righteous paths,
  So that my desire may wholly partake of Thy will.[41]

No less devoid of outright antirationalist biases was the other great Spanish poet-philosopher, Yehudah Halevi. He, too, felt the insufficiency of speculation in solving the riddles of existence. While criticizing extreme rationalism along the lines of Ghazzali's "Incoherence of the Philosophers," he nevertheless deeply approved of the ultimate need and value of knowledge. He merely contended that the human quest for knowledge, if unsupported by revelation, was doomed to failure, because revelation alone opened up avenues to absolute truths without error or defect. Time and again his Jewish spokesman assured the king of Khazaria: "Heaven forbid that there should be anything in the Bible to contradict that which is manifest or proved [by reason]." Yet the "philosophers" erred not only because their quest for knowledge was cold and impersonal—in one of his famous poems, Halevi decried Greek wisdom as bearing "no fruit, only flowers"—but also because their knowledge itself had no direct relationship to the essence of things. Compared with a genuinely religious thinker in his innermost religious experience, the philosopher resembles but the author of a travelogue or of an *ars poetica,* who can never furnish more than a mere inkling of the living experience of the traveler himself or of the creative joy of the gifted poet at work. That is why all speculative arguments fall flat in the presence of revealed truths. Just as only the internal senses have access to incorporeal perceptions, so can only a divinely revealed word or vision communicate to man the knowledge of mysterious essences. For this reason, the great prophetic visions,

> which cannot be approached by speculation, have been rejected by Greek philosophers, because speculation negates everything the like of which it has not seen. Prophets, however, confirm it, because they cannot deny what they were privileged to behold with their mind's eye. . . . These statements were borne out by contemporary sages who had witnessed their prophetic afflatus. Had the Greek philosophers seen them when they prophesied and performed miracles, they would have acknowledged them, and sought by speculative means to discover how to achieve such things.[42]

We shall see how fundamental a role prophecy and miracles played in the entire outlook on life of these medieval thinkers. Even those who, like Maimonides, held the cogitative abilities of man in higher esteem than did Halevi nevertheless recognized the prophetic visions and miracles as historic facts which could not be disputed. Only when the two lines of evidence seemed completely irreconcilable was one entitled to use the harmonistic method of allegory to make the prophetic truth identical with that secured by reason.

However, even in this respect there is an essential difference between Philo and Ibn Gabirol or Maimonides, who went further in this direction than any other medieval Jewish philosopher. Unlike Greek philosophy, medieval thought was basically dynamic. History had become a permanent force in the outlook of man. Consequently, the new allegory did not try to eliminate all historical factors and to replace them by abstract moral ideas. Even Maimonides, the most systematic of Jewish sages and consequently nearest to the Greek mode of thinking, does not allegorize away each historical reference in the Bible. Undoubtedly, myths and the more anthropomorphic expressions often receive a new moral meaning in his *Guide;* his cryptic suggestion that Adam represents the ever-active form, Eve passive matter, and the serpent imagination, may serve as one such illustration. But historical narratives in Scripture, which "many consider as being of no use whatever," he accepts as historical facts which were described for "a necessary reason." [43]

The more exaltedly nationalistic among the philosophers, such as Abraham bar Ḥiyya and Halevi, derived much more inspiration from the flowing stream of Jewish history than did their less emotional confreres. Abraham bar Ḥiyya, the mathematician, visualized the divine government of the universe under the aspect of great historical periods corresponding to the days of the Creation. His contemporary, Halevi, also had an irresistible, intuitive feeling that history was the primary element in Judaism. In his famous dialogue between the representatives of the three creeds and the king of the Khazars, the Jew at the outset startled his interlocutor by defining his religion not as a belief "in the Creator of the world, its Governor and Guide and in Him who created and keeps" men, a definition which the king expected to hear from the lips of every religious man, but by declaring, "I believe in the God of Abraham, Isaac and Israel, who led the children of Israel out of Egypt with signs and miracles; who fed them in the desert and gave them the land, after having made them traverse the sea and the Jordan in a miraculous way; who sent Moses with His law and subsequently thousands of prophets, who confirmed His law by promises to the observant and threats to the disobedient." Through this paradoxical accentuation of the historical theme, Halevi opened a lengthy discussion which always reverted to the ideas of the chosen people, of Israel's past, of its mission, and of its laws and observances. Indeed, in all his poetic and philosophic writings, the Jewish nationality occupies the central position. Perhaps that is why he could, without giving up his nationalist orientation, declare that acceptance or rejection of the

Aristotelian belief in the eternity of this world was comparatively irrelevant, while most of the other Jewish as well as Arab philosophers devoted a good deal of energy to proving by philosophic reasonings that the world must have been created by God.[44]

GOD AND THE UNIVERSE

Halevi was not the only one to concede the admissibility of the eternity of the universe from the standpoint of reason. In fact, while he eventually declined to accept this belief, because it contradicted the higher truth of Revelation, Ibn Gabirol contended that matter is the great metaphysical stuff of all creation, material as well as spiritual. Going beyond Plotinus and his own Spanish Jewish successor, Pseudo-Baḥya, both of whom admitted matter only into the fourth emanation, Ibn Gabirol assigned to it a supreme position within the first emanation itself. Abraham ibn Ezra likewise distinctly hinted that creation in time referred only to the sublunary world, which renews itself every twenty-five thousand years, while the upper spheres as well as the angels are eternal. Even Maimonides eventually had to admit that creation *ex nihilo* could not be proved, and to acquiesce in the assertion that he would "by philosophical reasoning, show that our theory of the Creation is more acceptable than that of the Eternity of the Universe; and although our theory includes points open to criticism, I will show that there are much stronger reasons for the rejection of the theory of our opponents." [45]

In all these speculations the Platonic-Aristotelian doctrine of primordial matter and primordial form, which in ancient times had already received a variety of detailed formulations, reigned supreme. Hardly any medieval Jewish thinker ventured to contradict the fundamentals of this hypothesis. The farthest some of them ventured to go was to postulate, as did Ibn Daud, that this assumption did not presuppose any real existence of either matter or form but was merely a method of making the origin of the Universe more nearly comprehensible to the human mind. "In all that we have mentioned here," Ibn Daud declared, "about this order of things, we did not wish to convey the idea that God had created matter, which remained void of any form, and that only later did He invest it with a corporeal form, and still later with the [specific] forms of the elements. For there is nothing in God's work in which the object does not have a definite existence in accordance with its determined aim. . . . All that I wish to indicate by this order is that it exists in this way in the mind, not in the real sequence of time." This existence in the mind only had by then become a frequent refuge of the medieval Jewish thinkers, and not of them alone. They postulated such purely conceptual, rather than real, existence whenever they had to bridge the conflict between a theory reached by reasoning but not borne out by direct observation. This was particularly true in their discussions of space and time. In connection with his discussion of the time argument for Creation, Saadiah combated an heretical view by saying that "the infinite divisibility of a thing can occur so far as we are concerned, only in thought, not in fact, because it is too subtle to be realized in actuality." Abraham bar Ḥiyya declared bluntly, "It [time] does not exist except in the mind." [46]

Most Jewish thinkers, on the other hand, with the exception of Abraham ibn Ezra, conceived of space as an objective reality. The school of agnostics, mentioned by Saadiah, which altogether denied any objective reality, seems to have found no literary exponent among Jews. Because of their belief, as Israel Efros explained it, that "unextended matter is an impossibility," the Jewish philosophers uniformly rejected the Arabian atomist hypothesis. Israeli's scientific mind rebelled against the idea that mathematical points, themselves devoid of magnitude, should ever produce an extended object. Saadiah, to be sure, was somewhat less certain. He discussed the atomistic theory as the very first of the aforementioned divergent theories of creation. Among his four specific objections he also mentioned that advanced by Israeli, but added, "If, however, they hold that these transformations and changes are possible, it is because the All-Wise Creator is able to effect them," in which case he would rather believe in creation out of nothing at all. But this concession in no way weakened the gaon's conviction of a spatial reality called into being by the divine act of creation.[47]

Saadiah's discussion of these arguments was but a part of his analysis of the twelve theories apparently controverting his own four proofs in favor of creation *ex nihilo.* These proofs, originating with the Arabic Mutakallimun, were then widely debated. Even a simple pietist like Baḥya felt obliged to pay homage to the expectation of many readers and to insert into the section dealing with the unity of God a chapter beginning:

The premises which clearly lead to the inference that the world has a Creator who created it *ex nihilo* are three: 1. that a thing does not make itself; 2. that causes are limited in number; and since their number is limited, they must have a First Cause unpreceded by a previous cause; 3. that everything that is a compound must have been brought into existence. When these premises will have been established, the inference from them will be clear to everyone who knows how to combine and apply them, that the world has a Creator who created it *ex nihilo,* as will, with God's help, appear from our exposition.

Maimonides went further and debated seven such arguments, only in part overlapping those presented by Saadiah and Baḥya. Summarizing these and other data, Harry A. Wolfson marshaled a total of nine basic arguments which, at one time or another, members of the school of Kalam had advanced in favor of creation, namely from (1) finitude; (2) composition; (3) accidents; (4) time or the generations of man; (5) the revolutions of the celestial bodies; (6) immortal souls; (7) analogy; (8) determination; and (9) preference. These arguments were driven home to the educated readers in the wide expanse of Islam in all forms of writings. According to Maimonides, Arab authors frequently employed "rhyme, rhythm, and poetical diction, and sometimes mysterious phrases which perhaps are intended to startle persons listening to their discourses, and to deter those who might otherwise criticize them." Only few contemporaries ventured, like Maimonides, to reject them outright as purely verbal. "I will not deceive myself," the latter wrote, "and consider dialectical methods as proofs; and the fact that a certain proposition has been proved by dialectical argument will never induce me to accept that proposition, but, on the contrary, will weaken my faith in it." Nevertheless, long beyond Maimonides' time, indeed almost to our day, these arguments, in ever new modifications, have enlivened all debates on the problems of the origin and structure of the Universe.[48]

Yet one cannot escape the impression that, despite all this furor, the problems of creation *ex nihilo* touched deeply but a few individuals. Although there doubtless existed in the Jewish community, as among the Muslims and Christians, persons who were prepared to follow Aristotle to his last logical consequences and to postulate an eternal Universe coexisting side by side with the Unmoved Mover, they seem to have kept such ideas to themselves. Not only do we possess no writings by medieval Jews publicly defending these theories, we possess almost no records of private debates along these lines. Most of the serious students were merely "perplexed" by the convincing and intrinsically consistent views of the Stagirite. For such persons it seemed sufficient to show the difficulties inherent in the Aristotelian concepts, in order to persuade them that they might peaceably accept the traditional outlook.

Greater unanimity prevailed in regard to the existence of God. Even agnostics tried to prove mainly the eternality of motion and the unchanging character of natural laws, and to deny God's knowledge of particulars and especially of the actions of man. Few, however, ventured to defy tradition, upheld by Plato and Aristotle just as much as by Scripture, and to become professed atheists. Discounting the equivocal religious outlook of Ḥivi, we possess no record of Jewish followers of the atheistic school of Dahriya. Nevertheless, almost every one of the religious thinkers in the Middle Ages exercised his intellect to prove anew the existence of God. Usually proceeding from the known to the unknown, according to the prevailing epistemological principle, they argued from the actuality of the physical world for the necessity of a creation in time, from which they then easily deduced the existence of a creator. Abraham ibn Daud and Maimonides followed in the footsteps of Aristotle and tried to establish the existence of God from the mere existence of the universe, omitting the link of creation. The existence of the physical world in motion, they taught, in itself leads through a causal chain to an unmoved mover, which must be God, just as behind the merely possible existence of the universe unavoidably looms, if one pursues logical reasoning to the end, a Supreme Being endowed with necessary existence.[49]

Precisely this assumption, however, created another difficulty, namely the transition from God the Creator to the created universe. The old question, which had already faced Philo of Alexandria, reemerged now with redoubled intensity. How could an imperfect, finite, and corruptible world emerge from any action by the absolutely perfect, infinite, and incorruptible Creator? Once again the answer which suggested itself was that of some intermediary powers which, though sharing some of God's qualities, are nevertheless sufficiently removed from Him to mark the transition to our world of perdition.

Probably without any direct knowledge of the works of his Alexandrian predecessor and of such of his possible medieval disciples as Benjamin Nahawendi, Ibn Gabirol developed another comprehensive theory of such mediation through a *Logos,* or rather through the divine *Will.* This entity created by God holds, in Ibn Gabirol's opinion, an intermediate position between a divine attribute (a part of the Deity Himself and as such eternal and incorruptible) and an independent hypostasy with somewhat inferior characteristics of its own. Combining the Logos doctrine with Plotinus' theory of emanations—this theory became quite influential in the Middle Ages especially through the impact of a spurious "Theology of Aristotle" and an equally spurious work attributed to Empedocles, with both of which Ibn Gabirol seems to have been familiar—our poet-philosopher postulated a process of creation through emanation. He compared this process with light, which penetrates other objects without losing itself. Although devoting, in a typically scholastic manner, no less than sixty proofs to demonstrating the Will's necessary existence, and although equating it at times with the divine Word and with Wisdom and Largesse (his special tract, *Origo Largitatis,* mentioned in the Latin translation, is unfortunately lost), Ibn Gabirol insisted that "it is impossible to describe the Will. One may only approximate its definition by saying that it is a divine power, creating matter and form and holding them together, and that it is diffused from the highest to the lowest, as is the soul in a body. It is this power which moves and directs everything." In another context, our poet-philosopher combined the ancient hypostasy of Wisdom with his doctrine of Will, and he sang in his "Royal Crown":

Thou art wise. And wisdom is the fount of life and from Thee it welleth
And by the side of Thy wisdom all human knowledge turneth to folly.
Thou art wise, more ancient than all primal things,
And wisdom was the nursling at Thy side.
Thou art wise, and Thou hast not learned from any beside Thee,
Nor acquired wisdom from any save Thyself.
Thou art wise, and from Thy wisdom Thou hast set apart Thy appointed Will,
As a craftsman and an artist,
To cause the continuity of Being to emanate from Nothing,
As light emanates when darting from the eye.

Although the impression created here is that the Will emanated from Wisdom, Ibn Gabirol makes it perfectly clear in his main work that these are really but two designations for the same original divine tool.[50]

Ibn Gabirol's solution, which because of the old Christological reinterpretation of the Logos doctrine was soon greatly to appeal to medieval Christian thinkers, carried little conviction in the Jewish camp. Ibn Daud's venomous attack would not have by itself succeeded in suppressing the "Fountain of Life" as a living part of Jewish literature, especially in the case of so highly revered a poet as Ibn Gabirol, were it not that the contention that "the whole work betrays his [Ibn Gabirol's] weakness in philosophic attainment, and his searching like one who gropes in the dark" sounded convincing to the general run of students by that time trained in the more rigid discipline of Aristotelian dialectics. For example, some of the fifty-six proofs adduced by Ibn Gabirol for the existence of intermediary entities (which Ibn Daud reduced to forty) sounded the less conclusive for being based on a double syllogism, which made the final conclusion dependent on the acceptance of two successive sets of premises.[51]

After rejecting Ibn Gabirol's solution, Ibn Daud and the other Jewish philosophers still had to answer the basic dichotomy between the perfect Creator and the imperfect world. They fell back on the old Aristotelian doctrine of the intermediary world of Intelligences, as it had been modified in the subsequent Hellenistic and Arab schools of philosophy. To harmonize this doctrine with the teachings of Judaism, they merely had to equate these Intelligences with the Angels, so frequently mentioned in the Bible and the Aggadah, the latter itself having absorbed no small number of Hellenistic teachings. To quote Ibn Daud once more (who does not fail on this occasion to attack Ibn Gabirol again): "From the First [Cause] blessed be He, emanated the first emanation, without any intermediary. This first thing is called, by their [the philosophers'] agreement, Intelligence, and in the language of the Torah, Angel. This first emanation is undoubtedly one only, but its oneness is not like the oneness of the First [Cause], for the First is, as was explained, in His essence of necessary existence, one in every respect, whereas the first emanation, . . . being dependent on someone else, . . . possesses only possible existence." Combining these philosophic teachings with the Aristotelian-Ptolemaic astronomic world outlook, Ibn Daud, Maimonides, and most of their confreres postulated the existence of eight other Intelligences, together governing the nine Spheres (the all-encompassing sphere, the fixed stars, and the five planets, the Sun, and the Moon), whose motion they direct by their perpetual desire toward the higher Intelligence of the preceding stage. The lowest of these Intelligences, governing the sphere of the Moon, gives rise to the final, the tenth, called Active Intelligence, which governs the sublunary world. Each of these stages becomes the more imperfect, the more remote it is from the First Cause.

There is nothing [Maimonides declared] in the opinion of Aristotle on this subject contrary to the teaching of Scripture. The whole difference between him and ourselves is this: he believes all these beings to be eternal, coexisting with the First Cause as its necessary effect; but we believe that they have had a beginning, that God created the Intelligences, and gave the spheres the capacity of seeking to become like them; that in creating the Intelligences and the spheres, He endowed them with their governing powers.[52]

In fact, as we recall, some philosophically less rigid Jewish thinkers saw no irreconcilable conflict with tradition in the acceptance of a primordial Matter, which God invested with its first

Form, and thus "created." He thereby set in motion all the other forces leading to the world of Intelligences and, ultimately, to the sublunary world of perdition. Even more strongly than Halevi, his friend Abraham ibn Ezra clearly intimated that he saw in such a doctrine of the eternality of Matter nothing contrary to Judaism. In his cryptic way he interpreted the word *bara* (created) in the biblical story of Creation as etymologically derived from setting limits, which may well have meant that God merely "delimited" Matter, that is invested it with Form. "The enlightened person," he concludes, "will understand." At the same time Ibn Ezra postulated the existence not only of the two worlds, that of Intelligences and Spheres and that of sublunary life, but divided the former into two: an uppermost world of Intelligences or Angels, and an intermediary world of the Spheres. Since he merely hinted at this division as a correlative to the division of the desert Tabernacle into a Holy of Holies, a Holy section, and an outer court, we cannot be too certain of his motivation in separating the Intelligences from the Spheres, which they were supposed to govern. Possibly he saw in this separation a way of reconciling his astrological determinism, presupposing the decisive influence of the motion of stars on the sublunary world, with the occasional miraculous irruption of the divine will, modifying that influence by the operation of the higher Intelligences or Angels.[53]

An intermediary position was taken by Abraham bar Ḥiyya. Although of little influence among philosophers, his doctrine, by penetrating the German pietist circles, exercised considerable influence on the formation of a focal doctrine of the later medieval Kabbalah. The distinguished scientist utilized old Neoplatonic concepts (his terminology reveals that he had before him a Hebrew text which had utilized Arabic sources), but he gave them a genuine Jewish coloring by interpreting them in a penetrating fashion into the biblical story of creation.

We say [he wrote] that on the first day the upper light arose by God's word, which is His will. . . . That light, however, which arose on the first day, did not shine upon the earth, for the original bright light [*or bahir*] had neither corporeality nor matter. . . . But you will find in this chapter [in Genesis, on the creation during the first day] the mention of light five times and of darkness three times. We do find indeed that on the first day were created five light stages, or light worlds which are above heaven. These correspond to the five stages or, in the words of philosophers, five worlds.

Bar Ḥiyya calls these worlds: (1) the wonderful *Light* which appeared on Sinai; (2) the *Voice* which Moses heard among the cherubs—these two worlds correspond to the Throne of Glory and the Holy Spirit; (3) Wisdom and Torah, which the philosophers called the world of intellect; (4) the world of the Soul and Spirit; and, finally, (5) that of Creation (the *yeṣirah*), which is the light preserved for the pious in the world to come. This division, as Gershom Scholem has shown, was utilized already in Pseudo-Saadiah's commentary on *Yeṣirah* and, through it, began influencing the crucial kabbalistic doctrine of the four worlds.[54]

DIVINE ATTRIBUTES

The main attention of the medieval metaphysicians, however, was directed not to the existence of God, which few disputed, nor to the problem of creation, which most thinkers were eventually ready to admit as insoluble by logical reasoning, but to the question of the divine attributes. In this realm manifested itself most clearly the contrast between the colorful designations of the divine essence and activity found in Scripture, and the rarified concepts of God's sublime spirituality derived from philosophic speculation. Here, moreover, the various attitudes of the three great denominations, as well as some of the social forces behind them, came distinctly to the fore, no matter how much they seemed to be divested of their earthbound character in their metaphysical garb. The problem of attributes was especially vital for Christians, whose thinkers saw therein a means of reconciling monotheism with the Trinitarian dogma. Even in the pre-Islamic age, the Syriac sectarians engaged in heated controversies about the homiletical explanation of Old Testament passages in the Trinitarian sense. Saadiah, for example, felt prompted to reject the Christian interpretation of the verse in II Samuel 23:2, "The spirit of the Lord spoke by me, and His word was upon my tongue," which served to prove the three separate entities: the Lord, the spirit, and His word (Logos, "son"). Translated into philosophic terminology, the Trinitarian creed usually assumed the form of the three attributes of God's Life, Omnipotence, and Omniscience. Once this theme was raised in the Syriac schools of the pre-Islamic age, it never rested until it found its final medieval (as well as its first modern) formulation in Spinoza.[55]

Of course, the fundamentals of the doctrine of attributes are much older; they go back to the early patristic literature, even to Philo. However, not until the rise of Islam and the sharp attacks by its spokesmen on Christian Trinitarianism did the issue loom large in the minds of eastern Christians, especially Nestorians, who had long lived peaceably under the dualistic Sassanian regime. We may thus understand also why, to cite A. S. Tritton, "the attributes of God appear suddenly in Muslim theology in the middle of the second century [A.H.]." Rationalist Muslims, especially Mu'tazilites, readily seized upon the attributes as a means of reinterpreting rationally the various adjectives associated with God in the Qur'an. That is why one of their early leaders, Ibn Hudail, did not mind accepting even the particular three attributes stressed by Christians, calling forth Shahrastani's censure that he had thus unwittingly incorporated in his doctrine the three Christian "persons." But one must not lose sight of the intervening great Almohade upheaval, which had brought into much sharper focus the idea of purifying the doctrine of God's unity from all possible encumbrances.[56]

Saadiah, who quoted the Christian interpretation of the passage in Samuel, as well as of Job 33:4, blamed the misunderstanding on the interpreters' unfamiliarity with the Hebrew language. Despite his realization, however, that the assumption of the three attributes of Life, Power, and Knowledge brought grist to the mill of Christian Trinitarianism, he, like Ibn Hudail before him, did not hesitate to employ them himself as clear derivatives from the belief in Creation. He merely argued that the Christians "erred" in concluding therefrom "the existence of distinction in God's personality." In fact, he contended, these attributes have no independent existence even in human thought. They "are grasped by our minds at one blow [though] our tongues are unable to convey them with one word, since we do not find in language an expression that would embrace these three connotations." Similarly, Nissim bar Jacob ibn Shahin of Kairuwan insisted in the introduction of his commentary on the Talmud on the identity of the three attributes with God's essence. Other Jewish, as well as Muslim theologians altogether abandoned the limitation to three attributes. Many Mutakallimun first increased their number to four by adding Will; others added still another attribute by subdividing Life into two: Existence and Life; still others felt that Unity, Truth, and Eternity likewise belonged to the integral attributes, making a total of eight. With perfect insouciance Baḥya wrote of "our faith that He exists, is one and eternal, who was and will be, the first and the last, mighty, wise and living." The latter three attributes were here combined with those of Existence, Unity, and Eternity in a way which, if David Neumark's interpretation is correct, foreshadowed the doctrine of attributes as "processes without a substratum or a bearer," since Baḥya seems to have denied that God had any kind of substance, spiritual or physical.[57]

Still others, however, concluded that all attributes were but derivatives of human traits ascribed to the Deity, and decided that only "negative" attributes were really justified. Not surprisingly it was David al-Muqammiṣ, the first Jewish philosopher, who reached that conclusion. Having returned to Judaism after years of association with leading Syriac theologians, he argued that "this is the error of Christians to contend that the Lord lives with a Life which is the Holy Spirit, and knows with Wisdom which is the Word, called Son." In contrast to any such views,

> We say that the Lord is One, not like the One of the large kind, or the One of the small kind, not like the One in number, nor like the One in the Creation, but in its correct simplicity in which there is neither change nor composition [of various elements]. He is One in his Glory and there is no other resembling Him. All this means that He is the First but has no beginning, the Last but has no end, that He is the occasion for all that happens, and the cause for all that is caused.

Al-Muqammiṣ, finally, invoked the authority of Aristotle, viewed through the spectacles of the Neoplatonic commentators, as to the preference one ought to give to negative over positive attributes while speaking about God. Ibn Gabirol seems to have taken a similar position and, in his philosophic book, rather carefully avoided any discussion of divine attributes. This did not prevent him from using certain adjectives in describing the First Cause. He did not even hesitate to follow the fashion of the age and to introduce his ethical treatise with the formula: "Blessed be the Lord, the mighty and wise, the near one who answers, the one and everlasting, the first and the creator, and may He be exalted on high." The poet-philosopher, and most of his listeners, readily drew a line between such "loose" terminology used in prayers or in ordinary parlance, and the deliberate use of attributes in a work of disciplined philosophic thought.[58]

Behind all these formulations lay one fundamental assumption: the absolute unknowability of God. While all existence, contended Ibn Gabirol, consists of the elements of That, What, How, and When, God as the absolutely existent one (the absolute That) has nothing of the other three. Hence all attributes referring to God can mean only a negation of the nonexistence of these features in the divine essence. This doctrine of essentially "negative" attributes was, in fact, ascribed in contemporary Muslim letters to Plato and Aristotle. Following Al-Muqammiṣ, Ibn Ṣaddiq expressly quoted "the philosopher" as saying that "it is more correct to remove all affirmative assertions from the Creator." Building on all these foundations and, as we recall, personally animated with a crusading spirit against any form of anthropomorphism or anthropopathism with respect to God (in some respect doubtless a reflection of his and his family's tragic experiences under Ibn Tumart and his cohorts' uncompromising unitarianism), Maimonides finally developed his magnificent exposition of the theory of "negative attributes." After a discussion extending over several chapters, he declared: "Know that the negative attributes of God are the true attributes; they do not include any incorrect notions or any deficiency whatever in reference to God, while positive attributes imply polytheism and are inadequate." He was convinced, therefore, that anyone affirming positive attributes "unconsciously loses his belief in God." On the other hand, the human mind looks for some approximation of the divine essence and its manifestations in the Universe. Hence, it adopts a number of descriptions chiefly derived from God's observable actions. This is, indeed, the import of the numerous divine attributes found in Scripture. One must always bear in mind that, on account of the poverty of human language, homonyms are necessary. They mean one thing when applied to men, and another when applied to God. None of Maimonides' Jewish successors ventured thereafter seriously to undermine a solution which seemed to offer complete reconciliation of the idea of pure spiritual monotheism with the scriptural descriptions of God's power and greatness. Whenever a Jewish philosopher thereafter spoke of positive attributes, he immediately emphasized their purely subjective character (Gersonides: in "discourse"; Albo: "intellectual conceptions").[59]

To what extent the medieval Jewish thinkers were influenced by Islamic theology can also be seen in their emphasis on one or the other attribute. Nowhere in Jewish or Islamic theology of the day, for example, do we find God's holiness as a supreme attribute. Power and justice are those divine elements which really matter—obviously a reflection of the Islamic expansion and of the time-honored Semitic heritage of God as the Lord and Supreme Judge. The Muslim emphasis on God as the God of Mercy and Lord of Judgment, embodied in the Qur'an (especially Sura 14) and from it in the Muslim daily prayers, also penetrated Jewish theology, displacing the great prophetic pronunciamentos of holiness. Only a poet like Ibn Gabirol, ever cognizant of the supreme importance of the *qedushah* in Jewish liturgy, stressed the attribute of holiness in his philosophic work, as when he taught that "the Creator *ex nihilo* is only the First Agent, high and holy." [60]

One of the most vital issues confronting the followers of the three scriptural revelations was that of anthropomorphism. The Bible, representing in its various cultural strata different stages in the ancient Israelitic and Jewish religion, contained many expressions which sounded strange to a philosophically trained medieval thinker. Even sharper objections were raised by the rationalist opponents of the rabbinic Aggadah and of the Jewish gnostic writings. The minute descriptions of God, his throne, and the angels as imagined by the populace in a religiously exuberant age were subjected to a most ruthless scrutiny. There was no end to the repercussions provoked, as we recall, by books of the type of the *She'ur qomah* (Measure of the Divine Stature). Although cherishing a tradition which ascribed the original rejection of anthropomorphism to a Jew, Labid ibn al-Asam, Muslim rationalists ridiculed every pertinent utterance in Jewish writings. The fratricidal hatred of Karaites injected further venom into the controversy. The generally moderate Qirqisani merely reechoed the prevailing opinion of his fellow sectarians when he said that the Rabbanites "attribute to Him [human] likeness and corporeality, and describe Him with most shameful descriptions" (*K. al-Anwar,* I.3, 2, p. 15; *HUCA,* VII, 331).

It was a natural reaction for the enlightened Rabbanites vigorously to deny the belief in God's corporeality. Saadiah, in replying to the Karaite, Ibn Saqawaihi, pointed out that the accusation was wholly based upon quotations from the Aggadah, apocryphal writings, or *piyyuṭim,* rather than from the official works, such as the Mishnah, the Mekhiltot, and the Targum. "Moreover," he added, "all these passages have a figurative meaning just as much as the analogous passages of the Bible." From the time of Saadiah on, indeed, medieval philosophers made it a point to interpret allegorically all suspicious passages in the Bible and in subsequent literature. Ḥananel, for example, though mainly a halakhist rather than a philosopher, was greatly wrought up over the Karaite accusation.

Nowhere in the Talmud [he asserted] is mention made that any Israelite whatever ascribes human likeness to his Creator, blessed be His name and memory. Some of the world's wicked men, the heretics, however, invent false stories in order to debase [us]. He who repaid to the generation of the flood, will pay back to them.

In this respect Maimonides went further than his predecessors. Abandoning his usual calm, he concluded his philosophic argument: "Therefore bear in mind that by the belief in corporeality or in anything connected with corporeality, you would provoke God to jealousy and wrath, kindle His fire and anger, become His foe, His enemy and His adversary in a higher degree than by the worship of idols." He even codified it as a matter of law that a Jew who believes in corporeality is a heretic—a statement which naturally provoked the caustic rebuttal of Abraham ben David of Posquières, that "greater and better men than he have followed that trend of thought." [61]

Despite these objections, Maimonides' inclusion of the noncorporeality of God among the thirteen articles of faith made it a permanent fixture of Jewish liturgy. Before long even persons who unperturbedly took many biblical descriptions of divine moods or actions in their literal sense began reciting daily, "I believe with complete faith that the Creator, may His name be blessed, is not a body and cannot be reached by corporeal senses, nor does He possess any likeness whatsoever." Of course, as is usual with deep-rooted prejudices, protestations of this type made little impression on anti-Jewish opinion. Long before Maimonides, Moses ibn Ezra complained that the "tyranny" of Gentile nations was preventing the Jews from giving a decisive reply to their accusations of Jewish anthropomorphism.[62]

MAN AND HIS SOUL

This wholly transcendent and unknowable God must have had a purpose in creating the world. Even Ibn Gabirol who, as we recall, was prepared to place Matter in the very realm of intelligible entities and to look for it in the First Emanation, adopted the principle of the Will as the supreme instrument in both the Creation and the subsequent government of the world. In this way he reconciled a theory of the Godhead and its emanations, which tended to become a purely naturalistic process and logically pointed to a pantheistic doctrine, with the teachings of Judaism of a God acting out of His free will when He brought the world into being.

Ibn Gabirol's teachings, to be sure, generally exercised little influence on the later evolution of Jewish thought. Even among his numerous Christian disciples it was only his admirer, William of Auvergne, who took up his doctrine of the Will, largely because of its associations with Wisdom and the Word and its ensuing affinity to the Christian doctrine of the Logos. However, almost all other Jewish thinkers likewise looked for some ultimate teleological motivations. Maimonides' exclamation, "I contend that no intelligent person can assume that any of the actions of God can be in vain, purposeless or unimportant," was shared by the overwhelming majority of his confreres. True, the savant of Fusṭaṭ himself warned his readers against mistakes in the inquiry into the purpose of existence, usually arising from man's "erroneous idea about himself . . . that the whole world exists only for his sake," and from his deep ignorance "about the nature of the sublunary world, and about the Creator's intention to give existence to all beings whose existence is possible, because existence is undoubtedly good." Considering these passages as crucial to the teleological doctrine of Maimonides, despite apparent contradictions in other statements, Zevi Diesendruck has ingeniously reconstructed that doctrine and pointed out the great role of Will and Wisdom in the Maimonidean cosmology and its underlying objective, the cosmic importance of morality.[63]

Maimonides' statement about the goodness of all things did not mean that he and the other Jewish philosophers paid no heed to the existence of evil in the world. In fact, their predominant transcendental optimism went hand in hand with a deep immanent pessimism, that is with a conviction that what they called the sublunary world was full of physical and moral degeneration. Apart from the cosmological aspects of this dichotomy between a perfect Creator and an imperfect Creation, which, as we recall, was one of the mainsprings of their philosophical speculations, the medieval thinkers were much concerned with its ethical implications. The ancient problems of theodicy appeared now in a new light, and they challenged the ingenuity of the thinkers of the three faiths.

Jewish philosophers were familiar with the answers furnished by the ancient prophets and the authors of Job and Ecclesiastes. They also knew of the talmudic sages' rejection of Elisha ben Abuyah. Led, we are told, by his observation of two successive similar incidents, in one of which a lawbreaker escaped unscathed, while in the other a boy, who in the process fulfilled two commandments for which the biblical lawgiver had promised long life, died instantaneously, Elisha became a "different man" (*aḥer*) and joined the Gnostics. The rabbis had explained such frequent experiences of "the righteous man faring badly, while the evildoer prospers" by their doctrine of retribution after death, where the balance is easily restored in favor of the just (Ḥagigah 14b–15b; j. II.1, 77b).

Nevertheless, the medieval thinkers still were deeply concerned with this problem of apparent divine injustice. They unanimously repudiated the Epicurean doctrine that every happening in the Universe is the result of mere chance, as well as its Aristotelian modification that at least in the sublunary world chance reigns supreme. Maimonides discussed both these views at some length and rejected them outright. Similarly, he found Muslim fatalism, especially in its Ash'arite version, totally inacceptable. He was less sharply opposed to the Mu'tazilite view, which, he admitted, was shared by some geonim (including Saadiah and Samuel ben Ḥofni), and which postulated ultimate divine compensation for the sufferings of every being, including children and animals. Like Ibn Ṣaddiq and others, Maimonides rejected the latter view as going too far. He contended that God's supervision outside humanity extends only to species, while chance alone determines the fate of individual animals and plants. He explained this difference by the fact that "divine Providence is connected with divine intellectual influence, and the same beings which are benefited by the latter so as to become intellectual, and to comprehend things comprehensible to rational beings, are also under the control of divine Providence, which examines all their deeds in order to reward or punish them." Man alone, moreover, other thinkers might have added, shares in this way the spiritual as well as the physical elements making up the Universe which entitles him exclusively to be styled the Microcosm. This doctrine expatiated by Shabbetai Donnolo in his commentary on similar concepts adumbrated in the "Book of Creation," furnished a peg for another scientist, Ibn Ṣaddiq, to attach to it his encyclopedic work on all facets of the life of that Microcosm on earth.[64]

All these and similar teachings by other philosophers presupposed the existence of a world to come, where the ultimate reward or punishment retrieves the distorted balance in this world. In fact, for Saadiah, as for many Mu'tazilites before him, the very problem of divine justice served as eminent proof for the existence of a Hereafter. "We see," he contended, "the godless prospering in this world, while believers are in misery therein. There can, therefore, be no escaping the belief that there exists for the former, as well as for the latter, a second world in which they will be recompensed in justice and righteousness" (*Beliefs and Opinions,* IX.1, p. 257; Hebrew, p. 131; English, p. 326). The possibility of such recompense depended, on the other hand, on the survival in some form of the individual to be so rewarded or punished. While the Mu'tazilites and their Jewish followers had difficulty in explaining the possibility of ultimately rewarding guiltless animals, believers of all three faiths agreed on the survival of the soul in the case of man. With the established Jewish belief in ultimate resurrection, even bodies could be made to partake of some form of the final bliss.

Al-Muqammiṣ was the first strongly to argue in favor of the body's sharing in the eschatological retribution, although he conceded his inability to explain how this could be accomplished. He also insisted on the infinite duration of rewards and punishments, disregarding the often quoted rabbinic sayings concerning the limit of twelve months established for the sufferings of evildoers in Hell. More remarkably, Saadiah accepted both doctrines, arguing only that rewards and punishments are graded in magnitude according to the number and quality of man's deeds on earth. Neither doctrine, however, enjoyed undisputed acceptance among the other medieval theologians. None of them questioned the fact that resurrection could come about only as a result of a miraculous intervention, although here, too, Saadiah tried to supply a rationalistic explanation by postulating the existence of some special ethereal substance in which God preserves the bodies of the righteous, and even more so of the wicked, for permanent ultimate retribution. While few thinkers were ready to follow the gaon in his minute speculations concerning the nature of the Hereafter, they all agreed that immortality of the soul could be proved by rational argument. At the same time, few of them, except for some mystics, subscribed to the doctrine of the transmigration of souls. Sharply combated by Saadiah, this doctrine found few protagonists among later thinkers, although it offered great temptations to attribute certain weird psychological manifestations to a carry-over from some previous existence, and also to give undeserving individuals some new chances for self-redemption in another life span in this world.[65]

The medieval rationalists could not subscribe to the widespread popular conceptions of the physical pleasures or sufferings in the Hereafter, so glowingly described in both the Aggadah and the Qur'an. The less corporeal they conceived the soul to be, the less could they imagine it partaking of physical delights or inflictions. The scientist Israeli suggested that the souls of the just ascended unscathed into the world of the celestial spheres to which they intrinsically belonged, whereas the souls of evildoers, unable to rise to those heights, remained suspended on their way and were "burned" by the spheres' fiery substance. This doctrine, evidently an adaptation of the ancient concepts of the soul's ascent to heaven which had become a *leitmotif* of *merkabah* mysticism, was further elaborated by Saadiah with reference to biblical phrases. Like the sun, he contended, the spheres emanate both light and heat. The just souls are the beneficiaries of the light only, or, in the words of the psalmist, "Light is sown for the righteous" (97:11). The impious suffer the torments of heat alone, for, as Isaiah had said, "Fire shall devour Thine adversaries" (26:11). This explanation was briefly repeated also by Ibn Ṣaddiq and others, only Pseudo-Baḥya indulging in a detailed description of the different punishments inflicted on the various categories of sinners. On the other hand, the reward of a penitent transgressor is depicted by Abraham bar Ḥiyya, in adaptation of an Avicennian doctrine, as consisting in a celestial vision of his enjoyment of precisely those delights which he had missed while overcoming his evil spirit.[66]

Here too, unavoidably, emerged the teleological problem of the purpose of man's creation and his endowment with the ability to live justly or to sin. One of the most noteworthy answers was offered by Baḥya in his remarkable dialogue between the Soul and the Intellect, the latter an ambiguous entity, oscillating between individual human reason and the world *nous*. Although in many details indebted to ancient Hermetic prototypes and in its denunciation of worldly pleasures going beyond the accepted doctrines of Judaism, its teleological reasoning is fairly representative of regnant Jewish philosophic opinion.

It is clear to you [the Intellect tells the Soul] and firmly fixed in your mind that you are pledged to your Creator for His goodness and belong to Him because of the multitude of His kindnesses and His favors. . . . If your longing proceeds from a clear realization how great is your obligation to God, how little it is in your power to fulfill it, and that your neglect of it involves your ruin, while your endeavor to fulfill it will secure your salvation, your longing is genuine and your desire urgent; if not, it is false. . . . The reprehensible dispositions in you are many. But the root and stock from which they spring are two. One of them is love of physical pleasures. . . . This disposition you have acquired from your bad neighbor, the body. The second disposition is love of domination and superiority—pride, haughtiness, jealousy. . . . This disposition you have acquired from your associates, among whom you have grown up.[67]

On his part Ibn Gabirol began his philosophic work with the inquiry into the purpose of man's creation, and came up with the fairly typical answer that man was created for the sake of knowledge. The latter, beginning with the knowledge of oneself, must proceed to the knowledge of the final Cause, and thus fulfill man's chief mission in life. Ibn Gabirol's ethical treatise, too, starts out with the assertion that "man is the object aimed at in the creation of all substances and beings," explains how the senses are so constituted that man may wisely order them, and finally develops the main theme of how man can best proceed to the "improvement of his moral qualities." Even more in line with the accepted doctrines of rabbinic Judaism was the poet's moving prayer in the "Royal Crown," emphasizing man's duty to provide during his short span of life for the day of reckoning. "For if I go out of my world as I came, / And return to my place, naked as I came forth, / Wherefore was I created? And called to see sorrow? / Better were it I had remained where I was." [68]

Such ethical considerations added zest to the intensive preoccupation of the medieval Jewish philosophers with the nature of the soul and its manifestations. Not only Ibn Gabirol, whom Abraham ibn Ezra admiringly called "a great expert in the mystery of the soul," but most other thinkers paid considerable attention to basic psychological problems. With his usual studied obscurity, Ibn Ezra himself once declared that "the knowledge of the soul [*ruaḥ*] is a profound subject requiring demonstration. No one can comprehend even a part thereof, except those enlightened persons whose thought has been clarified through the scales of wisdom and its four elements." Israeli and Pseudo-Baḥya devoted special treatises to this subject, as did Saadiah, whose essay was subsequently incorporated as a chapter (VI) in his philosophic work. In his lengthy discourse on psychology, Halevi's spokesman well summarized the regnant opinion of the time when he postulated the existence of three different divisions in the human soul. "The first," he stated, "is that which is common to animal and plant-life, and is called *vegetative power;* the second, which is common to man and the rest of living beings, is called *vital power;* the third, specific of man is called *rational power.*" Needless to say, these three divisions were not considered three distinct souls existing separately of one another, although in his arguments against ten erroneous schools of thought concerning the nature of the soul Saadiah mentioned a contemporary theory, according to which the rational soul was permanent and located in the heart while the vital soul was transient and spread over the rest of the body. As to the actual location of the soul, opinions differed. 'Anan the Karaite, with his general penchant for literal interpretation of Scripture, accepted verbatim the Deuteronomist's assertion that "the blood is the soul [*ha-nefesh*]" (12:23). Saadiah, rejecting this view, asserted that the blood "is only the seat and center of the soul." At the same time, recalling the frequent juxtaposition of heart and soul in the Bible (Deut. 6:5, 11:13, and elsewhere), he contended that the soul's seat is "in the heart, since it is definitely known that the nerves [veins] which endow the body with the powers of sensation and motion, all have their roots in the heart." The gaon was not blind to the fact of the nerves' ramifications from the brain, but he considered them merely as sinews and ligaments of the body, unconnected with the soul.[69]

The stuff from which the soul was made was likewise subject to differences of opinion. Saadiah and many others, as Philo before them, believed that the soul consisted of some ethereal substance which was, to quote the gaon again, "clearer and purer and simpler than that of the spheres." To Maimonides, as to most Arab philosophers of his day, even such a view sounded too materialistic. Although nowhere devoting special treatment to this "profound subject," the Fusṭaṭ sage clearly intimated his agreement with those philosophers who viewed the immortal souls as not being "substances which occupy a locality or a space," but rather as mere "abstract beings" or "ideals." He also emphasized the homonymous nature of such scriptural designations as *nefesh* or *ruaḥ,* and admiringly commented on certain biblical statements.

How sublime is this idea to him who understands it! for the soul that remains after the death of man is not the soul that lives in a man when he is born; the latter is a mere faculty [and disposition], while that which has a separate existence after death, is a reality; again, the soul and the spirit of man during his life are two different things; therefore the souls and the spirits are both named as existing in man; but separate from the body only one of them exists.

Some scholars believed that only that higher soul, acquired by man in the course of his growth into maturity, achieved immortality, but they failed to state clearly what happened to the souls of deceased innocent babes. Equally controversial was the relationship between the soul and the senses, both internal and external. Going further than any of his predecessors or successors, Ibn Gabirol postulated an actual correlation between the individual senses, as well as the four humors and the four elements accepted by medieval physiology and physics, and the great ethical virtues.[70]

DIVINE GUIDANCE AND LOVE

Partisan fervor thus tinged discussions of the relation of man to God and the universe, even more than it did those of the divine attributes. In the focal point of the most heated controversies was the fateful problem of predestination or free will. All three great religions united in teaching the omnipotence and omniscience of God. On the other hand, religious ethics demanded the responsibility of man for his actions. The medieval mind, not satisfied with the answers given in the early controversies among the Sadducees, Pharisees, and Essenes, sought new solutions for this inherent contradiction. Islam's strong fatalistic ingredients added stimulus to the quests for some new resolution of these difficulties. While the oldest school of Islamic philosophy, the Jabariya, and after them the orthodox Ash'ariya, clung to the doctrine of predestination as the decisive factor, the various rationalistic schools of the Mu'tazila searched for some compromise solution which would give much free rein to man's personal decisions and yet not infringe on God's foreknowledge of everything that is happening or is going to happen.

Jews had even stronger reasons for searching for some such middle-of-the-way solutions. Their entire traditional outlook had been colored by the ancient Pharisaic teaching, so pithily expressed in the famous phrase by R. 'Aqiba, "Everything is foreseen, and yet freedom is given." In fact, their ancient exponents of determinism, the Essenes, had all but been forgotten among the medieval Jews. Equally significant was the absence among them of that political background which colored so many of these debates among their Muslim neighbors. If the Jabariyite insistence on a fatalistic interpretation of pertinent Qur'anic passages carried within it the acceptance of things as they were, and was highly conducive to political quietism—which helps explain the early 'Umayyad support of that school of thought—there was no such incentive in the Jewish camp. On the contrary, the minority status of the Jews and their frequent oppression by their masters bred serious questioning of the established order and a growing recognition of the individual. Political aloofness or indifference, rather than quietism, on principle, was the less likely to foster determinist trends, as internally, too, the powerful social control of the central Jewish agencies in Babylonia was increasingly giving way to the autonomy of local communal groups.

Difficulties inherent in any compromise between predestination and free will came clearly to the fore in the teachings of Halevi, who, after brief and inconclusive discussions by Saadiah, Al-Baṣir, and Baḥya, was the first Jewish philosopher to come to grips with this subject. He was unable to accept, for instance, Baḥya's pietistic warning against indulging in speculations on this difficult and much-debated problem of reconciliation of necessity with justice, and his advice to the good man to act as if he were free to choose his course, leaving the rest to divine justice. "For God has rightful claims on man, but man has none on the Lord may He be blessed." Halevi, on the contrary, devoted to this topic the entire conclusion of his work. Here he tried to classify all happenings in the world as being "either of divine or of natural origin, either accidental or arbitrary." Only the arbitrary actions are within the realm of Free Will. Although Free Will, too, has its intermediary causes, which attach it chain-like to the Prime Cause, the entire realm of arbitrary actions is potential, the human mind being "permitted to turn where it chooses." [71]

This solution was, of course, likewise beset with enormous difficulties and was in essence self-contradictory. Ibn Daud, though adopting Halevi's fourfold classification, denied that the fourth realm of arbitrary actions still is attached to God as the Prime Cause, but rather intimated that, by God's own will, there exists no foreknowledge of the merely contingent. Ibn Daud was so perfectly convinced of man's complete freedom of will that he demanded that all biblical passages contradicting it be allegorically interpreted. In his time and environment this was a radical solution, which, understandably, did not satisfy most of his confreres, including even his no less daring fellow-Aristotelian, Maimonides. In this point Maimonides took refuge behind the old orthodox evasion, namely God's transcendence and ultimate unknowability. The very conflict between God's foreknowledge and man's freedom is based, he contended, on the assumption that God's knowledge is similar in nature to that of man. However, it is in fact entirely different in kind, "for He is His knowledge, and His knowledge is He." Through processes beyond our cognition, God knows what man is going to do without affecting his choice. Whatever the explanation, however, none of the Jewish philosophers before Crescas, not even Baḥya, dared to accept outright determinism. Not even Abraham bar Ḥiyya, despite the incontestable presence of Augustinian and Isidorian elements in his philosophy of history, preached anything resembling the doctrine of predestination when he taught that there exist four kinds of man's souls: wise and pious, wise and wicked, stupid and pious, stupid and wicked. Apart from stressing, more strongly than any of his compeers, that wisdom as such is not necessarily a safeguard against wickedness, he agreed with them, and indeed with the mainstream of Jewish tradition, that, as the ancient sages had phrased it, "everything is in the hands of heaven, except the fear of heaven." [72]

None of these thinkers doubted the influence of natural causes on the actions of man. Some like Ibn Gabirol, and even more strongly Abraham ibn Ezra, postulated man's ultimate dependence on changes taking place in the Universe, particularly in the realm of the celestial spheres. Since man's soul, they argued, is but part and parcel of the world of Intelligences, it must necessarily partake of whatever course these Intelligences impose upon the spheres. Ibn Ezra declared succinctly: "Know that every newborn child will be affected by accidents as shown by the constellation of stars at the time of his birth." Hence the importance of the science of astrology, for by tracing the course of the stars from the moment of one's birth one may divine the fate of each individual. To the majority of Jewish thinkers this sort of astral determinism appealed even less than outright divine predestination. The scholars of southern France, especially, doubtless familiar with Ibn Ezra's writings, were so deeply concerned about this problem that they addressed an inquiry to the highly revered jurist-philosopher of Fusṭaṭ. Maimonides answered with perfect frankness that he had himself in his youth been misguided by the pseudo-science of astrology, which must be distinguished from the real science of astronomy. But he now regarded indulgence in such studies as utter foolishness.[73]

Although the issue was far from settled, and astrology continued to dominate the minds of mystically minded Jews, few Jews doubted that it was man's duty to overcome nature wherever it lay athwart his superior ethical and religious obligations. To be sure, Halevi alone came close to the full recognition of the perennial conflict between history and nature. The other thinkers were too deeply permeated with the static and naturalistic way of Greek thought of the peripatetic or Neoplatonic variety to pay sufficient heed to this inherent conflict so significant in the entire history of their people. In fact, viewing man as a microcosm, mirroring in his composition of body and soul the macrocosm of the Universe, became one of the clichés of the age. Yet even such a detached philosopher as Ibn Gabirol in his "Fountain of Life," could not escape the conclusion that, if our soul wishes to contemplate the intelligible substances, we "must purge our intellect from the contamination of our sensations and free it from the control of nature." Moses ibn Ezra actually pointed out that "the Hebrew language had no term for nature nor any description that would fit it." [74]

Here we perceive the crucial difference between Jewish and Muslim, and even some Christian, mystics. By its very nature, its deep emotional involvement in the mysteries of Godhead and the universe, mysticism was apt to transcend traditional denominational lines. Since mystic categories of thinking, and the social forces behind them, were very much alike under most diverse civilizations, borrowings from one mystic school to another were often completely unconscious and aroused relatively little opposition even where they were entirely deliberate. There coursed, indeed, innumerable lines connecting Jewish with Christian, Zoroastrian, and Muslim mysticism on both the popular level of the magic arts and the more refined mystic speculations of the often saintly dreamers and visionaries.

Not surprisingly, therefore, such early Muslim mystics as Malik ibn Dinar often quoted extensively from Jewish writings, just as later, from the tenth century on, many mystic thinkers in Judaism, including Baḥya and Abraham Maimuni, learned a great deal from the Muslim Brethren of Purity and such distinguished mystics as Ḥussain ibn Manṣur al-Hallaj, who died a martyr's death in 922. But while Muslim fatalism tended to reduce greatly the distance between the Creator and the universe or man created by Him, thus opening the road to unrestrictedly pantheistic identification, Jews (even the Ṣufis among them) had retained enough of their traditional awe before the divine Holiness and its inherent transcendence to draw a sharp line of demarcation between them. Exclamations, like that by Hallaj, "I am He Whom I love, and He Whom I love is I,"—that is, "I am God"—would have sounded as execrable blasphemies in the ears of the most confirmed Jewish followers of Ṣufism. This did not mean that they did not venture to argue with God about certain alleged injustices and imperfections in His world order. This had been done with perfect equanimity by Job and many aggadic homilists. But in their most daring dialogues and visions they never forgot the chasm which separated the Infinite from all His creatures, even those belonging to the highest emanations, which alone the "descenders of the Chariot" ever dared directly to approach. In the ultimate sense, even these mystics resigned themselves in their diverse ways, to the acceptance of the inscrutable tortuousness of the divine guidance of man and history. Individually, too, they sought mere communion, not actual union, with the Deity.[75]

Understandably, too, no Jewish philosopher was ready to follow the lead of the Ash'arites, who fatalistically taught the relativity of good and evil and their dependence upon the will of God only. So universal were the Jewish belief in absolute moral values and the Jewish conviction that ethical conformity is in full accordance with the postulates of reason, that Saadiah could dismiss without much ado the assumption that the prohibition of murder and adultery was one of God's arbitrary commandments, rather than a restraint prescribed by human reason. Not only did such pure intellectualists as Maimonides proclaim the supremacy of the dianoetic virtues, but even some of the main protagonists of emotionalism, such as Baḥya and Halevi, bowed before reason. In Baḥya's major distinction between the duties of the "limbs" and those of the "heart," even the latter appear stimulated by rational rather than emotional motivations. Indeed it is one of his significant assertions that none of these higher duties has an irrational character. While criticizing extreme rationalism along the line of Al-Ghazzali's *Incoherence of the Philosophers* and trying to prove the inadequacy of human cognition, Halevi, too, finds the supreme and ultimate aim in knowledge. His contention is merely that human knowledge, unsupported by revelation, is doomed, because revelation alone opens the avenues to absolute truth without error or defect. Even the mystic, Ibn Gabirol, saw the chief purpose of the existence of the human soul in its striving for the knowledge of God. Granted that ecstasy, rather than deliberate reasoning, will lead to the goal, the primary aims remain knowledge and the unison with the world of Intelligences. In fact, Ibn Gabirol went out of his way, as we have seen, to find a physiological correlative to human virtues and vices. Anselm of

Canterbury's motto, *credo ut intelligam* (based on a homiletical interpretation of Isa. 7:9, "If ye will not have faith, surely ye shall not understand" [*te'amenu* = *intelligetis*]), may thus be said to render also the prevailing mood even of the more mystically minded among the medieval Jewish philosophers.[76]

Connected with knowledge is also the love of God, or, as Maimonides so pithily expressed it, "man's love of God is identical with his knowledge of Him." Curiously, this *amor Dei intellectualis* is almost invariably discussed by the medieval Jewish philosophers in terms of man's love of God, rather than of God's love of man or the Universe. This is understandable mainly because of the fashion of the age, since neither the Greek nor the Arab thinkers paid much attention to the element of divine love, although here and there they, like their Jewish followers, intimated that it was such love alone which brought about God's investment of matter with form, that is, its conversion from potential to actual existence. Such reticence, fully intelligible from the standpoint of the prevailing spiritualization of the God idea and the removal from God of any kind of human affects, was facilitated in the case of Muslim thinkers by the relative paucity of Qur'anic references to God's love of the world or of man. The Bible, however, is filled with such expressions. These were greatly elaborated in Talmud and Aggadah, as well as in the patristic letters. Hence the relative silence on this score on the part of Jewish philosophers, in contrast to Jewish preachers, is doubly meaningful.[77]

Many thinkers devoted considerable space, however, to the discussion of the love of God, with God as the object. Here, too, the Bible, and particularly the Deuteronomic injunction (6:5) which became part of the basic Jewish credo, offered much food for thought. In some respects, such love of God, or desire toward Him, was often considered, in Aristotelian terms, the main universal force motivating the propulsion of the spheres by their respective Intelligences. Ibn Gabirol, especially, built around this universal principle much of his cosmology. "This desire toward the First Agent and this movement toward him is common to all things, but they differ in accordance with their propinquity, or distance from him." That this desire was not completely unconscious, but based on knowledge, appeared even to this mystic philosopher a matter of certainty. His "teacher" took pains, therefore, to explain to the "disciple" how matter could have a desire toward form, if its knowledge itself was secured only through its form (*Fons,* v.33–34).

Even more widely accepted was the nexus between man's knowledge of God, together with his fear of Him arising from such knowledge, and his love of God. Saadiah concluded his lengthy philosophical discourse on the unity and attributes of God by saying that a person achieving such knowledge through speculation would find his soul "filled with completely sincere love of God, a love which is beyond all doubt." Abraham ibn Ezra and Ibn Daud likewise interpreted the commandment to love God "with all thy heart" (Deut. 6:5) as referring to the prerequisite of intellectual cognition. "For we cannot love strongly without knowing Him," explained Ibn Daud succinctly. Ibn Ezra, who on one occasion seems to have expressed doubt in the possibility of such love, nevertheless came around to explaining it as the result of man't total immersion in and communion with the Active Intellect, and thus with the World Soul. The medieval Jewish philosopher, however, who devoted more attention than any other to the subject of the *amor Dei intellectualis* was Maimonides, who referred to it in every one of his major works. "Thou shalt make," he stated succinctly, "His comprehension the very aim of all your activities," to which his commentator, Moses Narboni, added, "for this [pursuit] is the very purpose of his [man's] existence." Typical of Maimonides' general attitude was his enumeration of the six hundred and thirteen commandments, beginning with the ten commandments concerning man's attitude toward God. The interrelated first four commandments, we recollect, consist of: (1) knowing that there is a God; (2) believing that He is one; (3) loving Him; and (4) fearing Him. Maimonides then proceeded to spell out what is involved in the third commandment.

It means [he wrote] that we ought carefully to observe and meditate on His commandments, words, and works, until we grasp Him and enjoy such recognition with the profoundest of pleasures. It has already been said that this commandment also includes our obligation to urge all men to the service of God, and the belief in Him. . . . Just as Abraham who was a loving person (as it is written, "Abraham, My friend" [Isa. 41:8]) and endowed with great power of cognition, had called on all men to the faith, on account of his great love, so you, too, must love Him so as to attract men to Him." [78]

This was not necessarily a missionary interpretation, for the fellow men to be attracted to God may have been Jews. Yet an example set for Gentiles was by no means ruled out. In any case, a propagandistic approach of this kind was quite exceptional in Jewish letters of the period. In fact, Maimonides himself usually demanded from the true lover of God such total absorption in the contemplation, and secondarily also in the active service of God, that at times he preached a rather asocial behavior. Even in his early *Commentary* on the Mishnah he not only reiterated the absolutely disinterested character of the *amor Dei,* but also demanded exclusive concentration on it in every detail of one's daily life, even during one's hours of rest.

In the antisocial mood in which he composed his major philosophic work during the declining years of his life, the sage of Fusṭaṭ came to the conclusion that genuine love of God could generally be secured only "by seclusion and retirement. Every pious man should therefore seek retirement and seclusion, and should only in case of necessity associate with others." These were ascetic sounds, more appropriate for Baḥya than for the great jurist and communal leader. Baḥya had, indeed, devoted in his book a long discourse to the importance of the love of God which included the statement that "once love of God had filled their [men's] hearts, they derive no pleasure from talking to people, nor find any delight in their conversation." This sentence is an almost verbatim citation from a discourse attributed to the Muslim mystic, Dhu'l-Nun al-Misri (d. 859), and perfectly expressed the sentiments of many Ṣufi conventicles. Even Baḥya, however, refused to go the whole length of the radical Muslim or Christian mystics and see in the ecstatic love of God a means of real union with God. As Georges Vajda so well expressed it in terms of Christian mysticism, "Baḥya has described, in his own fashion and more or less successfully, the stations on the purgative and illuminative roads, but he deliberately stopped at the entrance to the unitive road." In short, Baḥya, Maimonides, and the other Jewish thinkers but restated in philosophic terms the traditional teachings of the talmudic sages on the theme of the Deuteronomic love of God "with all thy heart." They only added the new emphasis on knowledge as both the prerequisite for, and the ultimate aim of, that love. Hermann Cohen was, therefore, right in asserting that "the knowledge of God is the love of God, and the love of God is the knowledge of God—these are the two facets of the same basic idea, through which Maimonides became the perennial teacher of Israel." [79]

ETHICAL CONDUCT

Knowledge of God is, in Maimonides' view, also the ultimate source of any truly ethical behavior—the concluding note of his great philosophic work. The only perfection "in which man can truly glory," he declared, is the knowledge of God and the Divine providence. "Having acquired this knowledge he will be determined always to seek loving-kindness, judgment, and righteousness, and thus to imitate the ways of God." Somewhat more broadly, Saadiah insisted on psychological grounds that, since the human soul possesses three basic faculties, "the appetitive, the impulsive, and the cognitive," any truly disciplined person will give "his cognitive faculty dominion over his appetites and impulses." This supreme intellectualism was the more necessary for Jewish thinkers, the more they strove to rationalize their adherence to Jewish law and to the peculiar system of Jewish ethics. Like many Muslim and Christian philosophers, Maimonides tried to synthesize the religious ethics of his creed with the Aristotelian system. Even more than in the realm of pure metaphysics, however, this was an almost hopeless endeavor. True, the conditions in Athenian society of the fourth century were not altogether different from those in Jewish society of Palestine and Babylonia in the talmudic age. Consequently the Stagirite's postulates of practical behavior were not as far from those of the rabbis as from the other-worldly early Christian and Augustinian moral standards. Nevertheless, Maimonides, in his extreme intellectualization of the moral demands of Judaism, could do full justice neither to the rabbinic nor to the Aristotelian ethics.[80]

Abandoning the great achievement of Saadiah, whose distinction between rational and traditional commandments allowed for the historical justification of certain elements in Jewish behavior, and abandoning also Baḥya's reservation that at least some of the inferior duties of the limbs are of an irrational character, he went to extremes in his search for the "reasons of the commandments" (*ṭa'ame ha-miṣvot*). Of course, even he could not attempt to rationalize each detail in Jewish law. Often enough he emphasized the point that "the repeated assertions of our sages that there are reasons for all commandments, and the tradition that Solomon knew them, refer to the general purpose of the commandments, and not to the object of every detail." We have seen above how he adduced an historical precedent for the justification of sacrifices. Nevertheless, he firmly believed it possible to explain the rational purpose of almost all of the six hundred and thirteen commandments.[81]

Maimonides' extremism was far from typical even for the medieval Jewish philosophers. Although his argument that to assume that God enacted irrational laws would presuppose that man alone is a rational being and, as such, superior to the Deity, doubtless carried much conviction among his confreres, most of them were ready to admit the existence of rules of behavior beyond human comprehension. Even Ibn Daud, every bit as rationalistic as his great successor and, as we have seen, outdoing him in the boldness of his classification of laws according to the degree of their importance, nevertheless admitted that there are many laws which can be accepted only on the basis of faith. Unreasoned obedience is itself a mark of a genuine believer, whereas excessive "smartness" in speculating on the reasons of incomprehensible commandments, like the prohibitions of consuming certain animals or fish, leads man away from the road of his self-dedication to full compliance with the Lord's wishes (*Emunah,* end).

None of these thinkers, however, doubted that, to cite Maimonides again, it is among the objectives "of the perfect Law to make man reject, despise, and reduce his desires as much as is in his power. He should only give way to them when absolutely necessary." After extolling in the accepted vein the great virtue of the knowledge of God, Ibn Ṣaddiq climaxed his teaching by referring to Jeremiah 9:23 and exclaiming: "This is what I [the Lord] demand of you, nothing else; for all creatures exist altogether through righteousness." Here we find, indeed, an illustration of the Jewish "ethical gnosis," which so greatly differed from the ancient metaphysical gnosis, pagan, Jewish, or Christian. The more optimistic among the Jewish philosophers, who like Maimonides believed that good and evil are well balanced in the world, thought that the individual himself can determine the course of his actions and find his way to salvation. Pessimists like Ibn Gabirol, on the other hand, were too deeply persuaded of the essential sinfulness of human nature to believe in the possibility for man to escape sin without special aid divine. The great poet indeed composed many prayers imploring God for such assistance. Yet even he was far removed from the Christian doctrines of original sin, redemption, and grace. Abraham bar Ḥiyya, too, though more than any other Spanish-Jewish thinker before the *Reconquista* betraying familiarity with Christian modes of thinking, remained convinced of the basic freedom of the human will. For this and other reasons he did not hesitate to preach enjoyment of worldly pleasures with moderation and in consonance with the accepted law. Much as he generally appreciated the disciplinary merits of fasting, he interpreted Isaiah's prophetic exclamation, *U-mi-besarekha lo tit'alem* (And that thou hide not thyself from thine own flesh; 58:7), as referring not to one's relatives, but literally to one's own flesh, which one must not allow to starve.[82]

In this renunciation of the ascetic way of life, Bar Ḥiyya spoke for the majority of his fellow Jews, including the philosophers. Not that Bar Ḥiyya failed to share in the general admiration of self-imposed solitude. In a remarkable passage he placed the true anchorets at the head of three human groupings. For them and them alone the Ten Commandments offer sufficient guidance. A second group of pious men, living in an unorganized community, like that of Israel in the desert, requires the fuller instruction of the books of Exodus, Leviticus, and Numbers, while the third group, living within an organized state, needs also the book of Deuteronomy. But, however visionary his own outlook may have been in his astrological interpretation of history and his messianic computations, this distinguished scientist doubtless realized that the overwhelming majority of his Jewish contemporaries lived within organized communities, and hence required the guidance of the whole Torah and all its legal derivatives.[83]

Generally the Aristotelian golden mean found widespread acceptance among Jewish thinkers, because it lent itself easily to a reconciliation with rabbinic ethical ideals. Saadiah summed up the prevailing opinion when, after classifying the thirteen main motivations for human behavior, he declared that "everybody should adopt from each class such a measure as is proper for him according to the teachings of reason and of the Torah," at the same time adding, however, that he "should love life in this world not for its own sake but for the sake of the world to come." Even Baḥya advocated asceticism merely for a selected few who would inwardly separate themselves from the world, but outwardly take their full share in the life and labors of the people. Here again Maimonides was the chief systematizer. Opposing pessimistic tendencies of the age as exemplified by Ibn Gabirol, he built in his various writings a magnificent structure of values and countervalues, aimed at establishing a full equilibrium in the actional life of a Jew. The "middle way," a correlative to the primacy of society over the individual, certainly was a postulate inherent in the life of a struggling minority. Halevi, the nationalist, voiced this doctrine most sharply when he described it as "the duty of the individual to bear hardships, or even death, for the sake of the welfare of the commonwealth." Halevi did not preach here the fascist doctrine of total submersion of the individual in society and its interests. Although viewing society as an organism of which the individual members are like limbs in the human body, he made it clear in the same context that "a community will never pray for a thing which is hurtful for the individual." [84]

Needless to say, neither the ancient rabbis nor their medieval successors wished in any way to discourage leaning backward to lead a life holier than the middle-of-the-way sort. In this respect, Maimonides' statement in his *Code* well describes not only his own view but also that of most of his confreres:

> Not only the tribe of Levi, but every person from the world's inhabitants whose spirit moves him, and his intellect makes him understand, to dedicate himself to the service of the Lord . . . so that he removes from his neck the yoke of the numerous calculations pursued by men, such an one becomes the holy of holies and the Lord is his portion for ever and ever more.

However, particularly in the realm of ethics and practical conduct, even the philosophers had to insist on the validity of the solutions long achieved by rabbinic Judaism against extremes in either direction. Typical in this respect is Halevi's definition of the pious individual. Being a prince obeyed by his senses, Halevi contends, such a man "subdues his [appetitive forces], keeping them in bonds, but giving them their share in order to satisfy them as regards food, drink, cleanliness, etc. He further subdues the [impulsive forces striving] for power, but allows them as much expansion as avails them for the discussion of scientific or mundane views, as well as to warn the evilminded." [85]

Social equilibrium of this type, and the recognition of a golden mean in the relation between society and its members as well, accounts also for a characteristic exception. Hermann Cohen once pointed out that humility is the only virtue for which Maimonides sets no bounds, not even those of the golden mean. Quite different from the Islamic dervish's and the Christian monk's solitary unworldly humility, the Jewish ideal looks for humility in the active leader. Maimonides merely followed the Aggadah, which praised Moses as "the humblest of all men," and looked for the element of humility even in God himself. The misery of Jewish national life, its humiliations and sufferings, found its most complementary ideal in the humble person, humble because of his supreme inner worth. Baḥya, who devoted an entire chapter to the doctrine of man's "submission" to the divine will, found no less than ten synonyms for "humility" in Scripture, and tellingly cited the psalmist's assertion: "The sacrifices of God are a broken spirit; a broken and contrite heart, O God, Thou wilt not despise." [86]

Because of this constant intermingling of individual and social ethics, the medieval Jewish thinkers felt little inclination to devote special treatises to society and its problems. Although they usually accepted without demurrer the regnant Graeco-Arabic classification of sciences, and Abraham ibn Daud, for example, recognized that the attainment of "happiness," the objective of "practical philosophy," depended not only on individual ethics but also on economics and politics (*Emunah,* III, pp. 98, 126), he and his confreres paid but scanty attention to the economic, political, and other social theories. Even their Arab neighbors, though often in charge of a vast empire with its manifold political, administrative, and economic ramifications, were so preoccupied with the religious and ethical aspects of individual and mass behavior that their first genuine social scientist, Ibn Khaldun, did not appear until the fourteenth century. Before that time Farabi and others made some significant contributions to political theory, but these were always incidental to some general philosophic discussions. Economic and sociological thinking remained altogether rudimentary, and appeared largely as but a byproduct of jurisprudence. If the general advance of Arab and Jewish philosophy had been made possible precisely because of the emancipation of philosophic thinking from the shackles of the *shari'a* or *halakhah,* no such divorcement ever took place in the field of economics or most of the other social sciences. Ibn Daud voiced the regnant opinion when he concluded his aforementioned discussion of the fields of practical philosophy by saying, "But we shall show that this is found in our Law in the fullest possible way."

Even Baḥya's extremely individualistic piety, however, was not the expression of any antisocial or even asocial attitude. All medieval Jewish thinkers, as members of a closely-knit community fighting for its survival in the midst of a hostile world, agreed on preaching communal solidarity. Without necessarily joining Halevi in his assertion of the submission of the individual as but a limb in an organic body, they all subscribed to the Aristotelian doctrine, as restated by Maimonides, that "man is naturally a social being and that, by virtue of his nature, he seeks to form communities." He is not only in need of love and recognition by his fellow men, but he usually lives also by following the example of others. His life ought, therefore, also to be so regulated that it would accrue to society's benefit. In the Maimonidean restatement of rabbinic teachings, communal solidarity went so far that "he who can protest and does not do so, is himself guilty of the transgression for which he had failed to reprimand the transgressor." Particularly in cases which endanger the community's survival, as in the case of false prophecy, failure to prevent the crime, if need be by the assassination of the pretender, because of fear or any other motive, makes one guilty of a grievous sin.

In short, by balancing against one another the legitimate requirements of the individual and his community, Jewish law, in the unanimous opinion of the medieval Jewish thinkers, prescribed for the Jews a way of life which went very far in satisfying the requirements of their individual and social ethics.[87]

THE CHOSEN PEOPLE

Into these sublime metaphysical and ethical systems, the Jewish philosophers tried to fit, not without difficulty, the traditional concepts of the Jewish people, endowed with special grace divine as mankind's "Chosen People," having a special attachment and claim to its ancestral Holy Land, living under the specific obligations and privileges of its traditional law, and looking forward to its ultimate messianic goal. We have already analyzed in various connections the defense of this long-accepted set of beliefs by Jewish apologists in their extended socioreligious controversies with the spokesmen of the Gentile religions. In another context we have presented the various philosophic rationalizations of the Jewish messianic doctrine, alongside the sentimental yearnings toward that messianic ideal—sometimes expressed by the very same philosophers when they wrote Hebrew liturgical poems—and the more extravagant dreams of the apocalyptic visionaries. In connection with our review of the magnificent achievements of the Jewish jurists during the High Middle Ages an effort was made also to summarize concisely the various strands of fundamental legal thinking on the part of both codifiers and philosophers, which in their aggregate might be called a philosophy of Jewish law. Reference has also been made to the manifold approaches to a philosophy of Jewish history. Hence we need discuss here but a few additional aspects to round out that picture of an attempted reconciliation of faith and reason in the areas of Judaism's greatest distinctiveness.

Philosophers realized, of course, the inherent dichotomy between their universalist religious thought and their particularist religious tradition. This question came into focus, especially, in their attitude to proselytism and proselytes. True, rabbinic law had long tried to overcome the racial barriers and to integrate the proselyte as fully and speedily as possible into the body politic of the Chosen People. In fact, expatiating on the very term *'am* (people), an early homilist connected it with the *'amito* of Leviticus 25:17 ("And ye shall not wrong one another"), and taught that anyone who is "with you" (*'am itkha*) with respect to the Torah and good deeds, is a member of the people. Maimonides drew from this doctrine the radical conclusion that there is absolutely no difference in this respect between a native-born Jew and a proselyte. In reply to an inquiry by one of the few contemporary converts to Judaism, he taught him to recite regularly in his prayers "the God of our Fathers," because Abraham had taught to all men the religion of truth, and anyone recognizing this religion is the disciple of Abraham. Moreover, quoting Isaiah (44:5), one may well say that "if our descent is from Abraham, Isaac, and Jacob, thine is from God himself." Even more formally Maimonides included in his *Code* the following sweeping assertion:

> Any man from among the world's inhabitants, whose spirit has freely prompted him and whose mind has taught him to segregate himself from the others and to stand before God in order to serve him and worship him, so as to attain to the knowledge of God; anyone who walks upright just as God has made him, and has thrown off his neck the yoke of the "many inventions" sought out by man [a reference to Eccles. 7:29]—such a man is sanctified in the sanctity of the holy of holies, God will be his portion and his inheritance for ever and ever more and will also provide him in this world with a sufficient livelihood.[88]

This view, based upon sound talmudic sources and shared by the majority of medieval Jewish sages, was of course not pure humanitarianism, not even of the kind preached by such "rugged individualists" among the Arabs as the eastern poet Al-Ma'arri or the western mystic Ibn al-Masarra at the height of Muslim liberalism in the tenth century. Cosmopolitanism, pure and simple, then as before and after, could more readily be indulged by members of majority peoples than by spokesmen of a minority fighting for survival. Like atheism or agnosticism, unadulterated humanitarianism was in the case of many Jews merely a step toward assimilation to the majority. Many Jews, including their intellectual spokesmen, were not even ready to follow the lead of the ancient sages or of Maimonides in preaching full equality for Gentiles accepting conversion on Jewish terms. They clung the more ardently to the doctrine of the "chosen people" as limited to the physical descendants of the ancient Hebrew patriarchs, because they saw therein the supreme compensation for the unavoidable price they had to pay for their minority existence. While unable to resist the combined impact of an ancient tradition and a regular practice, both of which recognized descendants of proselytes after a generation or two as full-fledged Jews, they liked to feel superior at least to the proselytes themselves.

In Halevi, with his awareness of history-made differences, these popular sentiments found a spokesman of great frankness and penetration. Arguing on the basis of historic facts rather than mere reasoning, as in his general philosophy, the great poet insisted that Israel was physically, as well as spiritually, the chosen people. Its very longevity, contrasted with the rapid disappearance from the scene of history of many more powerful nations, was, in his opinion, a clear indication of the divine will to set them apart from all other peoples. That is why a proselyte may well become pious and learned, but he cannot attain the gift of prophecy reserved for born Jews. Just as the people of Israel are superior among the nations, so is the land of Israel superior to all other countries. It is distinguished not only because of its physical features and its location in the center of the earth, but also because it was the exclusive land of prophecy. "Whosoever prophesied," Halevi's spokesman exclaimed, "did so either in the [Holy] Land, or concerning it, viz. Abraham, in order to reach it, Ezekiel and Daniel on account of it." With consummate artistic skill, Halevi brought his dialogue to its climax when the king asked the rabbi why he stayed in the dispersion. Halevi admitted that this was a serious reproach; one, moreover, which could already have been leveled at the majority of Jews in the Babylonian Exile who, by their refusal "to leave their houses and their affairs" and to join the resettlers under Zerubbabel, prevented the fulfillment of the earlier prophecies that the Second Temple would fully equal the First. This is, indeed, in Halevi's opinion, the real meaning of the talmudic enumeration of the seven preexistent things: Paradise, Torah, the Just, Israel, the Throne of Glory,

Jerusalem, and the Messiah. In philosophic terms, he took this talmudic assertion to connote that the original preexistent divine thought unfolded itself in these seven final deeds.

> It was the object of divine wisdom in the creation of the world to create the Torah, which was the essence of wisdom, and whose bearers are the just, among whom stands the Throne of Glory, and the truly righteous who are the most select, viz. Israel, the proper place for them was Jerusalem, and only the best of man, viz. the Messiah, son of David, could be associated with them, and they all entered Paradise. Figuratively speaking, one must assume that they were created prior to the world.[89]

Whatever conviction arguments of this type carried with non-Jews, they certainly helped strengthen the morale of the Jewish people, then being ground between the millstones of warring Islam and Christendom. The problem of exile loomed very large in the eyes of all contemporaries. Arguing from the standpoint of a national theodicy, Saadiah had already pointed out that the fact that Israel was punished for its transgressions with the loss of national independence, while other sinful nations continued to prosper in this world, is itself a mighty argument for the existence of a world to come where the balance is restored. Ibn Gabirol, the pessimist, was weighed down by the burden of exile—a major keynote of his poetic works. His philosophic tractate, on the other hand, was in many ways for him an escape into an ideal, almost other-worldly reality. In the following century Maimon ben Joseph, forced out of his native Cordova by Almohade intolerance and living for many years the life of a wanderer trying to conceal his religion, felt the need of comforting his coreligionists who were in danger of surrendering to utter dispair. While graphically describing the desperate situation of his brethren, which he likened to that of a shipwrecked seaman floating on a plank amidst stormy seas, he expatiated particularly on Psalm 90. Considering that psalm an original "prayer of Moses," Maimon interpreted it as pointing toward a distant future; the great lawgiver was holding out a beacon of hope for the darkest days of his people. Following his father's example, Moses Maimonides later composed a similar "Epistle on Conversion," which was to serve the double purpose of comforting the recipients and of offering them legal guidance.[90]

Here again Halevi produced the most eloquent and sweeping rationale. Israel's selection and sufferings, he declared—particularly its political powerlessness, originally introduced as the reason why the king of the Khazars had not even wished to consult a Jewish spokesman—are part of the same divine plan. Pointing out, as we recall, that both Christian and Muslim traditions were glorifying the martyrs for their faith far above the conquerors, he argued that the nation of martyrs likewise towers high above the conquering empires. He also referred to the numerous religious compensations for the Jew's sufferings, such as "being cleansed from his sins; . . . the reward and recompense awaiting him in the world to come, and the attachment to the divine Influence in this world." Nor will he pay too much heed to his people's numerical inferiority. Remembering, in particular, the miraculous exodus from Egypt, he will realize "how we may recover our greatness, though only one of us may have remained." In short, despite all sufferings—indeed because of them—he will never waver in his firm belief in the ultimate messianic redemption.[91]

PROPHECY AND MIRACLES

Such beliefs in the people's selection and its messianic future obviously were religious credos rather than the effects of detached philosophic reasoning. Yet they too demanded at least an *a posteriori* justification by philosophic argument. Since, in the ultimate sense, they depended wholly on the acceptance (or rejection) of the word of God as revealed to Moses and the Israelitic prophets, the medieval thinkers were forced to seek justification for this entire system of revelation before the court of reason by ascribing to prophecy certain special supreme powers. That the prophet was a divine instrument to carry God's word to his people, and thus make available to them knowledge otherwise inaccessible, was the common belief of the religious thinkers of the three great denominations. But the Jewish philosophers had a more urgent need to elevate prophecy, and especially that of Moses, to a supreme position. Unlike the Christians, for whom Jesus was more than a prophet, Islam and Judaism maintained the human character of their founders. They endowed Moses and Mohammed with certain superhuman, but not truly supernatural, qualities. Against Islam, however, which was ready to acknowledge the prophetic character of the Old Testament *nebi'im,* Judaism insisted upon its exclusive claim to prophetic distinction. Various theories were propounded rationalistically to explain the gift of prophecy as a higher type of dream, and especially as a higher type of thinking, which the Aristotelians regarded as directly inspired by the Active Intelligence governing the sublunary world. But since all of human reason was directed by the Active Intelligence, indeed was part and parcel of the world of Intelligences, prophetic inspiration, while extraordinary, did not inescapably presuppose any breach in the course of nature.

Not that most philosophers objected to the possibility of such a breach. In fact, there was a fairly universal acceptance of "miracles" among the theologians of the three faiths, however much they may have differed in details. Saadiah sounded the keynote of all medieval Jewish philosophy when he declared that miracles were needed as signs to persuade the populace that a particular messenger was a true prophet. Among Saadiah's geonic successors a lively debate was carried on as to whether such evidential miracles were limited to regular prophets or could also be performed, with divine assistance, by extraordinarily pious persons. Running counter to express talmudic narratives, Samuel ben Ḥofni denied the possibility of miracles by anyone except genuine prophets. By implication he thus repudiated the possibility of miracles in any period between the conclusion of biblical prophecy and the messianic era. His son-in-law, Hai, stressed with equal fervor the ability of pious men to create situations in which God would produce miracles. To reconcile, moreover, the prophet's ability to foretell the future even in matters contingent on the subsequent decision by another individual's free will, Hai argued that God's foreknowledge embraces also the consequences of alternative decisions, and the inspired prediction merely emphasizes the ultimate results of a certain anticipated behavior. As Julius Guttmann pointed out, this doctrine adumbrated the speculations of later Spanish Jesuits, ridiculed by Leibniz, on what they were to call God's *scientia media.*[92]

Such miraculous signs given by God for the verification of prophecies may, according to Saadiah, consist of the subjection of natural elements to some unusual changes; for instance, of preventing fire from burning, or of the transformation of an animate into an inanimate object, or vice versa. God's will had preordained that such alterations in natural processes, on certain occasions willed by Him, should be part of the normal course of events. That is why He can also communicate His will to prophets chosen by Him without Himself becoming visible or audible to man. Familiar with the extensive discussions on this score among the various schools of *Kalam,* the gaon nevertheless chose his own explanation, largely borrowed from both the Aggadah and the *Merkabah* literature. He believed that the biblical reference to Moses' desire to view the divine Glory really related to "a special light which He [God] creates and makes manifest to His prophets in order that they may infer therefrom that it is a prophetic communication emanating from God that they hear." This divine Glory appeared, however, to Moses alone, while the other prophets had to be satisfied with a created divine Speech which they heard. This compromise between somewhat conflicting traditions pointedly rejected the Christian doctrine of a Logos being part of the divine essence and all dualistic conceptions. At the same time it enabled the gaon to adhere rather closely to the literal meaning of many phrases in Bible and Talmud. He was ready on this score to overlook the objections of some Muslim rationalists who repudiated even the assumption of a created speech telling Moses "I am God" as perilously bordering on dualism.[93]

Apart from such philosophic arguments against the accepted doctrine of prophecy, the Jewish, like the Muslim, public evinced concern about the criteria which might be drawn between the true and the false prophet and about the distinction between prophetic visions and ordinary dreams. Attacks by agnostics such as the school of Ar-Rawandi, who lumped all prophets together with other brands of magicians, could the less readily be dismissed, as the public at large had long been nurtured on the belief in the efficacy of magic arts. The simple answer that true prophets have been attested as such by an authentic tradition not only created a vicious circle between the verification of tradition through authentic prophecy and the verification of the latter through tradition, but ran straight into the major topic of controversy between the Rabbanites and the antitraditionalist Karaites. The latter, of course, likewise sought for some rationale to justify the authenticity of biblical prophecies.

In so far as anyone may be considered a representative spokesman of Karaism in the first chaotic two centuries of its evolution, Qirqisani's discourses on the subject may well have voiced the prevailing opinion among his coreligionists. "The true prophet," Qirqisani wrote succinctly, "is distinguished from the false prophet by means of miracles, not by tradition. Moreover, if anyone contends that a true prophet is the one who does not perform miracles, whereas the miracle worker is a false prophet, he could be answered by an appeal to reason only, not by one to tradition." Qirqisani himself took pains to explain in considerable detail the difference between the prophetic miracles and the magic arts of his day, to which, as then practiced by the Rabbanite masses, he took sharp exception. To this subject, in fact, and to that of dreams he devoted lengthy passages in the "Book of Lights." These problems agitated the minds of Rabbanites no less. Even orthodox students who were wont to think of all philosophic and theological subjects principally in terms of Jewish law and, hence, looked for guidance by the leaders of the Babylonian academies, addressed a large number of questions on this score to Sura and Pumbedita. Among the most noteworthy replies was Samuel ben Ḥofni's rejection of the literal interpretation of the biblical narratives concerning Saul's vision at Endor and Hai's endeavor to set up criteria as to how to distinguish a prophet from a magician. He declared that the miracle attesting to true prophecy must be distinguished (1) by being the work of God himself in a fashion which no man could possibly duplicate; (2) by obviously lying outside the ordinary course of nature.[94]

Answers of this type understandably failed to satisfy the more sophisticated groups in Jewry, and the interrelated problems of prophecy and miracles had to be discussed anew by almost all the leading medieval thinkers. More penetratingly than any other medieval philosopher, Maimonides took up the psychological implications of the phenomenon of prophecy, which he too recognized as being of crucial importance to any philosophy of religion.

> Prophecy is in truth and reality [he declared] an emanation sent forth by the Divine Being through the medium of the Active Intellect in the first instance to man's rational faculty, and then to his imaginative faculty; it is the highest degree and greatest perfection man can attain; it consists in the most perfect development of the imaginative faculty. Prophecy is a faculty that cannot in any way be found in a person, or acquired by man, through a culture of his mental or moral faculties; for if these latter were as good and perfect as possible, they would be of no avail, unless they were combined with the highest natural excellence of the imaginative faculty.

To be sure, by arduous training man could prepare himself for a prophetic calling, as was done in the ancient schools of prophecy. A prophet must attain, however, not only mental perfection, but also "perfection of the natural constitution of the imaginative faculty" and moral perfection through the suppression "of every thought of bodily pleasure and every kind of foolish or evil ambition" (*Guide,* II.36).

Clearly, the imaginative faculty here envisaged was not the simple imagination, which Maimonides generally held in rather low esteem, but something approximating the Spinozian ideal of the *scientia intuitiva.* Even Maimonides thus broke away from his predominantly intellectualistic patterns and recognized prophetic imagination, or rather prophetic intuition, as the supreme psychic power. In this respect he abandoned the teachings of both Aristotle and Ibn Daud, whom he usually followed, and adopted a theory which had decidedly Platonic, as well as Judaistic, overtones. His great stress on the importance of the moral perfection for the genuine prophet is likewise significant. That is why, he taught, even the greatest of prophets, including Elijah, Elisha, or Isaiah, suffered at least a temporary eclipse of their prophetic faculties when they allowed their short tempers to overcome their usually judicious approach to matters affecting the welfare of their people. In fact, moral turpitude, especially in the form of sexual licentiousness, is, in Maimonides' opinion, the hallmark of the "false" prophet, who either transmits an invention of his own or plagiarizes a genuine prophetic message revealed by God to someone else. Quoting Jeremiah 29:21–23, the sage of Fusṭaṭ pointedly illustrated both these kinds of false prophets and their moral shortcomings. For greater emphasis he added, "Note what is meant by these words." It did not require too much imagination on the part of the reader to apply these criteria to the founder of Islam.[95]

Not all prophets, however, were equal in rank. In the Maimonidean classification of eleven degrees in prophecy, that given to Moses is in a category by itself, on the ground that the lawgiver had been the only man on earth to receive his inspiration directly from God, and not from an angel. That is why Moses stood as high above the other prophets as the prophets stood over ordinary men, and the term "prophet" is applied to him only as a homonym. On the other hand, the first two degrees of prophecy are merely the equivalent of general divine assistance in the performance of certain acts or of divine inspiration in writing and the like. Neither of these degrees really deserves the designation "prophecy." The former is illustrated by the work of Joseph or Samson, while the latter is exemplified by David, Solomon, or Daniel. For this reason, too, in Maimonides' opinion, the book of Daniel was placed in the Hagiographa rather than among the "Prophets." While, following some Muslim rationalists, Ibn Daud acknowledged merely a superiority of degree of the prophet over the wise man, Halevi emphasized a difference in kind. To him, the prophet's knowledge is absolute, that of the philosopher relative; the prophet is a servant of God, the philosopher only the seeker after God. That is why reason may confirm the utterances of the ancient prophets, but never can disprove them. Thus the talmudic apothegm "A wise man is superior to a prophet" was radically reversed! One may perceive the historic reasons for this reversal. At a time when Christianity and sectarian currents threatened the existence of the Jewish people, the talmudic leaders had to fall back upon the representatives of the rational Jewish law and stress their superiority over the new preachers and prophets. Now that agnostic rationalism became the serious menace to national survival, Halevi and Maimonides invoked with increasing vigor the testimony of revelation and glorified above all its spokesman, the prophet.[96]

In prophecy lies one of the great distinctions of the chosen people. To be sure, biblical and talmudic traditions were far from exclusive in this respect, the Talmud itself listing seven Gentiles who, according to the biblical record, had prophetic visions. This recognition, running counter to the insistence on Israel's chosenness in the whole talmudic literature, is understandable only in the light of its comparative disparagement of prophetic gifts. Christian leaders, on the other hand, such as Justin Martyr and Clement of Alexandria, who justified the displacement of the old dispensation by virtue of a new prophetic revelation, were ready to concede the exclusive possession of prophetic gifts by ancient Israel. But they insisted that, because of its repudiation of Christ, the Jewish people had lost that distinction.[97]

With the new appreciation of prophetic visions among their neighbors, the Jewish thinkers sought to establish in various ways the exclusivity, or at least the unique character, of Old Testament prophecy. Ibn Daud, for example, who argued for the basic difference in kind between prophecy conceived in a dream and one received while the prophet was wide awake, also drew a sharp line of demarcation between the former's prophetic messages according to their scope. A dream vision, he contended, "which relates to an individual person, or a special matter, we shall not call prophecy; or if we do, we shall consider it but a weak portion of prophecy. Only if it relates to major matters, affecting nations and extending over long periods of time, is it a real prophetic dream." Abraham bar Ḥiyya and Halevi went further. They pushed the doctrine of the chosen people to the extreme of postulating that Israel stands as high above the nations as man above the other animals. Although admitting, as we recall, that a Gentile, through repentance and conversion, can become an Israelite, Halevi insisted that the gates of prophecy would still remain shut to him forever. Evidently sharing this point of view, Abraham ibn Ezra felt prompted to interpret away the biblical statements concerning the prophecies of Balaam, and declared him to be a simple magician inspired by God solely for the glorification of Israel. To such lengths were some of the Jewish thinkers ready to go in undermining the foundations on which had rested the claim to prophecy of Mohammed, the "madman." [98]

A similar purpose underlay Halevi's historical theory of prophecy, according to which the prophetic soul was transmitted from Adam, through Seth, to one man in each generation until the days of Patriarch Jacob, when all his twelve sons became "worthy of the divine influence, as well as of the country distinguished by the divine spirit." Here Halevi seems to have combined Augustinian and other patristic teachings, which may have reached him through Abraham bar Ḥiyya (or one of the latter's Spanish-Jewish sources, such as seems to have influenced also the Maimonidean gradation of prophecy), with Muslim concepts of the impact of the divine Influence (*amr illahi*) on man, old Isma'ili controversies over seven or twelve great imams in history, and some Iraqi claims to regional superiority because of the alleged prophecies in that country of Noah, Idris (Enoch), Abraham, Moses, Jesus, and Mohammed.[99]

In fact, this idea of selection permeates all medieval Jewish philosophy, whether it be amply discussed, as in Halevi, or merely referred to or implied, as in most of the other writers. Against the two international creeds, Islam and Christianity, the Jewish thinkers could easily point out the peculiarity of their ethnic religion. Certainly, they were well aware that their God idea had much in common with similar teachings of Islamic and Christian theologians. They were also ready to acknowledge that the strivings of all mankind are toward the same one and only God. To cite the prayer of Ibn Gabirol:

Thou art God and all things formed are Thy servants and worshipers.
Yet is not Thy glory diminished by reason of those that worship aught
 beside Thee,
For the yearning of them all is to draw nigh Thee,
But they are like the blind
Setting their faces forward on the king's highway,
Yet still wandering from the path.

Since the day of Sinai, however, it has been the great mission of the Jewish people to point out the right way, devoid of error and doubt. Halevi's idea of the central position of the Jewish people and Palestine in Jewish theology might not have found other equally eloquent protagonists, but all thinkers agreed that "Israel amidst the nations is like the heart amidst the organs of the body;

it is at one and the same time the most sick and the most healthy of them." What better simile could have been found for the humiliations of the present and the glorious messianic expectations of the future! [100]

PHILOSOPHY AND APOLOGETICS

Taken as a whole, philosophy as such was not the major concern of these Jewish thinkers. True, the statement of Ibn Sa'id, the Spanish Arabic writer of the eleventh century, that the Jews "did not distinguish themselves in philosophical sciences, but centered their attention on the legal sciences and biographies of the prophets," was written before the efflorescence of medieval Jewish philosophy in Spain. But his statement represents at least the prevailing opinion among the Arabic contemporaries of Ibn Gabirol, who in the Muslim era was the first Spanish-Jewish, and apparently the first Spanish, philosopher of distinction in any creed, with the exception of the mystic Ibn Masarra. There is no way of ascertaining whether such opinions influenced the great poet-philosopher to produce a philosophic work altogether divorced from Jewish law and prophecy. At any rate, although he did not accept Neoplatonic teachings regarding an impersonal and necessary cosmic process, and stressed above all the will of God, his *Fountain of Life* remained (next to the early and less significant attempt by Israeli) a singular example of philosophic detachedness in medieval Jewish letters. The other writers, even if distinguished by great independence of mind and an insatiable thirst for objective knowledge, sought in philosophy mainly a weapon for the defense of their traditional creed, which they cherished above all else. Maimonides himself, at least under the pressure of a growing opposition, professed to have utilized the sciences only in so far as they served "as spice mixers, cooks, and bakers" for the Torah, "in order to show to the peoples and princes her beauty, for she is very fair to look on." His immediate predecessor, the pedantically logical Ibn Daud, tartly stated: "The aim of all philosophy is action." [101]

Following the trend of the age, Ibn Daud and his confreres wrote in the Arabic philosophic jargon, even when their own proficiency therein was rather limited. It made little difference whether Baḥya wrote a popular treatise on ethics and Ibn Ṣaddiq a general compendium of mathematical and philosophical science for beginners, or whether Maimonides addressed himself expressly to the intellectual minority; the fundamental purpose remained the same: to justify Judaism before their own people and especially before the Arabic-speaking Jewish intelligentsia. The entire literature was directed much less at Gentile opinion than at a defense of the traditional creed for the Jews themselves. Maimonides, in fact, is said to have prohibited the transliteration of his *Guide* from Hebrew characters, in which it was written, into the Arabic alphabet. The self-styled definition of Arabic *Kalam* as "the science of the foundations of the faith and the intellectual proofs in support of the theological verities" may thus be applied to the entire medieval Jewish philosophy, although it soon became outspokenly critical of the teachings of the Mutukallimun. This is not only true of Halevi, whose work has an Arabic title which may be translated as "The Book of Argument and Demonstration in Aid of the Despised Faith," but of all the others, including Ibn Gabirol. This does not mean, of course, that some of the great thinkers such as Ibn Gabirol or Maimonides were not genuinely possessed of the beauty of purely theoretical speculations. How much the philosophic arguments had come into fashion can be seen in the example of Hai Gaon, who, though hardly a trained philosopher, applied the results of philosophy to the discussion of one or another halakhic problem.[102]

In short, it was a reformulation of one's own stand, rather than a missionizing attack upon other creeds, or an apologia to the nations. Even the theologians of the dominant creed (for instance, Ibn Ḥazm), had by that time realized that the differences between the three revealed religions were slighter than those separating them all from radical atheism and skepticism. They thus opened the road to mutual respectful toleration, which went far beyond the legal "tolerance" of the infidels. Although subdued soon, and for centuries to come, by the rising fanaticism of the Crusaders and the Almohades, this attitude was bound to have some effect upon the advanced thinkers of the nonmissionary minority.

The Jewish people supported these attempts at reformulation only in a certain degree. There were some agnostic Jews in Islamic lands to whom such a defense was too dogmatically limited. On the other hand, the masses of Jews, especially in Christian lands, needed no such defense. Even in the countries of Islam, the Jewish people were prone to disregard all the more objective scientific endeavors, and to cherish only those which restated the old tenets of Judaism in a fashion plausible to the new generation. They cast aside Israeli's and Ibn Gabirol's philosophic works, because these contained no direct defense of Judaism. Ibn Gabirol's *Fountain of Life,* because it was dogmatically so colorless, was practically eliminated from Jewish life, until fragments of Ibn Falaquera's Hebrew epitome were discovered in the nineteenth century. Of Israeli's philosophic treatises, neither originals nor translations were printed until 1871. This neglect contrasted with the popularity of Ibn Gabirol's strictly Judaistic, though intellectually much inferior, ethical writings, and of Israeli's medical books. Even Ibn Ṣaddiq's and Ibn Daud's more pronouncedly Jewish tracts were less accepted by the people than the outspokenly nationalistic works of Halevi or Baḥya. Maimonides had merely heard of Ibn Ṣaddiq, and he superseded Ibn Daud so completely that the latter was soon practically forgotten until the Hebrew translation of his work appeared in 1852. It is owing to the extraordinary position of Saadiah and Maimonides in other fields of Jewish learning, in addition to the sufficient modicum of apologetics in their two major works, that their two philosophic classics became part of a widely read literature in subsequent ages. Nonetheless, Maimonides' findings did not pass unchallenged. Outside of Islamic lands, Judaism was not ready to make even such minor concessions to a doctrinaire and static view of life as were demanded by the great thinker of Fusṭaṭ.

XXXV

SCIENTIFIC EXPLORATION

WITH the same passionate faith in the power of reason that characterized their quest for metaphysical and theological certainty, the Jewish thinkers under Islam began coping with the expanding horizons of scientific knowledge. True, for a long time they were, like their Christian and Muslim neighbors, overawed by the magnificent achievements of Greek science, which, through the ever multiplying translations of ancient classics, both authentic and spurious, opened up to them untold new vistas. In some respects, the awakened scientific curiosity could be satisfied with fewer misgivings than could that relating to philosophic problems. Here the pagan-secularist metaphysics of the Greek thinkers could be fully integrated into the overridingly theological medieval systems only through the frequently forced, if not incongruous, mediation of Alexandrine and Neoplatonic restatements of the original teachings. The scientific achievements of a Euclid, Ptolemy, or Galen, on the contrary, could be reproduced, continued, and expanded with far closer adherence to the original doctrines.

As in philosophy, the extreme reverence toward the great ancients proved to be a formidable obstacle to independent exploration. Learning in all phases was still rather bookish, and the invocation of an accepted authority readily replaced the fruits of personal observation and original reasoning. In the various branches of science, however, this evil was partly mitigated by the broadening geographic horizons and contacts with a variety of old cultures, especially the Iranian, Indian, and Chinese, which had developed in relative independence from Greek scientific endeavors. Integration of these diverse literary traditions into a new, more or less consistent whole was bound to produce new and valuable scientific discoveries.

Practical application likewise helped many scientific disciplines to progress far beyond the knowledge obtained by the great Hellenic explorers. For example, in communicating the fruits of his observations over forty years, the astronomer Al-Baṭṭani (d. 929), a Sabian of Raqqa, where Greek traditions had long been kept alive, submitted detailed astronomical tables which marked a substantial advance over those of Ptolemy, just as the latter had improved on those of Hipparchus. "For such is the majesty of this celestial science," commented this older compatriot of Al-Muqammiṣ, "and such is its breadth that no one individual can encompass it all." With growing self-assertion, nurtured from such tangible advances, many contemporaries began sharing the views expressed by the poet Hariri and the scientist Al-Asturlabi (d. 1139–40) that the ancient sages were only prior in time, not in their innate gifts, to their medieval successors. "The ancients distinguished themselves," Al-Asturlabi contended, "through their chance discovery of basic principles, and the invention of ideas. The modern scholars, on the other hand, distinguished themselves through the invention of a multitude of scientific details, the simplification of difficult (problems), the combination of scattered (information), and the explanation of (material which already exists in) coherent form." The convert, Samau'al ibn Yaḥya argued similarly that, just as Archimedes had known more than Euclid, so might another mathematician surpass Archimedes in the amount of information available to him. Samau'al concluded, therefore, that "no sage or well-informed historian will deny the fact that all the various disciplines of knowledge have manifested themselves through a process of gradual increase and ramification. This process stops at no final point, and tolerates no irregularity." [1]

Samau'al voiced here opinions widely held in progressive circles among his former coreligionists, as much as among the Muslims. True, because of the deeper roots of the Jewish tradition and the greater antiquity of its most authoritative sources, Jewish scholars found it even harder to justify departures from the views held by ancient authorities. While in the legal domain the gradation of Torah, post-Mosaic biblical tradition, tannaitic, and amoraic sayings, each with diminishing authority, had long been accepted, it could not be fully upheld in the realm of scientific fact, supported by direct observation or closely reasoned arguments. Discussing the difference between the rabbinic and the Aristotelian view concerning the alleged sound produced by the motion of heavenly bodies, Maimonides adopted the Aristotelian denial of such sounds and claimed that "our Sages have, in this astronomical question, abandoned their own theory in favor of the theory of others. . . . For speculative matters every one treats according to the results of his own study, and every one accepts that which appears to him established by proof." Before long the following rationale was added: The ancients may indeed have been giants, while the later generations produced only pigmies. But even a pigmy riding on the shoulders of a giant is taller and sees farther than the giant himself.[2]

Among the Jews there were additional incentives for rediscovering truths which, they believed, had been fully known to their ancient forefathers but had since been forgotten or inadequately transmitted by the latter's Greek disciples. Neither they nor the Muslims were completely free from obscurantist opponents of the pursuit of any scientific knowledge. While warning readers against excessive belief in mathematical achievements as a reason for equal acceptance of metaphysics, Ghazzali complained of some extremely orthodox objectors to the very study of arithmetic and logic. Manifestations of such exclusive devotion to theological and legal studies were not absent from the Jewish scene and were to increase in number and intensity in the Christian West. Nonetheless, opposition to scientific research could not be altogether consistent, since talmudic law itself had included many mathematical and medical teachings, albeit on the more popular level. Ghazzali's Jewish counterpart, Halevi, a practicing physician, did not include scientific investigations as such in his denunciation of "philosophy."

What was "Jewish" in the work of Jewish scientists living under the reign of Islam? This question, which was to become so troublesome in the nineteenth century, hardly disturbed the minds of the medieval contemporaries of Abraham bar Ḥiyya or Abraham ibn Ezra. In the case of these distinguished mathematicians and astronomers, of course, their use of the Hebrew language itself made their contribution eminently Jewish. Even the Jewish scientists writing in Arabic often used, like their colleagues in the field of philosophy, the Hebrew alphabet. Many utilized their mathematical calculations for such clearly Jewish purposes as the computation of dates in the Jewish calendar or the application of Jewish laws of inheritance. Medical men often tried to link their scientific findings with the accepted rabbinic legal or ethical doctrines. Most of these scholars, moreover, cited with predilection some supporting biblical or rabbinic passages. Even if they refrained from such outside signs of allegiance, Jewish authors were generally recognized as such by their own coreligionists, as well as by outsiders. In societies so deeply divided along denominational lines, as were the populations of both the Muslim and the Christian worlds, mere belonging to the Jewish minority colored one's entire personal status and was, at least indirectly, reflected also in one's literary or scientific contributions.

In fact, even converts to Islam and Christianity did not immediately wipe out all vestiges of their former allegiance. Not only was the fact of their conversion long remembered by friends and foes, but in many ways they unavoidably reflected their earlier training and experiences. That is why Steinschneider and others are not altogether wrong in counting the scientific work of such converts as Abu'l Barakat, or even the ardently anti-Jewish Samau'al ibn Yaḥya al-Maghribi, among the scholarly achievements of medieval Jewry. This form of belonging was not so much connected with one's racial origins as with the original environment and schooling, which could not be obliterated by a mere act of conversion in mature years. We are rarely in doubt as to whether an author was born and bred in a Jewish, a Christian, or a Muslim, environment.

CLASSIFICATION OF SCIENCES

Preoccupation with theology and law colored deeply the very appreciation of the respective scientific disciplines. Although generally following the ancient Aristotelian division of sciences, most medieval Jewish scholars could not withhold value judgments. Al-Muqammiṣ, as rationalistic a thinker as any of the more renowned Jewish scholastics, divided the sciences into practical or applied, and theoretical disciplines. The latter alone, in his opinion, merited the designation of branches of wisdom. Theoretical science, he added, is divided into three grades. "The first grade consists of the supreme science, called the divine science, which is the celebrated wisdom to comprehend the unity of God [a typical Mu'tazilite concept], and the understanding of His Torah and commandments. This is the highest and best of all the sciences. The middle grade is held by the science of propedeutics and the mind [probably referring to mathematics and logic], which strengthens men's opinions and leads them on the path of understanding. The third grade consists of the lowest and most inferior science, the science of the ways of the creatures and the essence of everything created [physics]" (cited in Yehudah bar Barzillai's *Commentary on Yeṣirah,* pp. 65 f.).

Such supreme appreciation of theology and law, for which no Aristotelian precedents could be invoked, was more than a bow toward established authority. It was substantially shared by the most authoritative expounders of Jewish rationalism. The greatest medieval Jewish mathematician, Abraham bar Ḥiyya, toying with the categories enumerated by Jeremiah (9:22–23), graded the sciences from the lowest to the highest in the following order: (1) "the science of propedeutics and the kalam," which he considered the equivalent of the biblical "wisdom" and included in it the five disciplines of arithmetic, geometry, music, astronomy, and logic; (2) "the science of created things [physics], which examines all existing things and explains the essence of their existence and the method of their creation" (this group of eight natural sciences, the equivalent of the biblical "might," includes in Bar Ḥiyya's opinion both the general principles of physics and the four disciplines of [a] mineralogy, [b] botany, [c] zoology, [d] physiology and psychology); (3) "the human science and the science of government," which, as the equivalent of the biblical "riches," consists of the three "pillars" of anthropology, economics, and politics; and (4) "the divine science, called by the Gentile sages the science of sciences," which includes all the preceding sciences viewed in the light of tradition, as well as the more strictly theological disciplines relating to the unity of God, the resplendent light, and all incorporeal beings. This science, to which the prophet alludes by saying "that he understandeth, and knoweth Me," can properly be grasped only through Scripture.[3]

Even more doctrinaire was the division of sciences suggested by the southern French grammarian, Joseph Qimḥi. He graded them by their usefulness for this world, or for the world to come. From this standpoint the "supreme science enthroned from of old in a place of honor is the divine science consisting of the knowledge of the unity of God, His teachings and commandments, which serves to secure the love of Him for the world to come," and one must not abuse it for this-worldly needs. In the second group are such disciplines as astronomy, mathematics, or medicine, "which serve both the purposes of this world and those of the world to come, and which one may utilize in this world." Finally the lowest position is held by the practical or technical sciences, such as the building of houses, cultivation of fields or vineyards, the production of garments, or work in precious metals or stones. These are exclusively devoted to the maintenance of this world. Qimḥi merely sharpened here a distinction already drawn by such mystics as Baḥya, for whom even mathematics, in its then accepted Aristotelian (Porphyrian) quadripartite division (called *quadrivium* by the later scholastics) of arithmetic, geometry, astronomy, and music, appeared only as a secondary or ancillary science. Curiously, even the more worldly Abraham ibn Daud considered intensive preoccupation with any science other than theology a mere waste of time. He admitted that, for instance, medicine had its good uses, particularly because, by prolonging human life, it enhances the opportunities for better preparation for the world to come. But one must not make it one's chief interest in life and "thus violate one's soul." Even less profitable was, in his opinion, concentration on grammar or language, while others wasted their time in arithmetical computations which are never likely to occur in life, or in equally fruitless geometrical subtleties. "The only really necessary part [of these sciences] is what accrues to the benefit of the science of astronomy." [4]

Remarkably, both Baḥya and Ibn Daud ventured to speak slightingly also of the excessive preoccupation of jurists with the minutiae of law, which under both Islam and Judaism represented the very core of religious studies. Ibn Daud conceded the social value of civil law, which "stems the transgressions occurring among men and ameliorates the social relations among them." Nevertheless, its function was, in his opinion, essentially less salutary even than that of medicine, for "assuming that all men would be just and harbor no evil, the science of the law would become almost unnecessary." Here again the pragmatic argument appeared most decisive: "He who spends his time and puts all his thoughts into far-fetched speculations and works on difficult problems and matters which had never happened and will never happen, thinks that all this refines and sharpens his mind, whereas he is really but wasting time." At the same time this Toledan scholar sincerely believed that theological speculations with respect to the riddles of the universe and the most obscure recesses of the soul, were of immediate practical benefit.

Some such bias was fairly universal. Few Jewish scientists and philosophers under medieval Islam actually paid concentrated attention to the classification of sciences as such; they usually mentioned it only in connection with precisely these value judgments. The relatively fullest analysis, because the least weighted down by such theological preconceptions, was found in Maimonides' "Treatise on Logical Terms." Although primarily motivated by his desire to explain some 175 terms currently used in philosophic and scientific circles, the then youthful author found among these terms numerous designations of sciences which he tried to define and classify. He spoke of "theoretical philosophy" as subdivided into mathematics, physics, and theology, and of "practical philosophy" (also called human or political philosophy) which included (1) "self-government [of the individual], (2) the government of the household, (3) the government of the city, (4) the government of the great people or the peoples." The latter divisions may roughly be equated with (1) ethics, (2) economics (the term is indeed derived from the Greek *oikonomia*), (3) politics, and (4) international relations. Of particular interest is the Maimonidean definition of mathematics and physics.

Mathematics studies material things not as they are but as abstracted from, though always existing in, matter. The parts of this science which are its roots are four: arithmetic, geometry, astronomy, and music; and these parts constitute what is called the propedeutic science. Physics studies material things existing, not as products of human will but in nature, e.g., minerals, plants, and animals. It studies these things and all that exists in them, I mean, their accidents, properties, causes, and also all in which they themselves exist, like time, space, and motion.

Logic, on the other hand, was not to be counted among the sciences, but rather to be considered as an instrument of all sciences, "and an instrument of something is not a part thereof." [5]

In popular parlance, however, one began hearing the phrase, "seven sciences," especially in medieval Europe, where Christian educators often spoke of the "seven arts" consisting of the *trivium* (grammar, dialectics, and rhetoric) and the mathematical *quadrivium*. But none of the medieval Jewish authors took pains to enumerate and clearly to define that heptad. One writer, Abba Mari Astruc of Lunel, actually placed all seven in the intermediary position between physics and theology, which he equated with the traditional works "of creation" and "of the chariot." More fully descriptive was Abraham ibn Ezra's comment on the biblical proverb, "Wisdom hath builded her house, she hath hewn out her seven pillars" (9:1). Although mentioning more than seven disciplines, Ibn Ezra seems to have intended to subsume them under the seven mainly Aristotelian categories: (1) logic, (2) theology (including psychology), (3) arithmetic (including what Ibn Ezra called the *ḥokhmat ha-ʿarakhim* or the science of proportions or perspectives), (4) geometry, (5) astronomy, (6) music, (7) physics (including astrology). Since Ibn Ezra himself failed to spell out his division, however, it is possible that he counted astrology as part of astronomy rather than physics, despite Nasiruddin aṭ-Ṭusi's clear assertion that "the decrees of the stars fall outside" mathematics and rather belong among the derivatives of "natural science." Certainly, the Hebrew terms used by Ibn Ezra, the *ḥokhmat ha-mazzalot* and the *mishpeṭe ha-mazzalot* (for astronomy and astrology respectively), indicate their intimate relationships. Characteristically, none of the medieval Hebrew authors separated the geographic, biological, and medical sciences as independent disciplines, notwithstanding the great role played especially by medicine in Jewish scientific life and letters. They were, as a rule, lumped together under the designation of physics.[6]

For practical purposes, however, especially in connection with educational programs, the medieval teachers had to segregate the individual branches of learning. In the extensive chapter devoted to education in his treatise on mental hygiene, Joseph ibn 'Aqnin suggested the following main stages in instruction: After teaching a pupil reading and writing, the teacher was to devote all his attention to imparting the knowledge of the Torah, Mishnah, and Hebrew grammar. These studies were to be followed by instruction in poetry and Talmud, and by general observations on religion. Only then was the pupil supposed to be prepared to take up the more intensive study of the philosophic disciplines, particularly logic and rhetoric. These studies were to be continued with instruction in arithmetic and geometry (both theoretical and practical), optics, astronomy, music, and mechanics, and lead up to intensive preoccupation with the physical sciences, in accordance with the eight divisions represented by eight specialized Aristotelian (or pseudo-Aristotelian) tracts. This entire course was to culminate in the teaching of Aristotelian metaphysics.[7]

In our analysis we shall follow none of these medieval classifications. The philosophic disciplines, theology, music, and political science, as well as the more specifically Jewish branches of Bible, law, and homiletics, have already been treated in various other contexts. Here we shall limit ourselves to an analysis of the more important contributions of medieval Jewish scholars to the mathematical and physical sciences, with special reference to aspects bearing on the general Jewish social and religious life of the period.[8]

MATHEMATICS AND NUMERALS

"By the end of the thirteenth century," comments M. Postan, "the mathematicians were tackling advanced problems of the geometry of Pythagoras, approaching the solution of cubic equations by the intersection of cones, discussing spherical trigonometry, and indeed approaching the very verge of differential calculus." This evolution was prepared by students of mathematics of various faiths in the Muslim world over a period of several centuries. The Islamic Renaissance was, in fact, principally a revival of ancient science and philosophy, unlike the Italian Renaissance which resurrected much of the ancient literature and arts. Adding to the Graeco-Roman heritage the mathematical and other scientific discoveries of the Babylonians, Jews, Syrians, Indians, and Chinese, forging ahead on the old, and opening up some uncharted new paths, the scholars of the ninth to the twelfth centuries—Jewish, Muslim, and Christian—greatly expanded the frontiers of human knowledge.[9]

Like their Syriac-Christian neighbors, Jews had a head start in the continuity of their scientific tradition which, however limited in scope and primitive in means, stimulated more advanced thinking. In the *Mishnat ha-middot,* possibly compiled as early as 150 C.E. by R. Nehemiah in connection with the measurements of the ancient Tabernacle, they possessed solid rudiments for geometric rules, which could subsequently be incorporated almost verbatim in the mathematical work of Mohammed ibn Musa al-Khwarizmi (about 820), one of the Muslim fathers of algebra. The so-called *Baraita de-Shemu'el,* ascribed sometimes to the Tannai Samuel the Little and sometimes to the scientifically trained third-century sage Mar Samuel of Nehardea, but evidently compiled from some older sources after the rise of Islam, likewise was largely devoted to analyses of mathematical and astronomic problems. The great emphasis laid upon numbers as basic cosmological entities in the *Book of Creation,* and such chronological-mystic lucubrations as were included in three chapters of the *Pirqe de-R. Eliezer,* also stimulated thoughtful students to speculate on numerical combinations and their mathematical as well as theological implications. More tangentially, the preoccupation of numerous contemporary students with problems of the Masorah, the fact that Hebrew letters also possessed numerical value, and the need for certain reliable mathematical computations in the adjustment of the Jewish calendar to astronomic facts as well as in the administration of the laws of inheritance, all combined to generate a fairly widespread interest in mathematical problems.[10]

Quite early, therefore, scientists of note emerged from among the Jews. According to a later report by Ibn Ezra, embroidered with the customary legendary threads, a Jew familiar with the Indian language (Sanskrit?), returning from a royal mission to India, brought back with him an Indian mathematician, Kankah, whose works he helped translate. The Indian scholar allegedly "taught the Arabs the bases of numbers, that is, the nine numerals" (the decimal system). The arrival of Kankah (or Mankah) and the translation of his scientific data are also recorded by the well-informed Al-Biruni as having occurred in the year 154 or 161 A.H. (771 or 778). Soon thereafter Masha'allah (fl. 750–800; the name, meaning What God Wills, was often misspelled in subsequent Latin translations or quotations into Messahala and the like) became one of the first distinguished Arabic-writing mathematicians of any faith. He is recorded to have assisted Al-Manṣur in drawing up the plans for the newly founded capital at Baghdad. Unfortunately, little of his extensive scientific output, recorded at length in An-Nadim's *Fihrist,* is extant today in either the original or translation. The same is true of his younger contemporary Sahl ben Bishr (fl. 820–30), who, under the misspelled name of Zahel, was considered one of the leading authorities on astrology throughout the Middle Ages. The almost immediate recognition extended to his "Algebra" and other works was indicated by An-Nadim in the following century. Many successors fared worse, their names alone having come down to us. How many are now altogether forgotten, no one can tell.[11]

Relatively more fortunate were the Spaniards, Abraham bar Ḥiyya Savasorda and Abraham ibn Ezra. Partly because of their geographic and chronological propinquity to Latin scholarship, which has maintained its unbroken continuity since its memorable twelfth-century Renaissance, and partly because their scientific works were written in Hebrew and thus remained accessible to the rapidly expanding western Jewries, they succeeded in weathering the ravages of time. True, some of their writings, too, are now either completely lost or extant only in translation or more or less extensive quotations. However, the fact that, for example, Abraham bar Ḥiyya personally collaborated with Plato of Tivoli in the translation of Arabic treatises into Latin, made it possible for the latter also to reproduce a major mathematical work by Bar

Ḥiyya himself in an almost "authorized" Latin version. The works by "Savasorda" thus became the fountainhead of much subsequent scientific research among both Jews and Christians, and Martin Levey rightly called him a "true pioneer of mathematical science in Europe." On the other hand, mathematical teachings, often expounded in connection with legal problems by such leading rabbinic authorities as Saadiah or Maimonides, were long limited to Jewish circles only. However, precisely this association with one or another aspect of Jewish law, and the great prestige of their authors, enabled these doctrines to penetrate much wider groups of Jewish students. Did not Bar Ḥiyya himself, like Ibn Daud after him, consider exclusive preoccupation with mathematics an undue waste of time? In a rather melancholy vein he also reminisced in his encyclopedic treatise, "Because I had formerly been engaged in purely secular matters, I have now treated of this subject [theology]. Perhaps I shall purify the profane by the sacred subjects." [12]

Apart from their preoccupation with law, adepts of traditional Jewish learning had long become aware of arithmetical problems arising from the intensive study of the Bible. Deep concern for numbers of any kind naturally aroused interest in mathematical methods and techniques. Al-Khwarizmi was not merely voicing a scholar's prejudice, when he started his *Algebra* with the sweeping declaration, "When I considered what people generally want in calculating, I found that it always is a number." There was a grain of historic truth in the talmudic etymology of the term *soferim* (scribes) as derived from the counting of letters in Scripture. True, the full evidence of such preoccupation comes to us from the later masoretic schools, when much of this oral tradition was confided to writing. Here we find exact figures given, for instance, for the total number of verses in the Pentateuch (5,845), the Prophets (9,294), and the Hagiographa (8,064), a total of 23,203. But precisely the long era of oral transmission doubly required mnemonic aids. While the total figure could be impressed on the student's mind by the phrase *Adam zakhar,* which combined the 930 years of Adam's life (Gen. 5:5) with the 22,273 firstborn "males" recorded in the book of Numbers (3:43) to yield the sum of 23,203, the other figures could readily be memorized with the aid of three- or four-letter words in which each letter represented a figure corresponding to its numerical value. An especially ingenious example of such complex techniques is the aforementioned alphabetic poem by Saadiah, in which the gaon succeeded in conveying to the reader the number of occurrences of each letter in Scripture. At the same time this poem had meaning without reference to the hidden artifice, expressing the usual messianic hopes. No wonder that the gaon himself found it necessary to add a brief commentary, explaining his technique and supplying the resulting numbers.[13]

Clearly, a generally accepted use of letters as numerals in an ascendent decimal order was presupposed, so that the eleventh letter, *kaf,* did not have the numerical value of eleven but of twenty, while the nineteenth letter, *qof,* began the series of hundreds. The Greeks, who had introduced this system as early as the fifth pre-Christian century, had no difficulty in using the twenty-seven letters of their alphabet to pursue this sequence up to 900. But users of the Hebrew alphabet, possessing only twenty-two letters, were forced to resort to the expedient of double letters to indicate five or more hundreds. In the Middle Ages there appeared the occasional use of the five final letters *KMNPṢ* to indicate figures ranging from 500 to 900. But, by their very nature, final letters looked very awkward at the beginning or in the middle of a word which usually represented numerical values in a descending order. That is why even Saadiah utilized these final forms only in such exceptional works as his aforementioned poem. Despite these handicaps the Jews continued to employ their own letter numerals, which underlay also the numerical value attached to the Syriac and Arabic letters, although the sequence of the Arabic alphabet soon followed a somewhat independent order. On the other hand, when the eastern Arabs adopted the Hindu numbering, while in Spain they modified the original Roman into so-called *ghubar* numerals (the real basis of our so-called "Arabic" ciphers of today), the Jews followed suit only in their Arabic writings. In Hebrew writings they continued to use their own numerals exclusively to the very end of the Middle Ages, and these predominated long thereafter. The first, rather timid, use of "Arabic" numerals in a Hebrew context seems to be that found in the writings of the fifteenth-century Constantinople mathematician, Mordecai Comtino.[14]

Numerical values of letters and words readily lent themselves to exploitation for a variety of purposes. We recall the extent to which *gemaṭrias* and other arithmetical expedients were utilized for homiletical and magical purposes. Mystics, especially, of all denominations were inclined to place numbers very high in their scheme of existence. Harking back to old Pythagorean doctrines, popularized among the Near Eastern intelligentsia particularly by the popular writings of Nicomachus of Gadara (*ca.* 100 C.E.), the author of the Book of Creation counted, as we recall, the Number among the three chief instruments of Creation. In his *Commentary* thereon, Saadiah analyzed nine cosmological schools of thought, each of which may have had some followers among his own coreligionists, too. The gaon approved fully of only the ninth interpretation, but he admitted that the latter also embraced some true elements from the seventh and eighth theories. According to the seventh school, which admitted the doctrine of Creation, "the numbers were the first things to be created. In fact, through the numbers we differentiate the substances, as well as the parts, and from them stem geometry and figures. . . . In the order of things the figure precedes the object shaped according to that figure." Saadiah objected to this extreme formulation on two grounds. First, because it postulates the existence, besides the Creator and the created object, of a third element, the figure as an independent substance. Secondly, the very idea of an absolute composition or abstract mensuration is self-contradictory, "for composition and mensuration and things like that require at least two things or even more in number," and, by presupposing their existence, they lose their abstract character. The gaon himself envisaged numbers, like letters, as merely piercing the air during the process of instantaneous creation and there forming a variety of figures which God simultaneously shapes into objects composing the Universe.[15]

Saadiah himself, however, could not refrain from speculating on the excellencies of the number "one," both by itself and as the beginning of a series of odd numbers, whose superiority over the even numbers had ever since Greek times been accepted in philosophic and popular circles. Commenting on *Yeṣirah's* exclamation "And all are hanging on the One," the gaon explained: "First, every odd number is noble, for adding one to the other produces perfect squares" (1 + 3 = 4, 4 + 5 = 9, 9 + 7 = 16, and so forth). Secondly, the figure "one" attaches itself to any other number, such as one dozen, one hundred, one thousand, and, ultimately, one universe. Thirdly, unity has an absolute character, which cannot be compared with that of any other figure and hence can be applied to God (*Commentary on Yeṣirah,* p. 68; French, pp. 89 f.).

While the gaon still refrained from extensively utilizing *gemaṭrias* for the justification of some of his pet theories, his admiring follower Abraham ibn Ezra had no such compunctions. Though evidently superior to the gaon as a mathematician, this polyhistor did not mind intermingling the various disciplines which he had mastered, in order to throw some light by mathematical formulas on problems of grammar and biblical exegesis. In his cosmological speculations in the philosophical *Yesod mora,* he stressed the importance of the four letters *AHWJ,* the components of the two divine names (the Tetragrammaton and the *Ehyeh* of Exodus 3:14) by referring to their numerical values of 1, 5, 6, and 10, that is at the beginning, the middle, and the end of the decade. Together they also amount to 22, the number of letters in the Hebrew alphabet. When written out, the numerical value of the four letters of the Tetragrammaton equals 72, and that is, in Ibn Ezra's opinion, what the rabbis had in mind when they spoke of a divine name of seventy-two letters. Even the shape of these four letters in the square Hebrew script had some such basic meaning, that of *he* and *vav,* especially, representing the female and male principles—food for thought, indeed, for some modern psychoanalysts. Similar lines were pursued in Ibn Ezra's "Book of Unity," his "Book of the Number," and even in his biblical commentaries. For instance, his comment on the ever mysterious divine revelation of the name *Ehyeh* begins with the observation:

Know that the One is the mystery and foundation of every number, Two the beginning of the even, Three of the odd numbers. Thus the numbers up to Nine follow one way, while number Ten follows another [dependent on the inclusion or exclusion of the first number]. If you write Nine in a circle and multiply it by any other number, you will find that the units appear on the left side, and the tens on the right side [18, that is $1 + 8 = 9$, 27, etc.] until the middle number five, when the reverse is true; here the tens become units and the units tens [54, 63, etc.]. On the other hand, "Ten *sefirot* are completeness" [*Yeṣirah*] . . . , for . . . ten is like one, and every number is part of a decade, or comes from its multiple, or from its addition to units, or both.[16]

Modern students have often been amazed by the extent to which letter and number symbolism was taken seriously by this sharp-witted and disciplined philologist and scientist. Because of their brevity, such allusions often appeared doubly cryptic, and they have mystified many readers of Ibn Ezra's Bible commentaries, even where the author himself did not stress their mysterious character (*sod*). Hence arose the need of those numerous super-commentaries with which his exegetical work was provided by admiring disciples. Despite such sustained efforts of generations, however, many puzzling passages, especially those borrowed from the mathematical domain, have not yet been satisfactorily explained. They may indeed remain obscure until all of Ibn Ezra's mathematical and astrological writings, and some of those by his contemporaries and immediate predecessors, are published and fully investigated.

ALGEBRA AND GEOMETRY

Jewish law, too, occasionally employed mathematical techniques. Under the impact of the Muslim laws of inheritance, which raised complex problems of distribution of landed property among heirs and legatees, there arose the need of placing in the hands of judges and executors convenient mathematical formulas for the calculation of the respective shares. Such an "algebra of inheritance," or as it was called in Arabic *'ilm al-fara'idh* (science of the legal shares), produced a fairly large outcropping of pertinent Arabic monographs. Al-Khwarizmi devoted the last section of his treatise on algebra to methods used in this phase of judicial mathematics. According to Yaqut, the last words spoken by the dying Al-Biruni concerned the solution of a difficult problem in calculating shares of respective heirs.

Arab examples spurred Saadiah to the writing of one of his aforementioned halakhic monographs, the *Kitab al-Mawarit* (in

Hebrew *Sefer ha-Yerushot,* or Book of Inheritance), in which he discussed the arithmetical and geometrical, alongside the juridical, problems of distribution of estates. As in other domains, the gaon did not merely follow his Arabic prototypes, but injected many new ideas of his own and reformulated others from the rich storehouse of Jewish tradition. Since the mathematical instruments were subservient to legal objectives, the differences between Muslim and Jewish laws required the applications of different techniques and the modification of many others. "The extraction of roots," comments Solomon Gandz, "and the transformation of rectangular fields into square fields of the same areal contents utilized and introduced here for the further elucidation and elaboration of the talmudic law, are original ideas of Saadiah. Such disquisitions never occur in the Muslim treatises, as there is no basis for such investigations in the Muslim law." So closely did the gaon adhere to his talmudic prototypes, which, incidentally, had doubtless exercised considerable influence directly or indirectly on some aspects of Muslim law of inheritance in its formative stages, that he often overtly disregarded the more advanced and accurate mathematical facts known in his day and reverted to the rather primitive patterns of his talmudic sources. For instance, he must have known that the crucial figure π, so indispensable for the accurate computation of any circular area, more nearly amounted to $3\frac{1}{7}$, a figure used already by the author of the *Mishnat ha-middot,* than to the round number of 3, casually mentioned in the Talmud's juridical discussions. Nevertheless the gaon retained that round figure, as he did also the more primitive methods of multiplication which he had found in his talmudic sources.[17]

Saadiah's chief aim doubtless was to place in the hands of practitioners of Jewish law a convenient summary and a few simple techniques for the application of the long-accepted laws. This practical angle also helps explain his use of arithmetic, rather than the more advanced algebraic methods applied to problems of inheritance by Al-Khwarizmi and others. Whatever mathematical knowledge Saadiah himself may have possessed—to judge from this work it was neither extensive nor profound—he probably could not take much for granted in the case of ordinary Jewish judges and executors of estates. Despite its hoary antecedents in ancient Babylonian mathematics, the algebra of inheritance, like all algebra of the type expounded by Al-Khwarizmi, was still too young a discipline to have been mastered by more than a few rabbis. It appears that even the purely arithmetical errors and inconsistencies, in which Saadiah's little monograph abounds, do not stem entirely from badly blundering copyists, but may well have come in part from the author's own insufficiency. This is particularly true of the introductory computation, where an initial error is consistently pursued through an entire paragraph, although it is abandoned in a later context. In any case, the audience of juridical students whom the gaon addressed would have resented the slightest substantive deviation from talmudic law much more than any number of arithmetical errors. He therefore clung closely to the talmudic regulations, even where they were obviously lacking in precision.[18]

On the other hand, concern for exactitude in the measurement of land parcels resulting from division of estates, as well as from commercial transactions, was the avowed reason for the composition of the main geometric treatise written by a medieval Jew, namely the *Ḥibbur ha-meshiḥah ve-ha-tishboret* (Treatise of Mensuration and Calculation) by Abraham bar Ḥiyya. Translated into Latin by Plato of Tivoli under the title of *Liber Embadorum,* this treatise, though originally conceived merely as a nontechnical textbook for the use of informed landholders and judges, exerted a very great influence on the mathematical progress in the West. In his brief introductory apologia the author invoked the Isaianic prophecy about the Lord "who teacheth thee for thy profit" (48:17), to show that anything useful to man in the pursuit of his worldly career, as well as in the fulfillment of commandments, is worthy of study. Savasorda felt that one of the great shortcomings of contemporary society was its inadequate information about geometrical techniques, which alone vouchsafed an equitable allotment of land to various claimants.

I see [he added] that arithmetic, in so far as it is needful to the world and proves helpful in its dealings and the performance of many commandments, is not difficult to understand, and most persons have some grasp of it and are in the habit of using it. For this reason no one feels the need of composing a Hebrew treatise on this subject. As to geometry, on the other hand, the need for it in many areas is equal to that of arithmetic in matters pertaining to the business of this world and numerous commandments of the Torah. Yet it is difficult to understand, and its subject matter exceeds the capacity of most people. That is why someone must put his mind to explaining it, for its need is great in the measurement of land and its distribution among heirs or partners. Unless one relies on this discipline, one can never measure and distribute land justly and in accordance with true judgment.

Abraham found that the French communities were particularly negligent and even distributed property by sheer guesswork, giving one entitled to a third but a quarter, and vice versa. "There is no greater robbery and cheating than this procedure!" [19]

In his encyclopedia, especially in its mathematical sections, Savasorda likewise professed to cater to practical needs. After discussing, for instance, the several major arithmetical operations of multiplication, division, resolution (of ratios between numbers), subtraction, addition, and reduction—this sixfold division and its order were followed also by Ibn Ezra and the great Italian mathematician, Leonardo Fibonacci of Pisa—he added: "Since I wish to facilitate the task for the student of this work I explain the general principles in calculations for commercial transactions, so that anyone may apply them by analogy and derive from them all his own business calculations." [20]

Professions of this kind, to be sure, need not always be taken at their face value; they frequently served merely as rationalizations for personal intellectual curiosity, and as a justification before the unenlightened masses of such "wasteful" pursuits. In all his scientific and philosophic works Bar Ḥiyya himself evinced such an overpowering passion for knowledge that he doubtless would have indulged in these studies without any reference to their practical aspects. In his handbook of geometry he devoted only Section II to problems of mensuration and Section III to those of land division, but he preceded them by an initial section dealing with general concepts and terms and concluded with the briefer Section IV in which the methods of measuring bodies were analyzed.

In all these matters, Savasorda went far beyond the practical needs of elementary land measurements. He utilized many Euclidean teachings partly included in a work since lost and only partially preserved in Arabic translation (Bar Ḥiyya's text has indeed proved helpful in reconstructing some views of the ancient Greek mathematician), and reached some independent conclusions which proved fruitful for the subsequent scientific progress. His answer, for instance, to a problem of measuring a rectangle was based on an earlier theoretical computation, and led him to the formulation of the equation: $x^2 + ax - b = 0$ and its various derivatives and correlations, such as $(a + x)^2 + x^2 = 2(\frac{a}{2})^2 + 2(\frac{a}{2} + x)^2$ or $xy = a; x + y = b; x = \frac{b}{2} \pm \sqrt{\frac{b^2}{4} - a}$. These formulas, and the underlying concept of two roots, marked an important step forward. Although at times in order to facilitate actual measurements Abraham disregarded some tiny fractions, his results as a rule stand up well against modern calculations. For example, in measuring an equilateral triangle he suggested shortcuts which involved but a negligible error of 0.001 of the measured area. He believed that by treating of squares and triangles only, he could help the surveyors to measure areas of any other shape as well, in so far as the land could be divided into square or triangular strips. Even for circular fields he suggested a rather novel, none too adequate, method of cutting it into strips which was adopted by the French Tosafists but otherwise left practically no traces in the geometrical science of the age.[21]

On the other hand, as pointed out by Michael Guttmann, Bar Ḥiyya greatly neglected the various methods of mensuration made possible by angle geometry and only occasionally discussed computations based on simple, right angles. This failure can hardly be accounted for by the absence of appropriate instruments. Certainly, the so-called gnomon, based on the same principle as the carpenter's square but extended to general mathematical and astronomic use, had long been known in Hebrew letters. In fact, Bar Ḥiyya himself mentioned that different methods of mensuration employed by surveyors were dependent upon the shape of the land, and he explained by this very fact the reluctance of the local rabbis to adopt such "inconsistent" procedures. He seems also to have been one of the first Europeans to mention the Heronian formula $S = p(p - a)\ (p - b)\ (p - c)$, and it was probably from him, rather than from Gerard of Cremona's translation of Al-Khwarizmi's geometry, that Leonardo Pisano took it over—an important step forward in the progress of Latin geometry. According to Maximilian Curtze, the editor of Savasorda's *Liber Embadorum,* Leonardo not only followed closely the arrangement of that book, but he, as well as the West in general, had learned from it and not from Al-Khwarizmi "how one might solve the problem of quadratic equations." Perhaps because of his familiarity with the rabbinic leaders' general conservatism in the use of new implements, Savasorda preferred to discuss the entire problem in mathematical rather than technological terms. Intrinsically, however, this very disregard of instruments, and exclusive reliance on computations and somewhat abstract mathematics, reflects his own main concern for the spread of theoretical knowledge, the practical implications serving as but incidental incentives.[22]

If such preeminently theoretical concerns also characterized Bar Ḥiyya's works in astronomy and philosophy, he was by no means an exception among his coreligionists. Gone is the time when scholars tried to explain the great role played by Spanish and Provençal Jewish mathematicians during the twelfth and thirteenth centuries by the Jews' concentration on trade and banking and the ensuing need of improved arithmetical techniques. True, businessmen undoubtedly looked for methods of facilitating their growingly complex commercial transactions. But these techniques had been fully developed during the economic upsurge of the preceding centuries, in which the eastern and, later, the Spanish Jews had participated fully. From the standpoint of mathematical science these techniques, such as those included in the *regula mercatorum* and explained by Bar Ḥiyya and others, were quite elementary. They could hardly have created more than a superficial response from the public at large to advanced mathematical work.

Curiously, at the height of Jewish mathematical learning the best scientists were concerned with such "impractical" subjects as the Computation of the Courses of Stars, Astronomical Tables, Books of Intercalation (Calendar)—all these are titles of works by Bar Ḥiyya—or with the astrological interpretation of history and the computation of the prospective advent of the Messiah. There is, for example, no Jewish book on mechanics. Not that Jews required no technological knowledge for the building of houses, the digging of canals for irrigation, or the utilization of implements in their crafts. Jewish builders of all kinds are, indeed, mentioned in the sources of both East and West. We recall, for one example, Masha'allah's significant contribution to the planning of the new capital of Baghdad. We even have reasons to believe that western Jews performed pioneering services in introducing new types of masonry and architectural designs into England and other countries. Yet they did not seem to find it necessary to describe and elaborate these techniques in special monographs. They apparently relied either on works written in Arabic or Latin or, even more, on the living transmission of actual practices from one generation to another through the training of apprentices. In any case, there would hardly have been sufficient demand for such books in the Jewish market, which had only slowly learned to extend the meaning of Torah to a few domains of secular learning essentially theoretical in nature.[23]

At the same time, such Jewish authors as Bar Ḥiyya and Ibn 'Aqnin paid at least lip service to the value of mechanical studies, particularly optics, in their classifications of sciences and their educational curricula. Although pointing out their great utilitarian purpose, Ibn 'Aqnin merely suggested that it would do no harm if a teacher were to instruct his pupils in this science "of heavy things" (mechanics), and he concluded with this characteristic remark: "However, the larger part of the study of these sciences turns [the pupil's] attention away from the [truly] useful theoretical sciences." A curious inversion of the concept of usefulness, indeed! [24]

Not that pure theory reigned supreme. Judaism was too much an activist religion, Jewish life too greatly beset with a host of practical problems, for the leaders to indulge in abstract thought completely unrelated to Jewish reality. Pragmatic, if not practical, considerations colored much of the thought of both Bar Ḥiyya and his younger contemporary, Ibn Ezra. Even astrology, to which, as we shall see, the latter devoted most of his scientific writings, was generally considered an unfailing guide for human behavior. Understandably, one could also far more easily enlist the financial support of the numerous patrons of that age for astrological work, especially if it was combined with personal horoscopes for the patrons, their families, and entourage, than for more detached astronomical and mathematical investigations. However, the thinking of most Jews, Muslims, and Christians of the period was so deeply permeated with religion that, like philosophy, science largely remained but the handmaiden of theology.

For this reason a versatile mind like Ibn Ezra's could so readily turn from mathematical subjects to the symbolism of numbers and letters and from these to biblical exegesis, grammar, and lexicography, winding up in the rarefied atmosphere of metaphysics in order finally to reemerge with some new mathematical insight. Such blending of various disciplines and approaches, rather than discouraging the educated student, proved for him a major attraction. The quest for all-inclusive solutions, so characteristic of the Christian even more than the Muslim Middle Ages (during the Islamic Renaissance one heard sporadic advocates of specialization), endeared works like those by Ibn Ezra to later generations. This polyhistor was among the best known and most admired Jewish authors in the Christian world, long before Browning sang his praises to receptive modern worshipers of scientific progress. Among Jews his prestige was further enhanced by his scintillating, though often consciously and provocatively tantalizing, Hebrew style, his satirical humor, and his poetic gifts. His poetic works included many a brief mathematical and astronomic treatise in verse. Even a poem on the then very popular, though apparently not yet fully standardized, game of chess is attributed to him—a game, incidentally, which often helped sharpen the minds of its adepts for mathematical thinking.[25]

IMAGE OF THE UNIVERSE

Mathematical methods were also used for astronomical computations, helping to explain to inquisitive minds some of the riddles of the universe. Apart from the problems of calendaring which, as we shall see, exerted a powerful influence on promoting astronomic studies among the Jewish intelligentsia, there was enough astronomical material in the biblical and talmudic tradition to intrigue exegetes as well as jurists and to remove whatever objections to the study of "Greek wisdom" had still lingered from ancient times. Even the most orthodox could not controvert such clear-cut statements as that of the second-century sage, Bar Qappara: "He who possesses the ability to compute the paths of the sun [controlling the seasons] and the planets but fails to do so" commits a sin of omission and is alluded to in the prophet's saying, "But they regard not the work of the Lord, neither have they considered the operation of His hands" (Isa. 5:12). R. Johanan went further and declared it to be an outright commandment for Israel to compute the course of the sun and planets, "for this is your wisdom and your understanding in the sight of the peoples" (Deut. 4:6; Shabbat 75a). Referring to statements of this kind, Ibn Ezra also pointed out that no intelligent person can understand the brief allusions to the moon's nativities in the Talmud, "unless he studies astronomy and knows the movements of the sun and the moon. Nor can he understand astronomy, unless he first learns geometry, for it is like a ladder set up on the earth, and the top of it reaches to heaven" (*Yesod mora,* p. 7; German trans., p. 18).

At the same time, Jewish students were seriously handicapped in their astronomical work by the lack of facilities for observation, and by their preeminently theoretical bent of studies. The relatively small and tax-ridden Jewish communities even in the populous East could not afford to maintain such large-scale astronomic observatories as were established for Muslim scholars by their powerful rulers. One need but peruse Maqrizi's amusing account of the construction of an observatory near Cairo in 1119 to realize how impossible it would have been for a Jewish communal academy to embark on such an ambitious venture. Only few Jews could secure access to these governmental institutions, except to a minor extent in Spain, and even there mainly in connection with astrological services. The very Alphonsine Tables had to be prepared by their chief Jewish compilers at the court of Alfonso X the Sage of Castile from books, rather than on the basis of observation with refined instruments. Even alert students of philosophy, moreover, talked disparagingly of the astronomer's empirical work, "for he does not profess to tell us the existing properties of the spheres, but to suggest, whether correctly or not, a theory in which the motion of the stars is circular and uniform, and yet in agreement with our observation." Maimonides, who wrote these lines, was himself an informed student of astronomy, as it was represented in his native Spain by such Muslim scholars as Jabir ibn Aflaḥ, with whose son he had associated in his youth. He had also studied together with a pupil of Ibn Bajja (called Avempace by the Latins) and others. Nevertheless, he himself remained extremely skeptical about the ability of man to penetrate the mysteries of the superlunary world. He was prepared to follow the regnant doctrines of contemporary scientists only in so far as they did not disagree with either the Jewish tradition or his own philosophic preconceptions. Even the distinguished Arab astronomer, Al-Bitruji, considered it his major claim to fame that his system, incidentally largely a restatement of older doctrines, had been derived not from observation or even speculation, but from divine inspiration.[26]

Modern man finds it difficult to place himself mentally in the position of Maimonides and his predecessors, and to view the universe as they saw it. He must first try to disregard some basic assumptions which have become deeply ingrained in his mind from the early stages of his education. He must forget, for example, such simple concepts as that stars are large bodies traveling through "empty" spaces, following the laws of gravitation, on courses determined by the attraction of other bodies.

Some medieval thinkers, to be sure, improving upon the knowledge of the Hellenistic schools, increased Hipparchus' list of 850 fixed stars to a total of 1,022. Al-Farghani (9th cent.) also taught that, while the moon was only $1/39$ and Venus $1/37$ the size of the earth, the sun was 166, Saturn 90, and Jupiter 95 times as large. Estimates by other astronomers, including Abraham bar Ḥiyya, differed considerably from those of Al-Farghani. Citing the observations instituted at the order of Caliph Al-Ma'mun, the famous promoter of scientific studies and experiments, the Spanish Jewish scientist devoted the entire ninth section of his handbook on cosmography to measurements of the distances of the various celestial bodies from the earth, and their respective sizes. He reached the following conclusions: the sun is more than $166\frac{1}{3}$ times the size of the earth, while the moon equals only $\frac{1}{39}$, Mercury $\frac{1}{19,000}$, and Venus $\frac{1}{36}$ of its displacement. On the other hand, the magnitude of Mars is $1\frac{1}{3}$, Saturn 79, and Jupiter 81 times that of the earth. Fixed stars, finally, are to be classed in six divisions, ranging from 16 to 105 times the size of the earth. Bar Ḥiyya counted in addition fourteen stars whose magnitudes had not yet been ascertained. "You will find," he concluded, "that the body of the sun is the largest in the entire host of heaven, that Mercury is the smallest star visible from the earth, and that this is their size according to the experts who have investigated this matter." These calculations, he insisted, however, referred only to stars visible to men. In addition to the 1,022 (or rather 1,025) fixed stars ascertained by observation, there doubtless existed millions of others which, because of their lesser size and the distance of the eighth sphere from earth, remained unseen. That is why, in Savasorda's opinion, the Bible was justified in speaking of countless celestial bodies, and the Midrash could mention even the hyperbolical figure of 291,600,000 stars.[27]

Despite the sun's admitted superior size, it was generally believed that it rotated around the earth. It supposedly traveled in a special sphere of its own, which was a more or less rigid crystalline body, propelled by a special Intelligence. The medieval man could not conceive of anything moving, or even continuing to move by a sort of inertia, without some such propelling force in immediate contact with the moving body. He conceded that, unlike the stars, the spheres in which they were supposed to move were invisible. Yet he postulated the existence of spheres, just as we postulate the presence of an invisible automobile when on a dark night we perceive tail-lights moving ahead of us. Being made of an ethereal substance, which, though lighter than fire, did not possess the latter's tendency to escape upwards, the heavenly bodies were said to proceed in an eternal circular motion. In this way the medieval man explained to himself their often changing positions in the skies.

No medieval scientist, except Al-Biruni following Indian sages, seriously took up the old suggestion by Aristarchus of Hippo and Seleucus of Babylon (!) that, appearances to the contrary, the earth rotated around the sun. Even the idea of the earth rotating around its own axis was but briefly alluded to; it was neither stressed nor explained in detail by Al-Biruni and the author of the *Zohar*. The majority entertained no doubts that the earth, though a globe, was stationary and placed, by the very weight of its main component, the earthly element, at the bottom of things; that is, in the center of the universe. Generally surrounded by the second-heaviest element, water—we shall see how the emergence of a limited land mass above the surface of the surrounding oceans was explained—and above it by air and by the lightest element, fire, the earth allegedly stood still. Around it moved the nearest celestial body, the moon, traveling in a sphere of its own. Opinions were divided as to whether the next sphere was that of the sun, or, as most students believed, that of Venus, followed by that of Mercury. Maimonides referred to this controversy, mentioning especially Jabir ibn Aflaḥ's "famous book" which restored the allegedly pre-Ptolemaic view that the spheres of all five planets were above that of the sun. This view was substantially accepted by Maimonides himself, despite Ibn Bajja's arguments showing the improbability (Maimonides emphasized *improbability,* not impossibility) of Venus and Mercury being above the sun. Everybody agreed, however, that the other planets moved in spheres located above the sun, being in turn surrounded by the sphere of the fixed stars, and finally, by one often called the *primum mobile,* which was supposed to keep the entire universe in motion.[28]

Such a simplified view, more or less shared by all thinking persons, did not satisfy the experts. Their observations of the existing irregularities in the motions of the celestial bodies could not be fully explained even by the assumption that the *primum mobile* moved in the opposite direction than that of the other spheres. From ancient times the Ptolemaic system had supplemented, therefore, this simple image by a complicated structure of epicycles and eccentric cycles, which were said to cause the observable deviations. However, closer observation had demonstrated the inadequacy of even that correction. Nor did the theory of "trepidation" of the stars, suggested in the ninth century by Ṭabit ibn Qurrah, remove more difficulties than it created, and hence it enjoyed but a passing vogue. Moreover, some thinkers, including Maimonides (who knew of Ṭabit), objected to these significant variants on principle.

> Let us first consider [Maimonides wrote] an epicycle, such as has been assumed in the spheres of the moon and the five planets, rotating on a sphere, but not round the center of the sphere that carries it. This arrangement would necessarily produce a revolving motion; the epicycle would then revolve, and entirely change its place; but that anything in the spheres should change its place is exactly what Aristotle considers impossible. . . . I have heard that Abu-Bekr [ibn aṣ-Ṣaij ibn Bajja] discovered a system in which no epicycles occur; but eccentric spheres are not excluded by him. I have not heard it from his pupils; and even if it be correct that he discovered such a system, he has not gained much by it; for eccentricity is likewise as contrary as possible to the principles laid down by Aristotle.

In another context, as we recall, the sage of Fusṭaṭ was ready to deny the Stagirite's authority in all matters concerning the superlunary world. Quoting the psalmist's exclamation "The heavens are the heavens of the Lord's but the earth hath He given to the children of man" (115:16), he contended that "of the things in the heavens man knows nothing except a few mathematical calculations, and you see how far these go" (*Guide,* II.19, 24; Friedländer, pp. 186, 196, 198). Thus, as in many crucial points of his theology, Maimonides took refuge in epistemological skepticism, in order to preserve intact the fundamental teachings of his religious tradition.

We must bear in mind, however, that, like Saadiah and Halevi, Maimonides was interested in astronomic facts only in so far as they were related to some of his philosophic theories. For the gaon the main issue was the finite character of the universe which presupposes the existence of a Creator and a First Mover. He debated therefore with some contemporary skeptics the problem of the possibility of the earth and the heaven, as we know them, not being the only ones to exist. Saadiah arrived at the "unshakable conclusion" that heaven and earth are both unique and finite. He also argued that "the eastern movement of the uppermost sphere is carried out once every day and night, whereas the western movement of the fixed stars traverses every hundred years a distance of one degree," and hence requires 13,140,000 days to complete its revolution. "How, then, canst thou say that a force, the movement of which varies so widely, is not finite?" Halevi adduced the testimony of the sun, whose astronomic reality is so different from what it appears to be, and whose diurnal and annual motions are "in two opposite directions from west to east, and from east to west, under conditions it would lead us too far to discuss," merely in order to demonstrate the insufficiency of man's sensory perceptions.[29]

ASTRONOMIC RESEARCH

Not all Jewish scientists were equally vacillating. Some of them doubtless pursued their astronomic studies in considerable detachment from theological preconceptions. This seems to be particularly true of the early savants, Masha'allah and Sahl ben Bishr. More numerous than their mathematical treatises, their astronomic works enjoyed considerable vogue throughout the Middle Ages, perhaps because of the intimate association of astronomy with astrology. In his writings, Ibn Ezra was frequently critical of Masha'allah's views. He nevertheless found it necessary to reproduce in Hebrew translation two Arabic essays (on "interrogations" and "eclipses") by this author. Latin versions of several tracts are still extant; some were printed as late as 1493–1583 for the benefit of modern students of astronomy and astrology. Others were merely quoted, sometimes in terms so obscure that it is impossible to reconstruct their subject matter, or even to ascertain whether the passages quoted belong to different works. Masha'allah's known writings, however, include a comprehensive treatise on the Elements and the Celestial Bodies, and others on Planets, Nativities of the Moon (of great importance for the computation of lunar months by both Arabs and Jews), the Eclipses of the Sun and the Moon (which seems to have dealt also with the influences of stellar conjunctions on countries and religions), and the Annual Revolutions of Stars. In 1583 students still found interest in his treatise on the Astrolabe, although many great improvements made in the intervening nine centuries had rendered Masha'allah's instrument practically obsolete. On the other hand, the essay he wrote on the so-called armillary sphere, connected with the astrolabe, was merely mentioned by later medieval authors.[30]

Like Masha'allah, with whom he was sometimes confused, Sahl ben Bishr was an extremely prolific writer. Many of his works, too, were subsequently translated into Latin, and some of them were printed as late as the sixteenth century. They were, in fact, among the earliest Latin translations of Arabic astronomical works; Hermann of Dalmatia translated his *Faticida* in 1138. Under the name Zahel, often further misspelled (a later Hebrew paraphrast gave him even the Hebrew name of Sha'ul [Saul] ben Baṣar), he is quoted as an outstanding authority by many Western scholars, beginning with Albertus Magnus. Regrettably, the Western scientists were far more interested in Sahl's astrological works than in those dealing more strictly with astronomy. Hence, most of the latter are totally lost. A treatise bearing the intriguing title *Kitab Hayya wa-'ilm al-ḥisab* (Book of Astronomy and the Science of Arithmetic) would doubtless have supplied us with many new insights into the early medieval relations between mathematics and astronomy. Another book, apparently called the "Tenth," offered a comprehensive summary of his astronomic teachings and, according to the generally reliable An-Nadim, enjoyed already in the tenth century a great reputation among the *Rumi* (Byzantines). On the other hand, the extant fragments of his astrological works contain many astronomic teachings which would merit further detailed exploration.[31]

We are even worse off with respect to the writings of Sahl's younger contemporary, Sind ben 'Ali. Because Sind's works were mainly astronomic in character, they were of less interest to the "pragmatic" Westerners. We are restricted, therefore, almost entirely to a few brief references in the *Fihrist* and other Arabic works. From these it appears that Sind served as court astronomer to both Al-Mu'izz and Al-Ma'mun. Originally sufficiently orthodox to maintain a synagogue at Al-Mu'izz's residence, he was later converted to Islam. Perhaps for this reason he was quickly forgotten among the Jews. Sind actively participated in the scientific expeditions arranged by Al-Ma'mun. According to the Egyptian, Ibn Yunus (d. 1009), himself one of the greatest astronomic observers of the Middle Ages, Sind left behind a description of a significant mission he had performed, together with several associates, for the caliph in measuring the distance between Wasit and Palmyra. This mission doubtless was part of Al-Ma'mun's endeavor to verify and bring up to date, by using Eratosthenes' own techniques, the observations which were the basis of ancient measurements of the earth's surface.[32]

Sahl ben Bishr was one of the earliest scientists to yield to the ever-growing love for poetry and compose a poem on the movements of stars. This poem, known only from a partial Latin translation preserved in a fifteenth-century manuscript, bears the nondescript title *Carmen de planetarum aspectibus*. It may have been but an astronomical tract in verse, such as were especially popular in India. Al-Biruni was not alone in objecting to these artificial shackles which must needs sacrifice clarity and precision to exigencies of form. However, when a gifted poet like Ibn Gabirol decided to versify on astronomic themes, he produced a poetic masterpiece, which, though contributing relatively little to the advancement of knowledge among specialists, greatly helped to popularize their discoveries among the general intelligentsia. Moreover, by integrating the astronomic facts into his indubitably original philosophic and theological system, Ibn Gabirol, especially in his celebrated "Royal Crown," presented the astronomic findings of contemporary scientists as part and parcel of a total world outlook. When, for example, the poet sang

Who shall understand the mysteries of Thy creations?
For Thou has exalted above the ninth sphere the sphere of Intelligence,
It is the Temple confronting us, "The tenth that shall be sacred to the Lord,"
It is the Sphere transcending height, To which conception cannot reach,
And there stands the veiled palanquin of Thy glory.
From the silver of Truth hast Thou cast it, And of the Gold of Reason hast Thou wrought its arms,
And on a pillar of Righteousness set its cushions, And from Thy power is its existence,
And from and toward Thee its yearning, "And unto Thee shall be its desire"

he alluded to his concept of the supreme world of Intelligences directing the highest sphere and setting in motion all the other spheres—all that because of the "desire" of the Intelligences toward God.[33]

Less theologically oriented were the astronomic works by Abraham bar Ḥiyya, especially his Hebrew trilogy, the *Ṣurat ha-areṣ* (Cosmography), the *Ḥeshbon mahalekhot ha-kokhabim* (Computation of the Courses of Stars), and *Luḥot* (Astronomical Tables). This trilogy seems to have been completed in 1136, possibly in a revised edition of an earlier draft. The latter two parts were later annotated by Ibn Ezra. The reason for this tripartite division is explained by the author in the introduction to his first work, whose very title indicates its indebtedness to similar Arabic treatises from Al-Khwarizmi on. Despite the evident interest of Jews in the movements of stars, he asserted, quoting the aforementioned rabbinic homilies, he had found no Hebrew work on the subject. He decided, therefore, to supply information on what he called the *ḥokhmat ha-ḥizzayon* (the science of observation; that is, astronomy), in contradistinction to the *ḥokhmat ha-nissayon* (the science of experience; that is, of contemplating the effects of stellar movements on the earth and on man, or "natural" astrology). The former is subdivided into two disciplines: "that of the shape [*ṣurat*] of the structure of heaven and earth, the order of the progression visible in the skies and the stars, the course and measure of each, and the proofs demonstrating all that. The second part deals with the way of computing the course of these moving celestial bodies, and how you can ascertain the position of the stars from the sky at any time you may wish." The Tables were, of course, to serve merely as a handy appendix to facilitate such computations.[34]

Savasorda seems to have been interested far more in astronomy than in astrology, particularly of the "judicial" kind. At least none of his published statements betray any direct acceptance of man's ability to foretell the fate of individuals from personal horoscopes. In this respect he differed greatly from Ibn Ezra, whose ardent belief in judicial astrology was to color posterity's judgment on Bar Ḥiyya's attitude as well. At times, it seems, the Latin translators actually confounded the views of the two Abrahams, and either under the influence of Ibn Ezra's own interpretation of Savasorda's teachings or as a result of the translators' or copyists' lack of discrimination, often attributed to Bar Ḥiyya views held only by his younger contemporary.[35]

Even Bar Ḥiyya's relative detachment, however, was not altogether in tune with the temper of the more orthodox Jewish circles in Christian Spain. As we recollect, he had to defend himself before the conservative faction, led by Yehudah bar Barzillai, for venturing into the field of astrology at all, though only astrology of the "natural" variety, or for suggesting the avoidance of certain "unlucky" days. In his letter of apology he reminisced that "from my childhood until today I have studied the science of stars, made use of it, studied and thought about it, while believing that I was acquiring wisdom and knowledge in which there is neither sin nor transgression." He also pointed out that this work had earned him recognition among rulers and princes—a telling argument indeed among a people whose destinies were often deeply affected by governmental good will secured by some such influential members. More directly than this letter Savasorda's ethical and philosophic writings, especially his astrological-messianic *Megillat ha-megalleh,* must have persuaded all judicious persons of his genuine piety.[36]

Not on dogmatic, but on purely scholarly grounds, Savasorda was sometimes criticized by his otherwise admiring successor, Ibn Ezra, with whom he was frequently confused because of the medieval habit of quoting either as "Abraham Judaeus" without further identification. On one occasion, Ibn Ezra censured his predecessor for following the astronomical tables of Al-Baṭṭani while claiming that these were the tables compiled by Ptolemy. But even in this instance the critic, who must have known that Al-Baṭṭani himself had offered but a corrected version of the work of the Alexandrian astronomer, did not name Bar Ḥiyya but merely voiced his amazement at the "great man's" error.

Perhaps yielding to popular pressures, Ibn Ezra himself devoted more attention to astrology than to astronomy proper. On his peregrinations during the declining years of his life he was often forced by popular demand, or by that of wealthy patrons, to elaborate quickly on some astrological or astronomic theme. Although perfectly familiar with the use of the astrolabe, to which he devoted two monographs, he had little opportunity for astronomic observations. He derived most of his knowledge from the few books available to him in the scientifically backward communities of Italy, France, and England. In fact, in Italy, later a major center of Jewish enlightenment, little scientific progress had been made since the days of Shabbetai Donnolo, who had found and copied a considerable number of the "writings of the ancient sages of Israel," but which none of his neighbors had been able to explain. Only the arrival of a visitor from Babylonia made it possible for him to receive instruction, at a high price, in such technical works as the apocryphal "Baraita of Samuel." Two centuries later Ibn Ezra still had to defend himself before his superorthodox Italian coreligionists, who viewed with suspicion any studies outside strictly rabbinic fields of learning. Nor did the northern Italian Christians of the time have access to any comprehensive scientific literature in Latin. Under the circumstances, Ibn Ezra must evidently have cited many data from his prodigious memory, which explains not only occasional slips, but also the frequency with which he corrected some of his earlier statements. For this reason, as well as because of his general predilection for revising earlier works, some of his writings are now available in more than one recension. Since the manuscripts are often incomplete and undatable, there is no certain way of separating the author's own revision from changes, unconscious or willful, inserted by later copyists.[37]

While among the Jews Ibn Ezra's popularity rested chiefly with his exegetical, grammatical, and poetic works, he speedily attracted a large following among Christian students of mathematics, astronomy, and astrology. He seems to have maintained such active personal contacts with Italian and French scientists that his "Pisan Tables," one of his major astronomic treatises, was apparently never written in Hebrew, but was directly dictated to a Latin-writing inquirer. This work, sometimes confused with Ibn Ezra's *Yesode ha-luḥot* or Fundamentals of Astronomic Tables, offered a revised version of the "Toledan Tables," prepared by Al-Zarqali (in cooperation with Jewish scientists) in 1089–90. It was composed, or revised from some earlier draft, by Ibn Ezra in Pisa and centered around the year 1149, that is, three twenty-year cycles after Al-Zarqali's Tables. Only under the assumption of such direct dictation can we readily understand the consistent use throughout this tract of the Christian era and the sequences of the Christian calendar, as well as the peculiar transliteration of Arabic names, which the writer must have heard pronounced by Ibn Ezra in the Spanish dialect of his time. True, there is no way of telling how much or how little Latin Ibn Ezra himself knew, even though he may have been familiar with the dialectal Castilian of his mother country, and hence how far he could go in checking his Christian translator's Latin phrasing. He certainly could not have approved of such a system of dating as "this year 1154 since the Lord's incarnation in which we have prepared this edition." That is also why there is no record of that work in Hebrew in either a manuscript fragment or any subsequent quotation. Be this as it may, the "Pisan Tables," like other treatises by Ibn Ezra, were frequently quoted thereafter by such outstanding authorities as Roger Bacon, Nicolaus of Cusa, and Pico della Mirandola. Even today a critical edition of a complete corpus of Ibn Ezra's scientific writings would undoubtedly shed considerable new light on the evolution of Western science, for, apart from his own contributions, his great erudition has helped salvage many an important older historic record since lost. For one example, his brief sketch of the early history of Arabian mathematics, and his emphasis on the great impact of Indian science allegedly communicated to the Arabs by a Jewish intermediary long before Ptolemy's *Almagest* had become available in an Arabic version, contains many detailed data and suggestions worthy of further exploration.[38]

Unlike the scientists, the public at large was often impatient with the slow and painful progress in the acquisition of knowledge, and was particularly disgruntled over the endless differences of opinion among the scholars. In its eternal quest for certainty, the medieval mind readily bowed to authority, and hence was doubly bewildered when recognized authorities controverted one another's findings. Such differences of opinion were particularly grist for the mill of the obscurantist opponents of independent research. If even Maimonides could advance arguments for the unreliability of human cognition in all matters relating to the superlunary world, how much more readily could ignorant or willfully antiscientific persons point to the contradictory and constantly changing views held by leading scientists as proof positive of the vacillations of human knowledge, in contrast with the certainties offered by the "revealed" texts!

To appease such doubts Ibn Ezra, addressing himself to an audience more deeply inured to philosophic than scientific debates, pointed out the basic similarity between the scientists' and the philosophers' quests for truth. In both cases the search is made more arduous, but not obviated, by the existing honest differences of opinion. Moreover, he emphasized, "such discord is of but minor importance [in practice], and is no obstacle to astronomic work and the understanding of the eclipses of the sun and moon, or to judicial astronomy [astrology]." He also stressed the genuine improvements constantly made in the techniques of actual observation, and underscored the confirmation of many of his data by the astrolabe. For this reason he devoted his aforementioned special treatises to a discussion of this important instrument, usually made of copper, and hence called in Hebrew the *Keli neḥoshet* (Copper Instrument).[39]

Evidently because of these universally recognized differences of opinion, Ibn Ezra felt obligated to quote his authorities far more amply than was customary in his day. After pointing out that there had been many opposing doctrines among the Indian, Persian, Egyptian, and Greek astronomers, especially with reference to the motions of the ninth sphere of fixed stars, he quoted the latest Muslim authorities, including Al-Zarqali. While generally following the latter's lead, he differed from him in two fundamental aspects. He rejected both Al-Zarqali's doctrine concerning the computation of the sun's apogee, and the then much debated hypothesis concerning the "trepidation" of stars, which was to help explain the divergences between the observable motions of the stars and the Ptolemaic theory.

Apart from the two Abrahams, twelfth-century Spanish Jewry included several other distinguished scientists, some of whom, however, were to find their way to the baptismal font. Among the Christian converts whose influence on medieval science was fairly enduring are Petrus Alphonsi (or Pedro Alfonso), and Johannes Hispalensis (Avendeath or Ibn Daud). Petrus, as we recall, was the former Moses ha-Sefardi, who, upon his conversion at the age of forty-four, joined the ranks of the leading controversialists against his former faith. Like his younger contemporary Ibn Ezra, he spent the last decades of his life away from his mother country, satisfying the awakened scientific curiosity of the French and English from the fruits of his earlier Arabic and Hebrew studies. Although at times likewise suffering from an insufficiency of books, Petrus was able to instruct, among others, Walcher the abbot of Malvern in England in the fundamentals of astronomy. He taught the abbot the proper use of the astrolabe and the quadrant (one of Walcher's letters expresses naive rejoicing over the use of these implements), and he composed, with Walcher's assistance, an astronomic treatise entitled *De Dracone* (*ca.*1120). He also seems to have assisted in, and possibly even taken the initiative for, Adelard of Bath's translation (in 1126) of Al-Khwarizmi's astronomical tables in the form revised by Maslama al-Majriti. Here, too, such collaboration helps explain the transliteration of Arabic names and terms in the current Spanish dialect, hardly known to the English translator, who apparently had never visited Spain. In all these works Petrus espoused vigorously the need of observation, and constantly referred to the force of "experimental arguments." In his opinion, the importance of astronomy could not easily be exaggerated, and he considered it his duty to spread its knowledge among his new coreligionists north of the Pyrenees. "Indeed innumerable other things," he wrote on one occasion, "happen on earth in accordance with the courses of the stars and pass unnoticed by the senses of most men, but are discovered and understood by the subtle acumen of learned men who are skilled in this art." To buttress his learned arguments, he often invoked scriptural passages, which he explained in a homiletical vein, sometimes betraying his earlier training in rabbinic modes of interpretation.[40]

Avendeath, on his part, was active in his native Spain as both an independent author and translator. He seems to have written, for instance, a philosophic-scientific *Liber de causis,* long considered of unknown authorship. His translations, especially, often in collaboration with Dominicus Gundissalinus (or Gundisalvus), opened up many treasures of Eastern science to eager Europeans.

On the whole, such translations were never slavish, but involved a good deal of reinterpretation, even modification, of the original teachings. In fact, in view of the great dependence of medieval scientists on recognized authorities, the difference in originality between author and translator often was but one of degree: the translator reproduced the contents of a single book, the author those of a number of books.[41]

ASTROLOGY

Astronomy led imperceptibly into astrology, both natural and judicial. Natural astrology is even today legitimately pursued by astronomers and meteorologists, and extensively employed in weather forecasts, navigation, or calendar computations. According to Lynn Thorndike, John of Saxony was delighted to have Ibn Ezra's support for his contention "that when the moon entered the aquatic sign of the Zodiac under certain circumstances, it would begin to rain and continue to rain so long as the moon remained in that sign" (*History of Magic*, III, 264 f.). It is to this branch that the term *ḥokhmat ha-nisyonot* applied with particular force. Starting from the observation of the obvious influences of the moon and stars on such natural manifestations on earth as the ebb and flow of seas, and postulating a strong nexus also between these motions and human behavior, even the most sober astronomers believed that there must exist a key to these correlations. By predicting the course of the stars, therefore, they believed, they might also help to unravel the otherwise admittedly unpredictable future fate or actions of men. For this reason even judicial astrology had attracted many disciplined thinkers, as well as practitioners of occult arts, from the days of ancient Babylonia and Egypt.

Pious Jews, to be sure, had to contend against the old prophetic injunction "Learn not the way of the nations, and be not dismayed by the signs of heaven" (Jer. 10:2), which was often interpreted to mean that, in contradistinction to other nations, Israel was not subject to the influence of stars. This pointed negation of the Babylonian astral religion did not, however, prevent Jews living in both the Graeco-Roman and the Persian worlds from making a living by the practice of this occult science. Nor did it weaken the widespread attribution of the origins of astrology to Enoch, Noah, or Abraham. Nevertheless, fierce denials of the value of all astrological predictions by outright rationalists were sufficiently reinforced by the lingering suspicions carried over from the biblical age to force even such independent thinkers as Bar Ḥiyya and Ibn Ezra to search for rationales. In the introduction to the fifth chapter of his "Scroll of Disclosure" Bar Ḥiyya argued that, while data taken from astrology cannot in any way compare with the force of his proofs derived from the authoritative Jewish sources, they served, at least, to persuade doubting Jewish intellectuals of the veracity of these predictions. "Another benefit will arise from this method that we shall be able to prove through it [our contention] against the Gentile nations, who do not believe in the Torah, and before whom one cannot argue from the words of Jewish law." Moreover, certain talmudic passages themselves reveal basic approval of the astrological approach. Ibn Ezra, too, the most prolific and influential of medieval Hebrew writers on astrology, prefaced his works with some such pious mouthings as "the fear of the Lord protects him [man] from the decrees of the heavenly bodies and from their sway as long as he lives." It is this very idea that inspired Ibn Ezra to call his main astrological treatise the "Beginning of Wisdom," reminiscent of the ancient proverb that such beginning consists in the fear of the Lord.[42]

At the same time, this very treatise shows the extent to which purely astronomic investigations were intermingled with the quest for divination of the future fate of groups and individuals. To quote Ibn Ezra's own summary:

> This book is divided into ten chapters. The first chapter deals with the form of the firmament and with its parts, its signs, and its figures, and with the seven wandering stars, their position, and influence, their motion, and power. The second chapter treats of the influence of the signs, their position, their action, the conjunction of the stars, and their forms. The third discusses the aspects of their position, and the influence of the quarters of the sphere, and the twelve "houses." The fourth tells of the conjunction of the seven planets and their influence, and all that which they prognosticate for all creatures which exist on earth. The fifth pertains to the qualities of the planets, when their influence increases, and when it wanes. The sixth describes the in-

fluence of the planets by themselves, and according to their position in front, or in back of the sun. The seventh takes up the aspect of the planets, their conjunction, or separation, and in general the things in which there is a conjunction of their mutual influence over all that which they prognosticate. The eighth relates the effects of the planets with regard to interrogations, nativities, and the seasons. The ninth refers to the lots of the planets, the lots of the houses, and the other lots mentioned by the experts on signs [astrologers]. The tenth bears upon the radiation of the light of the seven planets, the path of their course, their movements through the degrees of the sphere, and everything pertaining to them.

Clearly, this was a mixture of judicial with natural astrology, and even with pure astronomy. From the outset, the author realized that in the brief compass of a short treatise he could mention but the basic "facts" and "laws" pertaining to so many different phases, and that many statements would require further elucidation. He added, therefore, immediately a booklet on the "Reasons" of these phenomena (*Sefer ha-Ṭe'amim*), extant as much else in Ibn Ezra's literary work, in two different versions. This treatise which, despite its brevity, succeeded in documenting from the sources much of what was merely stated in the larger work, was followed in quick succession by five other astrological tracts and the aforementioned book (or books) on the "Astrolabe." These eight tracts together formed a distinct collection, and they frequently appear as a unit in medieval manuscripts. Although no general title embracing this "astrological encyclopedia," as Millás Vallicrosa has aptly called it, is recorded—the title *Ḥuqqot ha-shamayim* (Laws of Heavenly Bodies) doubtless is but a later invention based on the opening paragraph of the first work—these eight essays were treated as a unit by many Latin translators as well. A quarter century ago, R. Levy was already able to list thirty-three Hebrew manuscripts embracing the entire collection, side by side with forty-three manuscripts containing individual works.[43]

Ibn Ezra, as well as his innumerable readers, both Jewish and Christian, in the following centuries were perfectly convinced that birth under a particular conjunction would necessarily affect the mental and physical characteristics of any new-born child. After describing the constellation Taurus in its various manifestations, the polyhistor explained that "its beginning points to winds and darkness, its middle is cold and moist, and its end denotes tempest, fire, lightning, and firebrand [*lappid*]." Hence man born under one or another of its "faces" will develop peculiar characteristics. "He who is born in the third face will have a beautiful body and head; there will be a mark in his left eye; he will be a man suffering from overwork; and he will have no luck with women." Such assertions sounded the less incongruous even to pious Jews, as they found similar dicta in the Talmud; for instance, R. Ḥanina's assertion concerning the impact of birth under a particular planet on man's character and choice of occupation. Nor did Ibn Ezra disdain preparing horoscopes for newly born children; two such calculations attributed to him are still extant. Quoting Ptolemy, Masha'allah, and others, he also advised his readers as to the time when the most propitious constellations favored the purchase of an object for profit or the building of a house.[44]

Most astonishingly, these medieval students of astrology were firmly convinced that such connections between human fate and the constellations of stars had been borne out by thousands of years of actual observation. Ibn Ezra had no doubt that the numerous astrological teachings attributed to Enoch in contemporary Arabic letters, many of them going far beyond the mystic speculations of the apocryphal book of Enoch, had come down the ages from the biblical Enoch, Methuselah's father, who had "walked with God, and he was not; for God took him" (Gen. 5:24). Unperturbed by the conflicting traditions in the sources themselves, which made him quote the "ancient Enoch," the "first Enoch," and the "Egyptian Enoch," he was convinced that that mysterious biblical patriarch "had composed many books in various sciences, and they are extant today." He also freely invoked the testimony of ancient Babylonians, Egyptians, Persians, and especially Indians. A voracious but critical reader of the existing literature, he observed, on occasion, that even the revered Enoch "had not adduced any proof," or "In my opinion, Enoch could not have said that." Ibn Ezra was even less restrained with respect to a passage of Ptolemy's major work, the *Tetrabiblos,* which he once bluntly dismissed as "a great error." Ibn Ezra's general procedure is, indeed, best described in his as yet unpublished

"Book of Nativities": "It is appropriate that I should describe in this book everything agreed upon by the ancients, and which I myself have tried a sufficient number of times." He was even ready to accept a contention of experts, without a satisfactory explanation, because of their assertion, "We have tried it thus, and found it to work." Ibn Ezra then proceeded to add the missing rationale.[45]

Ibn Ezra's criticisms, though more independent than those of most of his contemporaries, rarely extended to the historical critique of sources, however. True, in his exegetical work he dared to question some basic assumptions concerning the authorship of certain biblical works, but he did it on the basis of general concepts rather than historical criteria. He did not hesitate, therefore, to recognize the authenticity of the various works attributed to Enoch, just as he unquestioningly cited the statement of the mystical *She'ur qomah:* "R. Ishmael said, He who knows the measurements of the Creator of the Universe is assured of partaking of the world to come. I and 'Aqiba guarantee it" (*Yesod mora,* p. 50; German, pp. 136 f.). At the same time he was careful enough to deny the authenticity of such apocryphal books as the Chronicle of Moses, the Book of Zerubbabel, and the Book of Eldad ha-Dani, and to proclaim the general theory that "if any book is not written by prophets or sages, according to dependable tradition, we do not rely on it" (*Commentary* on Exod. 2:22).

If predictions did not come true, as was often the case, the astrologers were never short of explanations. A conjunction determining the fate of an individual could readily be in conflict with what an earlier constellation had decided concerning the fate of mankind or a particular nation. Such a general determination easily overruled the dictates of the stars concerning individual destinies. Even astrology-minded Jews, moreover, always less fatalistic than their Muslim neighbors, firmly believed that human conduct, particularly the fulfillment of commandments and repentance, often evoked direct divine intervention altering the natural course of events. Ibn Ezra himself, like Naḥmanides after him, quoted Samuel ibn Nagrela's explanation of the divine name, Shaddai, which, the Nagid felt, connoted God's power to withdraw man from the influence of stars. Moreover, Ibn Ezra's general philosophic doctrine, which as we recall had postulated the existence of a world of spirits and intelligences above the world of spheres or stars, tied up the human soul with that highest spiritual world, which could under circumstances override the stellar influences emanating from the second intermediary world. In fact, the study of astrology itself could lead in some way to the alteration of the course indicated by the stars, for, in Ibn Ezra's opinion, "he whose soul is filled with a knowledge of mathematics and astronomy advances greatly towards the knowledge of the divine Being, and secures for it eternal existence, becomes like the angels who minister unto God, and sings praises to Him together with His angels." [46]

There were, of course, also sharp opponents of astrology, like the Karaite Yehudah Hadassi and, particularly, Maimonides. The latter regretfully remembered his youthful preoccupation with what in more mature years he came to consider a pernicious pseudo-science. Ultimately, in his letter to the scholars of southern France, he equated astrology with idolatry, although even here he had to admit that in his earlier years he had himself come close to committing this mortal sin by studying practically the entire, rather sizable, Arabic literature on the subject available in Spain. Now, however, with a zeal of a missionary, he tried to persuade even the communities of Yemen and of southern France, then living on the periphery of Jewish life, to give up their deeply ingrained belief in astrology. "You should dismiss such notions from your thoughts," he urged his Yemenite correspondents, "cleanse your mind as one cleanses dirty clothes." He argued especially against their inferiority complex, which resignedly ascribed the prevailing ignorance in their country to the influence of the conjunctions of the earthly trigon, that is Taurus, Virgo, and Capricorn. Apart from the widespread lack of learning in other countries as well, Maimonides pointed out, such an attribution was clearly controverted by the historic fact that the three great patriarchs of ancient Israel, as well as King Solomon, declared by Scripture to have been "wiser than all men" (I Kings 5:11), had all lived during the earthly trigon. To drive this lesson home the sage of Fusṭaṭ added the following astronomic computation:

There is first, the smaller conjunction, that is, the meeting of Saturn with Jupiter, which occurs once in approximately twenty solar years. These conjunctions continue to take place twelve times within the same trigon. Hence the conjunctions which occur in the same trigon, take place over a period of two hundred and forty solar years. The shift to the next trigon is known as the medium conjunction, which continues for another two hundred and forty years. According to this calculation an interval of nine hundred and sixty years will elapse between the first and the second meeting of two planets in the same point of the Zodiac. This is termed the great conjunction, and occurs once in nine hundred and sixty years. This is the time that must elapse between the first and second meeting of Saturn and Jupiter in the same degree of Aries. If you will calculate back, you will understand my statement above that Abraham, Isaac, and Jacob, as well as David and Solomon, lived during the earthly trigon.

Maimonides also denied the contention of some Yemenites that all the seven planets would soon meet in one of the constellations of the Zodiac. "Such an event will not happen even in ten thousand years, as is well known to those who are familiar with the astronomical law of equation." [47]

Ignorance of the true findings of astronomy was, of course, not characteristic of the more expert astrologers. Certainly, men of the caliber of Masha'allah, Bar Ḥiyya, or Ibn Ezra, and their confreres among Muslims and Christians, made sure that their astrological predictions followed accepted astronomic doctrines. Moreover, in his determined opposition to both the theory and practice of this occult science, Maimonides had to combat not only deep-rooted popular beliefs, but also a tradition of immemorial antiquity and even positive talmudic statements friendly to astrology. His opponent, Abraham ben David, certainly was more in line with the genuine halakhic record when he wrote, "All happenings in life, the smallest as well as the greatest, have been handed by God to the control of the stars"; although, he hastened to add, man's intellect and free will to choose good or bad behavior largely frees him from that control (on *M.T.* Teshubah v.5). Even Yehudah Halevi, personally averse to astrological practices, did not deny that "the heavenly spheres exercise influence on terrestrial matters." He merely doubted man's ability to fathom these connections. He was also ready to accept astrology, "if we find that any element of this science is based on divine law" (*K. al-Khazari,* IV.9, 23, pp. 248 f., 266 f.; English, pp. 215, 228).

We may understand, therefore, a certain ambivalence also in Bar Ḥiyya's attitude. This sober scientist, who in the middle of an ethical treatise written for the edification of pious readers warned them not to believe that prayers offered by mourners affected the fate of the deceased, nevertheless strongly believed in astral forces governing human history. Nor was he loath to warn a bridegroom against going to the wedding at the stated time because that hour, being under the constellation of Mars, boded ill for the future. His aforementioned popularity with the ruling circles, too, was more likely the result of individual astrological services than of purely theoretical scientific contributions, although the latter did not completely lack in patronage and, of course, accrued also to the benefit of more "pragmatic" observers. Certainly, Bar Ḥiyya's occasional discussions of the various "houses" in the position of stars could be put to very good use in judicial astrology as well. Yet his own interests as exemplified in his extant works, including the "Scroll of Disclosure," ran principally in the direction of "natural" rather than "judicial" astrology. He mainly tried to gauge the influence of stellar movements on the destinies of mankind and the Jewish people. Such a distinction between "small particular accidents" affecting individuals and "great universal accidents" involving large groups was well known in the Middle Ages. Albertus Magnus actually attributed to Ptolemy himself two treatises under these very titles.[48]

Perhaps the best explanation of this restraint is found in Bar Ḥiyya's own distinction between the relatively safe interpretation of past events with the aid of astrological observations and the ever tenuous predictions for the future. After quoting numerous biblical passages, he declared:

We shall find on the basis of all these verses that an expert in the course of stars is able to predict the events occurring in the world before their occurrence, but he is unable to guarantee their fulfillment. He can only say that the time is propitious for such a happening, if it finds response from heaven. This is the way of the students of this discipline among the men of faith when they investigate the future. However, if they interpret the signs of past events they may say that this matter or this event happened as a result of the movement of stars in such and such a fashion during that time. In this case one need not add the stated condition, since this fact had already been aided by heaven and brought to fruition [*Megillat*, v, p. 115].

Such a distinction, which to all intents and purposes undermined the entire judicial astrology, should certainly have disarmed conservatives of the type of Yehudah bar Barzillai.

In any case, Savasorda seems to have refrained from writing outright astrological treatises of the kind composed by Ibn Ezra. When in his "Cosmography" he announced his intention to write a sequel devoted to astrology, he made it clear that he had in mind only natural astrology, which was not considered by the sages on a par with astronomy, for "its proofs are not [logically] demonstrable proofs, but are all derived from opinions and experimental observations." What Savasorda considered here to be the main drawback of astrology was, from the standpoint of history, its main and lasting virtue. Precisely because it had induced man, curious about his own or his nation's destiny, to try to correlate it with the course of celestial bodies by close observation, he accumulated through the toil of generations a tremendous number of observable facts which in the long run accrued to the benefit of the genuine science of astronomy to a far greater extent than did the speculations and deductive processes of theoretical and dispassionate astronomers, however disciplined.[49]

The general ambivalence of the belief in astrology is best documented by the fact that Abraham ibn Ezra, its staunchest and most influential exponent deservedly called "the great astrologer" by Azariah de' Rossi, was one of the very few Jewish scholars to deny the existence of spirits. He also denied the possibility of foretelling the coming of the Messiah by astrological computations —the very method employed by the more moderate Bar Ḥiyya. It was also Ibn Ezra himself who suggested eight different circumstances, which either delimit or totally nullify the operation of individual horoscopes, and concluded that "there is no question that the righteous man is better protected than the expert in the laws governing celestial bodies." This did not prevent him, however, from blaming his personal misfortunes and the necessity of living the life of a wanderer on the influence of unpropitious stars at his birth. On the other hand, Naḥmanides viewed the very month of Tishre with its annual days of judgment as prefigured in the signs of the Zodiac, in which this month stands under the sign of the constellation of Libra. In this very context, however, the thirteenth-century Barcelona rabbi insisted on the power of repentance to alter an evil decree, and, though a confirmed mystic, he refused to accept messianic computations based on astrology. Similarly, those Jewish artists and printers who decorated synagogues and books with the signs of the Zodiac did not necessarily believe in the usual astrological implications of those symbols. Nor does orthodox Jewry even today hesitate to congratulate newlyweds and other family celebrants with wishes of good luck by invoking a *mazzal tob* (a good star).[50]

SOLILUNAR HARMONIZATION

Much popular interest in mathematical and astronomic studies stemmed from their usefulness for the exact computation of the Jewish calendar. Since this work affected a vital area of Jewish law and had particular bearing on dates set for Jewish holidays, it became of direct concern to all communities. More, as Samuel Langdon correctly observed, "the calendar is the framework of any civilization, the time index for all business transactions and religious observances, the rule by which all daily life is regulated" (*Babylonian Menologies and the Semitic Calendars,* p. 18). At times, as in the rise of the Karaite schism or the struggle between Saadiah and Ben Meir, calendar controversies loomed large as overt expressions of some deeper social and political, as well as religious, divisions.

Concern for the astronomic background of the Jewish calendar reached back to remote antiquity. Quite early the Jewish sages evinced interest in the relations between their seven-day week, culminating in the Sabbath, and the seven planets. They subscribed to the aforementioned view of the planets' respective distances from the earth: namely, in an ascending order, the Moon, Mercury, Venus, Sun, Mars, Jupiter, Saturn. Assuming that these planetary movements affected all happenings on earth, and that they governed in particular the days and the hours, the third-century Palestinian Amora, R. Ḥanina, taught that each day had its "regent" and each hour its "controller." Beginning with the time of the creation of these luminaries on the fourth day, which, according to the Jewish night and day sequence had started on Tuesday at 6:00 P.M., and assigning to each hour in succession its regent from the highest planet Saturn, down to the Moon, anyone could easily figure out that the morning hours of the first day of creation began under the control of the Sun, those of the second day under that of the Moon, of the third day under that of Mars, and so forth. The Graeco-Roman world, which had accepted the Jewish seven-day week without its crowning glory in the Sabbatical day of rest, also began calling the days by their planetary regents, Sunday, Monday (Moon day), Mars day (French: Mardi), and so on. But, unfamiliar with the origin of that sequence in the biblical story of creation, the Romans found an acceptable rationale in beginning the week with Saturday at 6:00 A.M. and assigning the first hour to Saturn. This explanation was offered as an alternative by the third-century historian Dio Cassius, who believed that the entire system had been "instituted by the Egyptians, and is now found among all mankind." It was subsequently widely accepted in the Western world, and even penetrated Jewish letters through Shabbetai Donnolo's *Commentary* on the "Book of Creation." The original Jewish tradition was not forgotten, however. Although quoting Donnolo, Rashi repeatedly reverted to the original Jewish rationale. The latter was more fully elaborated by Bar Ḥiyya.[51]

Since every week of 168 hours covered 24 such 7-hour cycles, there was little difference in the actual computation whether one started counting from Saturday morning or Tuesday evening. More complicated, and practically significant, were the astronomic problems relating to the lunar and solar years. Throughout their history the Jews appear to have faithfully adhered to the lunar months, but, unlike their Muslim neighbors, they had to reconcile the short lunar year with the solar seasons, because Scripture had expressly enjoined them to observe the Passover as a spring, and the Feast of Tabernacles as a harvest, or autumnal, festival. We recall that so long as the Palestinian center remained intact, its leadership could authoritatively proclaim the onset of a new month and the intercalation of an additional month whenever conditions warranted it. For a long time such decisions could be reached by the purely empirical method of observation, that is, by the testimony of witnesses who saw a new moon on the horizon, and by watching signs of approaching spring in the Holy Land. Even when the advance of astronomical knowledge had placed in the hands of Jewish leaders an easy method of calculating the sequence of months and years, the prevailing conservatism enforced adherence to this time-honored procedure. However, with the calendar reform of Hillel II in 359, the main burden was placed on long-range predictions based upon accurate calculation.

Not that the "secret of intercalation" was now completely divulged, or that the sequences of the calendar were established once for all. Many important details were purposely left out of the public proclamation, partly in order the better to guard whatever still remained secret, and partly doubtless because of the leaders' inability to furnish definitive data without further progress in the astronomic observations and calculations. The fourth-century Palestinian leaders could the more confidently leave the ultimate determination on this score to future generations, as they retained a great measure of control in their hands. They could also entrust to their successors the task of making whatever minor adjustments might prove necessary during the following centuries. The general spirit of the age likewise militated against making provisions for some dim and distant future. The very factors which had generated the uncertainty concerning the survival of the Palestinian patriarchate and the growing oppression under which Jews lived in the then nascent Christian Roman empire also strengthened their undying messianic hopes. Certainly, few Jews of the time were prepared to envisage many more centuries of exilic existence. After the coming of the Messiah, they confidently felt, the calendar would be based once again on actual observation.[52]

From such a short-range point of view it did not seem imperative to pay attention to small fractions of hours in the respective duration of the lunar and solar years, whose aggregate of twenty-four hours made itself felt only after several decades. Nor could earlier experiences serve as a warning. For, according to the testimony of witnesses, one could readily add or subtract a day by making two successive lunar months either full (of thirty days each), or defective (of twenty-nine days each). On one occasion, Judah the Patriarch did not hesitate to proclaim nine defective months within a single year ('Arakhin 9b). This freedom of choice extended over the entire year, including the summer months, which only at a later time were made to follow a rigid sequence of alternation between the full and defective months. In emergencies one could even depart from the long-established custom of adding the thirteenth month, the second Adar, at the end of the leap year. In a cryptic letter the Palestinian authorities informed the fourth-century Babylonian sage, Raba, that, prevented by the Roman seizure of messengers from notifying distant communities of their proclamation of the leap year on time, they decided to add a second Ab five months later (Sanhedrin 12a). Nor was the "spring" festival of Passover originally determined exclusively by the astronomic factor of the spring equinox. The latter served only as one of three criteria. The other two, the ripening of barley and of fruit trees in Palestine, and especially in Judaea, often occurring simultaneously at an earlier date, could well bring about the celebration of Passover a number of days before March 21.

Gradually, however, the effort to observe Passover invariably after March 21 gained ground. This transition probably occurred first among Christians, both on dogmatic grounds, via the computation of the dates of Christ's crucifixion and resurrection, and because of the early loss of leadership by the Palestinian church which could no longer dictate to the far-flung Christian world. While direct imitation by Jews of an example set by Christians in ritualistic matters is extremely unlikely, the underlying similarity of lessening Palestinian controls necessarily produced similar effects. Among the scholars of both faiths, moreover, simple adherence to tradition began to be undermined by the increase in verifiable astronomic knowledge and the growing popularity of works by such Greek astronomers as Hipparchus and Ptolemy. True, there is no evidence that any of these works were studied by the Palestinian leaders. In fact, we do not even hear of any learned Jewish astronomer in Alexandria itself, center of both Greek science and intellectual Graeco-Jewish rapprochement. Nevertheless the findings of the Hellenistic astronomers must have in some fashion or other percolated to intellectuals of all faiths throughout the Graeco-Roman world.[53]

Difficulties in calculating exactly the solar year and reconciling it with the readily observable changes in the sequences of the lunar months were aggravated by ritualistic considerations. In order not to inconvenience Jewish worshipers with two successive days of rest, one had to arrange the calendar so that no Day of Atonement fell on either Friday or Sunday. Jews also sought to avoid the celebration of the seventh day of the Feast of Tabernacles (*Hosha'anah rabbah*) on a Sabbath, because of the considerable amount of work involved in that day's ceremonies. Hence they adopted the principle that no New Year should be set for Sunday, Wednesday, or Friday (*lo adu rosh*), for which Ibn Ezra, with his delight in punning, readily supplied a biblical reminiscence in Ezra (8:17), "And I gave them commandment unto Iddo the chief" (spelled like *Adu ha-rosh*). With the acceptance of a stable six-months period of 177 days, or 25 weeks and 2 days for the first half year from Nissan 1 to Tishre 1, this rule automatically presupposed that no Passover would fall on a Monday, Wednesday, or Friday (*lo bedu pesaḥ*). These rules obviously complicated both the process of intercalating the preceding Adar and the decision concerning the duration of individual months, particularly of the seventh and eighth months (Marḥeshvan and Kislev). In fact, once relying on computations, the leaders had to bear in mind not only the immediately forthcoming Passover, but also their effects on the following years.[54]

Considerations of this type led to increasing reliance on astronomic cycles, that is, to the intercalation of a fixed number of lunar months within a stated number of solar years. Such cycles (*maḥzorim*), employed already by the ancient Babylonians, were increasingly refined by Greek astronomers. However, there was no complete uniformity in the Hellenistic world. Trying to reconcile their own traditional methods with these newly developed techniques, Jews long wavered between the application of such diverse cycles as those of 2, 3, 5, 8, 14, 24, 30, 49, 76, 84,

95, and 532 years. Assuming roughly that a solar year of 365¼ days exceeds by 11¼ days a lunar year of six full and six defective months totaling 354 days, one could try, by the intercalation of three full lunar months in eight years, to make up the ensuing deficiency of ninety days. This Jewish practice, objected to by the author of Enoch under the erroneous assumption that a solar year had a duration of but 364 days, is attested for the early third century by the Christian writer Julius Africanus. However, this cycle disregarded the small surpluses of some 44 minutes in excess of 29½ days in each lunar month, and the slight deficiency of less than five minutes in the duration of a solar year. This difficulty came to the fore in time also with respect to the twenty-four year cycle, recorded by Al-Biruni as adopted from Jewish prototypes by the heathen Arabs two hundred years before Mohammed; the thirty-year cycle, for whose observance among the Jews in 343, or shortly before Hillel's proclamation, we have interesting testimony from a western Christian leader; and the eighty-four year cycle, which for a time enjoyed considerable vogue among both Jews and Christians.[55]

For this reason leaders of both faiths adopted the more accurate nineteen-year cycle with seven intercalations. Known as the "Metonic cycle," because it was introduced into the West by a Greek astronomer of the fifth pre-Christian century who had possibly been familiar with similar Babylonian efforts, this cycle met far better the exigencies of the situation. When the Jews adopted the formula, attributed to the talmudic sage R. Adda, that the lunar month amounted to 29 days, 12 hours, and 793 parts of an hour (*ḥalaqim,* each equal $\frac{1}{1080}$ of an hour or $\frac{1}{18}$ of a minute; thenceforth abbreviated here by *d, h,* and *p*), it was readily recognized that 12 lunar months aggregating 354 days, 8*h*, 48 minutes, and 40 seconds (abbreviated *m* and *s*) were short of a solar year counted by "R. Adda" as the equivalent of 365*d,* 5*h,* 997-$\frac{48}{76}$*p* (the latter figure equals Al-Biruni's fraction of $\frac{3791}{4104}$ of an hour for the Jewish solar year, and our 55*m,* $25\frac{25}{57}$*s*) by 10*d,* 21*h,* 6*m,* $45\frac{25}{57}$*s*. The difference amounted, therefore, to precisely $\frac{7}{19}$ synodic months. In other words, by inserting seven such months every nineteen years one would achieve 235 months totaling 6,939*d,* 16*h,* 33*m,* 3⅓*s,* or the exact equivalent of the

19 solar years. Except for the general agreement not to let two intercalated years follow one another, there was still considerable leeway in the determination of particular years within each cycle to which a second Adar was to be added. Three opinions on this score were attributed to ancient rabbis, among which that of "Rabban Gamaliel" ultimately prevailed. Until today the Jewish calendar is based on the intercalation of the years 3, 6, 8, 11, 14, 17, 19 (according to the mnemonic Hebrew formula *guḥadzat*) in each cycle. This formula differs in two years from that attributed to "R. Eliezer" and adopted for the Christian Easter, namely the years 3, 5, 8, 11, 14, 16, 19 (*gahaḥ advat*) which were wittily differentiated from the Jewish system by Ibn Ezra with the biblical phrase "And they were [*ve-hayu,* a reference to 5 and 16] as if they had not been." [56]

R. Adda's formula, to be sure, does not fully square with our present-day astronomic knowledge, which postulates the duration of a solar year of only 365*d,* 5*h,* 48*m,* 46*s.* The discrepancy of 6*m,* $39^{25}/_{57}s$ each year adds up to approximately a day every 218 years (in the Gregorian calendar this discrepancy is reduced to one day in 3,323 years). Too small to become practically noticeable before the passage of centuries, it has nevertheless within the last millennium and a half since Hillel II's reform already played havoc with the ancient insistence that Passover be celebrated within the first month after the Spring equinox, or between March 21 and April 20. Because the sum total of Jewish intercalations since 359 has added seven days beyond the required equalization with solar years, Passover has already been celebrated twice on April 25 (in 1815 and 1929) and, unless some reform is adopted, will thus be celebrated 38 times in the course of the seventh Jewish millennium. More, quite a few Passovers will then be observed on April 26–29—a matter specifically prohibited in the Christian Easter—and once, in the year 3031, as late as April 30.

Considering, however, the enormous resistance which all calendar reforms encounter in conservative circles, the prospects for an early adoption of corrective measures for the Jewish calendar are not very good. As is well known, the Gregorian calendar, introduced in 1582, is astronomically decidedly superior to the old

Julian calendar. And yet it took nearly two centuries to persuade the British Parliament to adopt it formally (1750) and a communist revolution to introduce it into Russia. Even today millions of Orthodox worshipers still observe their holidays according to the Julian computations. If the Catholic West speedily adopted that reform, this was entirely owing to the prestige of the Papacy. In Judaism the absence of such an authoritative organ is further aggravated by the preliminary requirement of the restoration, in some form, of the ancient ordination, which might then lead to the reconstitution of a recognized Sanhedrin of seventy-one members so ordained. Only such an authoritative body would be in a position to institute a calendar reform which would have a chance of more or less universal acceptance.[57]

In their perennial lucubrations on the meaning of numbers and letters, mystics sometimes guessed better than their scientifically trained confreres. Trying to explain in his poem *Az ra'itah* (Thou Hast Then Seen) the world's expected duration for 6,000 years, Eleazar Qalir mentioned still another cycle, namely one of twenty-two jubilee years. This cycle of 1,078 solar years, going beyond the scheme of simple jubilee cycles of 7 × 7 years underlying the ancient Book of Jubilees, is almost the precise equivalent of 13,334 lunations according to R. Adda's formula. If the Jewish people had adopted that cycle, it would have added but some 6 hours and 19 minutes in the course of a millennium, instead of almost a whole day every two centuries. However, this computation seems to have been restricted to esoteric circles, some of which had assigned to the world a duration in excess of the round number of 6,000 years. At least the "Alphabet of R. 'Aqiba" mentioned a tradition that the world would be destroyed twice, once during the Deluge, and the second time at the end of 6,093 years. Of course, all these eschatological speculations were based on the psalmist's equation of the day of the Lord with a thousand years, which also led the author of the *Pirqe de-R. Eliezer* to regard the cycle of eighty-four (or 12 × 7) years as but the Lord's hour, namely the long hour of a twelve-hour day. It was possibly also the acceptance of some such cycle in repudiation of the Metonic cycle of nineteen years, rather than ignorance thereof, which caused the author of the "Book of Creation" to abstain from the alluring parallel between the years of this cycle and the letters of the alphabet. The contrast between the seven so-called double letters and the twelve ordinary letters, on which he speculates at length, would otherwise have offered an almost irresistible temptation for him to compare it with the seven intercalated (pregnant) years and the twelve ordinary years of the Metonic cycle. It did not, however, escape the eagle eye of such a Bible exegete as Samuel bar Meir that Scripture begins with a verse of seven words and concludes with one of twelve words.[58]

Curiously, the "circle" (*'iggul*) of 247 years, suggested by Naḥshon Gaon (d. 880) after two centuries of considerable scientific advances beyond the state of knowledge in Qalir's day, was far less accurate. Taking a total of thirteen 19-year cycles, or 12,888 weeks, included in that "circle," the gaon seems to have attempted to establish the exact recurrence of weekdays in new moons and festivals of certain years. However, on closer examination there appeared a discrepancy of 905*p*, which induced later students to abandon that formula completely. Punning on the word *remez*, which stood for both "hint" and the figure 247, Ibn Ezra voiced the gratitude of many informed students that "the first tables thou didst break," that is that they were allowed to sink into oblivion.[59]

CALENDARY STABILIZATION

While homilists and poets thus speculated on the astral movements and their influences on the world of man, other thinkers continued their quiet, more precise calculations of these movements and their particular bearing on the Jewish calendar. The same obscure centuries which witnessed such calm and painstaking research, out of which ultimately emerged the great structures of biblical Masorah, Hebrew grammar, and liturgy, also saw the first comprehensive formulations of the astronomic foundations of the Jewish calendar and chronology.

Like most other literary products of the period, these formulations cannot be accurately dated. Apart from the aforementioned three astronomic chapters in *Pirqe de-R. Eliezer*, we possess the *Baraita de-Shemu'el*, which seems to have been composed in 777, the year 776 being expressly mentioned by the author as the year "when they have equalized the sun and the moon, the sabbatical cycles and the periods [of the 84-year cycles]." It is noteworthy that that Hebrew date corresponds exactly with the completion of 54 of the latter cycles, and also fits into the chronological setting of the penetration of Indian mathematics to the centers of the Caliphate through Jewish mediation. The "Baraita of Samuel" is the first to mention clearly R. Adda's formula, which, though largely in agreement with the calculations in Ptolemy's "Almagest," was independent of it. In fact, it is clearly connected with a similar formula advanced by R. Gamaliel II half a century before Ptolemy. This leader of the Yabneh academy, who had built an astronomic observatory in his attic, quoted a tradition from his grandfather, R. Gamaliel I, that "the renovation of the moon takes place in no less than 29½ days ⅔ and 73*p* of an hour." Unequivocal statements of this sort lent substance to the claim of Savasorda and other medieval astronomers concerning the rabbis' priority in this field as well, and on the other hand induced some hypercritical modern scholars to view these talmudic passages as mere interpolations from a later, better informed age. Apart from such occasional flashes, however, the astronomic teachings of the talmudic sages are shrouded in willful obscurity. They were orally transmitted to later generations to reappear, with many accretions and modifications, in such writings of later vintage as the so-called *Midrash Sod ha-'ibbur* (Homily on the Mystery of Intercalation), and other medieval midrashim.[60]

"Mystery" of intercalation is, indeed, an apt designation for the process of formally declaring the onset of new months or leap years even after the proclamation of the fixed calendar by Hillel II. Like other ancient nations, the Jews had long preferred to keep their calendar calculations as official "top secrets," restricted to a closed circle of scholars at the central academy in Palestine. Even in the period of communal disintegration under the Christian Roman Empire, Jews generally recognized that to divulge the underlying mathematical formulas, even if these had been worked out in minutest detail, would have robbed the Palestinian leaders of their major prerogative. For a long time the actual "sanctification" of the new moon required the personal consent of the chairman of the Sanhedrin. This system essentially continued after Hillel II. The compiler of *Pirqe de-R. Eliezer* bluntly stated, "Even if prophets live in other countries, and only uneducated persons dwell in the land of Israel, the latter alone are entitled to proclaim a leap year," and he claimed that even Patriarch Jacob and the Prophet Ezekiel had been prevented by God from issuing such proclamations in Babylonia. To underscore the solemnity of the occasion, this proclamation, originally arranged only by a court of seven, was later performed in the presence of ten elders. In a remarkable letter written in 835, a Babylonian exilarch himself described the difficulties in deciding the duration of the respective months, and concluded: "Therefore I and the heads of the academies and the rabbis and all Israel rely on the intercalation as dispatched by the scholars [of the Holy Land]." [61]

Such closing of ranks had become doubly necessary as a result of the growing Karaite agitation. Doubtless prompted by the Muslim practice, 'Anan, as we recall, sharply denounced the Rabbanite reliance on calculations and insisted upon celebrating new moons on the basis of direct observation. The fact that Jews in their far-flung dispersion necessarily saw the arrival of a new moon at different times, and hence would diverge in their celebration of festivals, little disturbed the heresiarch and his early successors, prepared as these were generally to stress individual conscience and individual interpretation of Scripture even at the price of the much-dreaded fragmentation of the people. Al-Biruni noted that

> he ['Anan] gave up the system of computation of the Rabbanites, and made the intercalation of a month depend upon the observation of barley-seed in Iraq and Syria between 1st and 14th Nîsân. If he found a first-fruit fit for friction and reaping, he left the year a common year; if he did not find that, he intercalated the year . . . the 'Ananites mostly used Shefaṭ [as the additional month] not Adhâr, whilst the Rabbanites use exclusively Adhâr. This system of prognosticating the state of the corn is a different one according to the difference of the air and the climate of the countries. Therefore it would be necessary to make a special rule for every place [*Chronology*, p. 69].

Such territorial divergences did not appear too menacing so long as the majority of the Karaite schismatics was concentrated in either Babylonia or Palestine. In the ninth century Daniel al-Qumisi, securely ensconced in the Holy Land, could still afford to be particularly vehement in denouncing all mathematical calendar computations as pagan borrowings, derived from biblically forbidden astral speculations. In time, however, the spread of Karaism into the Balkans and other lands led to discrepancies ranging up to one month. Local differences of this kind had been quite common among the early Christians before the authoritative settlement of the Easter controversy. According to Augustine, in 387 the churches in Gaul celebrated their Easter on March 21, while the Italian churches observed it on April 18, and those of Egypt as late as April 25, which later became the terminal date for the celebration of any Christian Easter. In the case of the Jews, however, a divergence in dates was far more serious. Those who considered a certain day to be the proper date for observing Passover, or the Day of Atonement, necessarily viewed others who dared consume unleavened bread on the former, or any food whatsoever on the latter day, as outright lawbreakers. We need but remember the consternation caused in the Rabbanite camp when, as a result of the Saadiah–Ben Meir controversy, it was noticed that Palestinian Jews observed the New Year of 4683 (922) on Tuesday, and those of Babylonia on Thursday. As a result some local leaders complained that they "had become an object of shame among the Gentiles, and of derision among the heretics." To obviate such overt inconveniences, the Babylonian Karaites, as in many other areas of Jewish law, reverted at least partially to Rabbanite teachings and adopted the Metonic cycle. The young Byzantine community of the eleventh century still followed the lead of the Palestinian "searchers for the Spring maturation" of barley. On one occasion, it observed Tishre a month after the Rabbanites, and "there arose great enmity and hatred" between it and the majority, forcing the government to intervene. Three centuries later (1354), however, Aaron ben Elijah admitted that his Byzantine coreligionists had adopted the Rabbanite system, finding themselves at variance with their fellow sectarians of the Holy Land.[62]

Long before these internal Karaite divisions, however, the self-assertion of the Babylonian rabbis had begun undermining the Palestinian controls. Some time after 835 the Babylonians sent delegates to Palestine to arrange for some permanent, universally valid calculation. According to a letter written at the height of the sharp controversy between the two countries in 922–24, and hence not devoid of bias, the Babylonian representatives had many years previously

> gone up to Palestine and investigated closely, together with the Palestinian sages, the mystery of intercalation. They had studied it so attentively that for many years past they have been proclaiming new moons in Babylonia on their own. The Palestinian sages likewise calculated and set new moons on their part. During all these years these respective calculations led to the same results, and no difference arose between them. In this way the computation was staunchly upheld, and the holidays have uniformly been observed at the same time. For all these computations have been given us by the same shepherd.

The latter statement reflected the then growing conviction that the essential astronomic calculations had been handed down by immemorial tradition, reaching back to the first "shepherd," Moses. We recall that in his anti-Karaite zeal Saadiah, possibly a co-author of the letter here quoted, expressly invoked biblical sanctions for the accepted methods of mathematical calculation.[63]

Nor was this question of ancient origins a major issue in his great controversy with Ben Meir. Apart from the natural discrepancy in the respective latitudes of the two countries, which resulted in the difference of some fifty-six minutes in the time of their sunset, there also was basic disagreement on a point of law, namely the permissibility of proclaiming a new month, if the conjunction (*molad* or nativity) of the new moon occurred shortly after the noon hour. Saadiah, more fully in consonance with the extant older sources, insisted that, unless such nativity preceded noon, the new month had to be postponed for a day or even two, dependent on the ultimate effects on the following Passovers and New Years. Ben Meir, on the other hand, invoked his own Palestinian tradition, unattested from other sources, which allowed the leeway of 642*p*, or some thirty-six minutes, for the moon's nativity after noon without enforcing postponement. Neither leader referred any longer to actual observation, but rather to the moon's nativity calculated at the median time elapsing between its conjunctions. Since the nativity of the first of Tishre, 4684 (September 923) was to take place some fourteen minutes after noon, Ben Meir suggested two years in advance that that New Year not be postponed. For this purpose he wished to shorten the year 4682 by making both Marḥeshvan and Kislev defective. Saadiah, on the contrary, argued for a longer year 4682, with both Kislev and Marḥeshvan given thirty days each, so as to allow for the postponement of the New Year of 4684 by the necessary two days.

It seems that in the eighty-seven years which elapsed between the exilarch's letter of 835 acknowledging the supremacy of Palestine and the Saadiah–Ben Meir controversy, Babylonian hegemony had become so firmly established that Ben Meir himself was no longer fully aware of the roots of his own tradition. His allowance of 642*p* was evidently related in some way to the 9*h*, 642*p* on which, it was generally agreed, the nativity of the moon of the first Nisan of creation had occurred. Palestinian Jewry, adhering to its traditional view that the world had been created in Nisan, took the nativity of that month as the basis of all its computations. The Babylonians, on the other hand, long believing in the creation of the world in Tishre, simply figured out that by adding the then already standardized interval of 177*d*, 4*h*, and 438*p* to the first of Nisan, one could push the permissible limit to 18*h* and 642*p* without eliminating the possibility of the moon's visibility on the same day. For simplicity's sake they dropped the fraction and established the noon hour (18*h* after the beginning of the day at 6:00 o'clock on the preceding evening) as the ultimate limit. Matters proceeded smoothly for several decades, until 923, when, for the first time in 140 years, the nativity of Tishre was due to arise shortly after noon.

Ben Meir was prepared to make various concessions to the Babylonians, and even accepted Tishre 1 as the actual date of creation, although the scriptural story of the creation of the two great lights on the firmament of the heaven during the fourth day (Wednesday) better fit the Nisan date, and although opposition to creation on Tishre had not been completely silenced even in Babylonia. He only inconsistently invoked the tradition allowing for a margin of 642*p* after noon, without realizing its close relation to that fundamental chronological question. Saadiah and his party, on the other hand, simply assumed that the Babylonian standpoint ought to prevail under all circumstances, especially since it was not controverted by any clear statement in the Talmud. As if the talmudic sages had been prepared to disclose fully the "mystery of intercalation"! [64]

Whatever the historic merits of the controversy, however, Saadiah and his associates were right in warning the Jewish people against the dangers of separatism and holiday observance on different dates. Since one of the parties had to yield, they naturally preached in this, as in other matters, the primacy of the Babylonian academies.

Even in this famous controversy, however, the main issue did not concern astronomic calculations as such. Neither scholar, for example, denied the underlying contention that it required six hours for a new moon, visible to some witnesses from a particular point of vantage, to become generally noticeable. They merely argued whether the median nativity must come before noon, or whether it sufficed, as Ben Meir claimed, if only 5*h* and 25*m* remained before the theoretical end of that day. Two centuries later Ibn Ezra still had to argue against the so-called *tequfah* (solar season) of Samuel, based on the round figure of 365¼ days for the solar year. After pointing out that the Indians and Persians had postulated an even longer average duration, whereas Ptolemy and the Arabs had come more closely to R. Adda's formula, Ibn Ezra adduced seven "witnesses" to show that Mar Samuel of Babylonia, whose authorship he did not doubt, had merely offered a round figure for use by the uninitiated (*Sefer ha-'Ibbur,* fols. 8 f.). But this entire debate was largely academic. Evidently none of Ibn Ezra's contemporaries suggested any readjustment of the calendar along "Samuel's" formula.

Owing to their ritualistic conservatism the Jewish leaders long repeated R. Adda's formula, even though they had undoubtedly become familiar with the measurements conducted by some of their own coreligionists participating in Al-Ma'mun's expeditions. According to Ibn Yunus, these measurements had led to the fixing of the solar year to the duration of but 365*d,* 5*h,* 47*m,* 4*s,* which is some 8 minutes and 21 seconds less than the solar year envisaged by R. Adda or Ptolemy. Although this discrepancy is slightly greater than even that of nearly 6*m,* 40*s* accepted by modern astronomy's 48*m,* 46*s* and hence the accrual caused the addition of a whole day within little more than 170 years (according to Ibn Ezra, Arab opinion wavered between 106 and 130 years), this long-range surplus did not seem to disturb the medieval Jewish savants. In fact, neither Bar Ḥiyya nor Ibn Ezra, each of whom devoted a special monograph to the calendar, evinced any concern about it. In general Ibn Ezra was perfectly convinced that "we alone are on the right path. Blessed be our God, who has separated us from the errant [peoples], and given us the true Torah." Nor is there any reference to this divergence in the works of Maimonides who, at the age of twenty-three, wrote a little treatise on the calendar and two decades later assigned an entire section in his *Code* to the laws concerning the "sanctification of the moon." In a subsequent recension he added nine purely astronomic chapters based on Bar Ḥiyya and other sources. Such silence is doubly remarkable, as both Ibn Ezra and Maimonides always insisted that, in scientific matters, one must accept the evidence of mathematical calculations and the astrolabe, regardless of their provenance. On one occasion, the sage of Fusṭaṭ gave the usual excuse that, while the writings of Greek sages are still extant, those "composed by the Israelitic savants from the children of Issachar in the days of the prophets are lost." But he emphasized that "since all these matters have been demonstrated by clear and unmistakable proofs which no one can controvert, we do not hesitate [to accept them] whether their author is from among the prophets, or from Gentiles." Nevertheless Bar Ḥiyya and Ibn Ezra expressly, and Maimonides by implication, fully subscribed to the basic validity of R. Adda's formula. They all merely sought to elaborate the existing computations in their manifold minute implications for both astronomy and Jewish law. The need of such elaboration was the more keenly felt, as some dates recorded on extant manuscripts and deeds from that period still show certain deviations from the "official" calendar which, largely owing to these sages' efforts, has since come into common use.[65]

In this later period of the evolution of the Jewish calendar, the influence of the new astronomy developed by the schools of Al-Baṭṭani, Al-Farghani, Ibn Yunus, and Al-Zarqali made itself fully felt. While Al-Biruni could still report a variety of Jewish chronological formulas, the teachings on calendar as represented by Bar

Ḥiyya, Ibn Ezra, and Maimonides differ only in some minor details, because they all lean heavily on the same halakhic tradition on the one hand, and on the same astronomic systems on the other hand. There also seems to have developed in Spain, ever since the days of Ḥisdai ibn Shapruṭ, an independent tradition which, though originally nurtured from Eastern sources, now made use of the Western astronomic researches as well. Remarkably, even Maimonides, who in his later philosophic work expressed serious reservations concerning the basic Ptolemaic assumptions with reference to the movements of the planets along eccentres, epicycles, and the like, adhered to these accepted categories without demurrer in both his early monograph on the calendar and his section in the *Code*.

All these scholars recognized that their calculations, beginning with that of R. Adda, were based upon median figures and not upon actually observable changes in the position of the sun and the moon. To square such discrepancies with the facts derived from actual observation and the testimony of witnesses, the rabbis had long developed an appropriate rationale. Unlike Sabbaths, they taught, which become automatically binding as a result of the passage of time, new moons and leap years depend on a formal declaration by Jewish authorities. Utilizing older homilies, Bar Ḥiyya pointed out that the Levitical lawgiver himself had qualified his injunction concerning the holidays "which ye shall proclaim in their *appointed* season" (Lev. 23:4), indicating that "the appointed time depends on the declaration, to show us that it is our right to fix the holidays." For this reason, as Maimonides stated, a new moon, even if erroneously proclaimed by the Palestinian authorities, retained its validity. Leap years could from the outset be proclaimed, or postponed, out of deference to urgent social needs connected with famines or some sudden interruption of traffic for pilgrims.[66]

Nonetheless, when median calculations replaced the old latitude given by adjustments to actual observations, the sequences of the Jewish calendar became much more rigid, and qualified scholars could calculate them in advance for years to come. They also could figure back more exact dates for past events. Informed students knew, in particular, that the prevailing assumption that the four seasons of the solar year lasted equally 91*d*, 7½*h* each, was inexact. Maimonides first stated more precisely that, astronomically, "the spring season [*tequfat nisan*] begins on the hour and the part thereof when the sun enters into the sign of Aries, the summer season [*tequfat tammuz*] when it enters the sign of Cancer, the autumnal season [*tequfat Tishre*] when it enters that of Libra, and the winter season [*tequfat Tebet*] when it enters that of Sagittarius." Almost in the same breath he added, however, that by counting backwards to the days of Creation one could readily figure out the beginnings of the spring season of each particular year, after which "you need but count ninety-one days and seven and a half hours for each [subsequent] season." Addressing himself to a reading public more interested and better trained in law than in astronomy, he often resorted to such simplifications of complicated mathematical formulas. He anticipated carping criticisms by pedants, but he insisted that these shortcomings were quite willful, made no difference in practice, and were only motivated by his desire not to frighten away astronomically less informed students of the law. At the same time he felt prompted to warn his readers that the mystery of intercalation must not be taken lightly, although, with the progress of science and the introduction of ever more simplified methods, the calendar, "as it is computed today, can be fully grasped even by schoolchildren in three or four days." Combining the results obtained by such Muslim astronomers as Al-Baṭṭani with some independent reexamination of Greek sources available to him in Arabic translations or summaries such as those produced by the Spaniard Jabir ibn Aflaḥ, he looked for clarity, rather than absolute precision. This did not prevent him from coming, on occasion, closer to the truth as we know it today than had his predecessors.[67]

In all that Maimonides followed well-established patterns. Even an exact scientist like Savasorda always catered to the broader reading public. Although never compromising his scientific facts, he liked to present them in a spiritual, even theological context. After underscoring the difference of median times and the actual range of 88 to 92½ days between seasons, he observed that this inequality, and especially the sharply drawn contrasts between the six seasons mentioned in Genesis (8:22), was intended to bring home the God-willed eternal changes in nature and human affairs. Such constant flux ought to serve as a lesson to man never to despair when things go wrong, nor to feel too secure when he enjoys good fortune, for things may change even within a single day. More realistically, Savasorda pointed out that in the prayers for dew or rain the sages had taken cognizance of the longer combined duration of the spring and summer seasons over those of the fall and winter, although during occasional leap years the latter last seven months. Thus the prayer for dew is always recited during 185 days, extending from the beginning of Passover to the end of the Feast of Tabernacles, while that for rain averages only 180 days throughout the years.[68]

CHRONOLOGY

Calendary computations and controversies had numerous other ramifications, both historical and practical, which because of their complex and technical content often escaped the attention of the wider public. In connection with his aforementioned advice to readers concerning the computation of any spring season, for example, Maimonides pointed out that the very beginning of the era of Creation had not coincided with the conjunction of the moon. According to a long-accepted view, he claimed, the season (*tequfah*) of the year One preceded the actual nativity of the moon by 7*d,* 9*h,* 642*p* (*M.T.* Qiddush IX.3). This discrepancy disturbed nobody's peace of mind, however, as the first Passover, if one had been observed, would still have occurred in the first month after the spring equinox.

Nor was there any serious concern evinced about the exact chronology of the process of Creation itself. Although a gaon, R. Joseph (ben Jacob?) of Sura (942–44) had already taken pains to explain the basis for the growing practice of starting all chronological computations from the second day of Creation at 5*h* and 204*p* (Sunday, 11:11 P.M.), there was little debate on the answer suggested by him.

The reason is [he replied] that the lights were created on the fourth day at hour One [according to some students more precisely at 1*h* and 286*p,* or Tuesday, 7:16 P.M.], which was the beginning of Ellul 28.

For on Ellul 25, the world had begun to be created, and on Friday with the creation of Adam began the New Year. . . . During the first hour [Thursday, 6:00–7:00 P.M.] the idea [of man's creation] was conceived, on the second he was created, and thereby the world was completed, and no creature was absent from it.

Some exegetes expatiated on ancient mythologumena, and claimed that the sun was created long before the moon, but that they were suspended together in heaven on the fourth day. Because of their intensive rivalry, God "shouted at the moon and diminished its size." By figuring out that this event took place on Wednesday at 20*h* and 408*p* (2:23 P.M.), one could derive therefrom the accepted formula that the moon's first nativity occurred on Monday at 5*h*, 204*p*. This conclusion was evidently drawn by the author of the "Scroll of Abiathar," and before him by "Jonathan," the Aramaic translator of the Bible. Although repudiating the validity of all mathematical computations, even the Karaites were unable to depart completely from this Rabbanite chronology. According to Jephet ben 'Ali, some of his coreligionists claimed that the moon, created on the fourth day, remained invisible until after the creation of Adam two days later, and that the first man therefore began counting the month as of that day. Others, however, agreed with the Rabbanites that the moon had become visible on the fourth day and had had its nativity two days earlier. Adam, later informed of this fact by the Lord, considered accordingly the day of his own creation as the third of the month.[69]

Even these abstruse speculations were not devoid of practical consequences. When Saadiah wrote his *Kitab at-Tamyiz* in the year 1238 Sel. era, he contended that that year really corresponded to 4686, and not "as some claimed," to 4687 *Anno Mundi.* The latter date, based on the ancient chronology of *Seder 'Olam rabbah* but evidently not yet in common use, reflected the prevailing notions. Its underlying computation may have been followed ever since the first appearance of that era, possibly in a Crimean inscription of 376, and more definitely in a talmudic passage of 471. The protagonists of 4686, on the other hand, explained their lower figure by the fact, recorded already in a debate between two talmudic sages, that the year of the Deluge had been skipped in the chronology of the *Seder 'Olam.* Among Saadiah's contemporaries there was still another school of thought, represented by the otherwise unknown Joshua ben 'Ilan. Joshua, called by the Karaite Ben Mashiaḥ "the most erudite among the Rabbanites in the knowledge of calendar," claimed a theoretical deficiency of two years, namely the year of the Deluge, and that of Creation itself. Even in Savasorda's day there existed still another, though related, division among Jews, along geographic lines. Assuming that the world was really created in Nisan, or the Nisan season—an opinion which, Bar Ḥiyya unjustifiedly claimed, was agreed upon by the sages—but that the era was nevertheless counted as of Tishre 1, they argued as to whether that computation started on the Tishre preceding, or on that following the Nisan of Creation. The Spaniards counted from the Tishre before Creation and, by calculating backwards, reached the theoretical figure that the first nativity had occurred on the second day (Sunday night) at 5*h,* 204*p* (11:11 P.M.). They used this figure as the starting point of all their chronological computations. The Easterners, on the other hand, insisted on beginning with the nativity of the following Tishre which (in line with the accepted duration of a lunar year of 354*d,* 8*h,* and 876*p*) allegedly occurred on a Friday at 14*h* (8:00 A.M.) precisely.[70]

In Bar Ḥiyya's time, these different theoretical beginnings no longer involved any practical dispute. Once most Jews had begun to date their business documents, funeral inscriptions, and historical records by the new era—a practice which may indeed have become prevalent first in Italy, as suggested by Bornstein—the system of dating accepted by Shabbetai Donnolo, Hai Gaon, and Savasorda, in agreement with that previously recorded in the Venosa inscriptions and elsewhere, became uniform throughout the Jewish world. The divergence was now reduced to a theoretically different sequence in the declaration of leap years within the nineteen-year cycles. The Easterners celebrated the same leap years, though placing them in the years 2, 5, 7, 10, 13, 16, 18 (*behaziguḥ*) of their respective cycles, instead of a year later, according to the *guḥadzat* formula prevailing in the West. However, it seems that even this distinction was known to Savasorda from hearsay only, and doubtless already was but an historical reminiscence in his day. Although himself living and writing in an Eastern land, Maimonides did not feel impelled to mention it at all, but simply assumed that both the beginning of the era, and the sequence of the leap years, unquestioningly followed the Spanish rule.[71]

Perhaps because this uncertainty about the era of Creation was grist for the mill of the Karaite opponents of the Rabbanite calendar and because Joshua ben 'Ilan's statement concerning the existing three schools of thought could be cited with glee by these sectarians (we owe indeed its preservation to the Karaite polemist, Ben Mashiaḥ), Saadiah insisted with redoubled vehemence that 1238 Sel. era corresponded to 4686. He cited in his support the talmudic passage ('A.Z. 9b, but only according to a version which was also later recorded in the name of R. Ḥananel) that the difference in the last figure between the "Greek" and the Jewish eras invariably amounted to two. Of course, the very facts that the talmudic text itself was uncertain, and that the dating of both eras and their mutual relations often depended on whether one started either or both in the fall or the spring, could only nurture the flames of sectarian controversy.

Nevertheless, Saadiah not only felt that all basic calendar computations went back to Moses, indeed had already been known to the Patriarchs, but, with perfect assurance, asserted that the era of Creation as such had been well known to the first lawgiver. Al-Biruni's Jewish informants likewise spoke of "an era of Moses and David" which, at Alexander's order, the Jews had been forced to replace by the era of the conqueror. "The rabbis allowed them such a change at the end of each millennium after Moses. And at that time just a millennium had become complete, and their offerings and sacrifices ceased to be practiced." This figure was based on the prevailing Jewish calculations that from the Exodus to the building of the First Temple 480 years had passed, that the Temple had lasted 410 years, and that it was followed by the 70 years of the Babylonian Exile, and by 40 years from the Restoration to Alexander's conquest of Palestine. According to Saadiah, the entire system of observation of the new moon was first introduced during the Second Commonwealth, as a reaction to the rise of the Sadducee sect, the lineal ancestor of the Karaite schism. Such extremism understandably caused great consternation among the gaon's successors. Hai, who excused his illustrious predecessor by the compelling need of answering heretics, admitted that the fully developed calendar, as known in his day, had been an innovation by Hillel (II) ben Yehudah of 670 Sel. era (359 C.E.), and that formerly the Sanhedrin had enjoyed considerable leeway in the proclamation of leap years. Yet he too was certain that Moses had already disclosed to an intimate circle of his followers the fundamentals of the calendar, and particularly the number of intercalations which had been inserted before his time, and therewith had revealed to them the number of years which had elapsed since the day of creation.[72]

The Jewish era of Creation was a battle ground for sectarian controversies not only within the Jewish community, but also between it and Christians or Samaritans—all using their respective texts of the Bible. According to Al-Biruni, his Jewish contemporaries had computed the interval between Adam's expulsion from Paradise and the Deluge at 1,656 years. This figure was reduced to 1,307 by the Samaritans, but increased to 2,262 years by such Christians as (Sextus) Julius Africanus. The latter were guided not only by the textual variants in the Septuagint, but also by dogmatic motivations. Extending also the duration of the interval between the Deluge and Abraham to 1,015 years, Africanus found that Joseph's death occurred in the year 3565 after Adam. Adding the 210 years of Israel's sojourn in Egypt, the 1,235 years, which allegedly elapsed from Moses to Cyrus, and the 490 (70 × 7) years since Cyrus (in accordance with the prophecy of Daniel), Africanus postulated the birth of Jesus precisely in the year 5500 of the era of Creation, that is in the exact middle of the messianic millennium. True, there still were minor differences of opinion among the Alexandrine, Byzantine, and other Christians as to the era's exact date. Even the "unanimous supposition" (to cite Al-Biruni) of both Jews and Christians that Jesus had been born in 304 Sel. era (or 7 B.C.E.) was not quite so unanimous. Yet the issue appeared significant enough for the controversialists of both faiths to try to buttress their respective computations of the messianic era by reference to the prophecies of Daniel. Nor was astrology left out of sight. Using a combination of the Christian calendar and astrological speculation, one Anianus, as reported in Ibn

Al-Bazyar's "Book of Conjunctions," figured out that between the creation of Adam and the Deluge exactly 2,226 years, 23 days, and 4 hours had elapsed.[73]

Going beyond his geonic predecessors whom he cited, Bar Ḥiyya tried to explain to his readers also the nature of such other Jewish eras as those dating from the Exodus from Egypt, or from the destruction of the Second Temple. He also provided them with formulas for the conversion of these dates into those of the era of Creation. More, he even devoted the last two, rather lengthy, chapters to an analysis of the eras used by Muslims, Christians, ancient Greeks, Persians, and Egyptians. He refrained, with obvious reluctance, from discussing in any detail still other eras then known, all of which were based on the movements of either the sun, or the moon, or a combination of both like the Jewish soli-lunar calendar. As in most other works pursuing also eminently practical purposes, he consistently tried to place in the hands of readers mathematical formulas enabling them to convert given dates into months and years of the era of Creation. Further to facilitate their use, he illustrated these formulas by reference to Tishre of the year of his writing, namely 4883 A.M. or 1122 C.E., and showed how one could deduce therefrom the month and year then counted among Persians, Egyptians, Greeks, or Arabs.

> If you wish to know [he wrote in regard to the era of the *Hejira*] which month it is among the Arab months, subtract from the number of years [4882 of Creation] 4,382. You will be left with 500 full years, that is 26 nineteen-year cycles plus six years. Take 7 months for each cycle [of the seven leap years intercalated by Jews but not by Arabs], or a total of 182 months, add two months for the six years from the 13th year [in the cycle] when the Muslim era began, to the 18th year which you count at present [namely the 14th and the 17th year within the cycle], and another two months by which the first Muslim year had preceded the then month of Tishre, and you will obtain a total of 186 months, or 15 lunar years and 6 months. You will thus find that Tishre of the year 4883 would coincide with Ragab, the seventh Muslim month of the year 73 [515] of their era.

Savasorda concluded this discussion by explaining that he did not go into even greater detail, "for we do not need the computations of Gentile nations, since they do not intermingle with Israel." [74]

Jewish calendar problems, on the other hand, Bar Ḥiyya taught, should be of concern to every faithful member of the community. He believed that, by utilizing the methods presented in his book, every reader could figure out effortlessly the sequence of Jewish holidays, the recitation of special lessons during the four Sabbaths preceding Nisan, the succession of weekly lessons for every Sabbath including the times when some of the latter were to be read together or separately, the days on which prayers for rain were to be inserted, and the like. "It is a duty," he concluded, "of every honorable and experienced man in Israel to know [these matters] from his own mind, and not to rely on others."

Bar Ḥiyya's exhortations did not fall on receptive ears. Relatively few Jewish intellectuals found the mathematical and exegetical exercises underlying calendar computations sufficiently exciting to pay them more than passing attention. Apart from their technical difficulties, these studies must also have appeared too academic to a majority of students. Only where differences of chronological opinion had serious practical repercussions, as in the sequence of Sabbatical cycles and Jubilee years, they elicited deep interest under the Second Commonwealth. If as early as the third century B.C.E. the Alexandrian Jewish historian, Demetrius, had tried to marshal the biblical data for the construction of the first comprehensive chronological scheme based upon the era of Creation, a Palestinian author sought to achieve the same results by computing the number of Jubilee and Sabbatical cycles, which had elapsed since the beginning of history. The entire Book of Jubilees, in many ways divergent from the growing body of Pharisaic, and for that matter also, Sadducean traditions, was arranged according to this chronological system. To be sure, not this author but Demetrius found influential followers in Josephus and R. Jose ben Ḥalafta. The latter's world chronicle, the *Seder 'Olam,* though differing in many details from both predecessors, helped establish the era of Creation as a practical chronological instrument in Jewish life. Yet the problem of Sabbatical cycles remained a serious preoccupation of many talmudic and post-talmudic sages, since the Sabbatical laws still had considerable ritualistic significance.

Of course, years of fallowness were never observed in the dispersion, and even in Palestine they had been suspended, as we recall, by R. Yannai under the pressure of Rome's fiscal policies. However, pious Jews living in the Holy Land, then and later, hesitated to abandon entirely this biblical commandment. Even Jews of other lands took seriously the cancellation of debts during that year, restated as a universally binding law in the Maimonidean *Code,* and from time to time resorted to the ancient method of evasion through the deposit of a *prosbol* in court. From talmudic days, however, it was realized that only an historical chronology based on an accepted interpretation of the biblical record might justify the existing observance of certain years as Sabbatical years. The brief and often ambiguous statements in the Talmud were subsequently elaborated in books on the calendar.[75]

Nor did the prevailing assumption that the Jubilee and Sabbatical cycles permanently coincided enjoy unanimous acceptance. In fact, Al-Biruni reported the opposite as the official Jewish view. The Arabian chronologist discussed the practical importance of the two cycles not only because on them depended such ritualistic performances as the release of a Hebrew slave who had refused freedom at the end of his sixth year of bondage, but also because "in their [the Jews'] sales the higher and the lower prices should always correspond to the remaining number of years of the cycle." He supplied, therefore, a regular table of coincidences between them based on the larger cycle of 350 years. "Now, if you want to know," Al-Biruni added, "how many years have elapsed of each of the two cycles (at a certain time) take the years of the *Aera Adami,* including the current year, subtract therefrom 1,010, or add thereto 740; divide the sum by 350, and neglect the quotient." [76]

Following the example set by Saadiah, Hai, and Al-Biruni, and in turn closely followed therein by Maimonides, Bar-Ḥiyya tried to reconstruct briefly the original computations underlying the *shemiṭṭah* and Jubilee years. He concluded that it was not enough simply to follow the era of Creation or any other starting point, because there had been three major changes in the course of history, which must be taken into consideration. The first cycle was introduced in the year 2502 A.M., or fourteen years after the conquest of Palestine by the ancient Israelites. Hence the first year of fallowness occurred in 2509, and the first Jubilee year in 2552. So long as Jubilee years were observed, that is, until the fall of

Samaria in 3037, these years were simply superimposed upon the seven Sabbatical cycles, so that the new cycle started again every fifty-first year. When the two and a half tribes were exiled, however, and the Jubilee years were discontinued, the Sabbatical cycles ran without interruption every forty-nine years, until the fall of Jerusalem in 3338. Restored to Palestine seventy years later, the Jews of the Second Commonwealth resumed the counting by fifty-year cycles, in order to underscore the basic similarity between the return of the exiles and the earlier occupation under Joshua. But they could not actually observe the Jubilee years as such in the absence from Palestine of large segments of their people, and hence counted the fiftieth year as both the completion of the first Jubilee cycle and as the beginning of the next cycle. Since the Restoration took place in the 28th year of a Jubilee cycle, it did not alter the sequence of the Sabbatical cycles, which began in the following year and ran straight through the ages. Savasorda supplied simple arithmetical formulas for speedily ascertaining a particular year in a Jubilee or Sabbatical cycle during each of these three periods (*Sefer ha-'Ibbur,* III.6, pp. 95 f.).

In this interpretation of the talmudic passages Bar Ḥiyya followed an old tradition, expatiated on by Hai Gaon and others. Maimonides, in his own studies of the Jewish calendar, first reached somewhat divergent conclusions. But when it came to practical application he bowed before the traditional method and advised a zealous student to follow the accepted rule rather than his own.[77]

Even more theoretical was Maimonides' effort to reconstruct the sequence in the transmission of the oral law from generation to generation. Evidently conscious of the great importance of the *isnad* as a reassurance for the authenticity of tradition, the sage of Fusṭaṭ elaborated in his *Commentary* on the first Mishnah in Abot the chain of tradition recorded in that Mishnah. In the introduction to his *Code* he made the even more ambitious attempt to reconstruct a complete succession of forty generations of authorized transmitters from Moses to R. Ashi. Like Bar Ḥiyya, he accepted the general chronology of the *Seder 'Olam,* and hence counted only some fifteen centuries from the death of Moses to that of the fifth-century leader of the academy of Sura. Nevertheless he succeeded in obtaining the round figure of "forty" generations only by such desperate expedients as postulating that between the generation of Moses' immediate disciples Eleazar, Phineas, and Joshua, and that of Eli there had been only one generation of "elders." He evidently bridged the biblical gap of some three hundred and fifty years only by accepting the rabbinic homilies concerning Phineas' extraordinary longevity. On the other hand, similar gaps between Jeremiah and Ezra, and between the latter and Simon the Just, likewise glossed over by the insertion of a single generation each, required no further explanation, in view of the long-accepted telescoping of the Persian period during the Second Temple to but thirty-four years.[78]

GEOGRAPHY AND ETHNOLOGY

Compared with the intense interest of Jewish scholars in astronomy and cognate disciplines, that in geography and related subjects such as ethnology was rather limited. Most of the theoretical discussions on geography were related to the astronomic features of the earth's position in the universe. At the same time, popular interest in remote countries and civilizations never died down. In fact, with the growth of popular literature appealing to the less educated masses, stories of adventure and travelogues blending folkloristic tales with fruits of observation found voracious readers among the fancy-loving youth and adults.

Scholarly aloofness of this kind is doubly remarkable, as the Jews had sound practical reasons for gathering reliable geographic data. True, they lacked the impetus for travel information, which their Arab neighbors derived from Islam's religious requirement of a pilgrimage to Mecca at least once in a lifetime. Nevertheless many Jewish pilgrims from all over the world succeeded in overcoming all obstacles and in paying personal homage to the remnants of their ancient glory in the Holy Land. The required orientation toward Jerusalem in daily prayers forced even the least curious travelers to secure some rough approximation of their temporary position in relation to Palestine. On the other hand, the general freedom of movement within the vast expanses of the Islamic empire greatly encouraged commercial and educational journeys among both Muslims and "protected subjects." Certainly the vigorous participation of Jews in world trade must have stimulated careful investigations of trade routes, economic resources, and the output, both agricultural and industrial, of the various countries among which they mediated. And yet not a single full-fledged geographic treatise by a medieval Jew is extant, or even recorded. Had, as is often alleged, the Jewish mathematical literature, and not only that concerned with the comparatively unimportant *regula mercatorum,* been largely the effect of Jewish commercial needs, this neglect of basic geographic information would have been doubly incongruous.

Obviously, the best Jewish minds were so deeply engrossed in the study of law, philosophy, and Bible exegesis that they paid but scant attention to those facets of science which were not directly related to these Jewish disciplines. Travelogues and tales of adventure were ignored, if not viewed with disdain, by the Jewish intelligentsia. There certainly existed nothing in Hebrew or Judeo-Arabic letters that could be compared with the numerous Arabic "Books of Routes" from Ibn Khurdadhbah down, or even remotely resembled such crowning achievements of Muslim geographical science, as Idrisi's *Kitab al-Rujari* (Book of King Roger) of the twelfth century and Yaqut's thirteenth-century *Kitab Mu'jam al-Buldan* (Geographical Dictionary). Evidently, Jewish pilgrims, students, and merchants living under Muslim domination were satisfied with the available geographic handbooks in the Arabic language, often prepared by high government officials like Ibn Khurdadhbah with the support of generous monarchs. The denominational distinctions appeared the less disturbing, as the subject matter had little bearing on theological fundamentals, and as most Muslim authors themselves tried to present the geographic data in a purely descriptive, unbiased fashion.[79]

In his "Shape of the Universe" and his "Book of Intercalation" Bar Ḥiyya briefly formulated the prevailing outlook among his fellow scientists. The spheric character of the earth was no longer seriously debated. While talmudic sages and the author of the "Book of Creation," still viewed the earth as a disk surrounded by water and gravely discussed the problem as to how it was supported, later teachers, beginning with the fourth-century Palestinian Amora R. Jonah, unequivocally regarded the earth as "resembling a ball." R. Jonah's more famous Babylonian contemporary, Raba, was evidently familiar with the measurements of Hellenistic geographers from Eratosthenes to Ptolemy, and he declared that the world, or rather the earth's circumference, amounted to 6,000 parasangs. The English equivalent of 24,872 miles is indeed a good approximation of the modern measurements for the equator.[80]

Backed by this segment of rabbinic opinion, Saadiah did not hesitate to controvert the author of *Yeṣirah.* Though conceding that that venerable writer, whose great antiquity he never doubted, had much support among the ancient sages, the gaon claimed that the rabbis had conceded this point to the Gentile scholars. "The opinion accepted among us," he wrote, "is that the [celestial] sphere and the earth are both like a ball, and that the earth rests in the middle of heaven like a point. The sun moves above the earth during the day, and under it during the night. It is the opacity of the earth which prevents us from seeing the sun during the night, and half of the celestial sphere at any time." From these motions and the finite character of both the earth and the celestial sphere, Saadiah derived another argument for the existence of an outside mover: God. He also argued that the law of nature forcing heavier objects downwards militated against the assumption of many coexisting universes. Had there been, he contended, even a small body of earth or water anywhere above the sphere of fire surrounding the earth, it would have necessarily penetrated that sphere and fallen down to earth. He ventured even to estimate the size of that sphere separating the earth and the lowest celestial sphere; it amounted, he believed, to 1,008 times the size of the earth. In another connection, however, he presented it as a matter of common scientific knowledge that "the aerial space between the earth and the first part of the heaven has 1,089 times the volume of the entire earth, including its soil, mountains, seas, plants, and animals, because its measurements are thirty-three by thirty-three times [the earth's diameter]."[81]

The earth's diameter was, of course, computed from the measurements of the equator. Saadiah and his confreres readily disregarded here the various old aggadic measurements; for example, that of Midrash Konen which claimed that "[the distance around] the earth equals a journey of 500 years. One third of it consists of desert, one third of habitable land, and one third of sea." Since the average day's journey was supposed to cover 10 parasangs, a journey of 500 years would be the equivalent of 1,825,000 parasangs, or some 7,564,625 miles—clearly a legendary figure. Similarly, the proportion here given between the earth, desert, and sea, was almost totally neglected. Doubtless derived from a homiletical misinterpretation of the Isaianic ode to Him who had "comprehended the dust of the earth in a measure [*shalish,* which could also mean a third]," it was echoed only by such medieval conservatives as Rashi and the Tosafists. Ibn Gabirol and Bar Ḥiyya unhesitatingly declared the globe to be equally divided between water and dry land, Bar Ḥiyya only making the slight concession that the land mass was in turn subdivided into equal portions of habitable land and deserts. In his penchant for exact symmetries he even postulated the precise spatial equivalence of the surface of islands in the seas with that of lakes and other inland waters. Ibn Ezra went further. He not only denied the accepted view that one large ocean surrounded the entire globe, but also radically taught that the dry land in its totality did not exceed one twelfth of the area of the earth.[82]

Curiously, none of the Jewish scientists or rabbinic students referred to the ancient theory, expounded by the author of IV Ezra, that in creating the earth God had gathered in all waters to constitute but a seventh part of the earth's area. This neglect of medieval Jewish scientists was undoubtedly owing in part to their conviction, taken over from Arab travelers and geographers, of the immensity of the Indian, Pacific, and Atlantic Oceans. The latter, especially, inspired unholy awe among Arab sailors. "No navigator," commented Al-Idrisi, "dares to sail into the Atlantic Ocean, and to navigate out into the open sea. They are satisfied with cruising on it without ever losing sight of its shores. . . . Nobody knows what lies behind it. Hitherto no one has ascertained anything reliable about that Ocean on account of the difficulties of navigation on it, its lack of light [fogs], and the frequency of storms." That is why Idrisi himself, though born in

Spain and, through his cooperation with King Roger of Sicily, in possession of data of Christian sailors as well, seems to have known even of the Canary Islands only through Ptolemy. Nevertheless, the theory of the ancient apocryphon, accepted as authoritative by such Western scientists as Roger Bacon, was destined to become one of the most fruitful Great Illusions of history. Because Columbus implicitly believed it and hence readily underestimated the westerly distance separating Europe from the Far East, he dared to undertake his memorable "short-cut" to the East Indies.[83]

Not that the Jewish scholars were fully aware of the vast expanses of the Atlantic and Pacific Oceans. Even the great Arab geographer Mas'udi seems to have been misled by a Jewish student of the Talmud into accepting some fanciful guesses concerning the earth's surface. In his classical "Meadows of Gold" (I, 368) he quoted a scholar, "dedicated to the study of geography," who had not only reported to him the aforementioned estimate of the earth's length as tantamount to a 500-year journey, and the threefold division into equal parts of sea, desert, and habitable land, but had also asserted that "Ethiopia and the whole of Sudan cover a distance of a seven-year journey, that Egypt is but a sixtieth of the land of Sudan, which is a [sixtieth] part of the whole earth." Mas'udi's informant failed to mention only the Palestinian Talmud's further contentions that Egypt's length amounted to a journey of forty days. Evidently either he or Mas'udi himself readily noticed the discrepancy between 60×40 days and the round figure of seven years for the combined size of Ethiopia and the Sudan, and the still greater disparity of 60×7 and 500 years for the earth's surface.

Despite the combined authority of the Talmud and Mas'udi, none of the Jewish students of geography followed them along these fanciful paths. Without committing himself to any figures, Savasorda explained that

> human habitation extends over the whole [length of the] earth, from the line at the beginning of the east until it reaches the end of the west. But it does not extend over the whole breadth [of the globe]. Beginning with the equator, it spreads out northward to the 66th

parallel of the 90 covering the northern latitude. Beyond that parallel there is no habitation on account of the cold. Similarly, beginning from the equator it extends southward only to the 16th parallel of the 90 in the southern latitude. From there on no habitation exists on account of the heat. . . . All these 82 parallels are inhabited from the extreme east to the extreme west. Hence the students of secular science have concluded that the habitable area amounts to only one-quarter of the earth, for half the globe is immersed in the sea, and the other half is divided between desert and habitation.

Accepting a much-debated ancient theory, Bar Ḥiyya subdivided further this habitable area into seven "climates," disregarding entirely, however, the settlements south of the equator. In an ethnological aside he explained that those lands "are inhabited by the children of Ham whom Scripture had cursed, and whose ways differ in everything from the ways of the northern settlements." To begin with, they have summers when the north has winters, and their longest days coincide with the shortest days in the north. "For this reason the specialists in this discipline have neglected them, and failed to elucidate the peculiarities of their territory." These seven climates, extending over varying latitudes—Savasorda himself was not consistent in the number of degrees he assigned to each—are characterized by the differing durations of the longest days and nights. The inhabitants of the northernmost settlements at the 66th parallel have in the summer and winter of each year certain days and nights which last the entire twenty-four hours.[84]

Neither Bar Ḥiyya nor any of his Jewish colleagues went much beyond these geographic and climatological generalities. We shall look in vain for a description of conditions in individual countries, or of the nations inhabiting them. In the same context Bar Ḥiyya merely spoke of the "seventy nations" living in the northern hemisphere. He not only failed to analyze more specifically this generic term inherited from the ancient Aggadah, but he nowhere intimated how he squared this number with the rich ethnographic data accumulated in the contemporary Arabic letters. He and his Jewish fellow students may have been discouraged from going more deeply into geographic details by the latter's obvious discrepancies from the biblical and talmudic world picture. They may also have caught some of the aversion to geographic studies animating their Christian neighbors from the days of Ambrose and Augustine, the latter equating scientific quests with magic arts (*Confessiones,* x.35, 55, in *PL,* XXXII, 802; *CSEL,* XXXIII, 268).

Philosophers, too, were satisfied with vague generalities. In describing, for example, the era of redemption, Saadiah merely paraphrased the Isaianic prediction of the ingathering of the Jews from the "islands of the seas" on ships laden with silver and gold, without in any way indicating which more distant islands were then inhabited by Jews. He only added the interesting observation that if, upon the arrival of the Messiah, a Jew should "happen to be" in Ethiopia, he would be transported to Egypt in a boat of bulrushes, because protruding mountains make ordinary navigation on the upper Nile extremely hazardous. Although India was focusing considerable attention in his day, all Saadiah had to report about it was that, according to a popular adage, anyone going there gets rich quick, and that certain Hindus harden themselves against fire. In physical geography, too, the gaon was primarily intrigued by such religiously relevant facts as the relation between water and wind. Though finer in substance than water, he observed, winds are nevertheless able to set the latter in motion and even cause it to move upwards. But he was contented with the general assumption that all winds have their "fixed abode in the upper and lower regions," from which they come forth to do the Lord's bidding.[85]

Maimonides, too, evinced little interest in geographic and ethnological facts, even where they had some bearing on his discussions of theological or legal problems. His frequent references to the Sabean religion reveal little direct acquaintance with the existing remnants of that faith, and a rather uncritical acceptance of the antiquity of such spurious writings as Ibn al-Waḥshiya's *Kitab al-Filaḥa al-nabaṭiya* (Nabatean Agriculture). The sage of Fusṭaṭ avoided the talmudic phrase of "seventy languages," as a rule substituting for it the noncommittal expression of "most languages." But he unhesitatingly subscribed to the prevailing assumption of the innate superiority of Hebrew, Arabic, Aramaean, Greek, and Persian over all other languages, just as he accepted the regnant prejudice, also voiced by Farabi and others, that the inhabitants of the middle climates were natively endowed with greater intellectual gifts than the southern populations or the Nordics. India aroused in him no more scholarly curiosity than it did in Saadiah, although its intensive commercial relations with Egypt are frequently reflected in his responsa and even caused him great personal grief through the shipwreck of his brother David.[86]

THEORY VERSUS PRACTICE

In restrospect we note how these scientific explorations revealed a curious dichotomy between practical objectives and theoretical interests. Wherever practical needs were altogether absent, as in the case of political or physical geography and ethnology, Jewish scientists found few stimuli to write tractates of their own. Their contributions in these fields were largely limited to aspects of biblical and talmudic exegesis, where scientific discoveries shed new light on puzzling passages in these older sources, or when apparent conflicts between the traditional views and the newly established scientific verities had to be resolved. Similarly, wherever scientific findings had direct bearing on communal practice and the adjudication of the law, Jewish savants felt it incumbent upon themselves to supply the necessary factual underpinnings. This was particularly true in such fields as calendar computations, the precise chronological setting of Sabbatical years, the algebra and geometry involved in the distribution of estates among heirs, and the astrological predictions affecting communal or individual actions.

No sooner did many Jewish scientists start investigating these natural phenomena, however, than their predominantly theoretical bent of mind reasserted itself to the full. Instead of merely detecting the scientific facts for their own sake, they began philosophizing about them. They looked with actual disdain on the pursuit of purely practical disciplines, such as mechanics, and did not even rank them with economics and government as branches of "practical philosophy," the limited value of which, as we recollect, they were prepared to concede. To most of these scientists themselves science had thus become a mere "handmaiden" of law and exegesis.

Not all of their statements to this effect, however, are to be taken at their face value. Confronted by an obscurantist wing among the orthodox leaders and the uninformed public alike, which resented any diversion of the time allotted to study from the traditional talmudic learning, these scholars often went to great lengths in trying to prove not only the legitimacy of scientific inquiries, but also their direct relevance for talmudic studies. They also took great pains to demonstrate that, rather than leading to skepticism and unbelief, scientific pursuits were apt to deepen one's religious convictions and trust in God. Not only in his geometric and cosmographic treatises, but also in his "Scroll of Disclosure" and even his purely ethical "Contemplation of the Soul," Savasorda untiringly reassured his readers that mathematical and astronomic studies, though largely based on the works of the ancient Greeks, would do no harm to their orthodoxy. These pagan savants, he asserted, may not have had the benefit of the truth found in the Torah, but by relying upon their own tireless pursuits of learning they succeeded in "finding the right way." Contending further that "when thou understandest with all thy heart the order of the celestial movements above thee and of the earth under thee, thou immediately realizest that the Creator had created them according to His wise plan, and that He is the one and only God," Bar Ḥiyya concluded with a typical rabbinic homily on Job 19:26 and declared that "through this passage Scripture has permitted us to search after the words of the ancients and their ways of explaining all that exists." [87]

It is doubly remarkable, therefore, that acting under so many restraints, the medieval Jewish scientists made such signal contributions to human, especially Western knowledge. Strategically located in the Eastern centers during the upsurge of the Renaissance of Islam and again in the Western lands during the twelfth-century Renaissance, they served as a cementing force between the ancient traditions and the newly evolving scientific interests, and between the Eastern and Western civilizations. The poor state of preservation of the early medieval documents does not allow us to perceive the individual stages in the evolution of most of these disciplines, particularly during the crucial period of transition under the early Caliphate. Only a small fraction of the voluminous scientific output of Masha'allah and Sahl ben Bishr has come down to us. We hardly know the names of those numerous other Jews who undoubtedly fostered the scholarly exchanges between the Graeco-Roman or Christian worlds and those of Persia and India. We are somewhat better informed about the Jewish role in the transmission of Eastern science to the West, but much scholarly research is still needed before the story of that cultural diffusion will become fully known.

Historically of equal importance was the influence of those innumerable unnamed individuals who neither wrote nor translated books, but whose zest for new knowledge communicated itself to others, in their own and other religious communities, through constant oral exchanges. Nor shall we ever know the names of that host of teachers who, employing curricula akin to that outlined by Ibn 'Aqnin, instilled in their numerous disciples that scientific curiosity and relative openmindedness which alone made possible the discovery or rediscovery of valid scientific facts. Since the average level of education was undoubtedly higher among the Jews than among their neighbors even in the East, the mass impact of such a new orientation must have made itself felt much beyond the Jewish numerical ratio in the respective populations. In short, as investigators in their own right, or as transmitters of the fruits of one civilization to another—this distinction was not quite so pronounced in that period of predominantly "bookish" learning—and abetted by the creative *élan* of the masses, medieval Jews were able to make momentous contributions to the development of learning in that crucial intermediary period between ancient and modern science.

XXXVI

MEDICAL SCIENCE AND PRACTICE

ONE scientific discipline which eminently combined practical utility with vast opportunities for theoretical speculation, and hence greatly appealed to Jewish students, was medicine. Although, as we shall see, opposition to scientific forms of healing was never completely silenced, the pursuit of ever more intensive studies in this field and their application in practice steadily gained ground among the Eastern Jews under Islam and soon spread also to the Western lands. Sirach's ancient epigram typifies far more accurately the attitude of the Jewish intelligentsia and public alike than the occasional objections raised by the few extremists. "Honor the physician," the ancient sage enjoined his readers, "with the honor due unto him for the uses which ye may have of him, for the Lord hath created him. . . . And He hath given man skill that He might be honored in His marvelous works." Moreover, the opportunities for earning a living in the medical profession always were far greater than in any other scientific discipline. While mathematics, astronomy, and even astrology could furnish employment only to a limited group of specialists, the art of healing filled a more or less universal need. It also more easily transcended the denominational bounds, which often impeded the initial training and subsequent professional careers of Jewish students in other branches of science. It is small wonder, then, that most medieval Jewish scientists and philosophers derived their livelihood from the practice of medicine while independently pursuing their theoretical studies in other fields as well.

Such broader preoccupations were characteristic not only of those universal geniuses who conferred the great luster on the Renaissance of Islam, as their counterparts were later to enhance the glory of the Italian Renaissance. Despite the continued growth of specialization in the Muslim world, the scholarly and literary disciplines frequently overlapped, since some interest in, and knowledge of, law, poetry, and philology, as well as of philosophy and science, was expected from every educated person. Physicians, in particular, were keenly aware of the effect of various religious and social factors on the behavior of their patients. They also often sensed the peculiar interrelations between their own branch of learning and the other natural sciences, especially alchemy (or chemistry), zoology, and botany, in the preparation of drugs. Hence it was they who often pioneered in the accumulation and careful analytical sifting of vast factual data in these cognate sciences as well.

NATURAL SCIENCES

Understandably, Jewish interest in certain branches of science was less keen than in others. For example, the study of physics and chemistry, or rather the latter's forerunner, alchemy, attracted far less interest than mathematics or the study of stars. Of course, in their all-embracing quest for truth, philosophers had to take cognizance of the fundamental physical phenomena, too. They not only discussed physics and the related sciences within their general classification of scientific disciplines (always emphasizing the superiority of metaphysics), but they also had to pay some attention to the four elements of which the sublunary world was supposed to be composed, and their relation to the superlunary "fifth" element, as well as to the world of man. In their cosmological discussions they had to take a stand on such basic physical theories as the atomic doctrines, which had been cropping up in the philosophic literature since ancient times. However, even here the main focus was on philosophic speculation, rather than on naturalistic *realia.*

Typical of these discussions is the "Book of Elements" by Isaac Israeli. Although written by a distinguished scientist, it stressed the philosophic implications of the physical phenomena. Debating, for example, the relationship between fire and heat, Israeli stated:

The heat, not being separated from fire, is natural to it but not essential. If someone should ask, "What difference does it make whether a matter is natural or essential?" we would explain that a matter which is natural [to one object] may be found in other objects by accident as in the case of heat. While being natural to fire, heat can also be found in a man suffering from fever, in hot springs, or in iron which is accidentally hot. But an essential characteristic is found in no other objects, either essentially or accidentally, either potentially or actually. For instance, speech and mortality, because they are essential to man, cannot be found in any other being, either essentially or accidentally. If anyone should object by pointing to the presence of speech in the superior [angelic] beings and of death among animals, we would reply that such presence is diffused, not concentrated. For if speech is found among the superior beings, they cannot be affected by death at all. If, on the other hand, animals are mortal like man, they do not possess the quality of speech. Whereas in man both these characteristics are found together.

Such purely scholastic arguments indeed much too frequently took the place of detailed scientific elaborations of physical laws.[1]

To be sure, a man of encyclopedic mind, such as Abu'l Barakat, even before his conversion to Islam may have stumbled across a significant series of phenomena which made him foreshadow the modern doctrine of the impetus. But there was little incentive in either Jewish law and ritual, or in the practical problems facing the Jewish people at that time, for scholars to dedicate themselves wholeheartedly to the study of the physical sciences from their theoretical or technological aspects. There undoubtedly were some Jews who studied these subjects, and others who made practical use of some new technological discoveries based on them. But these men did not write treatises on the subject, and they evidently made no novel, independent contributions worthy of recording by the Arabian biographers of scholars, usually our main source of information.[2]

Not even alchemy seems to have exercised any particular attraction on Jewish minds. Their relative aloofness from this semi-scientific and semi-occult discipline is particularly remarkable, as its secret lore had had deep roots in remote Near Eastern and Greek antiquity. In fact, during the Middle Ages both Jews and non-Jews believed that Moses and Solomon had been among its founders and had each contributed several works, such as Moses' *Diplosis* (On the Transmutation of Gold) or Solomon's *Labyrinth*. The wise king was also supposed to have discovered a way of artificially producing silver through a process lasting forty days. The stimulus of Arab interest and scientific preoccupation was likewise present. Even before the end of the seventh century, the 'Umayyad prince Khalid ibn Yazid, grandson of Mu'awiya, sought solace in the study of alchemy for the loss of the throne to his cousin 'Abd al-Malik. The interest among Arab scholars increased tremendously in the subsequent three centuries, so that An-Nadim could devote an entire, fairly substantial chapter of his bibliography to this discipline.[3]

Nevertheless, most Jewish intellectuals seem to have held aloof. It has been suggested that among the most violent opponents of this quest for a method of transforming elements into one another, and particularly into gold, were wealthy owners of precious metals who lived in constant dread of their sudden depreciation by a successful alchemistic operation. Jewish bankers, merchants, and mintmasters, who, as we have seen, had invested a considerable part of their holdings in these readily convertible and easily hidden commodities, might have been doubly sensitive. However, one must not overestimate such fears. On the contrary, persons whose main preoccupation was with gold, would normally be the first to search for some secret means to produce it artificially and inexpensively. They doubtless would often have deluded themselves into believing that they could readily control the supply of artificial metal so as to avoid the sudden drop in value of their original holdings.[4]

Indeed there seems to have been no dearth of Jewish alchemists, although the Hebrew sources are remarkably silent on this score. Only incidentally do we catch a glimpse of some Jewish practitioners of that hidden art, as the convert Paul, to whom Adalbert of Hamburg-Bremen, the notable eleventh-century German statesman, was supposed to have "listened," according to the chronicler Adam of Bremen. Nor did Baḥya ibn Paquda, who introduced an alchemist as the exponent of naturalistic calculations, intimate in any way that this representative was a non-Jew. Probably the ancient connection of alchemy with magic arts discouraged some

Jews from indulging in these obscure practices, and it may have prevented others from recording them. We need but remember that the entire realm of magic, though flourishing among the masses and attested by numerous magic bowls, was rarely reflected in contemporary Jewish letters. Only mystics often felt the attraction of such manipulation of the physical world, especially if man achieved that mastery by invoking divine, angelic, or demonic names. Transfer of elements could, moreover, be envisaged as a prototype for the soul's progression toward ultimate perfection. Hence that combination of alchemy with ṣufism which was apparent already in the teachings of Dhu an-Nun (d. 860), and the great respect with which Baḥya, the nearest approximation of a Jewish ṣufist, spoke of alchemists. The majority of Jewish scholars, however, evidently had little use for both the discipline and its practitioners, at least until the thirteenth century.[5]

Nor were there sufficient practical inducements. Unlike astrology, which appealed to both the ruling classes and the populace at large, alchemy by its very nature was restricted to small circles of initiates. There certainly were no influential posts open to Jewish alchemists similar to those of court astrologers. Few of the alchemists themselves—not even such distinguished scientists as the physician Muḥammad ben Zakariya ar-Razi (known in European letters as Rhazes)—realized that the by-product of their investigations, namely the direct observation of the properties of the various metals, would prove historically far more significant than their quest for the artificial production of gold. The few Jews who had a scientific interest, akin to that of Ar-Razi himself, as a rule could study his *Secretum secretorum* or the alchemistic treatises by Jabir or others in their Arabic originals. The same was largely true in the case of those students of mineralogy who believed in the medicinal value of precious stones.[6]

Much greater was the scholarly interest in biological sciences, including zoology and botany. True, biological sciences had made little progress since Aristotle and his pupil Theophrastus; yet knowledge of biological factors was significant for almost all phases of medicine, and hence was of direct concern to its Jewish practitioners. Abraham ibn Daud inserted into his major philosophic tractate a lengthy and important biological discussion.

Here he rejected the largely mechanistic explanation of the relations between body and soul offered by the schools of Hippocrates and Galen and argued in favor of a "vitalistic" interpretation. He also analyzed in some detail the physiology of the external and the psychology of the internal senses. Comparing, for instance, the factors characteristic of animal as against plant life, he stated:

> These are the twelve forces which the animals have in addition to those of the plants: five external and five internal senses, and two forces of movement, in addition to the seven forces of the plants. Altogether nineteen forces of the soul are thus to be found in animals. Now we will prove that the forces are truly existing, that every act is the consequence of a force, and that the same act does not spring from two (different) forces. We maintain that the differences of the external senses are based upon a (qualitative) difference of the forces.

Special medical treatises devoted to dietetics and climatic influences on human bodies also constituted significant contributions to the study of biological factors. Among the works of the eleventh-century Egyptian Jewish physician Salama (Solomon) ibn Mubarak (Meborakh) ibn Raḥamun was one discussing the meteorological reasons and biological effects of the scarcity of rains in Egypt, and another explaining the obesity of most middle-aged Egyptian women. A century later the distinguished Jewish physician Hibbat Allah (Nathaniel?) ibn Jumay' wrote "An Epistle on the Nature of Alexandria, Its Air, Water, and Inhabitants," as well as special treatises on the use of lemon and rhubarb.[7]

Zoology and botany, moreover, were studied not only by philosophers and scientists, but also by philologists, Bible exegetes, and jurists. The biblical story of Creation itself offered many a challenge to naturalistic expounders. Isaac Israeli, for example, who had devoted two books, or lengthy chapters, to the exposition of Genesis 1, tried to elucidate the individual steps in Creation through contemporary scientific findings. His commentary is lost, but Abraham ibn Ezra, a rather hostile critic, cited Israeli as suggesting a harmonistic explanation for the apparent conflict between Genesis 1:20 and 2:19 by stating that fowl had been created from a mixture of water and earth. The Bible, Talmud, and other rabbinic writings were filled with names of animals and plants. While later generations of students were often satisfied with some generic explanation such as "a wild beast," "a tree," or "a vegetable," most of the earlier medieval students evinced a healthy curiosity about the specific identity of each. Translators, such as Saadiah, were forced by the exigencies of their task to furnish Arabic equivalents for the Hebrew or Aramaic animal or plant names, which often required much intensive research and personal acumen. Authors of Hebrew or talmudic dictionaries, especially Nathan ben Yeḥiel of Rome, likewise made valiant efforts to reproduce for the benefit of their readers the meaning of the less well-known designations or technical terms used in the older literature. In his attempt to clarify the talmudic texts, Rashi often had to resort to the French translation of such terms, thereby enriching, as we recall, the knowledge of modern students of medieval French dialects.[8]

In their attempt at identification of talmudic terms, the western scholars, such as Gershom bar Yehudah and Rashi, had at their disposal excellent traditions from the talmudic age. But they were often unable to verify them through direct observation, since many eastern animals or plants were unavailable in western Europe. According to Immanuel Löw, Nathan ben Yeḥiel was the first European to mention sago, some three centuries before Marco Polo. Wherever they could, Rashi and many other commentators or lexicographers went beyond mere translation and offered detailed descriptions of particular plants and animals, showing that they valiantly tried to familiarize themselves with the external appearance and specific characteristics of the biblical-talmudic fauna and flora.

Jurists had equally valid reasons for acquainting themselves with some zoological and botanical *realia*. The ancient rabbis had already had to decide whether certain animals met the specific criteria for Jewish consumption set up by Scripture. Close observation of animal life, and especially of the anatomy of domesticated livestock, resulted also from such ritualistic requirements as the proper slaughtering of animals. Ever since ancient times ritual law had required the application of certain humane methods assuring the quick death of the slaughtered beast and subsequent detailed examination showing whether or not it had previously suffered from any fatal disease. Hence the Talmud included a great many anatomical observations of great interest which were subsequently elaborated in the juristic and exegetical literature. The ritualistic differences between Palestine and Babylonia kept the debate constantly alive, precisely because they often related to mere minutiae; so did various other local customs or prejudices. We recall the stir created in western lands by Eldad ha-Dani's tantalizing reports about the laws of slaughtering allegedly practiced in his country. Incidentally, Eldad also presented his readers with a number of puzzling Hebrew designations of a zoological and botanical nature. So certain was Yehudah Halevi of the profundity of these Jewish laws that he cited them as illustrations of the ancient heritage of natural sciences among Jews, a heritage which had become the common property of a large number of scholars. "Whatever element of those sciences," he concluded, "was embodied in the talmudical law codes was thus protected and preserved by the zeal of many students. . . . A large amount of this remained unknown to Galen. If this were not so, why does he not mention easily recognizable diseases to which the Law calls attention?" [9]

On the other hand, the great learning which had accumulated in the priestly schools of Jerusalem in connection with the minutely elaborated rituals of the sacrificial worship was gradually forgotten. Scholars like Maimonides may have tried to perpetuate the laws of sacrifices on a par with other talmudic laws but their knowledge evidently consisted only in what they had read in the Talmud or had learned from a few oral traditions kept alive in the academies. However, the chain of living practice was broken. One need but compare the vivid, detailed, and authoritative statements in the Maimonidean *Code* relating to the Sanctification of the New Moon with the rather pale and bookish restatement there of the talmudic laws of sacrifices to realize how much scientific knowledge, based on ramified experience of centuries, had gone into total oblivion.

With the constant broadening of the geographic horizons, ever new animals came to the attention of the sages who had to issue formal rulings. New plants, if ritualistically less significant, aroused considerable medical and culinary interest. That is why the geonic responsa, particularly those by Sherira and Hai, contain so many attempts at correct identification of names and their relation to the previously known species. We also occasionally find there actual recipes for the preparation of vegetables, taken from Babylonian practice. Moreover, not only Maimonides, the physician, but also Rashi knew of the aesthetic-therapeutic value of gardens and landscapes. Commenting on the biblical proverb "The light of the eyes rejoiceth the heart" (15:30), Rashi observed that everything which delights the eye, for instance a green garden or a flowing stream, gladdens the heart and softens its worry. Maimonides was even more outspoken about the impact of beautiful objects on mental well-being.[10]

Identification of plant and animal names was greatly facilitated in the eastern lands by the Arabic language's great indebtedness in these domains to Aramaic prototypes. In the course of their rapid conquests the Arabs came across many new species, for which they usually adopted the readily available Aramaic-Syriac designations. If in some cases they resorted to Greek and Persian loan words, some of the former had already been incorporated in the Aramaic of the Talmud and Midrash, or in the Syriac spoken by the eastern Christians. Moreover, Jews never lost contact with the Greek-Byzantine world. Byzantine scholars continued to supply pertinent information through personal contacts or correspondence, or through their biblical and talmudic commentaries which sooner or later became the common property of the Jewish people. Spanish and Provençal Jewry, on the other hand, served in this respect, too, as a natural bridge between the eastern and western vernaculars.

Even animal life, however, was studied primarily for the understanding of man, his physical structure, and wants. If in his all-embracing quest for knowledge Abraham ibn Ezra devoted a special chapter, or "treatise," of his encyclopedic *Sefer ha-'Aṣamim* (Book of Substances) to animals, he did it mainly in order to comprehend better the human body. "We count," he declared, "365 veins and 365 arteries in every body, according to the number of the days of the year, the other corresponding to the number of the nights. This is not the place to compare all details of the structure of the human body with the structure of the world; but this is the reason why man has been called a 'small world' by the philosophers, as well as by our own sages." Even a self-avowed student of anatomy like Maimonides merely warned against the frequent confusion of nerves with veins and arteries, but neither he nor any other medieval Jewish scientist or exegete ever stopped to reexamine in detail the long-accepted rabbinic computation of 365 veins and 248 limbs or bones. Some of these scholars were undoubtedly familiar with the far lesser number of but 91 (together with finger and toe nails, 111) bones counted by Hippocrates, and the rather vague figure of over 200 offered by Galen. They also knew of the experiment conducted by the pupils of R. Ishmael on the corpse of a harlot executed by the government which, according to the Talmud, revealed a total of 252 bones. They were evidently prepared to accept the Talmud's evasive distinction between male and female anatomy, and its explanation that the figure 248 represented merely an average, from which one would find many deviations in life. In their purely philosophic and theological discussions the Jewish scholastics were much more interested, as we recall, in the problems of the animals' responsibility for their actions, and of their receiving reward or punishment in the Hereafter. This man-centered approach also accounts for the preponderance of psychological over strictly biological facets of the science of life.[11]

VICISSITUDES OF HEALING

Animal and plant life played a major role, however, in all fields of medicine. Precisely because both Muslim and Jewish law strenuously opposed dissection of human bodies, the medieval physicians, in their search for more precise knowledge of human anatomy and physiology, had exclusive recourse to the minute study of animals. Since both talmudic and Alexandrian science had long legitimized this type of experimentation, medieval physicians seem to have applied the technique of post mortem examination of animal organs with telling effect. There is no evidence that Jews ever practiced vivisection, although they did not formally outlaw it as did the Muslims. Their numerous ethical injunctions concerning the humane treatment of animals certainly ran counter to any cruelty inflicted upon them without good cause. Yet there was enough leeway for legitimate experimentation with carcasses and, within certain limits, with living animals.[12]

Jewish physicians looked back on a long and memorable tradition of their craft. True, God's promise to the ancient Hebrews during their desert migrations, that, if they would listen to His voice, He would safeguard them against the diseases He had put on the Egyptians, "for I am the Lord that healeth thee," was often taken in later ages as a warning against relying upon human advice. More unequivocally, the chronicler blamed King Asa because in his "exceeding great . . . disease he sought not to the Lord, but to the physicians." Yet such pious utterances did not really detract from the recognized necessity of applying human remedies. The ancient legislator of the "Book of the Covenant" simply took it for granted that, after committing assault and battery, the assailant "shall pay for the loss of his [the victim's] time, and shall cause him to be thoroughly healed." These passages were subsequently bandied back and forth by both adherents and opponents of the medical profession. But they never led to such a deep distrust of medicine as was evinced, for example, by Pope Gregory the Great. Nor do we find in Jewish or Muslim law any parallels to the canon (22) adopted by the Fourth Lateran Council in 1215, prohibiting physicians from attending to patients' needs without prior consultation with the appropriate ecclesiastical authorities, and from prescribing remedies forbidden by religious law. This is obviously to be distinguished from the licensing of physicians to engage in medical practice either by the state, or by a Jewish court, such as was recorded already in tannaitic times. In fact, the talmudic rabbis so thoroughly approved of skilled physicians (some of them, like Mar Samuel, exercised that profession) that the ultrapietistic opponents of human interference with God's will were permanently but an insignificant minority. The entire rabbinic literature mirrors widespread acceptance of the craft. By culling these stray data modern scholars have succeeded in reconstructing a rather imposing picture of talmudic medicine.[13]

In later periods communal interest actually dictated the promotion of Jewish medical practice as a major stepping stone to positions of power and influence at the courts of kings and ecclesiastical leaders. No one objected to Maimonides' great preoccupation with such highly placed practice during the last two decades of his life. Although frequently quoted, Maimonides' letter to Samuel ibn Tibbon (*Qobeṣ,* II, 27 f.), trying to discourage the latter from visiting Egypt for the purpose of personal consultation with him, may be partially cited here as an example of the life of a busy Jewish physician of the period.

I live in Fusṭaṭ [Maimonides wrote], while the king resides in Cairo at a distance of two permissible journeys on Sabbath [about three miles]. My duties at the royal court are very exacting: I must see the king early every day. But if he feels unwell, or if one of his children or concubines falls ill, I must spend most of the day at the royal palace in Cairo. Similarly if one or another official is sick, I must attend to his medication. . . . In any case, I do not return home before noon, quite hungry [and exhausted]. But I find my waiting rooms filled with people, Jews and Gentiles, distinguished and common, judges and surveyors, friends and enemies, a mixed multitude awaiting my return.

When he wrote this letter in 1199, Maimonides was some sixty-four years old, his body weakened by many preceding illnesses and by overwork. We may indeed believe him that when, after a hasty repast, he resumed his practice, which often lasted until eight o'clock, he had to attend to his patients while stretched out on a couch. And yet it was in these very years that he managed to write most of his medical, and a few of his lesser philosophic and juristic treatises. At the same time he was the recognized spiritual leader of Egyptian Jewry, and was consulted orally or in writing on many important communal or legal problems even by leaders of distant communities.

Nevertheless the pietistic masses long offered manifold obstacles to the development of a large professional class of physicians. There has always existed an inherent conflict between healing the sick in performance of a good deed, and the charging of fees for such services. The same factors which militated against the commercialization of the scholarly profession—we have seen that only after a protracted struggle there emerged a professional class of "rabbis"—also long operated against the professionalization of medicine. While a popular adage, repeated in the Talmud, insisted that "a physician who charges nothing is worth nothing," the story told with relish about a surgeon named Abba well reflects that polarity in the people's attitude. Abba allegedly not only allowed his patients to deposit their fees in a box according to their own desires and with perfect anonymity, but, if the patient was poor, he even provided him with food and medicine. In practice most physicians charged customary, some even exorbitant, fees. This undoubtedly was a contributory cause for the popular animosity toward the medical profession, which found an outlet in a number of irate rabbinic epigrams, such as that coined by R. Judah bar 'Ilai, "The best of doctors deserves to go to Gehenna." Nor was the pietistic theory that the physician must not charge for his skill and his studies, but only for the time lost from other gainful employment, ever formally abandoned. It was clearly restated in the "Book of the Pious" and by Joseph Karo. Nevertheless, even in talmudic times, and still more under Islam, medicine became an honored and financially rewarding profession, silencing all traditional objections. Still strenuously attacking the growing commercialization of rabbinic learning, Maimonides himself unperturbedly lived from the practice of medicine among Jews and Gentiles.[14]

On the other hand, the medical profession had to contend with the severe competition of a great many quacks. We have seen how popular were the magic arts during several centuries preceding and following the rise of Islam. With the rest of the populace, Jews believed in the efficacy of amulets and magical formulas in staving off attacks by demons, considered the major source of human diseases. Typical of a great many others were, for example, the four magic bowls, written in Judeo-Arabic for the benefit of one Muḥibb ben 'Atiqa. Here the demons were conjured "by the Great Name" to restore the patient's health and to release his "knots" placed upon him by the ruse of a Jew, Muslim, or Christian, sage or learned man, human being or demon. Objection to the use of any kind of magical implements for therapeutic use, occasionally voiced by such enlightened leaders as Hai, Samuel ben Ḥofni, and Maimonides, were not shared by the majority of rabbis. They were clearly controverted by such outstanding later leaders of Spanish Jewry as Naḥmanides and Solomon ibn Adret.[15]

In his competition with the magic healer, to be sure, the doctor was aided by the biblical prohibitions of occult arts. Although the population had long become inured to disregarding such injunctions in vital matters like health or the safeguarding of property, reference to them must have given a certain edge to the physician. On the other hand, the latter was necessarily restrained in the promises he made to patients. He certainly could neither give absolute assurances that he would stave off diseases by prophylactic treatment nor prognosticate instantaneous and permanent relief from any malady, as could the sorcerer with his magic formulas and fantastic brews. Some physicians were even warned against a modicum of self-praise. Isaac ben Solomon Israeli quoted the saying of the Christian doctor Masawaih, "If you find a physician ready to give prompt information about every disease and to praise his own treatment, regard him as a fool." [16]

We must bear in mind, however, that the distinction between the magical and the scientific healer long was far less obvious than today. The belief that many diseases were caused by evil spirits entering the human body and playing havoc with its customary functions was the ancient and medieval mind's closest approximation to the modern doctrine of germs and viruses. Even the verbal remedies of exorcisms, incantations, and amulets must have proved effective in many cases, if merely because of their psychological impact on the patient. Had not Maimonides himself, in the very course of his sharp denunciation of magic healing, admitted that verbal charms often give a person bitten by a snake "peace of mind and strengthen his heart"? These benefits were sufficiently frequent and observable for mankind to continue cultivating them during untold generations. In many cases, the "sorcerers" and "witches" administered a variety of herbs and special concoctions which, in their and their patients' experience, had proved helpful before. In some respects approximating the experimental functions of the astrological observation of stars and the alchemistic attempts to transform metals, magic healing, too, was part of that general "scientific twilight" which served as an important corrective to the pure book learning of many ancient and medieval physicians. Had not Galen already objected to those Jewish and Christian doctors who had countered many of his scientific arguments by invoking the authority of Moses? This attitude persevered in many medical circles throughout the Middle Ages, and only some of the great clinicians, like Ar-Razi, Israeli, Avicenna, and Maimonides, succeeded in escaping the overwhelming pressure of accepted authority.[17]

Most medieval Jewish physicians were perfectly aware, on the other hand, of the necessity of constantly reexamining their therapeutic methods. In his famous "Ethical Will," Yehudah ibn Tibbon enjoined his son to develop the habits of testing his drugs anew every week and of not applying any medicine whose properties he did not fully understand (I. Abrahams, *Hebrew Ethical Wills,* p. 68). But even Ibn Tibbon would doubtless have admitted that a citation from a recognized medical authority was sufficient proof for the correctness and efficacy of a particular treatment. Clearly, busy practitioners like Maimonides learned much from observing the effects of various treatments. They then transmitted such knowledge to their pupils, who in turn handed it down to later generations.

Modern historians of Jewish medicine during the transitional period from the Graeco-Roman to the Islamic civilizations are beset by the nearly total disappearance of the few Jewish sources which may have been written during that largely inarticulate period. Those generations did not even care to reproduce such older writings from the tannaitic age as the *Sefer Sammanim* (Book of Spices), which, long in the possession of a priestly family, seems to have listed medicinal drugs alongside spices for cultic uses (Yomah 38a). We recall that the dramatic political and military events, including the Jewish share in the Perso-Byzantine wars, the rise and evolution of Islam, and the large-scale economic changes, must be reconstructed almost exclusively from non-Jewish records. That is why the few books which have come down to us from that age, for example those by the physician Asaph Judaeus, have given rise to so many debates.

Although, with the exception of Asaph, we hear very little about Jewish medical writers before the tenth century, we may assume that there were Jewish practitioners in the field. Certainly, Byzantine Jews had access to the numerous medical tracts in Greek, while they and their Sassanian coreligionists could readily consult the scientific literature, original as well as in translation, available in their Aramaic-Syriac dialects. Jews seem to have collaborated, for instance, quite early in the great Nestorian school of Jundeshapur. Since most students obtained their training from individual physicians, medical lore could even more easily be transmitted by word of mouth than were halakhic teachings, which often required authoritative decisions by an academy.[18]

Denominational lines were easily crossed. Isaac Israeli was trained by the famous Muslim physician Isḥaq ibn 'Imran, and he in turn taught Muslim as well as Jewish pupils, including the later medical authors Dunash ibn Tamim and the Muslim Ibn al-Jazzar. Similarly the most distinguished medieval historian of Arabian medicine, Ibn abi Uṣaibi'a, to whom we owe much of our information about Jewish medical writers of the period as well, received instruction in Damascus from the Jewish doctor 'Imram ben Sedaqa, who, together with two Muslim doctors, served at the famous Nuri Hospital, and in Cairo from Ibn Mubarak (about 1200). True, some extremists felt compunctions about such easy crossing of the denominational boundaries. The pietistic Caliph 'Umar II, we are told, wrestled with his conscience for forty days and sought divine guidance on whether he ought to allow Muslims to consult a medical work then written by the Jew Masarjawaih. But even in this case calmer counsels ultimately prevailed.[19]

Little doubt exists, therefore, that there were many Jews among the *dhimmi* physicians in the early Islamic age. Muqaddasi's oft-quoted assertion that, in his day, most of the "assayers of coin, dyers, bankers, and tanners are Jews, while it is usual for the physicians and the scribes to be Christians," was only a facile generalization which applied exclusively to northern Syria, where Jews had long been a small minority. More truly reflecting the contemporary realities was the aforementioned decree of Al-Muqtadir (1073–94). While renewing the old prohibition of employing either Jews or Christians in public office, the caliph stipulated a specific exception in favor of physicians and scribes of both faiths, revealing how indispensable they had been in the ninth century. Nor did the tales spread by competitors about alleged intrigues between Jewish physicians and dissatisfied Muslim wives and similar other denunciations deter too many patients. Long before Muqtadir, a Baghdad Muslim physician complained to Al-Jaḥiẓ of his lack of success with patients because he had no Christian-sounding name and spoke Arabic without a Syriac accent. The number, financial standing, and prestige of non-Muslim and particularly Jewish physicians doubtless rose further in the subsequent generations. In his aforementioned illuminating letter of about 1230, Ibn Fadhlan commented,

There are among them [Jews and Christians of Baghdad] physicians with large incomes, for they frequent the houses of the grandees and the wealthy, and are often seen in the homes of high government officials. It is customary for people to pay doctors more than their due as a gift. These persons do not refrain from donning magnificent garments; they collect huge sums of money. On their holidays and festivals they appear in their costly attire. All that despite their lowering the dignity of the medical profession and catering badly to the health of the people, both mental and physical.

Much as we may discount such reckless assertions by an outspoken polemist, the fact evidently remains that there were at that time in Baghdad and elsewhere many prosperous Jewish physicians. In Cairo, Ibn abi Uṣaibi'a reports, a Jewish eye-doctor, Abu'l Fadail ibn an-Nagid (son of a Nagid) was so busy with his practice before his death in 1188 that he had to instruct his pupils in a peripatetic fashion by taking them with him during his calls on patients. Of course, there also were a great many who eked out a living with some difficulty.[20]

Ibn Fadhlan's concluding statement is obviously controverted by the very success of these doctors, of which he so bitterly complained. Patients would hardly have consistently patronized physicians of other faiths, while Muslim doctors were available, had they not had greater confidence in their ministrations; probably as a rule with good reason. Not that medical quacks were altogether absent from the medieval Jewish communities. Apart from the magic healers, there undoubtedly were quite a few ill-trained, greedy, and even fraudulent practitioners. Such incompetents were often the target of satirical writers like Ibn Zabara, whose *Book of Delight* includes several pertinent witty descriptions and dialogues. With typical self-irony some medically trained Hebrew poets themselves joined the chorus. Only Al-Ḥarizi, who had personally experienced the instability of human fortunes and the hard struggle for subsistence, sympathetically presented a highly successful medical swindler. When called to account, the quack offered the excuse of hard times. "Truly, I go about in quest of a living. Perhaps in His mercy God will provide it for me." For a long time there was nothing in the laws of the various countries, nor in Jewish law, effectively to counteract such abuses. Apparently the only safeguard offered by the rabbis against incompetent doctors consisted in their general responsibility for damages owing to negligence. Such responsibility, stressed in the Tosefta, was never fully elaborated, however. The Tosefta itself was far from consistent, which made it possible for the fourteenth-century jurist, Simon bar Ṣemaḥ Duran, to try to weaken that responsibility in the case of regular physicians. According to Duran, these sanctions fully applied to surgeons, but not to qualified doctors using drugs and other external medicines rather than surgical instruments.[21]

In fact, one of the outstanding features of the medieval Jewish medical literature is its unceasing emphasis on medicine as a service to the community, and on the physician's ethical and social behavior. Asaph left behind a remarkable admonition to his pupils, from which we need but quote the following passages:

> Beware of causing death to anyone by administering the juices of poisonous roots. Do not administer to an adulterous wife an abortifacient drug. Let not the beauty of woman arouse in thee the passion of adultery. Divulge not any secret entrusted to thee and do no act of injury or of harm for any price. Do not close thy heart to mercy toward the poor and the needy. . . . Allow no one to persuade you in any manner to produce disease in anyone. Take heed lest ye cause any bodily deformity whatsoever and be not too much in haste to apply the knife. . . . Beware lest the spirit of pride come upon you and lest ye bear revengeful hate against any sick one.

Medical aphorisms stressing ethical conduct, and incidentally teaching forbearance of the manifold weaknesses of human beings, were universally popular among physicians and public alike. We shall see that almost every major medical author from Asaph to Maimonides either composed aphorisms of his own or wrote a commentary on Hippocrates' *Aphorisms* or on some other recognized classic of that genre. In this field, too, a commentary did not pursue purely exegetical purposes, but rather served as a vehicle for the exposition of one's own cherished views.[22]

Jews also composed from time to time formulas of solemn oaths, largely variations on the theme of the Hippocratic oath, to be taken by physicians bent on the ethical exercise of their profession. One such formula is attributed to Asaph, another to Maimonides. The latter is undoubtedly apocryphal. It may have been composed as late as 1783 (possibly on the basis of a manuscript by Jacob ben Isaac Zahalon, 1630–93) by the first editor of its German translation (Marcus Herz?) "from a Hebrew manuscript of a renowned Jewish physician of the twelfth century in Egypt." Whoever the author, he caught the spirit of medieval inwardness, and he presented at least "poetic truth" in claiming the medieval origin of his oath.[23]

With the increase in medical knowledge grew also the communal responsibility for providing medical assistance particularly to poor members. We have no information of permanently salaried Jewish physicians until more recent centuries. But in ancient times there already existed not only some communal supervision, including the licensing of qualified men by the courts, but also certain provisions for hospitalization. True, although the biblical lawgivers had originally pioneered with the idea of quarantining patients suffering from communicable diseases, hospitalization of other patients had developed more slowly. Evidently, permanent residents were as a rule well taken care of by their large and cohesive families. A real need for care outside one's own home was felt only by strangers to a locality, whose number increased significantly toward the end of the Second Commonwealth. That is why the early communal hospices frequently took care of both transients and sick persons. This double-purpose institution was attached to the local synagogue, the center of all communal life. No one seems to have objected to the proximity of the two establishments, recorded already in the oft-quoted inscription from the synagogue of Theodotos, son of Vettenos, in Jerusalem before 70 C.E., which apparently catered to Italian-Jewish pilgrims. Certainly, few communities were wealthy and large enough to afford two independent buildings. The high estimate of this type of charity is evidenced by the increasing use for it by Maimonides and other rabbis of the ancient designation *heqdesh,* originally connoting sacred offerings to the Temple of Jerusalem.[24]

Curiously, however, the large and prosperous communities of the Great Caliphate or the Faṭimid Empire felt less need of independent institutions of their own than did the small communities of western Europe. Here the more rigid segregation between Jews and Christians and the purely ecclesiastical character of all charities led to frequent denominational duplication of charitable institutions. In the East, Muslim and possibly also Byzantine hospitals were open to the sick of all denominations. Even the aforementioned order given by the vizier to Sinan to heal Muslims before attending to Jews in pestilence-stricken Sura seems to have been but an emergency measure. Nor was the need of providing ritual food for Jewish patients, in modern times a major stimulus to the erection of Jewish hospitals, apparently serious enough in the Muslim world, whose own dietary rigidity made it respect ritualistic diversity. That is probably why so few records of Jewish hospitals in eastern lands have been preserved, while in the West even a tiny frontier community like Jerez de la Frontera boasted in 1266 of a Jewish "house of mercy." [25]

MEDICAL AUTHORS

Distinguished as some practitioners of medicine undoubtedly were, we rarely learn about them from chance historical or biographical records. Our information about medieval Jewish contributions to medicine is, therefore, mainly derived from the relatively few extant writings of Jewish physicians, original or translated. In view of the then prevailing unbounded admiration for the written word, it was the medical littérateur, even if he only repeated accepted doctrines, rather than the independent clinician whose discoveries enriched medical science, who achieved the greatest reputation among his contemporaries. That is why not only bibliographers like An-Nadim, but also historians of science and medicine like Ibn al-Qifṭi and Ibn abi Uṣaibi'a, transmitted to us mainly information concerning medical writers.

In modern times, too, it was a great bibliographer like Moritz

Steinschneider who unearthed most of the relevant sources. Equally significant spadework consisted in the securing of good, carefully edited texts of major Jewish medical tracts in so far as they still were available in the world's manuscript collections and in early Latin editions. But penetrating expert analyses of the substantive contributions of these works to one or another branch of medical science still are few and far between. Even excellent physicians, like Max Meyerhof and Harry Friedenwald, much too frequently limited their learned observations to biographical and bibliographical externals, rather than to critical analyses of contents and their scientific import. Of course, the latter task is doubly difficult so long as vast masses of contemporary materials remain unavailable in print. It would certainly be foolhardy, at this stage, to attribute to a particular author the introduction of certain diagnostic or therapeutic methods. But, leaving aside the as yet insoluble problem of originality, which was not the major prepossession of medieval thinkers, one could go much further along the road of scientific analysis of their theoretical teachings and practical applications.

The Hellenistic civilization had apparently failed to bring forth any Jewish authors of medical works comparable to those in philosophy, mathematics, and various branches of literature. Theudas of Laodicea or Agapios of Alexandria are possible exceptions. Described by Suidas as an "exegete of medical works," Agapios, who may have been a Jewish refugee from Alexandria after 415, settled in Constantinople and acquired great wealth through a successful medical practice. Nor do we know to what extent Domninus and Marinus, the Jewish thinkers at the famous academy of Athens at the time of its closing by Justinian in 529, were medical experts as well. We cannot even tell whether they were among the emigrés to the Sassanian Empire who, cordially received by Khosroe I, helped develop the great philosophic and medical academy of Jundeshapur.[26]

The first better known Jewish physician is Asaph Judaeus. Despite arguments to the contrary voiced by many scholars, his career in some Near Eastern country, perhaps Babylonia, not later than the seventh century, as espoused by L. Venetianer, I. Simon, and S. Muntner, the main specialists in this field, seems the most acceptable. At that time Arabian science still was in its infancy; it depended entirely on translations from Greek and Syriac. Not astonishingly, therefore, Asaph shows no acquaintance with either Arabic terminology or the findings of early Arabic-writing physicians. He is familiar, however, with some Syriac works and terminology. His comprehensive medical work, extant in several manuscripts (some incomplete) has not yet been published in full. But the analyses and citations offered by Venetianer and I. Simon show that the work covered a wide range of medical subjects. It dealt with anatomy, physiology, and the influence of climate, with dietetics and drugs, embryology, uroscopy, and other branches of medicine. It included also a medical calendar, the aforementioned prefatory statement on "medicine for the poor," and a personal variant of the Hippocratic oath. Simon even claims to have detected in Asaph an adumbration of the later Harveyan doctrine of the circulation of the blood, and of the Mendelian theory of hereditary transmission.[27]

Asaph's successors, whether themselves living under Muslim or Christian domination, maintained intimate contacts with the marvelously expanding Arabian medicine. To the Caliphate's "melting pot" of Western and Eastern science and the ensuing rapid scientific advances during the eighth and ninth centuries, Jews injected a few ingredients of their own. The earliest medical writer in Arabic of any faith was, as far as we know, the Jew Masarjawaih, living at the turn of the seventh to the eighth century. We know his works only from occasional citations by later medical and pharmaceutical writers, especially Ar-Razi in his great medical encyclopedia *Kitab al-Ḥavi,* which has long been familiar to the Western world in the Latin translation (*Liber Continens*) by the thirteenth-century Sicilian Jew Farragut (Faraj ibn Salim). It appears that Masarjawaih contributed greatly to the rise of Arabian medical science as both a translator and an independent author. He reproduced in a somewhat inelegant Arabic, which he had acquired in his later years, the encyclopedic *Pandects* by the pre-Islamic Egyptian priest Aaron, allegedly the first physician to describe the symptoms of smallpox. This disease had never been diagnosed as such in the Graeco-Roman world, although it had long been known in China, and although two of the five great pestilences which decimated the Mediterranean countries during the first Christian centuries were owing to its severely contagious nature. Its most devastating attack came during the Arab expansion, which doubtless contributed to Masarjawaih's interest in Aaron's work. Rather than merely offering a translation, Masarjawaih added two chapters and inserted other statements of his own, which can no longer be separated from the original text. He is also mentioned as the author of independent monographs on dietetics, on the medicinal usefulness as well as harm of certain plants, and on the diseases of the eye. He was followed by his son 'Isa, and by Christian physicians such as the apologist 'Ali aṭ-Ṭabari, author of a renowned medical work "Paradise of Wisdom." Just as 'Ali, long before his conversion to Islam, could instruct many Muslim pupils, including Ar-Razi, so could the Jewish physician Furat ben Shahnata become a disciple of a Christian doctor, while Yehudah ben Joseph ibn abi'l Thanna, hailing from the famous center of learning in Mesopotamian Raqqa, received much of his training from the distinguished Sabean mathematician, Ṭabit ibn Qurra. We know little about Yehudah's writings, but Mas'udi recorded some of his discussions with the Jewish savant on medical as well as philosophic subjects.[28]

Much better known than these early pioneers are the tenth-century authors Isaac ben Solomon Israeli of Egypt and Kairuwan, and Shabbetai Donnolo of southern Italy. Because his lifespan extended over a hundred years, the last decades of Isaac's activity coincided with the sudden effervescence of Jewish scientific interests on the European continent, represented by Donnolo. Both authors were interested in philosophy as much as in medicine, and we have had frequent occasion to refer to them in other contexts.

Israeli's medical writings made a strange career in medieval Europe, where they first became known in the Latin version by Constantine Africanus (*ca.*1020–87), the earliest translation of any Arabic medical book into Latin. This translator, a native of Kairuwan and probably either a Muslim or a Jew, became a Christian after his arrival in Salerno. In his translation he suppressed the identity of the real author, creating the impression that the work had stemmed from his own pen. Nevertheless, Israeli's name soon became generally known and admired. The publisher of his book of dietetics in Padua, in 1487, described it tellingly on the title page as the work *Eximii Isaac medicine monarce.* Israeli's treatises on urine and the fevers enjoyed a particularly great reputation in the later Middle Ages, the former being used for medical instruction at many European universities from Oxford to Vienna. Of importance also were his "Book of Foods and Simple Remedies," and his aforementioned ethical tractate, the "Guide for Physicians." All of these works, except the last mentioned, were later included in a Latin edition of Israeli's collected writings, published in 1515, which served as a vademecum for many European scholars far into the seventeenth century. Nor was his fame in the Muslim world completely eclipsed by his distinguished Muslim contemporaries Razi and Avicenna. Centuries later an Arab author, Mulla Yaḥya, still listed three of his books among the outstanding fourteen medical works in the Arabic language.[29]

To judge from the numerous extant Hebrew manuscripts, Israeli's medical tracts also enjoyed a great reputation in Jewish circles. Some were actually translated more than once, but at times only from the more readily accessible Latin versions. Unlike his philosophic essays, however, none of these Hebrew renditions, except that of the more ethical than medical *Musar ha-rofe'im,* has thus far been published. This is doubly regrettable, as Steinschneider, perhaps the first man to have studied them attentively, claimed that the Hebrew versions were generally better than the Latin. Moreover, whatever one thinks of Israeli as a philosopher, there is no question about his merits as a medical writer. Maimonides' patronizing remark that Israeli "was merely a physician" had but the same relative validity as his and Ibn abi Uṣaibi'a's similar disparagement of the fairly significant philosophic work of Ar-Razi. Conversely, Saadiah interspersed various medical observations in his philosophic and juridical works. Only occasionally did he devote a more elaborate statement to a medical subject as in his "Commentary on *Had al-insan* (The Anatomy of Man, or rather The Definition of Man). But Saadiah's authorship of this tract is debatable.[30]

Donnolo was less prolific. Apart from his occasional scientific excursuses in his *Commentary on Yeṣirah,* his main medical contribution consisted of a small Hebrew treatise, the *Sefer ha-Yaqar* (The Precious Book), a title probably inserted by an admiring copyist. Far more descriptive is Donnolo's introductory statement, "This is the Book of Drugs, Potions, Powders, Emulsions, and Unguents . . . to teach Jewish physicians, and to inform them of the way to prepare drugs in accordance with the science of Israel and Macedon [Hellas], and out of the author's practical experience acquired in the deep study and practice of medicine over forty years, by the will of God." Here the Italian doctor, whose ministrations were once rejected by Abbot Nilus of Rossano for no other reason than the fear of an adverse reaction among the Christian populace, analyzed the various qualities of certain drugs and their preparation for a variety of uses. He naturally had to create some new Hebrew terms, while extensively utilizing the current Latin, Greek, and Italian terminologies. Curiously, although he had become an assiduous student of Arabian science, Donnolo mentioned only three Arabic terms in this treatise which, according to Suessmann Muntner, its latest editor, listed a total of 118 drug names. In many ways Donnolo was the harbinger of the new scientific interests dawning in southern Italy, which were ultimately to blossom in the great cultural centers created by such enlightened monarchs as Roger the Norman and Frederick II, last of the Hohenstaufen emperors. While no direct link between Donnolo and the famous medical school of Salerno has thus far been established, the Jewish author undoubtedly was the first important exponent in southern Italy of the newly awakened scientific curiosity which soon led to the formation of that academy. Another Jewish doctor, Judah, is, in fact, recorded in Salerno's Jewish quarter in 1005, while Constantine Africanus, one of the school's chief founders, may have been a converted Jew. There is, indeed, a kernel of truth in the medieval adage that that school had been founded by "four masters, a Greek, a Latin, an Arab, and a Jew." [31]

Among the Jews of the Iberian Peninsula it was the statesman Ḥisdai ibn Shapruṭ who not only served as the great patron of learning in all its manifestations, but also personally collaborated in one of the major translation projects of the time. For various reasons an earlier Arabic translation of the Greek work on the *materia medica* by Dioscorides, then extremely popular throughout the eastern Mediterranean world, had been found inadequate. When therefore Emperor Romanos II sent Caliph 'Abd ar-Raḥman III a beautifully illustrated copy of the Greek text in which the individual drugs were realistically depicted in coloful illustrations, Ḥisdai joined hands with the Byzantine Monk Nicholas (dispatched shortly after the manuscript in 951–52) and six Muslim scholars in translating that work into Arabic, or at least in thoroughly revising the former rendition. Many beautifully illuminated Arabic manuscripts of the new translation memorized by the geographer Idrisi are now found in the world's leading libraries, and especially in the eastern mosques, where there are invaluable manuscript treasures not yet fully known to the scholarly world.[32]

Ḥisdai's claim to fame, however, did not derive from this translation. Even Israeli's pupil Dunash ibn Tamim, who left behind an apparently original medical treatise no longer extant today, was primarily distinguished as a philologist and astronomer. Some other Jewish medical men, like Musa ibn al-Azar (ben Eleazar) and his sons and grandsons, attained a high reputation for medical expertness while serving as court physicians to the Faṭimid caliph Mu'izz and his successors. But only Musa himself seems to have left behind some medical treatises, including an Antidotarium, a Pharmacopoeia, and a tract on coughs, all known only from subsequent quotations. One of Musa's sons, however, was converted to Islam and assumed the name of Awn Allah. There were many other converts to either Islam or Christianity among the Jewish doctors, including one Ibn Kusin who practiced in Mosul about 970, and 'Abd al-Masi'h, a disciple of the Christian physician Manṣur ben Sahlan (980–1000). But their major literary efforts were devoted to the defense of their new faiths and attacks on Judaism, rather than to medical subjects.[33]

Understandably, such apostates added nourishment to the general orthodox suspicions of secular learning. Among contemporary Karaites, particularly, though generally belonging to the intellectually most alert groups in the Jewish community, these manifestations of doctrinal unreliability reinforced the old aversion to medical ministrations stemming from their literal interpretations of biblical passages. Even a scholar of the rank of Jephet ben 'Ali could exclaim, "And they shall not busy themselves with books of Gentile scholars" (*Commentary* on Psalms, ed. by Bargès, pp. 17, 75 f.)—this at a time when Arabian scholarship had celebrated its greatest scholastic triumphs. Probably for this reason we find few Karaites among the distinguished physicians and scientists of the period. They pursued even mathematical studies mainly for the ritualistic purposes of calendar computations, although here, too, their attempt to revive the ancient proclamation of the new moon on the basis of direct observations fostered an antiscientific attitude.

Among the distinguished Karaite jurists of the tenth century it was only Qirqisani who evinced a healthy, if not altogether detached, curiosity about basic philosophic and scientific problems and betrayed good familiarity with the medical teachings of his time. In his encyclopedic "Book of Lights" there are, indeed, a number of interesting physiological discussions. For example, he objected to the doctrine "that vapors are minute particles detaching themselves from the (odiferous) body; that when they reach the nasal region, they are sensed as odors; and that (when originating in unclean things) they must not be permitted to reach (clean) food, since they would become mixed with it." Qirqisani sneeringly declared these teachings to be characteristic of those "who apply speculation to natural phenomena." He was equally outspoken, on the other hand, in his condemnation of obscurantist efforts to delimit scientific research. Among his major criticisms, leveled against the very founder of the Karaite sect, was that aimed at 'Anan's prohibition of the practice of medicine. At the same time this distinguished heresiologue was sufficiently influenced by the Karaite ritualistic concepts to prohibit the mixing of vipers' flesh into medical "theriacs," a practice specifically permitted for medical purposes by Rabbanite law.[34]

Not before the late twelfth century, therefore, do we hear of a distinguished Karaite physician unperturbedly pursuing his medical career. Even then he had to go outside his own community in order to receive his medical training. David ben Solomon (As-Sadid ibn abi al-Bayan, born in Cairo in 1161) was a pupil of the Rabbanite Ibn Jumay', and a coworker of Ibn abi Uṣaibi'a at the Nasiri Hospital founded by Saladin in the Egyptian capital. Ibn abi Uṣaibi'a praised Ibn abi al-Bayan's pharmacological treatise. There also were several distinguished Samaritan physicians among David's Egyptian contemporaries.[35]

Antirationalist trends of this kind gained momentum in the eastern lands, as a result of the general pietistic reaction connected with the Asha'rite movement. In Ghazzali they found a spokesman of superlative depth and eloquence. Although the Jews were not immediately affected, in the long run they could not remain immune. We recall how clearly such leading defenders of Jewish theology as Baḥya and Halevi reflected these new trends. However, antirationalism in the Jewish camp seems to have produced less retardation of the study of medical science than it did among the Muslims. In Spain, particularly, the number of Jewish physicians seems to have increased by leaps and bounds, Halevi himself exercising that profession without compunctions. But relatively few felt impelled to write on medical subjects. Among the medical authors one might mention especially Junus (Jonah) ben Isḥaq ibn Buklarish of Almeria (*ca.*1085–1100), whose work on simple remedies gives their names in Arabic, Syriac, Persian, Greek, and even Spanish and Berber. Extant in a Rabat manuscript, it is known through frequent quotations by a distinguished Arab contemporary, Ghafiqi, and through a more recent study by H. P. J. Renaud. Its title shows that Ibn Buklarish had written it at the instance of Al-Musta'in, ruler of Saragossa (d. 1109). Polyhistors like Abraham ibn Ezra may also have included one or another medical essay in their prolific output. Ibn Ezra's authorship of the medical *Sefer Nisyonot* (Book of Experiences) has been disputed, however. The famous grammarian Jonah ibn Janaḥ also wrote a medical dictionary. But the most prolific among the Spanish Jewish medical authors, Joseph ben Aḥmad ibn Ḥisdai, had evidently left both Spain and Judaism before he engaged in medical research and wrote several treatises under the patronage of the Egyptian vizier, Ma'mun al-Amiri (executed in 1128).[36]

Among the numerous other Jewish physicians of that period one need but mention Al-Ḥaqir an-Nafi' (the Useful), court physician and surgeon to Al-Ḥakim (probably also during the latter's intolerant outburst); Ephraim ibn az-Zaffan, likewise a Faṭimid court physician and particularly famous for his large library; and Hibbat Allah (Nathaniel) ibn Jumay' (d. 1198), author of an "Antidotarium" written in a fine Arabic style and highly esteemed by both Saladin and Ibn abi Uṣaibi'a. This distinguished historian of Arabian medicine mentioned a conversation he once had with the vizier Yaḥya ibn Matruḥ of Damascus, "master of both the sword and the pen." The vizier had asked him whether he did not consider Ibn Ridhwan the greatest of all Egyptian physicians of former times, and Ibn Jumay' the greatest of those of the more recent period; Ibn abi Uṣaibi'a answered in the affirmative. Ibn Jumay', who bore the title "Sun of Authority," also wrote a comprehensive treatise in four books entitled "Instruction for the Health of Souls and Bodies," a commentary on the "Secrets" of Avicenna's *Canon,* and an epistle resembling our first-aid manuals. Nor need we completely overlook in this connection the medical works by such eminent converts as Samau'al ibn Yaḥya al-Maghribi, Abu'l Barakat or, for that matter, even by the son of a convert like Gregory Barhebraeus, who may well have received part of his medical training while still a member of the Jewish community. In the case of Abu'l Barakat, we are told that he, who was to live ninety solar years, "was afflicted with leprosy, treated himself and was healed, but became blind and remained so for a certain time." [37]

MAIMONIDES

Far overshadowing all these men in popular recognition, if not necessarily in medical attainments, was another Spanish exile in Egypt, Moses Maimonides. Quickly achieving a reputation also as a physician at the court of Saladin and his successors, he met there several other Jewish court physicians, including his double brother-in-law, Abu'l Ma'ali ibn Hibbat Allah. We recall his graphic description of his busy days in medical practice in Cairo and Fusṭaṭ. Even earlier his reputation had been so well established in the Egyptian capital that he was called to the sickbed of a Christian prince (perhaps Amalric, not, as legend has it, Richard Lion-Heart) in Acco. But he declined that invitation. His medical successes attracted scholars, like Ibn al-Latif of Damascus, who came to Egypt for the express purpose of meeting Maimonides and two other famous doctors. An admiring Muslim poet, Sa'id ibn Sina al-Mulk, called him "the physician of the century." On the other hand, this extraordinary reputation aroused the envy of some Muslim colleagues, one of whom denounced the great sage to the authorities as a backsliding Muslim. Apparently, only Maimonides' excellent connections at court saved him from what might have become a prosecution for a capital offense. He himself was not altogether happy over having to waste much of his time on the minor or imaginary ailments of his highly placed patients. In his letters to his favorite disciple, Ibn 'Aqnin, in 1190, he emphasized how little he cared for the worldly successes "open to Jews nowadays," which he considered the acme of hard work and worry. He complained with particular bitterness of the trivia of his medical practice, which left him little time for study, even for careful reading of essential medical literature. "For you know how exacting and difficult is this profession," he added, "for any person of conscience and precision, who refuses to make a statement without knowing how to prove it, or else how to indicate its source, or the kind of analogy [*heqqesh*] leading up to it. . . . Hence I read only on the Sabbath day." [38]

Whatever sympathy contemporaries may have felt for this overburdened and sick old man, we must nevertheless be grateful for these court connections which gave the impetus to almost all of Maimonides' medical monographs. Even after the completion of his two masterpieces, the *Code* and the *Guide,* he himself evidently enjoyed spending all his free time on philosophic and theological speculations. If left to his own devices he might have composed only his "Medical Aphorisms" and his *Commentary* on similar aphorisms by Hippocrates, which ever since Ḥunain ibn Isḥaq's Arabic translation had been extensively discussed throughout the Muslim world. In a preliminary way Maimonides might also have compiled a small treatise containing extracts from Galen's voluminous and often diffused works. In all these studies he could give free play to his flair for the philosophic fundamentals and his well-tested exegetical method. Although not stating his conviction as bluntly as had his countryman Ibn Ridhwan, whom he occasionally quoted, he was a firm believer in the supreme achievements of Graeco-Roman medicine. Without accepting uncritically all the teachings of Hippocrates or Galen—he frequently ventured to criticize especially the latter on formal as well as substantive grounds—he evidently made far less use of the more recent Arabic literature.[39]

All his specialized medical monographs, however, namely those on Hemorrhoids, Sexual Intercourse, Asthma, Poisons, Fits [of Melancholia], and even the more general treatise on the Regulation of Health, were written by order of a ruler, prince, or vizier. Understandably, in such *ad hoc* monographs addressed to laymen there was greater stress on salutary lessons for them than on scientific innovations. There also was a good deal of repetition. "For all my discourses," the author himself apologized for the latter shortcoming, "have been composed by personal demand, and not with the purpose of giving all people instruction in the medical art." It was not easy for him to meet the high-strung expectations of his august patients, as we may gather from the Introduction to his Discourse on Sexual Intercourse, requested by Al-Muzaffar 'Umar ibn Nur ad-Din, Saladin's nephew and sultan of Syrian Hama (1179–92).

Our lord His Majesty—may Allah make his power last long!—ordered me to compose for him a treatise on behavior which would help to increase his sexual power, as he mentioned that he had some hardship in this way. At the same time he informed the humble servant of the falling away of the lord's body so that he is near to abate in his flesh; and that his temper is a little inclined to heat. He mentioned, moreover, that he does not wish to depart from his custom concerning sexual intercourse and wishes for that purpose a regulation, being alarmed by the abatement of his flesh, as he desires an augmentation [of the sexual power] on account of the increasing number of female slaves. He informed me that what he wants is a regulation easy of execution and of little difficulty.

Nor could Maimonides, or any other Jewish physician at a Muslim court, forget for a moment that he was a Jew. He not only had to refer rather gingerly to teachings of his own tradition, but when he prescribed wine or music, shunned by orthodox Muslims, he had to apologize that he was only stating what he considered the best medical advice.[40]

More technical, but essentially paramedical was Maimonides'

"Glossary of Drug Names," recovered and published only in recent years. This work is extant in a copy made by Ibn al-Bayṭar, later the leading pharmacologist of the Muslim world, soon after his arrival in Egypt from Spain about a dozen years after Maimonides' death. Its 405 entries of varying lengths, too, although largely dealing with names of some 2,000 drugs then used in the western as in eastern lands, reveal the author's marvelous erudition and exactitude in medical philology. We know practically nothing, however, about the particular circumstances which induced Maimonides to compose this tract which is so different from all his other works. His own introduction is quite informative as to the methods he had pursued in compiling this largely alphabetical glossary, designed for facile memorization. He also mentioned there his main sources (Ibn Juljul, Ibn Janaḥ, Ghafiqi, Ibn Wafid, and Ibn Samjun), to which he added material derived from the practical usages he had observed in Maghrib-Morocco, where he had received most of his medical training. But he said little about the objectives of his work. It may not be too venturesome to suggest that this booklet was one of his earliest medical works composed at the beginning of his medical practice in Egypt. Perhaps disturbed by the differences he had noticed in the administration of drugs between the western masters under whom he had studied and his Near Eastern contemporaries, he may have sought to establish for himself, as well as for his pupils and colleagues, the extent to which these differences could be reduced to divergent nomenclature. The same drugs were often designated by different names in various parts of the Arab world because of local differences in their preparation, different linguistic backgrounds, or mere chance. More, many drugs readily available in antiquity, and hence recommended by Hippocrates or Galen, were scarce and expensive in the Middle Ages, particularly in certain regions. Hence the constant quest for substitutes, which explains the relentless outpouring of ever new pharmacopoeias. Renaud and Colin's remark concerning the Moroccan "Glossary of Drugs," that it "is less a list of synonyms than a glossary of substitutes," applies with equal force to most other works of this kind, including the tracts by Donnolo and Ibn Buklarish. An emigré physician like Maimonides must doubly have felt the need of such a comparative study of "synonyms." [41]

MEDICAL CONTRIBUTIONS

Surveying the totality of medical writings by early medieval Jewish authors, of which, as we have seen, only a small segment has thus far been published, one is struck by its great richness and variety. But how much of it was Jewish in nature? While the study of mathematics and astronomy had important implications for the Jewish calendar, and anatomy or physiology had some bearing on the Jewish laws of *sheḥiṭah,* there was little in the study of various human diseases and remedies that had particular import on Jewish law and tradition.

Nor can one detect any clear line of continuity between the ancient biblical and talmudic medicine and that of the medieval Jewish authors. Shabbetai Donnolo, to be sure, after deciding in his youth to study medicine and astronomy, claims to have copied some ancient Jewish books in these fields. He admitted, however, that he had found no Jewish scholar who could explain them to him. On the contrary, he was told that "the books of astronomy are found only among Gentiles, and that their books do not agree with similar works among Jews." Donnolo himself dissented from this view, but the only Jewish work he expressly mentioned was the ancient "Baraita of Samuel," which, as we recall, was primarily concerned with astronomic observations relating to the calendar. Even great experts in all phases of Jewish lore, like Maimonides, rarely referred to medical teachings reflected in Jewish sources but usually quoted non-Jewish authorities like Hippocrates, Galen, or the more "modern" Arabian physicians. Only occasionally did they mention pertinent ethical teachings of their own sages. In discussions, principally philological, concerning names of drugs, they also tried to identify some Hebrew or Aramaic names of plants and minerals recorded in their ancient literature. Characteristically, while quoting Greek authors they knew nothing about the ancient Jewish writers in that language. To quote Donnolo again, he knew that ancient Judaea had possessed a precious variety of balsam. But, as his authority he cited only the special chapter devoted to it in Pliny's *Natural History,* failing to mention the illuminating story told by Josephus.[42]

Nevertheless, there was something in the very socio-economic position of the Jewish people which gave a peculiar tinge to their medical contributions. The very segregation of religious communities throughout Islam, though far less stringent than in Christian Europe and leaving ample room for scholarly cooperation between members of various denominations, was sufficiently marked to distinguish Jewish and Christian doctors in the eyes of both their patients and the Arabian medical historians and biographers. The latter rarely missed the opportunity of designating a particular author as "al-Isra'ili" or "al-Yahudi," even when they pursued no discriminatory objectives. At that time everything a Jew did, or failed to do, ultimately accrued to the benefit, or disadvantage, of his community.

Economic and educational factors too, which induced an increasing number of Jews to choose the medical career, had originated from the political status and cultural traditions of their people and reciprocally reflected on both. The pronounced drive to reach the top of their profession, natural with most individuals, was reinforced in the case of Jews by the vast opportunities offered them for the acquisition of wealth and prestige in this domain, from which they were not so tightly shut out as from the more influential positions in public service. Those Muslim extremists who, like Ibn 'Abdun of Seville, tried to discourage their coreligionists from calling on *dhimmi* physicians and even from giving or selling scientific books to "unbelieving" scholars, represented but a small minority. Certainly no occupation, except an extremely successful but always risky business career, made it possible for a man to earn annually more than 20,000 dinars ($80,000 in gold, but easily three times that amount in purchasing power), the reputed income of a Christian physician in Baghdad in the middle of the twelfth century. Some Jewish physicians, to be sure, took seriously their leaders' untiring ethical injunctions, and charged smaller fees to less wealthy patients. A delightful story narrated by Ibn abi Uṣaibi'a about the extremely busy ophthalmologist Abu'l Fadail is probably illustrative also of the charitableness of many other Jewish physicians with respect to both revenue and distribution. Having promised a poor Jewish acquaintance, we are told, to give him that entire day's earnings, Abu'l Fadail upon his return home opened the small envelopes containing the fees he had collected. "In some of them were dinars and in others *nasiriyya* dirhams [coined by An-Nasir Saladin], and in many were copper dirhams. The total amount was about 300 copper dirhams, which he gave that man, and told him: 'I do not know who gives me gold or dirhams, be they many or few.' " But even the 300 copper dirhams thus indiscriminately collected as a daily average doubtless placed their recipients within the highest income brackets in the Jewish quarter. Many a patriotic Jewish doctor must also have believed that, by serving as court physician to a high dignitary of the State (in the West, also of the Church), he was helping his entire community. Under the conditions of medieval society, indeed, mere access to the seats of the mighty could often help turn the tide in crucial decisions affecting the lives of untold thousands.[43]

There is no way of estimating even remotely the number of Jewish physicians in the early medieval period. The few extant records usually refer only to leaders of the profession, or to some persons incidentally involved in the events narrated by the chronicler. However, the facts that already in the talmudic age the rabbis had advised Jews against settling in a city without a doctor, and that, where the records flow in larger quantity as in Christian Spain, the number of Jewish physicians appears very large, would seem to indicate their presence in ever larger numbers also in Muslim lands. Here quantity turned into quality. The mere fact that so many Jewish individuals practiced the medical arts helped them accumulate living experiences which, only rarely recorded in medical works, were transmitted from master to pupil in the course of generations. This cumulative experience of a great many unnamed individuals often enriched medical science far more than did the formal writings, which less frequently dared to depart from the sacrosanct words of ancient masters.

Equally significant was the Jewish intermediary position between the hostile worlds of Islam and Christendom. In the early Middle Ages the future of all science, indeed of all culture, largely depended on the degree in which the great achievements of the ancient Near Eastern and Graeco-Roman worlds would be maintained in unbroken continuity and serve as a basis for further advances. The Renaissance of Islam was mainly such a renascence of Greek philosophy and science, enriched by the heritage of ancient Babylonia and Persia and the now far more accessible fruits of Indian and Chinese thinking. From Islam this Renaissance spread to western Europe to set there in motion forces of unparalleled intensity and creativity. In this entire evolution the ubiquitous Jews played a special role precisely because of their vast dispersion. Just as Masarjawaih, and perhaps Asaph, at the beginning of the Muslim period, so did Jewish physicians and translators of medical works of the twelfth and thirteenth centuries in the West help construct those invisible bridges over which many vital ingredients of the older scientific heritage crossed from one civilization to another.

Once again we must not limit our vision, as is often done, to the formal works of translation, or, in fact, to any literary documents. No less significant was the oral transmission by Jewish immigrants of the fruits of learning, first from Byzantine lands to the Caliphate, and later from the Near East, North Africa, and Spain to Christian Europe. European Jewish pupils returning there after the completion of their studies under an eastern master likewise served as a leaven to awaken the scientific curiosity of the native majority, and to acquaint the local professionals with some more recent diagnostic or therapeutic methods. Donnolo probably needed to travel only across the Strait of Messina to find in Sicily, if not in his southern Italian home, a "Babylonian" teacher, named Bagodes, as well as bearers of the living Graeco-Byzantine tradition. Under the conditions of mutual Christian-Arab hostility, especially during the era of Crusades, non-Jewish easterners rarely visited any western land, while Jewish visitors and immigrants grew in number and scholarly attainments. Here, too, we may not be able to document by chapter and verse the influence of particular eastern teachings on the southern Italian or other European medical pioneers. But western physicians must have learned so much by word of mouth, or by observing the practices of recent arrivals from the eastern centers, that the whole atmosphere became, so to say, charged with new scientific findings and approaches.[44]

Nor must we overlook the international Jewish trader as still another channel for the transmission of eastern medical learning to the western countries, and even for the spread of new therapeutic methods from one country to another within the same civilization. Every trader who brought with him some new drugs for sale must have described their uses to both doctors and laymen. While many of these claims were undoubtedly spurious, whether because of the traders' dishonesty or because the new prescriptions had been introduced by medical charlatans, others were perfectly genuine and stood the test of experience.

Maimonides had to warn his readers to be extremely careful in accepting untested medications even from a reputable doctor. "Do not allow your mind," he wrote in an aphorism whose importance he underscored by an unusual prefatory remark, "to be swayed by the 'novelties' which he tells you, but look well into his theory and belief, just as you should do concerning the things which he declares that he has seen; look into the matter without letting yourself be persuaded easily." Even rich Egypt, however, was suffering from both a paucity of doctors and the unavailability of many important drugs. This was, indeed, the main reason for Maimonides' composition of his important Antidotarium, according to his Introduction, where he described the great difficulties encountered by the Egyptian government in assembling the necessary drugs for the so-called Great Theriak and Mitridates Potions, considered the most efficacious antidotes for snake bites and other poisons. His purpose, Maimonides declared, was to list the most effective and readily found remedies, which one could prepare even without the help of a physician. In the more backward and sparsely populated provinces of the Caliphate and western Europe, the number of physicians was still smaller and the availability of drugs far more limited. Hence came the great popularity of compilations of names and characteristics of drugs, and the procedures employed in their preparation. Nor is it a mere accident that the most widely read book on the "Management of the Drug Store" was written in 1260 by the Jewish druggist, Abu'l Mina ha-Kohen al-'Attar. It still is widely used throughout the Near East today.[45]

From the point of view of content, on the other hand, there is little in medical science that may be called peculiarly Jewish, Greek, or Arab. Only the preponderance of ethical teachings and the great emphasis on mental hygiene, so characteristic of most medieval Jewish medical works, may have partially been influenced by the Jewish tradition. We recall that three of the four chief medical writers here reviewed, namely Asaph, Israeli, and Maimonides, devoted much space to aphorisms and other literary devices to convey ethical lessons. Concentrating exclusively on a technical pharmacopoeia, Donnolo had less opportunity for ethical digressions. But even he saw the main objective of his treatise in teaching physicians and surgeons the proper ingredients and preparation of drugs, so that they might use them in their purity, "without any prevarication and underhandedness, for the traders often cheat them." At the same time he warned his readers carefully to check the place of origin of certain plants, "for there are locations where they raise deathly [poisonous] plants, or such as cause intoxication or vomiting" ("Book of Drugs," ed. by Muntner, p. 8).

Uniformly, Jewish physicians exhorted one another to set aside much time for charity practice. In his homely "Guide for the Physician" Israeli knew well enough human weaknesses, such as the great appreciation by patients of a physician charging high fees, while they think little of one treating them for nothing. He merely echoed therein the old popular adage of the Talmud. He also advised, on practical grounds, wherever possible to attend to upper classes rather than to common men, because the latter were in the habit of resenting even part payments of doctors' fees. Moreover, he counseled collection while the patient was still quite ill and appreciative of the service rendered him by the doctor. Nevertheless, even Israeli insisted, "Make it thy special concern to visit and treat poor and needy patients, for in no way canst thou find more meritorious service." Similar injunctions were emphasized by Yehudah ibn Tibbon in the "Will" addressed to his son. The author of the "Book of the Pious" actually counseled, "If a rich man and a poor man be sick and thou seest all the world going to see the rich man, go thou to the poor one, even though he be ignorant and unlettered." As we recall, Asaph had already made a special effort to designate for his fellow physicians a number of inexpensive and readily accessible remedies, which even the poor could afford.[46]

Preoccupation with ethical and philosophic problems—practically all Jewish medical writers were also students of philosophy—naturally increased the tendency to argue by logical reasoning and on the basis of established authority, rather than to rely on practical experience. True, not professing a fatalistic religion, the Jewish physicians and philosophers evinced far less concern about either the philosophic or the medical aspects of the *ajal,* the doctrine of the predetermined duration of human life. The Mutakallimun had long sought for some resolution of the difficulty of squaring God's omniscience, which included God's advance knowledge of when a particular individual was going to die, with man's ability, through proper behavior or medical treatment, to prolong his span of life or to foreshorten it by wrong actions. Under the overpowering impact of these kalamistic discussions, not only Saadiah, in his philosophic work, but even Hai, in a special responsum, tried to find some philosophic answers to that dichotomy. Maimonides, on the other hand, could the more readily evade that question, as he was always insisting that God's knowledge is different in kind from human knowledge, and that hence one must not apply to it the usual human epistemological criteria. For this reason he did not find it necessary to discuss *ajal* in his *Guide.* Only in a reply to his beloved pupil Joseph ben Yehudah did he take up the problem from its philosophic and medical angles. He clearly formulated the official Jewish position in his introductory paragraph:

> Among us Jews [he wrote] there exists no predetermined end of life. On the contrary, each living being lives so long as it replenishes whatever it loses from its natural humors and the latter remain uncorrupted. As Galen describes it: "The cause of death consists in the disturbance of the balance of one's naturally born warmth." This disturbance is the result of factors influencing that warmth from within, and of others which affect it from without.

Maimonides reinforced his naturalistic arguments by a series of theological demonstrations, to which, because of "their loftiness and weight," he attributed primary value.[47]

At the same time this combination of science and theology helped stem the opposite trend toward the physicians' exclusive concentration on mere techniques, without the knowledge of fundamentals, and without consideration of the patient's whole personality against his social and cultural background. Maimonides voiced prevailing opinion when he wrote that "medical practice is not knitting and weaving and the labor of hands, but it must be inspired with soul, filled with understanding, and equipped with the gift of keen observation. These faculties, combined with accurate scientific knowledge, are the indispensable requisites for proficient medical practice." For this reason, too, many eminent Jewish doctors preferred to apply as little surgery and prescribe as few drugs as possible. In the treatment, for instance, of hemorrhoids, Israeli and Maimonides agreed that surgery was indicated only as a last resort, and that the physician should try to cure most ailments by a properly regulated diet and mode of living. These Jewish doctors also had great faith in the healing power of nature. As Israeli phrased it, "the physician does not bring about the cure, but he prepares and paves the way for nature; nature is the actual healer." At times "nature" could readily be replaced by "God," as in the aforementioned prayer of Yehudah Halevi. To make the patient implore God's grace meant for the physician to advise him to live a pious, ethical life.[48]

Out of these theological and ethical concerns arose also the Jewish physicians' clear recognition of the importance of mental factors for man's health and well-being. Mental therapy was, of course, well known already to the ancients, and was given careful consideration also by Christian and Muslim physicians. However, one cannot escape the impression that to many Jewish doctors psychogenic factors appeared of even greater significance. They accepted the long regnant theory of physiological "humors" affecting the operations of the human body and reacting on man's mentality. But, in their theological preoccupation with the soul and its survival, they had to probe so deeply into mere psychological manifestations that they readily stressed mental hygiene as a supreme preventive and therapeutic instrumentality. In answering Sultan Al-Afdhal's complaints concerning his frequent dejectedness, unsociability, forebodings of death, and weak digestion, Maimonides in his "Regimen Sanitatis" prescribed principally psychological cures.

> The humble servant [he wrote] only gave advice by these regulations in order to explain how the soul may become accustomed to resist passion by considering the ethical books, the literature on the rules of the religious law, and the sermons and the wise sayings of the sages, until the soul is strengthened and sees the right as right, and the idle as idle. In this way the passions diminish, the bad thoughts disappear, the unsociableness is removed, and the soul is gladdened in spite of all the conditions which may happen to a man.

He advised especially that the patient avoid worry, as most detrimental to his health. When confronted by some untoward prospects, he should take the philosophic view that, since there usually exist various possible alternatives, a favorable turn of events would remove the cause of his anxiety. Israeli and others also felt that the physician's function was to forestall illness by proper guidance as much, as to cure it after it occurred. The author of the "Book of the Pious" even compared preventive medicine to avoidance of sin. "Just as a man who is careful not to sin," he declared, "is wiser than one who sins and repents, so is that doctor to be called an expert who knows how to advise one to escape illness." [49]

Needless to say that this great preoccupation with mental health did not diminish these physicians' interest in other aspects of disease. Although, generally speaking, the scientific evolution under the Caliphate created many specialists who looked with disdain upon the scientific "littérateurs," all of medicine, rather than any of its subdivisions, was considered a specialized discipline.

For this reason comprehensive works, like Maimonides' "Aphorisms," or Hippocrates' similar work and the commentaries thereon, covered a wide range of medical subjects. The division of the twenty-five chapters of that Maimonidean work is sufficiently descriptive. The first three chapters deal with human organs, humors, and general methods of medicine, or with basic anatomical, physiological, and pathological problems. The following six sections discuss the pulse, the urine, and other symptoms revealing certain general or specific diseases, and indicate some cures. These are followed by five chapters devoted to the consideration of fevers, and the effects of purgation by bloodletting, cathartics, or emetics. Chapter xv discusses surgery, while Chapter xvi describes female ailments. The following four chapters are set aside for a discussion of hygiene, including exercise, baths, and diet. Two chapters discuss the effects of various drugs. The remaining three chapters (XXIII–XXV) take up critically certain teachings of Galen, including some rare diseases described by him. This division gave Maimonides the opportunity to discuss, for example, diabetes, which was rather uncommon at that time. While Galen admitted to having seen only two cases in his lifetime, the sage of Fusṭaṭ asserted that, while living in Morocco, neither he nor any of his teachers seem ever to have come across a patient afflicted with that disease. On the other hand, after his arrival in Egypt, he had observed twenty male and three female diabetics. Evidently that disease did not then strike such a high ratio of Jewish patients as it has in more recent generations, unless we assume that the medieval physicians often failed to diagnose it properly. Maimonides even had the occasion here to refer to some diseases of the teeth, and thus shed some light on the state of dental research in his time.[50]

Nor must we totally neglect the impact of ritualistic ablutions on general hygiene. The following passage, quoted from Asaph by the twelfth-century halakhist, Eliezer bar Nathan, may serve here as a typical illustration:

Shivta [= meningitis, according to Mazie] is a bad spirit: at the time the woman comes from the river or the privy, or when she discharges faeces and does not wash her hands and gives bread to her son or milk, and nurses without washing her hands, there is a bad ghost, Saturn by name, which seizes youths, and bends and breaks the neck. The name of this sickness is called in a foreign language 'Sterneodiossi' and there is no cure but to burn with fire. The same explanation is given by Asaph in his Book of Medicine [*Eben ha-'Ezer:* a halakhic treatise, Prague ed., p. 52; in Muntner's English translation in *Bulletin of the History of Medicine,* XXV, 126].

INCIPIENT ENLIGHTENMENT

Jewish participation in the great intellectual movements of the "Renaissance of Islam" had many of the features of the modern era of Enlightenment. To be sure, a slogan like that which epitomized the *haskalah* movement of the nineteenth century, "Be a man outside, and a Jew in thy tent," could not have been coined by the intellectual leaders of eastern Jewry in the tenth century, or by those of the Spanish Golden Age in the eleventh or twelfth century. The very concept of an all-embracing humanity, of an abstract "man," divorced from his religious and ethnic moorings, was to reemerge only in the cosmopolitan eighteenth century, to a large extent as the result of the tragic stalemate in the preceding Wars of Religion. In the Middle Ages, eastern as well as western, the heritage of the Graeco-Roman *philanthropia* or *humanitas,* which even in the ancient world never became a dominant intellectual trend, was a mere literary reminiscence with no basis in reality. Al-Ma'arri, the poet, may have sung about the wholeness of mankind, and stressed its unity above its religious differences. But in reality everybody belonged first and foremost to his religious community, and only secondarily to society at large. Loyalty to the state and its ruler was considered on all sides as decidedly secondary to one's religious allegiance. High treason for religious reasons was violently suppressed by the state having the power to do so, but it was not seriously condemned by public opinion on moral grounds, and was more or less expected as the natural behavior of oppressed minorities. Certainly, a Jew could not dream of becoming a "man," that is, part and parcel of the regnant civilization, without giving up his religion and community.

In most other aspects, however, Jewish culture of its "Golden Age" adumbrated the manifestations of modern Enlightenment. Linguistic assimilation, as we recall, had gone so far that rabbis addressing legal inquiries to other rabbis, or replying to such inquiries, used Arabic as their medium, although both sides were well versed in talmudic lore and could readily employ its Hebrew-Aramaic idiom. Substantively, too, Arabian learning and modes of thinking, themselves largely a synthesis of the manifold cultural ingredients taken over from the earlier civilizations, including the Jewish, dominated the thought processes of the Jewish intellectual leaders and gradually percolated also into the masses.

Above all there was a newly awakened intellectual curiosity about man and the world, and a new reliance upon human reason to master the riddles of existence. Starting with investigations directly related to the Jewish religious tradition, like the calendar and chronology, and continuing with efforts to predict the destinies of individuals and nations by watching the stars, alchemistically to manipulate the forces of nature, and to control human diseases through medical ministrations, many Jews began specializing in the related sciences of mathematics, astronomy, and astrology, while others branched out into physical and biological disciplines, and a still larger number devoted themselves to the study and practice of medicine. These studies were interrelated, and the same men often attained mastery in more than one branch of learning. All these pursuits, moreover, were diffused with some basic philosophic approaches combining the findings of reason with ancestral traditions. They were also frequently given ethical directions greatly influenced by the Jewish heritage, even where the verbiage seemed to have been borrowed from other civilizations.

These processes required lengthy maturation, and often escaped the attention of outsiders. Ibn Sa'id's aforementioned remark that the Jews had centered their studies on law and the biographies of prophets, but had not distinguished themselves in philosophic sciences, was decidedly a retrospect summary of what had become known to the Arab world of ancient Jewish intellectual activity. Slightly behind the times even with respect to tenth-century Spain where this Toledan judge wrote his famous "Categories of Nations," it certainly was unjustified in regard to the Near East of that time, and was wholly controverted by the philosophic and scientific contributions of Spanish and eastern Jews in the following two centuries. Preoccupation with all branches of science soon became such a passionate concern of the Jewish intelligentsia in the Mediterranean lands that even the enthusiastic affirmation of the apologist, Yedaiah ha-Penini of Béziers, did not altogether overshoot the mark.

> We cannot give up science [this eloquent defender of Maimonidean rationalism wrote]; it is as the breath of our nostrils. Even if Joshua were to appear and forbid it, we should not obey him. For we have a warranty which outweighs them all, namely, Maimuni who recommended it, and impressed it upon us. We are ready to set our goods, our children, and our lives at stake for it.

True, when these words were written (in 1305–6) the great anti-intellectual reaction among western Jewry had set in. But we shall see in a later context that, unlike the similar reaction in the Arabian world, this new opposition was not aimed so much at scientific pursuits, as such, as it was at the study of non-Jewish works of any kind, in which Orthodox leadership saw a danger to Jewish survival. Considering the large number of Jewish scientists and medical experts who had found their way to the dominant faiths in both East and West, these fears were by no means unjustified.[51]

Even the Orthodox, however, usually halted in their opposition before the study of medicine. Appreciation of human life had been too deeply rooted in the biblical and talmudic tradition, care for the ill had been too highly exalted as a personal and communal obligation, for even the conservative circles consistently to uphold objections derived from certain biblical passages extolling the Lord alone as the true healer. The very "Book of the Pious," we recall, merely enjoined doctors to repair first to poverty-stricken patients. Under the existing circumstances this toleration of medical studies led at least to tacit condoning of the study of non-Jewish medical works, as well as association with, and receiving of instruction from Gentile doctors. In fact, the more frequently Jews practiced medicine among Gentiles, the more need they felt to familiarize themselves with the existing state of medical knowledge among their Gentile colleagues. The later medieval author of *Sefer ha-Yosher* (Book of Justice) was not alone in voicing the fear that an insufficiently informed Jewish physician would draw upon himself the accusation of envious competitors that he was killing his Gentile patients. One can readily envisage what chagrin that accusation might have caused to the entire community.[52]

As a matter of fact, the issue was rarely raised in public. Even the active collaboration between Jews and Catholic priests or monks in the translation of major eastern works into Latin, often through the mediation of Hebrew, was on the whole silently tolerated, wherever the need was strongly felt and society at large made such collaboration possible. This combination of favorable circumstances occurred especially in Christian Spain, southern

Italy, and the Provence. Abraham bar Ḥiyya may have been called to task by the rabbinic leader Yehudah bar Barzillai for indulging in the study of astrology, but nobody seemed to resent his active collaboration with Plato of Tivoli in the task of translating Hebrew mathematical works, very possibly including his own.

Arabian Jewish Enlightenment was ultimately cut short, largely for external reasons, which will become clear from the general historical evolution of the later Middle Ages. But, while it lasted, it brought forth some magnificent contributions to Jewish and human learning. In this great transitional period between the ancient and modern civilizations, which goes under the somewhat misleading names of the Renaissance of Islam or the Twelfth-Century Renaissance, Jews injected significant ingredients of their own. If, moreover, the major function of medieval culture from the standpoint of world history was to preserve, elaborate, and transmit to the modern world the main achievements of the ancient civilizations in both East and West, the Jews certainly played an important role in this process, far more important indeed than was warranted by their relatively small numbers.

NOTES

ABBREVIATIONS

Abrahams Mem. Vol.	Jewish Studies in Memory of Israel Abrahams. New York, 1927.
AHDL	Archives d'histoire doctrinale et littéraire du moyen âge
AIHS	Archives internationales d'histoire et des sciences
'A.Z.	'Abodah Zarah (talmudic tractate)
b.	Babylonian Talmud
B.B.	Baba Batra (talmudic tractate)
BJRL	Bulletin of the John Rylands Library, Manchester
B.M.	Baba Meṣiah (talmudic tractate)
B.Q.	Baba Qamma
BSOAS	Bulletin of the School of Oriental and African Studies (University of London)
CSEL	Corpus Scriptorum ecclesiasticorum latinorum
EJ	Encyclopaedia Judaica
Festschrift Harkavy	Festschrift zu Ehren des Dr. A. Harkavy. St. Petersburg, 1908.
Festschrift Israel Lewy	Festschrift zu Israel Lewy's siebzigstem Geburtstag. Breslau, 1911.
Festschrift Jakob Freimann	Festschrift Dr. Jakob Freimann zum 70 Geburtstag gewidmet. Berlin, 1937.
Festschrift Steinschneider	Festschrift zum achtzigsten Geburtstag Moritz Steinschneider's. Leipzig, 1896.
Ginzberg Jub. Vol.	Louis Ginzberg Jubilee Volume. 2 vols. New York, 1945. A volume each of English and Hebrew essays.
Goldziher Mem. Vol.	Ignace Goldziher Memorial Volume. Vol. I Budapest, 1948.
G.S.	Gesammelte Schriften
HTR	Harvard Theological Review
HUCA	Hebrew Union College Annual
IC	Islamic Culture
j.	Palestinian Talmud
JA	Journal asiatique
JAOS	Journal of the American Oriental Society
JBL	Journal of Biblical Literature and Exegesis

JJS	Journal of Jewish Studies
JQR	Jewish Quarterly Review (new series, unless otherwise stated)
JRAS	Journal of the Royal Asiatic Society
JSS	Jewish Social Studies
KA	Korrespondenzblatt . . . Akademie für die Wissenschaft des Judentums
Kaplan Jub. Vol.	Mordecai M. Kaplan Jubilee Volume. 2 vols. New York, 1953. A volume each of English and Hebrew essays.
Kohut Mem. Vol.	Jewish Studies in Memory of George A. Kohut. New York, 1935.
KS	Kirjath Sepher, Quarterly Bibliographical Review
Löw Mem. Vol.	Semitic Studies in Memory of Immanuel Löw. Budapest, 1947.
M.	Mishnah
Magnes Anniv. Book	Magnes Anniversary Book. By Staff of the Hebrew University. Jerusalem, 1938.
MGWJ	Monatsschrift für Geschichte und Wissenschaft des Judentums
Miller Mem. Vol.	Essays and Studies in Memory of Linda R. Miller. New York, 1938.
MJC	Mediaeval Jewish Chronicles, ed. by A. Neubauer
M.T.	Moses ben Maimon's Mishneh Torah (Code)
MW	Moslem World
MWJ	Magazin für die Wissenschaft des Judentums
PAAJR	Proceedings of the American Academy for Jewish Research
PG	Patrologiae cursus completus, series Graeca
PL	Patrologiae cursus completus, series Latina
Poznanski Mem. Vol.	Livre d'hommage à la memoire du Samuel Poznanski. Warsaw, 1927.
r.	Midrash Rabbah (Gen. r. = Bereshit rabbah; Lam. r. = Ekhah rabbati, etc.)
REJ	Revue des études juives
Resp.	Responsa (*Teshubot* or *She'elot u-teshubot*)
R.H.	Rosh ha-Shanah (talmudic tractate)
RHMH	Revue d'histoire de la médecine hébraïque
RHR	Revue d'histoire des religions
Rosenheim Festschrift	Festschrift für Jakob Rosenheim. Frankfort, 1931.
RSO	Rivista degli studi orientali
Saadia Anniv. Vol.	American Academy for Jewish Research, Texts and Studies, Vol. II. Saadia Anniversary Volume. New York, 1943.

SB	Sitzungsberichte der Akademie der Wissenschaften (identified by city: e.g. *SB* Berlin, Heidelberg, Vienna)
Schwarz Festschrift	Festschrift Adolf Schwarz. Berlin, 1917.
Sokolow Jub. Vol.	Sefer ha-Yobel li-khebod Nahum Sokolow. Warsaw, 1904.
T.	Tosefta, ed. by M. S. Zuckermandel
VT	Vetus Testamentum
Y.D.	Yoreh de'ah (sections of Jacob ben Asher's *Turim* and Joseph Karo's *Shulḥan Arukh*)
Yellin Jub. Vol.	Minḥah le David: Jubilee Volume in Honor of David Yellin. Jerusalem, 1935.
ZDMG	Zeitschrift der Deutschen Morgenländischen Gesellschaft
ZHB	Zeitschrift für hebräische Bibliographie

NOTES

CHAPTER XXXIII: MAGIC AND MYSTICISM

1. Halevi's *K. al-Khazari,* II,60 (the bracketed words are found only in Ibn Tibbon's trans., ed. by D. Cassel, pp. 167 f., and in some manuscripts—they do not occur in the Arabic original, ed. by Hirschfeld, p. 120; see the latter's Notes, p. xxxi n. 72; and his English trans., p. 120); Pseudo-Maimonides' *Peraqim be-haṣlaḥah* (Chapters on Bliss), in the *Qobeṣ teshubot,* ed. by Lichtenberg, II, fol. 32a; and the more recent edition by S. D. Dawidowicz, p. 7. This alleged epistle to Ibn 'Aqnin was given all the earmarks of a testamentary injunction. Its authenticity has often been doubted, however. Although defended by W. Bacher in "The Treatise on Eternal Bliss," *JQR,* [o.s.] IX, 270–89, it has quite conclusively been proved a forgery by Dawidowicz in the introduction to his edition, pp. xiv f. Even the counsel to keep on singing pleasant tunes to the Lord is out of keeping with the Fusṭaṭ sage's general attitude to music. See *supra,* Chap. XXXII, n. 94.

2. M. Ḥagigah II.1; b. 12a ff. (the Talmud quotes in this context a similar statement by Sirach; see Ecclesiasticus 3:21 ff.); j. II.1, 77c; Shabbat 88b f.; Berakhot 55a; *Abot de-R. Natan,* XXXI.3, ed. by Schechter, p. 91. The Torah's preexistence was generally accepted, although its creation in time was never subject to doubt. Next to the computation of 974 generations, we find R. Johanan and R. Simon ben Laqish contending that it antedated creation by two thousand generations. See *supra,* Chap. XXIV, n. 13; and W. Bacher's comments in *Die Agada der palästinensischen Amoräer,* I, 362 n. 1. Nor was the Torah the only preexistent creation. According to a tannaitic assertion, "seven things were created before the creation of the world, namely the Torah, repentance, the Garden of Eden, Gehennah, the Throne of Glory, the Temple, and the name of the Messiah" (Nedarim 39b). The reference to the Throne of Glory is particularly significant in our context. "The Discussions of Angels with God," often with an antihuman bias, are a frequent theme in the Aggadah. They are analyzed, with reference to a passage in *Midrash Tanḥuma,* VIII.2, ed. by Buber, p. 73, in a Hebrew essay by A. Marmorstein under this title in *Melilah,* III–IV, 93–102. On the angels' opposition to the creation of man altogether, see A. Altmann, "The Gnostic Background of the Rabbinic Adam Legends," *JQR,* XXXV, 371–91.

3. Gen. r. VIII.2, pp. 57 f. The same explanation of Bezalel's name is found also in Philo's *Legum Allegoria* (III.96, ed. by Colson and Whitaker, I, 365 f.), where, however, the term "shadow" is equated with the Logos, in the sense that in Bezalel's mind there arose the "image" of the Tabernacle to be built, just as God had made use of the Word "like an instrument, and so made the world." See also H. A. Wolfson's *Philo,* I, 238 f.; II, 83 f. An ingenious interpretation of some of these and other passages is offered by D. Neumark in his *Toledot ha-pilosophiah be-Yisrael*

(A History of Jewish Philosophy), I, 44 ff., which is vitiated in part, however, by the author's insistence on subsuming these talmudic discussions under the evidently alien Platonic and Aristotelian categories of matter and form. See also the data and literature cited *supra,* Vol. II, pp. 314 ff., 434 ff., to which add R. Marcus's brief discussion of "Judaism and Gnosticism," *Judaism,* IV, 360–64; G. Scholem, "Some Problems of Jewish Gnosticism," *Atti* of the Eighth International Congress for the History of Religions, V, 283–85; A. Neher, "Le Voyage mystique de quatre," *RHR,* CXL, 59–82 (on the four who had entered the Orchard; Ḥag. 14b); G. Quispel, "Der gnostische Anthropos und die jüdische Tradition," *Eranos-Jahrbuch,* XXII, 195–234 (denying the widely postulated impact of the Iranian idea of primordial man); and, on the newly discovered gnostic library of Chenoboskion, whose relations to the gnostic currents in Judaism have not yet been fully examined, J. E. Ménard's bibliographical study, "Les Manuscrits de Nag Hamadi," *Bibliotheca orientalis,* XIII, 2–6. Of course, protagonists of the ancient origin of the *Zohar,* the chief book of Jewish mysticism, could argue, as did A. Kaminka, for "Additional Ancient Sayings in the *Zohar* from Which Were Derived Aggadot in Talmud and Midrash." See his Hebrew essay in *Sinai,* XVII, Nos. 147–48, pp. 103–4 (supplementing his earlier Hebrew essay "On the Antiquity of the Book *Zohar*"). But a discussion of this still somewhat controversial problem must be postponed until we take up the thirteenth-century kabbalistic evolution.

4. Lewin, *Otzar ha-gaonim,* IV, Part 2, p. 20 (on Ḥagigah 14b, a responsum by Hai Gaon); E. H. Weiss, *Dor dor ve-doreshav,* IV, 195 f.; J. A. Montgomery, *Aramaic Incantation Texts from Nippur;* E. Peterson, "Das Amulett von Acre," *Aegyptus,* XXXIII, 172–78 (syncretistic-Jewish with a curious reference to Ez. 9); S. Reich, "Quatre coupes magiques," *Bulletin d'études orientales* of the Institut français de Damas, VII–VIII, 159–75; J. David-Weill, "Un Papyrus arabe inédit du Musée de Louvre," *Semitica,* IV, 67–71 (a magic papyrus referring to both Isa ibn Maryam and to Jews); and other writings listed *supra,* Vol. II, pp. 335 f. n. 23. See in general *ibid.,* pp. 15 ff., 334 ff., 434 ff.; and the interesting comparative materials assembled by Sir E. A. Budge in his *Amulets and Superstitions* (includes also a chapter on Hebrew amulets, pp. 212 ff.); A. Dupont-Sommer's interpretation of *La Doctrine gnostique de la lettre "wâw" d'après une lamelle araméenne inédite* (includes an interesting chapter "De la mystique des lettres en général et de celle du "wâw" en particulier," pp. 35 ff.); G. Vajda's "Sur quelques éléments juifs et pseudo-juifs dans l'encyclopédie magique de Bûnî," *Goldziher Mem. Vol.,* I, 387–92 (Aḥmad Buni died in 1225).

A comprehensive and careful examination of the interrelations of these documents of daily life with the more lofty formulations in the mystical literature of the outgoing ancient and early Muslim times is likely to yield some striking insights into the character of both. Certainly the differences between theoretical and applied mysticism did not loom large in the eyes of contemporaries, and magic arts were frequently counted among the "sciences" in contemporary letters. On Muslim literature, see the few striking illustrations cited by I. Goldziher in his *Stellung der alten islamischen Orthodoxie zu den antiken Wissenschaften,* p. 4. On the underground persistence of many outlawed forms, see *supra,* Chaps. XXIV, n. 32; XXV, n. 41; and on the relation between magic arts and experimental science, see *infra,* Chap. XXXVI, nn. 3 ff.

5. C. H. Gordon's "Aramaic Incantation Bowls," *Orientalia,* X, 117 f.; J. A. Montgomery's *Aramaic Incantation Texts from Nippur, passim.* On the theurgic use of the divine names, see the illustrations given by S. S. Cohon in "The Name of God, a Study in Rabbinic Theology," *HUCA,* XXIII, Part 1, pp. 592 ff. We do not possess, to be sure, any Jewish counterpart to the Nestorian Narsai's sermon "On the Function of the Angels." Cf. P. Krüger's German translation and analysis of the Syriac text (ed. by Mingana) in "Das älteste syrisch-nestorianische Dokument über die Engel," *Ostkirchliche Studien,* I, 283–96. Yet Jewish students of occultism seem quite early to have had definite ideas about the specific functions performed by individual angels. On the multitude of angelic and demonic names in Jewish literature, see M. Schwab's "Vocabulaire de l'Angélologie d'après les manuscrits hébreux de la Bibliothèque Nationale," *Mémoires* of the Académie des Inscriptions, X, 113–430; R. Margulies's more recent list of *Mal'akhe Elyon* (Angels on High); and H. Bietenhard's more searching analysis of *Die himmlische Welt im Urchristentum und Spätjudentum,* which might profitably be elaborated through study of the even richer medieval materials. A magic formula awaiting insertion of a name is included in the three strips published in Mann's *Texts and Studies,* II, 94. The name Hindoy on the bowl cited in the text (elsewhere Hindu, Hinduita), seems to have been quite common in these magic texts, although it was rarely recorded in the literary sources. See Montgomery, *Aramaic Incantation Texts,* pp. 23, 205, 244, 246, 253 f. Such frequency may be indicative of much closer relationships between the Babylonian Jews and India than is evident from other sources.

Other names recorded in the various texts would likewise deserve careful attention. For example, in Montgomery's text No. 12 (pp. 174 f.), "salvation from Heaven" is implored in behalf of Dadbeh bar Asmanduch, Sarkoi bat Dada, his wife, and their seven children. Only one of the latter bears the Hebrew name Abraham, while the other children, the parents and grandmothers all have Persian names. This ratio reveals an unsuspected degree of onomatological assimilation under Sassanian domination not only on the Iranian Plateau, but also in Babylonia. For this reason the attribution of a particular magical text to Jews often remains entirely conjectural. Not even the occurrence of the divine name *Iao* stamps a text as of definitely Jewish origin. This name appears frequently in inscriptions, for instance one on the shield of the cock-headed anguipede in military costume, whereby the ancient pagan soldiery expressed its idea of an all-embracing cosmic God. On the other hand, even occasional misspellings of the Tetragrammaton are no proof of non-Jewish origin, since there is no uniformity in its orthography even in the ancient Hebrew manuscripts. See M. Delcor, "Des diverses manières d'écrire le tétragramme sacré dans les anciens documents hébraïques," *RHR,* CXLVII, 145–73; and M. P. Nilsson, "The Anguipede of the Magical Amulets," *HTR,* XLIV, 61–64.

6. Shabbat 66b (a saying by Abbaye); and *supra,* Vol. I, p. 22. Examples of older usage of the metronymic are cited by Montgomery, p. 49 n. 1. See also C. H. Gordon's note on "The Aramaic Incantation in Cuneiform," *Archiv für Orientforschung,* XII, 109 n. 13. Whether or not we see in this procedure one of the few surviving vestiges of the ancient matriarchate (see *supra,* Vol. I, p. 310 n. 20) in the consciousness of the medieval Jews, the quest for certainty was paramount. This is indeed the explanation still given today for the use of the metronymic in special prayers for the dangerously ill in older orthodox congregations.

7. See esp. the texts published by C. Wessely in his "Griechische Zauberpapyri von Paris und London," *Denkschriften* of the Vienna Academy, XXXVI, 129 ff. lines 109 f., 144; the foreign words used in the formula given in Yoma 84a; and the references to Hermes in J. A. Montgomery's *Aramaic Incantation Texts,* Nos. 2, 7, 11, 19, 25, 27 (see also the comments *ibid.,* pp. 99, 123 f.); in Gordon's text No. 11 (*Orientalia,* X, 273 ff.; the author uses here the mystically significant term *lebusha de-Ermes,* or the garb of Hermes); and Moses ibn Ezra's *'Arugat ha-bosem,* in the excerpts, ed. by L. Dukes in *Zion* (ed. by M. Creizenach and J. M. Jost), II, 123. See *infra,* Chaps. XXXIV, nn. 14, 67; XXXV, n. 45; and, more generally, A. D. Nock's and A. J. Festugière's remarks in their edition and translation respectively, of the *Corpus Hermeticum* and the latter's *La Révélation d'Hermès Trismégiste.* Now that this vast body of Hermetic materials is available to scholars, a fuller re-examination of the pertinent references to Jewish bowls and other texts is clearly indicated. Particularly the equation of Hermes with Meṭaṭron (see below) is fraught with enormous implications for both ancient syncretism and Jewish mysticism. See also A. E. Affifi's brief review of "The Influence of Hermetic Literature on Moslem Thought," *BSOAS,* XIII, 840–55; H. Ritter, "Picatrix, ein arabisches Handbuch hellenistischer Magie," *Vorträge der Bibliothek Warburg,* 1921–22, pp. 94–124 (followed by his edition in cooperation with M. Plessner of the Arabic text and German trans. of the *Ghayat al-ḥakum* or The Goal of Philosophers attributed to Majriṭi); *supra,* Vol. II, p. 334 n. 17; and *infra,* n. 20. All this despite the general prohibition of "sorcery" and the protracted debates among Muslim jurists as to whether Jewish and Christian sorcerers were to be condemned to death on a par with Muslim practitioners of that art. See G. H. Bousquet, "Fiqh et sorcellerie (Petite contribution à l'étude de la sorcellerie en Islam)," *Annales* of the Institut d'Etudes Orientales of the University of Algiers, VIII, 230–34. Nor are the magic bowls of clearly Mandaean provenance altogether devoid of Jewish interest, since, despite their deep hatred of Jews and Judaism, Mandaeans continued to reflect not only biblical, but also talmudic practices and phrases. See J. N. Epstein's succinct illustrations in his "Mandäische Glossen," *Archiv orientalni,* XVIII, 165–69; and *supra,* Vol. II, pp. 347 n. 59, 433 n. 18.

8. Montgomery, *Aramaic Incantation Texts,* esp. pp. 80, 242 f., 244 f.; Gordon's "Bowls" in *Orientalia,* X, 273 ff. Here a passage blurred in the photographic reproduction (p. 282) is rendered by Gordon by "which I brought on Mount [Hermon]." This translation makes little sense, especially when brought in connection with the Leviathan. The word *tura,* even if incorrectly spelled with a *ṭet* by the uneducated medicine man, more likely stands for the mythological Wild Steer (*shor ha-bar*), which, sometimes under the better known biblical name, *behemot* (Job 40:15, etc.), shared with the Leviathan in being "the proper objects for hunting by the pious in the world to come." See B.B. 75a; Lev. r. XIII.3, ed. by M. Margulies, pp. 277 f. These concepts, based on ancient Near Eastern mythology (see, e.g., *supra,* Vol. I, p. 357 n. 5; Chap. XXV, n. 10; and G. R. Driver's "Mythical Monsters in the Old Testament," *Studi orientalistici in onore di Giorgio Levi della Vida,* I, 234–49, equating *behemot* with a crocodile, and the Leviathan with a whale) became popular ingredients of medieval Jewish eschatology. See also E. Zbinden, *Die Djinn des Islam und der altorientalische Geisterglaube.*

9. Montgomery, *Aramaic Incantation Texts,* p. 115. That author's argumentation, however, that Nippur was destroyed by the onrushing Arabs and that, hence, the bowls are all of pre-Islamic origin (pp. 102 ff.) is far from cogent. There is neither any reason for postulating the total destruction of a town which had long lost its former glory, nor for the speedy disappearance of the Aramaic medium or the Persian names from the community after its occupation by the Muslims. On the former, see Hai's testimony as late as the eleventh century, cited *supra,* Chaps. XXIX, n. 28; XXX, n. 4. The survival of Persian names, too, is the less astonishing since Persian culture in general was before very long to stage its memorable revival. Even conceding the absence of Arabic names, therefore, the *terminus ad quem* of these magic bowls may readily be pushed a century or two beyond the date of 600 C.E. suggested by Montgomery. However, a great many bowls probably date from the Sassanian period.

10. Qirqisani's *K. al-Anwar,* I.4, 5–6, ed. by Nemoy, I, 32 f. (in his English trans. in *HUCA,* VII, 351 f.); Hai's aforementioned responsum in Lewin, *Otzar ha-gaonim,* IV, Part 2, p. 21. The formerly equally obscure blend of *Merkabah* mysticism and magic, however, called *Sefer Raza rabbah* and quoted by Daniel al-Qumisi (see Mann's *Texts and Studies,* II, 75 f., 80 ff.), has in part been recovered by Scholem. See his *Reshit ha-Qabbalah* (Beginnings of Kabbalah, 1150–1250), pp. 195 ff.; and *infra,* n. 36. *Sefer Yeṣirah* has long been available in numerous editions, as a rule with extensive commentaries, and even in three independent English translations. These editions and Western translations are in part mentioned in our previous notes, but are more fully listed in G. Scholem's *Bibliographia Kabbalistica* (see the nearly twoscore entries in the Index, p. 228). Most of the other mystical writings of that period were published nearly a century ago by A. Jellinek in his *Bet ha-Midrasch* and reprinted in J. D. Eisenstein's *Ozar Midrashim.* For example, the *Hekhalot rabbati* and *Hekhalot zuṭra* (Great and Lesser Palaces) appeared in Jellinek's collection, III, 83–108, 161–63 (also Introduction, pp. xx–xxv); and II, 40–47 (Intro., pp. xiv–xvii); and in Eisenstein, pp. 111–22, 108–11, respectively. *The Otiot* [or *Alphabeta*] *de-Rabbi 'Aqiba,* in two versions, ed. by Jellinek, III, 12–49, 50–64 (also Intro., pp. xiv–xvii), and in Eisenstein, pp. 407–31, appeared in a fuller ed. by A. S. Wertheimer. This treatise includes also (under the letter *ḥet*) an important excerpt from *She'ur qomah* (Measure of the Divine Stature), while another longer passage has been preserved in the important *Sefer Reziel* (first published in Amsterdam in 1701 and frequently thereafter), which is to be distinguished from *Sefer Reziel ha-mal'akh* (Book of the Angel Reziel). See also the text reproduced in the kabbalistic anthology, *Merkabah shelemah,* fols. 34–44; and the excerpts from an important commentary on the *She'ur,* extant in Rome and New York MSS, in Scholem's *Reshit ha-Qabbalah,* pp. 196 ff., 210 ff., 220 ff. On the meaning of the term *qomah* (stature), see Scholem's *Major Trends,* p. 360 n. 81. Scholem's insistence upon translating it as "body" emphasizes even more sharply the treatise's anthropomorphism (see *infra,* n. 28). We certainly must not lose sight, however, for example, of the enormously important doctrine of the mystic body of Christ, which, in medieval Christian thought, had long lost its anthropomorphic features.

Of independent value are the aforementioned publications of the Hebrew Enoch and of such mystic midrashim as *Eleh ezkerah* (On the Ten Martyrs), and *Midrash Tadshe,* with its pronounced Philonic associations (see *supra,* Vol. II, pp. 335 n. 22;

370, n. 9; and Chaps. XXI, n. 67; XXIV, n. 4; XXIX, n. 65); as well as the *Ḥarba de-Mosheh* (Sword of Moses), ed. by M. Gaster, and reprinted in his *Studies and Texts,* I, 288 ff. (Intro. and English trans.), III, 69 ff. (Hebrew text, preceded by a facsimile page of the MS); *The Apocalypse of Abraham,* trans. into English by G. H. Box, and the *Pereq Re'iyot Yeḥezqel* (Visions of Ezekiel), ed. by J. Mann in *Ha-Zofeh,* V, 256–64. Quite a few early works of this type are still unpublished, however. See esp. those mentioned in Scholem's *Major Trends in Jewish Mysticism,* pp. 353 n. 11, 364 n. 134. On the other hand, one must beware not only of apocryphal writings attributed to ancient masters—perhaps the majority of extant writings fall within this category—but also of outright modern forgeries. See, e.g., H. Albeck's attestation (in his comment on Zunz's *Ha-Derashot be-Yisrael,* p. 334 n. 69) concerning the so-called *Baraita de-ma'aseh bereshit* (a Tannaitic Treatise on the Works of Creation), ed. by L. Goldschmidt in 1894.

The line of demarcation between these mystic tracts and supernaturally oriented midrashim is often extremely tenuous. Technically, to be sure, most of the former do not consist of a sequence of aggadic interpretations of biblical passages, although the *Zohar* was to appear as precisely such a mystic midrash on the Pentateuch. Most of the earlier treatises belong to the category of aggadic monographs, such as the historical homilies on Zerubbabel, Antiochus, or Mordecai's Dream, or the special aggadic collections on ethical topics like charity. See *supra,* Chap. XXVIII, nn. 6, 18. The same persons, for example Zerubbabel, who appear in these midrashim were often used by the "descenders of Merkabah" and other mystics for their purposes as well. Certainly, many later midrashic apocrypha, such as the Chronicle of Moses, the Midrash on the Death of Moses, or one on the Death of Aaron, could well qualify as mystic writings, too. Nor is there any basic distinction between these lucubrations and those included in the more standardized aggadic commentaries on biblical books. For example, the comments on the mystically provocative saying "The Lord by wisdom founded the earth; by understanding He established the heavens" (Prov. 3:19), included in the regular *Midrash Mishle,* contain nothing in either form or substance that could not find its place also in any mystic tract. See the extensive data in Zunz and Albeck's *Ha-Derashot,* pp. 71 ff., 325 ff. That is why the ancient and medieval Jews rightly included all these writings among the aggadic midrashim, unless they considered them outright tannaitic collections, in which case they dignified them by the designation *Mishnayot.* This was indeed the term used by Hai Gaon with respect to the *Hekhalot* (see *infra*).

These intriguing problems have produced a considerable secondary literature. Apart from those already referred to in our notes and those listed in Scholem's *Bibliographia* and his *Major Trends, passim,* we need but mention P. Bloch's brief summary of "Die jüdische Mystik und Kabbala" in J. Winter and A. Wünsche's *Jüdische Literatur,* III, 217–86, including excerpts in German translation; and the more recent general surveys by E. Müller, *History of Jewish Mysticism,* and by H. Sérouya, *La Kabbale, ses origines, sa psychologie mystique, sa métaphysique,* esp. pp. 115 ff. See also G. Scholem's succinct summary of "Caractères généreaux de la mystique juive," *Revue de la Pensée juive,* I, 81–99; L. Gardet's "Pour la connaissance de la mystique juive," *Cahiers sioniens,* VII, 50–62; and G. Vajda's bibliographical surveys, chiefly of G. Scholem's work, "Les Origines et le développement de la Kabbale juive d'après quelques travaux récents," *RHR,* CXXXIV, 120–67; and "Recherches récentes sur l'ésoterisme juif (1947–1953)," *ibid.,* CXLVII, 62–92. Although most of these publications are primarily concerned with the kabbalistic doctrines developed after 1200, they shed considerable light also on the earlier period. Of some interest also is J. Bernhart's succinct survey of *Die philosophische Mystik des Mittelalters von ihren Ursprüngen bis zur Renaissance.*

11. *Hekhalot r.* XI.5, ed. by Jellinek, III, 84 (ed. by Eisenstein, p. 112). See *supra,* Chaps. XXXI, n. 18; XXXII, n. 63. The *Hekhalot* are indeed full of hymns of adoration. On one occasion the author describes a "descender of the Chariot" finally reaching the Throne of Glory; he "opens up and sings a song which the Throne of Glory intones every day" (XXIV.1 in Jellinek, pp. 100 f.; Eisenstein, p. 119). This statement is followed by perhaps the largest collection of synonyms for song in Hebrew letters (18 terms for the song as such and an additional 69 terms for the various attributes of God forming the main content of these chants). This nexus between religious song, particularly hymns, and mystic exaltation remained a permanent feature of Jewish mysticism, as it was a major characteristic of much of non-Jewish mysticism as well. See the illustrations cited from the later kabbalistic and ḥasidic literatures by S. A. Horodetzky in "The Religious Hymn in Jewish Mysticism" (Hebrew), *Keneset,* I, 416–29.

12. *Hekhalot r.* IX.1–3, XXVI.7; and *Alphabeta* [or *Otiot*] *de-R. 'Aqiba,* to letters *alef* and *gimmel,* ed. by Jellinek, III, 12 ff., 21, 90, 103 f. (ed. by Eisenstein, pp. 114 f., 120 f., 408 ff., 412). The widespread inclusion of *Ha-Adderet ve-ha-emunah* in the High Holidays ritual is well illustrated by the sources listed in I. Davidson's *Oṣar,* II, 116 f. See the English translation in Scholem's *Major Trends,* pp. 57 f. The connection between *Hekhalot* and the *qedushah* is so obvious that the so-called *Pirqe hekhalot* (Chapters in the Book of Palaces) are almost entirely devoted to a homily stressing Israel's precedence over the angelic hosts in the recitation of this hymn. This homily is characteristically attributed to R. Ishmael, the alleged chief author of the entire cycle (see the passage quoted *supra,* Chap. XXXI, n. 20). In the main book of *Hekhalot r.,* too, several early chapters (II, III, VII–XI) and many other passages are concluded with this Isaianic refrain. One might almost contend that the entire work was originally composed as but a mystic midrash on the *Trishagion.* The *Alphabet of R. 'Aqiba,* without any self-consciousness in the face of Christian Trinitarianism but possibly in tacit opposition to it, adduced the *qedushah* as proof for a threefold prayer with which one must praise the one and only God (Jellinek, p. 17; Eisenstein, p. 410).

13. *Sefer Yeṣirah,* I, ed. by Goldschmidt, p. 51 (ed. by Kalisch, pp. 10 f., 47 n. 4); *Otiot de-R. 'Aqiba,* in both versions published by Jellinek, III, 12–49, 50–64; and his so-called *Midrash* in Jellinek, V, 31–34 (ed. by Eisenstein, pp. 408 ff., 424 ff., 431 ff.); and *supra,* Chap. XXIX, n. 8. The interpretation of the concluding three words in the opening statement of *Yeṣirah* depends on the vowels with which these consonantally identical terms were provided by the readers. There was already considerable confusion in both reading and interpretation in the eleventh century, when Yehudah bar Barzillai composed his commentary. See Halberstam's ed., pp. 138 f. Although Yehudah's explanation of the reason for the sequence of "book, number, and word," as reproduced in our text, namely that "one first writes down letters, then counts them, and only thereafter pronounces them," is obviously forced, it seems still more acceptable than the interpretations and corresponding spellings of either Goldschmidt or Kalisch. It is still more meaningful when we

equate, with Saadiah, the middle category, "number," with "idea," so understood, for example, by Abraham ibn Ezra. See Saadiah's *Commentary on Yeṣirah,* ed. by Lambert, pp. 22 f. (Arabic), 42 f. (French); and H. A. Wolfson's analysis in "The Classification of Sciences in Mediaeval Jewish Philosophy," *HUCA,* Jub. Vol., pp. 275 ff. In any case, our author could not have brought home more poignantly to his readers the ambiguity of Hebrew consonantal texts without the aid of an accepted vocalization, which was indeed a major preoccupation of the masoretic schools.

The intellectual connection between *Yeṣirah* and *Masorah* by no means presupposes the former's composition in the early Muslim age. Both the exact study of the biblical text and the mystic interpretations based thereon had been cultivated intensively throughout the talmudic and saboraic ages. The period between 300 and 600 C.E. seems, indeed, the most likely date for the composition of that mystical classic. However, such a nexus could also have existed in the second century, were we to accept A. Epstein's dating of *Yeṣirah* (see his Hebrew essay, in *Mi-Qadmoniyot ha-Yehudim;* and his "Recherches sur le Séfer Yeçira," *REJ,* XXIX, 75 ff.), for many Tannaim had likewise evinced great interest in masoretic problems. On the other hand, placing *Yeṣirah* in the second pre-Christian century, as does Goldschmidt (in the intro. to his ed., p. 12), merely because the book was written in Hebrew, and hence before the Aramaization of Palestinian Jewry under the Seleucids, is not to be taken seriously. On a summary of the conflicting chronologies and other controversies, see G. Scholem's article, "Jezira," *EJ,* IX, 104–11; and more generally, his "Kabbala," *ibid.,* cols. 630–732; L. Baeck's "Zum Sepher Jezira," *MGWJ,* LXX, 371–76; and "Die zehn Sephiroth im Sepher Jezira," *ibid.,* LXXVIII, 448–55; M. E. Müller's "On Sefer Yeṣirah" (Hebrew), *Metsudah,* II, 105–10; and more succinctly his *History of Jewish Mysticism,* pp. 46 ff., 62 ff. See also E. Bertola's brief observations on "Il 'Sefer Yezirah' nella storia del pensiero," *Rivista critica di storia della filosofia,* VIII, 584–96.

14. Lewin, *Otzar ha-gaonim,* IV, Part 2, p. 14. On the mystic posture of the head bent between the knees, see the parallels, both talmudic and Chinese, quoted by Scholem in his *Major Trends,* pp. 48 f.; and, more generally, H. Thurston, *The Physical Phenomena of Mysticism* (ed. by J. H. Crehan). Intermingling of ideas was but slightly less pronounced in works of mystical thought than it was in the practical realm of incantations. See *supra,* n. 9. Palestinian mystics living under Byzantine domination understandably used common Greek words, particularly when they referred to God, Heaven, or the four elements. See Johanan Lewy's felicitous reconstruction of "Vestiges of Greek Sentences and Names in *Hekhalot Rabbati*" (Hebrew), *Tarbiz,* XII, 163–67. The deviations from the literary Greek are not only owing to copyists' errors or willful alterations by mystics bent upon secrecy, as suggested by Lewy, but also to dialectal differences, as in the Hebrew transliteration of *aer* and corruptions arising from protracted oral transmission.

15. See the excerpt in Syriac of the *Gannat bussamé* (Garden of Delights), used liturgically in Syriac churches, ed. and trans. into French by J. Vosté in J. Bidez and F. Cumont's *Mages hellénisés,* II, 113 ff.; Scholem, *Major Trends,* p. 362 nn. 105–7. The designation "Little Lord" (*Adonai qaṭan,* or even *YHWH qaṭan*) was fairly widespread in Jewish as well as in Christian gnostic circles. As early as the second century, sectarians like Elisha ben Abuyah saw in Meṭaṭron a second deity

and, hence, an embodiment of the dualistic principle. See Ḥagigah 15a; Sanhedrin 38b; and other data assembled by H. Odeberg in the introduction to his ed. of *3 Enoch,* pp. 125 ff., 188 ff. Odeberg devotes here an entire chapter to an analysis of the various views on the name and function of Meṭaṭron. See also Odeberg's earlier "Fragen von Metatron, Shekina und Memra," *Bulletin* of the Société Royale de Lettres de Lund, 1941, pp. 31–46 (even discounting the authenticity of the Yiddish work here cited, the essay is not devoid of merit; cf. G. Scholem's strictures in his Hebrew "Collectanea to the Bibliography of the Kabbalah," *KS,* XXX, 412); the more recent studies by M. Black, "The Origin of the Name Metatron," *VT,* I, 217–19; and by A. Murtonen, "The Figure of Meṭaṭrôn," *ibid.,* III, 409–11 ("a kind of counterpart to Jesus"); and *supra,* Vol. II. p. 335 n. 22.

In any case, we find in the Talmud (Sanhedrin 38b) the significant designation of Meṭaṭron as *sar ha-penim* (Prince of the Interior) or, more likely, *ha-panim* (Prince of the Presence). But whether we consider any of the medieval derivations of that name from the Latin *metator* (measurer), first suggested by Eleazar of Worms and supported by many modern scholars including Black, who cites a pertinent Philonic passage, or *maṭronita* (a synonym for the divine Presence, the *Shekhinah*), proposed by Gersonides, or accept some of the modern equations with the Persian Mithra or with a Greek derivative of *meta thronon* (behind the throne), the medieval mystic doubtless was most impressed by the numerical equivalence of that name with the old divine name of *Shaddai* (the *gemaṭria* of both amounts to 314). That venerable name, already known to the Hebrew patriarchs, lent itself more readily to the designation of a demiurge as, according to the story in Exodus (7:3), God did not reveal his superior, truly "ineffable" name until the days of Moses. At the same time the name *Shaddai* figured prominently both in the mystically intriguing discussions of Job and his friends, and in Ezekiel's vision of the Chariot, during which the prophet "heard the noise of their [the angelic living creatures'] wings like the noise of great waters, like the voice of the Almighty [*Shaddai*]" (1:24). It is small wonder, then, that the writers of the magic incantations likewise made extensive use of it. One of them, for example, tried to have "all the idols, male and female, . . . bound and sealed in the name of Ah, Ah, Ah, amen, amen, amen, YHWH, YHWH, YHWH, El Shaddai, El Shaddai, El Shaddai." See C. H. Gordon's Text 6 in *Orientalia,* X, 124 ff. In another syncretistic text Meṭaṭron is called "the Great Healer of mercies . . . who vanquishes devils and demons." See C. H. Gordon's "Two Magic Bowls in Teheran," *Orientalia,* XX, 307. The extent to which both the names *Shaddai* and *Meṭaṭron* had penetrated Muslim magic may be noted from Aḥmad Buni's aforementioned encyclopedia, cited by Vajda in *Goldziher Mem. Vol.,* I, 388 f. Here Meṭaṭron appears also in the possession of a "crown" and a "sword," the latter reminiscent of the Sword of Moses. See also, more broadly, L. Gardet, "Un Problème de mystique comparée: La Mention du nom divin (*dhikhr*) dans la mystique musulmane," *Revue thomiste,* LII, 642–79; LIII, 197–216.

16. *Hekhalot r.* XIII.2, XX.1–2, XXVIII.1, ed. by Jellinek, III, 93, 98, 105 (ed. by Eisenstein, pp. 116, 118, 121); R. A. Nicholson in his essay on Islamic "Mysticism" in *The Legacy of Islam,* ed. by Arnold and Guillaume, pp. 232 f. The mention of "sound wisdom" (*tushiyyah*) in *Hekhalot r.* doubtless conjured in the minds of many readers the paean on "wisdom" in Prov. 8 (particularly v. 14), and probably also the homily on God taking "counsel with the Torah whose name is *tushiyyah*

with reference to the creation of the world." See *Pirqe de-R. Eliezer,* III, in Higger's ed. in *Horeb,* VIII, 88 (in Friedlander's trans., p. 12). The antinomian trends in the Shabbetian movement and its artificial rationalization as "a commandment fulfilled through sin" will be analyzed in their modern context.

17. *Hekhalot r.* IV.5 ff.; *Kisse ve-ippodromin shel Shelomoh ha-melekh,* ed. by Jellinek, III, 86 ff.; V, 34, 38 (ed. by Eisenstein, pp. 113 f., 527 f.). See also J. Perles's detailed interpretation in his "Thron und Circus des Königs Salomo." *MGWJ,* XXI, 122–39, which, however, fails to take cognizance of that midrash's apologetic aims. See also R. Guilland's analysis of the shape and decoration of "The Hippodrome at Byzantium," *Speculum,* XXIII, 676–82 (part of a larger study). In the *Alphabet of R. 'Aqiba,* too, the usual descriptions of the present inferior position of Israel and its total reversal in the messianic age are interspersed with passages stressing the kingdom of God. For example, when the letter *kaf* appeared in the contest for the leading role in Creation, "the Throne shook and the wheels of the Chariot began to tremble" merely because that letter is the initial for such mystically fraught terms as *keter* (crown), *kabod* (glory), and *kisse* (throne). See the first version under *alef* and *dalet* and the second version under *mem* and *kaf,* ed. by Jellinek, III, 14, 22, 52 f. (ed. by Eisenstein, pp. 409, 412, 425). In the Hebrew Enoch, Meṭaṭron, here identified with the ancient hero of the Bible who when "God took him" (Gen. 5:24) up to heaven during the Flood was allegedly elevated there to the post of divine viceroy, and his regime are usually described in military-bureaucratic terms. He appears as the commander of the angelic hosts, in charge of the divine treasury, and the like. See *3 Enoch,* XIV ff., ed. by Odeberg, pp. 18 ff. (Hebrew), 36 ff. (English); Ginzberg's *Ginze Schechter,* I, 183 f., 187. On the rabbinic doctrine of the divine "cosmocrator," see *supra,* Vol. II, pp. 394 n. 50; 435 n. 27. However unacceptable Graetz's theories concerning the historical background and doctrinal significance of the Merkabah literature may be in other respects, his classification of it as "basileomorphism" has much to commend itself. See esp. his century-old but still valuable essay, "Die mystiche Literatur in der gaonäischen Epoche," *MGWJ,* VIII, 67–78, 103–18, 140–53. See also *supra,* Chap. XIX, n. 7.

18. *Alphabet of R. 'Aqiba,* letter *'ayin,* ed. by Jellinek, III, 41 f. (ed. by Eisenstein, pp. 420 f.); *Midrash Tehillim,* ed. by S. Buber, p. 35; *Hekhalot r.* XXX, ed. by Jellinek, III, 107 (ed. by Eisenstein, p. 122). In his recent analysis of "The Meaning of the Torah in Jewish Mysticism," *Diogenes,* XIV, 36–47; XV, 65–94, G. Scholem has shown the great sublimation of that meaning and its divestment of magical ingredients in the works of the thirteenth-century Kabbalists.

19. *Alphabet of R. 'Aqiba,* letters *ṣadi* and *qof,* ed. by Jellinek, III, 43 ff. (ed. by Eisenstein, pp. 421 f.). In this connection Moses is said to have viewed much of the course of future history in the divine "Curtain" which, playing a role already in talmudic mysticism, appeared to the "descenders of the Chariot" to contain in its texture a panorama of world history down to the messianic age. See Scholem's *Major Trends,* p. 71. The various midrashim expatiating on the life and death of Moses and Aaron are conveniently reproduced in Eisenstein's *Ozar,* pp. 11 ff., 357 ff., and are briefly scanned in Zunz and Albeck's *Ha-Derashot,* pp. 66 f. The elaborations were not limited to the great biblical heroes, although, like the

Aggadah generally, or for that matter also the ancient Alexandrian Jewish historiography, they laid the main stress on the "sacred" history of the biblical age. In a brief homily included in his *Alphabet*, R. 'Aqiba saw the past mainly as extending from the Creation to Sennacherib. See Jellinek's ed., III, 115 (Eisenstein, p. 409). On the other hand, among the talmudic sages and the mystic writers after them there was great idealization, especially of the Ten Martyrs, including the four tannaim commemorated in *Hekhalot*. This glorification of the ever actual Jewish martyrdom led to the composition of the intriguing semimystic Midrash *Eleh ezkerah*. See *supra*, n. 17; and Vols. I, pp. 197 f.; II, p. 370 n. 9.

20. See the conclusion of the brief fragment of the Hebrew Book of Enoch, ed. by Jellinek, II, 114 ff. (ed. by Eisenstein, p. 185); *3 Enoch*, end, ed. by Odeberg, pp. 73 f. (Hebrew), 177 ff. (English); Montgomery's *Aramaic Incantation Texts*, No. 7 line 9, and his intro., pp. 47, 57. There also were several aggadic collections commemorating in rational or mystic terms those among the great talmudic sages (Eliezer ben Hyrcanus, 'Aqiba, Ishmael, Simon bar Yoḥai, Joshua ben Levi) who had been the reputed grandmasters of ancient mysticism as well. In this way many old folkloristic concepts of unknown authorship, as well as many newly invented teachings or stories, were supplied with authoritative paternity. Even the remarkable apocalypse, written at the beginning of the Muslim age, in which Meṭaṭron, the "Prince of the Interior," informs Israel that "the Holy One, blessed be He, brought the reign of Ishmael only in order to save you from that of the evil one," is attributed, as we recall, to R. Simon bar Yoḥai. See his *Nistarot*, ed. by Jellinek, III, 78 (ed. by Eisenstein, p. 555); and *supra*, Chap. XVII, n. 27. What is truly astonishing in all these proceedings, however, is not so much the existence of so large a body of medieval apocrypha and pseudepigrapha, but rather the fact that even the most popular mystics sought additional validation through the sanction of history.

21. See the remarkable conversation which allegedly took place between R. Ishmael and R. 'Aqiba, in the excerpt from an Oxford MS published by Scholem in his *Major Trends*, p. 364 n. 136; and trans. into English, *ibid.*, p. 77; the *Alphabet of R. 'Aqiba*, under *alef, gimmel, dalet, ḥet* and *ṣadi*, ed. by Jellinek, pp. 14, 20, 22, 29 f., 43 (ed. by Eisenstein, pp. 409, 411 f., 415, 421); and *supra*, Chap. XXIX, nn. 65–66. The relative paucity of erotic incantations emanating from the Jews of Nippur and elsewhere (Montgomery's text, No. 28, p. 213, invoking the aid of the goddess of love Dlibat evidently was of pagan origin) testifies to the strong hold of the regnant Jewish ethics over the popular masses and their miracle-working agents even in the obscure realm of sex. This does not mean that human weaknesses were absent from the Jewish community. Daniel al-Qumisi's accusation doubtless had a solid grain of truth when he blamed the Rabbanites for using "many magic books, whether one wanted to arouse a man's love for a woman or make them hate each other, or else one wished to leap across a large distance, and other such numerous abominations; may the Lord keep us away from them!" (*Commentary* on Mal. 3:5, in Mann's *Texts and Studies*, II, 80 f.). However, the early medieval mystics seem, on the whole, to have continued the ancient tradition of allowing ethical categories to dominate even the supernatural world, as when, in the Testament of Solomon, the seven demons were designated Strife, Deception, and so forth. For talmudic practices, see L. Blau's illustrations in *Das altjüdische Zauberwesen*, *passim*.

22. Halevi's *K. al-Khazari,* IV.25, ed. by Hirschfeld, pp. 266 ff. (in the latter's English trans., pp. 230 f.); *Exod. r.* XV.22. See also Rab's statement cited *supra,* n. 3; and Chap. XXIX, n. 9. The antiquity of the numerical principle as an ordering, even creative, element in the cosmic structure needs no further elaboration. It was fully developed by the ancient Pythagoreans and the schools of thought influenced by them, and it was a basis for many astral speculations of the ancient Babylonians. Hence the *sefirot,* as understood in the Book of Creation, had many old and venerable antecedents. The origins of letter mysticism, on the other hand, are more controversial. While scholars were long prepared to accept Jewish priority in this area, F. Dornseiff argued with considerable erudition and acumen in favor of ascribing that innovation, too, to the fertile minds of Greek thinkers. See his interesting array of data in *Das Alphabet in Mystik und Magie.* However, more recent investigations have shown that letter symbolism and other mystical uses of the alphabet probably antedate the Greek period, and that, in any case, the Jews, who were perhaps the original inventors of the alphabet for the Greeks as well and clung more tenaciously than any other people to each letter of the divine revelation, had every inducement to cultivate this technique above anyone else. See esp. D. Diringer's comprehensive work on *The Alphabet;* Dornseiff's own remarks in his *Das Alphabet,* pp. 133 ff.; and the vast literature on this subject listed *supra,* Vol. I, p. 307 n. 13.

Numerical symbolism of a different kind was involved in the quest for measurement of the divine limbs and other forms of the divine appearance; even the author of *Hekhalot r.* (x) claimed to know that it extended beyond the Throne of Glory by 180,000,000 parasangs in height and 700,000 parasangs in width. Of still another order was the ritualistic import of repetition of formulas and rituals. Disregarding the staggering figures concerning the number of particular ministrations allegedly performed before the Deity by the Angel of Divine Presence (*ha-panim*), often identified with Meṭaṭron (XI.1), one had to take seriously the injunction for a prospective "descender of the Chariot" to adjure that Prince of the Presence (here called Suriah) 112 times in the name of Totressia, that is the Tetragrammaton. "He shall neither add to, nor subtract from the 112 times, and anyone who does add or subtract, his blood shall fall on his own head" (XIV.4–5). See the text, ed. by Jellinek, III, 91, 94 (ed. by Eisenstein, pp. 115 f.).

23. The mystic concept of the soul's ascent to heaven had venerable ancient antecedents. It was given a new impetus, however, throughout the world of Islam by Mohammed's reputed ascension (Qur'an 5:1–18, 53:4–18, etc.). See the data assembled from various civilizations in the lectures delivered at the Warburg Library in 1928–29, which were subsequently edited by F. Saxl under the title *Ueber die Vorstellungen von der Himmelsreise der Seele.* One lecture by R. Hartmann was devoted to an analysis of "Die Himmelsreise Muhammeds und ihre Bedeutung in der Religion des Islam" (pp. 42–65). See also A. E. Affifi's briefer account of "The Story of the Prophet's Ascent (*Mi'raj*) in Sufi Thought and Literature," *Islamic Quarterly,* II, 23–27. While there is no question about the priority of the Judeo-Christian speculations and their decisive impact on the Muslim concepts (see esp. J. Horovitz's "Mohammeds Himmelfahrt," *Der Islam,* IX, 159–83), the novel emphasis placed by leading circles in the new religion on these mystical aspects undoubtedly helped bring out into the open what had theretofore been essentially but a cherished doctrine of the mystically minded minority alone. The reciprocal

influences of *Merkabah* and early Muslim teachings on these peregrinations of the soul would, therefore, decidedly deserve a more careful examination.

The task is facilitated now by the new materials from both the East and the West accumulated by G. Widengren in *The Ascension of the Apostle and the Heavenly Book* (includes also Israelitic, Samaritan, and Jewish-gnostic data and an extensive bibliography); and by E. Cerulli in *Il "Libro della Scala" e la questione delle fonti arabo-spagnole della Divina Commedia.* This mystical Arabic "Book of the Ladder," a detailed description of Mohammed's ascension, has also been made available in a well-annotated Spanish translation by J. Muñoz Sendino, published almost simultaneously with that of Cerulli and entitled *La Escala de Mahoma.* See also G. Levi della Vida's significant corrections and observations relating to both books in his "Nuova luce sulle fonti islamiche della Divina Commedia," *Al-Andalus,* XIV, 377–407; his more popular survey, "Dante et l'Islam, d'après de nouveaux documents," *Revue de la Mediterranée,* XIV, 131–46; and L. Olschki, "Mohammedan Eschatology and Dante's Other World," *Comparative Literature,* III, 1–17. Despite the concentration of these debates on the old problem of the influences of Muslim eschatology on Dante, they have helped clarify many obscure points in the Muslim tradition itself and opened the road for a careful reexamination of the latter's antecedents, including those among the *Merkabah* mystics.

24. *Sefer Yeṣirah,* ed. by Goldschmidt, I.6; IV.4 (pp. 50, 60, 88 n. 58; ed. by Kalisch, I.5; IV.4; pp. 12, 24); *Alphabet of R. 'Aqiba,* letter *he* (Jellinek, III, 23 ff.; Eisenstein, p. 413). Yehudah bar Barzillai came closer to the meaning of the latter passage in *Yeṣirah* when he interpreted the "palace" as referring to that on high, and only in parallel to the earthly Temple in Jerusalem. See his *Perush* (Commentary), ed. by Halberstam, pp. 231 ff.

25. *Sefer Yeṣirah,* ed. by Goldschmidt, I.8, p. 51 (ed. by Kalisch, I.7, pp. 12 f.), with reference to Job 26:7. The number of 3,300 words is a vague approximation, based on Goldschmidt's edition, in which the doublets and alleged interpolations are distinguished by smaller print and occupy more than half the space. Decisions on the genuineness of individual passages are necessarily arbitrary, and in view of the great divergences in the extant manuscripts and early prints the reconstruction of the original text of *Yeṣirah* seems rather hopeless. In the passage cited here the author goes even further; he demands that a pious man should also refrain from thinking about the *Sefirot,* or, as Yehudah bar Barzillai interprets this passage (pp. 165 f.), he should not try to find out the reasons for the various commandments. Needless to say, neither mystics generally nor rational philosophers were ready to submit to such rigid thought controls, although these had behind them a long and revered tradition. In addition to the exegetical work by this Barcelona scholar, we have had frequent occasion to refer to Saadiah's and Dunash's commentaries on *Yeṣirah.* On the latter's compilation in the middle of the tenth century, see G. Vajda's essays "Quelques notes sur le commentaire kairouanais du Sefer Yeṣira," *REJ,* CV, 133 ff., 140; "Le Commentaire kairouanais sur le 'Livre de la Création,'" *ibid.,* CVII, 99–156; CX, 67–92; CXII, 5–33; and "Nouveaux fragments arabes du commentaire de Dunash b. Tamin sur le 'Livre de la Création,'" *ibid.,* CXIII, 37–61. Those by Abraham ben David and Naḥmanides, however, are of very dubious authorship. The former seems not really to have been composed until the fifteenth century by one Joseph ha-Arukh (il Lungo), while the commentary published under

Naḥmanides' name stems from teachings by the distinguished, though somewhat less famous, Gerona mystic 'Azriel. See A. Jellinek's *Beiträge zur Geschichte der Kabbalah,* I, 75 f.; and J. Tishbi's remarks in the introduction to, and the list of sources cited in, his edition of 'Azriel's *Perush ha-Aggadot* (Commentary on Talmudic Legends), pp. 25, 137 f. There exists, however, also a genuine exegetical work by Naḥmanides. Similarly, the genuine *Commentary* by Saadiah, ed. by Lambert, had long been displaced by a spurious work of the same kind, attributed to the gaon but probably written by a German pietist of the fourteenth century. See *infra,* Chap. XXIV, n. 6. The fact that some of these works happen not to have been written by their alleged authors does not deprive them of their great intrinsic and historical value.

26. Saadiah's introduction to his Arabic commentary on *Yeṣirah,* ed. by Lambert, pp. 12 f. (Arabic), 28 f. (French). See G. Vajda's fresh analysis of "Le Commentaire de Saadia sur le Sefer Yeṣira," *REJ,* CVI, 64–85. The *Sidre de-shimmushe rabba ve-sidre hekhalot* was published by Jellinek, VI, 109–11 (by Eisenstein, pp. 547 ff.). See *infra,* n. 30. The replies on the subject of mysticism by Sherira and Hai are fully commented upon by E. E. Hildesheimer in his "Mystik und Agada im Urteile der Gaonen R. Scherira und R. Hai," *Rosenheim Festschrift,* pp. 259 ff. (see the list of sources *ibid.,* pp. 274 f. n. 6). See also Lewin's *Otzar ha-gaonim,* IV, Part 2, pp. 13 ff.

27. Ḥagigah 13a; Pesaḥim 94ab; Agobard of Lyon's epistle, *De Judaicis superstitionibus* in *PL,* CIV, 77–100 (see *supra,* Chap. XXIV, n. 57); Qirqisani's statement cited *supra,* n. 10; and *infra* n. 31; Salmon ben Yeruḥim's *Milḥamot,* ed. by I. Davidson, pp. 114 ff. One should bear in mind, however, that the term *superstitio* was used by medieval Christian controversialists not only with reference to specific irrational concepts or observances of Jews, but often embraced the entire Jewish faith.

28. *She'ur qomah* in the *Alphabet of R. 'Aqiba* under letter *ḥet* (ed. by Jellinek, III, 29 f.; ed. by Eisenstein, p. 415); j. Berakhot, I.1, 2c; Gen. r. xv.6–7, ed. by Theodor and Albeck, pp. 138 ff.; b. Ḥagigah 13b; Maimonides' *Guide,* II.30 (in Friedländer's English trans. p. 217), according to Efodi's and Shem Tob's interpretation, followed by S. Munk in his French trans. of the *Guide,* II, 251 n. 3. Cf. I. Finkelscherer's dissertation, *Mose Maimuni's Stellung zum Aberglauben und zur Mystik.* With his vague terminology, the author of the *She'ur qomah* may even have had in mind not God himself, but His appearance created especially for the benefit of the seekers after Him from among the "descenders of the Chariot." Nevertheless these detailed descriptions shocked even such a literalist as Moses Taku (13th cent.), who otherwise sharply attacked the Jewish philosophers, including Maimonides, for denying the corporeality of God. See also *infra,* Chap. XXXIV, n. 61. On a Muslim parallel to the anthropomorphism of the *She'ur,* see I. Friedlaender, *Heterodoxies,* p. 28 (59).

29. Lewin, *Otzar ha-gaonim,* IV, Part 2, p. 14 (a continuation of the passage cited *supra,* n. 14); Hildesheimer's comments thereon in *Rosenheim Festschrift,* pp. 262 ff.; see also *infra,* Chap. XXXIV, nn. 50 ff. It seems that we possess no pertinent

inquiry antedating Saadiah, and that the great gaon himself had to answer such a query only once. Perhaps as a result of the Karaite onslaught, the problem appeared more serious in the eleventh century, and Hai, as well as his father-in-law, Samuel ben Ḥofni, felt prompted to deal with it at greater length. Samuel, whose works unfortunately are preserved only in fragmentary form, went further in his rationalist denial than Hai. It is to be regretted that Yehudah bar Barzillai limited himself to a general reference to this portion of the literary activity of the last gaon of Sura, because his and Saadiah's works "are not frequently found among us [in Barcelona]." Yehudah himself denied the literal interpretation of the relevant scriptural passages and blamed it on "the heretics and the Gentile nations who had before them the Torah written in foreign languages." See his *Commentary on Yeṣirah*, pp. 76 f., and other passages analyzed by W. Bacher in his "Matériaux pour servir à l'histoire de l'exégèse biblique en Espagne dans la première moitié du XIIe siècle Jehuda b. Barzilai de Barcelone," *REJ*, XVII, 272–84.

30. *Hekhalot r.*, I; *Alphabet of R. 'Aqiba*, letter *vav*, ed. by Jellinek, III, 26, 83 f. (ed. by Eisenstein, pp. 111 f., 413 f.); and *supra*, Vol. II, p. 21. See also the brief tract on magic uses, cited *supra*, n. 25. On the technical meaning of the terms *shimmush* and *hishtammesh* as the equivalents of magic use, see Scholem's *Major Trends*, p. 354 n. 17, with reference to Ḥagigah 15b.

31. Qirqisani's *K. al-Anwar*, VI.9–11, 14, ed. by Nemoy, III, 575 ff., 600 ff. (esp. 9, 33, pp. 586 f.; also available in the French translation by G. Vajda in his "Etudes sur Qirqisani," *REJ*, CVI, 39 ff.); Saadiah's Commentary on *Yeṣirah*, pp. 94 (Arabic), 114 (French); Maimonides' *Guide*, I.62 (English, p. 93), with reference to Prov. 14:15. Maimonides seems to have thought of specific "papers," but he did not identify their author. In all these cases he probably had Byzantine rather than West European homilists in mind, contrary to Holzer's suggestion in his edition of Maimonides' *Commentary* on M. Sanhedrin x, p. 28 n. 47. On the interrelated problems of prophecy and miracles, see *infra*, Chap. XXXIV, nn. 92 ff. The talmudic and posttalmudic practices are illustrated especially by the data assembled by Blau and Trachtenberg in their works cited *supra*, Vol. II, p. 337 n. 26, while the specific divinatory function of dreams is analyzed in L. Nemoy's Hebrew and English rendition of "Al-Qirqisani's Essay on the Psychophysiology of Sleep and Dreams," *Harofé Haivri*, 1949, Part 2, pp. 88–95 (Hebrew), 158–65 (English); R. J. Z. Werblowsky's "Kabbalistische Buchstabenmystik und der Traum," *Zeitschrift für Religions- und Geistesgeschichte*, VII, 164–69 (although mainly analyzing the views of the thirteenth-century Kabbalist Joseph ben Abraham Chiquitilla, this essay sheds light also on the earlier period); and, on the talmudic antecedents, A. Kristianpoller's study of *Traum und Traumdeutung* in *Monumenta talmudica*, IV, 2, 1, pp. 25 f. (Traum und Prophetie), 38 ff. (Traumdeuter). A good general survey of the *Wandlungen in der Auffassung und Deutung des Traumes von den Griechen bis zur Gegenwart* is offered by A. L. Binswanger.

32. Maimonides' *Resp.*, p. 343 No. 373; and *supra*, Chap. XXIV, *passim*. The Fusṭaṭ sage's aversion to the "Greek" communities came to the fore also in many other utterances. See his *Commentary* on M. Sanhedrin x, ed. by Holzer, p. 8; his *Guide*, II.29 (in Friedländer's trans., p. 211); and *supra*, Chap. XXIII, n. 70. But such deprecation of Byzantine Jewry's intellectual achievements need not cast doubt

upon the authenticity of the Maimonidean testimony, reinforced as it is by general historical considerations.

33. Tobiah ben Eliezer's *Midrash Leqaḥ ṭob* on Deut. 4:12, ed. by A. M. Padwa, p. 14; A. Scheiber's "Eléments fabuleux dans l' 'Eshkôl ha-Kôfer' de Juda Hadassi," *REJ,* CVIII, 41–62; the sacred poetry by Amittai ben Shefaṭiah cited *supra,* Chaps. XXV, n. 4; XXXII, n. 63; and, more generally, *supra,* Chaps. XXVII, nn. 91–92; and XXVIII, nn. 27–28. We may recall in this context the interrelations between Byzantino-Slav and Jewish apocalyptic writings, discussed particularly in connection with the various "Visions of Daniel," *supra,* Chap. XIX, n. 6. See also, from another angle, *infra,* Chap. XXXV, n. 25.

34. The strong survivals of gnostic-Manichaean influences in all Byzantine civilizations have become much clearer in recent years. See esp. the studies by S. Runciman, *The Medieval Manichee,* and D. Obolensky, *The Bogomils: a Study in Balkan Neo-Manichaeism.* Unfortunately, we have little information about the medieval Jewish communities in Asia Minor, the main focus of the ancient mystery religions and Marcionite gnosticism, on whose long-range impact see E. C. Blackman, *Marcion and His Influence.* Much as Anatolian Jewry undoubtedly hated Marcionite antisemitism and that sect's rejection of the Old Testament, it could not remain totally immune to the powerful spiritual forces and the underlying social factors of which that great "heresy" was both effect and cause. We must be grateful for such incidental glimpses as are offered by A. Dupont-Sommer's interpretation of "Deux lamelles d'argent à inscription hebréo-araméenne trouvés à Āğabeyli (Turquie)," *Jahrbuch für kleinasiatische Forschung,* I, 201–17. We are no better informed about the ancient Jewries in such border regions as Armenia, which gave rise to the powerful sect of Paulicians. Through their very opposition to the Old Testament, as well as their dualist teachings, they must have raised many questions among the inquiring minds of their Jewish compatriots, too. Despite the paucity of relevant Jewish materials, a careful reexamination of all extant data by both Byzantinists and students of mysticism might, therefore, yield some interesting clues to the transition from Eastern to Western Jewish mystic lore.

35. The relations between the nascent Provençal center of the newer forms of Jewish mysticism and the twelfth-century Christian heresies still are far from clarified. On the one hand, as we shall presently see, the teachings of the Provençal Jewish mystics have emerged from age-old obscurity only in recent years as a result of the intensive researches by Gershom Scholem and his disciples. On the other hand, many important documents concerning the rise and doctrines of the Christian Catharii have likewise but recently become available to students. There has also arisen a newly awakened interest among Western scholars, stimulated by the social unrest of our time, in the "subversive" nature of these heretical movements and their meaning within the general context of Franco-Italian history of that period. See esp. the numerous documents, published since 1949 by D. Roché and others in the successive volumes of *Cahiers d'études cathares,* and the careful analytical studies by H. Söderberg, *La Religion des Cathares,* and by A. Borst, *Die Katharer.* The latter volume contains not only ample bibliographies of earlier researches and a good survey of Catharist doctrines, but also valuable notes on A. Dondaine's edition of the Catharist *Liber de duobus principiis.*

On the eleventh-century antecedents and the impact of Byzantine heterodoxies through the mediation of the returning Crusaders, see also Ilarino da Milano, "Le Eresie popolari del secolo XI nell' Europa occidentale," *Studi Gregoriani,* ed. by G. B. Borino, II, 43–89; the essay by C. Thouzellier and other analytical and bibliographical studies listed *supra,* Chap. XXI, n. 54. The ever increasing literature on the Albigensian Crusade and the subsequent history of the southern French Inquisition has also brought forth some relevant new materials useful in retrospect also for the understanding of the earlier evolution. Since most of that information stems from the thirteenth century or later, a fuller consideration of the light these new researches shed on Provençal Jewish life and thought must be relegated to a later volume.

36. See Mann, *Texts and Studies,* II, 75 f., 80 f.; and *supra,* n. 27. In his *Reshit ha-Qabbalah* G. Scholem devoted a lengthy appendix (pp. 195–238) to the study of that anonymous commentary on the *She'ur qomah,* including its quotations from the *Raza rabba.* How many more passages the commentator borrowed from the "Great Mystery" without indicating his source is impossible to ascertain today. We cannot be absolutely confident that that book reached him in its approximately original form, nor, for that matter, do we know that he himself was exactingly accurate in his citations. But we have at least an idea of the content and style of *Raza rabba,* whereas most of the other writings bunched together by Qumisi in his wholesale censure have thus far remained mere titles. There is no way of telling, therefore, to what extent they may have served as sources for the compiler of *Bahir* and other Western mystics.

37. Relatively the best, though not technically critical, edition of the *Sefer ha-Bahir* (Book of the Bright Light) is that edited by Reuben Margulies. Based upon four manuscripts and on many quotations in subsequent letters, this edition is provided with commentaries by one of Solomon ibn Adret's pupils, by Mordecai Jafeh, and by the editor, as well as (in part) with concise marginal notes by Elijah Gaon of Vilna. Of great value also is G. Scholem's earlier German translation of *Das Buch Bahir,* based principally on the Munich MS and likewise provided with illuminating comments. Scholem has also repeatedly analyzed that book's historical framework, its leading ideas and their origin. See esp. his "Zur Frage der Entstehung der Kabbala," *Korrespondenzblatt . . . Akademie für die Wissenschaft des Judentums,* IX, 5–26; and his more recent *Reshit ha-Qabbalah,* pp. 23–65. Here Scholem points out that particularly the *Bahir*'s explanation of *Tohu va-bohu* in the cosmogeny of the Book of Genesis closely follows the theories expounded by Abraham bar Ḥiyya in his *Hegyon ha-nefesh,* fol. 3ab; and his *Megillat ha-megalleh,* pp. 16 f. It is not at all surprising that this remarkable scientist, who combined a rigorously scientific approach to geometrical problems with an astrological conception of history and actual computations of the date of the arrival of the Messiah, should also have influenced the final formulation of the book *Bahir.* See *supra,* Chaps. XXV, n. 23; XXVIII, nn. 97–98; and *infra,* Chap. XXXIV, nn. 13, 54. However such borrowings from twelfth-century thinkers were probably interpolations into already existing texts, rather than part and parcel of the original formulation.

38. *Sefer ha-Bahir,* ed. by Margulies, fols. 1ab No. 1 (the editor cites here Solomon Labi's explanation from the latter's commentary on the *Zohar*), 8b No. 13; in

Scholem's German trans. pp. 1 ff. No. 1, 12 f. No. 10. On the problem of light and darkness, which so deeply agitated the minds of all dualists and affected also the thinking of their neighbors, see esp. the anonymous midrashim ed. by Mann, and Saadiah's views mentioned *supra,* Chaps. XXIV, n. 33; and XXIX, n. 66. Despite the lack of clarity and even inherent contradictions in the formulas here cited, our author is by no means sympathetic to any form of dualism. This becomes doubly clear in his treatment of the related doctrine of Satan, the Evil principle in the universe. In a bluntly antidualistic vein he answers his own query, "What is Satan? It is to teach us that the Holy One, blessed be He, possesses an attribute whose name is Evil. . . ." Even though in the continuation he combines this definition with some of the ancient mythologumena of the Evil coming from the north, which had found a distinct echo already in the Bible, he leaves not the slightest doubt of his conviction that Evil as well as Good ultimately stems from God alone. See the text, ed. by Margulies, fol. 71a No. 162; in Scholem's trans., pp. 116 f. No. 109; his *Reshit ha-Qabbalah,* pp. 55 f.; and *supra,* Vol. I, pp. 338 f. n. 45. True, in his "Kabbalah und Mythus," *Eranos-Jahrbuch,* XVII, 295, Scholem points out how much further the author of *Bahir* went in his attribution of the Evil principle to God Himself than, for example, Yehudah bar Barzillai. Nevertheless, even he never seriously overstepped the bounds of traditional Jewish lore, and in this respect he diverged sharply from the overtly dualistic Christian sectarians.

39. *Bahir,* ed. by Margulies, fols. 2b ff. Nos. 3, 14, 15, 18 (all on letter *bet*), 17 (on *alef*), 19–20 (on *gimmel*), 27, 36 (on *dalet*), 28–29 (on *he,* includes R. Amorai's angry exclamation), 30 (on *vav*), 34 (on *ḥet*). A somewhat different arrangement appears in the Munich MS followed in Scholem's trans., where the important discussion on *he* is found on p. 25 No. 20. The omission of the seventh letter *zayin* is no more meaningful than our author's failure to include comments on the subsequent letters of the alphabet, except for *nun* and *mim* (in that order) in Margulies' edition, fols. 36b f. Nos. 83–86. Such comments may indeed have been included in the original compilation and dropped in the final selection. Similarly, the relative neglect of the first letter of the alphabet, which because of its numerical value of one lent itself particularly well to mystic speculations on the oneness of God and related subjects and indeed plays a great role in the letter symbolism of other mystics, may have been owing to such later selectivity or even to purely accidental causes. As a matter of fact, our author attaches to *alef* the utmost importance: "R. Amorai [some versions have Reḥomai] sat and preached, Why is *alef* placed at the head? Because it precedes in time everything else, even the Torah." This primordial nature of the first letter, contrasting with the *bet* of *bereshit* (In the beginning; Gen. 1:1) which merely marked the beginning of the present world, lends it permanent distinction. In another context our author declares bluntly that without the opening of the letter *alef* the universe (or man) could not persist. No wonder that this symbolism was open to a variety of interpretations, even a variety of readings. Cf. the commentators on *Bahir,* fol. 9ab Nos. 15, 17; and Scholem's comments on his trans., pp. 13 ff. Nos. 11, 13. On the origin and the multifarious aspects of the doctrine of the divine Presence (*Shekhinah*) in the Aggadah and Jewish mysticism, see Scholem's penetrating study, "Zur Entwicklungsgeschichte der kabbalistischen Konzeption der Schechinah," *Eranos-Jahrbuch,* XXI, 45–107. See also *supra,* nn. 13 and 18.

40. *Bahir,* fols. 53ab Nos. 121–22, 88a No. 195 (in somewhat different formulations in Scholem's trans., pp. 93 No. 86, 148 ff. No. 135). The meaning of this passage, reinforced by many other passages, is quite clear, and Ibn Adret's pupil did no violence to the text (though he did not hesitate to do so on other occasions) when he summed up its meaning that the "generation cometh" relates to the generation "which had previously come in an earlier transmigration. Because of its misconduct then it came to the world again to correct its misdeeds" (Margulies' edition, *loc. cit.*). This interpretation of the verse in Ecclesiastes may indeed have already been in the mind of the talmudic sage who had first furnished a similar explanation of the apparent reversal of the natural order in the related verse in Ecclesiastes (12:7). See Shabbat 152b; and the comments thereon cited by Scholem in his *Reshit,* p. 44, n. 1. See also, more fully, Scholem's detailed reexamination of "Seelenwanderung und Sympathie der Seelen in der jüdischen Mystik," *Eranos-Jahrbuch,* XXIV, 55–118. Nonetheless, to confirmed opponents of the doctrine of metempsychosis, this reiterated emphasis must have carried with it a strongly heretical connotation. On 'Anan's and the philosophers' attitude to that doctrine, see *supra,* Chap. XXIV, n. 24; and *infra,* Chap. XXXIV, n. 65. The studied obscurities in the *Bahir*'s views on transmigration of souls are matched by similar ambiguities in the pertinent teachings of the Balkan Bogomils. See D. Obolensky, *The Bogomils,* p. 215.

41. Meir ben Simon's letter, excerpted from a Parma MS and trans. by A. Neubauer in "The Bahir and the Zohar," *JQR,* [o.s.] IV, 358 f.; and cited in Scholem's *Reshit ha-Qabbalah,* p. 19. Characteristically, neither the protagonists nor the opponents of the *Bahir* during the twelfth and early thirteenth centuries have left behind much articulate literary material. Evidently, the mystic lore was cultivated at that time in very restricted circles and created no stir even among the intellectuals until it achieved complete respectability through the distinguished halakhists of Narbonne and Posquières. See note 42.

42. Cf. Yehudah bar Barzillai al-Barceloni's oft-quoted *Commentary on Yeṣirah,* ed. by Halberstam, with the editor's comments (pp. ix f.) on the insufficiencies of the existing manuscripts. On Abraham ben Isaac's great dependence on Yehudah's juristic work, the *Sefer ha-'Ittim,* see *supra,* Chap. XXVII, n. 81. That Yehudah had visited Lunel, and not associated with Abraham ben Isaac in Barcelona as is usually assumed, is asserted on the basis of a rather forced reasoning by B. Z. Benedikt in his "The History of the Provençal Center of Jewish Learning" (Hebrew), *Tarbiz,* XXII, 109. Benedikt also doubts the long-accepted teacher-pupil relationship between Yehudah and Abraham, although he does not impugn the authenticity of Abraham's statement that he had "seen Yehudah bar Barzillai many times." See his Hebrew review of the *Entsiklopediah le-toledot gedole Yisrael,* Vols. I–II, ed. by M. Margulies, *KS,* XXIV, 8. Regrettably, too few mystic teachings by Abraham are transmitted even at second hand for us to judge to what extent he may have deviated, at least occasionally, from Al-Barceloni's doctrines expounded in that extensive commentary. Yet it stands to reason that, since the deviations in the homiletical-hermeneutic field of the Provençal communities, as represented by the school of Moses the Preacher, were apparently greater than the halakhic differences, Abraham departed from his Barcelonian model more extensively in his mystic teachings than in his *Eshkol.* The secret nature of these teachings was also

conducive to greater deviation, especially since they were unlikely to generate a different practical behavior which mattered most to the leaders.

43. Jacob ben Moses of Bagnoles in A. Neubauer's "Documents inédits," *REJ*, IX, 55; Shem Tob ben Abraham ibn Gaon's *Sefer Badde ha-aron* (Staves of the Ark; a commentary on the mystical-masoretic *Sefer Tagin* or *Liber Coronalarum*), in the excerpt, ed. from an Oxford MS by G. Scholem in his "A New Document for the History of Early Kabbalah" (Hebrew), *Sefer Bialik,* ed. by J. Fichman, p. 153; Moses Taku's aforementioned *Ketab tamim* (Unblemished Work), ed. by R. Kirchheim in *Ozar nechmad,* III, 71; Yehudah ibn Tibbon's Hebrew trans. of Baḥya's *Duties of the Heart,* Preface and Chap. 1 end, ed. by Zifroni, pp. 2 f., 55 f.; English trans. by Hyamson, I, 51; G. Scholem, "Zur Frage der Entstehung der Kabbala," *KA,* IX, 18; and his *Reshit ha-Qabbalah,* pp. 66 ff. In his Hebrew essay on "R. Moses ben Joseph of Narbonne" in *Tarbiz,* XIX, 23 n. 53, B. Z. Benedikt rejects Neubauer's interpretation that Jacob ben Moses' statement refers to the Narbonnese leader as "one of the first kabbalists." He thinks that the term refers only to Moses as one of the fountainheads of the tradition in Oral Law. Since none of Moses' works are extant, it is difficult to judge what his attitude to secret lore was. In any case, he undoubtedly applied to himself the restraints characteristic of the entire Provençal school, including his own pupil Abraham ben David, and kept his mystic teachings within the restricted circle of devotees while publicly discussing only halakhic and ritualistic questions. Even in this area he evidently was a pioneer, who through his literary work tried to safeguard the continuity of Provençal traditions against the incursion of geonic, African, and Spanish patterns which, through the works of Ḥananel and Alfasi, soon began to dominate the thinking of the southern French jurists as well. Hence also his leanings toward the juridical doctrines of the schools of Gershom bar Yehudah and Rashi which represented northern French traditions akin to those current in southern France. This clear-cut separation between the explicit and the secret lore was certainly characteristic of Moses' senior colleague, Abraham ben Isaac, although it began breaking down in the works of his pupil Abraham ben David. On the connections between these Provençal mystics and their counterparts in Germany, from whom they must have received more than an early version of *Bahir,* see *supra,* n. 36; and *infra,* n. 48.

44. Abraham ben David in the introduction to his *Ḥiddushim* (Novellae) on the talmudic tractate 'Eduyot, with the comments thereon by H. Gross in his aforementioned biographical sketch, "R. Abraham b. David," *MGWJ,* XXIII, 169; and Scholem in his *Reshit ha-Qabbalah,* pp. 71 f. On Ben David's great self-assurance in the juridical field, see *supra,* Chap. XXVII, esp. nn. 82, 99, 122. No comprehensive analysis of the mystical teachings scattered through the numerous halakhic and exegetical works of this distinguished Provençal scholar has thus far been published, but one may be expected in I. Twersky's forthcoming biography.

45. Abraham ben David's *Hassagot* on *M.T.* Teshubah III.7; Yesode ha-torah I.10; Bet ha-beḥirah XIV.16. The latter passage struck the copyists of the Maimonidean Code and Ben David's strictures thereon as so incongruous in a purely juridical work that they eliminated it from most MSS and editions. It has been preserved, however, in a citation by Joseph Karo, as mystically minded a halakhist as any, in his *Kosef mishneh* (Double Desire; a commentary on the Maimonidean Code),

Yesode ha-torah I.10. This passage had already been quoted by Shem Tob ibn Gaon, who had lived much closer to Abraham both geographically and chronologically, in his *Migdal 'oz* (Tower of Strength; a commentary on the Maimonidean Code), *ad loc.* (The reversal of that quotation in the usual editions, which make it appear as if Ibn Gaon had quoted Karo, is of course chronologically untenable.) This citation gave Ibn Gaon the opportunity to record the legend that in his old age the revered master of Fusṭaṭ had himself seen the light and been converted to mysticism. On this legend, in part the outgrowth of the anti-Maimonidean controversy, see G. Scholem's succinct review of these later data in his "From Philosopher to Kabbalist (a Legend of the Kabbalists on Maimonides"; Hebrew), *Tarbiz,* VI, Part 3 (The Maimonides Book), pp. 90–98; and R. Margulies's more recent, but less critical, analysis of "Maimonides and the *Zohar*" (Hebrew), *Sinai,* XVI, No. 193, pp. 263–74; XVII, Nos. 195–200, pp. 9–15, 128–35, 219–24; Nos. 201–7, pp. 227–30, 386–95.

46. Asher ben David (Abraham's grandson), in a MS excerpt from his "Commentary on the Thirteen Divine Attributes" communicated by M. Soave in his "RABD the Fourth" (Hebrew), *Ozar nechmad,* IV, 37; Meir ibn Sahula, *Be'ur* (Explanation; a supercommentary on Naḥmanides' Commentary on the Pentateuch), 1875, fol. 4c and the excerpt cited from British Museum and Oxford MSS by Scholem in his *Reshit ha-Qabbalah,* p. 79 n. 2. Like his friend, Shem Tob ibn Gaon, Meir is not an altogether reliable witness for mystic statements allegedly made by revered predecessors. Nor is the homely parable of the complete harmony between man and woman and the similar intertwining of the divine attributes of Mercy and Justice (supported by the homily that it was YHWH, standing for the attribute of Mercy, who nevertheless is recorded to have "caused to rain upon Sodom and upon Gomorrah brimstone and fire" [Gen. 19:24], a function usually associated with the attribute of Justice) quite in keeping with what we know about Abraham ben David's style even in his homilies. Yet, the substance of that discourse may well have been authentic.

47. See *supra,* Chaps. XXIII, n. 72; XXVII, n. 149. We know too little about the inner life of German Jewry during the Merovingian age to judge to what extent the barbarian migrations had interrupted the continuity of the socioreligious patterns of life developed during the Roman occupation. But it stands to reason that there were at least some underground folkloristic survivals in the communities of Treves, Cologne, and others from the ancient period. Cf., however, *supra,* Chap. XX, n. 83.

48. Eleazar Roqeaḥ of Worms, *Perush ha-tefillot* (Commentary on Prayers), cited from a MS by Joseph Solomon Delmedigo of Candia in his *Maṣref le-ḥokhmah* (Refinement of Wisdom), Odessa ed., 1865, pp. 41 f. See also B. Klar's ed. of the *Chronicle of Aḥimaaz,* pp. 57, 128, 151; A. Neubauer's "Abou Ahron, le Babylonien," *REJ,* XXIII, 230 f.; and *supra,* Chap. XXIII, n. 69.

49. Yehudah bar Samuel's *Sefer ha-Kabod* (Book of [Divine] Glory), cited by Moses Taku (of Tachau) in his *Ketab tamim,* ed. by R. Kirchheim in *Ozar nechmad,* III, 65. On Yehudah's indebtedness in this point to the genuine Saadiah and Yehudah bar Barzillai see V. Aptowitzer's *Mabo,* pp. 345 ff.; and *supra,* n. 42. See also *infra,* Chap. XXXIV, n. 54. In his more popular "Book of the Pious" Yehudah bar Samuel generally steered clear of such metaphysical problems, although he fre-

quently referred to the duty of fearing the Lord and its manifold implications. Even in his homily on the mysterious theophany to Moses, he limited himself to such mystical teachings as the following: "It is written 'I will all my goodness [*kol ṭubi*] pass before thee' [Exod. 33:19], *kol* is by *gemaṭria* the equivalent of fifty. This refers to the fifty gates of Understanding. Over each gate an angel *kol ṭubi* is appointed, which is by *gemaṭria* [77] the equivalent of *mazzal* [*omen*]." Here Yehudah intimates that all the secrets which future scholars were going to discover and write up in books were included in the Torah given to Moses, the prophets resembling in this respect the angels overseeing the gates of Understanding. See his *Sefer Ḥasidim,* ed. by Wistinetzki, pp. 369 f. No. 1514. It is primarily these excursions into angelology and, more frequently, demonology which give the book the aura of mysticism, since for the most part it deals only with simple ethical and folkloristic concepts.

50. Eleazar of Worms, *Hilkhot ha-kabod* (Laws of Glory), cited in Scholem's *Major Trends,* p. 91; A. Borst, *Die Katharer,* p. 94 n. 19; *supra,* Chap. XXI, n. 18. In his penetrating essay "The Religious-Social Tendency of 'Sepher Ḥasidim'" (Hebrew), *Zion,* III, 15 f., Y. Baer adduces several other examples of such appearances of ghosts of dead persons and contends that this belief had penetrated Jewish folklore from the German. However, antecedents of such beliefs in the intervention of underworld forces in the affairs of living men are very ancient; they were widely held throughout the ancient Mediterranean world. Aḥimaaz of Oria, too, relates the weird story of the Babylonian visitor Aaron (or Abu Aaron), who by attentively listening to the precentor during a synagogue service noticed that the latter omitted the divine name. From that omission of a single word in an otherwise impeccable performance, Aaron deduced that the precentor had been dead for some time. As a ghost he had refrained from mentioning the name of God in accordance with the Psalmist's assertion that "the dead praise not the Lord" (115:17). Exposed by the Babylonian visitor, the ghost acknowledged his fraudulent action. See *The Chronicle of Ahimaaz,* ed. by Salzman, pp. 4 (Hebrew), 64 (English); ed. by Klar, p. 15. It would seem that this story originated from Aaron's Babylonian background but was subsequently embellished by the imagination of its South Italian narrator. In any case, the latter expected no serious objections from his compatriots. In this entire obscure domain of folk beliefs and superstitions concepts traveled far and wide, and it is next to impossible to trace either their origin or the way in which they were transplanted from one civilization to another. See also *infra,* n. 52.

51. *Sefer Ḥasidim,* ed. by Wistinetzki, p. 76 No. 211; *supra,* Chap. XXXII, n. 64. See B. Rosenfeld, *Die Golemsage und ihre Verwertung in der deutschen Literatur,* and esp. G. Scholem, "Die Vorstellung vom Golem in ihren tellurischen und magischen Beziehungen," *Eranos-Jahrbuch,* XXII, 235–89.

52. *Sefer Ḥasidim,* pp. 76 f. Nos. 210, 212; and *supra,* Chap. XXVIII, n. 91. From passages like these N. H. Simchoni had concluded that Yehudah the Pious and his circle had tried to tone down the eschatological elements in Judaism. This view had not entirely been controverted by Scholem's arguments in his *Major Trends,* pp. 87 f. Of course, none of the German pietists ever abandoned the messianic hope as such, for it had become too deeply ingrained in the entire mental outlook of all medieval Jews. The "Book of the Pious" itself contains a number of passages relating

to the belief in the ultimate advent of the Redeemer. It even describes certain actions of man, for instance allowing another person to suffer the penalty for one's own misdeeds, as delaying that advent (p. 63 No. 147). But it is quite possible that Yehudah and his immediate associates, aware of the ravages caused by the messianic frenzy in the daily life of numerous individuals during the age of the Crusades and cognizant of the old Judeo-Christian controversy on the messianic issue, tried to deemphasize this element of the traditional lore. Other pietists, however, from the days of Eleazar of Worms felt no compunction about playing up the messianic theme to the full.

53. *Sefer Ḥasidim,* pp. 276 No. 1086, 305 f. No. 1233, and *passim.* See *supra,* Chaps. XXI, nn. 43–44; XXII, n. 72; XXIV, n. 58. Needless to say, these leading pietists, although themselves belonging to the upper classes, did not seek to justify wealth, but rather viewed it as but a necessary component of the divinely instituted world order. Every page in the "Book of the Pious" testifies to their deep concern for the poor and the humble. In their attempt to level social differences they were even prepared to lower the barriers separating the learned from the illiterate and to emphasize again and again the limited value of learning, which is to be truly appreciated only if it is combined with, and leads to, good deeds. If their attitude toward both wealth and learning sometimes appears ambivalent, even contradictory, we must remember that these men were enthusiastic preachers, not logicians.

54. See Baer's aforementioned essay in *Zion,* III. Here the impact of the Christian pietistic concepts, at that time propagated especially by Franciscan preachers, is demonstrated by plausible arguments and illustrated by a number of telling quotations. It must be borne in mind, however, that the "Book of the Pious" agrees with these contemporary Christian approaches only in such ethical and folkloristic teachings as are in full accord with the traditional Jewish legal and ethical doctrines. Wherever there had previously existed a chasm between the two religions, it was by no means bridged over by the medieval German pietists. In fact, conversion to Christianity was constantly treated by Yehudah and his associates as both the sin of sins and a personal calamity for the individual and the community. Nor were they ever ready to compromise with any of the antinomian tendencies carried down from the early centuries of Christianity. The similarities—these are more frequent than direct influences—and the detailed effects of the new climate of opinion in both camps touch the periphery more than the core of Jewish life and leave all its truly differentiating manifestations wholly unimpaired. For this reason even the most devoted of halakhists—and Eleazar of Worms certainly was one—could not take issue with the practical lessons of German Ḥasidism. See also *supra,* n. 49.

55. See T. W. Danzel's pertinent, though only preliminary, remarks on *Magie und Geheimwissenschaft in ihrer Bedeutung für Kultur und Kulturgeschichte.*

CHAPTER XXXIV: FAITH AND REASON

1. See the sources cited *supra,* Chap. XXIV, n. 1. Much of the material discussed in that chapter, "Socioreligious Controversies," naturally has a bearing on our present discussion. However, there the emphasis lay principally on the issues dividing the representatives of the three faiths; here it is on those which were of common concern to them all. Even the Manichaeans, *zindiqs,* and dualists, briefly referred to in that chapter, offered far less of a challenge to all established religions, not only because of their relatively small numbers and limited influence, but also because in many essentials they, too, shared the monotheistic religious concept which had overcome ancient paganism. By emphasizing two, rather than one, principles, the dualists themselves were far closer to the monotheistic outlook than to that of ancient polytheism.

2. See the brief studies on Domninus, as well as Marinus, cited *supra,* Chap. XVI, n. 9; and P. Tannery, "Un Manuel d'introduction arithmétique du philosophe Domninos de Larissa," *Revue des études greques,* XIX, 359–82 (includes French trans. of text and references to earlier publications); and more generally, *supra,* Vols. I, p. 387 n. 48; II, p. 391 n. 38. See also I. Heinemann's data, largely medieval, on "The Struggle against Anthropomorphism in Greece and in Israel" (Hebrew), *Eyoon* (*'Iyyun*), I, 147–65; and on "Die wissenschaftliche Allegoristik des jüdischen Mittelalters," *HUCA,* XXIII, Part 1, pp. 611–43.

There is, of course, an enormous literature on the religious philosophy of the medieval Arabs and, to a lesser extent, of the eastern Christians. For our purpose we need but refer to the aforementioned general histories of the respective literatures by Brockelmann, Graf, Baumstark, Chabot, and Krumbacher and the numerous monographs mentioned in our earlier and forthcoming notes. See also the brief review of *La Philosophie byzantine* by B. Tatakis, in E. Bréhier's *Histoire de la philosophie,* Supplementary Vol., and the good general survey and bibliographical documentation in L. Gardet and M. M. Anawati's *Introduction à la théologie musulmane: essai de théologie comparée,* where the comparison, however, extends to works of Christian rather than medieval Jewish thinkers. This shortcoming is doubly regrettable, as H. A. Wolfson, in his series of studies ranging from Philo to Spinoza, has shown the intrinsic affinities between the ideas formulated by the Arabian philosophers and their Jewish as well as Christian predecessors and successors. Other writings are conveniently listed in P. J. de Menasce's bibliographical guide to *Arabische Philosophie.* Since the main contacts of Jews with Western Christian scholasticism came after 1200, their fuller consideration will have to be relegated to a future volume. From the vast array of pertinent publications we need mention here only G. B. Ladner's "Bibliographical Survey: the History of Ideas in the Christian Middle Ages from the Fathers to Dante in American and Canadian Publications of the Years 1940–1952," *Traditio,* IX, 449–514; and J. Isaac's or P. M. de Coutenson's reviews, "Bulletin d'histoire de la philosophie médiévale" in the *Revue des sciences philosophiques et théologiques,* XXXV, 255–81; XXXVII, 343–71; XXXVIII, 777–91.

Medieval Jewish philosophy, too, has been studied by modern scholars for the last several generations with great intensity and acumen. A good general survey may be obtained from I. Husik, *A History of Medieval Jewish Philosophy*, 2d ed.; supplemented by several of his *Philosophical Essays, Ancient, Medieval and Modern*, ed. by M. C. Nahm and L. Strauss. A penetrating, although in many ways one-sided, analysis was offered by D. Neumark in his *Geschichte der jüdischen Philosophie des Mittelalters, nach Problemen dargestellt;* and, with considerable modifications, in the incomplete Hebrew translation of this work, under the title *Toledot ha-pilosophiah be-Yisrael* (both unfinished). These volumes are supplemented by a number of papers included in his collected *Essays in Jewish Philosophy*. In *Die Philosophie des Judentums* Julius Guttmann has restated the vital issues in an independent fashion. See also his "Religion und Wissenschaft im mittelalterlichen und modernen Denken," *Festschrift der Hochschule für die Wissenschaft des Judentums*, pp. 145–216; his collection of studies trans. into Hebrew by S. Esh under the title, *Dat u-madda'* (Religion and Knowledge); and some of his other essays listed by B. Schochetmann in his Hebrew bibliographical study of "The Writings of Isaac (Julius) Guttmann," in *Eyoon ('Iyyun)*, II, 11–19, supplemented by J. Fleischmann's notes *ibid.*, pp. 182–84. More recently another, more up-to-date but unfortunately undocumented, summary has been presented by G. Vajda in his *Introduction à la pensée juive du moyen âge*. The selected bibliography appended to this volume, however, as well as his even more recent (1950) bibliographical introduction to *Jüdische Philosophie*, will offer the student some guidance in the main primary and secondary sources. See also K. Schubert's concise review of "Die Problemstellung in der mittelalterlichen jüdischen Religionsphilosophie vor Maimunides," *Zeitschrift für katholische Theologie*, LXXV, 55–81.

3. While Benjamin's legal teachings are succinctly summarized in his *Mas'at Binyamin*, his theological and philosophic doctrines (on which see *infra*, n. 50) are expanded in a series of biblical commentaries, of which only a small portion has been published. The same holds true for the works of his immediate successor, Daniel al-Qumisi. See *supra*, Chaps. XXVI, nn. 20, 24; XXIX, nn. 54, 65–66. Fuller publication of their manuscripts still available in the world's libraries and detailed analyses of their teachings by competent students of medieval Jewish thought are likely to shed much new light on the first stirrings of constructive Jewish rationalism during the crucial ninth century. In contrast thereto, the vestiges of the evidently more destructive rationalist critique by Ḥivi have been subjected to repeated careful scrutiny. See *supra*, Chap. XXIX, nn. 87 ff.

4. The fragments of Al-Muqammiṣ' *Ishrun maqalat* (Twenty Tractates), included in Yehudah bar Barzillai's *Commentary on Yeṣirah*, pp. 65 f., 77 ff., 151 f., have thus far been the basis of practically all the analytical comments by modern students. However, the much larger text, preserved in the Arabic original in a Leningrad MS, though announced by Harkavy as far back as 1898, has never been made available to scholars. Only a few pages therefrom have been published with a Russian translation by M. J. [I.] Ginzburg in the *Zapiski Kollegii Vostokovedov*, V, 481–506. Another passage, doubtless part of the "Tractates" but bearing the separate title "Book Containing Questions as to the Unity of God and the Rational and Traditional Explanation of the Ten Sephirot," was published with an English translation by E. N. Adler and I. Broydé in "An Ancient Bookseller's Catalogue," *JQR*, [o.s.]

XIII, 60 f. In so far as they cover the same ground, this section bears out the accuracy of the Hebrew rendition. Also to be mentioned are Al-Muqammiṣ' "Fifty Queries in Refutation of the Christians," of which only a few lines have been recovered by Hirschfeld (in "The Arabic Portion of the Cairo Geniza at Cambridge," *JQR,* [o.s.] XV, 682, 688 f.); and his commentary on the Bible, whose very title is unknown to us. The recovery of the latter text would undoubtedly shed new light on both the early philosophic and exegetical studies among Jews. See also I. Goldziher's introduction to his ed. of "Pseudo-Baḥya" (see *infra,* n. 11), pp. 18 f.; and J. Mann's denial of Al-Muqammiṣ' authorship of a fragment previously published by A. Marmorstein. See Mann's own more extensive publication of that and additional fragments of "An Early Theologico-Polemical Work" in *HUCA,* XII–XIII, 411 ff. Although not from Al-Muqammiṣ' pen, this work, too, testifies to the awakened philosophic curiosity among the Jews of the tenth century. Our author rejects the views of some Jewish adherents of the Mu'tazilites Al-Jubai and his son Abu Hashim (see *infra,* n. 8), but he follows Mu'tazilite patterns in devoting the entire first book in seven chapters to a discussion of the central problem of the Unity of God (pp. 449 ff.), which was also Al-Muqammiṣ' main concern. Unfortunately, only a small part of that book has thus far come to light. See *supra,* Chap. XXIX, n. 67.

Like Benjamin, Al-Muqammiṣ, the second distinguished pioneer in medieval Jewish philosophy, would certainly have deserved more concentrated attention on the part of modern specialists, particularly in view of his connections with the Syriac scholars. On the latter's historic influence, see, e.g., G. Klinge's analysis of "Die Bedeutung der syrischen Theologen als Vermittler der griechischen Philosophie an den Islam," *Zeitschrift für Kirchengeschichte,* LVIII, 346–86; and V. Ryssel's detailed older study, "Ueber den textkritischen Werth der syrischen Uebersetzungen griechischer Klassiker" in *Programm des Nikolaigymnasiums in Leipzig, 1880–81.* A careful study of Al-Muqammiṣ' fragments may, therefore, retroactively even shed some light on those vital, but hitherto obscure, relations between Syriac and Jewish theologians before and soon after the rise of Islam. Certainly such interrelations were not restricted to the mere techniques of Masorah, Bible exegesis, law, and poetry.

5. Isaac ben Solomon Israeli's *Commentary* on Genesis and Dunash ibn Tamim's *Commentary on Sefer Yeṣirah* have been discussed *supra,* Chaps. XXIX, n. 63; and XXXIII, n. 25. Of Israeli's Book of Definitions (*K. al-Ḥadud;* in Hebrew *Sefer ha-Gebulim*), which in its Hebrew translation by Nissim ben Solomon bears the nondescript title, *Ḥibbur* (Tractate), we possess small fragments in both Arabic and Hebrew, published by H. (N.) Hirschfeld in "The Arabic Portion," *JQR,* [o.s.] XV, 682 f., 689–93; and in *Festschrift Steinschneider,* Hebrew section, pp. 131–41, respectively. See also Hirschfeld's introductory remarks, *ibid.,* German section, pp. 233 f.; and A. Altmann's more recent "Isaac Israeli's *Book of Definitions:* Some Fragments of a Second Hebrew Translation," *Journal of Semitic Studies,* II, 232–42. The title, *Liber de definitionibus,* is borrowed from a much longer designation in the medieval Latin translation by Gerard of Cremona, critically edited by J. T. Muckle in *AHDL,* XII–XIII, 299–340. Of the "Book of Elements" we have a fairly comprehensive medieval Hebrew translation by Abraham ben Samuel ibn Ḥisdai, entitled *Sefer ha-Yesodot,* which was edited by S. Fried in 1900. An old Latin translation by Gerard (?) was included in the *Omnia Opera* of Isaac (Ysaac), published in Lyons, 1515. More recently S. M. Stern and A. Altmann have published, respectively, "The Fragments of Isaac Israeli's 'Book of Substances' " and "Isaac Israeli's 'Chapter

on the Elements' (MS Mantua)," the latter in the anonymous Hebrew rendition, with an English trans., in *JJS,* VII, 13–29, 31–57. It must be admitted, however, that Israeli's authorship of that "Chapter" still is somewhat in doubt. One must await further elucidation from the forthcoming volume on Israeli's philosophy, now in preparation by these two authors. Of comparative interest are also "Les Notes d'Avicenne sur la 'Théologie d'Aristote,'" discussed by G. Vajda in *Revue thomiste,* LI, 346–406; and A. J. Borisov's essay cited *infra,* n. 16. The older literature includes M. Steinschneider's data in *Die hebräischen Uebersetzungen des Mittelalters,* pp. 388 ff.; Jakob Guttmann's still useful analysis of *Die philosophischen Lehren des Isaak ben Salomon Israeli;* and *infra,* Chap. XXXVI, n. 29.

6. See S. J. Halberstam's introduction to his edition of Yehudah bar Barzillai's *Commentary on Sefer Yeṣirah,* p. x; and the text, p. 237. Saadiah's *K. al-Amanat w'al-I'tiqadat* (in Hebrew: *Emunot ve-de'ot;* in English: *Beliefs and Opinions*), is available in a critical ed. by S. Landauer (with some important textual corrections by I. Goldziher in his review thereof in *ZDMG,* XXXV, 773–83), and in a good English trans. by S. Rosenblatt. The gaon's *Commentary on Yeṣirah* (*Tafsir K. al-Mabadi*) was edited with a French translation by M. Lambert. It is, of course, to be sharply differentiated from the commentary in Hebrew attributed to the gaon, which appeared in many older editions of the "Book of Creation," and which most likely stemmed from a German pietist. See *supra,* Chap. XXXIII, n. 25. The critical editions, the translations therefrom, and the host of secondary writings on the gaon's historic achievements in the field of Jewish philosophy have frequently been mentioned here in various contexts. See also the rich bibliographical data supplied by H. Malter in his *Saadia Gaon,* pp. 355 ff.; supplemented by I. Werfel in *Rav Saadya Gaon,* ed. by J. L. Fishman, pp. 652 ff.; and by A. Freimann in *Saadia Anniv. Vol.,* pp. 327 ff. Yehudah ibn Tibbon's Hebrew version of the *Emunot ve-de'ot* (quoted here regularly from David Slucki's edition) has likewise been subjected to frequent textual criticisms. See esp. D. Kaufmann's "Sa'adja 'Alfajjûmîs Einleitung zum *Kitab al-Amanat w'al-I'tiqadat* in Ibn Tibbons Uebersetzung," reprinted in his *G.S.,* III, 432–53; and B. Klar's Hebrew "Notes on the Book of Beliefs and Opinions (On the Basis of Early Prints and the Arabic Original)," reprinted in his *Meḥqarim ve-'iyyunim,* pp. 220–42 (lists also earlier publications, but covers only the first 38 pages of Slucki's text).

Unfortunately, a critical edition of that translation prepared by H. Malter has never been published. Yehudah Kaufman (Ibn Shemuel), who intended to publish Malter's critical edition, as well as the text of a medieval Hebrew translation of Saadiah's genuine *Commentary on Yeṣirah,* never got around to issuing more than Chap. VIII of *Beliefs,* relating to the messianic hope, which appeared in his *Midreshe ha-ge'ulah,* pp. 117–28 (here followed by a brief excerpt from Saadiah's commentary on the Song of Songs, entitled "Essay on Armilus," pp. 129–32). As we recall, this chapter enjoyed great popularity throughout the Middle Ages and early modern times in a pre-Tibbonide Hebrew translation which first appeared in Mantua in 1557. It was often reprinted under such expressive titles as *Ha-Galut ve-ha-pedut* (Exile and Redemption), or *Ha-Pedut ve-ha-purqan* (Redemption and Release). See Steinschneider's *Hebräische Uebersetzungen,* I, 440 ff.; *supra,* Chap. XXV, n. 21; and N. M. Zobel's remarks in *Rav Saadya Gaon,* ed. by Fishman, pp. 175 f. On the much-debated meaning of the two terms used in the title see the various theories summarized by M. Zucker in his "Meaning of the Title *Emunot ve-de'ot*" (Hebrew), *Bitzaron,* VII, 257–70. Zucker himself reached the conclusion that these terms were intended to contrast "traditional beliefs" with "logical perceptions." B. Klar, on the other hand, has strongly argued in favor of considering the two terms as neutral and complementary rather than as theologically weighted and contrasting designations, and hence of rendering the title "Book of Views and Opinions." See his Hebrew essay on "Four Book Titles" reproduced in his *Meḥqarim ve-'iyyunim,* pp. 338 ff.

That the work had originated from independent monographs has long been recognized. This fact was confirmed by Saadiah's express statement in a New York MS described by E. Mittwoch in "An Unknown Fragment by Gaon Saadya," in Rosenthal's *Saadya Studies,* p. 119. Even S. Landauer's suggestion (in the introduction to his edition, pp. xix ff.) that the first nine chapters followed a preconceived plan, and that only the tenth chapter was added as an afterthought, appears rather dubious. Chaps. VII and IX are, in fact, known to us in two different versions (Landauer, pp. viii f.; Mittwoch, pp. 121 ff.), evidently stemming from the gaon's own revision. See also the general analytical studies by Jakob Guttmann, *Die Religionsphilosophie des Saadia,* and by M. Ventura, *La Philosophie de Saadia Gaon;* G. Vajda's briefer comments on "Le Commentaire de Saadia sur le Séfer Yeçîra," *REJ,* CVI, 64–86, and his "Etudes sur Saadia," *ibid.,* CIX, 68–102; and the studies mentioned in the succeeding notes.

Regrettably, our information concerning Saadiah's Rabbanite successors in the Eastern philosophic circles is extremely limited. Only here and there do we hear something about a Jewish thinker from one of his Arab contemporaries. For example, Ibn Ḥayyan at-Tawḥidi refers on several occasions to a Jewish skeptic, Wahb ibn Ya'ish ar-Raqqi, but these citations are insufficient to give us the picture of either the evidently unusual personality or the philosophic outlook of this late tenth-century native or resident of Raqqa. See F. Rosenthal, "A Jewish Philosopher of the Tenth Century," *HUCA,* XXI, 155–73, which includes five excerpts from At-Tawḥidi's work in English translation.

7. The relationship between Saadiah's and Donnolo's commentaries on *Yeṣirah* has not yet been made clear. Donnolo's Hebrew work, entitled *Ḥakmoni,* was written about 946 and hence Saadiah's *Commentary,* as well as some or all of the gaon's philosophic chapters, could have been available to him. But no one has thus far shown any definite traces of the gaon's teachings. The text of *Ḥakmoni* has long been available in a critical edition with an extensive Italian introduction, by D. Castelli in *Il Commento di Sabbatai Donnolo sul libro della creazione,* with an additional chapter published by A. Neubauer in "Un Chapitre inédit de Sabbatai Donnolo," *REJ,* XXII, 213–18. See also A. Scheiber's notes on the related text of "A New Fragment of Shabbetai Donnolo's Commentary on 'Let us make man in our image' [Gen. 1:26]" (Hebrew), *Sinai,* XV, Nos. 177–79, pp. 62–64 (from a Kaufmann MS). This comment is found in the introduction to the *Ḥakmoni,* republished in the new critical edition of Donnolo's medical works prepared by S. Muntner together with that author's biography entitled *Rabbi Shabtai Donnolo,* I, 24 ff. See E. Ivánka's pertinent remarks in his *Hellenisches und Christliches im frühbyzantinischen Geistesleben.*

8. Halevi's *K. al-Khazari,* v.15, ed. by Hirschfeld, pp. 330 f. (in his English translation, p. 274); Maimonides' *Guide,* 1.71 (in Friedländer's English translation, p. 108). By including "some geonim" in his condemnation, Maimonides may even

have had Saadiah in mind. See D. Cassel's comments in his edition of the *Kuzari,* pp. 407 n. 2, 409 n. 3. Except for Qirqisani's *K. al-Anwar* (Book of Lights), which has fortunately found in L. Nemoy both an editor (be it only in facsimile and without the usual critical apparatus and detailed introduction) and a partial translator into English (see esp. his essays mentioned *supra,* Chaps. XXVI, nn. 9, 37, 60–61; XXXVI, n. 34), none of the philosophic works written by the Karaite sages in the tenth and eleventh centuries have been made fully available to scholarship. Even Qirqisani's exegetical works, as we recall, have remained largely unpublished. Nothing but the title is known of Qirqisani's treatise on the Decalogue, which included a discussion on the existence of God, although it may have been but a distinct section of one of his larger works. See Steinschneider's *Arabische Literatur,* pp. 79 f.; and the partial analysis of his philosophic teachings in G. Vajda's "Etudes sur Qirqisani," *REJ,* CVI, 87–123; CVII, 52–98; CVIII, 63–91 (to be continued).

Joseph al-Baṣir (ha-Ro'eh, or the Seer) was a leading Karaite jurist and theologian. His death *after* 1048 was proved by Alexander Marx from a MS he had dictated in that year; see Marx, "Die Bücher und Manuskripte der Seminar-Bibliothek auf der Ausstellung der New Yorker Stadtbibliothek," *Soncino-Blätter,* II, 116. He left, among other writings, an extensive *K. al-Muḥtawi* (Comprehensive Book; in Hebrew, *Sefer Ne'imot*), of whose Hebrew translation, however, only a few fragments were published by P. F. Frankl in "Ein mu'tazilischer Kalam aus dem 10. Jahrhundert," *SB* Vienna, LXXI, 217 ff. These were republished together with some other chapters and a Hungarian translation in the Budapest dissertations by M. Klein and E. Morgenstern. If the Hebrew title, given in some manuscripts and possibly stemming from the original translator, Tobiah ben Moses (?), is to be regarded as truly descriptive, then this *Zikhron ha-datot* (Memorial on Religions) doubly deserves the attention of scholars. It may belong in the category of those comparative religious studies of which the works of Ibn Ḥazm and Shahrastani are the outstanding examples. In any case, in contrast to the aforementioned anonymous author of the theologico-polemical work, ed. by Mann (see *supra,* n. 4), Al-Baṣir frequently quoted both Al-Jubai and Abu Hashim with full approval. We are but slightly better informed about his pupil Yeshu'a ben Yehudah, through some extant fragments made available, together with a fine analysis, by M. Schreiner in his *Studien über Jeschu'a ben Jehuda.* But these represent only a small fraction of that scholar's prolific output, little of which has survived even in manuscript. Apart from his commentaries and homilies on the Bible he wrote, for example, an ethical-dogmatic treatise, known only under the Hebrew title *Meshivat nefesh* (Restoration of the Soul). See Steinschneider's *Arabische Literatur,* pp. 89 ff., 91 ff. Little of significance has been added in the course of the last half century to our knowledge of this keen and independent thinker. Jephet ben 'Ali, Abu'l Faraj Harun, and others who made their principal contributions to Karaite thought through their influential Bible commentaries have been treated *supra,* Chap. XXIX.

9. These environmental influences have often been studied, and still form a more or less important fixture in every handbook on medieval Jewish philosophy. In fact, with the general penchant of scholars a generation or two ago to make out of every *post hoc* a *propter hoc,* influences have often been postulated because of a certain similarity of ideas, where the basic rationalizations arising from a similar social background and cultural outlook make independent origins far more likely. Moreover, even today only such a small fraction of the early Muslim and Jewish

theological treatises and of the Bible or Qur'an commentaries incorporating theological and philosophical doctrines has been published that most statements on direct indebtedness appear quite hazardous. Despite these intrinsic difficulties, which naturally were greater sixty years ago, M. Schreiner's study of *Der Kalâm in der jüdischen Literatur* may still be consulted with much profit. Of value also are the studies relating to individual Jewish philosophers, such as S. Horovitz's "Ueber die Bekanntschaft Saadias mit der griechischen Skepsis," *Judaica* (Festschrift Hermann Cohen), pp. 235–52; M. Wittmann's *Zur Stellung Avencebrol's (Ibn Gebirol's) im Entwicklungsgang der arabischen Philosophie;* and M. Ventura's thesis cited *infra,* n. 39; as well as the comparative studies relating to specific problems by H. A. Wolfson and others which will be mentioned in the following notes. The almost inevitable distortion of the original thought of a Greek author by his Arab translators is well illustrated by Farabi's translation of Plato's *Nomoi.* See F. Gabrieli's lecture, "Un Compendio arabo delle leggi di Platone," *RSO,* XXIV, 20–24; and the preface to his edition with a Latin translation of Farabi's *Compendium legum Platonis.* See also, more generally, R. Klibansky's succinct comments on *The Continuity of Platonic Tradition during the Middle Ages;* F. Rosenthal's "On the Knowledge of Plato's Philosophy in the Islamic World," *IC,* XIV, 387–422; and the pertinent data on the survival of Hellenistic learning in eleventh-century Egypt and Iraq, in J. Schacht and M. Meyerhof's analysis of *The Medico-Philosophical Controversy between Ibn Butlan of Baghdad and Ibn Ridwan of Cairo.*

10. Ibn Gabirol's *Meqor ḥayyim* (Fountain of Life) is known only in the Hebrew epitome of Shem Tob ibn Falaquera, in S. Munk's *Mélanges de philosophie juive et arabe,* pp. 1–38 (Hebrew), 3–148 (French). The Latin translation by Avendeath and Gundissalinus entitled *Fons Vitae,* has been edited from three MSS by C. Baeumker. See also B. Getler's description of "A New Manuscript of the Latin Epitome of 'Fons vitae'" (Hebrew), *Tarbiz,* VI, 180–89 (referring to a Prague MS of the so-called Epitome Campilliensis). A fuller Hebrew translation from the Latin by J. Bluvstein appeared in Jerusalem, in 1926. Ibn Gabirol's *K. Islaḥ al-akhlaq* (in Hebrew: *Tikkun Middot ha-Nefesh;* in English: *The Improvement of the Moral Qualities*), however, is extant in Arabic. It was edited and translated into English by S. S. Wise. The Hebrew translation by Yehudah ibn Tibbon has long been known and frequently reprinted. On his "Choice of Pearls," see *supra,* Chap. XXXII, n. 43. The two important Latin translators of his *Fons* will be discussed in a later volume, in connection with their other significant translations from the Arabic. Jakob Guttmann's older general survey, *Die Philosophie des Salomon ibn Gabirol;* and R. Seyerlen's still older analysis "Avicebron, De materia universali (Fons Vitae)," *Theologische Jahrbücher,* XV, 486–544; XVI, 109–46, 258–95, 332–81, are still quite useful. See also F. Brunner's notes to his French translation of *La Source de Vie, Livre III;* and the aforementioned studies by I. Simchoni, K. Dreyer, and J. M. Millás Vallicrosa, referring especially to the philosophic ideas included in Ibn Gabirol's poetry, though Millás also has a lengthy chapter on the "Fountain of Life." See *supra,* Chap. XXXII, nn. 27, 50.

11. Baḥya's *K. al-Hidaya 'ila fara'id al-qulub* (in Hebrew: *Torat ḥobot ha-lebabot;* in English: *Duties of the Heart*), extremely popular in Hebrew, has been edited in Arabic by A. S. Yahuda, in the Hebrew translation of Yehudah ibn Tibbon by Zifroni, and (incompletely) in the English translation by M. Hyamson. For the date

of its composition (*ca.*1070–90), see the plausible arguments of Kokowzoff (Kokovtsov) in "The Date of the Life of Bahya ibn Paqoda," *Poznanski Mem. Vol.*, pp. 13–21. In "La Patria de Bahya ibn Paquda," *Sefarad,* XI, 102–7, C. Ramos Gil has confirmed, on the basis of a MS of 1340, L. Zunz's suggestion that Baḥya was a native or resident of Saragossa. There are numerous European translations, including three in German by R. Fürstenthal, E. Baumgarten, and M. E. Stern. On the Hebrew translation entitled *Torat ḥobot ha-lebabot,* begun by Yehudah ibn Tibbon, perhaps as early as 1161, see *supra,* Chap. XXX, n. 5. It appeared in numerous editions and was provided with several commentaries. See also A. Chouraqui's French translation, *Introduction aux Devoirs des coeurs* (with a Foreword by Jacques Maritain; includes the translation of Baḥya's three poems); A. M. Habermann's "On the Study of the *Duties of the Heart* and Its Hebrew Texts" (Hebrew), *Sinai,* XIV, Nos. 169–70, pp. 315–29; Nos. 171–72, pp. 58–79; and the analytical studies by D. Kaufmann, "Die Theologie des Bachja Ibn Pakuda" in his *G.S.*, II, 1–98; and by G. Vajda, *La Théologie ascétique de Bahya ibn Paquda.* See also C. Ramos Gil, "La Toqeḥa de Baḥya ibn Paquda," *Homenaje a Millás,* II, 197–216; *supra,* Chap. XXXII, n. 54; and *infra,* n. 31.

Pseudo-Baḥya's *K. Ma'ani al-nafs* (Investigation of the Soul), was edited in the Arabic original by I. Goldziher, six years after it had first been translated into Hebrew from the Arabic MS by I. Broydé under the title *Torot ha-nefesh* (Les Reflexions sur l'âme). See also S. Dörfler's dissertation, *Untersuchung der Autentie und des Inhalts der Schrift "Kitab Ma'ani al-Nafs"* (typescript; summarized in *Jahrbuch der Dissertationen der Philos. Fakultät . . . Berlin,* 1923–25, pp. 294–95); A. J. Borisov's "New Materials on the Question of Pseudo-Baḥya" (Russian), *Bulletin* of the Academy of Sciences of the U.S.S.R., Humanistic Division, 7th ser., 1929, pp. 775–97 (pointing out, among other matters, that the Leningrad MS, in contrast to that of Paris, upon which Goldziher's edition is based, does not contain the reference to Baḥya's authorship); and Jakob Guttmann's brief analytical study, based only on the Hebrew translation, "Eine bisher unbekannte dem Bachja Ibn Pakuda zugeeignete Schrift," *MGWJ,* XLI, 241–56.

12. Halevi's *K. al-Khazari* (Book of Argument and Proof in Defense of the Despised Religion), whose composition about 1140 seems indicated in I.44–47 (ed. by Hirschfeld, p. 23; English, p. 49), has frequently been referred to in our earlier chapters. It appeared in a critical edition by H. Hirschfeld and was provided with textual corrections by I. Goldziher in his review thereof in *ZDMG,* XLI, 691–707. See also L. Nemoy's "Contributions to the Textual Criticism of Judah Ha-Levi's Kitab al Khazari," *JQR,* XXVI, 221–26 (based on Ibn Kammuna's quotations); and G. Vajda's "Remarques sur le texte arabe du 'Kuzari,'" *REJ,* CIII, 102–4. Hirschfeld published a German translation, and followed it with an English translation from the Arabic. The old Hebrew translation by Yehudah ibn Tibbon, prepared in 1167 and printed many times, is available in a good edition by D. Cassel, accompanied by both a German translation and extensive critical and explanatory comments. The Hebrew text, too, has been carefully reviewed by S. Horovitz in his "Zur Textkritik des Kusari," *MGWJ,* XLI, 264–73, 312–21; and by I. Efros in his "Some Textual Notes on Judah Halevi's Kusari," *PAAJR,* II, 3–6. A new edition, revised "in accordance with the Arabic text and provided with a commentary, notes and indexes by A. Zifroni and vocalized by J. Toporowski" appeared in 1948. A Spanish translation from the Hebrew, prepared by Jacob Abendana, appeared

in Amsterdam in 1663 and was reissued in 1910 by Don Adolfo Bonilla y San Martín. More recently, I. Heinemann published an "abridged edition" in English, valuable mainly because of his introduction and commentary. See also Heinemann's Hebrew essays, "The Philosopher-Poet: an Interpretation of Selected Poems," *Keneset,* IX, 163 ff., and "The Historical Picture of R. Yehudah Halevi," *Zion,* IX, 147 ff., which, like M. Millás's *Yehudá Ha-Levi como poeta y apologista* and many other writings, are concerned with Halevi, the poet, as much as with Halevi, the philosopher. Among the numerous analytical studies one need mention here only those by D. Kaufmann, "Jehuda Halevi," reissued, with some corrections, in his *G.S.,* II, 99–151 and by D. Neumark, "Jehuda Hallevi's Philosophy in Its Principles" reprinted in his *Essays in Jewish Philosophy,* pp. 219–300. See also M. Ventura's analysis of *Le Kalâm et le Péripatétisme d'après le Kuzari* (showing the influence of the former on Halevi's doctrine of God and Free Will, and of Aristotelianism, via Farabi and Avicenna, on his cosmological and psychological theories); I. Epstein's briefer analysis of "Judah Halevi as Philosopher," *JQR,* XXV, 201–25; M. Wiener's "Judah Halevi's Concept of Religion and a Modern Counterpart," *HUCA,* XXIII, Part 1, pp. 669–82 (referring to Isaac Breuer, *Der neue Kusari: Ein Weg zum Judentum*); and the numerous monographs and collective works listed *supra,* Chap. XXXII, nn. 29, 46.

13. Abraham bar Ḥiyya's *Sefer Hegyon ha-nefesh* (Contemplation of the Soul) has been known for almost a century in E. Freimann's edition, provided with extensive introductions by both the editor and S. J. L. Rapoport, but his *Sefer Megillat ha-megalleh* (Scroll of Disclosure, or more literally: Of One Who Discloses), became public property only in 1924, when it was edited posthumously for A. Poznanski, with an introduction by Julius Guttmann. It was soon thereafter translated into Catalan by J. M. Millás Vallicrosa, under the title *Llibre revelador.* Two decades earlier, however, Jakob Guttmann, who had already previously analyzed "Die philosophischen und ethischen Anschauungen in Abraham bar Chijja's Hegjon ha-Nefesch," *MGWJ,* XLIV, 193–217, also wrote "Ueber Abraham bar Chijja's 'Buch der Enthüllung'," *MGWJ,* XLVII, 446–68, 545–69. See also G. Vajda's more recent "Les Idées théologiques et philosophiques d'Abraham bar Hiyya," *AHDL,* XXI, 191–223; and I. Efros's terminological study cited *infra,* n. 57. However, Abraham's perhaps most significant philosophic contribution on which he brought to bear his full scientific equipment, namely what we may call his "astrological conception of history," has not yet been sufficiently elucidated. See *supra,* Chaps. XXV, n. 23; XXVIII, nn. 97–98.

14. Abraham ibn Ezra's *Astrological Works,* still largely unpublished, have been critically reexamined by R. Levy with special reference to the old French translation of Hagin and other versions. Several of his aforementioned briefer tracts like *Yesod mora* and *Sefer ha-Shem,* likewise include philosophically relevant materials. So do his numerous poems, both secular and liturgical. See *supra,* Chap. XXXII, nn. 30 and 52. A careful student of Ibn Ezra's life and poetry, D. Rosin, contributed also a comprehensive analysis of "Die Religionsphilosophie Abraham Ibn Esra's," posthumously published in *MGWJ,* Vols. XLII–XLIII. See also L. Orschansky's *Abraham ibn Esra als Philosoph;* and L. G. Lévy's briefer restatement of "La Philosophie d'Abraham ibn Ezra," *REJ,* LXXXIX, 169–78. A new, up-to-date study is, however, clearly indicated.

The Arabic original of Ibn Ṣaddiq's "Microcosm" has never been recovered. The Hebrew translation, however, long known under the title *'Olam qaṭan*, was critically edited and introduced by S. Horovitz in *Der Mikrokosmos des Josef ibn Ṣaddiḳ*. Ibn Ṣaddiq's authorship, questioned during the overcritical generation of the late nineteenth century by L. Weinsberg in his dissertation *Der Mikrokosmos . . . nach seiner Echtheit untersucht*, has since been almost unanimously upheld. The analytical study, however, by M. Doctor, *Die Philosophie des Josef (Ibn) Zaddik, nach ihren Quellen, insbesondere nach ihren Beziehungen zu den Lauteren Brüdern und zu Gabirol untersucht*, has not quite fulfilled the ambitious program indicated in the title. More satisfactory is G. Vajda's interpretation of "La Philosophie et la théologie de Joseph ibn Çaddiq," *AHDL*, XXIV, 93–181. On Ibn Ṣaddiq's treatise on logic mentioned in his "Microcosm," see Steinschneider's *Arabische Literatur*, p. 152; and, on his poetic works, *supra*, Chap. XXXII, n. 54. Incidentally, one might also mention Moses ibn Ezra's semiphilosophic tract, *K. Makâlat al-hadîka* (in Hebrew *'Arugat ha-bosem* or Bed of Spices; on the metaphoric versus the real meaning of biblical terms), of which we possess but a small fragment in the original, communicated from a St. Petersburg MS by A. Harkavy in *MGWJ*, XLIII, 133–36. An old anonymous Hebrew translation has been much better preserved. See Y. (L.) Dukes's edition in his "Collectanea from Moses ibn Ezra's *Sefer 'Arugat ha-bosem*" (Hebrew), *Zion*, II, 117–23, 134–37, 157–59, 175–76.

15. Abu'l Barakat ibn Malka's main work on logic, physics, and metaphysics, bearing the characteristic title of *K. al-Mu'tabar* (The Appreciated Book), was but recently published in three substantial volumes in Hyderabad. See S. Pines, "Etudes sur Awḥad al-Zamân Abu'l Barakât al-Baghdâdi," *REJ*, CIII, 3–64; CIV, 1–33; and H. Z. Ulken's brief summary "Un Philosophe de l'Islam: Ebu-l-Berekat Bagdadi," *Proceedings* of the Tenth International Congress of Philosophy (Amsterdam, 1948), I, 270–73. Pines has argued that our philosopher, also bearing the forenames Ḥibbat Allah 'Ali ibn Malka, must have been converted after Isaac ben Abraham ibn Ezra had in 1143 written a poem in his honor (see Isaac's *Shire*, No. 3; Abu'l Barakat is called here in Hebrew Netanel), and that he probably died after 1164–65 at the age of eighty or ninety. However, a contemporary Arab acquaintance attributes Abu'l Barakat's conversion to his imprisonment by Caliph Al-Mustarshid (1118–35) and claims that he had lived ninety solar years. See M. Meyerhof's " 'Ali al-Bayhaqi's Tatimmat Ṣiwan al-Ḥikma: A Biographical Work on Learned Men of the Islam," *Osiris*, VIII, 191 f. No. 93. Unfortunately, only Abu'l Barakat's encyclopedic *K. al-Mu'tabar*, but not his commentary on Ecclesiastes nor, for that matter, any of his other works, has as yet been published in full. On the older publications by and on Abu'l Barakat, see Steinschneider's *Arabische Literatur*, pp. 182 ff.

16. Ibn Daud's *Emunah ramah* (Exalted Faith) is available only in the Hebrew translation by Solomon ben Labi (*ca.*1400), edited with a German rendition therefrom by S. Weil. Another, almost simultaneous, translation (1392) by Samuel Motot is extant only in a Mantua MS. According to Steinschneider, this translation is more elegant, if less precise. See his *Arabische Literatur*, p. 154. In his *Bibelexegese der jüdischen Religionsphilosophen*, pp. 137 f., W. Bacher has argued that the fuller title stressing the concordance of philosophy and religion stems from the author himself, and not from the translator. Abraham's harmonistic attitude may also help explain his failure to quote the anti-philosophical Halevi, whom he otherwise

greatly admired. See also Hirschfeld's comments in the introduction to his translation of Halevi's work, pp. 23 ff. Weil's publication was soon followed by Jakob Guttmann's analytical study of *Die Religionsphilosophie des Abraham ibn Daud aus Toledo;* and half a century later by M. König's comparison of *Die Philosophie des Jehuda Halevi und des Abraham ibn Daud.* Weil's edition leaves much room for improvement in the light of present-day knowledge.

Nor do we as yet have any comprehensive investigation concerning the particular works of Aristotle and his ancient and medieval commentators which were available to each of the successive Jewish philosophers and what use they had made of them. On the difficulties of such an undertaking, cf., however, *infra,* n. 27. Apart from the general handbooks on medieval Jewish philosophy see S. Horovitz's brief lecture on *Die Stellung des Aristoteles bei den Juden des Mittelalters.* M. Grabmann's extensive essays on "Aristoteles im Werturteil des Mittelalters," in his *Mittelalterliches Geistesleben,* II, 63–102; and "Aristoteles im zwölften Jahrhundert," *ibid.,* III, 64–127, deal only with Christian, not with Jewish-Muslim scholasticism, and hence offer merely a few interesting parallels for our period. Among these the legend of Aristotle's ultimate conversion (*ibid.,* II, 92 ff.) is particularly noteworthy. The earlier legend of Alexander's conversion to Christianity may have paved the way to similar contentions regarding his teacher, Aristotle. Around this theme is woven a Christian Alexander Romance, antedating the seventh century, which was available also in a Syriac translation of a Pehlevi rendition from the Greek, edited in 1889 with an English translation by E. A. W. Budge and entitled *The History of Alexander the Great.* See also the Hebrew and Arabic sources referred to *ibid.,* pp. lxxxiii ff.; and in Zunz and Albeck's *Ha-Derashot,* p. 321 n. 154; G. Cary's "Alexander the Great in Mediaeval Theology," *Journal of the Warburg and Courtauld Institutes,* XVII, 98–114 (analyzing the medieval Latin interpretations of the references in Daniel, Maccabees, and Josephus); E. N. Adler's "Aristotle and the Jews," *REJ,* LXXXII, 91–102; A. J. Borisov's Russian essay on "The Arabic Original of the Latin Version of the Treatise Called 'The Theology of Aristotle,'" *Zapiski Kollegii Vostokovedov,* V, 83–98; *supra,* n. 5; and Chap. XXVIII, n. 48.

17. Maimonides' *K. Dalalat al-ḥairin* (in Hebrew: *Moreh nebukhim;* in English: *The Guide of* [or *for*] *the Perplexed*), known in two Hebrew translations by Samuel ibn Tibbon and Yehudah al-Ḥarizi, has been published in Arabic, with a French translation by S. Munk. The Arabic text, somewhat revised by I. Joel and provided with an Appendix containing several excerpts from extant Maimonidean autographs, was reissued by J. Junovitch. But interesting new manuscripts of the *Guide* are still coming to light. See, e.g., F. Rosenthal's brief description of one written in Yemen in 1477–80 in his "From Arabic Books and Manuscripts V: a One-Volume Library of Arabic Philosophical and Scientific Texts in Istanbul," *JAOS,* LXXV, 15 (this MS is doubly remarkable as it was written by a Muslim). There also exists an English translation of the *Guide* by M. Friedländer, and a German one by A. Weiss. Y. Kaufman published a vocalized Hebrew text of the Ibn Tibbon translation, with a running commentary for more popular use. Selections in English have been edited by L. Roth, and in Spanish by J. Llamas in his biography of *Maimónides, siglo XII.* To be sure, Al-Ḥarizi's translation, made from the Arabic original though after consultation of Ibn Tibbon's somewhat earlier version, underlay the anonymous Latin translation, perhaps by a member of Frederick II's circle, and thus greatly influenced Christian scholasticism. See the new impression of Ḥarizi's version with

comments by S. Scheyer and S. Munk issued in Tel Aviv in 1953; D. Z. Baneth's Hebrew essay on "R. Yehudah al-Ḥarizi and the Three Translations of Maimonides' Treatise on Resurrection," *Tarbiz,* XI, 260–70; and W. Kluxen's "Literargeschichtliches zum lateinischen Moses Maimonides," *Recherches de théologie ancienne et médiévale,* XXI, 23–50 (written in preparation of the critical edition of the Latin text, begun by J. Koch and J. O. Riedl, and listing fourteen MSS extant in European libraries). Nevertheless that by Samuel ibn Tibbon has enjoyed greater popularity among the Jews.

Ibn Tibbon's version was among the first Hebrew incunabula printed in Italy (before 1480), and was provided with extensive commentaries by Efodi (Profiat Duran), Shem Tob ben Joseph, Asher Crescas, and Don Isaac Abravanel. These four commentaries were published, together with Ibn Tibbon's text, in the Warsaw edition of the *Moreh.* Like those independently published by Shem Tob ibn Falaquera (entitled *Moreh ha-moreh,* or Guide to the Guide, edited by M. L. Bisliches), by Joseph ben Abba-Mari ibn Kaspi (entitled *'Ammude Kesef u-Maskiyot Kesef,* or Pillars of Silver and Settings of Silver, with reference to their author's residence in Argentière, and edited from Munich and Leipzig manuscripts by S. Werbluner), and by Moses ben Joshua Narboni (*Be'ur* or Commentary, edited by Jakob Goldenthal, or an earlier Sulzbach edition, 1828), these commentaries are major philosophical works in their own right and will be treated in their respective contexts. Other commentaries, some still unpublished, are enumerated in Steinschneider's *Arabische Literatur,* pp. 206 f. Neither Ibn Tibbon's text nor those of most commentators have been critically edited, however. S. Rawidowicz's plea to this effect in 1935 has thus far remained unheeded. See his Hebrew essay on "Our Scholarly Duty to the Guide of the Perplexed" in *Haaretz,* Octocentennial issue, No. 4797, pp. 39–44.

Some Muslim scholars, too, studied the *Guide* intensively, and At-Tabrizi even wrote a commentary on its twenty-five propositions. "On the Date of Completion of the More Nebukim," see Z. Diesendruck's searching study in *HUCA,* XII–XIII, 461–97, reaching the conclusion that this work, which had required many years of arduous labor, was completed about 1185. Although differing in many details, D. Z. Baneth substantially agreed with this date. See his edition of Maimonides' *Iggerot* (Epistles), pp. 31 ff.; and *supra,* Chap. XVIII, n. 7. Much of the debate hinged on the dating (1191 or 1190) of the important letter to Joseph ibn Shime'on concerning the controversy with the Baghdad academy (reedited *ibid.,* pp. 49 ff.). Radically denying its authenticity altogether, J. L. Teicher reached the conclusion that the first authentic intimation concerning the compilation of the *Guide* is found in its author's letter on astrology, dated in 1195. See A. Marx's edition of "The Correspondence between the Rabbis of Southern France and Maimonides," in *HUCA,* III, 311–58, slightly revised but with the omission of the text in his *Studies in Jewish History and Booklore,* pp. 48 ff.; S. M. Stern's "Maimonides' Correspondence with the Scholars of Provence" (Hebrew), *Zion,* XVI, 18–29; and Teicher's "Maimonides' Letter to Joseph b. Jehudah—a Literary Forgery," *JJS,* I, 35–54 referring to that crucial epistle No. VI. Teicher's critique, however, stands or falls with the validity of his related attack on the authenticity of Maimonides' *Treatise on Resurrection,* to be discussed presently.

The lesser philosophical and theological treatises by Maimonides are also available now for the most part in good critical editions, especially those issued by the American Academy for Jewish Research:

(1) On Logic, written in Maimonides' youth and entitled *Maqâla fi sina'at al-*

manṭiq (in the Hebrew translation by Moses ibn Tibbon called *Millot ha-higgayon*), edited by I. Efros in both languages (also in the Aḥitub and Vivas versions) and provided with an English translation in *PAAJR,* VIII (it had also appeared, slightly earlier, with a French translation by M. Ventura entitled *La Logique d'Aristote*).

(2) On Conversion or Martyrdom, written before 1165 and entitled in the anonymous Hebrew translation *Iggeret ha-Shemad* or *Ma'amar Qiddush ha-shem,* available only in the older Hebrew version, edited from several MSS by A. Geiger in his *Moses ben Maimon, Studien,* Vol. I; and again in *Qobeṣ teshubot ha-Rambam,* ed. by Lichtenberg, II, fols. 12–15; and in the more recent well-annotated Hebrew popular edition with vocalized texts by M. D. Rabbinowitz, entitled *Iggerot ha-Rambam,* Vol. I.

(3) On Messianic Movements, addressed to Yemen about 1172 and entitled *Risala* (Epistle to Yemen), available also in three Hebrew translations under the title *Iggeret Teman,* all critically edited by A. S. Halkin, with an English translation by B. Cohen.

(4) On Resurrection, written in 1191, and entitled *Maqala fi teḥiyyat ha-metim* (in Samuel ibn Tibbon's Hebrew translation, *Ma'amar Teḥiyyat ha-metim*), critically edited by J. Finkel in *PAAJR,* IX. See also his comparative study thereof in my *Essays on Maimonides,* pp. 93–121; J. L. Teicher's attack on its authenticity in his "Maimonides' Treatise on Resurrection, a Thirteenth-Century Forgery" (Hebrew), *Melilah,* I, 81–92; with additional observations in the same vein in *JJS,* I, 41 ff.; I. Sonne's convincing reply thereto in "A Scrutiny of the Charges of Forgery against Maimonides' Letter on Resurrection," *PAAJR,* XXI, 101–17; D. Z. Baneth's suggested corrections in his "On the Text of Maimonides' Treatise on Resurrection and Its Translation" (Hebrew), *Tarbiz,* XIII, 37–42; and his aforementioned discussion of Al-Ḥarizi's translation of that treatise in *Tarbiz,* Vol. XI. Baneth's defense of Al-Ḥarizi's authorship of the translation, avowedly made from an Arabic retranslation from Ibn Tibbon's Hebrew version, because the original Maimonidean text sent by the author to his Provençal translator was kept by him and remained inaccessible to other readers, is not as far-fetched as it sounds. The availability of texts written by authors in distant lands was often very limited, indeed. See *supra,* Chap. XXVII, n. 68.

(5) On the Unity of God, the Arabic original of which is lost, but whose Hebrew translation by Isaac ben Nathan (*ca.*1350), entitled *Ma'amar ha-Yiḥud* (*ha-Jichud,* or *Abhandlung über die Einheit*), edited with comments by M. Steinschneider.

(6) The aforementioned Epistle on Felicity (*Peraqim be-haṣlaḥah*), edited with a Hebrew translation by S. D. Dawidowicz, which is, however, of questionable authorship (see *supra,* Chap. XXXIII, n. 1).

The various editions of Maimonides' *Commentary on the Mishnah,* including the "Eight Chapters," and his lesser "Epistles" and responsa, some of philosophic content, have already been mentioned *supra,* Chap. XXVII, esp. nn. 65 and 137. Of course, like other great ancient and medieval masters, Maimonides was made responsible for works written by disciples and imitators. See, for instance, the so-called *Tish'ah peraqim me-yiḥud* (Nine Chapters on the Unity of God), attributed to him and ed. from a Paris MS by Y. A. (G.) Vajda in *Qobeṣ 'al-yad,* XV, 103–37, showing the indebtedness of that work to the thirteenth-century mystic, Joseph ben Abraham ibn Chiquitilla. See also Vajda's analysis of "Le Traité pseudo-maïmonideen 'Neuf chapitres sur l'unité de Dieu'," *AHDL,* XXVIII, 83–98.

In the aforementioned notes of Chap. XXVII (also in n. 114) the reader will find most of the necessary references to the general biographical literature, the various collective works, and the bibliographies dealing with the sage of Fusṭaṭ. Many monographs on special phases of Maimonides' thought, some of a high order, will be mentioned in succeeding notes. It will suffice, therefore, to add here but L. G. Lévy's and F. Bamberger's comprehensive analyses, *Maïmonide;* and *Das System des Maimonides, eine Analyse des More Newuchim vom Gottesbegriff aus;* Julius Guttmann's searching observations on "Die religiösen Motive in der Philosophie des Maimonides," *Entwicklungsstufen der jüdischen Religion,* ed. by H. Gressmann, pp. 61–90; D. Baumgardt's succinct observations on "Maimonides the Conciliator of Eastern and Western Thought," *Transactions* of the Indian Institute of Culture, XXI; the Maimonides issue of the *Boletín de la Academia de Ciencias . . . Cordoba,* XIV, whose publication was delayed from 1935 to 1950; and the interesting collection of Arabic documents pertaining to Maimonides assembled by D. B. Lewis in his Hebrew essay on "Hebrew in Arabic Letters," *Metsudah,* III–IV, 171–81. See also *infra,* n. 25. On Maimonides' influence on Thomas Aquinas and other scholastics, see W. Kluxen's recent essay, "Maimonides und die Hochscholastik," *Philosophisches Jahrbuch,* LXIII, 151–65; J. Strulovici's dissertation, *Der Einfluss Moses Maimonides' in der Schrift "de veritate" des Thomas von Aquin;* and *infra,* nn. 45, 60. This subject will be more fully discussed in a later volume.

Of the major works of Maimonides' father and son, see especially "The Letter of Consolation of Maimun [Maimon] ben Joseph," edited in Arabic with an English translation by L. M. Simmons in *JQR,* [o.s.] I, 62–101, and Arabic section, after p. 334; in the new Hebrew translation entitled *Iggeret ha-Neḥamah,* by B. Klar, with an introduction and notes by J. L. Fishman; and *infra,* n. 90. Abraham Maimonides' *K. Kifayat al-'abadin* (Adequate Guide for God's Servants) was, in part, critically edited in Arabic with an English translation by S. Rosenblatt under the title *The High Ways of Perfection* (covers only 4th section, Part 2, Chapters XI–XXIII). Abraham's semiphilosophic *Milḥamot Adonai* (Wars of the Lord), long known from his father's *Qobeṣ,* ed. by Lichtenberg, III, fols. 15–21, has been reissued on the basis of an old MS with a biographical sketch and notes by R. Margulies. Needless to say, both Maimon's and Abraham's exegetical works likewise contained many philosophical, especially ethical, teachings. See *supra,* Chap. XXIX, n. 85; and, more generally, S. Eppenstein's older but still useful biographical study, *Abraham Maimuni, sein Leben und seine Schriften* (republished from the *Jahresbericht* of the Rabbinerseminar in Berlin for 1912–13). In passing one may also mention a similar work on the borderline between philosophy and homiletics written by Maimon's Yemenite contemporary Nathanael ibn al-Fayyumi (d. before 1172). His work, the *Bustan al-ukul* (The Garden of Wisdom) was edited with an English translation and somewhat scanty notes by D. Levine.

18. Maimonides, *Qobeṣ,* II, fol. 27c; M. Steinschneider, *Die arabischen Uebersetzungen aus dem Griechischen, passim.* On the astrological works of Abraham ibn Ezra, including his translations from Arabic, see Chap. XXXV, nn. 43–45. In his Hebrew essay on "Maimonides' Letter to Samuel ibn Tibbon according to an Unknown Text in the Archives of the Jewish Community of Verona," *Tarbiz,* X, 135–54, 309–32, I. Sonne offers both interesting variants and searching explanatory comments.

19. The nearly total absence of careful investigations of Jewish translations and paraphrases of, and commentaries on, older works of philosophy in the early centuries of Islam is truly disconcerting. We still must rely principally on the purely bibliographical data assembled by that grandmaster of Jewish bibliography, Moritz Steinschneider, especially in *Die hebräischen Uebersetzungen des Mittelalters;* and in *Die arabische Literatur.* Despite frequent flashes of insight, only occasionally marred by polemical outbursts, these works offer in essence only the raw materials for a series of analytical studies. Of course, any analytical endeavor will be hampered by the relative absence of printed texts, since much of that material still rests in the world's manuscript rooms. A closer examination of these manuscripts is likely to reveal, however, as it did for example in the case of Shem Tob ibn Falaquera's compilations, that here are buried treasures yet to be dug out by enterprising excavators. On the Jewish part in the Latin translations of Arabic philosophic works, see J. L. Teicher, "The Latin-Hebrew School of Translators in Spain in the Twelfth Century," *Homenaje a Millás,* II, 403–44; and the literature listed *infra,* Chap. XXXV, n. 41.

20. See 'Erubin 19a; Maimonides' *M.T.* Teshubah III.14. At moments of great stress, of course, the issue of apostasy loomed large on the Jewish horizon. This was indeed the main import of Maimonides' own "Epistle on Conversion." On the general impact of the religious disputations and apologias, see *supra,* Chap. XXIV.

21. Ibn Ṣaddiq's *'Olam qaṭan* (Microcosm), III, beg., ed. by Horovitz, p. 43; Mann's text in *HUCA,* XII–XIII, 433 ff.; S. D. Goitein's "New Information about Jewish Philosophers of R. Saadiah's Period" (Hebrew) in *Rav Saadya Gaon,* ed. by Fishman, pp. 567–70; F. Rosenthal's fuller data on "A Jewish Philosopher of the Tenth Century," *HUCA,* XXI, 155–73 (both relating principally to Wahb ibn Ya'ish of Raqqa); Halevi's *K. al-Khazari,* I.1, 4, 10; Peter Abelard's *Dialogus inter philosophum, Judaeum et Christianum,* in *PL,* CLXXVIII, 1609–82; Maimonides' *Guide,* III.16, in Friedländer's trans., p. 280. In Hirschfeld's trans. of *K. al-Khazari,* I.1, p. 36, the philosopher is even more sharply asked to state his "religious persuasion." The Arabic term *amanat,* like Ibn Tibbon's precise rendition, *emunah,* lends itself to either translation (in I.10, Hirschfeld uses "belief"). See also *supra,* n. 6. Curiously, the representatives of both Christianity and Islam were not asked to state their beliefs, but rather their "doctrine and observance" (I.5; in I.4 rather inconsistently rendered by "the theory and practice of his faith"). This contrast aroused the curiosity of Halevi's sixteenth-century commentator, Yehudah Muscato. Cf. the rather forced explanation offered by Cassel in his ed., p. 16 n. 1. Nor should we be misled by the frequent designation of the Mu'tazilites as "liberal theologians." As a rule, these thinkers were as insistent on unflinching adherence to their respective systems, as were any orthodox persecutors of "heresies." Did not even Averroës advocate capital punishment for any denial of the existence of God, or of a world to come? On the difficulties of this point of view within the general philosophic system of that thinker, see T. J. de Boer, *Die Widersprüche der Philosophie nach Al-Ġazzali, und ihr Ausgleich durch Ibn Rošd,* pp. 91, 95 f.; and *infra,* n. 22.

In "The Law of Reason in the Kuzari" (reprinted in his *Persecution and the Art of Writing,* pp. 103 ff.) L. Strauss rightly pointed out that Halevi's treatise is directed far more against the "philosophers" than against Christianity, Islam,

Karaism, or the *Kalam*. While all these points of view are attacked, only philosophy "is coherently discussed twice (in I.1–3 and V.2–14). Besides, the occasional polemical references to philosophy are more numerous, and much more significant, than the corresponding references to any other" of the above positions (p. 103 n. 23). Halevi also expressly stated that followers of Jeroboam (possibly an allusion to the Karaites), as well as Muslims and Christians were closer to pious Jews than the "philosophers" (IV.12–13). This fact, however, should not mislead us into assuming that Halevi viewed philosophy as a greater menace to Judaism not only than Karaism, which played a minor role in his native Spain, or *Kalam*, which after all was only a less popular brand of philosophy there, but also than the two world powers of Islam and Christendom. See my remarks in *JSS*, III, 259 ff. Only because the main import of the book was to argue against "philosophy" on its own plane, the author had to give it this somewhat distorted emphasis. In part, moreover, Halevi followed the fashion of his age among Muslim traditionalists, including Ibn Ḥazm and Ghazzali. Even those among them who, like Halevi himself, appreciated the importance of human reason, nevertheless often attacked "the learning of the ancients," and especially Greek logic, as prejudicial to orthodoxy. It almost became proverbial among the Arab masses that "he who studies logic, becomes a heretic." See the interesting illustrations, largely from the literature of the eleventh to fifteenth centuries, assembled by I. Goldziher in his *Stellung der alten islamischen Orthodoxie zur den antiken Wissenschaften*. Even an enlightened gaon like Hai, as we shall presently see, advised restraining children from the study of logic. In any case, the philosophers within the Jewish community made up in vocal self-assertion for their lack of numbers and constituted a factor to be reckoned with. See also *supra*, Chap. XXIX, n. 90.

22. J. Finkel's trans. of "A Risala of al-Jaḥiẓ," *JAOS*, XLVII, 326; Joseph ibn Kaspi's "Testament" called *Sefer ha-Musar* (Guide to Knowledge) in Abraham's *Ethical Wills*, I, 146 ff.; Isa. 2:6; Berakhot 28b, with the comment thereon by Hai in Lewin's *Otzar ha-gaonim*, I, Part 2, p. 39; Hai's alleged resp. published by H. Graetz in "Ein pseudoepigraphisches Sendschreiben," *MGWJ*, XI, 37–40 (denying its authenticity); Saadiah's *Beliefs and Opinions*, Intro., ed. by Landauer, pp. 20 f. (Hebrew, pp. 10 f.; English, p. 26); and, more generally, *supra*, Chap. XXVIII. "Die rabbinische Kritik an Gott" is illustrated by a number of telling examples in E. A. Dietrich's pertinent essay in *Zeitschrift für Religions- und Geistesgeschichte*, VII, 193–224. It goes without saying that this type of questioning was motivated by fervent faith and the feeling of closeness to the Creator rather than by skepticism. The subsequent reversal of the antiphilosophic attitude may not have gone as far as our one-sided sources would seem to indicate. Yet the general tolerance of the Spanish-Jewish communities toward philosophic speculation and interpretation was sufficiently well established for Averroës (Ibn Roshd) to invoke Solomon's early contributions to religious philosophy, although he added that when heretics "have really the power to destroy religious belief both theologians and philosophers will no doubt kill them." See his *Tahafut at-tahafut* (The Incoherence of Incoherence), ed. by M. Bouyges, pp. 583 ff.; in S. van den Bergh's English trans., I, 360 ff., with the notes thereon II, 205 f. Incidentally see also G. Vajda's brief discussion, "Averroès a-t-il cité le Talmud?" *AHDL*, XXIV, 267–70, attributing such citation in the Latin trans. of his *Tahafut* (*Destructio destructionis*) to an alteration by the

Jewish translator Calo Calonymus and his summary of the Hebrew translation. Even later, the anti-Maimonidean controversy had some rather exceptional features, as will be explained in a future volume.

23. Baḥya's *Duties of the Heart,* Intro., ed. by Yahuda, p. 13 (Hebrew, ed. by Zifroni, p. 12; Hyamson, I, 7, offers a somewhat different translation). Such basic divergence in approach should have warned scholars against glibly asserting Baḥya's indebtedness to this Muslim mystic even before Kokovtsov's chronological study (see *supra,* n. 11) had proved its impossibility. Of course, both masters had before them a vast array of literary sources, many no longer extant, from which they could freely borrow what fitted their needs. An example of such borrowing, by both Baḥya and Ghazzali from a ninth-century work by Al-Jaḥiẓ, has been shown by D. H. Baneth in "The Common Teleological Source of Bahye Ibn Paqoda and Ghazzali," *Magnes Anniv. Book,* pp. 23–30. We know too little about Baḥya's life confidently to make any biographical assertions. However, the fact that he is consistently called in the older sources *ha-dayyan* (the judge), makes very likely his service at a Jewish tribunal, perhaps in Saragossa, where the name Baḥya is found later on several occasions. See C. Ramos Gil's discussions of "La Patria de Bahya ibn Paquda," *Sefarad,* XI, 102–7, supporting Baḥya's Saragossan residence or nativity. See *supra,* n. 11. Needless to say, there probably were also some philosophers who had no communal ties. The intriguing case of Al-Muqammiṣ may serve as an illustration. But these men were decided exceptions.

Even among the Karaites there existed universal reverence for the law in all its ramifications. While we know next to nothing about the personal careers of Qirqisani, Joseph al-Baṣir, or Yeshu'a ben Yehudah—most of them seem to have earned a living as physicians or in other independent occupations—their passionate attachment to the accepted law is evidenced by the fact that so many of them wrote Books of Commandments. See *supra,* Chap. XXVI, nn. 28 f., 36 ff.; and, on the absence of serious antinomian tendencies even among the early Jewish mystics, *supra,* Chap. XXXIII, n. 54.

24. Saadiah's *Beliefs,* Intro., ed. by Landauer, p. 4 (in Ibn Tibbon's trans., ed. by Slucki, p. 3; English, p. 7); Maimonides' *Guide,* Intro. (in Friedländer's trans., p. 29); Abraham Maimuni's *Milḥamot Adonai* (Wars of the Lord), in his father's *Qobeṣ,* III, fol. 17d. Maimonides himself so strongly believed in his appeal to a single wise man against a thousand fools that he repeated this statement also in his "Treatise on Resurrection," ed. by Finkel, p. 18*. Friedländer's translation fails to reproduce the crucial characteristic expected from the *Guide*'s prospective reader, namely his ability to understand by himself (the author uses, I, fol. 3b, the talmudic phrase: *ḥakham u-mebin mi-da'ato*), obviously a reference to the talmudic requirement for a pupil of the works of Creation. It was quite in the Maimonidean spirit that, in his commentary on this passage, Shem Tob ben Joseph developed seven qualities which a reader must possess before he may be considered a proper reader of the *Guide* (ed. Warsaw, 1872, I, fol. 4a).

25. Sukkah 28a. The contrast between the designation, *ḥibbur* (work), or *ha-ḥibbur ha-gadol* (the great work), consistently applied by Maimonides to his Code, and the more modest designation of the *Guide* as *maqala* (treatise), which Ibn Tibbon consistently rendered by *ma'amar,* has frequently been noted. See L. Strauss's

ingenious study of "The Literary Character of the Guide for the Perplexed," reprinted in his *Persecution and the Art of Writing,* especially pp. 38 ff., 47, 78 ff., 82 n. 129; J. Becker's related "new interpretation" of *Sodo shel "Moreh nebukhim"* (The Mystery of the Guide for the Perplexed); and on the equation between *ḥibbur* and *summa,* as well as the translation of the first book, *Madda'* by "religious knowledge," see L. Blau's and S. Rawidowicz's essays mentioned *supra,* Chap. XXVII, nn. 114, 116. Not surprisingly, the commentators departed from Ibn Tibbon's term and called the *Guide* by the more dignified term *Sefer* (book); Shem Tob even termed it a "book great in quality and usefulness" (see the Intro. to his commentary).

26. Ibn Ṣaddiq's *'Olam qaṭan,* ed. by Horovitz, p. 22; Baḥya's *Duties,* Intro., ed. by Yahuda, p. 25 (Zifroni, p. 19; in Hyamson's English trans., I, 15). In his Intro. (p. 4; German trans., p. 6) Ibn Daud made it clear that he did not write for the benefit of confirmed, if naive, believers, since the chief aim of philosophy was practice, and these men already practiced their religion without it. Nor was his book needed by persons well-trained in philosophy, whose own researches should prove more satisfactory. "Only the beginner in the field of speculation, who is perplexed about matters which had reached him by tradition alone and whose [speculative] achievement does not yet enable him to detect the truth in whatever matter he had gone astray, such an one will find this book very useful." But neither the style nor the subject matter of the "Exalted Faith" could have attracted any real beginners. Nor was Ibn Ṣaddiq's encyclopedic treatise, which in brief compass reviewed all the main branches of philosophy and science, a real textbook for beginners. Discounting their author's customary professions of modesty, these works gave much food for thought to serious and fairly advanced, if still groping, students. And how many of those who had squarely faced the conflict between reason and tradition had ceased groping?

27. Maimonides' aforementioned letter to Ibn Tibbon (see *supra,* n. 18); William of Auvergne's *De Legibus,* xv; and *De universo,* II, Part 2, c. CII, in his *Opera omnia,* Orléans, 1674 ed., pp. 47, 998 (written before 1249). See Jakob Guttmann's "Guillaume d'Auvergne et la littérature juive," *REJ,* XXVIII, 251. On the other hand, Maimonides did not mean literally that "all our Andalusian scholars followed the teachings of the philosophers, from whom they accepted those opinions which were not opposed to our own religious principles" (*Guide,* I.71, ed. by Munk, I, fol. 94a; Friedländer, p. 108 omits the crucial word "all" of the Arabic text and the Hebrew *kullam*). He doubtless knew that there were Spanish Jews uninterested in philosophy, and others who did not so readily reject teachings opposed to the principles of Judaism. One need only read the introduction to the philosophic tract of his immediate predecessor, Ibn Daud, to note that persons of the type described here must have been in a small minority even in the Iberian Peninsula. Maimonides merely invoked here a practice current in his Spanish homeland, as he often did in legal matters, in order to take the edge off the opponent's accusation that he was a radical innovator. These constant apologies sharply contrasted with the perfect insouciance with which Saadiah addressed the component monographs of his *Beliefs* to the public at large. In fact, he expressed the hope that his book would reach all intelligent Jews and fortify them in their faith. See his *Beliefs,* Intro., pp. 5 f. (Hebrew, pp. 3 f.; English, pp. 8 f.). There certainly was no basic difference between the audience he approached in his Bible commentaries and

that of the *Beliefs*, as suggested by Vajda in *REJ*, CVI, 67 n. 10. On the earlier rationalist trends among the eastern Jews see *supra*, Chap. XXIX, nn. 87 ff.; and on the situation in Muslim Spain, M. Asín Palacios's brief remarks on "La Indiferencia religiosa en la España musulmana," *Cultura española*, 1907, Part 5, pp. 297–301; and the references to contemporary Arabic sources in Pérès's *Poésie andalouse*, pp. 455 ff.

28. Maimonides' *Guide*, Intro. (in Friedländer's trans., pp. 3, 8); Strauss in his *Persecution*, pp. 73 ff.; Isaac Israeli's *Sefer ha-Yesodot*, II, ed. by Fried, pp. 51 ff.; Ibn Ṣaddiq's *'Olam qaṭan*, ed. by Horovitz, pp. 44, 53 f., with reference to the very delicate problem of the divine will. Maimonides was conscious not only of the likely opposition of conservatives in his own community, but also of the danger of denunciation to Muslim authorities. The latter might well share the view soon thereafter expressed by Saladin's court physician. "I have read," 'Abd al-Latif, Maimonides' younger contemporary, declared, "this work [the *Guide*] and found it to be a bad book, apt to undermine the principles and foundations of all religions with the very means it purportedly uses to strengthen them." The Muslim physician intimated that for this reason Maimonides had forbidden under curse its transliteration into Arabic letters, which would have made it accessible to all Arab readers. See his "Autobiography," cited in S. Munk's *Notice sur Joseph ben Yehoudah*, p. 29; and *supra*, Chap. XXX, n. 7. Evidently, some copies in Arabic script were soon available even to Samuel ibn Tibbon. See Friedländer's remarks in the introduction to his translation of the *Guide* (larger ed.), I, p. xxx n. 2. Despite such precautions, moreover, Maimonides realized that he was subject to prosecution at the denunciation of any of those "sinners and evildoers in Israel," about whom he expressed concern, for instance, in his *Resp.*, pp. 335 ff. No. 369; and in his letter to Ibn Shime'on in *Iggerot*, ed. by Baneth, I. 68.

One should not assume, however, that the order of the *Guide* is really confused. See S. Rawidowicz's apt observations on "The Structure of the 'Guide for the Perplexed'" (Hebrew), *Tarbiz*, VI, 41–89. Strauss's extremist interpretation of this deliberate planlessness, as another means to confuse the uninitiated, is, like his whole theory of this deliberate concealment by means of contradictions, in part self-defeating. If pursued to its logical conclusion, his thesis would leave it entirely to the reader's discretion to decide between the true parts of contradictions and those intended merely to conceal the truth. The sage of Fusṭaṭ himself must have sensed that; known as he was for his general orderliness and even pedantic planning of the sequences of his paragraphs (see *supra*, Chap. XXVII, n. 117), he would have aroused deep suspicions if he suddenly decided to produce an incoherent book. Does not even a modern scholar like W. M. Watt use clear-cut orderliness, or lack of it, as one of the three major criteria to establish "The Authenticity of the Works Attributed to al-Ghazali," *JRAS*, 1952, pp. 24–45? Nor could Maimonides, by placing such tremendous obstacles in the path of the unwary, legitimately entertain any hope "that those of my readers who have not studied philosophy, will still derive profit from many a chapter" (Intro., fol. 9a; in Friedländer's trans., p. 9). Such an invitation to nonphilosophers to read the book and to absorb the more conspicuously stated false assertions, made only in order to conceal the truth, would have been like "placing an obstacle before the blind," entirely different from the talmudic injunction merely to keep silent in the presence of unqualified persons. Nor would he have so eagerly collaborated with Ibn Tibbon in the Hebrew translation so that, to quote the translator's Preface, the treatise's "usefulness should spread among our nation." In Maimonides' own low estimation of the philosophic capacities of Western Jewry, he certainly could expect to find there but very few persons "able to understand by themselves." Much more moderately, Moses ben Solomon of Salerno, with special reference to the *Guide,* II.30, merely asserted that the "third Moses himself knew the secret, but refused to furnish illustration so as not to be a revealer of secrets. This he did in many passages relating to the Chariot, works of Creation, divine Names, and other innumerable matters." See the statement cited from a MS by M. Steinschneider in his review of J. Perles's study, *Die in einer Münchener Handschrift aufgefundene erste lateinische Uebersetzung des Maimonidischen "Führers,"* in *Hebräische Bibliographie,* XV, 88 f. See also J. Bergmann's "Maimonides als Erzieher," *MGWJ,* LXXIX, 89–101; and particularly I. Heinemann's "Maimuni und die arabischen Einheitslehrer," *ibid.,* pp. 102–48, analyzing the general Graeco-Arabic antecedents of the sharp division in communications to the intellectual élite and to the public at large, but at the same time showing how passionately Maimonides wished to spread his antianthropomorphic doctrines among the masses. The very success of Ibn Tumart and the Almohades, from which Maimon's family had suffered so severely, served as a powerful incentive to remove that stumbling block from the Jewish community.

29. Ibn Daud's *Emunah ramah,* edited by Weil, pp. 2 f. (Arabic), 3 f. (German); Abraham bar Ḥiyya's *Hegyon ha-nefesh,* ed. by I. E. Freimann, fol. 1ab. The contrast between the two works of Ibn Gabirol is clearly indicated by himself. Although we do not have his own formal introduction to the *Fons vitae,* the entire book is arranged in the form of a dialogue between a master and a very well informed pupil, or practically between two equals. In contrast thereto, his ethical treatise was avowedly written "for the benefit largely of the masses." For this purpose he not only fortified his arguments by scriptural quotations but, with a slight apology, also cited from the rhymed prose and poems by Gentile sages and poets. See his *Improvement of the Moral Qualities,* edited by S. S. Wise, pp. 15 f. (Arabic), 50 (English). The possibility that Bar Ḥiyya's ethical composition had been put to edificational, if not liturgical, use during the "days of repentance" between the New Year and the Day of Atonement was suggested by several scholars. See W. Bacher, *Die Bibelexegese der jüdischen Religionsphilosophen des Mittelalters vor Maimuni,* pp. 82 f.

30. The use of the talmudic "abbreviated form of argumentation" was first illustrated by H. A. Wolfson in his *Crescas' Critique of Aristotle,* pp. 27 ff.; and later expanded to cover even such diverse philosophers as Philo and Spinoza. See his *Philo,* I, 106 f.; and *The Philosophy of Spinoza,* I, 20 ff. On the peculiar features of the talmudic mode of thinking, see also H. Guggenheimer's pertinent observations in his "Ueber ein bemerkenswertes logisches System aus der Antike," *Methodos,* III, 150–64; and *supra,* Chap. XXVIII, nn. 1, 13. The curriculum of the medieval schools, practically all of which were devoted to the study of the Talmud, but only few to the teaching of philosophy even in the Mediterranean countries, will be discussed more fully in the general context of Jewish education in the later Middle Ages.

31. Prefaces of Moses ibn Chiquitilla and the two Tibbonides, mentioned *supra,* n. 44, and Chap. XXX, n. 5. "Contrary to the prevalent opinion among students of the history of philosophy," commented H. A. Wolfson with special reference to Crescas' ability to read the writings of Greek philosophers only in their secondary or tertiary Hebrew versions, "the translations of Aristotle both in Arabic and in Hebrew have preserved to a remarkable degree not only clear-cut analyses of the text of Aristotle's works but also the exact meaning of his terminology and forms of expression" (*Crescas' Critique of Aristotle,* p. 7). It should also be noted that with few exceptions (like "hyle" or "philosophy"), the translators succeeded in finding Hebrew, or at least Semitic, equivalents for all Greek terms. Nevertheless, even a rendition from Arabic into Hebrew, related though both languages were in structure and particular application to scholastic themes, created tremendous difficulties. Maimonides was not alone in admiring Samuel ibn Tibbon's acumen for finding proper equivalents for Arabic terms. Yet he had to make numerous corrections in the manuscript submitted to him. See his letter to Ibn Tibbon in *Qobeṣ,* II, fol. 27c f.; and Sonne's remarks thereon cited *supra,* n. 18.

These terminological problems have been subjected to careful scholarly scrutiny, not only in such general reviews as I. Friedlaender's aforementioned studies on Maimonides' Arabic language and style (see *supra,* Chap. XXX, n. 8), but also with special reference to the Hebrew terms employed by both translators and original authors. The most comprehensive reference work is J. Klatzkin's *Oṣar ha-munaḥim ha-pilosofiim* (Thesaurus philosophicus linguae hebraicae), which, despite certain valid criticisms voiced by Z. Diesendruck and I. Efros in their reviews of the first two volumes in *KS,* V, 338–44, and *JQR,* XXII, 191–98, has proved very useful to students. M. H. Gottstein's well-documented *Taḥbirah u-millonah shel ha-lashon ha-'ibrit* (Mediaeval Hebrew Syntax and Vocabulary as Influenced by Arabic) likewise goes beyond the realm of philology and sheds much light on the terms used in the "Translation Hebrew" of the Tibbonides and other writers. More specialized are the investigations by I. Efros, "Studies in Pre-Tibbonian Philosophic Terminology," *JQR,* XVII, 129–64, 323–68; XX, 113–38 (on Abraham bar Ḥiyya); his *Philosophical Terms in the Moreh Nebukim* (with notes by L. Ginzberg); his brief remarks in *PAAJR,* II, 3 ff.; D. Z. Baneth's "On the Philosophic Terminology of Maimonides" (Hebrew), *Tarbiz,* VI, 10–40; H. A. Wolfson's analysis of "The Amphibolous Terms in Aristotle, Arabic Philosophy and Maimonides," *HTR,* XXXI, 151–73 (explaining the meaning and sources of those intermediary terms between "homonyms" and "synonyms"); M. Sister's "Bachja Studien, I," *Fünfzigster Bericht der Lehranstalt für die Wissenschaft des Judentums,* pp. 33–75 (analyzes the ethical and ascetic terms); and his "Einige Bemerkungen über Bachjas Stil im Kitab al-hidaja . . . und dessen Uebersetzung durch J. ibn Tibbon," *MGWJ,* LXXXI, 86–93. Needless to say, the scholarly apparatus appended to critical editions of pertinent texts, and such critical comments thereon as are mentioned, e.g., *supra,* nn. 2, 5, and 7, often shed much light on terminological usage.

32. Halevi's *K. al-Khazari,* II.66, in Hirschfeld's translation, p. 124. The first medieval thinker to resume this hypothesis appears to have been Qirqisani, in whose day the Philonic traditions were still much alive. He found full evidence for it in the biblical description of the all-comprehensive wisdom of Solomon and also in the report of the clear-cut superiority of Hananiah, Mishael, and Azariah over the counselors of the Babylonian king. See Hirschfeld, *Qirqisani Studies,* p. 15;

and, on Jephet ben 'Ali's related philosophy of history, *supra,* Chap. XXVIII, nn. 74–75. Other older sources are quoted by Munk in his translation of Maimonides' *Guide,* I.71 (I, 332 n. 3) and Cassel in his note on Halevi's statement (in his ed., p. 172 n. 2). More surprisingly many Muslims and Christians agreed with this Jewish claim. See, e.g., the encyclopedia of the Brethren of Purity (*Ikhwan aṣ-ṣafa*), Tract XXI (pointed out by Munk in his *Mélanges de philosophie juive et arabe,* p. 466 n.1); and Roger Bacon's *Opus tertium,* III.10, in his *Opera quaedam hactenus inedita,* ed. by J. S. Brewer, pp. 32 f. See also my study of "The Historical Outlook of Maimonides," *PAAJR,* VI, 105 f. The claims of the ancient apologists, at times even more extravagant, have been discussed *supra,* Vols. I, pp. 198 f., 386 n. 43; II, pp. 157, 390 f. n. 36.

33. Ibn Daud's *Emunah ramah,* I.2; III, pp. 8, 102 (Hebrew), 11 ff., 131 (German). On Ibn Gabirol's and Maimonides' allegorical interpretations of Scripture, see *infra,* nn. 67, 69; and *supra,* Chap. XXIX, nn. 85–86. It ought to be noted, however, that despite their general acknowledgement of indebtedness to Greek and Arabic writers, relatively few of these philosophers directly cited their sources, or even mentioned names of authors from whom they borrowed certain ideas. Even Baḥya and Maimonides, relatively the most articulate on this score, frequently leave us in the dark on their most direct sources of information. That is why the important study of the sources of each of these thinkers, on which modern scholars have lavished so much care and attention, will necessarily remain largely conjectural. Certainly, many intermediary links between the now surviving Arabic writings of Greek and Muslim philosophers, and those then available to the Jewish thinkers, are irretrievably lost. We know, for example, that man's destiny, as taught by Ibn Daud and Maimonides, was not strictly Aristotelian in the sense of the later writings of the Stagirite. Similarly the Platonists, Israeli, Gabirol, and Ibn Ṣaddiq, have taken little, if anything, directly from Plato or even Plotinus, although some writings of each of these ancient thinkers had become available in Arabic translations. See I. Heinemann's observations on *Die Lehre von der Zweckbestimmung des Menschen, passim;* and Julius Guttmann's review of that book in *MGWJ,* LXX, 422–24. The limited availability of some Neoplatonic writings to the twelfth-century Muslim student of comparative religion, Shahrastani, is illustrated by the latter's *K. al-Milal,* ed. by Cureton, pp. 334–37, 345–47; and in Haarbrücker's German trans., *Religionspartheien,* II, 192 ff., 208 ff. See F. Gabrieli's intro. to his Italian trans. of these passages in his "Plotino e Porfirio in un eresiografo musulmano," *Parola di Passato,* I, 338–46. That the very notion of Platonism did not mean the same thing to the thinkers of various schools is well illustrated by the contrast, as well as the great similarities, between St. Bonaventura and Baḥya ibn Paquda, shown, in part in parallel columns, by E. Bertola in his "Platonismo escolástico-cristiano y arabe-judío," *Sefarad,* X, 385–400. On the translations of Aristotle's works, on the other hand, see *infra,* n. 80.

34. Saadiah's *Beliefs,* I.3, ed. by Landauer, pp. 63 ff. (Hebrew, pp. 33 ff.; English, pp. 75 ff.). In his summary of these views in "The Quest for Certainty in Saadia's Philosophy," *JQR,* XXXIII, 268 ff., A. Heschel explained the difference between the last two schools of thought as probably referring to the validity of sensations. While the agnostics denied it, the ephectics admitted the validity of such perception, but only for its duration. In *La Philosophie de Saadia Gaon,* pp. 148 ff., M.

Ventura has rightly pointed out, however, that only the last three schools of thought are properly treated within the domain of epistemology by such Arab authors as At-Tusi, Ibn Ḥazm, and Al-Baghdadi. The first school of materialists (in Saadiah's enumeration the tenth) represented really but a cosmological doctrine. One cannot deny, however, that the underlying theory of cognition, though incidental, is sufficiently strong for S. Horovitz (in *Judaica,* pp. 242 ff.) and his successors rightly to treat it as an independent epistemological school as well. Apart from these extreme schools of thought, Saadiah enumerated eight others holding erroneous views on the subject of the creation of the world, although their epistemological approaches were less radical. These included representatives of the Platonic cosmology, the eastern theory of emanation, gnostic-Parsee dualism, and the allegedly Hippocratic doctrine of the four cosmic elements (Ventura, pp. 116 ff.). Saadiah refuted them all one by one with logical arguments, and only secondarily mentioned the scriptural evidence. He exhorted his reader to "hold on to the following three points in every chapter of this book: namely, (*a*) that thy proofs are stronger than those of the others, (*b*) that thou art able to refute anyone that disagrees with thee, and (*c*) that the miracles of thy prophets are a part of thy advantage" (I.Intro., ed. by Landauer, p. 32; Hebrew, p. 16; English, p. 40). In this connection (I.1) Saadiah also referred to related discussions in his earlier works, such as the commentaries on the Bible and the Book of Creation, or his reply to Ḥivi. See also I. Efros's careful analysis of "Saadia's Theory of Knowledge," *JQR,* XXXIII, 133–70; A. Heschel's "Reason and Revelation in Saadia's Philosophy," *ibid.,* XXXIV, 391–408 (supplementing his aforementioned essay); A. Altmann's "Saadya's Theory of Revelation: Its Origin and Background," in Rosenthal's *Saadya Studies,* pp. 4–25 (see *infra,* n. 93); and I. Heinemann's "R. Saadiah Gaon's Rationalism" (Hebrew) in *Rav Saadya Gaon,* ed. by Fishman, pp. 191–240 (particularly interesting because of its methodological comparison with talmudic methods of interpretation).

35. Isaac Israeli's *Sefer ha-Yesodot,* II, ed. by Fried, pp. 53 ff. See H. A. Wolfson's careful analysis of "Isaac Israeli on the Internal Senses," *Kohut Mem. Vol.,* pp. 583–98; and, more generally, of "The Internal Senses in Latin, Arabic, and Hebrew Philosophic Texts," *HTR,* XXVIII, 69–133. To be sure, in his four definitions of "memory," Israeli, indirectly following John of Damascus, was concerned only with individual memory. However, his description of memory as a "continuous and uninterrupted conservation" of the results of earlier sensations and cogitation might apply, without its physiological background, to tradition as well. At least Saadiah seems to have reached that conclusion when, after discussing the three sources of knowledge, he emphasized as the fourth source "authentic tradition" and, in another context, stressed the fact that God had rendered "the human mind susceptible to the acceptance of authenticated tradition and the human soul capable of finding repose therein, so that his Scriptures and traditions might be acknowledged as true." See his *Beliefs,* Intro. and III.6, ed. by Landauer, pp. 14, 126 (Hebrew, pp. 7, 65; English, pp. 18, 156 f.). See also Efros's observations in *JQR,* XXXIII, 159 ff.; and, on the specific gifts of prophecy, *infra,* nn. 93 and 99.

36. Saadiah's *Beliefs,* Intro., pp. 3 f. (Hebrew, pp. 2 f.; English, pp. 6 ff.); Maimonides' "Treatise on Logic," VIII, ed. by Efros, pp. 17 f. (Arabic), 39 f., 113 (Hebrew), 47 f. (English). In his argument that "we are forced to affirm, although we have never seen it, that man possesses a soul, in order not to deny its manifest activity,"

and in the parallel reasoning for the existence of reason (*Beliefs,* p. 13; Hebrew, p. 7; English, p. 17), Saadiah found a significant answer to the doubters. One might see therein a somewhat inarticulate adumbration of Descartes's famous formula. Heschel (in *JQR,* XXXIII, 273 n. 40) cites some Augustinian parallels. But it is very unlikely that any views of the Bishop of Hippo percolated into the gaon's consciousness even through the mediation of the Arabic schools of philosophy. The great Latin Church Father's writings seem to have remained little known even in Byzantium down to the fourteenth century, when they were first translated into Greek. See Krumbacher's *Geschichte der byzantinischen Litteratur,* p. 40. However Saadiah's basic argument seems so obvious that one need not look for historical indebtedness. See also J. Teicher's observations, mainly with reference to Maimonides, on "Spunti cartesiani nella filosofia arabo-giudaica," *Giornale critico della filosofia italiana,* XVI, 101–30, 235–49.

37. Saadiah's *Beliefs,* Intro. and II.3, ed. by Landauer, pp. 14, 25 f., (Hebrew, pp. 7, 12 f., 44; English, pp. 18, 32, 100). See H. A. Wolfson's comparative study of "The Double Faith Theory in Clement, Saadia, Averroës and St. Thomas, and Its Origin in Aristotle and the Stoics," *JQR,* XXXIII, 230 ff.; D. Neumark's *Toledot,* II, 111; and Saadiah's statements in his various works, cited by Efros in *JQR,* XXXIII, 153. While generally accepting Wolfson's keen analysis, we must not lose sight of the serious reservations advanced against it by G. Vajda in *REJ,* CIX, 92 ff. Even in his remarkable plea for the justification of doubts, Saadiah merely argued that he who "desires that God endow him with a knowledge free from all uncertainty, such a one asks that his Master make him His equal" (*Beliefs,* Intro., p. 10; Hebrew, p. 5; English, p. 13). The gaon emphasized here only the limitations of the human mind to secure certainty without the arduous effort of careful research and meditation. This position was essentially held also by the most influential Muslim philosophers, ever since Al-Kindi, who had died a short time before Saadiah was born (after 870). See esp. his brief introduction to Aristotle in M. Guidi and R. Walzer, *Studi su Al-Kindi,* I (Chap. VI.2).

38. Maimonides' *Guide,* I.31; II.22, 25 (in Friedländer's trans., pp. 41 f., 194, 199); Wolfson in "The Double Faith Theory," *JQR,* XXXIII, 243. See also *Guide,* II.24 (p. 198). The Maimonidean theory of cognition, like most phases of the thought of that sage, has often been considered by modern scholars. It has been the subject of special studies by W. Mischel, *Die Erkenntnistheorie Maimonides';* and by A. J. Bombach, *Versuch einer systematischen Darstellung der Erkenntnistheorie des Maimonides.* See also S. Rawidowicz's analysis of the Maimonidean views on "Philosophy as a Duty" in I. Epstein's edition of octocentenary essays on *Moses Maimonides,* pp. 175–88. Of related interest, though broader in scope, are the numerous discussions on the relation between faith and reasons in the Maimonidean philosophy. See esp. the dissertations by C. Tirschtigel, *Das Verhältnis von Glauben und Wissen bei den bedeutendsten jüdischen Religionsphilosophen bis Maimonides,* and by A. Schück, *Glauben und Wissen nach R. Mose ben Maimon* (although dealing also with much irrelevant material, the latter offers a comprehensive accumulation of data on the sage of Fusṭaṭ and many of his ancient and medieval predecessors); B. Z. Bokser's briefer analysis of "Reason and Revelation in the Theology of Maimonides," *HUCA,* XX, 541–84 ("in all the crucial issues where philosophy and the Torah clashed he upheld the Torah," p. 582); G. Vajda's

"Quelques aspects du problème de la foi et de la raison dans la philosophie juive du moyen âge," *Revue de la Pensée juive,* I, 100–115; and, for comparative purposes, M. Horten's small collection of *Texte zu dem Streite zwischen Glauben und Wissen im Islam:* and W. C. Klein's more recent translation of Abu'l Ḥasan 'Ali al-Ash'ari's *K. al-Ibanah 'an Uṣul ad-diyanah* (The Elucidation of Islam's Foundation). Other aspects of the attitude of the medieval philosophers to human psychology, prophetic endowment, and revelation will be discussed later in this chapter.

39. Ibn Gabirol's "Royal Crown," cited *infra,* n. 76; his *Fons vitae,* II.6; V.13–15, ed. by Baeumker, pp. 34 f., 279 ff. (in Bluvstein's Hebrew translation, pp. 26 f., 184 ff.). See K. Dreyer's data in *Die religiöse Gedankenwelt des Salomo ibn Gabirol,* pp. 144 ff.; Heinemann's observations in *Die Lehre von der Zweckbestimmung des Menschen,* pp. 53 f.; and Julius Guttmann's brief remarks in *Die Philosophie des Judentums,* pp. 114 f. See also A. Heschel's somewhat modernizing reconstruction of "Das Wesen der Dinge nach der Lehre Gabirols," *HUCA,* XIV, 359–85. On the difference between "union" and "communion" with God, see also *infra,* n. 75.

40. Ibn Gabirol's *Fons,* I.2–5, ed. by Baeumker, pp. 3 ff. (Bluvstein, pp. 2 ff.); Jalalu'ddin Rumi's "Spiritual Couplet," cited by R. A. Nicholson in his "Mysticism" in *The Legacy of Islam,* p. 234; his selections from *Rumi, Poet and Mystic (1207–1273)*; Martin Luther's last Wittenberg sermon of January 17, 1546, in his *Werke,* Kritische Gesammtausgabe, LI, 126 (reason "is the greatest whore the devil has").

41. Ibn Gabirol's *Shire,* II, 48 (Zangwill, p. 13, offers a different translation); and *supra,* Chaps. XXV, nn. 15–16; XXXII, n. 47. In the concluding line of the poem we get a glimpse of Ibn Gabirol's "voluntaristic" doctrine, which, as we shall see, is one of his major contributions to Jewish metaphysical speculation. Even Maimonides, angry opponent though he was of all philosophizing poets (see *supra,* Chap. XXXI, nn. 55, 81), could not possibly have objected to obscure allusions of this type.

42. Halevi's *K. al-Khazari,* I.67, 89; IV.3, 6; V.16, ed. by Hirschfeld, pp. 28 f., 40 f., 242 ff., 248 f., 330 f. (in Hirschfeld's translation, pp, 54, 62, 206, 210 f., 214, 274 f.); his poem, *Debarekha be-mor* (Thy Words Are Compounded of Sweet-Smelling Myrrh) in his *Diwan,* ed. by Brody, II, 166 No. 6 (in N. Salaman's translation, p. 16). In his edition of the Hebrew *Kuzari* (p. 324 nn. 2–3), D. Cassel cites Muscato and others who referred to the legends concerning the meeting between Plato and Jeremiah in Egypt, to show that, in the opinion of Halevi and his contemporaries, philosophers often rationalized what they accepted as indubitable prophetic evidence. That Halevi was essentially a rationalist and believer in evidence, although in his opinion historical evidence outweighed that of fallible human speculation, has been convincingly argued by Julius Guttmann in "Das Verhältnis von Religion und Philosophie bei Jehuda Halewi," *Festschrift Israel Lewy,* pp. 327–58 (reproduced in Hebrew in his *Dat u-madda',* pp. 66–85). See also E. Berger's *Das Problem der Erkenntnis in der Religionsphilosophie Jehuda Hallewis.* The indebtedness of Yehudah Halevi's "rationalism" to the "anti-rationalism" of Al-Ghazzali, a problem long controversial, is judiciously analyzed by D. H. Baneth, in his "Jehuda Hallewi und Gazali," *KA,* V, 27–45. The argument is well summed up by the author's concluding sentence: "That is why he [Halevi] stands close to the aspirations of the present generation of Jews who look for a return to *living* Judaism, while Ghazzali

is much rather related to the mystic currents of our day." Baneth later expanded this study into a more fully documented Hebrew essay in *Keneset,* VII, 311–29. A spirited comparison with Halevi's great rationalist compeer is drawn by H. A. Wolfson in his "Maimonides and Halevi," *JQR,* II, 297–337. However, Wolfson's youthfully exuberant assertion—"Maimonides may be considered as swimming with the stream, he was the expression of his age; Halevi was swimming against the stream, he was the insurgent, the utterer of paradoxes" (p. 307)—is only correct if we limit the "stream" to the small circle of the intellectual élite in the Mediterranean countries. The masses probably made use of neither work, while the relatively large group of rabbinic students perused Halevi's book with far less misgivings.

43. Maimonides' *Guide,* II.30; III.50 (in Friedländer's translation, pp. 216 f., 380 f.). The allegory of Adam and Eve has been correctly recognized by such commentators as Efodi, Shem Tob, and Asher Crescas (on II.30), though Maimonides' own formulation was consciously obscure. "I will therefore not add long explanations," he forewarned the reader, "lest I make their statement plain, and I might thus become 'a revealer of secrets.'" And yet he was so certain of the correctness of his interpretation that he sharply attacked the great "ignorance of those who do not see that all this necessarily includes some" other than the ordinary meaning. See *supra,* n. 28. In the introduction to his *Commentary* on the Mishnah the sage of Fusṭaṭ went even further, and asserted that one must also study even the homilies of the rabbis with proper attention to the dictates of reason. "All these homiletical statements," he declared, "if studied with deep understanding, will be found to contain the truly good, above which there is none higher. One will detect in them the divine matters and their true nature, which the men of wisdom had concealed and did not wish to reveal, and over which the philosophers had labored for generations." See his *Commentary* on M. Berakhot, Intro., ed. by B. Hamburger, pp. 44 f. In short, where the accepted texts controvert reason they must be viewed as metaphors not to be taken too literally. In all this Maimonides was essentially anticipated by Saadiah who, without resorting to the strained allegories of Philo, Ibn Gabirol, or Maimonides, nevertheless felt, as we recall, that Scripture cannot possibly contradict reason. See esp. the passages referred to *supra,* n. 37; and, more generally, W. Bacher's two detailed monographs on the Bible exegesis of the medieval Jewish philosophers; and other literature cited *supra,* Chap. XXIX, *passim.* The Maimonidean influence made itself widely felt in this realm, as it did in the other fields of Jewish learning, and traces of it are still distinctly noticeable in the works of Spinoza. See I. Husik's brief comparison of "Maimonides and Spinoza on the Interpretation of the Bible," in his *Philosophical Essays,* pp. 141–59. The general impact of the Maimonidean teachings on Western thought will be discussed in their respective contexts.

44. Abraham bar Ḥiyya's *Megillat ha-megalleh,* II, edited by Poznanski, pp. 15 ff.; Halevi's *K. al-Khazari,* I.11–12, 67 (in Hirschfeld's translation, pp. 44 f., 54). In his interpretation of the six days of creation as an adumbration of the whole history of the world, Bar Ḥiyya followed not only notions long accepted in the Aggadah, but also certain basic views known among his Christian neighbors in Spain and stemming from Isidore of Seville. See Julius Guttmann's introduction to Poznanski's edition, pp. xiii f. In essence, however, his was a Jewish philosophy of history,

emphasizing above everything the error of those philosophers who believed that the universe was of infinite duration. In his basic approach, too, Abraham untiringly stressed the permissibility, from the standpoint of the Jewish tradition, of engaging in this sort of speculation. In fact, he believed that since the whole goal of creation is the ultimate messianic era, the proper computation of the date of the arrival of the Messiah would help solve many philosophic problems as well. This combination of speculative and practical objectives is fully indicated in the opening paragraph of his work. "Everything," he declared, "that is based on the Torah, and does some good to Israel in this exile, strengthens their heart through faith, or gives them additional confidence and hope, is a fit subject for research and devoted investigation of its hidden aspects." See *supra,* Chaps. XXV, n. 23; XXVIII, nn. 97–98.

45. Halevi's *K. al-Khazari,* I.67 (English, p. 54: "The theory of creation derives greater weight from the prophetic tradition of Adam, Noah, and Moses, which is more deserving of credence than mere speculation"); Ibn Gabirol's *Fons vitae,* I.10–13; II.12–13; V.27, ed. by Baeumker, pp. 12 ff., 43 ff., 306 (Hebrew, pp. 9 ff., 32 ff., 200 f.; cf. Falaquera epitome, V.64 ff., *ibid.,* pp. 263 ff.); Pseudo-Baḥya's *K. Ma'ani al-nafs,* XVI, edited by Goldziher, p. 54 (in Broydé's Hebrew translation, p. 72); Maimonides' *Guide,* II.16, 25 (in Friedländer's translation, pp. 178, 199). On Ibn Ezra's views, see his *Commentaries* on Exodus and Daniel, cited *infra,* n. 53. Among these doctrines that of Ibn Gabirol was the most revolutionary. It placed Matter in the very center of the spiritual world, as much as of the physical world. It is small wonder, then, that in the subsequent protracted debates among the medieval Christian scholastics on this issue, Avicebron's teachings were frequently quoted. Both Albertus Magnus and Thomas Aquinas wrote extensively in their refutation. See esp. the distinction drawn between Ibn Gabirol's concept and the related views of Plotinus in M. Bieler's dissertation, *Der göttliche Wille (Logosbegriff) bei Gabirol,* pp. 41 ff. See also H. A. Wolfson's examination of "The Meaning of 'Ex nihilo' in the Church Fathers, Arabic and Hebrew Philosophy and St. Thomas" in *Mediaeval Studies in Honour of Jeremiah Denis Matthias Ford,* pp. 353–70; and of "The Platonic, Aristotelian and Stoic Theories of Creation in Hallevi and Maimonides," *Essays Hertz,* pp. 427–42; A. Rohner's and M. Fakhry's comparative studies of *Das Schöpfungsproblem bei Moses Maimonides, Albertus Magnus und Thomas von Aquin;* and "The 'Antinomy' of the Eternity of the World in Averroës, Maimonides and Aquinas," *Muséon,* LXVI, 139–55 (postulating a rather tenuous distinction between creation *ex nihilo* and one of a world which had not always been). Of course, these debates had many ancient antecedents. On the earlier doctrines of both the Aggadah and the Muslim *ḥadith,* see esp. V. Aptowitzer's "Arabisch-jüdische Schöpfungstheorien," *HUCA,* VI, 205–46; E. Hahn's "Hadith cosmogonique et Aggada," *REJ,* CI, 53–72; and *supra,* Chap. XXIX, nn. 65 ff.

46. Ibn Daud's *Emunah ramah,* I.2, pp. 10 (Hebrew), 15 (German; S. Weil's translation here lacks precision); Saadiah's *Beliefs,* I.1, ed. by Landauer, pp. 36 f. (Hebrew, p. 20; English, p. 45; by translating "virtually," rather than "in thought," Rosenblatt gave this idea a somewhat different turn); Bar Ḥiyya's *Megillat ha-megalleh,* VI.23. Understandably, the extremely complex problems of the creation of time and the very difficulty of conceiving of something existing "before" its creation, had to be faced by many thinkers since ancient times. On Philo's pertinent query, see *supra,* Vol. II, pp. 158, 391 n. 37; and the literature listed there. Additional data may be

found in the following recent essays: M. M. Kasher, "The Concept of Time in Rabbinic Literature" (Hebrew), *Talpioth*, V, 799–827 (somewhat futilely trying to interpret into it certain assumptions of the modern theory of relativity); C. Tresmontant, "Création et temps dans la pensée hébraïque," *Cahiers sioniens*, VII, 25–49; and, for comparative purposes, R. Florez, "El Tema del tiempo en la filosofia de S. Augustin," *Ciudad de Dios*, CLXVI, 61–86; G. Le Bras, "Le Problème du temps dans l'histoire du droit canon," *Revue historique du droit français*, 4th ser., XXX, 487–513 (discussing also the distinction between eternal law and temporary adjustments, so significant also from the standpoint of Jewish law); L. Massignon, "Le Temps dans la pensée islamique," *Eranos-Jahrbuch*, XX 141–48; and *infra*, n. 47. The difference between real existence and one only in the human mind was to play a particularly great role in the doctrine of attributes, especially of "negative" attributes. See *infra*, nn. 55 ff. Neither did the doctrine of emanation by Ibn Gabirol and others imply any time sequence.

47. Israeli's *Sefer ha-Yesodot*, p. 43; Saadiah's *Beliefs*, I.2, p. 43 (Hebrew, p. 23; English, p. 52). See I. I. Efros, *The Problem of Space in Jewish Mediaeval Philosophy*, esp. pp. 49 ff., 72, 110 ff. According to H. A. Wolfson, the Kalam theory combated by Saadiah, though not otherwise fully documented, is based on the combination of atomism with antemundane matter and ideas. See his reconstruction of "The Kalam Problem of Nonexistence and Saadia's Second Theory of Creation," *JQR*, XXXVI, 371–91; and his further elaboration of the doctrine of "Atomism in Saadia," *ibid.*, XXXVII, 107–24. See also M. Ventura's more general analysis of the Graeco-Arabian sources in his Hebrew "Survey of the Cosmological Theories in the Writings of R. Saadiah Gaon and Creation Ex Nihilo" in *Rav Saadya Gaon*, ed. by Fishman, pp. 310–32. Maimonides, too, opposed sharply the atomistic theory which, at variance with that originally advanced by Epicurus and the other Greek Atomists, he considered the first of "twelve propositions common to all Mutakallimun" (*Guide*, I.73; English, pp. 120 f.), and which he proceeded to repudiate one by one. See M. Guttmann's analysis of *Das religionsphilosophische System der Mutakallimun nach dem Berichte des Maimonides*. See also Abu'l Barakat's noteworthy discussion of Space, the Void and Spatial Infinite, analyzed by Pines in *REJ*, CIII, 5 ff.; D. B. Macdonald's "Continuous Re-Creation and Atomic Time in Muslim Scholastic Theology," *Isis*, IX, 326–44; and, more generally, Pines's *Beiträge zur islamischen Atomenlehre*. On Abraham bar Ḥiyya's view of time and its possible Augustinian antecedents, see *supra*, Chap. XXVIII, n. 98.

48. Saadiah's *Beliefs*, I.1, pp. 32 ff. (Hebrew, pp. 16 ff.; English, pp. 40 ff.); Baḥya's *Duties*, I.5, ed. by Yahuda, p. 43 (ed. by Zifroni, p. 30; by Hyamson, I, 29); Maimonides' *Guide*, I.74 beg., II.16 (English, pp. 133, 178); and H. A. Wolfson's ingenious reconstruction of "The Kalam Arguments for Creation in Saadia, Averroës, Maimonides and St. Thomas," in *Saadia Anniv. Vol.*, pp. 197–245. On some of these arguments, see also Z. Diesendruck's "Saadya's Formulation of the Time-Argument for Creation" in *Kohut Mem. Vol.*, pp. 145–58; and I. Efros's "Saadya's Second Theory of Creation in Its Relation to Pythagoreanism and Platonism," *Ginzberg Jub. Vol.*, pp. 133–42. As Wolfson points out, the formulation of these proofs is "one of the legacies left by the Kalam to the history of philosophy" (p. 243). See also Wolfson's "Hallevi and Maimonides on Design, Chance and Necessity," *PAAJR*, XI, 105–63; his essay cited *supra*, n. 45; and E. L. Fackenheim's comparative study

of "The Possibility of the Universe in Al-Farabi, Ibn Sina and Maimonides," *PAAJR*, XVI, 39–70.

49. That all medieval Jewish philosophers limited themselves to the cosmological argument in its various stages, but definitely ignored those derived from the universal assent of man (reminiscent of the Arabic *idjma'*), as well as from the innateness of the God idea, and that they touched only slightly upon the teleological and ontological proofs, has been shown by H. A. Wolfson in his "Notes on Proofs of the Existence of God in Jewish Philosophy," *HUCA*, I, 575–96. It is evident that their strict monotheism prevented them from making full use of these lines of reasoning. See also C. Ramos Gil's analysis of "La Demostración de la existencia divina en Baḥya Ibn Paquda," *Sefarad*, XI, 305–38; S. Nirenstein's comparative study of "The Problem of the Existence of God in Maimonides, Alanus and Averroës," *JQR*, XIV, 395–454; and A. J. Wensinck's data on "Les Preuves de l'existence de Dieu dans la théologie musulmane," *Mededeelingen* of the K. Akademie van Wettenschappen, Section Letterkunde, LXXXI, Ser. A, pp. 41–67. Here Wensinck keenly analyzes the various proofs offered by the theologians of the eleventh and twelfth centuries, in part under the challenge of the "philosophers," and shows that only the ontological proof of later Christian scholasticism is absent. However, a related ontological argument had, indeed, been advanced by Avicenna in his later writings. See M. Cruz Hernández, "Algunos aspectos de la existencia de Dios en la filosofía de Avicenna," *Al-Andalus*, XII, 97–122. Of more tangential interest is the discussion of God as Prime Mover in Avicennian terms by an anonymous Judeo-Arab author of the thirteenth century, whose brief treatise was published with a French translation by G. Vajda in "Un Champion de l'avicennisme. Le problème de l'identité de Dieu et du premieur moteur d'après un opuscule judéo-arabe inédit du XIIIe siècle," *Revue Thomiste*, XLVIII, 480–508 (referring to Moses ben Joseph ha-Levi).

50. Ibn Gabirol's *Fons vitae*, v.38, ed. by Baeumker, p. 326 (Hebrew, p. 213); his "Royal Crown," in *Shire*, II, 64 No. 62 (ed. by Davidson, pp. 87 f.). Our translation of these verses follows closely that by I. Zangwill, except where he missed the two main points concerning the divine Will and emanation. See also Ibn Falaquera's epitome of the *Fons*, v.62–64 in Bluvstein's ed., p. 263. The *Origo largitatis et causa essendi*, mentioned in *Fons*, v.40, p. 330, as "treating of the knowledge of the Will" and able to give the reader "certainty about creation," has never been recovered even in a small fragment. This is doubly regrettable, as it might have helped us to clear up the fundamental question of the sources, to which Ibn Gabirol, however original he may have been, was indebted to some extent. He may have felt the less inclined to quote his sources directly in his main philosophic work, as it was written in the form of a semi-poetic dialogue. Even the three references to Plato and, a more oblique one, to the Book of Creation (*Fons*, II.21 end; IV.8, 20; V.17, 169, 190, pp. 63, 229, 256, 289; Hebrew, pp. 46, 151), come rather as a surprise. One cannot assert, therefore, with complete confidence that our poet-philosopher was familiar with Pseudo-Empedocles, as suggested by D. Kaufmann in his *Studien über Salomon ibn Gabirol*, pp. 7 ff. Certainly the old question as to why he followed essentially Plotinian doctrines, at a time when the Arab world itself had largely moved from Neoplatonism to Aristotelianism, requires qualification in two directions: (1) Ibn Gabirol was, in fact, greatly influenced by Aristotelian teachings, as was shown in the debate between Munk and Neumark in the latter's *Toledot*, II,

255 ff.; (2) he followed later Neoplatonists like Porphyry and Proclus even more than Plotinus; see I. Heinemann's brief hints in *Die Lehre von der Zweckbestimmung des Menschen im griechisch-römischen Altertum und im jüdischen Mittelalter,* pp. 49 ff. On the other hand, Farabi's influence, often postulated especially with reference to Ibn Gabirol's doctrine of the Will, becomes less certain if we deny the genuineness of his *Fuṣuṣ al-ḥikam* as does K. Georr in his "Farabi est-il l'auteur de Fuçuç al ḥikam?" in *Revue des études islamiques,* 1941–46, pp. 31–39. See also S. Pines, "Ibn Sina et l'auteur de la Risâlat al-Fusûs f'il hikma: Quelques données du problème," *ibid.,* XIX, 121–24 (likewise prefers attribution to Avicenna).

Regrettably, no serious effort has thus far been made to search for influences or even parallels in the contemporary Arabic poetry, which must have greatly impressed Ibn Gabirol also with its metaphysical doctrines. Here we have to consider not only the orthodox, but also the heretical poets, who had every reason to speculate about theological fundamentals. Considering how important the doctrine of Matter and Form are in the philosophic outlook of Ibn Gabirol, and how vital, in particular, is his concept of both being present already in the First Emanation, one may indeed gain an inkling from the perusal of the brief remarks by Jawad Masqati (or rather Kamil Hussain) at the International Congress of Orientalists on the "Theory of 'Matter' and 'Spirit' and Its Influence on the Egyptian Poetry of the Fatimid Period," published in *IC,* XXIV, 108–16. Of course, owing to official suppression, little of that Isma'ili and other heretical poetry has come down to us, especially from medieval Spain. On the more formal influences, see, e.g., *supra,* Chap. XXXII, n. 84.

Because of Ibn Gabirol's importance as both poet and philosopher, his teachings, and especially his doctrine of the divine Will, have been frequently analyzed. See esp. M. Bieler's aforementioned dissertation, *Der göttliche Wille . . . bei Gabirol* and the literature listed therein. See also A. J. Borisov's "On the Point of Departure of the Voluntarism of Solomon ibn Gabirol" (Russian), *Bulletin* of the Academy of Sciences of the U.S.S.R., Humanistic Div., 7th ser., 1933, pp. 755–68; A. Heschel's scrutiny of "Der Begriff der Einheit in der Philosophie Gabirols," *MGWJ,* LXXXII, 89–111; F. Brunner's "Sur l'hylémorphisme d'Ibn Gabirol," *Etudes philosophiques,* VIII, 28–38 ("does not introduce corporeality into the spiritual world"); his "La Doctrine de la matière chez Avicébron," *Revue de Théologie et de Philosophie,* 3d ser., VI, 261–79; and, for a comparison with other medieval philosophers, the monographs by A. Grünfeld, *Die Lehre vom göttlichen Willen bei den jüdischen Religionsphilosophen des Mittelalters von Saadja bis Maimûni;* and by I. Epstein, "Das Problem des göttlichen Willens in der Schöpfung nach Maimonides, Gersonides und Crescas," *MGWJ,* LXXV, 335–47.

51. Ibn Gabirol's *Fons vitae,* III.1–10, ed. by Baeumker, pp. 73 ff. (Hebrew, pp. 52 ff.); Ibn Daud's *Emunah ramah,* II.4, 2, pp. 62 (Hebrew), 78 (German). Ibn Daud's stricture that Ibn Gabirol had "left it to anyone who so desires to choose from the bad ones [arguments] whichever he needs," refers to Ibn Gabirol's own introductory disclaimer of any wish to present these proofs in any logical order. The numerical discrepancy between the actual number of fifty-six demonstrations, some of them decidedly repetitious, and the round figure of forty given by Ibn Daud, is rather forcedly explained by D. Kaufmann in his *Studien über Ibn Gabirol,* p. 106 n. 2, as the result of a copyist's error. See also Bieler's analysis of these proofs in *Der göttliche Wille,* pp. 32 ff.

52. Ibn Daud's *Emunah,* II.4, 3, pp. 63 f. (Hebrew), 80 (German); Maimonides' *Guide,* II.6 (English, p. 162). Ibn Daud's sanguine assertion in this context that Aristotle's assumption of the coexistence of an eternal world with God, made some fifteen centuries before, had long since been disproved, reflects more than mere wishful thinking. There were indeed few men among his contemporaries who still insisted upon that duality. The underlying astronomic and astrological teachings will be discussed more fully in connection with the general development of medieval science in the next chapter.

53. Abraham ibn Ezra's *Commentary* on Gen. 1:1; Exod. 3:15, 25:40, and Dan. 11:2. See D. Rosin's interpretation of these cryptic comments cited in part from a Breslau MS in *MGWJ,* XLII, 202 ff. Of course, this entire world outlook, based on the system of Intelligences and Spheres, has become so antiquated that not surprisingly it has exercised but little attraction on modern scholars. Hence the paucity of recent monographs on this subject.

54. Bar Ḥiyya's *Megillat ha-megalleh,* pp. 21 f. See G. Scholem's penetrating analysis in his "Reste neuplatonischer Spekulation in der Mystik der deutschen Chassidim und ihre Vermittlung durch Abraham bar Chija," *MGWJ,* LXXV, 172–91; and *supra,* Chap. XXXIII, n. 49.

55. See Saadiah's polemics against the Christian interpretation in his *Beliefs,* II.5, p. 88 (Hebrew, p. 46; English, pp. 105 f.). According to Shahrastani, these debates raged with particular vehemence among such Christian sectarians as the Nestorians. One Nestorius, living under the reign of Al-Ma'mun, taught that the three attributes of Life, Power, and Knowledge were actual persons in the Deity. This doctrine, Shahrastani asserts, was accepted even by some theologians who added other attributes, such as Will, but did not recognize them as distinct persons. See his *K. al-Milal,* II.1, 2, 2, ed. by Cureton, pp. 175 f.; in Haarbrücker's German translation, *Religionspartheien und Philosophenschulen,* I, 265 f. Although not impossible, D. Kaufmann's old suggestion that the diligent Arab compiler of data on all religious movements really had in mind the fifth-century founder of the Nestorian sect, but mistook the period of his activity, has little to commend itself. See Kaufmann's still unsuperseded *Geschichte der Attributenlehre in der jüdischen Religionsphilosophie des Mittelalters von Saadja bis Maimûni,* p. 43 n. 79. Here and in his "Elias von Nisibis und Saadja Alfajjûmis Äusserungen über die Trinität" in his *G.S.,* III, 64–66, Kaufmann has also shown the Nestorian background of Saadiah's polemics. See also *supra,* Chap. XXIV, nn. 49–50.

56. A. S. Tritton's "Foreign Influences on Muslim Theology," *BSOAS,* X, 841; Shahrastani's *K. al-Milal,* p. 34; in Haarbrücker's translation, I, 49. See also H. A. Wolfson's careful analysis of "The Muslim Attributes and the Christian Trinity," *HTR,* XLIX, 1–18. On the impact of the Almohade upheaval also on Jewish thought, especially that of Maimonides, see the sources assembled by Goldziher and others, and the remarks thereon by I. Heinemann in *MGWJ,* LXXIX, 102–48.

57. Saadiah's *Beliefs, loc. cit.;* Baḥya's *Duties,* I.7, p. 54 (Zifroni, p. 37; Hyamson, I, 36); D. Neumark's *Geschichte der jüdischen Philosophie,* II, Part 2, pp. 228 ff., 234 ff. The Kalam doctrine of four or five essential attributes, Life (Existence),

Power, Wisdom or Knowledge, and Will is effectively combated by Maimonides in his *Guide,* I.53, 56 (English, pp. 74, 79). On the other hand, Ibn Daud did not mind analyzing especially the eight attributes, while adding "We shall not stubbornly insist that there are no other attributes, which might be ascribed to Him blessed be He, provided that one will clearly understand them in a way which will not involve multiplicity in His essence." See *Emunah,* II.3 end, pp. 56 (Hebrew), 71 (German). Kaufmann's attempt to find in Al-Baṣir a protagonist of five attributes (*Geschichte der Attributenlehre,* p. 418 n. 87) is, however, decidedly forced. In fact, this Karaite teacher felt prompted to apologize for treating even the divine Word in the context of God's unity, rather than justice. He did it only, he declared, because some of his opponents insisted on considering the Logos an eternal entity on a par with the Christians. See the excerpt published by P. F. Frankl in *SB,* Vienna, LXXI, 181 (German), 218 (Hebrew).

58. David al-Muqammiṣ, "Twenty Chapters," IX–X, quoted in Yehudah bar Barzillai's *Commentary on Yeṣirah,* ed. by Halberstam, pp. 77 f., 80 f.; Ibn Gabirol's *Improvement of the Moral Qualities,* pp. 1 (Arabic), 29 (English; *Tikkun Middot ha-nefesh,* edited by N. Bar-On [Braun], p. 3). To judge from the brief excerpt in Yehudah bar Barzillai's *Commentary* (pp. 82 f.), it would seem that Al-Muqammiṣ' tenth chapter was mainly devoted to a refutation of the Christian doctrine of attributes. Ibn Gabirol's blunt declaration in his philosophic work, "The First and Holy Substance and its Attributes are altogether one thing, and not distinct" (*Fons,* V.42, p. 333; Hebrew, p. 218) remains of course unimpaired by any poetic descriptions even in the "Royal Crown." In this sense, Kaufmann, rather than Bieler, is right. See the former's *Geschichte der Attributenlehre,* pp. 110 ff.; and Bieler, *Der göttliche Wille,* pp. 24 f. See also A. Heschel's analysis of "Der Begriff des Seins in der Philosophie Gabirols," *Festschrift Jakob Freimann,* pp. 68–77; and *supra,* n. 29.

59. Ibn Gabirol's *Fons,* V.35, ed. by Baeumker, p. 321 ("iam constat apud me *quod* sunt, et *quid* sunt, et *quales* sunt, et *quare* sunt"; Hebrew, p. 210); Ibn Ṣaddiq's *'Olam qaṭan,* III end, ed. by Horovitz, p. 58; Maimonides' *Guide,* I.58, 60 (English, pp. 81, 88); Gersonides (Levi ben Gerson), *Milḥamot Adonai* (Wars of the Lord), V.12, Leipzig ed., pp. 278 ff.; Joseph Albo, *Sefer ha-'Iqqarim* (Book of Principles), VIII ff., ed. and translated by I. Husik, II, 43 ff. See H. A. Wolfson's "Maimonides and Gersonides on Divine Attributes as Ambiguous Terms," *Kaplan Jub. Vol.,* pp. 515–30; and *infra,* n. 60. The brief hints given here concerning Gersonides' and Albo's departures from the Maimonidean views will become clearer in the general context of their teachings in a later volume. In his *Commentary* on the *Guide,* I.60, Moses Narboni pointed out the exceptional promise held out by Maimonides' teachings to anyone who penetrates the meaning of negative attributes and who, therefore, will rejoice over his nearness to God. Such nearness can be secured, Narboni declared, by understanding alone, without the aid of divine grace, that essential prerequisite of prophecy. Ibn Daud, too, introduced his discussion of attributes with a blunt declaration, "Know that the most truthful statements or attributes concerning God blessed be He, are indeed, the negative ones." See his *Emunah,* II.2, 3, pp. 51 (Hebrew), 65 (German). On the ancient Greek antecedents of the doctrine of negative attributes as reflected in Shahrastani, and on its influence even on the early medieval kabbalists, see Kaufmann's *Geschichte der Attributenlehre,* pp. 330 n. 198, 345 n. 8.

We must bear in mind, however, that, without deviating from his general insistence on negative attributes only, Maimonides himself had to use, especially in his cosmological doctrine, the attributes of Wisdom and Will, both derived from divine actions. After a careful analysis of the Maimonidean views and their differences from those of Ibn Gabirol and other medieval thinkers, Z. Diesendruck concluded that, according to the sage of Fusṭaṭ, "Wisdom is the factual principle in Creation, its *order*, in the nature of *quid facti*. The Will is its ultimate principle, in the nature of *quid iuris*, the first *reason* for Creation. Both need each other to furnish the reason for the Universe from its teleological standpoint." See his "Maimonides' Theory of Teleology and the Divine Attributes" (Hebrew), *Tarbiz,* II, 37. See also *infra,* n. 63.

60. Ibn Gabirol's *Fons,* III.1, 25, ed. by Baeumker, pp. 73, 139 ("sed creator ex nihilo non est nisi factor primus, altus et sanctus"; Hebrew, pp. 51, 93). See also the other significant passages listed in Baeumker's index, p. 510, *s.v. Sanctus.* On the centrality of the prophetic doctrine of "holiness" in the Bible, see *supra,* Vol. I, pp. 138, 358 n. 7. See also I. Efros, "Holiness and Glory in the Bible: an Approach to the History of Jewish Thought," *JQR,* XLI, 363–77. Of course, justice is an ethical attribute and, as such, relates primarily to the world of man and his relations to the Creator. However, medieval Jewish and Arab philosophy were so deeply colored by their ethical concerns that the principle of justice had to affect also the universal order. Did not the Mu'tazilites stress above all divine justice and unity? See Mas'udi's description in his *K. Muruj adh-dhahab* (Prairies d'or), VI, 20 ff. Among the Jews we need but mention the example of Ibn Ṣaddiq. Quoting Jer. 9:23, which had often been invoked by philosophers as justification for philosophic inquiries into the nature of God and the Universe, he stressed righteousness as the main factor in the preservation of all creatures. See his *'Olam qaṭan,* p. 67 (cited *infra,* n. 79), and, more generally, *infra,* n. 61.

Clearly, the doctrine of divine attributes, including that of the incorporeality of God, which plays so large a role in all medieval philosophic systems, has often been discussed by modern scholars. Apart from being given much space in the general histories of medieval philosophy (Jewish as well as Muslim and Christian), and apart from forming important chapters in the various analyses of teachings by individual thinkers, it has been the subject of numerous specialized studies ever since Kaufmann's *Geschichte der Attributenlehre.* Among recent monographs, see esp. H. A. Wolfson's "Avicenna, Algazali and Averroës on Divine Attributes," *Homenaje a Millás,* II, 545–71, and his other essays mentioned before or to be mentioned presently; S. Rawidowicz's "Saadya's Purification of the Idea of God" in Rosenthal's *Saadya Studies,* pp. 139–65; Julius Guttmann's "Maimonides' Doctrine of God" in *Essays Hertz,* Hebrew section, pp. 53–69 (reprinted in his *Dat u-madda',* pp. 103–18); A. Altmann's "Essence and Existence in Maimonides," *BJRL,* XXXV, 294–315; J. Teicher's "Observations critiques sur l'interprétation traditionelle de la doctrine des attributs négatifs chez Maïmonide," *REJ,* XCIX, 56–67 (suggesting that this doctrine can be understood only out of the Maimonidean concept of God which, he believes, is related to that of Descartes as well as to the "substance" of Spinoza; see also his essay cited *supra,* n. 36). Cf., however, the legitimate rejection of this critique by Julius Guttmann in *Essays Hertz,* p. 62 n. 7 (*Dat u-madda',* p. 111 n. 7); and such still more specialized studies as Z. Diesendruck's "Maimonides' Theory of the Negation of Privation," *PAAJR,* VI, 139–51 (this crucial term is used by Maimonides in his *Guide,* I.58; Friedländer, p. 83, translates less precisely: "negation of the opposite"); and H. A. Wolfson's comparison of "The Aristotelian Predicables and Maimonides' Division of Attributes," *Miller Mem. Vol.,* pp. 201–34.

Wolfson reaches here the significant conclusion that "histories of philosophy or of logic which hitherto have assumed that nothing new had happened in the classification of predicables from the time of Porphyry to that of Kant, may now report that a new list of predicables was introduced in the 12th century by Maimonides, and by the side of Porphyry's five predicables of 'genus,' 'species,' 'difference,' 'property,' and 'accident,' they may now place Maimonides' five predicables of 'definition,' 'part of definition,' 'quality,' 'relation' and 'verb.'" This essay is supplemented by Wolfson's "Maimonides on Negative Attributes," *Ginzberg Jub. Vol.,* pp. 411–46, reaching the conclusion that this older doctrine is given here a new turn "as a means of justifying the affirmative form in which certain terms must be predicated by God" under strict logical rules. See also M. Springer's dissertation, *Die Attributenlehre des Moses Maimonides beleuchtet vom Standpunkt der modernen Logik;* and, from the standpoint of his own interpretation of medieval scholasticism, E. Gilson's brief remarks on "Homage to Maimonides" in my *Essays on Maimonides,* pp. 19–35; and, more specifically, his "Maïmonide et la philosophie de l'Exode," *Mediaeval Studies,* XIII, 223–25. Here the French neo-Thomist points out that the Maimonidean doctrine of the identity of God's essence and existence, going back to the name revealed to Moses (in Exod. 3:13), greatly impressed Aquinas, and may be considered a major contribution to human thought.

61. Saadiah's pamphlet against Ibn Saqawaihi in A. Harkavy's "Fragments of Anti-Karaite Writings of Saadiah in the Imperial Public Library at St. Petersburg," *JQR,* [o.s.] XIII, 664 (Arabic), 667 (English); and with some variants in his Hebrew essay, "From an Oriental Genizah in the Imperial Library at St. Petersburg," *Hakedem,* I, 127 f. (on the identity of this Karaite opponent see *supra,* Chap. XXVI, nn. 27, 43, 80); Ḥananel's *Commentary* on Berakhot 6a, in Lewin's *Otzar ha-gaonim,* I, Part 3, pp. 3 f.; Maimonides' *Guide,* I.36 (English, p. 52); his *M.T.* Teshubah III.7, with Abraham ben David's marginal comment thereon.

According to a modern ḥasidic legend, Maimonides' sharp declaration concerning the heretical nature of anthropomorphism caused the expulsion from the Garden of Eden of many souls of righteous Jews who, during their life on earth, had believed in God's corporeality. They were soon restored to Paradise, however, upon Abraham ben David's equally sharp denial. See Israel Berger's *Eser orot* (Ten Lights; biographies of Ḥasidic rabbis), p. 82, cited by Rawidowicz in *Saadya Studies,* ed. by Rosenthal, p. 163 n. 1; *supra,* Chap. XXXIII, n. 45; and, more generally, Rawidowicz's succinct summary of "The Problem of Corporeality in Saadiah and Maimonides" (Hebrew), *Keneset,* III, 332–77.

62. Moses ibn Ezra, *'Arugat ha-bosem,* ed. by L. Dukes in *Zion,* II, 137. On the role of anthropomorphism in Judeo-Muslim polemics, including the standard accusation of the alleged Jewish "falsification" of Scripture and the different emphases in the controversies with Christians, see *supra,* Chap. XXIV.

63. Maimonides' *Guide,* III.25 (English, pp. 308 f.). See Z. Diesendruck's comprehensive analysis of "Die Teleologie bei Maimonides," *HUCA,* V, 415–534; his additional remarks in his "Maimonides' Theory of Teleology" (Hebrew), *Tarbiz,* I,

Part 4, pp. 106–36; II, 27–73; and P. Brunner's *Probleme der Teleologie bei Maimonides, Thomas von Aquin und Spinoza.* See also A. Forest, "Guillaume d'Auvergne, critique d'Aristote," *Etudes médiévales offertes à Augustin Fliche,* pp. 67–79. On a more popular level, Baḥya argued that the very orderliness of the world suggests the existence of a Creator. He did not understand how a sane man who, seeing a wheel turning an irrigation machine in a field or a page written in orderly characters, has no doubt whatsoever that some person placed the wheel or wrote the page, yet can contend that the universe which is so much more complicated is a matter of sheer chance. Here Baḥya voiced the very opinion rejected by Maimonides (also in his *Guide,* III.13; English, pp. 275 f.) that this entire world so well ordered was created for the benefit of man. See Baḥya's *Duties of the Heart,* I.6, pp. 48 ff. (Hebrew, pp. 32 ff.; English, pp. 32 f.). This anthropocentric view represented indeed not only popular, but also regnant scholarly opinion of the time.

64. Ibn Ṣaddiq's *'Olam qaṭan, passim;* Maimonides' *Guide,* III.17 (English, pp. 282 ff., 287); Saadiah's *Beliefs,* V.3, p. 173 (Hebrew, p. 87; English, p. 214); Donnolo's *Ḥakmoni,* Introduction, ed. by Muntner, pp. 35 f. (see *supra,* n. 7). On Maimonides' sources, see S. Munk's notes on his French translation of the *Guide,* III, 115 ff. These contrasted, however, with various rabbinic sources clearly indicating that even animals were subject to the final judgment. See the sources cited by J. L. Fishman in his "Capital Punishment in Jewish Law" (Hebrew), *Sinai,* II, No. 16, p. 149 n. On his part, Saadiah discusses only the sufferings of innocent children, rather than those of animals. He explains these sufferings as a form of divine discipline similar to the punishments inflicted on minors by their fathers for their own good. Elsewhere (VIII.2, p. 234; Hebrew, pp. 119 f.; English, p. 295) he also attributes some such sufferings to God's desire to store up for man additional merits for which he would receive compensation in the Hereafter. Animal behavior is mentioned by Saadiah specifically only in connection with the prophetic predictions of the universal peace, which is to affect also the lion and the lamb, and which had thus far not been fulfilled (VIII.9, p. 251; Hebrew, pp. 127 f.; English, pp. 318 f.). Although less outspoken than the Mu'tazilites, their Karaite followers including Joseph al-Baṣir, and Samuel ben Ḥofni, Saadiah nevertheless seems to have shared their position with respect to the eschatological retribution of all living beings. But neither he nor any other medieval Jewish thinker entered more deeply into either the philosophic or the biological problems of living beings, other than man, such as had engaged the attention, for instance, of Avicenna. See J. Wilczynski's analysis of the "Contribution oubliée d'Ibn Sina à la théorie des êtres vivants," *AIHS,* VII, 35–45 (showing Avicenna's considerable independence from Aristotle's teachings). See also, in general, J. Ehrich's dissertation, *Das Problem der Theodizee in der jüdischen Philosophie des Mittelalters* (chiefly on Saadiah and Maimonides); and I. Wolfsberg's "R. Saadiah Gaon's Doctrine of Reward" (Hebrew) in *Rav Saadya Gaon,* edited by J. L. Fishman, pp. 442–58.

65. Al-Muqammiṣ' "Twenty Tractates," XVI, cited in Yehudah bar Barzillai's *Commentary on Yeṣirah,* pp. 153 f.; Saadiah's *Beliefs,* IX.5, pp. 265 ff. (Hebrew, pp. 137 ff.; English, pp. 336 ff.). The doctrine of metempsychosis, which Saadiah asserted to have found among "certain people, who call themselves Jews," was supported by them according to the gaon by four main arguments, including scriptural evidence, which he tried to disprove one by one. See his *Beliefs,* VI.8, pp. 207 ff. (Hebrew, pp.

103 ff.; English, pp. 259 ff.). Saadiah undoubtedly had 'Anan and some of his followers in mind. Beginning with Qirqisani, however, the Karaites, too, seem to have completely abandoned this doctrine. See his *K. al-Anwar,* III.18, ed. by L. Nemoy, II, 315 ff. This chapter, previously published by Poznanski, was translated into English by Nemoy in his "Biblical Quasi-Evidence for the Transmigration of Souls," *JBL,* LIX, 163 ff. The doctrine of Transmigration reappeared, however, obliquely in Ibn Gabirol's "Royal Crown," and more elaborately, in the Rabbanite Kabbalah, beginning with the book *Bahir.* See Ibn Gabirol's *Shire,* II, 71 (Zangwill's translation, p. 105, according to S. Horovitz's rather dubious interpretation in his *Psychologie,* p. 143 n. 165); M. Schreiner's excursus "Zur Geschichte der Lehre von der Seelenwanderung" in his still very valuable study of *Der Kalâm in der jüdischen Literatur,* pp. 62 ff.; the *Zohar,* Zhitomir edition, II, fol. 99b; and *supra,* Chap. XXXIII, n. 40.

66. Israeli's *Sefer ha-Yesodot,* II, edited by Fried, pp. 40 ff.; Saadiah's *Beliefs, loc. cit.* (IX.5); Ibn Ṣaddiq, *'Olam qaṭan,* ed. by Horovitz, p. 66; Pseudo-Baḥya's *K. Ma'ani al-nafs,* XXI, ed. by Goldziher, pp. 64 ff. (Broydé, pp. 85 ff.); Bar Ḥiyya's *Hegyon,* II, fol. 12ab. Israeli's explanation appears more understandable in the light of his general psychological concepts, explained in his *Sefer ha-Ruaḥ ve-ha-nefesh* (Book of the Spirit and the Soul and the Difference between Them), which is extant only in a small fragment of the Hebrew translation so entitled. See M. Steinschneider's edition from a Munich MS in *Ha-Karmel,* I, 400–405. On the mystic background of the doctrine of the soul's painful peregrinations, see *supra,* Chap. XXXIII, n. 22. On the related teachings by Ibn Gabirol and Bar Ḥiyya, see Julius Guttmann's "Zu Gabirols allegorischer Deutung der Erzählung vom Paradies," *MGWJ,* LXXX, 180–84; G. Vajda's observations in "Les Idées théologiques et philosophiques d'Abraham bar Hiyya," *AHDL,* XXI, 204 f.; and Jakob Guttmann's reconstruction in *Die philosophischen Lehren des Isaak ben Salomon Israeli,* p. 23 (citing a parallel conception of the Brethren of Purity). On Saadiah's otherwise often divergent psychological views, see *infra,* nn. 69–70. These and other aspects of the soul's immortality, as well as preexistence, were extensively aired in the subsequent literature. Nevertheless, Sa'd ibn Kammuna, writing in the latter part of the thirteenth century, could rightly claim that he had advanced many new and original ideas in his *Risala* (Epistle on the Immortality of the Soul), republished in a facsimile reproduction of a good Yale MS by L. Nemoy. See also I. Goldziher's earlier description of "Sa'd b. Manṣûr ibn Kammûna's Abhandlung über die Unvergänglichkeit der Seele," *Festschrift Steinschneider,* pp. 110–14. It goes without saying that philosophers rationalized here the people's deep spiritual yearnings which had long dominated Jewish funeral arts and epigraphy. See *supra,* Vol. II, pp. 286 ff., 423 f. nn. 59 ff.; and F. Cantera y Burgos's recent illustrations of "L'Idée de l'immortalité et de resurrection à travers les inscriptions hébraïques du moyen âge espagnol," *Atti* of the Eighth International Congress of the History of Religions, V, 287–91. Some interesting comparative data may also be secured from R. Eklund's well-documented Uppsala dissertation, *Life between Death and Resurrection according to Islam.*

67. Baḥya's *Duties,* III.5, pp. 150 ff. (Zifroni, pp. 96 ff.; Hyamson, II, 55 ff.). The Hermetic background of Baḥya's dialogue was aptly demonstrated by I. Heinemann in *Die Lehre von der Zweckbestimmung des Menschen,* pp. 37 ff.; revised only in some details by G. Vajda in "Le Dialogue de l'âme et de la raison dans les Devoirs des Coeurs de Bahya ibn Paquda," *REJ,* CII, 93–104. See also the latter's *La Théolo-*

gie ascétique de Bahya ibn Paquda, p. 59 n. 1. Both authors have argued, however, only on the basis of a single Hermetic text in Arabic (*De castigatione animae,* edited by O. Bardenhewer in his Bonn dissertation of 1873). Today a fuller reexamination in the light of the materials made available in A. D. Nock and A. J. Festugière's edition of the *Corpus hermeticum* is likely to yield substantial new insights. See also *supra,* Chap. XXXIII, n. 7.

68. Ibn Gabirol's *Fons,* I.1–2, pp. 2 ff. (Hebrew, pp. 1 ff.); his *Improvement of the Moral Qualities,* edited by Wise, pp. 2 f., 5 f. (Arabic), 29, 35 ff. (English); and his "Royal Crown" in his *Shire,* II, 74 (Zangwill's translation, p. 114). The similarity between Ibn Gabirol's and Baḥya's psychologico-ethical doctrines is even more pronounced in the enumeration of the ten pairs of positive and negative qualities of the soul. See Ibn Gabirol's *Improvement,* pp. 16 ff. (Arabic), 53 ff. (English); Baḥya's *Duties,* III.10, pp. 171 ff. (Zifroni, pp. 112 ff.; Hyamson, II, 76 ff.).

69. Abraham ibn Ezra's *Commentary* on Gen., First Draft, published by Marco Mortara in *Ozar nechmad,* II, 218; his *Commentary* on Eccles. 3:21; Halevi's *K. al-Khazari,* V.12, ed. by Hirschfeld, pp. 310 f. (English, p. 259); Saadiah's *Beliefs,* VI.1, 3, pp. 188 ff., 195 f. (Hebrew, pp. 95 ff.; English, pp. 238, 244). See also *infra,* n. 81. On the meaning of the four elements of knowledge required by Ibn Ezra, see H. A. Wolfson's plausible explanation in "The Classification of Sciences in Mediaeval Jewish Philosophy," *HUCA,* Jub. Vol., pp. 275 ff.; and *infra,* Chap. XXXV, n. 6. On the Hellenistic background of the seven, or rather eleven, doctrines concerning the soul listed by Saadiah, see Julius Guttmann's Hebrew essay, "The Views of Greek Philosophers on the Essence of the Soul, according to Saadiah Gaon" in *Magnes Anniversary Book,* pp. 80–88. Guttmann concludes that the gaon must have used, and modified, some such Greek listing, although his is more complete than any Greek text extant today. It is probably from the Greek sources through Arabic channels (not necessarily Farabi) that Qirqisani, too, took some ingredients of his psychological teachings so closely akin to those of Saadiah, although at least in one passage he seems to betray his direct indebtedness to the gaon. See Hirschfeld's *Qirqisani Studies,* pp. 21 f. See also *supra,* n. 65. Pseudo-Baḥya went too far, therefore, in accusing the entire "community of Karaites" of following the various Mu'tazilite sects in believing in the accidental and, hence, perishable nature of the souls. See his *Ma'ani al-nafs,* I, ed. by Goldziher, p. 4 (Hebrew, pp. 4 f.). See also M. Ventura's citation of numerous more or less relevant sources in *La Philosophie de Saadiah Gaon,* pp. 227 ff.

In view of the great importance of the psychological doctrines within the medieval philosophic systems, modern scholarship has subjected them to frequent careful scrutiny. The most comprehensive work still is S. Horovitz's older series of monographs on individual philosophers entitled *Die Psychologie bei den jüdischen Religionsphilosophen des Mittelalters von Saadia bis Maimuni* (the four published parts discuss only the psychological doctrines of Saadiah, Ibn Gabirol, Ibn Ṣaddiq, and Ibn Daud). See also P. D. Bookstaber's more recent semipopular analysis of *The Idea of Development of the Soul in Medieval Jewish Philosophy* (exclaiming with abandon that "if you took out the concept of soul in the discussions of the various philosophers you would, thereby, take out the centripetal force of all their systems and utterances"; p. 103); the detailed older study by S. B. Scheyer, *Das psy-*

chologische System des Maimonides; A. Litwak's psychoanalytical comments on "Les Conceptions de Maïmonide sur l'âme et leur comparison avec celles de notre temps," *RHMH,* I, 30–41 (with special reference to the teachings of Freud and Henri Baruk); and J. Leibowitz's succinct medical interpretation of "The Influence of Mental Factors on Physical Processes according to Maimonides" (Hebrew), *Dappim refuiim,* X, 150–52. Closely related, of course, are the modern studies devoted to medieval doctrines concerning internal and external senses and the then very popular teachings related to "Mental Hygiene." See esp. D. Kaufmann's comprehensive analysis of *Die Sinne: Beiträge zur Geschichte der Physiologie und Psychologie im Mittelalter;* H. A. Wolfson's essays on "Internal Senses" mentioned *supra,* n. 35; his "Maimonides on the Internal Senses," *JQR,* XXV, 441–67; and, on mental hygiene, *infra,* Chap. XXXVI, n. 49. Interesting comparative insights may be gleaned from J. Bakoš's ed. and French trans. of the *Psychologie de Grégoire Aboulfaradj dit Barhebraeus d'après la huitième base de l'ouvrage Le Candélabre des sanctuaires;* and from the Western data going back to Boetius analyzed by P. Michaud-Quantin in "La Classification des puissances de l'âme au XIIe siècle," *Revue du moyen âge latin,* V, 15–34.

70. Saadiah's *Beliefs,* VI.3, p. 194 (Hebrew, p. 97; English, p. 242); Maimonides' *Guide,* I.70, 74 (English, pp. 106, 137; on the bracketed words, see Munk's note in his French translation, I, 328 n. 1); Ibn Gabirol's *Improvement, passim.* On Baḥya's rather noncommittal definition, see his *Duties,* X.1, p. 379 (Zifroni, p. 261). The extremes to which Ibn Gabirol went in his artificial correlation may be illustrated by his ascription of Pride, Meekness, Pudency, and Impudence to the sense of vision, merely because "thou perceivest the haughty glance of the proud and boastful of spirit" and because in ordinary parlance these qualities are frequently so expressed (e.g., Isa. 2:11, 5:15). See his *Improvement,* pp. 7 (Arabic), 37 f. (English). That this weird construction was not a mere extravagance on the part of the poet-philosopher, but rather stemmed from his valiant effort to connect all the qualities of both body and soul with the World Soul and the World Intellect, is mentioned but not well elaborated by S. Horovitz in his *Psychologie,* pp. 141 f.

The confusion which prevailed in the contemporary Muslim and Jewish circles concerning the nature and activities of the soul is well illustrated by Saadiah's aforementioned enumeration of the various schools of thought on this subject. One of these schools, postulating that the soul is but an accident, was subdivided, according to the gaon, into five distinct groups. These debates calmed down in the following two centuries. The fairly prevalent earlier view, as expressed by the Ash'arite, Abu'l-Ma'ali Juwayni (Imam al-Haramein; 1028–85) that the soul "is composed of subtle substances embedded in intelligible substances" (see his *K. al-Irshad* [El-Irchad; a Guide toward Certain Proofs for the Principles of Faith], XXVII.1, ed. and translated by J. D. Luciani, p. 320) was almost universally abandoned. Its place was taken by the insistence on the soul's exclusively spiritual substance, such as was argued by Ghazzali and Maimonides. See L. Gardet and M. M. Anawati's *Introduction,* p. 73 n. 3.

71. Baḥya's *Duties,* III.8, pp. 164 f. (Zifroni, pp. 106 f.; Hyamson, II, 69; this is indeed the climactic part of the aforementioned dialogue between the Intellect and the Soul); Halevi's *K. al-Khazari,* V.20, pp. 336 ff. (English, pp. 279 ff.). In many ways, Halevi's solution was in part anticipated by Saadiah. Without delving deeply into

the subject, the gaon argued that man's freedom of choice is attested by the observation of the senses and can be proved from the standpoint of reason, Scripture and tradition. He also denied the basic assumption of the determinists that "God's knowledge of things is the cause of their coming into being." See his *Beliefs,* IV.4, pp. 152 ff. (Hebrew, pp. 78 ff.; English, pp. 186 ff.). It is obvious that both Saadiah and Halevi were more concerned with the doctrine of determinism advocated by the most influential Muslim theologians, than by the Mu'tazilites' championship of free will, which most of them, too, tried to reconcile in one way or another with divine Providence. See L. Stein's older, but still useful dissertation, *Die Willensfreiheit und ihr Verhältnis zur göttlichen Präscienz und Providenz bei den jüdischen Philosophen des Mittelalters;* and, for comparative data, W. M. Watt's *Free Will and Predestination in Early Islam,* with W. Thomson's critical observations thereon in *MW,* XL, 207–16, 276–87; and M. Fakhry's "Some Paradoxical Implications of the Mu'tazilite View of the Free Will," *ibid.,* XLIII, 95–109, concluding that the Mu'tazilite claim that "man was the creator of his deeds" was purely verbal, and that this concept was "emptied of any content through their [the Mu'tazilites'] adherence to the occasionalist metaphysics of atoms-accidents" and their interest in safeguarding the unity of God and His transcendence (pp. 105, 109). See also, from other angles, J. Wochenmark's somewhat too general observations on *Die Schicksalsidee im Judentum;* and H. Ringgren's *Studies in Arabian Fatalism.*

72. Ibn Daud's *Emunah,* Intro., and II.2, pp. 2, 96 f. (Hebrew), 2 f., 124 f. (German); Maimonides' *Eight Chapters,* VIII end (in Gorfinkle's translation, pp. 101 f.); his *Guide,* III.20 (English, pp. 293 f.; see also Munk's note in his translation, III, 149 n. 3); Abraham bar Ḥiyya's *Sefer Hegyon ha-nefesh,* fol. 5ab; his *Megillat ha-megalleh,* p. 7; Berakhot 33b. The inadequacies of Halevi's theory have already been pointed out by Joseph Albo in his *Sefer ha-'Iqqarim,* IV.1, ed. by I. Husik, IV, 6 ff. Husik himself, after briefly reviewing the theories of both Halevi and Ibn Daud, came to the judicious conclusion that "in the final outcome of their respective analyses, Halevi maintains God's foreknowledge at the expense of absolute freedom, or rather he does not see that his admissions are fatal to the cause he endeavors to defend. Ibn Daud maintains absolute freedom and frankly sacrifices foreknowledge; though his defense of freedom is secured by blinding himself to the argument most dangerous to that doctrine," namely that God's inability to foresee the contingent is a mark of imperfection. See Husik's *History of Medieval Jewish Philosophy,* p. 231. Only the pressure of the Muslim environment and its impact on wavering Jewish souls can explain why an orthodox rabbinic scholar like Ibn Daud chanced upon this radical doctrine. We may, indeed, believe him that the debates on the conflict between Predestination and Free Will gave the main impetus to the writing of his philosophic treatise, where, for the purposes of a more complete answer, he started by building up the necessary metaphysical premises. In this sense the last pages of the *Emunah,* although comparatively brief and overshadowed by the preceding extensive discussions, represent the very core of Ibn Daud's concern with philosophic problems, a point overlooked by Julius Guttmann in his *Philosophie des Judentums,* pp. 164 f. On the parallels, but also dissimilarities, of Bar Ḥiyya's teachings of predestination and original sin and those current among Christian theologians in his environment, see F. Baer's penetrating observations in "Eine jüdische Messiasprophetie auf das Jahr 1186 und der dritte Kreuzzug," *MGWJ,* LXX, 120 n. 1. See also *supra,* n. 66.

73. Ibn Gabirol's *Improvement,* Intro., pp. 3 (Arabic), 30 (English); Ibn Ezra's *Commentary* on Exod. 23:25; Maimonides' *Guide,* II.12; III.37 (English, pp. 170, 332 f.); his "Correspondence between the Rabbis of Southern France and Maimonides about Astrology," ed. by Marx in *HUCA,* III, 311 ff. Abraham ibn Ezra's astrological concepts will be discussed in connection with his and the other Jewish scientists' contributions to astrological and astronomical science, *infra,* Chap. XXXV. Although Maimonides' rejection of astrology had been fully anticipated by the rationalistic gaon Samuel ben Ḥofni, as well as by Qirqisani (see the former's Responsum in Ginzberg's *Ginze Schechter,* I, 304 ff., and Qirqisani's *K. al-Anwar,* VI.11, pp. 590 ff.; this passage is translated into French and commented on by G. Vajda in *REJ,* CVI, 103 ff.), believers in astrology persisted among some very learned and orthodox rabbis. See, e.g., Abraham ben David's comment on Maimonides' *M.T.* Teshubah v.5. See also, more generally, the data discussed in A. Schmiedl's older *Studien über jüdische, insbesondere jüdisch-arabische Religionsphilosophie,* pp. 299 ff. (under the expressive chapter heading of "Astrologische Trübungen").

74. Ibn Gabirol's *Fons,* III.56, p. 204 (Hebrew, p. 136; cf. A. Harkavy's reconstruction, "Aus dem Original von Mose Ibn Esra's 'Arugat ha-bosem," in *MGWJ,* XLIII, 134 ff.); Ibn Ezra's Hebrew text of *'Arugat ha-bosem* in Dukes's edition in *Zion,* II, 158 f. Like his namesake, Abraham (*Commentary* on Exod. 23:25, etc.), Ibn Ezra's translator occasionally used for nature the Hebrew term *toledet,* just as Yehudah ibn Tibbon employed the related word *toladah* in his translation of Baḥya's *Duties,* I.6, ed. by Zifroni, p. 33 (Hyamson, I, 31), but as a rule he and most other writers applied the Arabic loan word *ṭeba'.* We also find the use of the word *yeṣirah.* See H. Malter's "Medieval Hebrew Terms for Nature," *Judaica* (Festschrift H. Cohen), pp. 253–56; and J. Klatzkin's *Oṣar ha-munaḥim,* II, 9 ff., 46 f.; IV, 182. The meaning of this term oscillated between that of human nature, usually seen in its bodily extensions, and Nature at large. Saadiah, for example, spoke interchangeably of (1) the laws of Nature, as opposed to chance, which cannot be overcome by man, except by a miracle; (2) human nature and its passions which the reason of a moral person is able to overcome; and (3) man's physical nature which is coarsened by inappropriate food and the like. See his *Beliefs,* I.3; III.4; IX.1; X.14, pp. 62, 120, 256, 310 (Hebrew, pp. 33, 62, 130 f., 156 f.; English, pp. 74, 147, 325, 394) and other passages here and in his Bible commentaries. On the latter see E. I. J. Rosenthal's remarks in *BJRL,* XXII, 173. See also, from another angle, M. D. Chenu, "Nature ou histoire? Une controverse exégétique sur la création au XIIe siècle," *AHDL,* XXVIII, 25–30 (with reference to Guillaume of Conches' *Philosophia mundi,* I.21 in *PL,* CLXXII, 53, here attributed to Honorius of Autun). It must also be borne in mind that to Ibn Gabirol himself (a belief in which he was closely followed by such other disciples of Neoplatonism as Pseudo-Baḥya) Nature held, together with Intelligence and the Soul, an intermediate position between God and the physical world. See his *Fons,* III.56; V.20, pp. 203, 294 (Hebrew, pp. 136, 193; incidentally the Latin term *natura* is used frequently also in other meanings, see Baeumker's index, pp. 493 f.); Pseudo-Baḥya's *K. Ma'ani al-nafs,* XVI, pp. 53 f. (Hebrew, pp. 71 f.). This Neoplatonic trinity between God and the world, however, seemed acceptable only to believers in emanation such as these two thinkers and the later kabbalists. It carried little appeal to exponents of a direct process of creation. It is unlikely, therefore, that the rather obscure reconstruction of the biblical story of creation in semiphilosophic terms, given by Abraham bar Ḥiyya in his *Hegyon,* fols. 2b ff.,

had anything to do with this particular trinity, as suggested by Husik (in his *History,* pp. 118 f.). Rather, it harkened back to the speculations of the role of water in the biblical cosmogony, found in *Yeṣirah* and other early commentators. See *supra,* Chap. XXIX, nn. 66–67. While the latter, too, were doubtless writing under some indirect inspiration of Plotinian and other schools of Hellenistic thought, they had little in common with that threefold, or rather fivefold, division of Ibn Gabirol. On the related theologico-medical problems of the allegedly predetermined duration of the individual human life, a debate in which even Hai Gaon felt obliged to participate, see *infra,* n. 92.

75. M. Smith, *Readings from the Mystics of Islam,* p. 37 No. 34; S. D. Goitein, "Isra'liyyat" (Hebrew), *Tarbiz,* VI, 89–101, 510–32 (on Malik ibn Dinar and his circle, showing their indebtedness to Jewish prototypes); his "A Jewish Addict to Sufism," *JQR,* XLIV, 37–49 (publishing a letter written between 1355 and 1367); his brief remarks in his *Jews and Arabs,* pp. 148 ff.; and F. Rosenthal, "A Judaeo-Arabic Work under Sufi Influence," *HUCA,* XV, 433–84 (likewise written in the fourteenth century). On Baḥya and Abraham Maimuni, see the writings by and on them listed *supra,* nn. 11 and 17. Despite the vast literature already produced on this subject, the investigations of the profound interrelations between Jewish and Muslim mysticism are still in their early stages, many of the primary sources themselves still lying dormant in the world's manuscript libraries. While Baḥya's main work has long been published, and was in its Hebrew version one of the leading Jewish "best-sellers" down to the twentieth century, only a relatively small part of Abraham Maimuni's standard work has been issued (in the Arabic text, with an English version by S. Rosenblatt; see *supra,* n. 17). Muslim mysticism, too, though much more familiar today than it was half a century ago, will require much scholarly effort before the more hidden lines of its historic evolution are uncovered sufficiently to enable specialists to see clearly its inner interrelations with the early schools of Jewish mystic thought. See, e.g., A. L. Tibawi's pertinent observations on the "Ikhwan aṣ-Ṣafa and Their Rasa'il: A Critical Review of a Century and a Half of Research," *Islamic Quarterly,* II, 28–46; L. Massignon, "Nouvelle bibliographie hallagienne," *Goldziher Mem. Vol.,* I, 252–79 (since 1922); and A. J. Arberry's brief but highly informative surveys, *Sufism: An Account of the Mystics of Islam* and *An Introduction to the History of Sufism* (a good historical survey of the researches in this field).

76. Saadiah, *Beliefs,* III.1–2, pp. 114 f. (Hebrew, p. 59; English, pp. 140 f.); Baḥya, *Duties,* Intro., pp. 8 ff. (Zifroni, pp. 9 ff.; Hyamson, I, 4 ff.); Anselm of Canterbury, *Cur Deus homo,* I.1–2 in *PL,* CLXVIII, 361 ff. (ed. by F. C. Schmitt, II, 47 ff.; see *supra,* Chap. XXIV, n. 42). On Ibn Gabirol, see *supra,* nn. 68, 70. One could also reverse the order and postulate *intelligo ut credam.* This was, indeed, the main purpose of all medieval Jewish philosophers, even apart from Maimonides, to fortify, through offering rational arguments, wavering souls in adhering to the faith of their forefathers and fulfilling its commandments. That is why, as Z. Diesendruck rightly observed, even in their doctrine of the soul, the Jewish thinkers invariably tried "to lift it out of the domain of mere metaphysics, and to anchor it firmly in ethics." See the brief summary of his paper on "Der Seelenbegriff in der jüdischen Religionsphilosophie des Mittelalters" in *Actes du Ve Congrès International d'Histoire des Religions à Lund . . . 1929,* pp. 320–26.

77. Maimonides' *Guide,* III.51 (English, p. 386). On the discussions in contemporary Muslim circles, see the data succinctly summarized by I. Goldziher in "Die Gottesliebe in der islamischen Theologie," *Der Islam,* IX, 148–58. The ramified doctrine of the love, as well as the fear of God, as expatiated by the biblical writers is carefully reviewed in the complementary studies by B. J. Bamberger and G. Nagel mentioned *supra,* Vol. I, p. 357 n. 6. No such detailed treatment of the later rabbinic teachings is as yet available, but enough information may be culled from the general works on rabbinic theology. See, e.g., G. F. Moore's *Judaism,* II, 98 ff.; III, 180.

78. Saadiah, *Beliefs,* II.13, 108 f. (Hebrew, p. 56; English, p. 132); Ibn Daud, *Emunah,* pp. 100 (Hebrew), 128 (German); Abraham ibn Ezra, *Commentary* on Deut. 6:5; Maimonides, *Guide,* I.39 (English, p. 55; the author himself refers here to his earlier elaborations of that idea in his *Commentary* on the Mishnah and his *Code*), with the explanation offered by Moses Narboni in his *Commentary* on that passage; Sulzbach ed., fol. 35a; Maimonides, *Book of Commandments,* ed. by Bloch, p. 61; ed. by Heller, p. 25; and *supra,* Chap. XXVII, n. 110. Cf. E. Hoffmann's dissertation, *Die Liebe zu Gott bei Mose ben Maimon.* It is to be regretted that this intelligent analysis of that important and much-neglected subject has been only partially published. To judge from the Contents (*ibid.,* pp. 77 f.), the more significant, truly analytical portion has not been printed. See also G. Vajda, "L'Amour de Dieu selon Moïse Maïmonide," *Trait d'Union,* IV, Nos. 39–40, pp. 3–16.

79. Maimonides' *Guide,* III.51 (English, p. 386); Baḥya's *Duties,* X.7, p. 393 (Zifroni, p. 271; this entire tenth section of Baḥya's treatise is devoted to the love of God); C. Ramos Gil, "Baḥya ibn Paquda: El puro amor divino," *Miscellanea de Estudios arabes y hebraicos* of the University of Granada, I, 85–148; G. Vajda, *La Théologie ascétique de Baḥya,* pp. 123 ff., 135 ff.; H. Cohen in his "Charakteristik der Ethik Maimunis" in *Moses ben Maimon,* ed. by Jakob Guttmann *et al.,* I, 104 f. (reprinted in his *Jüdische Schriften,* III, 261). There is no real conflict between Cohen's view and that expressed by Diesendruck in *HUCA,* V, 533 f., as suggested by E. Hoffmann, pp. 6 f. In fact, Diesendruck himself insisted on the significance of the ethical element in the entire teleological outlook of Maimonides. The nexus between the love of God as an incentive to knowledge and the knowledge of God as a prerequisite for true love was one of the constants in the otherwise often changing Maimonidean emphases on the individual ingredients of each.

80. Maimonides' *Guide,* III.54 (English, p. 397); and Saadiah's statements cited in the next note. Maimonides' familiarity at least with Aristotle's *Nicomachean Ethics* has long been noted. In fact, he quotes that work expressly three times in his own *Guide* (II.36; III.49; English, pp. 226 [reference omitted], 353, 377). Of course, he used an Arabic version somewhat akin to that represented by the MS of 1232, an excerpt of which (Chap. IX.1), was edited with an English translation by A. J. Arberry in "The Nicomachean Ethics in Arabic," *BSOAS,* XVII, 1–9. Hence we need not assume, as did S. Munk, that Maimonides quoted here from memory. See Munk's notes on his translation of the *Guide,* III, 343 n. 2, 403 n. 2. On the general impact of the Aristotelian ethics on Maimonides' teachings and the latter's numerous deviations, see D. Rosin's somewhat general observations in *Die Ethik des Maimonides,* pp. 6 ff.; A. Jaraczewsky, "Die Ethik des Maimonides und ihr Einfluss auf die scholastische Philosophie des dreizehnten Jahrhunderts," *Zeitschrift für*

Philosophie und philosophische Kritik, L, 5–24; and, from other angles, S. Rawidowicz, "On Maimonides' Ethics," *Kaplan Jub. Vol.,* Hebrew section, pp. 205–36. See also, more generally, R. Walzer's "New Light on the Arabic Translations of Aristotle," *Oriens,* VI, 91–142; and *supra,* nn. 16, 33.

81. Maimonides' *Guide,* III.26 (English, p. 312); Saadiah's *Beliefs,* III.2; IV.5; X.2, pp. 117 f., 155, 284 (Hebrew, pp. 60 f., 79 f., 145 f.; English, pp. 143 f., 192, 360 f.); Baḥya's *Duties,* Intro., pp. 8 ff. (Zifroni, pp. 8 ff.; Hyamson, I, 4 ff.). Both Saadiah and Maimonides indulged in biblical semantics in order to prove some of their points. To show, for example, that the three faculties of man are already intimated in Scripture, the gaon referred to the several Hebrew synonyms for *neshamah* (soul). In his opinion, *nefesh* stands for the appetitive, and *ruaḥ* for the impulsive faculty. Still two other designations found in the Bible convey other meanings. Thus *yeḥidah* (unique) indicates the totally unique character of the human soul, which has no parallel among other beings, celestial or earthly, while *ḥayyah* (living) serves as a clear reminder of the immortality of the soul. See *Beliefs,* VI.3, pp. 195 f. (Hebrew, p. 98; English, pp. 243 f.). The former distinction is fully accepted by Abraham ibn Ezra (in his *Commentary* on Exod. 23:25), except that, unlike Saadiah, who placed the seat of the soul entirely in the heart, Ibn Ezra attributed the cognitive *neshamah* to the brain, the impulsive *ruaḥ* to the heart, and the appetitive *nefesh* to the liver.

Of interest is also Ibn Gabirol's related allegory, communicated by Ibn Ezra (in his first *Commentary* on Gen. in *Ozar nechmad,* II, 218), according to which Adam represented the highest soul of wisdom, Eve (*Ḥavvah*) the *ruaḥ ḥayyah,* that is the living (probably also the impulsive) faculty, while the serpent stood for the appetitive *nefesh.* One can see how far the imagination of exegetes could range. With respect to the five Hebrew designations of soul, it was in particular the kabbalists who had a field day in classifying the different souls according to their chosen mystic categories. In this particular point Maimonides' semantics (*Guide,* I.40–41; English, pp. 55 f.), too, were imbedded in his general doctrine of the soul which saw in the human intellect, through its connection with the sublunary Active Intellect, "so to say the specific intellect of our star." See Diesendruck's "Seelenbegriff," p. 324, cited *supra,* n. 76; and *supra,* n. 69.

On the other hand, his related legal semantics were far simpler. He believed, for example, that the biblical term *mishpaṭim* designated laws whose reasons were obvious, while *ḥuqqim* represented ordinances whose object was not generally clear. It is with special reference to the latter that Moses told Israel, "For it is no vain thing for you" (Deut. 32:47), that is "the giving of these commandments is not a vain thing and without any useful object; and if it appears so to you in any commandment, it is owing to the deficiency in your comprehension" (*Guide,* III.26; English, p. 310). See also *supra,* Chap. XXVII, nn. 110, 111, 166.

82. Maimonides' *Guide,* III.31, 33 (English, pp. 321, 327); Ibn Ṣaddiq's *'Olam qaṭan,* ed. by Horovitz, p. 67; Abraham bar Ḥiyya's *Hegyon,* fol. 15a. See *supra,* n. 72; and I. Heinemann's *Lehre von der Zweckbestimmung,* p. 59. On Ibn Gabirol's doctrine of sin, see the data assembled chiefly from his poetic works by K. Dreyer in *Die religiöse Gedankenwelt,* pp. 88 ff. It lay in the nature of his major philosophic work that Ibn Gabirol failed to discuss there the problem of sin, and rather stressed in his triumphant finale the element of love and desire on the part of the human

soul to rejoin the World Soul, and through it its original source in God. On the latter point, see also *infra,* n. 87. The related subject of mental therapy or, as it was then called, "hygiene of the soul," will be discussed in the general context of medieval medicine *infra,* Chap. XXXVI. See also H. Goitein's study, *Der Optimismus und Pessimismus in der jüdischen Religionsphilosophie,* and J. Günzig's observations on *Das jüdische Schrifttum über den Wert des Lebens,* pp. 59 ff.

83. Abraham bar Ḥiyya's *Hegyon,* pp. 35 ff. Following Jakob Guttmann's suggestion, G. Vajda interpreted this threefold division in terms of Farabi's political theory. See his "Abraham bar Hiyya et Al-Farabi," *REJ,* CIV, 113–19. However, a closer examination reveals that the dissimilarities far exceed the similarities.

84. Saadiah's *Beliefs,* x.17, pp. 314 f. (Hebrew, pp. 158 f.; English, pp. 399 f., with minor variations); Baḥya's *Duties,* ix (this entire chapter is devoted to the analysis of an ascetic mode of life; it concludes with the admission that the overcoming of earthly desires had become increasingly difficult in the course of human history, and hence came the necessary multiplication of laws intended to aid the average human being in this struggle); Halevi's *K. al-Khazari,* iii.19, pp. 168 f. (English, pp. 155 ff.). Halevi's and especially Maimonides' doctrine of the golden mean, while following Aristotle's teachings, rather than the Platonic classification of virtues previously widely adopted in Jewish philosophic circles, is nevertheless essentially Jewish. In fact, this doctrine is firmly rooted in talmudic ethics, as pointed out by H. S. Lewis in "The 'Golden Mean' in Judaism," *Abrahams Mem. Vol.,* pp. 283–95.

85. Maimonides' *M.T.* Shemiṭṭah ve-yobel xiii.13; Halevi's *K. al-Khazari,* iii.5, pp. 142 f. (English, p. 137; the bracketed words in our quotation follow Ibn Tibbon's plausible distinction). Other reservations concerning the Maimonidean doctrine of the "golden mean" are advanced by S. Rawidowicz in his aforementioned essay, "On Maimonides' Ethics," *Kaplan Jub. Vol.,* Hebrew section, pp. 205–36. The tenth chapter of Saadiah's major work is clearly indicative of the radical tendencies current in certain Arab philosophic circles, and these were very likely reflected to some extent also among Baghdad's Jewish intellectuals. See, for example, the gaon's polemics against exaggerations of the importance of the erotic element in human life, exaggerations for which he found a protagonist in a contemporary Arab writer. See G. Vajda, "Une Source arabe de Saadia, le *kitab al-zahra* d'Aboû Bakr Ibn Dâwoûd," *REJ,* XCII, 146–50; and, more generally, the data assembled by G.-H. Bousquet in *La Morale de l'Islam et son éthique sexuelle* and by M. Papo in "Die sexuelle Ethik im Qoran in ihrem Verhältnis zu seinen jüdischen Quellen," *Jahrbuch für jüdische Volkskunde,* II, 171–291. Saadiah himself, on the other hand, found it necessary to buttress his religious motivation of ethical conduct as a matter of duty and compliance with the law by another, more worldly emphasis upon the eudaimonistic value of moral behavior for a rich and contented personal life. See Julius Guttmann's *Philosophie des Judentums,* p. 81.

86. Ps. 51:19; Maimonides' *M.T.* De'ot ii.3; H. Cohen's "Charakteristik der Ethik Maimunis" in Jakob Guttmann *et al., Moses ben Maimon,* I, 114 f. (also in his *Jüdische Schriften,* III, 269 f.); Baḥya's *Duties,* vi.2, p. 261 (Zifroni, p. 178). See also Maimonides' comment on the talmudic adage that "piety leads to humility,

humility to the fear of sin, and the fear of sin to holiness" ('A.Z. 20b) in his *Eight Chapters,* ed. by Gorfinkle, pp. 6 (Arabic and Hebrew), 34 (English). See also the variant in M. Soṭah ix.15 end, with no comment by Maimonides. On Moses' extraordinary humility, see Num. 12:3 and numerous aggadic elaborations thereof. It must be borne in mind, however, that non-Jewish moralists often likewise stressed the great virtues of humility. Following Muslim authors, both Joseph ibn 'Aqnin and Yehudah al-Ḥarizi cited, for example, the saying attributed to Ptolemy: "The scholars who are most outstanding for their humility are the richest in learning, just as the lowest place is the richest in water of all the valleys." See the collection of aphorisms from Ibn 'Aqnin's *Ṭibb* [or *Ṭubb*] *an-nufus,* ed. and trans. by A. S. Halkin in his "Classical and Arabic Material in Ibn 'Aḳnīn's 'Hygiene of the Soul,'" *PAAJR,* XIV, 67; and Al-Ḥarizi's *Musere ha-pilosofim,* ii.11, 14.

87. Maimonides' *Guide,* ii.40 beg.; iii.49 (English, pp. 232, 373), etc.; *M.T.* De'ot vi.7; 'Akum v.9; and other statements, as well as their talmudic antecedents cited in my *Essays on Maimonides,* pp. 134 f., 140. The doctrine of the "social animal" was, of course, borrowed from Aristotle, especially from his *Nicomachean Ethics.* See *supra,* n. 80. In his doctrine of love, on the other hand, as a major social as well as religious influence, Maimonides may have been impressed particularly by the teachings of Avicenna. See especially the latter's *Risalah fi'l 'ishq,* translated into English under the title, "The Treatise of Love," by E. L. Fackenheim in *Mediaeval Studies,* VII, 208–28 (includes significant data also on other Arab philosophers). In view of the great importance which Maimonides attached to social relations, notwithstanding the relatively small space he assigned to their analysis, we shall not be surprised to find him, like Farabi and other students of Plato's *Nomoi,* treat of Providence not in the context of his metaphysical teachings, but rather as part of political science. See L. Strauss's pertinent remarks on "Der Ort der Vorsehungslehre nach der Ansicht Maimunis," *MGWJ,* LXXXI, 93–105.

These observations on the ethical teachings, both individual and social, of the medieval Jewish philosophers under Islam, necessarily had to be very brief, even sketchy. Many other aspects, however, have already been more fully treated and documented in various other contexts, especially in our analyses of the economic and communal theories, socioreligious controversies, and legal philosophy, *supra,* Chaps. XXII, XXIII, XXIV, and XXVII. They will receive further close attention in a later volume dealing with the social institutions developed by the medieval Jewish communities. See also such monographs as D. Rau, "Die Ethik R. Saadjas," *MGWJ,* LV–LVI; D. Rosin, "The Ethics of Solomon ibn Gabirol," *JQR,* [o.s.] III, 159–81; A. Kahlberg, *Die Ethik des Bachja ibn Pakuda;* and the comparative data offered in D. M. Donaldson's *Studies in Muslim Ethics.*

88. B.M. 59a; Ginzberg, *Ginze Schechter,* I, 17; Maimonides' *Resp.,* ed. by Freimann, pp. 40 ff. No. 42; his *M.T.* Shemiṭṭah ve-yobel xiii.13. Of course, even in modern times, throughout the Near East national allegiance was measured principally by one's religious associations rather than by mere ethnic descent. That there was no unanimity, however, concerning the relations between these two principles even among the ancient and medieval Jewish sages has been correctly emphasized by I. Heinemann in his "Conflicting Views on Nationalism in the Aggadah and Medieval Philosophy" (Hebrew), *Sefer Dinaburg,* pp. 132–50. The status of the proselyte in medieval law and society will be more fully discussed in the con-

text of the later Middle Ages. See also *supra,* Vols. I, pp. 180 ff., 375 f.; II, pp. 147 ff., 387 f.; and Chaps. XXIV, n. 40; and XXVII, n. 168.

89. Halevi's *K. al-Khazari,* I.115; II.12 ff., 23 f., 33; III.73, pp. 64 f., 76 ff., 90 ff., 103 f., 222 f. (English, pp. 79, 88 ff., 99 f., 107, 196). In the enumeration of the seven preexistent things Halevi followed, with important variations, the listing of Nedarim 39b. See *supra,* Chap. XXXIII, n. 2; and Cassel's note in his edition, p. 304. Although preexistence of the Torah was the simplest and most direct answer to the Muslim claims of the preexistence of the Qur'an, Jewish thinkers rebelled against the idea of any kind of genuine primordial existence, however ideal, as bordering on the philosophic doctrine of an eternal universe. Even the ancient rabbis, and in their wake the medieval mystics, discussed the Torah's preexistence in terms of how many thousands of years before the creation of the world the Torah had already been created by God. This, of course, meant creation at a certain time. Halevi's mind, however, rebelled against the idea of placing Israel, Jerusalem, and the Messiah among things really created long before the creation of the physical world. Hence the solution of the gradual unfolding of the original will divine, where the final deeds proved the presence of the original thought. Jerusalem's presence in this list is fully in line with Halevi's glorification of the Holy Land, to which he devoted a substantial portion of his second book, as well as many of his best known poems. See *supra,* Chap. XXXII, n. 46. Palestine's intimate connection with prophecy was, in fact, a commonplace of the Aggadah and, following it, of medieval Jewish philosophy as well. See Saadiah's *Beliefs,* III.5, p. 125 (Hebrew, p. 65; English, pp. 153 f.); Ibn Daud's *Emunah,* pp. 74 (Hebrew), 93 (German). See also B. Z. Dinaburg's "Yehudah Halevi's Journey to Palestine and the Messianic Ferment in His Day" (Hebrew), *Yellin Jub. Vol.,* pp. 157–82; S. Abramson's reconstruction of "R. Yehudah Halevi's Letter on His Emigration to the Land of Israel" (Hebrew), *KS,* XXIX, 133–44; my remarks in *JSS,* III, 258 ff.; and *supra,* Chap. XXVIII, n. 96.

90. Saadiah's *Beliefs,* IX.2, p. 260 (Hebrew, p. 132; English, p. 329); Maimon ben Joseph's "Letter of Consolation," ed. by L. M. Simmons in *JQR,* [o.s.] II, 84 ff. (English), 14 ff. (Arabic, after p. 236); and in B. Klar's new Hebrew translation, pp. 37 ff.; Maimonides' *Iggeret ha-shemad* (see *supra,* n. 17). The importance of the feeling of despair over exilic existence permeating the poetic works of Ibn Gabirol is rather overstated by Dreyer in *Die religiöse Gedankenwelt,* pp. 36 ff., 155 f., but it is also unduly minimized by I. Heinemann in his review of Dreyer's work in *MGWJ,* LXXVI, 473. With respect to the date of Psalm 90 Maimon reminisced how, during his composition of a commentary on the weekly portion, *Ha'azinu,* he had concluded that Moses must have written that prayer shortly before his death, especially in view of the similarity between Deut. 32:36, and Ps. 90:13. Only later, while continuing his commentary on the final weekly lesson, he suddenly discovered that this argument had already been advanced a millennium earlier in *Sifre* on Deut. (No. 342, ed. by Friedmann, fol. 142a; ed. by Finkelstein, pp. 392 f.). Evidently during his period of wanderings Maimon had access to few Hebrew books, whose possession might have betrayed him to the intolerant Almohade authorities, and had to rely greatly on his and his friends' memory. In any case, so impressed was this former Cordovan judge with the eschatological import of the "prayer of Moses" that he decided to recite it every morning in conjunction with the "hundred benedictions," before *Barukh she-amar* (Blessed be He who spoke). On the difficulty of

squaring this number, see Fishman's comment on Klar's translation, p. 38 n. 44. However, the difficulty is removed if we do not press the term בעד (p. 15) as meaning "after," but rather as we have rendered it "in conjunction with," that is after the recitation of the portion relating to the hundred prayers in Amram's *Seder*. See the latter, ed. by Frumkin, I, fol. 25 ff. (ed. by Hedegard, I, 2 ff.); and *supra*, Chap. XXXI, nn. 64, 67.

91. Halevi's *K. al-Khazari*, I.4, 95, 113; II.36–42; III.11; IV.22–23, pp. 10 f., 42 ff., 62 f., 102 ff., 160 ff., 262 ff. (English, pp. 40, 64 ff., 78, 109, 150, 225 f.); *supra*, Chaps. XXI, n. 69; XXIV, n. 27. In the latter passage the Spanish poet-philosopher mentions "prominent men amongst us who could escape this degradation by a word spoken lightly, become free men, and turn against their oppressors, but do not do so out of devotion to their faith." This was a realistic appraisal of the position of Jewish converts under Islam. By merely verbal adherence to the new faith any Jew could get rid of his disabilities and even join the highest ranks of Muslim society. See *supra*, Chap. XVIII. In his eloquent plea, Halevi's spokesman naturally enough invokes here the prophecies of Deutero-Isaiah concerning the Servant of the Lord in whom he, like almost all medieval Jewish commentators, saw only Israel personified. See the large literature on this subject cited *supra*, Vol. I, p. 365 n. 29, and especially the studies by Hutterer and Fischel. On Israel's "chosenness" as a result of the "divine influence" resting on it since the days of the patriarchs, and on the meaning of this term, see *infra*, n. 99.

92. Saadiah's *Beliefs*, Intro., 6, p. 22 (Hebrew, p. 11; English, p. 28); Samuel ben Ḥofni's and Hai's responsa in Lewin, *Otzar ha-gaonim*, IV, Part 2, pp. 15 ff.; Julius Guttmann, *Philosophie des Judentums*, pp. 87 ff. The connection with the subsequent discussion in Leibniz's *Theodicy* was pointed out by D. Kaufmann in "Ein Responsum des Gaons R. Hâja über Gottes Vorherwissen und die Dauer des menschlichen Lebens (Aǵal)," *ZDMG*, XLIX, 73–84. G. Weil, "R. Hai Gaon's Responsum on Life's Predestined End" (Hebrew), *Sefer Assaf*, pp. 261–79, republishes the Arabic text with a Hebrew translation. See also M. Schreiner's more general observations, "Zur Charakteristik R. Samuel b. Chofni's und R. Hai's," *MGWJ*, XXXV, 314–19; and the literature cited *supra*, Chap. XXIX, n. 67.

93. Saadiah's *Beliefs*, Intro., 6; II.12; III.1–6, pp. 22, 105 f., 112 ff. (Hebrew, pp. 11, 54 f., 58 ff.; English, pp. 28, 128 ff., 137 ff.). We must bear in mind that next to his discussion, in his *Beliefs*, of the problems of creation including that of the media of revelation, Saadiah had also offered somewhat divergent explanations in his earlier *Commentary on Yeṣirah*. While we must ascribe part of that divergence to the text commented on, Saadiah often reinterpreted the latter sufficiently to make the product largely mirroral of his own views as well. Without altogether falling into the anthropomorphic snares offered by the mystic author of the Book of Creation, he nevertheless advanced here a doctrine of the "second air" created by God for the purpose of serving as medium for the revelation of God's will. See his *Commentary*, ed. by Lambert, pp. 72 (Arabic), 94 f. (French). It is small wonder that this doctrine appealed greatly to the German kabbalists. See G. Scholem's *Major Trends*, pp. 110 ff. Yet, as presented by the gaon himself, this concept appeared sufficiently equivocal not to elicit any protest even from the sharply anti-anthropomorphic Maimonides, who, by a queer irony of history, did not himself

escape being bandied around as a leading mystic authority by later kabbalists. See *supra,* Chap. XXXIII, n. 44. The evident compromise character of Saadiah's doctrine of the created Glory and Speech has been well demonstrated by A. Altmann in "Saadya's Theory of Revelation: Its Origin and Background" in Rosenthal's *Saadya Studies,* pp. 4–25.

In all these discussions the gaon had in mind the extensive debates conducted on this score among Muslim theologians, orthodox as well as sectarian. It is reported, for instance, that the Jahmiya taught "that when Moses heard a voice, he did not hear the speech of God or God speaking—the infinite God could not be restricted to the compass of finite words—what he heard was merely a speech created by God." See W. M. Watt's "Early Discussions about the Qur'an," *MW,* XL, 27–40, 96–105. As we recall, some Mu'tazilites did not hesitate to emend, on this score, the Qur'anic phrase "But Moses did God speak to" (4:162) into: "Moses did speak to God." See Goldziher, *Richtungen,* pp. 173 ff.; and *supra,* Chap. XXIX, nn. 53–54. Saadiah himself pointed out that, in one particular aspect of this doctrine, the Arabic language proved completely inadequate, namely in expressing also God's silence as the mere opposite of speech, or as its postponement. Such postponement is, however, clearly indicated in the Hebrew term, *heḥesheti* (I have held my peace; Isa. 42:14). This remark of the gaon was a distinct rejection of the Ash'arite doctrine (with reference to Qur'an 18:109, 31:26) of God's word flowing continually, since complete silence would have been a sign of divine imperfection. See the sources cited by Ventura in *La Philosophie de Saadia Gaon,* pp. 192 f. See also Julius Guttmann's "Zur Kritik der Offenbarungsreligion in der islamischen und jüdischen Philosophie," *MGWJ,* LXXVIII, 456–64 (with special reference to Baḥya's *Duties,* III.4, pp. 146 ff.; Zifroni, pp. 93 ff.; Hyamson, II, 50 ff.); and W. D. Zimmerli's succinct observations from a missionary standpoint on *Prophet im Alten Testament und im Islam.*

94. Qirqisani's *K. al-Anwar,* II.4; VI.9–10, ed. by Nemoy, I, 66; II, 575 ff.; Samuel ben Ḥofni's and Hai's responsa in Lewin's *Otzar ha-gaonim, loc. cit.* The pertinent passages by Al-Qirqisani are also available in the well-annotated French excerpts by G. Vajda in his "Etudes sur Qirqisani." See esp. *REJ,* CVI, 89 ff.; CVII, 62; and *supra,* Chap. XXIX, nn. 71–72; and, more generally, J. Kramer's study of *Das Problem des Wunders im Zusammenhang mit dem der Providenz bei den jüdischen Religionsphilosophen des Mittelalters von Saadia bis Maimûni.* Of some interest for comparative purposes is R. M. Grant's analysis of *Miracle and Natural Law in Graeco-Roman and Early Christian Thought.*

95. *Guide,* II.40 end (English, p. 234); and the other sources discussed in my essay in *PAAJR,* VI, 56 f. These moral emphases, as well as the stress on prophetic intuition, show the extent to which Maimonides departed from the purely Aristotelian standards. See Z. Diesendruck's ingenious reconstruction of "Maimonides' Lehre von der Prophetie," *Abrahams Mem. Vol.,* pp. 74–134. See also L. Strauss's comparative study of "Maimunis Lehre von der Prophetie und ihre Quellen," *Monde oriental,* XXVIII, 99–139 (comparing it especially with the teachings of Farabi and Avicenna); and, more generally, N. Sandler's dissertation, *Das Problem der Prophetie in der jüdischen Religionsphilosophie von Saadia bis Maimuni.* An interesting personal question is raised by A. J. Heschel in his "Did Maimonides Strive for Prophetic Inspiration?" *Ginzberg Jub. Vol.,* Hebrew vol., pp. 159–88. The arguments in favor of an affirmative answer are far from conclusive, however. On the relations between

Maimonides' concept of the prophetic imagination and Spinoza's *scientia intuitiva,* see L. Roth's observations in his *Spinoza, Descartes and Maimonides,* pp. 133 f.; and, with reference also to Ibn Gabirol, Halevi, and Ibn Daud, those by H. A. Wolfson in *The Philosophy of Spinoza,* II, 155.

96. *Guide,* II.45 (English, pp. 241 ff.); Ibn Daud's *Emunah,* II.5, 1, pp. 70 f. (Hebrew), 88 f. (German); Halevi's *K. al-Khazari,* IV.3, 11, 15–16; V.10 end (English, pp. 208 ff., 216 f., 220 ff., 259). See also the passage in III.73, cited *supra,* n. 89. Curiously, Balaam is also mentioned in this lowest Maimonidean group, but not Job and his friends, who figure prominently in the talmudic enumeration (B.B. 15b f.). Originally inclined to consider them all true prophets, Maimonides finally decided to follow that segment of the talmudic opinion which treated the entire book of Job as a mere allegory. See his *Guide,* III.22 (English, p. 296); and my remarks in *PAAJR,* VI, 57 n. 114. He was attacked on this score by his otherwise admiring commentator, Joseph ben Abba-Mari ibn Kaspi (of Argentière). See the latter's *'Ammude Kesef* on the *Guide,* II.48, ed. by T. Werbluner, p. 119.

Although refraining from discussing Moses' prophetic visions in the *Guide* and merely referring there to his earlier analysis in the *Code* (see *M.T.* Yesode ha-torah VII.6, and the intro. to his *Commentary* on M. Sanhedrin X, 7th principle, ed. by Holzer, pp. 23 ff.), Maimonides made it perfectly clear that one could not compare even Abraham to Moses. See the *Guide,* II.45 (English, pp. 244 f.). Without going the whole length of the Maimonidean glorification of Moses, Abraham ibn Ezra had likewise tried to explain the great lawgiver's superiority over the patriarchs. See his *Commentary* on Exodus 6:3. If this distinction clearly controverted the Muslim claim to restoration of the pure Abrahamitic faith, Maimonides' designation of Moses as *sof nebu'ah* (seal of prophecy; in his letter to Ḥisdai ha-Levi of Alexandria in *Qobeṣ,* II, fol. 23c) was an even more overt denial of Mohammed's assertions. On the talmudic (Amemar's) contrast between a wise man and a prophet, see B.B. 12a; and, more generally, *supra,* Vol. II, pp. 139, 383 n. 14; and Chap. XXIV, nn. 5 ff.

97. B.B. 15b; Justin's *Dialogue,* LXXXII (in *PG,* VI, 669); Clement of Alexandria's *Excerpta ex scriptis Theodoti,* LIV ff. (in *PG,* IX, 685). Quoting these passages in his "Hallevi and Maimonides on Prophecy," *JQR,* XXXII, 345–70; XXXIII, 49–82, H. A. Wolfson also pointed out that Philo, though less outspoken than the rabbinic Aggadah, nevertheless intimated that Gentiles, too, could be entrusted with genuine prophetic missions through angels, if not directly through God. See also Wolfson's *Philo,* II, 50 ff. Clearly, to Philo this distinction was not of major importance. Hardly cognizant of the incipient threat of the Christian or other sectarian claims, he doubtless considered it his major objective to persuade his Greek-speaking readers among Gentiles, and even more, among wavering Jews, of the authenticity and significance of Hebrew prophecy, rather than to argue about the validity of non-Jewish claims to prophecy.

98. Ibn Daud's *Emunah, loc. cit.* (p. 71); Bar Ḥiyya's *Megillat ha-megalleh,* pp. 72 f.; Halevi's *K. al-Khazari,* I.115, pp. 64 f. (English, p. 79); Ibn Ezra's *Commentary* on Num. 22:7–9. The similarities, and even greater dissimilarities, between these doctrines of prophecy and the prophetic nation and the Nietzschean (as well as Nazi) doctrine of superman (and superrace), are briefly indicated by I. Heinemann in

"Der Begriff des Uebermenschen in der jüdischen Religionsphilosophie," *Der Morgen,* I, 3–17 (with special reference to Philo, Halevi, and Maimonides), and in *Die Lehre von der Zweckbestimmung,* pp. 69 ff.

99. Halevi's *K. al-Khazari,* I.95 ff., pp. 42 ff. (English, pp. 64 ff.). See B. Ziemlich's "Abraham ben Chija und Jehuda Halewi," *MGWJ,* XXIX, 366–74; Julius Guttmann's introduction to Abraham bar Ḥiyya's *Megillat ha-megalleh,* pp. xvi, xxi f.; I. Goldziher's data in his "Mélanges judéo-arabes: Le Amr ilâhî (ha-'inyân ha-élôhî) chez Juda Halévi," *REJ,* L, 32–41; and the statement attributed to an Iraqi in a book stemming from the Brethren of Purity and edited by F. Dieterici under the title, *Thier und Mensch vor dem König der Genien,* p. 6, cited by Wolfson in *JQR,* XXXIII, 65 f. See also *supra,* Chap. XXIV, nn. 6, 16; and, on Saadiah's related doctrine of an outstanding leader of each generation, Chap. XXIII, n. 21. It should also be noted that the tenth-century author of "An Early Theologico-Polemical Work" had argued against both the rationalist followers of Barham, who altogether negated prophecy, and those who believed that revelation had begun with Noah. Citing Deut. 34:3, he declared that the Torah had been given not to an individual like Noah, but exclusively to the "congregation of Jacob" for the purpose that they should "learn and teach to all nations law and judgment." See Mann's edition of that text in *HUCA,* XII–XIII, 424 ff., 442 ff.

100. Ibn Gabirol's "Royal Crown" in *Shire,* II, 64 (in Zangwill's trans., pp. 86 f.); Halevi's *K. al-Khazari,* II.36, pp. 102 f. (English, p. 109). Maimonides went even further than Ibn Gabirol. Discussing the philosophically very difficult concept of the divine Glory, so frequently mentioned in the Bible, he explained that it sometimes referred merely to the glorification of the Lord by His creatures. Such glorification, he added, "consists in the comprehension of His greatness, and all who comprehend His greatness and perfection, glorify Him according to their capacity." In a sense, even inanimate objects like the bones of man or minerals may be said to glorify the Lord, because "they testify to the omnipotence and wisdom of their Creator, and cause him who examines them to praise God" (*Guide,* I.64; English, p. 96). This basic combination of Judaism's universalist aspirations with the martyrology of the Jewish people as their main vehicle, had long and venerable antecedents in ancient Jewish letters. Rashi voiced this long-accepted doctrine when in his *Commentary* on the Servant of the Lord (Isa. 53:4–5) he declared: "But now we see that all came to him [the Servant] not because of his inferiority. He was rather afflicted with sufferings, . . . so that the whole world may enjoy peace." See also *supra,* n. 86; and Vol. I, pp. 157, 365 n. 29.

101. Abu Qasim ibn Sa'id's *K. Tabaqat al-uman* (Categories of Nations), ed. by L. Cheikho, pp. 87 ff. (in J. Finkel's trans. in *JQR,* XVIII, 48); Maimonides' Letter to Jonathan of Lunel, reproduced in his *Resp.,* p. lx; Ibn Daud's *Emunah,* Intro., pp. 4 (Hebrew), 6 (German). Even the mystic Ibn Gabirol stated, "Knowledge brings forth action, and action keeps the soul away from the antagonistic, corrupting forces and returns it to its nature and substance" (*Fons,* I.2, pp. 4 f.; Hebrew, p. 3). On similar other statements by Ibn Gabirol and Pseudo-Baḥya, and their contrast to Plotinian concepts, see S. Horovitz's *Psychologie,* p. 145 n. 174. See also *supra,* n. 63. If in the same context Ibn Sa'id called the Jewish doctors well informed about

the story of creation, he may have had in mind their intensive preoccupation with the teachings of *Sefer Yeṣirah.* At least one of his Jewish compatriots, Yehudah bar Barzillai, indeed wrote a lengthy commentary on that work.

102. See A. Guillaume's "Philosophy and Theology" in *The Legacy of Islam,* ed. by T. Arnold and A. Guillaume, p. 265; and various statements by Hai, cited *supra,* nn. 92, 94, more fully analyzed by E. E. Hildesheimer. See also A. Altmann's data on "Das Verhältnis Maimunis zur jüdischen Mystik," *MGWJ,* LXXX, 305–30; and *supra,* Chap. XXXIII, n. 25. On the prevailing use of the Hebrew script in the Arabic Jewish philosophic works, see *supra,* Chap. XXX, n. 7. This safeguard did not, however, prevent such Muslims as 'Abd al-Latif and At-Tabrizi from making full use of the *Guide* within a few years or decades after its publication. See *supra,* nn. 17, 28. The general impact of Maimonidean teachings on both Muslims and Christians will be discussed in a later volume.

CHAPTER XXXV: SCIENTIFIC EXPLORATION

1. See Muhammad ibn Jabir al-Baṭṭani's *K. az-Zij* (Tables or Opus astronomicum), Intro., ed. with a Latin trans. and notes by C. A. Nallino, II, 1 ff. (Latin), III, 227 ff. (Arabic); F. Rosenthal's "Al-Asturlâbî and as-Samaw'al on Scientific Progress," *Osiris,* IX, 555–64. On Samau'al as author of mathematical and medical works, see H. Suter, *Die Mathematiker und Astronomen der Araber und ihre Werke,* pp. 124 f. No. 302. These mild apologies betray at the same time the inner insecurity of the progressives against the array of vigorous arguments advanced by the orthodox opponents of any imitation of the ways of the ancient scientists. See the data reviewed by Goldziher in his aforementioned study of the *Stellung der alten islamischen Orthodoxie zu den antiken Wissenschaften.* See also, from another angle, Rosenthal's observations on *The Technique and Approach of Muslim Scholarship.*

2. Maimonides' *Guide,* II.8 (Friedländer's trans., p. 163). Maimonides evidently referred here to Pesaḥim 94b. Although the passage, as quoted by him, perhaps from memory, is not recorded in any extant talmudic text, its meaning is, indeed, conveyed by R. Judah's declaration. See R. N. Rabbinovicz's *Diqduqe soferim* (Variae lectiones), *ad loc.;* and Munk's note on his translation of the *Guide,* II, 79 n. 1. Curiously, David Gans recorded private conversations with Tycho de Brahe and Johannes Kepler in which both famous astronomers had declared that the rabbinic sages had wrongly yielded this point to Aristotle. See Gans's astronomic treatise, *Neḥmad ve-na'im* (Desirable and Pleasant), XIII, XXV. The simile of the pigmy apparently was first employed by Zedekiah 'Anav, citing an ancient sage. See his *Shibbole ha-leqeṭ,* Intro., fol. 18a.

3. Abraham bar Ḥiyya's encyclopedic *Yesode ha-tebunah u-migdal ha-emunah* (Principles of Understanding and Tower of Faith), Intro., ed. by J. M. Millás Vallicrosa under the title *La Obra enciclopédica . . . de R. Abraham bar Ḥiyya ha-Bargeloni,* pp. 9 f. (Hebrew), 35 ff. (Spanish). See M. Steinschneider's earlier analysis of "Die Encyklopädie des Abraham bar Chijja" reprinted in his *G.S.,* I, 388 ff.; other literature listed *infra,* n. 12; and, more generally, F. S. Bodenheimer, "On Some Hebrew Encyclopaedias of the Middle Ages," *AIHS,* VI, 3–13; and F. Rosenthal, *The Technique,* pp. 60 ff. The Aristotelian background of this classification, as modified by both the ancient commentators and the Arab thinkers, esp. the mystic Brethren of Purity, is rightly emphasized by H. A. Wolfson in "The Classification of Sciences in Mediaeval Jewish Philosophy," *HUCA,* Jub. Vol., pp. 269 f. Not that Al-Muqammiṣ was familiar with the encyclopedic work of the Brethren which was not yet compiled in his day, or even with their general doctrines; he was in fact far more of a rationalist than a mystic. But the eclectic Brethren merely presented the then prevailing division of sciences. The very juxtaposition in the title of Bar Ḥiyya's encyclopedia, Principles of Understanding and Tower of Faith, clearly mirrors the author's sense of values. See also *infra,* n. 12. Bar Ḥiyya, the father of much of the medieval Hebrew scientific and philosophical terminology (see

I. Efros's aforementioned "Studies in Pre-Tibbonian Philosophic Terminology," *JQR*, XVII and XX; S. Gandz's data on "The Terminology of Multiplication in Arabic and Hebrew Sources," in his "Studies in History of Mathematics from Hebrew and Arabic Sources," *HUCA*, VI, 247 ff.; and *supra*, Chap. XXXIV, n. 31), seems also to have introduced the designation *musar* for the Greek propedeutic sciences, which had long been equated with the mathematical disciplines of arithmetic, geometry, astronomy, and music. In his translation of Baḥya's *Duties*, Yehudah ibn Tibbon closely followed Bar Ḥiyya's terms, and hence the remark "Some call it [the propedeutic science] the science of *musar*," may well be Ibn Tibbon's original explanation rather than a subsequent gloss, despite its absence in some early editions. See Wolfson's observations in *HUCA*, Jub. Vol., pp. 272 f., where, however, Bar Ḥiyya's classification is not mentioned. See also Klatzkin's *Oṣar ha-munaḥim*, II, 163 (referring to that usage already in Nissi ben Nuḥ's commentary on the Decalogue).

4. Joseph Qimḥi's *Sefer ha-Galui*, Intro., ed. by H. G. Matthews, pp. 1 f.; Baḥya's *Duties*, Intro., p. 4 (trans. by Hyamson, I, 1); Ibn Daud's *Emunah*, II. Intro., pp. 45 (Hebrew), 57 f. (German). Curiously, Ibn Daud thought that by playing up the mathematicians' superfluous experiments he would more easily expose them to deadly ridicule than by merely referring to their time-consuming calculations.

5. Maimonides' "Treatise on Logic," XIV, ed. by Efros, pp. 59 ff. (Ibn Tibbon's trans.), 61 ff. (English). In describing the fourth discipline of "practical philosophy," Maimonides is far from specific. Regrettably, the Arabic original of that concluding chapter has not been preserved, but on the basis of the Tibbonide translation Wolfson equated it with religious legislation, both Muslim and Jewish. This interpretation is controverted, however, not only by the contrast drawn here between the government of the "city," or rather city state, and that of a large people or peoples (another Hebrew translator, Aḥitub, uses the even less equivocal designation *'am*), but also by the sequel. Referring to the large literature which had accumulated in Arabic on the subject of the government of the city and other political *nomoi*, the author sweepingly declared: "But in these times we do not need all these laws and *nomoi*; for divine laws govern human conduct." In other words, both the third and the fourth disciplines of political science, devoted respectively to the governments of a city and of a great people, had become superfluous and been replaced by the study of the religious law. In Bar Ḥiyya's aforementioned tripartite division, too, the third discipline of his third group of disciplines dealing with the "human science" is clearly defined as "counsels of kings and princes of states" (*Yesode ha-tebunah*, p. 9; Spanish, pp. 36 f.). See *supra*, n. 3. There is a distinct likelihood that Maimonides was familiar with this encyclopedic work of his distinguished predecessor.

True, the term *ummah* could be used equally well for an ethnic or for a religious community, and in the mind of at least such thinkers as Farabi there was a strong nexus between theology and politics. See *supra*, Chaps. XXIII, n. 86; and XXXIV, n. 88. However, Maimonides' argument seems to have stressed the superfluity of the accepted disciplines of political science precisely because of the self-sufficiency of the revealed law. On the other hand, the distinction between the politics of the ancient Greek city state and that of a large empire or system of states and empires had been familiar already to the ancient Hellenistic writers and reappeared with redoubled force in the Great Caliphate and its successor states. Nonetheless, even several decades after Maimonides, Nasiruddin aṭ-Ṭusi still enumerated only three divisions of "practical philosophy," namely ethics, economics, and politics. See J. Stephenson's trans. of the passage pertaining to "The Classification of Sciences according to Nasiruddin Ṭusi," *Isis,* V, 334 ff.

6. Abba Mari ha-Yarḥi (of Lunel) *Sefer ha-Yareaḥ,* ed. by M. L. Bisliches, I, 125; Aṭ-Ṭusi in J. Stephenson's English trans. in *Isis,* V. 332 ff. A somewhat different grouping of the disciplines in Ibn Ezra's enumeration was suggested by D. Rosin in "Die Religionsphilosophie Abraham Ibn Esra's," *MGWJ,* XLIII, 231 ff. On the other hand, M. Güdemann, who altogether dismissed this comment by Ibn Ezra as mere mysticism, declared that the phrase "seven sciences" was of late medieval origin. He pointed out that Gersonides specifically interpreted away this proverbial reference to "seven pillars" of wisdom as a mere figure of speech indicating the multiplicity of disciplines without reference to any specific number. See Gersonides' *Commentary* on Prov. 9:1; and Güdemann's other data in *Das jüdische Unterrichtswesen,* p. 38 n. 1. The latter's own quotations indicate, however, that at least in the thirteenth century the phrase "seven sciences" had reached a certain vogue, Gersonides evidently finding it necessary to combat that widespread notion.

7. Ibn 'Aqnin's *Ṭubb an-nufus,* xxvii, in Güdemann's ed. and trans., in *Das jüdische Unterrichtswesen,* pp. 43 ff. and Appendix. This educational program bears the earmarks of pure scholastic theory. There is no evidence that it was ever put into practical operation in any Jewish school. This and related pedagogic problems will be discussed more fully in the far better known context of Jewish education in the later Middle Ages.

8. No effort will be made in this presentation to give a complete picture of the Jews' scientific contributions during the High Middle Ages. Neither the space allotted to this subject within the total framework of a social and religious history, nor the limited competence of the author—perhaps of any author whose specialized information rarely extends beyond the history of one or another of these branches of knowledge—allows more than a very general analysis. On the other hand, one must beware of taking the line of least resistance and offering but a series of biographical and bibliographical data concerning the leading Jewish scientists of that period. Important as these facts doubtless are, and deeply grateful as we all must be especially for Steinschneider's yeoman efforts to accumulate and carefully to sift the extant records in this field, they essentially touch the periphery and framework rather than the core of the early Jewish scientific endeavors. At the same time, in accordance with our main theme, we must treat also of the technical aspects of medieval Jewish scientific learning principally from the angle of their significance within the general cultural history of the period.

9. M. Postan's "Why Was Science Backward in the Middle Ages?" in the symposium on *The History of Science* of the British Broadcasting Company, p. 26. There is no comprehensive history of medieval Jewish contributions to science in general or the mathematical sciences in particular, although the main biographical and bibliographical data concerning the Jewish mathematicians and their works were assembled some sixty years ago by M. Steinschneider in a series of essays on "Die Mathematik bei den Juden," *Bibliotheca mathematica,* n.s. Vols. VII–XIII

(covering the period to 1440). This series was supplemented by his briefer sketches of "Die mathematischen Wissenschaften bei den Juden 1441–1500," *ibid.*, 3d ser. II, 58–76; and "Mathematik bei den Juden (1501–1550)," *Abhandlungen zur Geschichte der Mathematik,* IX, 473–83. See also A. Goldberg's brief index thereto, published under the title *Die jüdischen Mathematiker und die jüdischen anonymen mathematischen Schriften, alphabetisch geordnet mit Angabe ihrer Zeit.* While few publications and even manuscripts known at the end of the nineteenth century escaped Steinschneider's eagle eye, a number of additional sources, including the most important single work, Abraham bar Ḥiyya's treatise on geometry (see *infra*), have since appeared in more or less critical editions. A considerable number of analytical studies by S. Gandz, J. M. Millás, and others, published in the last decades and partly referred to in the following notes, have substantially advanced our knowledge of specific problems. The time may soon be ripe for a comprehensive work of synthesis. In the meantime students must be satisfied with data incorporated in the various general histories of science, or of individual disciplines. Many pertinent monographs will readily be found in *An Introduction to the History of Science* by the late George Sarton, of which Vols. I–II are particularly significant for the period here under review. Despite frequent repetitions resulting from its unusual organization, this work has served for a quarter of a century as a standard guide for the history of science. Until recently this work was kept up to date and frequently amplified and corrected in Sarton's running commentaries in his annual bibliographies in *Isis.* See also his more recent *Horus: a Guide to the History of Science;* and A. A. (Abraham ha-Levi) Frankel's brief popular survey, *Ha-Meḥqar ha-matemaṭi ve-ha-asṭronomi eṣel ha-Yehudim* (Mathematical and Astronomic Research among Jews).

10. *The Mishnat ha-middot,* ed. by S. Gandz; the *Baraita de-Shemu'el* in Eisenstein's *Ozar Midrashim,* pp. 542 ff.; the comments thereon by A. A. Akaviah in his "Baraitha de-Shemuel" (Hebrew), *Melilah,* V, 119–32 (analyzes chiefly its data on the Hebrew calendar); *Pirqe de-R. Eliezer,* v–vii, ed. by Higger in *Horeb,* VIII, 97 ff. (vi–viii in G. Friedlander's trans., pp. 31 ff.). See *infra,* n. 60; *supra,* Chap. XVII, n. 27; and Vol. II, p. 433 n. 19. The similarity between the *Mishnat ha-middot* and Al-Khwarizmi's geometry is quite evident and can readily be gleaned from a comparison of the numerous passages listed by Gandz in his edition, p. 85, and his study of "The Sources of Al-Khowarizmi's Algebra," *Osiris,* I, 263–77. Nevertheless many questions still remain open; they are perhaps unanswerable with the paucity of sources at our disposal. Not only are Al-Khwarizmi's omissions of data furnished by the Mishnah equally significant, but there is no record whatsoever of an intervening link in Arabic, whether translated directly from the Hebrew or through some Syriac medium, which alone might have been accessible to the Arab mathematician—unless, of course, that Mishnah was translated for him orally by some Jew in the Caliphate or in Khazaria, if indeed he had visited Khazaria. Doubts about the historicity of that reported visit have in fact been voiced by D. M. Dunlop in his "Muhammad b. Musa al-Khwarizmi," *JRAS,* 1943, pp. 248–50. Nor is there any evidence of that Mishnah's impact on Jewish mathematical thinking in the early Middle Ages. Further, no cogent reasons have thus far been advanced as to why this significant combination of geometric rules in five chapters with a brief description of the Tabernacle, if compiled by R. Nehemiah or another Tanna, should have been passed over in silence in both the Mishnah and the Tosefta, and have so completely

escaped scholarly attention for several centuries. The style of these first five chapters, too, being different from the general standards of the tannaitic collections, would require further explanation. These questions have not been satisfactorily cleared up by either M. Steinschneider's and H. Schapira's older, or S. Gandz's more recent investigations, and leave ample room for uncertainty. See also Albeck's observations on Zunz's *Ha-Derashot be-Yisrael,* pp. 273 f. Nevertheless, the *Mishnat ha-middot* does seem to have preserved some memory, even if more or less modified by later views, of the geometrical theories and practices in ancient Palestine.

11. Abraham ibn Ezra's text, published by M. Steinschneider in his "Zur Geschichte der Uebersetzungen aus dem Indischen in's Arabische und ihres Einflusses auf die arabische Literatur," *ZDMG,* XXIV, 356 ff. (see also D. E. Smith and J. Ginsburg's trans. and comments cited *infra,* n. 38); Al-Biruni's *Tariḥ al-Hind* (India), L, LV, ed. by E. Sachau, pp. 208, 233, and in the latter's English trans., II, 15, 67. The titles of some thirty works each by Masha'allah and Sahl are enumerated, in accordance with An-Nadim's *Fihrist* and quotations in later works, by M. Steinschneider in his *Arabische Literatur,* pp. 15 ff., 23 ff. See H. Suter's comments on his German trans. of the pertinent passages in *Das Mathematiker-Verzeichnis im Fihrist des Ibn Abi Ja'kub an Nadim,* pp. 27, 29. However, so little is preserved of these writings that we cannot ascertain their compass or size. In fact, some may have been but sections of larger works, either circulating under separate titles or being thus quoted by bibliographically less exacting successors. On the other hand, many Arab writers, like Greek or Syriac authors before them, excelled in the quantity of their output, so that even thirty titles, accidentally preserved, need not represent the totality of writings by these pioneers. See *supra,* Chap. XXIX, n. 63. None of the mathematical or astronomic treatises by Masha'allah have come down to us in their Arabic originals. We possess only a MS excerpt from his treatise on prices (see Steinschneider's *Arabische Literatur,* pp. 19 f.; and, more generally, *supra,* Chap. XXII, n. 84), one of the very earliest scholarly works in Arabic extant today. See also *infra,* nn. 30-32. Ibn Ezra, who translated two of Masha'allah's astrological treatises into Hebrew, seems to have been aware of his predecessor's Jewish faith. The Spanish savant was evidently less indebted to Sahl ben Bishr (Zahel), perhaps because the latter's designation "Israelita" was often misspelled "Ismaelita" in the Middle Ages. Sahl's Jewishness seems nevertheless well supported by Steinschneider's arguments in his *Catalogus* of the Bodleian Library (col. 2259) and later writings. The Arab scientist's alleged identity with the father of 'Ali aṭ-Ṭabari, however, likewise postulated by Steinschneider, has given way to the now prevailing assumption of 'Ali's Christian origin. See *supra,* Chap. XXIV, n. 10; H. Suter's comprehensive study of *Die Mathematiker und Astronomen der Araber,* pp. 14 f. Nos. 25–26; and V. Stegemann's more recent monograph on *Dorotheus von Sidon und das sogenannte Introductorium des Sahl ibn Bišr,* showing the influence of the Hellenistic poet-astrologer of the first (?) century on Sahl's "Book of Judgments." The Greek MS of the latter work used here (alongside a modern Arabic transcript and a medieval Latin translation) attests Sahl's prestige in Byzantium as well.

12. While both Abrahams devoted most of their scientific studies to astronomy and astrology (see *infra,* nn. 34–35 and 43), Bar Ḥiyya also wrote a significant work in the field of geometry. His *Ḥibbur ha-meshiḥah ve-ha-tishboret* (Treatise on Mensuration and Calculation), written in 1116 and translated by Plato of Tivoli in 1145

under the title *Liber Embadorum,* is now available in a critical edition by M. Guttmann of 1913. The Latin translation was edited a decade earlier (1902) by M. Curtze, while in 1931, J. M. Millás Vallicrosa published its Catalan version entitled *Llibro de geometria.* Additional information on Bar Ḥiyya's mathematical teachings has long been derived from the few extant fragments of his encyclopedic *Yesode ha-tebunah,* as summarized by Steinschneider (in his articles cited below). It still is a moot question whether this work was ever completed by its author, although the weight of evidence seems to favor the assumption that the existing fragments (a single MS of the Intro., and 4 MSS of Chapters I–II) are but parts of a much larger work. Even before the publication of his critical edition and translation (see *supra,* n. 3) J. M. Millás Vallicrosa offered brief preliminary studies of "La Obra enciclopédica *Yĕsodé ha-tĕbuna w-migdal ha-ĕmuná* de R. Abraham bar Ḥiyya ha-Bargeloni" in *HUCA,* XXIII, Part 1, pp. 645–68; and in a pertinent chapter of his *Estudios sobre historia de la ciencia española,* pp. 219 ff. Millás plausibly argued here (*Estudios,* pp. 221 f., 259) also against the accepted date (1136) of Bar Ḥiyya's death, largely based on Plato of Tivoli's failure to mention him in the translation of Ptolemy's *Tetrabiblos,* prepared in 1138. As a matter of fact, Savasorda seems to have assisted in the last of Plato's translations composed in 1145, including that of his own *Liber Embadorum.* See also M. Levey's observations on "The Encyclopedia of Abraham Savasorda: a Departure in Mathematical Methodology," *Isis,* XLIII, 257–64, stressing Bar Ḥiyya's remarkable blend of theory and practice, soon closely followed by Leonardo Fibonacci (Pisano). This view is well illustrated here by citations in parallel columns of passages from Savasorda's and Leonardo's geometrical treatises, and further elaborated in Levey's "Abraham Savasorda and his Allegorism: a Study in Early European Logistic," *Osiris,* XI, 50–64. See esp. p. 64. See also Millás's "Sumario" in the introduction to *La obra Forma de la tierra,* his Spanish translation of Bar Ḥiyya's *Ṣurat ha-areṣ.*

Ibn Ezra's main arithmetical treatise is entitled *Sefer ha-Mispar* (Book of the Number), and should be distinguished from his brief grammatical treatise, more frequently called *Yesod mispar.* The former was edited with a German translation by M. Silberberg. Less significant is Abraham's briefer tract called *Sefer ha-Eḥad* (Book of the Unit), ed. by S. Pinsker with a Hebrew commentary by him and M. A. Goldhardt. The German translation of this *Buch der Einheit* by E. Müller supplied not only a commentary but also numerous relevant excerpts from Ibn Ezra's other works. This is the more important as our author incorporated many mathematical discussions even in his Bible commentaries. Many of Ibn Ezra's works found admiring Latin translators and became very influential in the later Middle Ages. It is even possible that he himself collaborated in some of these Latin versions. See *infra,* n. 38.

Here, too, Steinschneider's biographical and bibliographical data have not yet been superseded, except in some details. See his "Abraham Judaeus—Savasorda und Ibn Esra," supplemented by "Die Encyklopädie des Abraham bar Chijja," and "Abraham ibn Esra,"—all written between 1864 and 1880 and reprinted, together with several shorter essays, in his *G.S.,* I, 327–506. Although Steinschneider came to grips with many mathematical problems as well, his was chiefly a bibliographical contribution, and a new detailed analysis in the light of the now far better known Arabian background and the additional information available for Latin translations is clearly indicated. See also L. Rodet's older study, *Sur les notations numériques et algébriques antérieurement au XVI*[e] *siècle* ("with reference to an arithmetical MS of Ibn Ezra"); the literature cited *infra,* nn. 37–39; and, more generally, F. Vera's semipopular *Historia de la matemática en España,* Vols. III–IV (devoted to Arabs and Jews); and *Los Judíos españoles y su contribución á las ciencias exactas.*

13. Al-Khwarizmi's *Algebra,* ed. by F. Rosen, pp. 3 (Arabic), 5 (English); Aaron Ben Asher's *Diqduqe ha-ṭe'amim,* p. 55; Saadiah's poem, *Ohel makhon binyanai* (The Tent [Temple], Foundation of My Buildings), readily available, with extensive notes thereon by S. Stein in his edition of "Saadya's Piyyuṭ on the Alphabet" in *Saadya Studies,* ed. by Rosenthal, pp. 206–26; and *supra,* Chaps. XXIX, n. 24; XXX, n. 2. This poem, understandably very popular with the students of Masorah ever since its first publication by Elijah Levita in 1538 (in his *Mesorat ha-masoret*), gave rise to extensive debates in the nineteenth century. Saadiah's authorship of the poem, although confirmed by the heading in a Genizah fragment published by Schechter (in his *Saadyana,* p. 52 No. XXVI) is still doubted by some scholars. See the data discussed in Malter's *Saadia Gaon,* pp. 154 ff., 339 ff., with I. Werfel's supplement in *Rav Saadya Gaon,* ed. by Fishman, p. 649; and Davidson's *Oṣar,* I, 78, No. 1685 (still considering Saadiah ben Joseph Bekhor Shor as the more likely author, although the very existence of the latter is quite problematical). Stein favors the gaon's authorship of the *piyyuṭ* itself, but raises doubts, not fully justified in our opinion, as to whether Saadiah also wrote the commentary. On its mathematical implications, see S. Gandz's "Saadia Gaon as a Mathematician" in *Saadia Anniv. Vol.,* pp. 151 ff.; and, more generally, his comprehensive study of the "Hebrew Numerals," *PAAJR,* IV, 53–112.

14. Saadiah's aforementioned poem; and Gandz's and Stein's comments thereon *loc. cit.* See also Gandz's general observations on "The Origin of the Ghubar Numerals, or the Arabian Abacus and the Articuli," *Isis,* XVI, 393–424, with M. C. Welborn's comments thereon in her "Ghubar Numerals," *ibid.,* XVII, 260–63. As pointed out by Gandz, one of the earliest mentions of the *ghubar* computation (*ḥisab al-ghubar*) is found in Yehudah bar Barzillai's *Commentary on Yeṣirah,* p. 140. This Barcelona rabbi was evidently familiar with both the ordinary finger reckoning and the use of a mechanical counter abacus, on which some of his compatriots were computing their figures silently. Similarly, Maimonides must have had the western, and especially Spanish, practice in mind when he referred to the "symbols and figures employed for computation in registers" and called them "Roman knots." See Gandz's analysis, with a minor emendation, of Maimonides' *Commentary* on M. Shabbat VIII.2 (ed. in Arabic by M. Katz) in "The Knot in Hebrew Literature, or, From the Knot to the Alphabet," *Isis,* XIV, 211 f.

15. Saadiah's *Commentary on Yeṣirah,* Intro., ed. by Lambert, pp. 9 f. (Arabic), 25 f. (French). This problem, intimately connected with the relationships between Matter and Form (see *supra,* Chap. XXXIV, nn. 46 ff.), also had mathematical implications, inasmuch as Form could be connected with Numbers in the abstract, as had long been done by the ancient Pythagoreans. Saadiah was, indeed, prepared to consider the "number" *qua* instrument of creation, as the equivalent of the thought or the idea, in contradistinction to the written or spoken word. But the term "number" did not thereby lose its original significance, as may be seen from the sequel, where Saadiah tried to explain the reference in the "Book of Creation" to God's

creation through the medium of ten numbers and twenty-two letters, the latter of course also having their numerical implications. See his *Commentary,* pp. 22 ff. (Arabic), 42 ff. (French); and *supra,* Chap. XXXIII, n. 13.

16. Abraham ibn Ezra's *Yesod mora,* XI, ed. by M. Creizenach, pp. 45 ff. (Hebrew), 118 ff. (German); his *Commentary* on Exod. 3:15. See *supra,* Vol. I, p. 295 n. 5. Among Ibn Ezra's other remarks on the numerical components of the divine name, one may note especially his emphasis on the number 15 as the equivalent of *Yah,* which is also the first half of the Ineffable Name. The letters from A to Ṭ (1 to 9) can be arranged in a perfect magic square of three lines, in which the sum total of figures added in any direction, horizontally, vertically, or diagonally, yields the same number 15. Such squares were clearly grist for the mill of magicians of all faiths, and had long been used by Jewish and Christian mystics. See J. Carcopino, "Le Christianisme secret du 'carré magique,'" *Museum helveticum,* V, 16–59. From the latter certain ingredients were taken over by Arabs, for example Al-Buni's magic encyclopedia. See W. Ahrens, "Studien über die 'magischen Quadrate' der Araber," *Der Islam,* VII, 186–250; his "Die 'magischen Quadrate' Al-Buni's," *ibid.,* XII, 157–77; XIV, 104–10; and G. Vajda's "Sur quelques éléments juifs et pseudo-juifs dans l'encyclopédie magique de Bûnî," *Goldziher Mem. Vol.,* I, 387–92. Reciprocally the Arabs began influencing Jewish students, including such otherwise sober thinkers as Ibn Ezra. See also G. Vajda, "Une Version hébraïque inconnue des 'cercles imaginaires' de Batalyawsi," *Löw Mem. Vol.,* pp. 202–4 (less literal than that by Samuel ibn Tibbon, previously ed. and analyzed by D. Kaufmann).

17. Saadiah's *K. al-Mawarit* (Book of Inheritance), ed. with S. Horovitz's Hebrew translation, under the title *Sefer ha-Yerushot,* by J. Müller and provided with notes by both translator and editor in Saadiah's *Oeuvres complètes,* IX, 1–53. See *supra,* Chap. XXVII, nn. 73 and 75. This is essentially a juridical treatise, following the patterns of similar Arabic works in form, rather than legal substance. See also S. Gandz, "The Algebra of Inheritance: a Rehabilitation of Al-Khuwarizmi," *Osiris,* V, 319–91 (pointing out, against Frederick Rosen's strictures, that the mathematical computations had to fit the existing laws of inheritance, a statement which essentially applies to Saadiah's treatise as well).

18. See Müller's introduction in *Oeuvres,* IX, p. xvii; S. Gandz's comments on and translation of the concluding section of Saadiah's treatise in his "Saadia Gaon as a Mathematician," *Saadia Anniv. Vol.,* pp. 166 ff., 173 ff.; and his broader investigation of the historic origins and nature of "The Algebra of Inheritance," *Osiris,* V, 319–91, which shows that even a great mathematician, when tied to an existing legal system, could not avoid those serious mathematical inconsistencies, which had long ago (1831) been pointed out by F. Rosen, the editor of Al-Khwarizmi's *Algebra.* See also Gandz's earlier studies on "The Origin of the Term 'Algebra,'" *American Mathematical Monthly,* XXXIII, 437–40; "The Sources of Al-Khowarizmi's Algebra," *Osiris,* I, 263–77; and their brief evaluation in M. Levey's obituary article, "Solomon Gandz, 1884–1954," *Isis,* XLV, 107–10.

19. Bar Ḥiyya's *Ḥibbur ha-meshiḥah,* pp. 1 ff. Bar Ḥiyya knew that the ancient sages themselves were not always precise in their geometrical data. They had been satisfied, for example, in stating, in accordance with the well-known Pythagorean

theorem, that a diagonal in a square exceeds the size of the side by two-fifths, disregarding the additional small fraction of 1/70. The sages' equivalent for π consistently was 3, instead of "somewhat less than 3 1/7." However, he explained, these rabbinic computations related only to ritualistic matters, where one could use round numbers in a more stringent interpretation without harming any person. Incorrect division of land, however, decidedly accrued to the injury of one party. That is why the rabbis themselves applied the biblical injunction "Ye shall do no unrighteousness in judgment" (Lev. 19:15) specifically to land measurements, particularly on rainy or hot days during which the measuring cords were apt to expand or to contract unduly (B.M. 61b). See W. M. Feldman's observations in his *Rabbinical Mathematics and Astronomy*, pp. 25 f.

20. Bar Ḥiyya's *Yesode ha-tebunah*, I.2, ed. by Millás, pp. 27 (Hebrew), 59 (Spanish); and in Steinschneider's *G.S.*, I, 395. Savasorda seems to have followed here some Arabic work on the *mu'amalat,* or what the Latins were to call, the *regula mercatorum,* which went back to Hellenistic sources. See D. E. Smith's *History of Mathematics,* II, 488; and J. M. Millás's brief remarks in "La Obra enciclopédica," *HUCA,* XXIII, Part 1, pp. 649 f. Most likely, our author was familiar with a work of this type written by the Spanish-Arab mathematician Maslama al-Majriti, on whose revision of Al-Khwarizmi's Astronomic Tables see *infra,* nn. 38, 40. Unfortunately, neither the Arabic original nor any translation of Maslama's own treatise is now extant. See H. Suter's remarks in the intro. to his ed. of Al-Khwarizmi's "Tables" ("Astronomische Tafeln"), p. ix. However, in so far as one can judge from the extant fragments, Abraham's encyclopedia, even more than the treatise on geometry, was permeated with a genuine quest for truth and the pedagogic passion for imparting it, regardless of its practical applications. Bar Ḥiyya also readily invoked the authority of his predecessors, especially among the Greek scientists, listing a large number of their contributions to the various branches of geometry at the end of the pertinent section of his geometrical handbook. See Millás's *Estudios sobre historia,* pp. 226 f.

21. Bar Ḥiyya's *Ḥibbur,* II.2, 58a; 4, 95, pp. 38, 60 f.; and Guttmann's reconstruction in his introduction, pp. xv ff. This reconstruction is largely followed by Millás in his Catalan translation, pp. vii ff.; and his *Estudios sobre historia,* pp. 230 ff., 236 f. The general accuracy of Bar Ḥiyya's computations is also evident from the table of equivalences (drawn up by Guttmann, p. xxvi) between the author's measurements of the arc and our own. Savasorda's results differ from ours as a rule only by some tiny fraction of up to plus or minus 4 seconds of a degree, which, moreover, was not so much the result of the author's error as the effect of his quest for simplification. See Bar Ḥiyya's table with its elaboration in his treatise, II.4, 113 ff., pp. 68 ff., and Guttmann's notes thereon. Cf., however, also the corrections suggested by Z. H. Jafeh, *ibid.,* pp. 127 ff. (Millás's Catalan version, pp. 149 f.). The origin of this particular table is still obscure. Since the author specifically mentioned that he had borrowed a method extensively used by astronomers, it stands to reason that he was indebted here, as in his astronomical tables, to such Arab predecessors as Al-Baṭṭani and Al-Farghani. But evidently he always injected some variants of his own.

22. Bar Ḥiyya's *Ḥibbur,* IV.190, pp. 111 f.; M. Curtze in his ed. of *Der "Liber Embadorum" des Savasorda,* pp. 5, 7. Cf. M. Guttmann's Intro., p. xiv; and S. Gandz's

more general observations on "The Origin of Angle-Geometry," *Isis,* XII, 452–81 (showing that neither the *Mishnat ha-middot,* nor the geometry of Al-Khwarizmi, though familiar with oblique as well as right angles, made any use of angle geometry); and "The Origin of the Gnomon," *PAAJR,* II, 23–38 (emphasizing that the term originated among the Hebrews and that the Arabs, long before Bar Ḥiyya, had developed a ramified science of gnomonics).

23. "At the very time," writes G. Sarton, "when Nemorarius and Bacon were groping for the principles of mechanics, the Muslims were still living on the inferior mechanical knowledge handed down to them from the Hellenistic age. Instead of being concerned with ideas, they had but a childish interest in automata and in mechanical toys and contrivances" (*Introduction,* II, 22). As to the Jews there is no evidence that they ever evinced a deep interest even in such gadgets. That some of them were active in the construction of houses and canals is occasionally mentioned in the sources. Doubtless more important was their contribution to Western architecture and methods of production, if for no other reason than that they settled in the Western lands after arriving there from the East with its superior standard of life and amenities. See *supra,* Chaps. XVIII, n. 39; XX, n. 112.

24. M. Güdemann's edition of Ibn 'Aqnin's text in *Das jüdische Unterrichtswesen,* pp. 35 (Arabic), 98 ff. (German). See also the section on optics in Bar Ḥiyya's encyclopedic *Yesode ha-tebunah,* pp. 43 ff. (Hebrew), 80 ff. (Spanish), which, as J. M. Millás has rightly observed, treated of the theoretical-mathematical aspects much more fully than of the physiological and psychological elements in vision. See "La Obra enciclopédica," *HUCA,* XXIII, Part 1, p. 651. In this respect Savasorda was evidently influenced not only by Euclid, but also by Farabi's *Iḥsa al-'ulum,* whose section on optics he closely followed. See the latter work in A. González Palencia's ed., especially p. 36; and, for a parallel from the philosophic angle, G. Vajda's remarks on "Abraham bar Ḥiyya et Al-Farabi," *REJ,* CIV, 113–19.

25. Abraham ibn Ezra's probably spurious poem on chess, beginning *Ashorer shir* (I Will Sing a Song of Battle), was first published by Steinschneider in 1873, and has been frequently reprinted since. It is available with a German translation and extensive comments by D. Rosin in his edition of Ibn Ezra's *Reime und Gedichte,* pp. 159 ff.; and in N. Davis's English version in her *Songs of Exile,* pp. 127 ff. See also Davidson's *Oṣar,* I, 356 No. 7863; and, for the sake of comparison, a similar Arabic poem written some two centuries later by a Moroccan poet and published by J. Robson in "A Chess Maqama in the John Rylands Library," *BJRL,* XXXVI, 111–27. The ingenious Hebrew poem which, if not from Ibn Ezra's pen, was written not very long after him, shows remarkable divergences from the present rules of the chess game. Evidently in its procession from India, through Persia (where according to Mas'udi it arrived as a gift to Khosroe I), to the Near East and Europe the game underwent many changes. It seems quickly to have captured the imagination of Jews in Christian lands as well, and was mentioned by the author of *Sefer Ḥasidim.* See Wistinetzki's edition, p. 306 No. 1236 (more clearly in the Sudzilkov ed., 1831, fol. 64a No. 400). Against the usual assumption that Spain had served as a cultural bridge to Germany, H. M. Gamer has rightly argued that "we must reckon more realistically with the fruits of direct contacts between Germany and Byzantine or Arabic lands under the Ottos and later." See "The Earliest Evidence

of Chess in Western Literature: The Einsiedeln Verses," *Speculum,* XXIX, 749 f.; and the parallel reasoning *supra,* Chap. XXXIII, nn. 33 ff., 47. Maimonides, on the other hand, was less sympathetic. Perhaps reflecting the greater degree of professionalization in Muslim lands, he classified a chess player for money among those indulging in games of chance, whom the ancient rabbis had disqualified from testifying as witnesses in court. See his *Commentary* on M. Sanhedrin III.3, ed. by M. Weisz, pp. 16 f.; and, more generally, M. Steinschneider's still far from obsolete chapter on "Schach bei den Juden" in A. van der Linde, *Geschichte und Litteratur des Schachspiels,* I, 155–202 (includes 6 Hebrew texts in the Appendix); and H. J. R. Murray, *A History of Chess.*

Of social, more than scientific, interest is the playful use of the numerical value of letters in the then popular riddles. Both Ibn Ezra and Halevi found, for example, that by subtracting 8 from 5 (that is the letter *ḥet* from the word *ḥamishah*) one gets the name of Mosheh (Moses). Similarly the four Hebrew letters of the name Aaron were, according to Ibn Ezra, so arranged that the fourth letter amounted to a quarter of the third, the second was a tenth of the fourth, and the first a fifth of the second letter. It was easy for him to compose a riddle around these ratios, and to challenge the ingenuity of students to find the appropriate name. See his *Reime,* pp. 203 No. 94, 210 No. 117; and Halevi's poem *Shemonah be-hasirkhah* (When You Subtract Eight from Five) in the *Diwan,* ed. by Brody, II, 208 (ed. by Zemorah, II, Part 6, p. 328). See also *supra,* Chap. XXXII, n. 38.

26. Maqrizi's *K. al-Khitat* (Description topographique et historique de l'Egypte), XLVI, in U. Bouriant's French trans., I, 363 ff.; Maimonides' *Guide* II.9, 24 (in Friedländer's trans., pp. 164, 198); Munk's *Mélanges,* p. 521 n. 2. See other data in B. Carra de Vaux's *Penseurs,* II, 202 ff.; and in F. Rosenthal's *Technique,* pp. 65 f. On Ibn Bajja's circle which included Abu Ja'far Yusuf ibn Ḥisdai, recipient of one of Ibn Bajja's "Missives" extant in a Bodleian MS and an astronomer in his own right, see D. M. Dunlop, "Philosophical Predecessors and Contemporaries of Ibn Bajjah," *Islamic Quarterly,* II, 100–116. Like all other aspects of Maimonides' scholarly work, his views on astronomic questions have been subjected to close scholarly scrutiny, especially in connection with his elaboration of the traditional regulations of the Jewish calendar. Apart from the still valuable older work by E. Baneth, well summarized in his "Maimonides als Chronologe und Astronom," in *Moses ben Maimon,* ed. by Jakob Guttmann *et al.,* II, 243–79, one need but mention the recent debate on "The Astronomy of Maimonides and Its Sources" between O. Neugebauer and S. Gandz in their two essays under this title in *HUCA,* XXII, 321–63; and *AIHS,* III, 835–55. See also *infra,* n. 65.

27. Abraham bar Ḥiyya's *Sefer Ṣurat ha-areṣ* (Cosmography), IX–X, Offenbach ed., fols. 38b ff.; and the talmudic data summarized by W. M. Feldman in his *Rabbinical Mathematics,* pp. 214 f. See the data analyzed by A. Mieli in *La Science arabe et son rôle dans l'évolution scientifique mondiale;* and H. Butterfield's brief remarks on "Dante's View of the Universe" in the British Broadcasting Company's aforementioned symposium on *The History of Science,* pp. 15 ff. The astronomic observations conducted under Al-Ma'mun's sponsorship have often been described. See S. B. Samadi's recent review of the "Literary and Scientific Development and the Growth of Rationalism in the Time of Al-Mamun," *IC,* XXX, 77–94, 309–29; and on the Jewish participant in Al-Ma'mun's expeditions, *infra,* n. 32. In "Les Sources de

l'oeuvre astronomique de R. Abraham Bar Ḥiyya de Barcelone," *AIHS,* II, 855–63, J. M. Millás Vallicrosa has shown that, while generally eclectic and, in many respects, indebted to Al-Farghani, as well as Al-Baṭṭani, Savasorda at times reached independent conclusions. He diverged especially from his Muslim predecessors in those points, where the medieval computations deviated from Jewish tradition. In some calendar problems particularly he often reverted to Ptolemy, in order to justify the traditional computation by R. Adda. Of course, Bar Ḥiyya's independence was restricted by his recognition of the decisive value of astronomic observations, to which he personally had but limited access. He certainly could not compare in this respect with his Muslim compatriot Al-Zarqali, a gifted inventor as well as astronomic observer, on whose Jewish collaborators and translators see Steinschneider's *Etudes sur Zarqali,* esp. pp. 16 ff., 61, 73 f., 92 ff.; his *Hebräische Uebersetzungen,* pp. 590 ff.; and *infra,* n. 38. See also Millás's *Estudios sobre Azarquiel,* which includes a photographic reproduction of a unique Paris MS of the anonymous Hebrew trans. of Al-Zarqali's "Tractate on the Movements of the Fixed Stars" (pp. 250 ff.); and his earlier ed. of *Don Profeit Tibbon. Tractat de l'assafea d'Azarquiel,* offering Don Profet's Hebrew trans. of Zarqali's treatise on the *assafea* (a corruption of the Arabic *as-sufiha*), that is a new astrolabe invented by the author. See also, more generally, E. S. Kennedy, *A Survey of Islamic Astronomical Tables* ("In the great majority . . . the basic theory is that of Ptolemy . . . ; the main Islamic contributions were in trigonometrical, computational, and observational techniques. A minority . . . [was] based on Hindu or pre-Islamic Iranian theory," p. 173).

The Hebrew names of stars, already recorded in the talmudic literature, were evidently indebted to Babylonian-Hellenistic prototypes. There is no way of telling, therefore, to what extent the early Jewish astronomers in the Caliphate contributed to the parallel naming of stars in Arabic, on which see A. Benhamouda, "Les Noms arabes des étoiles, essai d'identification," *Annales de l'Institut d'Etudes Orientales* of the University of Algiers, IX, 76–210.

28. Al-Biruni's *K. Tariḥ al-Hind,* XXVI, p. 139 (English trans., I, 276 f.); *Zohar,* III. fol. 10a (citing the "Book by R. Hamnuna"); Maimonides' *Guide,* II.9 (Friedländer, p. 164); and *infra,* nn. 67, 82 ff. Maimonides evidently had in mind Ibn Aflaḥ's *K. al-Hayya* (Book of Astronomy), which, because of its numerous corrections of the Ptolemaic theory, was later often called the "Rectification of the Almagest." Neither the Arabic original, nor Moses ibn Tibbon's Hebrew version of that work, although known in manuscript form for more than a century (see Munk's note on his trans. of the *Guide,* II, 81 n. 5; and Steinschneider's *Hebräische Uebersetzungen,* pp. 543 f.) have thus far been published, but the Latin trans. by Gerard of Cremona appeared in Nuremberg, 1534, under the telling title, *Gebri filii Affla Hispalensis de astronomia libri IX in quibus Ptolemaeum, alioqui doctissimum, emendavit.* Munk pointed out that the position of the spheres of Venus and Mercury was also discussed, with direct reference to Ibn Aflaḥ, in Averroës' "Outline of the Almagest." That, unlike Ibn Bajja, the sage of Fusṭaṭ was willing to accept Ibn Aflaḥ's theory, was doubtless owing to his own preference for grouping the five spheres of the planets together. This alone enabled him to reduce the total classification of spheres into four main groups of: (1) fixed stars; (2) planets; (3) sun; (4) moon, necessary for the advancement of his own theory of the correspondence between the spheres and the four earthly elements. It is to be regretted that these aspects of the Maimonidean outlook on the world have never been carefully examined, not even by the astute students of his astronomic teachings, listed *supra,* n. 26.

These teachings can properly be understood only against the background of the grand debate on the merits of the Ptolemaic system carried on in twelfth-century Spain from Ibn Aflaḥ and Ibn Bajja to Ibn Ṭufayl, his pupil Abu Isḥaq al-Biṭruji, and Averroës. See esp. L. Gauthier's data on "Une Réforme du système astronomique de Ptolémée tentée par les philosophes arabes au XIIe s.," *JA,* 19th ser. XIV, 483–510 (somewhat overstating his thesis that these philosophers rather than being innovators, largely criticized Ptolemy merely for his departures from Aristotle; this statement, questionable with respect to Ibn Bajja's critique of the theory of epicycles and Ibn aṭ-Ṭufayl's attack on the doctrine of eccentrics, is also controverted by Maimonides' rather independent appraisal of Aristotle's authority, especially in sublunary matters); and F. J. Carmody's more recent analysis of "The Planetary Theory of Ibn Rushd," *Osiris,* X, 556–86.

29. Saadiah's *Beliefs and Opinions,* I.1, 3, pp. 33 f., 60 f. (Hebrew, pp. 16 f., 32; English, pp. 41 f., 72 f.); Halevi's *K. al-Khazari,* IV.3, ed. by Landauer, pp. 236 ff. (English, p. 206). See *infra,* n. 33.

30. A full listing of Masha'allah's astronomic and astrological works, whether recorded by An-Nadim or in later writings and manuscripts, is found in Steinschneider's *Arabische Literatur,* pp. 15 ff. So great was the interest of medieval scholars in these works that one (his "Epistle on Eclipses") was translated almost simultaneously by Plato of Tivoli and John Avendeath (Ibn Daud). See L. Thorndike's *History of Magic and Experimental Science,* II, 82. Perhaps his most popular treatise was *De scientia motus orbis,* which, in Gerard of Cremona's Latin trans., was published twice in Nuremberg, in 1504 and 1547. Roger Bacon, it may be noted, specifically defended Masha'allah against the accusation that his astrological teachings attributed fatal necessity to the influence of stars (Thorndike, II, 669). The extant MSS give varying titles.

Masha'allah's influence transcended the narrower circles of Mediterranean mathematicians and astronomers. See, e.g., M. Power's edition of *An Irish Astronomical Tract Based in Part on a Mediaeval Latin Version of a Work by Messahala* (also referring to an earlier translation and analysis by M. Close); and R. T. Gunther's edition with the original illustrations, of *Chaucer and Messahalla on the Astrolabe.* Of course, the astrolabe had been well known long before Masha'allah's time. A plane astrolabe, though not the armillary sphere, was used already by Ptolemy and Theon, and a special treatise on the subject had been written in Syriac by Severus Sebokht before 660. See O. Neugebauer's observations on "The Early History of the Astrolabe," *Isis,* XL, 240–56. However, Severus' work seems to have remained unknown to the Jewish astronomer of the following century, and generally exerted little influence on Arabic authors, including Ibrahim al-Fazari, who had constructed an astrolabe some time before his death in 777. See J. M. Faddyan's remarks in "L'Etat actuel des études concernant les sciences exactes en Orient durant le Moyen-Age," *Archeion,* XIV, 375. See also D. M. Donaldson, "The Nomenclature and Common Uses of the Astrolabe," *IC,* XIX, 49–53; S. Gandz, "The Astrolabe in Jewish Literature," *HUCA,* IV, 469–86; and, on early astrolabes still extant in various museums, D. J. Price, "An International Checklist of Astrolabes," *AIHS,* VIII, 243–63, 363–81.

31. An-Nadim's *K. Al-Fihrist,* the passage translated by H. Suter in *Das Mathematiker-Verzeichnis* (*Abhandlungen zur Geschichte der Mathematik,* VI), pp. 28 f.,

62; Steinschneider's *Arabische Literatur,* pp. 23 ff.; his *Hebräische Uebersetzungen,* pp. 603 ff.; and L. Thorndike's reference to the MSS of Hermann's translation in *A History of Magic,* pp. 256, 389 f. Little has been added to the bibliographical knowledge of Sahl's works in the course of the past half a century. However, in the light of the general increase in our familiarity with early Arab mathematical and astronomic science, a careful investigation of all the extant editions and manuscripts of both Sahl's and Masha'allah's works by a competent specialist is likely to shed new light on the role played by Jews in the cultural life of the awakening Near East during that crucial period of transition under the early Abbasids.

32. See the sources cited in Steinschneider's *Arabische Literatur,* pp. 34 f. Remarkably, Sind's name is not even mentioned by Abraham bar Ḥiyya, who, although referring to the scientific expeditions under Al-Ma'mun, appears to have had no knowledge of any of the caliph's Jewish collaborators. See his *Ṣurat ha-areṣ,* IX, fol. 38b. A dim recollection of some such early Jewish contributions may have been retained in Ibn Ezra's aforementioned story of the Jewish mediation in the adoption of the "Indian" numerals. Sind not only bore a name easily associated with *Sindhind,* the Arabic designation for the astronomic methods of the Indians, but he also seems to have written one of the earliest Arabic treatises on *al-ḥisab al-hindi* (Indian Arithmetic). See Steinschneider's observations in his "Zur Geschichte der Uebersetzungen aus dem Indischen in's Arabische," *ZDMG,* XXIV, 328 f., 332 f., 356 f., 362 f.; *supra,* nn. 11 and 27; and *infra,* n. 84.

33. Sahl's *Carmen de planetarum aspectibus* (see Steinschneider's *Arabische Literatur,* p. 30 No. 27); Al-Biruni's *Tariḥ al-Hind,* pp. 9 f. (Arabic ed.); I, 19 (English ed.); Ibn Gabirol's "Royal Crown" in his *Shire,* ed. by Bialik and Rawnitzky, II, 69 f. (in Zangwill's trans., p. 100). In the preceding strophes, the poet summarized the prevailing astronomic doctrines concerning the other spheres. He gives, for example, the following sizes for the celestial bodies: (1) the moon is $1/39$ the size of the earth; (2) Mercury $1/22{,}000$; (3) Venus $1/37$; (4) the sun exceeds the earth by 170 times; (5) Mars by $1\frac{5}{8}$; (6) Jupiter by 75; (7) Saturn by 91; (8) each of the fixed stars by 107 times. The latter sphere requires 36,000 years to complete its revolution. It is remarkable that precisely with respect to the sun, about which opinions hardly differed, the poet chose to give the round number of 170. Even Halevi, who mentioned this matter in his philosophic treatise only in passing, preferred the figure of 166 times, although on another occasion he spoke more roughly of the earth being but "the one hundred and sixtieth part of the sun disc." See his *K. al-Khazari,* III.49; IV.3, pp. 198 f., 236 f. (in Hirschfeld's trans., pp. 178, 206, 305). The Hebrew translator, however, either had not found the latter figure in his text, or harmonistically corrected it to 166 as in iv.3. See Cassel's ed., p. 279 and his note 3 thereon; also Hirschfeld's note on his ed., p. xxxix n. 96. See also *supra,* n. 29.

34. Abraham bar Ḥiyya's *Ṣurat ha-areṣ,* fol. lab. On the title, see, e.g., Al-Khwarizmi's *K. Surat al-ard,* ed. and trans. into German by H. von Mžik. A critical edition of the *Ḥeshbon* with a Spanish trans. and full annotation has been prepared by Millás. See the brief analysis of its content in his *Estudios sobre historia,* pp. 243 ff. On the question of sources, Millás concluded that "in the trigonometrical section he [Bar Ḥiyya] decidedly follows Al-Baṭṭani; on certain subjects, for example lunations [*mansiones lunares*], he accepts the teachings of Al-Farghani; whereas

in fundamental problems, as well in those on which there is a difference of opinion among the authors . . . he follows Ptolemy" (p. 247).

The *ḥokhmat ha-nissayon* is usually interpreted as derived from "trying to secure a sign from God" similar to King Ahaz's reputed saying "I will not ask, neither will I try [*anasseh*] the Lord" (Isa. 7:12). See I. Efros's explanation of Bar Ḥiyya's term in his "Studies in Pre-Tibbonian Philosophic Terminology," *JQR,* XVII, 334; and Klatzkin's *Oṣar ha-munaḥim,* III, 45 f. However, this rendition does not do justice to the distinction between "natural" and "judicial" astrology. Even Ibn Ezra seems to have had principally the former in mind when he spoke of the *ḥakhme nissayon* (the experts in the science of experiment). For instance, in his *Sefer ha-Ṭe'amin* (ed. by Fleischer, p. 39) he referred to the alleged connection between the moon and the rise or fall in prices, reminiscent of Masha'allah's interest in the price structure. Incidentally, the term *nisyonot* could also be applied to knowledge derived from medical observation. In fact an evidently apocryphal book under this title, listing a long series of remedies partly of a magic character, was attributed to Ibn Ezra. See Steinschneider's *G.S.* I, 424 ff.; and *infra,* Chap. XXXVI, n. 36.

35. These statements about Bar Ḥiyya's attitude toward judicial astrology are made here with considerable diffidence, since only his "Cosmography" has been printed in its entirety. The two other works are known to us mainly from Latin translations, and even these are available only in manuscripts differing greatly from one another. Only the beginning paragraph of *Ḥeshbon* was published by H. Filipowski in the introduction to his edition of Bar Ḥiyya's *Sefer ha-'Ibbur* (Book of Intercalation), p. viii. This neglect is the more remarkable as, at least at the beginning of the fourteenth century, this "Computation" seems to have enjoyed considerable popularity in certain "enlightened" circles of Provençal Jewry. In his "Ethical Will," Joseph Kaspi recommended to his son, on reaching the age of fourteen, that he study mathematics by successively mastering (1) Ibn Ezra's *Sefer ha-Mispar;* (2) The Elements of Euclid; (3) those by Al-Farghani, and (4) Bar Ḥiyya's *Ḥeshbon.* See I. Abrahams's ed. of *Hebrew Ethical Wills,* p. 144. See also the still very useful data assembled by Steinschneider in his essay on Bar Ḥiyya, reprinted in his *G.S.,* I, 339 ff. On Bar Ḥiyya's "Tables" and their relation to similar earlier handbooks by Al-Farghani and Al-Baṭṭani, see J. M. Millás Vallicrosa's aforementioned study, "Les Sources de l'oeuvre astronomique de R. Abraham Bar Ḥiyya de Barcelone," *AIHS,* II, 855–63.

36. Bar Ḥiyya's letter, published by A. Z. Schwarz in *Festschrift Schwarz,* Hebrew section, pp. 23 ff., 36. Ironically, Yehudah bar Barzillai himself resorted to similar computations of the date of the Messiah's arrival. See *supra,* Chap. XXVIII, n. 97. We know nothing about the particular services rendered by Savasorda to powerful Gentiles, but his official title, *sa'hib ash-shurta,* misspelled by his friend Plato of Tivoli forever after into Savasorda, though literally meaning something like police commissioner and district attorney, may have included some work in geometry, astronomy, and astrology under official patronage. See *supra,* Chap. XX, n. 45.

37. Ibn Ezra's censure of Bar Ḥiyya is found in his *Sefer ha-'Olam,* ed. by J. L. Fleischer in *Ozar Hachaim,* XIII, 40. Donnolo's melancholy comment on the neglect of sciences in his immediate environment is part of the introduction to his aforementioned *Commentary on Yeṣirah,* ed. by Castelli, pp. 4 ff. See also S. Munt-

ner's "Cosmographic Introduction to the Book *Ḥakmoni*" in his ed. of Donnolo's *Kitbe ha-refu'ah* (Medical Writings), II, 105 ff. Neither of the two recensions of Ibn Ezra's treatise on the astrolabe (entitled *Keli neḥoshet* or Copper Instrument), written in 1145–46 and 1148 (the latter was published by H. Edelmann in a fashion sharply criticized by H. Filipowski and M. Steinschneider), has been subjected to careful scholarly scrutiny in the light of the numerous extant Latin manuscripts. Even the title *Keli* (Instrument), clearly indicated in the opening sentence, is sometimes misspelled into *Kele* (Instruments) by Millás and others.

On the other hand, Millás discovered "Uno Nuevo tratado de astrolabio de R. Abraham ibn 'Ezra," *Al-Andalus,* V, 1–29; with additional observations "Sobre un 'Tratado de astrolabio' atribuido a R. Abraham ibn 'Ezra," *Sefarad,* IV, 31–38. In the latter essay Millás defends his assumption of Ibn Ezra's authorship against R. Levy's serious doubts concerning "The Authorship of a Latin Treatise on the Astrolabe," *Speculum,* XVII, 566–69; and S. Gandz's article cited *supra,* n. 30. See also the debate mentioned *infra,* n. 43. This treatise, extant only in a Latin version, seems to have been written in England between 1158 and 1166. Millás also found another small Latin treatise on the Almanac, which he considers as an extension, probably by Ibn Ezra himself, of the teachings of the "Pisan Tables." See "Un Tratado de almanaque probablemente de R. Abraham ibn 'Ezra" in *Studies and Essays . . . in Homage to George Sarton,* pp. 421–32. At the same time, there is no evidence proving the existence of some alleged Arabic writings by Ibn Ezra in the field of mathematical and astronomic sciences. See Steinschneider, *G.S.,* I, 423 ff.

38. See J. M. Millás's critical ed. of *El Libro de los fundamentos de las Tablas astronómicas de R. Abraham ibn 'Ezra,* esp. pp. 77 f.; his earlier Hebrew analysis of "The Work of Abraham ibn Ezra in Astronomy," *Tarbiz,* IX, 306–22; the aforementioned text published by Steinschneider in *ZDMG,* XXIV, 356 ff.; and *supra,* nn. 11, 27. Of course, occasional insertions of Christian dates may have stemmed from the Christian translator or one of his copyists. Certainly neither Al-Khwarizmi nor his reviser Maslama al-Majriti dated segments of the "Roman" era *usque ad incarnationem domini,* a phrase clearly added by Adelard of Bath, their Latin translator. See the former's *Die astronomischen Tafeln,* ed. by Suter, p. 3, with Suter's observations, *ibid.,* p. 35; and *infra,* n. 40. But the frequency and consistency of such dating in Ibn Ezra's Latin version tends to support Millás's hypothesis of its original composition in Latin under the author's dictation.

According to Millás, the *Yesode ha-luḥot,* composed by Ibn Ezra in Anjou and its vicinity in 1154, was only a revised and much enlarged edition of his original *Tabulae Pisanae* of 1149, which in turn may have been based on a still earlier work composed in Lucca, near Pisa, some time between 1141 and 1145. See also *infra,* n. 43. We may thus understand the reference to Ibn Ezra's two astronomical tables, allegedly composed in Lucca and Narbonne, according to the supercommentary on Ibn Ezra's commentary on Gen. 33:10 by the fourteenth-century Spanish exegete and mathematician, Joseph ben Eliezer Bonfils (Tob 'Elem). See his *Ṣophenath pane'aḥ* (Revealer of Secrets, Joseph's name according to Gen. 41:45) ed. by D. Herzog, Part 1, p. 142; Steinschneider's *G.S.,* I, 346 f.; and L. Fleischer's "R. Abraham ibn Ezra and His Literary Activity in the City of Lucca, Italy" (Hebrew), *Ha-Soqer,* II, 77–85; IV, 186–94 (incomplete). It was probably only during some such longer sojourn in one locality that Ibn Ezra could make use of actual observations with the aid of the astrolabe, to which he referred in his comments in *Libro de los fundamentos,* p. 160. These comments reveal also their author's excellent familiarity with the earlier scientific literature. Now that this text is available, one must make a number of corrections in D. E. Smith and J. Ginsburg's otherwise very useful study of "Rabbi Ben Ezra and the Hindu-Arabic Problem," *American Mathematical Monthly,* XXV, 99–108, based on Steinschneider's aforementioned ed. of Ibn Ezra's text, here translated into English. See *supra,* n. 11.

Ibn Ezra seems to have made extensive use also of Bar Ḥiyya's earlier work on astronomical tables, although the notes now found in some manuscripts of that work do not seem to stem from Ibn Ezra, but rather from some less informed copyist. At the same time our polyhistor was also deeply indebted to Al-Zarqali, on whose Jewish collaborators and translators see *supra,* n. 27. Since Ibn Ezra, and not Bar Ḥiyya, wrote special studies on the astrolabe (see *supra,* n. 37), it seems likely that the notice concerning Rudolf Brugensis' Latin translation of an Arabic work on the astrolabe by Maslama al-Majriti, under the dictation of his teacher, Abraham, refers to Ibn Ezra, rather than to Savasorda. The former doubtless had more opportunity to work with Rudolf. See Steinschneider's *G.S.,* I, 494 f.; and the debate on "Abrahamismus" summarized *infra,* n. 43. On Ibn Ezra's considerable influence on the development of later medieval science, see esp. the data assembled by Millás in the introduction to his edition of *Libro de los fundamentos,* pp. 66 ff.; and, more generally, his comprehensive summary (in part repeated in that intro.) of "El Magisterio astronómico de Abraham ibn 'Ezra en la Europa latina" in his *Estudios sobre historia,* pp. 289–347.

39. Ibn Ezra's *Libro de los fundamentos,* Intro., ed. by Millás, p. 79; and *supra,* n. 37. Despite his aforementioned reliance on memory his quotations seem extraordinarily accurate, if one discounts the ravages of transmission through slipshod copyists. In the case of the "Pisan Tables," one is even unable to correct mistakes by the original translator through consultation of the Hebrew original, which perhaps was never confided to writing. See Millás's observations in "Uno Nuevo Tratado," *Al-Andalus,* V, 6 ff.; and *infra,* n. 43 end. See also, more generally, A. van de Vyer, "Les Plus anciennes traductions latines médiévales (X[e] et XIe siècles) des traités d'astronomie et d'astrologie," *Osiris,* I, 658–91; and F. J. Carmody's "critical bibliography" of *Arabic Astronomical and Astrological Sciences in Latin Translation* (includes sixteen entries under Masha'allah and fifteen under Sahl).

40. Neither the *De Dracone* nor a lengthy epistle addressed by Petrus Alphonsi, about 1115, to French and other Aristotelians ever appeared in print. In a British Museum MS of the late twelfth century discovered by L. Thorndike, that letter bears the characteristic title *Epistola de studio artium liberalium precipue astronomiae ad peripateticos aliosque philosophicos ubique per Franciam.* Petrus argued here very vigorously in favor of astronomic observation, as opposed to the mere book learning of many Christian contemporaries, particularly those whose "laziness" made them satisfied with the few works available in Latin. It appears that in order to help them get acquainted at first hand with the fruits of Arab scientists, he assisted Adelard of Bath in the translation of Al-Khwarizmi's handbook. Text and translation of that work are available in H. Suter's aforementioned critical edition entitled *Die astronomischen Tafeln.* Many of Moses-Petrus' observations relating to astronomy, astrology, and other sciences are also interspersed in his more folkloristic *Disciplina clericalis* and in his polemical *Dialogus* (see *supra,* Chap. XXIV, n. 43).

See the data supplied by L. Thorndike in his *History of Magic,* II, 68 ff.; and by J. M. Millás in his Hebrew essay on "The Work of Moses Sefaradi (Petrus Alphonsi) in Astronomy," *Tarbiz,* IX, 55–64, subsequently expanded in "La Aportación astronómica de Pedro Alfonso" (1943) included in his *Estudios sobre historia,* pp. 197–218.

41. M. Alonso, "El 'liber de causis,'" *Al-Andalus,* IX, 43–69 (arguing for Avendeath's authorship). It seems that more than one John of Spain participated in the vast enterprise of translating philosophical and scientific works from Arabic into Latin. Since the medieval copyists were not always specific enough, the attribution of one or another translation to Avendeath (a corruption of Avendehut, which in turn was a derivative of Ibn Daud or Ben David), is often debatable and depends largely on internal evidence. The relatively most reliable and complete enumeration of his translations which included astrological treatises by Masha'allah, still is M. Steinschneider, *Die europäischen Uebersetzungen aus dem Arabischen bis Mitte des 17. Jahrhunderts* (*SB,* Vienna, CLI), pp. 41–50. See also Thorndike's *History,* II, 73 ff., 269 ff.; and, on the other hand, the long list of medieval Johns mentioned in manuscripts, *ibid.,* pp. 94 ff. On Avendeath's collaboration with Gundissalinus and others, see *supra,* Chaps. XX, n. 35; XXXIV, nn. 10, 19; and, more generally, the recent studies by M. Alonso Alonso, "Traducciones del árabe al latin por Juan Hispano (Ibn Dawud)," *Al-Andalus,* XVII, 129–51; and "Traducciones del arcediano Domingo Gundisalvo," *ibid.,* XII, 295–338; and A. González Palencia, *El Arzobispo don Raimundo de Toledo,* esp. pp. 149 ff. It must also be borne in mind that, apart from reproducing works by others, Avendeath wrote treatises of his own, and an especially comprehensive work, *Epitome totius astrologiae,* was published in Nuremberg, 1548. This work was cited as authoritative by Albertus Magnus and others. Its author was mentioned among the leading authorities in this field by Michael Scot in the early thirteenth century, and was even plagiarized by some later writers—generally as high a compliment as a medieval author could receive (Thorndike, *History,* II, 183 n. 1, 322). As late as the sixteenth century the title page of the *Epitome* still extols its author as *astrologus celeberrimus.* See also J. M. Millás's analysis of "Una Obra astronómica desconocida de Johannes Avendaut Hispanus" (1936), revised in his *Estudios sobre historia,* pp. 263–88.

42. Bar Ḥiyya's *Megillat ha-megalleh,* v, p. 111; Ibn Ezra's *Sefer Reshit ḥokhmah* (The Beginning of Wisdom; an astrological treatise), ed. by R. Levy and F. Cantera, p. v; in R. Levy's English trans., p. 152; Ps. 111:10; Prov. 1:7. On the ancient Jewish attitudes, see G. V. Schiaparelli's *Astronomy in the Old Testament,* English translation; G. R. Driver's more detailed explanation of "Two Astronomical Passages in the Old Testament," *Journal of Theological Studies,* n.s. IV, 208–12 (on Amos 5:8–9 and Job 38:12–15); W. M. Feldman's *Rabbinical Mathematics and Astronomy;* and other data cited *supra,* Vols. I, pp. 15 f.; II, pp. 15 ff., 306 f., 334 n. 18, 433 n. 19. The connection of astrology with magic was obvious. That is why Daniel al-Qumisi counted a "Book of Stars," since lost, among the several objectionable Rabbanite writings used for purposes of sorcery. See J. Mann's *Texts and Studies,* II, 76; and *supra,* Chap. XXXIII, n. 36. With some justice, therefore, could Ibn Ezra stress in the same context that he was trying to describe the "laws of heavenly bodies in regard to their judgments, as the ancients have tried [*nissu*] to do generation after generation." These professions go beyond the usual pious introductory

formulas which, under the impact of an Arabian literary fashion, now appeared also in most Hebrew works of the period.

43. Ibn Ezra's *Beginning of Wisdom, loc. cit.* (the lengthy quotation here given is a variant of Levy's translation), and pp. 24 f. In his prefatory remark the author announced his intention to supplement this work by a treatise giving "the explanation of the reasons," just as the *Sefer ha-Ṭe'amim* (Book of Reasons) concludes with the promise, "I shall explain it further in the *Sefer ha-'Olam* [Book of the Universe]." A booklet bearing this title was, indeed, the third tract in the series. Cf., however, Fleischer's intro. to his recent ed. of *Sefer ha-Ṭe'amim* in which, summarizing his earlier researches, he considers the "Book of the Universe" as the latest of the series. But, quite apart from the wording of the aforementioned conclusion of the second treatise, Fleischer's dating presupposes the composition of all seven tracts within some four months (from Tammuz 4908 to Marḥeshvan 4909, or from June to October 1148), an extraordinary literary feat even were we to assume that the author spent all his time in Béziers writing these treatises and that he had before him some earlier drafts. Both these assumptions would yet have to be proved. The careful revision of but three treatises, with their enormous wealth of detail, would easily have absorbed all of the author's energies during that four-month period. Certainly, neither the concluding phrase in the "Book of the Universe" that "thereby are completed all the laws of astrology," nor the fact that this tract is placed at the end of the whole collection in most manuscripts, is conclusive proof that this arrangement followed the author's original plan.

Apart from these three tracts, Ibn Ezra's *Sefer ha-Me'orot* (Book of Luminaries) and his *Sefer ha-Mibḥarim* (Book of Selections) are now available in printed editions likewise issued by J. L. Fleischer in 1937 (in the Bucharest *Sinai,* V) and 1939 (in the *Emlékkönyv* [*Jubilee Volume*] *in Honor of Ferenc Lövy, et al.,* Hebrew section, pp. 3–19), respectively. The former deals with the influence of the Sun and the Moon on the destinies of man, while the latter primarily offers advice as to the choice of astrologically most propitious moments for the transaction of business. Since the treatise on the Astrolabe has also been published, however inadequately (see *supra,* n. 37), only two more tracts await publication, namely the *Sefer ha-She'elot* (Book of Questions) and the *Sefer ha-Moladot* (Book of Nativities), both concerned with the consultation of stars, especially at the birth of a child. Only the introduction to the latter is now published in N. Ben Menahem's Hebrew "Studies on Abraham ibn Ezra" in *Sinai* (Jerusalem), V, Nos. 60–62, pp. 283–86.

All these works, and the extant manuscripts and translations therefrom are briefly reviewed in R. Levy's "literary and linguistic study" of *The Astrological Works of Abraham ibn Ezra* which, however, concentrates principally on the medieval French translations, especially that of the *Beginning of Wisdom* by the Jew Hagin. Levy subsequently published that translation in full in his and Cantera's edition of that work in Hebrew, adding some "Errata et Addenda" to the *Astrological Works, ibid.,* pp. 24 ff. Since more than half of Levy's broader work is devoted to a glossary of medieval French terms, a contribution to French lexicography much more than to the understanding of Ibn Ezra's scientific work, a comprehensive analysis of Ibn Ezra's contributions to astronomy and astrology still is a major desideratum. Such an analysis will not only have to take account of all published Hebrew and Latin texts, especially the Peter Lichtenstein collection of Ibn Ezra's (Avenaris) *In re judiciali opera,* issued in Peter of Abano's translation in Venice (1507), but also of the so-called *Tractatus particulares,* whose likely Hebrew originals seem to be totally lost. In his *History of Magic,* II, 927, Thorndike quotes the following three fairly descriptive Latin titles: (1) *Tractatus de partibus horarum interrogationibus;* (2) *Tractatus in tredecim manieribus planetarum;* (3) *Tractatus de significationibus planetarum in duodecim domibus Abrahe.* All these translations are likewise attributed to Peter of Abano. The second or third treatise might be connected with the *Sullam ha-mazzalot* (Ladder of Stars), ascribed to Ibn Ezra in a dubious source according to Steinschneider's *G.S.,* I, 411 n. 6, 497 f.

As may be seen from this example, even the purely bibliographical problems of Ibn Ezra's astrological works still await full elucidation, despite Steinschneider's yeoman work, particularly also in the appendix on "Abraham ibn Esra's astrologische Schriften" in his *Verzeichniss der hebräischen Handschriften . . . der kgl. Bibliothek zu Berlin,* Part 2, pp. 136–50 (includes on p. 138 a brief description of two of the *Tractatus particulares* but expresses serious doubts concerning their authenticity). See also the three-cornered discussion between Thorndike, Birkenmajer, and Millás on "Abrahamismus" in *Isis,* XL, 34–35, and *AIHS,* III, 378–90, 856–58. Millás defends especially his assumption that Ibn Ezra's "Pisan Tables" were composed in 1154, and not in 1144, and that they, as well as the "Tractate on the Astrolabe" and possibly other works originally had appeared in Latin.

44. Ibn Ezra's *Beginning of Wisdom,* II, pp. 11 f. (Hebrew), 40 ff. (French), 159 f. (English); Shabbat 156a; J. L. Fleischer's Hebrew essay, "On Two Horoscopes Attributed to R. Abraham ibn Ezra" in *Zlotnik Jub. Vol.,* pp. 129–40; and his edition of Ibn Ezra's *Sefer ha-Mibḥarim,* II, IV, in *Emelékkönyv . . . Ferenc Lövy,* Hebrew section, pp. 11, 13. Some parts of a horoscope, allegedly prepared by Ibn Ezra for a child born during his stay in Narbonne in 1160, have been communicated and interpreted by Steinschneider as early as 1847 in his edition of the *Shene ha-me'orot* (Two Luminaries).

45. Ibn Ezra's *Commentary* on Gen. 5:29, 2d version, in M. Friedlaender's *Essays,* IV, Hebrew section, pp. 44 f.; his *Sefer ha-'Olam,* ed. by L. Fleischer in *Ozar Hachaim,* XIII, 43 f., 47; his *Sefer ha-Ṭe'amim,* especially pp. 37 ff., 58, 84; and *infra,* n. 48. The passage from the "Book of Nativities" is quoted from the Paris MS of Hagin's French trans. by R. Levy in *The Astrological Works,* p. 16. Here the reader will also find a rather motley list of authorities cited by Ibn Ezra. See also the relatively extensive list in Fleischer's introduction to his edition of the *Sefer ha-Ṭe'amim,* pp. 12 ff. Of course, the old identification of Enoch with Idris and Hermes, which many Muslim writers took over from the Jews, opened the gates for the incursion of Hermetic astrology into the Jewish letters as well. See A. J. Festugière, *La Révélation d'Hermès Trismégiste, I: L'Astrologie et les sciences occultes;* and *supra,* Chaps. XXXIII, n. 7; XXXIV, n. 67.

46. Ibn Ezra's *Commentary* on Gen. 17:1 (in Friedlaender's *Essays,* IV, Hebrew section, p. 63); and M. Friedlaender's English summary in his "Ibn Ezra in England," *JQR,* [o.s.] VIII, 145 f. See *supra,* Chap. XXXIV, n. 53.

47. Maimonides' aforementioned "Letter on Astrology," ed. by A. Marx in "The Correspondence between the Rabbis of Southern France and Maimonides about

Astrology," *HUCA,* III, 311–58; and his *Epistle to Yemen,* ed. by Halkin, pp. 64 ff. (Arabic and Hebrew), xiii f. (English; with minor variants). As pointed out by Halkin, Bar Ḥiyya, too, considered David and Solomon as living under the earthly trigon, though he drew no astrological conclusions therefrom. He did not even find it necessary to refer to the trigon of the period of the patriarchs. See his *Megillat ha-megalleh,* v, pp. 127 ff. On the Maimonidean chronological computations underlying his placing of the three patriarchs and the two kings under the same earthly trigon, see *infra,* n. 77.

48. Bar Ḥiyya's *Hegyon ha-nefesh,* fol. 32a; his aforementioned Letter to Yehudah bar Barzillai, ed. by Z. Schwarz in *Schwarz Festschrift,* pp. 24 ff.; Albertus Magnus' *De coelo et de mundo,* II.3, 5 in his *Opera,* Lyons, 1651 ed., II, 111. Albertus' knowledge of Ptolemaic astrology, needless to say, stemmed to a large extent from Latin translations of Arabic and Hebrew sources. On one occasion (*De meteororum libri,* I.3, 5, *ibid.,* p. 18), he expressly quoted "Abraham's" (Ibn Ezra's) comment. See Thorndike's *History of Magic,* II, 585 f. There is little doubt that Albertus and most other Christian students of medieval science studied at least Ptolemy's chief astrological work, the *Quadripartitum* (or *Tetrabiblos*), in the Latin translation by Plato of Tivoli. Plato's rendition was finished in 1138, and he may well have consulted his friend, Savasorda, on the meaning of various passages. See *supra,* n. 12; and M. E. Winkel's observations in his German trans. of the *Tetrabiblos.*

49. Bar Ḥiyya's *Ṣurat ha-areṣ* (Cosmography), Intro., fol. 1b. The general contributions of astrological observations to astronomical knowledge have long been recognized. Like the alchemists, astrologers were driven to empiricism, and became leaders in the empirical observation of stars, which prevented astronomy from petrifying around a set of accepted authoritarian theories. In this respect, astrology was not only the "mother of astronomy," but also continued to nurture this ever more independent child from the fruits of its rich experiences. See also M. E. Winkel's *Naturwissenschaft und Astrologie,* pp. 59 ff., which will prove suggestive even to readers who do not share the author's general appreciation of the contemporary revival of astrological quests.

50. Azariah de' Rossi's *Sefer Me'or Eynaim* (Light of the Eyes; Studies in Jewish History and Chronology), ed. by D. Cassel, p. 370; Ibn Ezra's *Commentary* on Lev. 17:7; the intro. to his "Book of Nativities," ed. by Ben Menahem in *Sinai,* V, Nos. 60–62, pp. 285 f.; Naḥmanides' *Commentary* on Lev. 24:23 end. In his suggestive analysis of "The Zodiac Theme in Ancient Synagogues and in Hebrew Printed Books," *Studies in Bibliography and Booklore,* I, 3–13, I. Sonne reached the interesting conclusion that in the sixth-century synagogue of Bet-Alpha and later decorations the Jewish artists had adopted the zodiac scheme from the Gentile world, but transformed its symbolic meaning into the very opposite. "Originally connected with the sun-cult, and aiming at the glorification of the triumphant Helios in his chariot, the zodiac was now turned into a representation of Helios' doom and final defeat. . . . The two constellations, *Cancer* and *Leo,* were in this way made a mirror of the struggles and aspirations of the Jewish people" (p. 12). At times, however, zodiacal illustrations were altogether devoid of symbolic meaning and merely served graphically to underscore the description of the zodiac in prayers or poems.

Not surprisingly, Ibn Ezra's denial of the existence of demons brought down on him the wrath of the defenders of the literal truth of the Aggadah. According to a popular tale, recorded by the arch-conservative Moses Taku (of Tachau), Ibn Ezra met his deserved punishment when, traveling in England through the woods, he encountered a large number of evil spirits disguised as a pack of black dogs. The ensuing shock allegedly caused the spiteful rationalist to contract an illness from which he never recovered. See Taku's *Ketab tamim* (The Unblemished Work; an apologia), ed. by R. Kirchheim in *Ozar nechmad,* III, 97. Although far closer in time and place, Moses is, of course, less reliable as a witness for the cause of Ibn Ezra's death than he is in his testimony about the earlier Karaite-Rabbanite arguments in the East mentioned *supra,* Chap. XXVI, n. 54.

51. Shabbat 156a; Dio Cassius' *Roman History,* xxxvii.18; Al-Biruni's *Chronology,* pp. 185 ff. (Arabic), 168 ff. (English); Donnolo's *Ḥakmoni,* ed. by Castelli, pp. 59 ff., 71 f.; Rashi's *Commentary* on Shabbat 129b *s.v. De-qayyema;* 'Erubin 56a *s.v. Ve-eyn tequfah;* Bar Ḥiyya's *Sefer ha-'Ibbur,* I.10, pp. 26 ff. See F. H. Colson's comprehensive study of *The Week: an Essay on the Origin and Development of the Seven-Day Cycle;* and especially S. Gandz's noteworthy essay on "The Origin of the Planetary Week or The Planetary Week in Hebrew Literature," *PAAJR,* XVIII, 213–54, where the aforementioned rabbinic passages and several others are reproduced in full in both their original texts and an English translation. The fact that Philo nowhere connects the Sabbath day with the planetary week certainly is not as serious an objection to that historic nexus, as Colson implies (p. 54 n. 1). In his Postscript (p. 254), however, Gandz, as well as Sachau (in his trans. of Al-Biruni, p. 412), apparently misunderstood the import of Al-Biruni's Table. The distinguished Arab astronomer had not chosen as the starting point for his calculations the time of the creation of the luminaries, but rather the beginnings of the respective *tequfot* (seasons). He made it clear that he followed here a Jewish informant who believed that the sun was created on Ellul 27 (see *infra,* nn. 69 and 71), and that accordingly the first Tishre season (autumnal equinox) "took place at the end of the third hour of the day of Wednesday the 5th of Tishre." The following Nisan *tequfah* (vernal equinox) being 182 days and 15 hours later, had to occur on the same day at 18:00 hours, that is at noon. This leaves, however, the starting point of the original computation "from the beginning of the night of Wednesday" unaffected. Only the attribution of the beginning of the vernal equinox to the control of Shabbetai-Saturn seems misleading. On these pagan names of stars, accepted also by the monotheistic religions, see *supra,* n. 27.

52. Origin and early evolution of the Hebrew calendar are still very obscure. In fact, the debates connected with the Dead Sea Scrolls, which have revived interest in the remarkable computations of the Book of Jubilees, have rather increased the existing confusion. Scholars resumed the discussion on the very question of whether ancient Israel observed principally a solar or a lunar year, J. Morgenstern favoring the former, while S. Gandz and J. B. Segal have strongly argued for the predominantly lunar origins of the Jewish calendar. The weight of evidence decidedly favors the latter point of view. See esp. J. Morgenstern, "The Calendar of the Book of Jubilees, Its Origin and Its Character," *Vetus Testamentum,* V, 34–76; A. Jaubert, "Le Calendrier des Jubilés et les jours liturgiques de la semaine," *ibid.,* VII, 33–61; J. B. Segal, "Intercalation and the Hebrew Calendar," *ibid.,* pp. 250–307; S.

Gandz, "The Calendar of Ancient Israel," *Homenaje a Millás,* I, 623–46; and the large literature cited in these essays.

There is no doubt, however, that the leaders of the talmudic age, long before Hillel II, had at their disposal scientific computations which helped them verify and correct the results of empirical observations. Yet for good reasons they refused to divulge their scientific findings, or even to discuss them publicly. Even the specific circumstances which led to the proclamation of the calendar by Hillel II are shrouded in darkness, its very date being far from certain. While modern scholars have long accepted the year mentioned in a responsum by Hai Gaon (cited in full in Abraham bar Ḥiyya's *Sefer ha-'Ibbur,* III.7, pp. 97 f., see Lewin's *Otzar ha-gaonim,* V, Part 3, pp. 16 ff.), namely 670 Sel. era (359 C.E.) as literally true, E. Mahler has argued with much conviction in favor of a slight emendation of that text (the replacement of the last letter *'ayyin* by *nun vav*) to yield the date of 656 Sel. era, or 344–45 C.E. See his *Handbuch der jüdischen Chronologie,* pp. 462 ff.; and *supra,* Vol. II, p. 209. Whatever the date, it is apparent that the patriarchs, who continued functioning for some three quarters of a century under the full protection of Roman public law, did not thereby proclaim an automatically operating perpetual calendar, but retained considerable authority on regulating the details as the occasion arose. This is evident from the subsequent story of the calendar computations, and is generally agreed upon by such modern scholars as A. Schwarz, whose *Der jüdische Kalender historisch und astronomisch untersucht* is still far from obsolete today; H. J. Bornstein in his specialized authoritative studies on the Jewish calendar (see especially his Hebrew essay on "The Latest Phases in the Story of Intercalation," *Hatekufah,* XIV–XV, 321–72; XVI, 228–92); and Z. H. Jaffe in his posthumous *Qorot ḥeshbon ha-'ibbur* (History of Calendar Computations: Studies for the Clarification of the Mystery of the True Intercalation), ed. by A. A. Akaviah. See also E. Frank's *Talmudic and Rabbinic Chronology.* The impact of the messianic hope on the protracted reticence in making public long-range computations deserves, however, further investigation.

53. As is well known, the controversy between the Christian *quatrodecimani,* who insisted on observing Easter on the 14th of Nisan, the *quintodecimani* who shifted it to the 15th of that month, and the western Christians who observed it on the following Sunday, was not settled until the Council of Nicea. That great assembly decided the issue in favor of the westerners, and forbade all the faithful "henceforth to follow the blindness of Jews." The trend away from Palestinian leadership was underscored by the Council's additional resolution that all churches follow the computations of the patriarchs of Alexandria, because of the city's reputation as a center of astronomic learning. That the controversies were not completely silenced by these canons, and that for centuries thereafter enough Christians were ready to follow the Jewish lead in this matter, further aggravating the existing Judeo-Christian tensions, has already been mentioned *supra,* Vol. II, pp. 209, 400 n. 21.

54. Abraham ibn Ezra's *Sefer ha-'Ibbur* (Book of Intercalation), ed. by S. Z. H. Halberstam, fol. 2a. The reason why Marḥeshvan and Kislev were selected for the adjustment of ordinary lunar years to range from 353 to 355 days, and that of leap years to vary between 383 and 385 days, has long been debated. The most plausible explanation is that any other combination of winter months might produce four consecutive full months in leap years. See Z. H. Jaffe's *Qorot,* pp. 19 ff.

55. Enoch 74:16; Julius Africanus, cited in Eusebius' *Demonstratio evangelica,* VIII.2, in *PG,* XXII, 612 (also in the excerpts of Africanus' works collected *ibid.,* X, 84); Al-Biruni, *Chronology,* pp. 12, 62 (Arabic), 14 f., 73 f. (English); E. Schwartz, *Christliche und jüdische Ostertafeln.* According to Al-Biruni, the pre-Islamic Arabs adopted the Jewish custom, because "they desired to perform the pilgrimage at such times as their merchandise (hides, skins, fruit, etc.) was ready for the market." They had their own intercalators, however, who instituted the particular *nasi'* (intercalation). One wonders whether this term did not originate from a mishearing of the Jewish reference to their *nasi* (patriarch) as the officer in charge of intercalation. See also the somewhat divergent description in the *K. at-Tafhim* (*The Book of Instruction in the Elements of the Art of Astrology*) by Al-Biruni, ed. from a British Museum MS and translated into English by R. R. Wright, p. 154 (Arabic and English).

It may be noted in this connection that the distinguished Muslim scientist had gathered much material not only for the chronological notions current among the pre-Islamic Arabs, Persians, and Indians, but also had found some well-informed Jewish confreres who supplied him with data on Jewish traditions in this field. These informants, including one Ya'qub ibn Musa al-Nigrisi, with whom he conversed in Jurjan about Jewish holidays and to whom he himself refers in his major chronological work, evidently came from eastern, probably Iranian, communities. There obviously were Jewish scholars of note, whether orthodox or sectarian, in those parts during the tenth century who may well have made significant contributions to Jewish scientific studies, although, as in other fields, the Jewish sources concerning these eastern communities are totally lost. See Al-Biruni's *Chronology,* pp. 52 ff., 275 ff. (Arabic), 62 ff., 268 ff. (English); and *supra,* Chap. XXV, n. 45. See also M. Schreiner, "Les Juifs dans Al-Beruni," *REJ,* XII, 259–66; and, more generally, K. Garbers, "Eine Ergänzung zur Sachauschen Ausgabe von Al-Biruni's Chronologie orientalischer Völker," *Der Islam,* XXX, 39–80 (offering a German translation from an Istanbul MS discovered by H. Ritter); D. J. Boilot, "L'Oeuvre d'Al-Beruni: Essai bibliographique," *Mélanges* of the Institut Dominicain d'Etudes Orientales du Caire, II, 161–256; and the various essays included in *Al-Biruni Commemoration Volume A.H. 362—A.H. 1362,* which includes a brief essay by V. Minorsky, "On Some of Biruni's Informants" (pp. 233–36, showing how keenly the great scientist collected information from travelers and envoys whom he met at the Khorasanian court and elsewhere). In any case, it was Mohammed who, at the time of his anti-Jewish reaction, denounced any interference with the natural course of the lunar year as a mark of infidelity (Qur'an 9:37). On these and other cycles recorded among the Jews and their neighbors, see esp. H. J. Bornstein's comprehensive analysis in his "Intercalations and Cycles" (Hebrew), *Hatekufah,* XX, 285–330.

56. Al-Biruni's *Chronology,* pp. 145 f. (Arabic), 143 (English); Ibn Ezra's *Sefer ha-'Ibbur,* fol. 6b, with reference to Obadiah 16. See O. Neugebauer, "The 'Metonic Cycle' in Babylonian Astronomy" in *Studies and Essays . . . in Homage to George Sarton,* pp. 433–48. It should be noted that, as late as 992 and 995, when Hai Gaon wrote his two lengthy replies, the *guḥadzat* formula still was under debate. See the texts in Lewin's *Otzar ha-gaonim,* V, Part 3, pp. 16 ff. (on R.H. 10b). The origin of the unusual division of the hour into 1,080*p,* each of which is further subdivided into 76 time atoms (*rega'im*), is discussed by S. Gandz in "The Division of the Hour in Hebrew Literature," *Osiris,* X, 10–34; and *infra,* n. 60. It should also be noted

that the controversy over the three different sequences of the seven intercalations during each cycle, goes back to the generation of Tannaim living soon after the fall of Jerusalem, according to a passage quoted from *Pirqe de-R. Eliezer* by Samuel bar Meir (in his unpublished "Book of Intercalation"), and by Isaac Israeli the Second in his *Yesod 'Olam* (Foundation of the World; an astronomic treatise), IV.2, fol. 63b. See *Pirqe,* VII, ed. by Higger in *Horeb,* VIII, 110; in G. Friedlander's English trans., p. 57 (Chap. VIII); and Bornstein's other citations in "The Latest Phases," *Hatekufah,* XIV–XV, 338. On the nexus between these sequences and the attribution of the origins of R. Adda's formula to R. Gamaliel II (indirectly even Gamaliel I), and their relation to the chronology of the era of Creation, see *infra,* nn. 60, 65, 69.

On the other hand, the situation in the pre-Hellenistic period, is well illustrated by the scattered data in the Elephantine papyri. These show conclusively that the reconciliation of the solar with the lunar calendars, was not yet as closely regulated as in the tannaitic period. See H. Y. Bornstein's careful analysis in his essay on "A Vestige from Ancient Times" in *Festschrift Harkavy,* Hebrew section, pp. 63–104. Bornstein's conclusions have on the whole been confirmed by the subsequent investigations, as well as by the new data supplied by E. G. Kraeling's recent edition of *The Brooklyn Museum Aramaic Papyri,* although the dating of Papyrus VIII is problematical. The discrepancy of a month between the accepted Babylonian and Egyptian chronologies may not have been owing to a scribal error, as Kraeling assumes (p. 228), but rather to a local variant in intercalation. See also S. H. Horn and L. H. Wood's more recent analysis of "The Fifth-Century Jewish Calendar of Elephantine," *JNES,* XIII, 1–20, in part controverted by R. A. Parker in his "Some Considerations of the Nature of the Fifth-Century Jewish Calendar at Elephantine," *ibid.,* XIV, 271–74.

57. See A. A. Akaviah's intro. to his ed. of Jaffe's *Qorot,* pp. 17 ff.; and Ibn Ezra's somewhat forced observations in his *Sefer ha-'Ibbur,* fol. 9ab. The futile sixteenth-century effort to reintroduce the ancient ordination has been reviewed anew by C. D. Regensberg in "The Controversy between R. Jacob Berab and R. Levi ibn Ḥabib concerning the Renewal of Ordination" (Hebrew), *Kerem,* I, 87–96. It, as well as the debate on the renovation of a Sanhedrin now being conducted in Israel, will be more fully discussed in their respective contexts. So intimate has always been the nexus between calendar and ordination that Bornstein was led by his researches in the history of the Jewish calendar to the writing of an extensive Hebrew essay on "The Rules of Ordination," in *Hatekufah,* IV, 393–426. See also *supra,* Vol. II, pp. 201, 419 n. 44; and A. Burstein's more recent Hebrew study, "On the Problem of Proclaiming Leap Years in the Dispersion," *Sinai,* XIX, No. 226, pp. 32–46.

58. Qalir's *Az ra'itah* (Thou Hast Then Seen, which is the concluding section VI of the *Az me-az zamotah;* see Davidson's *Oṣar,* I, 101 No. 2149; IV, 232); "Alphabet of R. 'Aqiba," under letter *bet* in Jellinek's *Bet ha-Midrasch,* III, 19 (in Eisenstein *Ozar Midrashim,* pp. 426 f.); Ps. 90:4; *Pirqe de-R. Eliezer,* VI, ed. by Higger in *Horeb,* VIII, 105 (in G. Friedlander's trans., pp. 36 f.); *Sefer Yeṣirah,* IV–V, ed. by L. Goldschmidt, pp. 59 ff. (in I. Kalisch's English trans., pp. 25 ff.); Samuel bar Meir's aforementioned MS commentary cited by Bornstein in *Hatekufah,* XIV–XV, 337 n. 2. A variant of Samuel bar Meir's observation is quoted by Aaron ben Elijah the

Karaite in the name of R. Israel ha-Ma'arabi. See Aaron's *Gan 'eden,* fol. 22b. The meaning of Qalir's poem was further elucidated by Bornstein in his "Intercalations and Cycles," *Hatekufah,* XX, 324 ff.; and, with some corrections, by Jaffe in his *Qorot,* pp. 117 ff.

Although adopted by the apocryphal Book of Jubilees, the Jubilee cycles seem never to have had any practical application among Jews. Even the recent attempt to find traces of its acceptance among the Qumran sectarians has not proved particularly successful. See A. Jaubert, "Le Calendrier des Jubilés et de la secte de Qumrân. Ses origines bibliques," *Vetus Testamentum,* III, 250–64. See also, from another angle, G. Lambert, "Jubilé hébreux et jubilé chrétien," *Nouvelle Revue théologique,* LXXXII (1950), 234–51. The tradition of that ancient chronological device was cultivated, however, in apocalyptic and mystic circles and generated, as we recollect, the belief that the Messiah would come during the eighty-fifth jubilee, or between 440 and 490 C.E. See *supra,* Chap. XXV, n. 28. Despite the ensuing disappointment, it persisted under the surface to the seventh century and reappeared in this Qalirian poem. Its connection with the mystic teachings is also borne out by the poem's context. According to Qalir's formulation, "The whole world [endures] six thousand years, which amount to five and two thirds cycles, each cycle amounts to twenty-two jubilees, and the jubilee to seven Sabbaths," the total (of $5\frac{2}{3} \times 1078$) is almost 6,109 years. This figure is far closer to "'Aqiba's" 6,093 years than to the round figure of 6,000. Incidentally, Al-Biruni's Jewish informants did not stress either figure for the duration of the world, as did, for instance, the Zoroastrians who insisted on a total duration of 12,000 years. But they, and their Christian counterparts, related to the Arab scientist numerous computations based on Sabbatical cycles which, in their respective opinions, explained Daniel's date of 1,335 years for the coming of the Redeemer. Al-Biruni was not impressed, however. See his *Chronology,* pp. 17 ff.; and, on the reasons for the Zoroastrian figures, *supra,* Vol. II, p. 435 n. 31.

59. Ibn Ezra's reply to three chronological questions by David ben Joseph Narboni (before 1139), published in *Shene ha-me'orot,* ed. by Steinschneider, containing his characteristic play on the words of Exod. 34:1. Meaning and origin of R. Naḥshon's "circle" are still obscure. Jaffe's theory that the 247-year cycle was actually in operation during 57 years (781–838 C.E.) and that it was rejected by an assembly of Palestinian and Babylonian scholars including R. Naḥshon himself (*Qorot,* pp. 155 ff., 159 ff., 202) is very questionable. It actually converts Naḥshon into an opponent, rather than the author of that "circle."

60. *Baraita de-Shemu'el,* v beg., in Eisenstein's *Ozar Midrashim,* p. 544 (on its date, see A. A. Akaviah's aforementioned Hebrew article in *Melilah,* V, 119–32); M. R.H. II.8; b. 25a; Bar Ḥiyya's *Sefer ha-'Ibbur,* ed. by Filipowski, pp. 37 f. Savasorda realized that, although prior to Ptolemy, the two Gamaliels might have borrowed the theory from Hipparchus (about 150 B.C.E.) who, in turn as we now know, was often indebted to Babylonian prototypes. The Spanish astronomer made, therefore, a desperate effort to prove that Hipparchus, who, as he believed, had lived some eighty years after Alexander and, hence, according to the telescoped chronology of the rabbis (see *supra,* Vol. I, p. 486 n. 44), 126 years after the building of the Second Temple, flourished after the ancestors of R. Gamaliel who, "as is well known lived at the beginning of the Second Temple." Ibn Ezra spoke more vaguely of a tradition

which was handed down in the family of David, "the man of God," alluding to the reputed descent of the two Gamaliels from the house of David. See his *Sefer ha-'Ibbur,* fol. 3a. Such a formulation, often repeated, could give rise to the popular fallacy that calendar computations had originated with that king-psalmist himself. See Isaac Israeli the Second's *Yesod 'olam,* IV.14, fols. 81 f. The confusion on this score even among modern scholars may best be illustrated by E. Mahler's attempt to explain the difference in views between R. Eliezer and R. Gamaliel with respect to the sequence of leap years in the nineteen-year cycles as going back to the divergence of these 73*p*. See his *Handbuch,* p. 374. However, there is no evidence that the computation of 29½*d* and ⅔ (or 720*p*) of an hour for the duration of the average lunation such as is used in *Pirqe* and the "Baraita of Samuel" was intended to deny the additional 73*p* included by R. Gamaliel. It may have been but a round figure disregarding what amounted to little more than four minutes each month.

These fractions, however, seem to have been responsible for the division of hours into 1,080 parts. According to the introduction to the medieval tractate, *Sefer 'Ibronot* (Book of Intercalations, of uncertain date), first ed. by Sebastian Münster and later, more fully, by Eliezer ben Jacob Belin, "when the children of Issachar went up to heaven, they introduced [the division into] 1,080 parts of an hour." This tradition evidently harkened back to the homiletical elaboration of the Chronicler's description of the children of Issachar as "men that had understanding of the times" (I Chr. 12:33) and also equated this description with expertness in calendar. See Gen. r. LXXII.18, pp. 842 f., and Theodor's notes thereon. To believers in the Mosaic origin of the Jewish calendar (see below) this statement seemed to relate to the very early members of the tribe of Issachar. Others like Maimonides (*M.T.* Qiddush XVII.25), viewed them as synchronous with the ancient prophets. Still others who denied the genuineness of the attribution of the formula to R. Gamaliel, claimed that there was no evidence for that division before the conclusion of the talmudic era. See Bornstein's data in *Hatekufah,* XIV–XV, 327 ff.; and Jaffe's *Qorot,* pp. 104 ff. (attributing it to the alleged assembly which reformed the Jewish calendar in the light of Ptolemy's *Almagest*).

Such skepticism seems decidedly exaggerated, however. We may, indeed, rightly attribute this division to the period around the beginning of the Christian era, when the confluence of Babylonian and Greek mathematical sciences sharpened the perception of Jewish leaders in the astronomic aspects of their ritualistic observances. Nor is it difficult to explain why that particular division into 1,080 parts, evidently based upon the Babylonian sexagesimal system, was adopted. Maimonides' explanation that the number 1,080 is divisible by all numbers from 1 to 10 with the exception of 7 (VI.2) is inadequate, since the smaller number 360 would likewise have met this requirement, as pointed out by Neugebauer in *HUCA,* XXII, 325. Ibn Ezra, from whom Maimonides had evidently taken his argument, had, indeed, offered this divisibility by nine numbers, as an explanation for the division into 360 only. But he added that, since the lunation required an additional subdvision of ⅔ thereof, the figure 1,080 was adopted. Cf. his *Sefer ha-'Ibbur,* fol. 3a. Pursuing his general pedagogic objectives, Maimonides submitted this reasoning in an abridged, if oversimplified, fashion. That is also why he failed to mention another explanation offered by Bar Ḥiyya, whose work he otherwise greatly admired. See his *Commentary* on M. 'Arakhin II.2. Savasorda had called attention to the Ptolemaic fractions of $\frac{6}{9}+\frac{3}{5\times 9}+\frac{1}{4\times 6\times 5\times 9}$, the latter fraction amounting to $\frac{1}{1080}$.

Hence also the reduction of the other fractions to the same common denominator. See his *Sefer ha-'Ibbur,* II.2, p. 37. See also Gandz's comments in "The Astronomy of Maimonides," *AIHS,* III, 837 ff.; and "The Division of the Hour," *Osiris,* X, 28 ff., where, however, Ibn Ezra's explanation is passed over in silence.

61. *Pirqe de-R. Eliezer,* VII, ed by Higger in *Horeb,* VIII, 108 f. (in G. Friedlander's trans., p. 49); Mann's *Jews in Egypt,* II, 41 f.; and other sources cited *supra,* Chaps. XXIII, n. 35; XXVI, n. 21. The solemn proclamation of the leap year in the presence of ten members is mentioned in *Pirqe, loc. cit.* p. 58, where it is deduced from the term *'edah* (congregation), which meant a minimum of ten (Mann, I, 273, is to be accordingly modified). However, the author of *Pirqe* made certain that the lack of a quorum would not prevent action. He added, therefore, that "if their number diminished, they bring in the scroll of law and spread it before them." This custom is otherwise unattested, but a membership of ten or less indicates that this was neither a "court," since all courts had to consist of an odd number of members in order to enable them to have majority votes, nor a liturgical assembly. Maimonides, evidently familiar with this procedure, tried to reconcile the various sources by postulating that the decision was to be made originally by a court of three. Only in the absence of unanimity the court was gradually increased to one of five, or seven judges. Only after the decision was reached, the actual proclamation of a new moon was accompanied by a modest feast in the presence of ten persons. See *M.T.* Qiddush III.7; IV.9–10, obviously referring to M. Sanhedrin I.2, VIII.2; b. 10b f., 70 f., but probably also bearing in mind the practice recorded in *Pirqe.* See also *supra,* Chap. XXIX, n. 101.

62. Al-Qumisi's "Book of Commandments," cited in Harkavy's *Zikhron,* VIII, 189; his *Commentary* on the Minor Prophets in Mann's *Texts and Studies,* II, 56 f., 76; Ben Meir's second letter of 922 in Bornstein's *Maḥloqet Rab Saadya Gaon u-Ben Meir,* No. v, p. 90 (*Sokolow Jub. Vol.,* p. 105; see also the text ed. by A. Guillaume in his "Further Documents on the Ben Meir Controversy," *JQR,* V, 552); Elijah Bashyatchi's *Adderet Eliyahu,* Qiddush ha-ḥodesh XL, fol. 36a; Augustine's *Epistles,* LIV–LV, ed. by A. Goldbacher in *CSEL,* XXXIII, 158 ff. (in *PL,* XXXIII, 199 ff.); Elijah of Salonica's (?) chronicle in Mann's *Texts,* I, 46 f., 49 f.; Aaron ben Elijah's *Gan 'eden,* fol. 22b. The sensation created among the Christians by this conflicting observance is well illustrated by Elijah of Nisibis' comments in *Fragmente syrischer und arabischer Historiker,* ed. by F. B. Baethgen, pp. 84 (Syriac), 141 (German). See also Bornstein's data, and particularly his interpretation of a decisive passage in Halevi's *K. al-Khazari* (III.38, pp. 188 f.; in Hirschfeld's English trans., p. 170) in *Hatekufah,* XIV–XV, 365 ff.; and *supra,* Chap. XXIII, n. 35.

It appears that the Karaites never ceased to celebrate, together with the Rabbanites, two New Moon days whenever the preceding month was considered "full." They were, of course, unable to accept the Rabbanite rationale that originally Jews celebrated only one day dependent on the proclamation of the Sanhedrin, whether astronomically correct or incorrect (see M. R.H. III.1; and Maimonides' remarks in *M.T.* Qiddush II.8; VIII.4), and that only after the proclamation of the fixed calendar each thirtieth day of the month became a holiday, followed by another holiday marking the beginning of a new month. Benjamin Nahawendi cited, therefore, the record of King Saul's celebration of such a double holiday (I Sam. 20:27) as an authoritative precedent. See his comment cited by Yeshu'a ben Yehudah in

Harkavy's *Zikhron,* VIII, 176 f. S. Gandz has plausibly argued that this was indeed the meaning of that biblical passage, and that ancient Israel had long adhered to this custom. Displaced some time during the Second Commonwealth, the double holiday reasserted itself after Hillel's calendar reform. See Gandz's "Studies in the Hebrew Calendar," *JQR,* XL, 157 ff. See also, more generally, A. S. Halkin's aforementioned Hebrew study, "History of the Sanctification of the New Moon in the Karaite Community," *Horeb,* II, 87–93, 208–36; and *supra,* Chap. XXVI, n. 46.

63. The Babylonian letter, probably dating from the beginning of the controversy, is reprinted in Bornstein's *Maḥloqet,* No. IV, pp. 73 f. (in the *Sokolow Jub. Vol.,* pp. 87 ff.). Saadiah's extremist views (cited *supra,* Chap. XXVI, nn. 3, 19, 81) found few followers among the geonim. See, e.g., Hai's oblique reference thereto in his aforementioned responsum of 995 in Lewin's *Otzar ha-gaonim,* V, Part 3, p. 21. Because of Saadiah's authority, to be sure, it was repeated by Ḥananel ben Ḥushiel, Meshullam ben Qalonymus, Yehudah ibn Bal'am (Bornstein's *Maḥloqet,* p. 147 n. 1), and, in a consciously equivocal formulation, by Maimonides (*M.T.* Qiddush I.1, 7; II.2). It was expressly rejected, however, by Isaac ben Baruch Albaliah, Bar Ḥiyya (*Sefer ha-'Ibbur,* II.8, pp. 60 ff.); and Naḥmanides (in his strictures on Maimonides' "Book of Commandments," Positive Comm. 153 toward end). See also Isaac Israeli's *Yesod 'olam,* IV.6, fol. 68b f. It must be borne in mind, however, that at least the ancient Babylonians were familiar with the times of the conjunctions of the moon, and that such knowledge may well have spread to some limited circles in ancient Israel as well. A cuneiform tablet dating from about 1000 B.C.E. presupposed sufficient popular knowledge of these astronomic factors to recommend the periods of the moon's conjunction as an auspicious time for bringing home a bride. See Langdon's *Babylonian Menologies,* pp. 50 f.

64. See esp. M. D. Cassuto's ingenious explanation of "What Was the Difference of Opinion between R. Saadiah Gaon and Ben Meir?" (Hebrew), in *Rav Saadya Gaon,* ed. by Fishman, pp. 333–64. Despite the extensive work done by scholars in explaining this memorable controversy, some of its astronomic ingredients are still obscure. The nexus, especially, between Ben Meir's latitude concerning the 642*p* and the date of creation would deserve further elucidation. Cassuto has rightly postulated Ben Meir's limit of 14*h,* 204*p* for a Nisan nativity as a natural consequence of his limit of 18*h,* 642*p,* for that occurring six months later. But he has thereby merely pushed back the riddle of the origin of that limit. His own explanation that it depended entirely on the importance of Nisan and Passover is not only astronomically forced, but would also allow for much later nativities during the following months, and hence also for the visibility of the moon a day later. Both protagonists, in any case, concentrated only on the effects of their respective rules on the nativity of the subsequent Tishre, although, as we learn from Bar Ḥiyya, even two centuries later, there still was a wide division of opinion between the Jews of East and West as to whether one was to count the beginning of the world from the Tishre preceding, or that following the first Nisan. See his *Sefer ha-'Ibbur,* III.7, pp. 96 ff. True, this difference of opinion did not affect their basic chronology. But it had some bearing on the computation of the "four gates," namely the various techniques employed in securing that the New Year would occur only on a Monday, Tuesday, Thursday, or Saturday. This system, however, lucidly explained by Savasorda (*ibid.,* II.9, pp. 62 ff.), seems to have still been debated in Saadiah's day, inducing the gaon to devote a

special monograph to the subject. Unfortunately this treatise is completely lost. See Malter's *Saadia Gaon,* p. 352; and the related data *ibid.,* p. 73 n. 151.

65. Ibn Ezra's *Sefer ha-'Ibbur,* fols. 7a, 8a; Maimonides' *Ma'amar ha-'Ibbur* (Treatise on Intercalation) in his *Qobeṣ,* II, fols. 17–23ab; *M.T.* Qiddush XVII.25. See also the literature listed *supra,* n. 26; and, on the problem of the additional chapters and their relation to the date of the composition of *M.T., supra,* Chap. XXVII, n. 114. It must be borne in mind, however, that the conclusion of the first part and the whole third part of Ibn Ezra's treatise, in which he repeatedly promised to discuss in greater detail the astronomic aspects of the "mystery of intercalation," are no longer extant. See N. Brüll's review of Halberstam's edition of that treatise in his *Jahrbücher für jüdische Geschichte und Literatur,* III, 165 f. Nor do we possess the writings of such other Spanish astronomers as Ḥasan ben Mar-Ḥasan, or Isaac ben Baruch. According to Ibn Ezra, the former had written three books on the mystery of intercalation. Although Ibn Ezra disposed of them curtly in his own treatise (for example, fol. 10b: "his words have no substance"), the few extant quotations therefrom in the works of Bar Ḥiyya and Isaac Israeli the Second reveal Ḥasan as a genuine pioneer in calendar research among Western Jews. It was he who had vigorously argued, long before Ibn Ezra, against the uncritical acceptance of Samuel's formula, although he failed to mention expressly that of R. Adda. However, to conclude from such silence that R. Adda's *tequfah* was altogether invented in the generation after Ḥasan, as does Jaffe (in his *Qorot,* pp. 138 ff.), is decidedly far-fetched. Certainly, Al-Biruni, writing at about the same time (1000 C.E.), knew of no other Jewish computation. See his *Chronology,* p. 143; and *supra,* n. 56. See also J. Vernet, "Un Antiguo tratado sobre el calendario judio en las 'Tabulae Probatae,'" *Sefarad,* XIV, 59–78 (publishing part of a well-known Escorial Arabic MS written in 1087–90).

66. Bar Ḥiyya's *Sefer ha-'Ibbur,* II.1, pp. 34 f.; Maimonides' *M.T.* Qiddush II.10, IV.4–7, 16. This was also the main import of Ibn Ezra's treatise. Doubtless with a view to Karaite criticisms, Ibn Ezra pointed out that the climatic seasons differ from one country to another, and that in the Holy Land itself they diverge from one year to another. Without reliance on human regulation, therefore, profound insecurity would permeate all Jewish life, the ancient sages having rightly claimed that "when the earthly court sanctifies a new moon, the court on high also sanctifies it." See his *Sefer ha-'Ibbur,* fols. 11b f. On another occasion he stressed the controversies regarding the duration of the lunar year among the Indian, Greek, and Arab astronomers, only Aṣ-Ṣufi agreeing with the Hebrew computation. See his *Libro de los fundamentos,* pp. 98 f. See also the modern formulas suggested by B. Cohn in "Die Vorausberechnung der Sichtbarkeit der neuen Mondsichel," *Jahrbuch der Jüdisch-Literarischen Gesellschaft in Frankfurt,* XVIII, 353 ff.; and, from a different angle, by L. A. Reznikoff in his "Jewish Calendar Calculations," *Scripta mathematica,* IX, 191–95, 274–77. Of comparative interest also is M. A. C. M. Saleh's parallel analysis of "The Crescent Moon of Ramadhan: the Use of Modern Scientific Methods to Determine Its Appearance," *Islamic Revue,* XL, No. 5, pp. 28–30.

67. Maimonides' *M.T.* Qiddush IX.3–4; XI.4–6. On Maimonides' relation to Jabir, see *supra,* n. 28. As pointed out by P. Duhem, Jabir's treatise so greatly ignores the work by Al-Baṭṭani and his successors, that it may indeed be but a translation of

some unknown Greek tract or else is "plagiarized from" some such translation made before the great discoveries from Al-Ma'mun's days on. See *Le Système du monde; histoire des doctrines cosmologiques de Platon à Copernic,* II, 177 ff. Comparing the Maimonidean figures for the ready computation of the sun's position on the basis of its daily mean movement of 59′ 8″, with Al-Baṭṭani's tables based on the same figure (trans. by Nallino, II, 75 ff.), O. Neugebauer suggested that, in order to obtain a figure for 100 days, the Fusṭaṭ sage had used Al-Baṭṭani's calculations for 3 × 30 days and added those for 10 more days. Since Al-Baṭṭani had already used a round figure for 30, Maimonides necessarily trebled his slight error. "It is an amusing accident," Neugebauer adds, "that the result agrees much better with modern values than any other value from Ptolemy to Copernicus" (*HUCA,* XXII, 339). One wonders, however, whether such cumulative errors were altogether unpremeditated. If Maimonides had wished to take the line of least resistance he might simply have multiplied by 10 Al-Baṭṭani's calculation for 10 days, and obtained a total only 3″ short of the one he furnished. He may have, indeed, decided to present the more precise value, because he found it thus given in some older source, or because he had independently compared various sources with one another. See E. Baneth's observations in *Moses ben Maimon,* ed. by Jakob Guttmann *et al.,* II, 259. See also A. A. Akaviah's commentary on his recent edition of Maimonides' *Hilkhot Qiddush ha-ḥodesh* (Laws Concerning the Sanctification of the New Moon; an excerpt from the *Code*); and the literature listed *supra,* n. 26.

68. Bar Ḥiyya's *Sefer ha-'Ibbur,* III.2, pp. 80 f. In the same context Savasorda distinguished clearly between the "pedagogues" who, for the sake of simplicity, applied the round figures of 365¼ days for the solar year according to Samuel's *tequfah,* and the "students and precisionists" who used the more exact smaller equation of R. Adda. But he in no way wished to express disapproval of the former method.

69. Lewin's *Otzar ha-gaonim,* V, Part 3, p. 15; *Megillat Abyatar* in Schechter's *Saadyana,* pp. 102 f.; *Targum Jonathan* on Gen. 1:16; Jephet ben 'Ali's *Commentary* on Gen., summarized by Bornstein in his *Maḥloqet,* p. 113 (*Sokolow Jub. Vol.,* p. 127). Because of this difficulty in identifying either Tishre or Nisan 1, as the actual beginning or the completion of the six days of Creation, some scholars, for instance Savasorda in his *Sefer ha-'Ibbur,* III.7, p. 96, preferred to speak more vaguely of the world's creation during the *tequfat Nisan,* or the spring season, which could start up to a fortnight earlier than the month of Nisan. According to Al-Biruni, however (see *supra,* n. 51), the process of creation had started on Ellul 24, indicating its completion on the Sabbath, Tishre 1, which was *followed* by the autumnal equinox. See, more generally, H. J. Bornstein's comprehensive analysis of the various systems current among Jews in his Hebrew essay on "Eras in Israel," *Hatekufah,* VIII, 281–338; IX, 202–64.

70. Bar Ḥiyya's *Sefer ha-'Ibbur,* III.7, pp. 96 ff.; Joshua ben 'Ilan's half Arabic and half Hebrew essay on the calendar, published by A. E. Harkavy in his "Old and New" (Hebrew), *Ha-Goren,* IV, 75 ff., 79; Maimonides' *M.T.* Qiddush VI.8–15; his earlier "Treatise on Intercalation" in *Qobeṣ,* II, fol. 17d; and *supra,* Chap. XXVIII, n. 93. Bar Ḥiyya quoted here extensively from both Saadiah's *Sefer ha-Hakkarah* (Book of Recognition), long identified with his polemical *K. at-Tamyiz* (see Malter's *Saadia,* pp. 380 ff.), and from a responsum by Hai Gaon of 992, reproduced in

Lewin's *Otzar ha-gaonim,* V, Part 3, pp. 14 ff. Hai's attempt to reduce the difference of opinion concerning the date according to the era of Creation to a merely theoretical inclusion, or exclusion, of one or two years, which so greatly appealed to Bar Ḥiyya, was doubtless correct for his own time, but hardly applied to the days of Saadiah. Early in the tenth century, it appears, the era of Creation, still used sparingly, had left some room for practical differences in dating.

71. See Bornstein's observations in *Hatekufah,* IX, 222 f. In his *Qorot,* pp. 86 f., Jaffe quotes Hai's responsum of 992 mentioning that another school of thought dropped two years from the total number from Creation so as to start the intercalations from the first year of each cycle, according to the formula *aduṭbehaz* (years 1, 4, 6, 9, 12, 15, 17 of the cycle). Jaffe's emendation of Hai's text to read only one, rather than two years, is refuted by a closer reading of that text which shows the gaon's familiarity with the *guḥadzat* system, and his previous reduction of the total by one year to secure the change to *bahaziguḥ*. Hence the further change to *aduṭbehaz* required, indeed, an additional reduction by another year. Hai could justify such a radical change by eliminating from the total years of the era the first half year from the Nisan of Creation to the following Tishre, and the year of the Deluge. Hai himself evidently preferred the middle system *bahaziguḥ* which, according to Joshua ben 'Ilan, had indeed been generally adopted by "the sages of this generation" (Harkavy's ed. in *Ha-Goren,* IV, 79). It was also given as the norm for the Jewish calendar by Al-Biruni's Hebrew informants in the days of Hai. See his *Chronology,* pp. 146 (Arabic), 144 (English). We have no information about the causes and the individual stages of its disappearance in the following two centuries, but the great prestige of the Maimonidean *Code,* particularly in the East, must have helped eradicate it completely from public consciousness.

72. Saadiah's and Hai's aforementioned responsa cited by Bar Ḥiyya, and in Lewin's *Otzar ha-gaonim, loc. cit.;* Al-Biruni's *Chronology,* pp. 18, 28 (Arabic), 21, 32 (English); Schechter's *Saadyana,* pp. 34 ff. No. x. So great, nevertheless, was Saadiah's prestige that, when Isaac ben Baruch found fault with some of the gaon's other views on the calendar, he prefaced his objections with a lengthy expostulation that even the very teachings of Moses had to be supplemented on occasion by Eleazar the priest (Num. 31:21). See the text cited by Bar Ḥiyya in his *Sefer ha-'Ibbur,* p. 60. See also the additional materials reprinted in Lewin's *Otzar ha-gaonim,* V, Part 3, pp. 35, 100 ff.

73. Al-Biruni's *Chronology,* pp. 15 ff. (Arabic), 18 ff. (English); Julius Africanus' aforementioned fragments in *PG,* X, 63 ff. See also H. Graetz's older note on "Fälschungen in dem Texte der Septuaginta von christlicher Hand zu dogmatischen Zwecken," *MGWJ,* II, 432–36; and *supra,* nn. 53, 55. The controversy over the era of Creation appeared the more important to the Christians even in Al-Biruni's time, as the Christian era had not yet enjoyed wide acceptance. Even in western Europe, where it did not encounter the stiff competition of the universally accepted Seleucid chronology, it only began to become popular at the beginning of the second millennium; in Spain considerably later. Just as the popularity of the Jewish era of Creation was at that time gradually spreading from Italy to other countries, so did the Christian era slowly gain ground in Italy and the Frankish empire. From there it

imperceptibly radiated into other lands. See, in general, F. K. Ginzel's still fundamental *Handbuch der mathematischen und technischen Chronolgie,* especially Vol. II; and B. Krusch, *Studien zur christlich-mittelalterlichen Chronologie; die Entstehung unserer heutigen Zeitrechnung* (also discussing the sixth-century scholar, Dionysius Exiguus, the "Begründer der christlichen Ära").

74. Bar Ḥiyya's *Sefer ha-'Ibbur,* III.9–10, pp. 100 ff., 108, 112. The author devoted also a special chapter (VIII) of his "Computation of the Courses of the Stars" to such comparative data on the various calendars. See Millás's *Estudios sobre historia,* p. 245. The fact that many writers exemplified their calculations by reference to contemporary dates, as was also done by Saadiah and Hai in their aforementioned responsa, has proved very helpful to later historians in dating their works. Bar Ḥiyya was quite exceptional, however, among Jewish authors in his analysis of non-Jewish calendars, offered in a form comprehensible to nonspecialists. Since most of the Jewish students of mathematical chronology had access to Arabic sources, he certainly did not need to duplicate those mathematically and astronomically elaborate formulas found in Al-Biruni's comparative study of chronological systems. But was not Al-Biruni himself an altogether singular exception even in the much wider Muslim and Christian worlds? See *supra,* n. 55.

75. Saadiah's *K. at-Ta'riḫ* (Book of Chronology), published from a Bodleian MS by A. Neubauer in his *MJC,* II, 89–110; *supra,* n. 58; Vols. I, pp. 332 n. 30, 377 n. 22; II, pp. 116, 263, 344 n. 45, 376 n. 33. There also exists a second MS in the Adler collection, now at the Jewish Theological Seminary of America. See E. N. Adler's *Catalogue of Hebrew Manuscripts,* p. 43 No. 713. Although neither manuscript mentions Saadiah as the author, its composition by the gaon has been unmistakably established. See Malter's *Saadia,* pp. 353 f.; and *supra,* Chap. XXVIII, n. 74. On Yannai's suspension of the Sabbatical year, and the vicissitudes of the institution of *prosbol,* see *supra,* Vol. II, pp. 262 f., 417 n. 39. Already in talmudic times there had existed considerable confusion concerning the historic computation of the Sabbatical cycles, which depended on their controversial framework within Jubilee years (see below), and their reputed operation under both the First and the Second Commonwealths. Their relation to the accepted eras, moreover, was not only subject to the existing general differences in dating, but also, because of the frequent misunderstandings by copyists, was often reflected in corrupt readings, which were to cause endless debates among medieval commentators. For example, the crucial statement by R. Huna son of R. Joshua ('A.Z. 9b) appears so altered in the existing versions of the Talmud as to become unintelligible. It is better reproduced in a responsum of 990–91 by Hai Gaon (*Teshubot ha-geonim,* ed. by Harkavy, p. 20 No. 45); and with minor changes, but fuller interpretation, in R. Ḥananel's commentary (in the Vilna ed. of the Babylonian Talmud, *ad loc.*). As reconstructed by Bornstein, R. Huna's statement counseled the reader how to ascertain quickly the particular year within the Sabbatical cycle, if he knew the date according to any of the three accepted eras: of Creation (in its Eastern version), of the destruction of the Second Temple, or of the Seleucides. See Bornstein's comprehensive analysis of "The Computation of Sabbatical and Jubilee Years" (Hebrew), *Hatekufah,* XI, 244 ff. See also S. J. Zevin's more recent observations in his *Le-Or ha-halakhah* (In the Light of Jewish Law: Problems and Elucidations), pp. 64 ff.; and on the laws governing the observance of Sabbatical years today, *ibid.,* pp. 79 ff.

76. Al-Biruni's *Chronology*, pp. 177 ff. (Arabic), 160 ff. (English). Apart from pointing out some talmudic antecedents of this theory (in j. Qiddushin I.2, 59a), Bornstein also suggested the obvious correction that the computation be made by the *addition* of 1,010, or by the *subtraction* of 740 years (*Hatekufah*, XI, 236 ff.).

77. Maimonides' *M.T.* Shemiṭṭah X.2–8; and his *Resp.*, pp. 221 ff. Nos. 234, 239. There also are scattered chronological remarks in other Maimonidean writings, for instance the round figure of "about" 2,500 years which elapsed from Adam to Moses mentioned in the *Guide* (II.50; in Friedländer's trans., p. 381), in lieu of the more precise date of 2503 given in *M.T.* Both referred to the beginning of the Sabbatical cycles in the fifteenth year after Israel's entry into Palestine. The date 2503 accorded with the view that the era of Creation had begun with Adam's nativity in the second year of the actual creation, which is in agreement with Maimonides' general teachings on calendar. See *supra*, nn. 65, 70; and Chap. XXVIII, n. 93. See also other data analyzed in my "Historical Outlook of Maimonides" in *PAAJR*, VI, 93 ff.; and E. Frank, "A Perplexing Passage from Maimonides: a Contribution to the Chronology of Sabbatical Cycles," *JQR*, XXXVII, 149–64 (on *M.T.* Shemiṭṭah X.2–6). A like divergence between theoretical argumentation and bowing before accepted tradition had also taken place some three decades earlier, probably unbeknown to Maimonides. See the extensive discussion in R. Jacob Tam's sharp reply to R. Meshullam bar Nathan in *Sefer ha-Yashar*, No. 44, 2, ed. by F. Rosenthal, pp. 76 f. See also Bornstein's somewhat daring amendments in *Hatekufah*, VIII, 317 n. 2; his further elaboration, *ibid.*, XI, 247 ff.; Isaac Israeli the Second's brief chronological survey in *Yesod 'olam*, IV.16–18, fols. 83a ff.; and, on the continued validity of the sabbatical laws, the data assembled in I. Z. Kahana's *Shemiṭṭat Kesafim* (Lapse of Debts).

78. Maimonides' *Commentary* on M. Abot, I, ed. in Arabic and Hebrew on the basis of Berlin and Paris MSS by E. (Y.) Baneth in *Jubelschrift . . . Israel Hildesheimer*, Hebrew section, pp. 57 ff.; and his *M.T.*, General Intro. On the talmudic sources of this artificial structure, and the difficulties of squaring many contradictory statements therein, see my remarks in *PAAJR*, VI, 96 ff. Apart from the general attractiveness of the round number forty to an oriental mind, this scheme also enabled the sage of Fusṭaṭ to claim the symmetry of twenty generations each for the periods before and after the first fall of Jerusalem. See *supra*, Chap. XXVIII, n. 95.

79. Modern scholarship, too, has evinced little interest in medieval Jewish geographical science. L. Zunz's "Essay on the Geographical Literature of the Jews from the Remotest Times to the Year 1841," published more than a century ago in A. Asher's edition of Benjamin of Tudela's *Itinerary*, II, 230–317 (the German original appeared later in Zunz's *G.S.*, I, 146–216) has since served as the main bibliographical guide. It was followed by neither comprehensive general treatments, nor detailed monographs on individual authors, except travelers like Benjamin of Tudela. See *supra*, Chap. XXVIII, nn. 88–90. In contrast thereto the Arabic geographical literature has been the subject of very extensive treatment for several generations. The main bibliographical data are readily available in the general handbooks by Brockelmann, Sarton, and Mieli. More analytical are the surveys by Cara de Vaux in *Les Penseurs de l'Islam*, Vol. II; and by Nafis Ahmad in *Muslim Contributions to Geography*.

80. Ḥagigah 12b; j. 'A.Z. III.1, 42c; b. Pesaḥim 94ab; *Sefer Yeṣirah,* I.11, ed. by Goldschmidt, p. 52 (in Kalisch's trans., pp. 14, 16; not necessarily indicating its early origin). See esp. Moses Botarel's comments on the latter passage in *Sefer Yeṣirah,* Warsaw ed., p. 62; and *infra,* n. 81. The statements in Pesaḥim are fully annotated by S. Gandz in his interesting analysis of "The Distribution of Land and Sea on the Earth's Surface according to Hebrew Sources," *PAAJR,* XXII, 41 ff. Cf. also W. M. Feldman's *Rabbinical Mathematics,* pp. 102 ff.; and, on the problem of the earth's rotation around its axis, *supra,* n. 28. It may be noted that neither the Hellenistic nor the Arab estimates generally agreed with those of Eratosthenes. Al-Ma'mun's memorable expedition, heavily relied upon by later scholars, yielded for the equator a total of nearly 30,000 miles, or, more precisely, 47,325 kilometers. See Carra de Vaux's *Penseurs,* II, 27 ff.; and the different figures culled from various sources by S. B. Samadi in his aforementioned "Literary and Scientific Development . . . in the Time of Al-Mamun," *IC,* XXX, 317; and Nafis Ahmad's *Muslim Contributions,* p. 76 n. 1, pointing out that the Arabian mile of 6,472.4 feet is larger than the English mile and that hence an estimate of 20,400 Arabian miles for the equator equaled 24,847.2 English miles.

81. Saadiah's *Commentary on Yeṣirah,* II.4, ed. by Lambert, pp. 48 ff. (Arabic), 71 ff. (French), with reference to Pesaḥim 94b (see *supra,* Chap. XXXIII, n. 13); his *Beliefs and Opinions,* I.1; VII.7, pp. 33 f., 221 (Arabic); 16 f., 107 (Hebrew); 41 f., 278, 412 ff. (English). The estimate of 1,089 times is given only in the variant version of Saadiah's seventh chapter dealing with resurrection which underlay Ibn Tibbon's translation. It was edited in Arabic by Bacher in the *Festschrift Steinschneider,* Hebrew section, p. 100, and therefrom translated into English in S. Rosenblatt's appendix. Evidently neither figure is intended to convey the *volume* of the aerial space, compared with that of the earth, since both are clearly based on the distance between the earth and the lowest celestial sphere raised to the *second* power. This means that Saadiah measured the two-dimensional surface of the area encompassed by the lowest celestial sphere, as compared with the surface of the globe cut at the equator. The gaon seems to have accepted the computation, recorded by Bar Ḥiyya (*Ṣurat ha-areṣ,* IX, fol. 39a), that at its greatest distance from the earth the moon is separated from the earth by a line 64 times the size of the earth's radius, or 32 times the earth's diameter. Apparently using the figure 33 to include the earth's diameter itself (instead of only the radius) and applying the ratio of $33d^2 \pi : 1d^2 \pi$, he reached the conclusion that the surface of the "atmosphere" is 1,089 times as large as that of the earth. But apart from his initial mistake, he also failed to reduce that surface by the size of the earth itself to 1,088 times. Perhaps disturbed by this omission, the substitution of the earth's radius by its diameter, and the replacement of the accepted figure of 32 diameters by 33, a copyist simply multiplied 32 by 31.5 (namely minus one radius), and obtained the strange figure of 1,008 times the size of the earth.

82. Midrash Konen in Jellinek's *Bet ha-Midrasch,* II, 27 (in Eisenstein's *Ozar Midrashim,* p. 255a); Isa. 40:12; Ibn Gabirol's "Royal Crown" in *Shire,* ed. by Bialik and Rawnitzky, II, 65 (in Zangwill's translation, p. 88); Bar Ḥiyya's *Sefer ha-'Ibbur,* I.1, pp. 6 f.; Ibn Ezra's *Commentary* on Gen., Intro. (on Method IV), and on Gen. 1:10. Gandz, who in "The Distribution of Land and Sea," *PAAJR,* XXII, sub-

jected this material to careful scrutiny, also pointed out (p. 39) that the idea of a threefold division of the earth and of its size extending over a journey of 500 years had penetrated the liturgical poetry of Qalir and others. These authors may well have confounded the figure, sometimes given in ancient aggadic sources and relating to the distance of 500 years between heaven and earth, with the size of the earth's surface. See Midrash Konen, *loc. cit.*

83. IV Ezra 6:42, 47 (in Charles's *Apocrypha,* II, 578 f.); Roger Bacon's *Opus majus,* ed. by H. J. Bridges, I, 290 f., and in R. B. Burke's English trans., I, 310 ff. See Gandz's "Distribution," *PAAJR,* XXII, 24 ff. The much-discussed attempt of eight Spanish-Arab adventurers, some time before 1147, to lift some of the obscurities surrounding the Atlantic, ended in almost total failure. We may understand, therefore, why Bar Ḥiyya in drawing a diagram of the human habitations, assigned to the eighth climate below the equator only the eastern section of central Africa down to the 16th parallel, but left the southwestern part of the Dark Continent entirely blank. At the same time he believed, as we shall presently see, that that southern region, too, was inhabited. Indeed, the contemporary knowledge of western equatorial Africa was extremely hazy. See Al-Idrisi's *K. al-Rujari* in the portion relating to the *Description de l'Afrique et de l'Espagne,* IV, ed. and trans. into French by R. Dozy and M. J. de Goeje, pp. 165, 184 f. (Arabic), 197, 223 ff. (French); K. Miller's analysis of *Charta Rogeriana, nebst Erläuterung Weltkarte des Idrisi;* R. Hennig's *Terrae incognitae,* 2d ed., II, 424 ff.; and Bar Ḥiyya's *Sefer ha-'Ibbur,* I.1, p. 8. See also C. Issawi's "Arab Geographers and the Circumnavigation of Africa," *Osiris,* X, 117–28.

84. Bar Ḥiyya's *Sefer ha-'Ibbur,* I.1, p. 7; and, more fully, his *Ṣurat ha-areṣ,* I.7, fols. 7a–8a. While agreeing, for instance, with Gregory Abu'lfaraj Barhebraeus that most of Egypt belongs to the first climate, Savasorda did not mention the legend that that climate includes the city of Meroe built by Moses in honor of Merris, Pharaoh's daughter. The Christian polyhistor also extended the northern limits of that climate to 20′ 14″ from the equator, instead of the 16′ given by Bar Ḥiyya. See Barhebraeus, *Le Candélabre du sanctuaire,* ed. and trans. into French by J. Bakoš, pp. 92 ff., 583 ff. The doctrine of the seven climates, widely accepted already in Hellenistic geography, became a byword among medieval scientists. The tenth-century author, Suhrab, for example, published his comprehensive treatise on world geography under the telling title, *K. 'Aja'ib al-aqalim as-sab'a* (Book of Marvels of the Seven Climates), ed. (with a proposed trans. into German) by H. von Mžik. The earliest Jewish discussion seems to be found in the physician Asaph Judaeus, on whose activity probably not later than the seventh century, see *infra,* Chap. XXXVI, n. 27. Additional data on the estimated measurements of the earth in Arabic letters may be found in Nafis Ahmad's *Muslim Contributions to Geography,* pp. 98 ff. See also Millás's comments on his translation of Bar Ḥiyya, *Forma de la tierra,* pp. 44 f.

85. Saadiah's *Beliefs and Opinions,* Intro., 4, 5; II.8; VI.8; VII.6, pp. 12, 21, 92, 211, 244 (Arabic); 6, 10, 48, 105 (Hebrew); 16, 26, 111 f., 263, 308 f. (English). The latter passage, not included in the version which underlay Ibn Tibbon's translation, refers to Isa. 60:9. On the relations of the earth's area to the magnitude of planets and fixed stars, see *supra,* nn. 27 and 33.

86. Maimonides' *Commentary* on M. Soṭah VII.3 (reproducing the Mishnah's "seventy languages" by "in the writing of each of these peoples"); *M.T.* Sanhedrin II.6; *Pirqe Mosheh* (Aphorisms), in the excerpt reproduced in his *Qobeṣ,* II, fols. 22d f. (see also his "Epistle" to Ibn Tibbon, *ibid.,* fol. 27c; in Sonne's ed. in *Tarbiz,* X, 310 ff.); his *Resp.,* pp. 207 No. 214; 243 ff. Nos. 265, 267, 272, 275; 299 ff. Nos. 331, 335; *Guide,* III.29 ff. (in Friedländer's translation, pp. 318 ff.). See my analysis in "The Historical Outlook of Maimonides," *PAAJR,* VI, 14, 92 n. 175, 101 f.; and *supra,* Chap. XXII, nn. 28–29.

87. Bar Ḥiyya's *Hegyon ha-nefesh,* fol. 1ab. This pious expostulation was not fundamentally different from the apologies often offered by Al-Biruni in the introductions to his works. See, e.g., S. H. Baraniy's "Kitab ut-Tahdid (An Unpublished Masterpiece of Al-Biruni on Astronomical Geography)," *IC,* XXXI, 168 f.

CHAPTER XXXVI: MEDICAL SCIENCE AND PRACTICE

1. Israeli's *Sefer ha-Yesodot,* ed. by Fried, fols. 30b f. This seems to be the tenor of another Hebrew work by that name, which purported to be a translation of parts of Aristotle's *Physics* but was in fact a fragment of some pseudo-Aristotelian encyclopedic work. Apparently extant only in a Mantua MS, its nature can be surmised from the two all-too-brief quotations communicated by M. Mortara to M. Steinschneider and cited in the latter's *Hebräische Uebersetzungen,* p. 324 n. 905.

2. See S. Pines's data on "Les Précurseurs musulmans de la théorie de l'impetus," *Archeion,* XXI, 298–306; and, on the general physical arguments advanced by Abu'l Barakat against Avicenna's theories, Pines's analysis in his "Etudes," *REJ,* CIV, 1 ff.; and, more generally, his *Beiträge zur islamischen Atomenlehre.* Abu'l Barakat, who became a convert at a fairly advanced age, must be counted also among the Jewish scientists as well as philosophers. See *supra,* Chap. XXXIV, n. 15. Nor must we overlook the work of Jewish translators, such as Moses ibn Tibbon, who translated Aristotle's *Physics* and the commentators thereon into Hebrew. See Steinschneider's *Hebräische Uebersetzungen,* pp. 108 ff. But the relative lack of interest of the Jewish intelligentsia in the physical sciences is mirrored in the paucity of both translations and extant manuscripts of the few works written by early medieval authors. Even the relatively best preserved writings from the Golden Age of Spanish Jewry include few contributions to these scientific disciplines. See F. Vera's aforementioned popular summary of *Los Judíos españoles y su contribución a las ciencias exactas.* This relative aloofness is the more remarkable, as the study of physics generally was largely bookish, and depended relatively little on direct experimentation in laboratories, for which Jews may indeed have had fewer opportunities than their neighbors. The dearth of manuscripts on the physical subjects contrasts sharply with the relative wealth of Hebrew and Judeo-Arabic copies in other scientific disciplines, especially mathematics, astronomy, and medicine. We need not be surprised that the latter have been preserved in much larger numbers than even, for example, the *Diwans* of the great poets, for poetic and rabbinic writings were of interest only to Jews, whereas Hebrew scientific literature appealed to many Christian students and bibliophiles, especially during the Renaissance age. It is doubtless the Christian Hebraists who were mainly responsible for the accumulation and preservation of most of the Hebrew manuscripts now extant, often representing merely various recensions of the same works.

3. An-Nadim's *Fihrist,* x, in J. W. Fück's fully annotated English translation in "The Arabic Literature on Alchemy according to Al-Nadim (A.D. 987)," *Ambix,* IV, 81–144. See J. Ruska's detailed analysis of Khalid ibn Yazid's work in *Arabische Alchemisten,* I. On its background, see also G. Goldschmidt's more recent "Ein Beitrag zur Ursprungsgeschichte der Alchemie," *Cahiers de Frontenax,* 1947, pp. 101–26, emphasizing the interrelations between the alchemist Stephanus of Alexandria and the New Testament or the mystic writings of Pseudo-Dionysius Aeropagita.

4. See H. H. Dabs's suggestion in "The Beginning of Alchemy," *Isis,* XXXVIII, 62–89. Dabs correctly points out, however, that the technique of assaying genuine gold in alloy is very old. As far back as the Amarna Age the Babylonian king complained to the king of Egypt that he had been short-changed, and that the twenty minas of gold sent him, after melting in the furnace, had yielded only five minas. See J. A. Knudtzon's *El-Amarna Tafeln,* I, 84 f. No. 7, 92 f. No. 10. Of course, no one objected to such tests. We have seen that in the early Muslim age many Jews actively engaged in money trade and banking in all its ramifications, including the exchange of money from one currency to another. Such money changers, as well as mintmasters, were forced constantly to refine their techniques to keep up with the ever-multiplying currencies and the widespread practice of coin clipping, official as well as criminal. Perhaps it was this daily preoccupation with the realistic problems of precious metals, rather than fear of a sudden metallic inflation, which cooled the interest of many Jews in the alchemists' mysterious manipulations.

5. Adam of Bremen's *Gesta Hammaburgensis ecclesiae pontificum,* III.36 scholia 77 or 78 (in *PL,* CXLVI, 585 f.; and in B. Schmeidler's German trans., entitled *Hamburgische Kirchengeschichte,* 3d ed., p. 178); Baḥya's *Duties of the Heart,* IV, pp. 177 ff. (Arabic), 116 ff. (Zifroni), III, 2 ff. (Hyamson). See, more generally, G. Scholem's "Alchemie und Kabbalah," *MGWJ,* LXIX, 13–30, 95–110, supplemented by his debate with R. Eisler in his "Nachbemerkung" on the latter's "Zur Terminologie der jüdischen Alchemie," *ibid.,* pp. 364–71. Scholem's denial, in particular, of the Jewish authorship of the great alchemistic *corpus* going under the name of Geber (Jebir) has since been fully borne out by P. Kraus's edition of some of the latter texts. See *infra,* n. 6; and *supra,* Chap. XXII, n. 86.

6. See esp. J. Ruska's introduction to his German translation of Ar-Razi's *K. Sirr al-asrar,* entitled *Al-Razis Buch Geheimnis der Geheimnisse;* and P. Kraus's comprehensive study of *Jabir ibn Ḥayyan. Contribution à l'histoire des idées scientifiques dans l'Islam.* The relations between alchemy and chemistry are well known, and, for instance, R. Steele could write about "Practical Chemistry in the Twelfth Century" while referring mainly to Ar-Razi's tenth-century *De aluminibus et salibus,* which became known in Europe through Gerard of Cremona's twelfth-century Latin translation. See his essay in *Isis,* XII, 10–46. See also, more generally, the Syriac and Arabic text, ed. and trans. (with the assistance of R. Duval and O. Houdas) by M. Berthelot in *La Chimie au moyen âge,* I, 311 ff.; E. O. von Lippmann's *Entstehung und Ausbreitung der Alchemie;* and F. S. Taylor's more recent survey of *The Alchemists: Founders of Modern Chemistry.* On "The Belief in the Curative Powers of Precious Stones among the Jews," see N. Shapiro's Hebrew essay in *Harofé Haivri,* 1952, Part 2, pp. 114–18 (Hebrew), 158–60 (English summary). See also, more generally, F. W. E. Roth's "Heilkräftige Sympathiewirkung der Edelsteine im XII. Jahrhundert," *Archiv für Geschichte der Medizin,* XI, 315–17.

7. Ibn Daud's *Emunah ramah,* I.6, ed. by Weil, pp. 31 (Hebrew), 39 (German; this passage was translated into English and provided with notes by F. S. Bodenheimer in "The Biology of Abraham ben David Halevi of Toledo," *AIHS,* IV, 55); Ibn abi Uṣaibi'a's *K. 'Uyun al-Anba'* (Choicest News on the Classes of Physicians, or a History of Arab Physicians). Regrettably none of these treatises by Ibn Raḥamun and Ibn Jumay' seem to be extant today. On the two authors, see *infra,* nn. 35, 37; and,

on the general retardation in biological studies, A. Mieli, *La Science arabe,* pp. 27 f., 30 ff.

8. See Ibn Ezra's *Commentary* on Gen. 1:20 in the version ed. by Friedlaender, p. 30; Naḥmanides' *Commentary* on Gen. 1:20 (citing older authorities including *Pirqe de-R. Eliezer*); and the numerous examples cited by I. Löw in his standard work on *Die Flora der Juden,* IV, 148 ff. Nor must we altogether underestimate the value of translations into new languages. Although leaning heavily on his illustrious predecessor Abu'l Walid ibn Janaḥ, David Qimḥi courageously tackled the problem of reproducing some Aramaic names, given by Ibn Janaḥ in Arabic, in the Romance dialect spoken in his Provençal home. He acquitted himself creditably of this task, incidentally contributing some further data to Romance philology and thus duplicating on a lesser scale Rashi's unwitting achievement. See *supra,* Chap. XXX, nn. 33, 62.

9. Halevi's *K. al-Khazari,* IV.31, pp. 288 ff. (Arabic, ed. by Hirschfeld), 363 ff. (ed. by Cassel), 243 ff. (English). The anatomical aspects of the Jewish method of slaughtering animals are carefully analyzed by S. I. Levin and E. A. Boyden in the appendix to their translation of *The Kosher Code of the Orthodox Jew.* See also A. Dubnove's review of that volume in *Harofé Haivri,* 1940, Part 2, pp. 134–35; and I. Simon's somewhat apologetical essay, "Les Bases physiologiques, anatomiques et humanitaires de la Shehitah, ou méthode juive d'abatage des animaux," *RHMH,* VI, No. 19, pp. 205–22; VII, No. 20, pp. 37–46, 159–72, 215–27 (with a bibliography, pp. 223 ff.). The humanity of this method, as compared with other contemporary methods of killing animals for human consumption, has often been heatedly debated in recent decades. Not only the Nazis, who made much ado about it, but even a democratic country like Switzerland was induced by obviously questionable arguments to outlaw Jewish *sheḥiṭah* in their territories. From the fiscal angle the Jewish meat tax was often a mainstay of communal budgets and, as in Russia, accrued also to the benefit of the state. In western countries problems of organization, accreditation, and proper supervision of producers and distributors of ritualistically permissible meat likewise engaged the frequent attention of communal leaders and governmental authorities. It is not surprising, therefore, that this problem has generated a vast literature. Many data, mainly from the modern period, are found in J. J. Berman's comprehensive volume on *Shehitah: a Study in the Cultural and Social Life of the Jewish People.* See also, more broadly, the various essays, though largely popular in nature, assembled in the volume *Hygiene und Judentum,* with an introduction by H. Goslar.

10. See Löw's data in his *Flora der Juden,* IV, 159 f.; Rashi's *Commentary* on Prov. 15:30; Maimonides' intro. to his *Commentary* on M. Abot (Eight Chapters), v, ed. by Gorfinkle, pp. 33 (Hebrew), 72 (English); my remarks in *Essays on Maimonides,* p. 157 n. 62. We have no record, however, of any Jewish monograph entirely devoted to zoological or botanical subjects, be it only of the kind produced by Al-Jaḥiẓ in his mainly philological study of zoology, and Abu Ḥanifa ad-Dinawari in his botanical treatise, richly interspersed with folklore. See the data supplied by M. Asín Palacios in "El 'Libro de los animales' de Jâḥiẓ," *Isis,* XIV, 20–54 (includes excerpts in Spanish trans. from Jaḥiẓ's *K. al-Ḥayyawan* or Book of Animals,

which is available in two Cairo editions); B. Silberberg in "Das Pflanzenbuch des Abu Ḥanifa Aḥmed ibn Da'wd ad-Dînawarî," *Zeitschrift für Assyriologie,* XXIV, 225–65; XXV, 39–88 (discussing also other Arabic botanical works and their relations to medical science); and M. Hamidullah in "Dinawariy's Encyclopedia Botanica (Kitab an-Nabāt) in the Light of Fragments in Turkish Libraries," *Fuad Köprülü Armeğani* (*Mélanges*), pp. 195–206. Of course, Jews assumed that the origin of these sciences, too, went back to ancient Israel. From the biblical reference that Solomon "spoke of trees . . . also of beasts, and of fowl, and of creeping things, and of fishes" (I Kings 5:13), Shem Tob ben Joseph ibn Falaquera deduced that the ancient Hebrew king had composed treatises on plants and animals. See his *Sefer ha-Ma'alot* (Book of Degrees in Human Perfection), ed. by L. Venetianer, p. 12. See also M. Meyerhof's "Esquisse d'histoire de la pharmacologie et botanique chez les musulmans d'Espagne," *Al-Andalus,* III, 1–41; J. Seide's "Early Jewish Medical Botany," *Harofé Haivri,* 1956, Part 1, pp. 82–90 (Hebrew), 161–70 (English); and the other, fairly substantial literature dealing with drugs and their medicinal qualities quoted *infra,* nn. 30 ff.

11. Abraham ibn Ezra's *Sefer ha-'Aṣamim* (Book of Substances), ed. by M. Grossberg, pp. 25 ff.; Maimonides' *Pirqe Mosheh* (Aphorisms), I, fols. 2 ff.; Bekhorot 45a. The Ibn Ezra passage here quoted is taken from F. S. Bodenheimer's English trans. in his "Studies in the History of Hebrew Natural History from the Middle Ages to the Beginning of the XIXth Century," *AIHS,* I, 670. Even more remarkably, many Arab physicians, including Avicenna, seem to have unquestioningly accepted the rabbinic figures of 248 limbs, although their Greek sources did not bear it out. Nor is modern science altogether unanimous on this score; the estimates given by modern anatomists vary between 200 and 226 limbs. See B. L. Gordon's *Medicine throughout Antiquity,* p. 729.

12. See Maimonides' *M.T.* Roseaḥ XIII; and numerous other passages quoted by J. Wohlgemuth in his instructive, though apologetically colored, essays, "Vom Tier und seiner Wertung (nach Bibel und Talmud)," *Jeschurun,* XIV, 585–610; "Das Leid der Tiere," *ibid.,* XV, 245–67, 452–68; and "Einfühlung in das Empfindungsleben der Tiere (nach Bibel und Talmud)," *ibid.,* XVI, 455–81, 535–67. Of even more direct interest to our subject is I. Jakobovits's recent analysis of "The Medical Treatment of Animals in Jewish Law," *JJS,* VII, 207–20. So powerful was this rabbinic tradition, especially in the juristic domain that, as we recall, even Maimonides disregarded more recent medical and veterinarian doctrines when they ran counter to the categories of *ṭerefot* (life-endangering illnesses of animals) set up by the talmudic sages. See *supra,* Chap. XXVII, n. 118; and, more generally, S. Muntner, "Maimonides' Views of Poisonous Snakes and the Treatment of Those Bitten" (Hebrew), *Dappim refuiim,* XIII, 361–64; and A. Shushan, "Maimonides and Veterinary Problems," *Refuah veterinarit,* XI, 144–47 (Hebrew), 166–67 (English summary).

13. Exod. 15:26, 21:19; II Chron. 16:12; Mansi, *Collectio,* XXII, 1010 f. (Hefele, *Histoire des conciles,* V, 1351 f.; subsequently this canon became part of the permanent *Corpus juris canonici*); T. Giṭṭin IV.6, ed. by Zuckermandel, p. 328. See the recent literature on ancient Jewish medicine listed *supra,* Vol. II, p. 412 n. 21, as well as the numerous older writings assembled in H. Friedenwald's comprehensive

"Bibliography of Ancient Hebrew Medicine," reprinted in his collected essays on *The Jews and Medicine,* I, 99–144; and his more popular review of "The Relation of the Jews and of Judaism to the Medical Art," reprinted *ibid.,* pp. 5–17.

14. B.Q. 85a; Ta'anit 21b; M. Qiddushin IV.14; *Sefer Ḥasidim,* ed. by Wistinetzki, p. 204 No. 810; Karo's *Shulḥan 'arukh,* Y.D., CCCXXXVI.2; *infra,* n. 46; and *supra,* Chap. XXIII. Maimonides actually considered it a moral and religious duty for a sick person to seek the advice of a physician. See his *Commentary* on M. Pesaḥim, IV.9; ed. by H. Kroner, pp. 15, 18 f.; and, more generally, J. Preuss, *Biblisch-talmudische Medizin,* esp. pp. 34 ff.; and I. Jakobovits, "The Physician in Jewish Law and Religious Literature," *Harofé Haivri,* 1956, Part 2, pp. 87–99 (Hebrew), 156–69 (English).

15. S. Reich's "Quatres coupes magiques," *Bulletin d'études orientales* of the Institut français de Damas, VII–VIII, 159–75; *supra,* Chap. XXXIII; and Solomon ibn Adret's *Resp.,* II, No. 281; V, No. 119. See also the data cited by A. A. Neuman in *The Jews in Spain,* I, 111 f.

16. See Israeli's *Sefer Musar* [or *Minhag*] *ha-rofe'im* (Book of Preparatory Instruction; or, Guide for the Physician), ed. in the medieval Hebrew trans. (from the MS used by the first translator, Moise Soave) and provided with a German trans. by D. Kaufmann in *MWJ,* XI, 100, and its Hebrew appendix, *Oṣar tob,* p. 11. On the disputed authorship of this collection of aphorisms, of which the Arabic original is totally lost, see *infra,* n. 29.

17. Maimonides' *M.T.* 'Akum XI.11; and other data analyzed by L. Nemoy in his "Maimonides' Opposition to Occultism," *Harofé Haivri,* 1954, Part 2, pp. 102–9 (Hebrew), 163–67 (English), pointing up certain similarities with views previously expressed by Qirqisani, though admitting that Maimonides may never have heard the name of the Karaite scholar. See also, more generally, I. Jakobovits, "Irrational Medical Beliefs in Jewish Law—Superstitions, Occult and Scatological Cures," *ibid.,* 1957, Part 1, pp. 98–109 (Hebrew), 166–77 (English; to be continued); and R. Walzer's *Galen on Jews and Christians,* pp. 10 f., 14, 18; and *supra,* Vol. II, pp. 19 ff., 158 f., 334 ff., 391 nn. 37 and 39, 432 n. 17; and Chap. XXVII, n. 118. The problem of authority vs. experience had indeed become the subject of heated debate between Ibn Buṭlan of Baghdad and 'Ali ibn Ridhwan (known to Europeans as Haly Rodoam) of Cairo (both died in the 1060's). While the former argued for the great value of the latest observations, Ibn Ridhwan insisted that study of ancient authors sufficed for the acquisition of sound medical knowledge. See J. Schacht and M. Meyerhof's ed. of *The Medico-Philosophical Controversy between Ibn Buṭlan of Baghdad and Ibn Ridwan of Cairo;* and the former's "Ueber den Hellenismus in Baghdad und Cairo im 11. Jahrhundert," *ZDMG,* XC, 526–45.

Not surprisingly, Galen's attacks irked patriotic Jewish and Christian readers. Notwithstanding his general reverence for the Roman physician, Maimonides repeatedly answered them in his "Medical Aphorisms." See the excerpts in English cited and analyzed by M. Meyerhof in his "Maimonides Criticizes Galen," *Medical Leaves,* III, 141–46; and *infra,* n. 38. Needless to say, neither Maimonides, nor any other medieval Jewish scientist ever took seriously the popular equation of Galen with the ancient sage Gamaliel, current among their more credulous contemporaries.

See the interesting data culled from several medieval sources by D. Kaufmann in *Die Sinne,* Intro., pp. 6 f.; and largely repeated by D. Margalith in "On Galen and His Hebrew Transmigration: Gamaliel" (Hebrew), *Harefuah,* XLII, 207–8. One wishes that some competent student of the history of medicine would cull from the vast Jewish magical and folkloristic sources the rich data pertaining to physical and mental therapy, and dispassionately reexamine them in the light of modern knowledge. L. Thorndike certainly was not wrong in calling his comprehensive review of the pertinent Western sources, *A History of Magic and Experimental Science.* See also C. Singer's essays in *From Magic to Science.*

18. There is little information about the methods of training and licensing physicians before and after the rise of Islam. It stands to reason that, as in other fields of education, the state allowed full leeway to the religious minorities. In any case, the prevailing system was for the candidate to secure instruction, both theoretical and practical, from one of the qualified physicians. See C. Roth's data, largely derived from later western sources, on "The Qualifications of Jewish Physicians in the Middle Ages," *Speculum,* XXVIII, 834–43; M. Meyerhof's somewhat tangential "Von Alexandrien nach Bagdad; ein Beitrag zur Geschichte des philosophischen und medizinischen Unterrichts bei den Arabern," *SB* Berlin, XXIII, 389–429; and J. L. Cassan's references to private instruction in "La Medicina romana en España y su enseñanza," *Cuadernos de historia de España,* XII, 51–69.

19. See Ahmed Ben Milad's observations in *L'Ecole médicale de Kairouan* (aux Xe et XIe siècles); M. Steinschneider's "Mose b. Zedaka, Imram b. 'Sadaka und Moses Dar'i," in A. Geiger's *Jüdische Zeitschrift,* IX, 172 ff.; S. B. Samadi, "Literary and Scientific Development . . . in the Time of Al-Mamun," *IC,* XXX, 81 f.; and *infra,* nn. 28, 43. 'Imram ben Sadaqa was probably identical with the physician Moses ben Sedaqa, so greatly extolled by Al-Ḥarizi in his *Taḥkemoni,* XLVI, L, ed. by Stern, fols. 57b, 65a (ed. by Lagarde, pp. 168, 194; ed. by Toporowski, pp. 350 f., 409). The absence of Jewish doctors among the attending physicians of the famous 'Adhud Hospital founded in Baghdad in 978, whose personnel included Christians and Sabians alongside of Muslims of various sects, was doubtless owing to mere chance, rather than any anti-Jewish animus, or the absence of qualified Jewish physicians, as suggested by Meyerhof in his "Von Alexandrien nach Bagdad," *SB* Berlin, 1930, pp. 424 f.

20. Muqaddasi's *K. Aḥsan at-taqasin,* ed. by De Goeje, p. 183 (in G. Le Strange's English trans. in *Palestine under the Moslems,* p. 77); Al-Muqtadir's decree discussed *supra,* Chap. XVIII, n. 22; Ibn Fadhlan's aforementioned letter in the Hebrew trans. by A. Ben-Jacob in *Zion,* XV, 63. See also *supra,* Chaps. XVIII, nn. 31–32; XXIV, n. 20. The number of Jewish physicians in any particular medieval country cannot be estimated, though M. Steinschneider and his colleagues early in this century were able to list by name some 3,100 Jewish physicians living before 1800. A significant number among them lived under medieval Islam. See his "Jüdische Aerzte," *ZHB,* XVII, 63–96, 121–67; XVIII, 25–57; supplemented in the "Nachträge und Berichtigungen," by S. Poznanski, *ibid.,* XIX, 22–36; XX, 69–71; the "Bemerkungen und Nachträge" by W. Zeitlin, *ibid.,* pp. 44–48; and in the "Nachträge und Bemerkungen" by L. Lewin, *ibid.,* XXII, 76–89; XXIII, 40–62 (was to be continued). A great many stray data may also be found in Steinschneider's other works, listed

by F. H. Garrison, in his "Bibliographie der Arbeiten Moritz Steinschneiders zur Geschichte der Medizin und der Naturwissenschaften," *Sudhoffs Archiv für Geschichte der Medizin,* XXV, 249–78 (giving 552 titles); and briefly analyzed by him in his "Moritz Steinschneider as a Contributor to the History and Bibliography of Medical Literature," *Emanuel Libman Anniversary Volume,* II, 473–79. More recent and detailed are M. Meyerhof's "Notes sur quelques médecins juifs égyptiens qui se sont illustrés à l'époque arabe," *Isis,* XII, 113–31; and his "Mediaeval Jewish Physicians in the Near East, from Arabic Sources," *ibid.,* XXVIII, 432–60 (had previously appeared in Hebrew, in *Harefuah,* XIII). A wealth of additional material is scattered in Meyerhof's other writings listed by J. Schacht in his "Max Meyerhof," *Osiris,* IX, 7–32 (a biographical sketch and bibliography). See also E. Ashtor-Strauss, "Saladin and the Jews," *HUCA,* XXVII, 309 ff. For the West see M. Ginsburger, "Un médecin juif à Paris au XIIe siècle," *REJ,* LXXVIII, 156–59. Of course, where Jewish communities were sparse and scattered, as in medieval Belgium and parts of northern France, there were few Jewish physicians. Only four are mentioned in F. Vercauteren's well-documented study of "Les Médecins dans les principautés de la Belgique et du nord de France du VIIIe au XIIIe siècle," *Moyen Age,* LVII, 71 f.

Many additional data are to be found in more general histories of Jewish contributions to medicine, including S. Krauss's *Geschichte der jüdischen Ärzte vom frühesten Mittelalter bis zur Gleichberechtigung;* and H. Friedenwald's collected essays. See also C. Singer's review of the latter work in "The Early Jewish Contributions to Medicine," *British Medical Journal,* 1945, II, 930 (unsigned); Friedenwald's *Jewish Luminaries in Medical History and a Catalogue of Works Bearing on the Subject of the Jews and Medicine from the Private Library of Harry Friedenwald;* and the general observations offered by I. Simon in "L'Histoire et le rôle de la médecine hébraïque," *Revue de la Pensée juive,* VII, 10–30. Of importance also are the general background materials assembled in the older works on Arab medicine and physicians by Wüstenfeld and Leclerc; the more recent surveys by E. G. Browne, *Arabian Medicine;* D. Campbell, *Arabian Medicine and Its Influence on the Middle Ages;* A. Castiglioni, *A History of Medicine* (English trans., 2d ed.); P. Diepgen, *Geschichte der Medizin,* Vol. I (to the middle of the eighteenth century); and the works on the general history of science by Sarton, Mieli, and others.

21. Al-Ḥarizi's *Taḥkemoni,* xxx, ed. by Stern, fol. 42a (ed. by Lagarde, pp. 123 f.; ed. by Toporowski, p. 257; in S. Solis-Cohen's English trans. of that chapter in "Of the Itinerant Physician and the Divers Medicines that He Cried in the Street," reprinted in his *Judaism and Science,* pp. 164 ff., 169); T. Giṭṭin IV.6; B.Q. VI.17; Makkot II.5, ed. by Zuckermandel, pp. 328, 355, 439. See the numerous citations supplied by Friedenwald in "The Ethics of the Practice of Medicine from the Jewish Point of View," and in "Wit and Satire about the Physician in Hebrew Literature," reprinted in *The Jews and Medicine,* pp. 18–30, 69–83; and S. Muntner's review of "The Ethics of Jewish Physicians in Ancient Hebrew Letters" (Hebrew), *Harofé Haivri,* 1946, Part 1, pp. 123–27. The problem of medical charlatans was universal. For example, it caused Ar-Razi to compose a number of *risalahs* (Epistles) on such subjects as "Why People Prefer Quacks and Charlatans to Skilled Physicians?" or "Why Ignorant Physicians, Laymen, and Women Have More Success than Learned Medical Men?" See M. Meyerhof's "Science and Medicine," in *The Legacy of Islam,* ed. by Arnold and Guillaume, p. 323. Incompetent doctors were, moreover, pro-

tected, then and later, by a somewhat exaggerated sense of professional ethics and solidarity. A great many skilled doctors were induced to condone shortcomings of their less qualified colleagues by injunctions like those sounded by Israeli: "Suffer not thy mouth to condemn when something [untoward] happens to a physician, for everyone has his evil day. Let thy deeds praise thee, and seek not thine honor in another's shame" ("Guide for the Physician," ed. by D. Kaufmann in *MWJ,* XI, 106 [German]; *Oṣar tob,* p. 14 [Hebrew]; in Friedenwald's trans. in *The Jews and Medicine,* p. 25). See also, in general, H. Higier's *Z dziejów etyki wśród lekarzy Żydów* (From the History of Ethics among the Jewish Physicians of the Early and Later Middle Ages).

22. Asaph Judaeus' admonition, quoted in Friedenwald's English trans. in *The Jews and Medicine,* I, 22 f. Cf. S. Muntner's "Classical Pronouncements on Medical Ethics by Asaph the Physician" (Hebrew), *Harofé Haivri,* 1947, Part 1, pp. 107–14 (Hebrew), 155–62 (English); and *infra,* n. 27. In his concern for healing the poor, Asaph actually composed a treatise, or a chapter on the "Medicine of the Poor," in which he assembled the necessary practical information as to how physicians could prescribe readily available drugs which the poor could afford. See the text in L. Venetianer's comprehensive work, *Asaf Judaeus: Der älteste medizinische Schriftsteller in hebraeischer Sprache,* p. 169 n. 1 (from the Munich MS); and the citation from a Friedenwald MS in A. Marx's informative survey of "The Scientific Work of Some Outstanding Mediaeval Jewish Scholars," in *Miller Mem. Vol.,* p. 127 n. 27. Many a Jewish doctor, moreover, approached his task with deep religious humility, such as was expressed by the poet-physician, Yehudah Halevi, in his beautiful short prayer on an occasion when he himself took some medicine. "Not on my power of healing," he concluded, "I rely; Only for Thine healing do I watch." See his poem, *Eli refa'eni* (My God, Heal Me), in his *Diwan,* ed. by Brody, II, 294 No. 71 (ed. by Zemorah, II, Part 5, p. 227; in N. Salaman's English trans., p. 113); and *infra,* n. 36.

23. The question of the authorship of "Maimonides' Prayer," first published in German trans. in the *Deutsches Museum,* 1783, Part 1, pp. 43–45, under the title "Tägliches Gebet eines Arztes bevor er seine Kranke besucht: Aus einer Hebräischen Handschrift eines berühmten jüdischen Arztes in Egypten aus dam zwölften Jahrhundert," is far from solved. See the more recent discussions by E. Bogen, "The Daily Prayer of a Physician," *Journal of the American Medical Association,* XCII, 2128; H. Keller, "Comparison between the Hippocratic Oath and Maimonides' Prayer," reprinted in his *Modern Hebrew Orthopedic Terminology and Jewish Medical Essays,* pp. 142–45; S. Muntner in the detailed introduction to his *Mishneh tefillah le-Mosheh* (The Deutero Prayer of Moses; with reference to Psalm 90); and I. Simon, "La 'Prière des médecins,' 'Tephilat Harofim,' de Jacob Zahalon, médecin et rabbin en Italie (1630–1693)," *RHMH,* VIII, No. 25, pp. 38–51. Translated into many languages, this prayer is readily available in English and is reproduced in Friedenwald's *Jews and Medicine,* I, 28 ff. See also J. Leibowitz's review, "The Physician's Prayer Ascribed to Maimonides," *Dappim refuiim,* XIII, 77–81 (Hebrew), vii–viii (English summary; includes a new Hebrew translation of the prayer).

24. Maimonides' *M.T.* Matenot 'aniyyim IX.11; his *Resp.,* pp. 77 f. No. 80, 139 f. No. 144. See also Isaac Alfasi's *Resp.,* No. 6; Joseph ibn Megas' *Resp.,* No. 207; and *supra,* Vol. I, pp. 214, 392 n. 5. In "The Origin of Hospitals" (in *Science, Medicine*

and History: Essays . . . in Honour of Charles Singer, ed. by E. A. Underwood, I, 122–30), G. E. Gask and J. Todd have rightly argued that there is no conclusive evidence for the existence of hospitals in the Graeco-Roman world or anywhere else before the Christian era. They relate, therefore, the origin of these institutions to the Christian *xenodochia.* But they neglect to mention that the Christian hospices for strangers clearly had predecessors and contemporaries in the Jewish institutions of the same kind. Our authors admit, moreover, that there is no record of Christian hospitals even in the writings of Eusebius, and that the first reference to them is found in Julian's envious reference to the way Jewish and Christian communities took care of their poor. See *supra,* Vol. II, pp. 269 ff., 274, 420 n. 49; and, on Theodotos' "hospice," *supra,* Vol. I, p. 214. Bearing in mind the old biblical legislation concerning segregation of persons suffering from communicable diseases, the growing sense of social responsibility characteristic of talmudic law, and the genuine social needs of a widely dispersed and often persecuted people, it would not be surprising if Jews had indeed pioneered also in the establishment of hospitals or their early forerunners. That combination of hospice for strangers and hospital for the sick continued to be reverently called *heqdesh* throughout the Middle Ages and early modern times, until the institution, owing to the overcrowding of the East European ghettoes, developed those appalling unsanitary conditions which, though characteristic of most Christian hospitals as well, brought it into deserved disrepute. It became the butt of innumerable satires by the progressive writers in the ever critical Enlightenment era. But in the Middle Ages proper, especially in the small western communities, it performed a highly beneficial service. See my *Jewish Community,* II, 328 f.; III, 211 n. 41.

25. See F. Baer's edition of the Jerez document in *Die Juden im christlichen Spanien,* I, Part 2, p. 58 No. 76. From the same century date also the references to a *domus hospitale Judaeorum* in Ratisbon (1210), and to a similar institution in Cologne (1248). See K. Baas's "Jüdische Hospitäler im Mittelalter," *MGWJ,* LVII, 452–60, exclusively dealing with conditions in medieval Europe. Even less informative for our period are H. Friedenwald's "Notes on the History of Jewish Hospitals," reprinted in *The Jews and Medicine,* II, 514–22. For that matter, our knowledge of non-Jewish hospitals in the medieval Muslim and Byzantine empires is far from adequate. See 'Isa Bey's communication on "Histoire de bimaristans (hopitaux) à l'époque islamique" to the International Congress for Tropical Diseases, in Cairo, 1928, published in its *Comptes rendus,* II, 81–210; and G. Schreiber's "Byzantinisches und abendländisches Hospital," in his *Gemeinschaften des Mittelalters,* I, 8–80 (with special reference to the Pantocrator monastery founded by John II Comenus *ca.*1136). This ramified problem would certainly merit further investigation.

26. R. J. Wunderbar's *Biblisch-talmudische Medicin,* I, 24 f.; M. Wellmann's "Agapios aus Alexandria" in Pauly-Wissowa-Kroll, *Realencyclopädie der classischen Altertumswissenschaft,* I, 735 (based on Suidas' report); and the articles on Domninus and Marinus, cited *supra,* Chaps. XVI, n. 9; and XXXIV, n. 2. The school of Jundeshapur continued in many ways the traditions of the academy of Nisibis. On the Jewish part in the development of the latter center of learning, see *supra,* Chap. XXIX, n. 7. It probably was from these quarters that some talmudic teachings percolated to the Arab scientists. See, e.g., A. Bloom's communication on "L'Ostéologie d'Abul Qasim et d'Avicenne; son origine talmudique suivie d'un chapitre sur l'ana-

tomie dans le Talmud" to the *Xe Congrès de l'histoire de la médecine à Madrid, 1935*, pp. 5–71.

27. See L. Venetianer's *Asaf Judaeus;* I. Simon's *Asaf ha-Jehoudi, médecin et astrologue du moyen âge* (based on several Paris MSS, while Venetianer had access only to a transcript of the Munich MS); and S. Muntner's more recent arguments in favor of "The Antiquity of Asaph the Physician and His Editorship of the Earliest Hebrew Book of Medicine," *Bulletin of the History of Medicine*, XXV, 101–31. See also the Friedenwald MS described by him (on the basis of A. Marx's notes) in *The Jews and Medicine*, I, 171 f.; S. Muntner's Hebrew bibliographical essay on "Asaph ha-Rofe" in *KS*, XXIV, 148–52 (especially valuable for its list of extant MSS); and *supra*, n. 22. I. Löw's main disagreement with Venetianer's dating of Asaph in the seventh century was based on Asaph's use of many Syriac terms for drugs which, Löw thought, indicated the Jewish physician's indebtedness to the ninth-century Syriac translation of Dioscorides' "Book on Simples." See *Die Flora der Juden*, IV, 167 ff.; and *infra*, n. 32. Venetianer and others believed that, on the contrary, the Syriac translator made use of Asaph. As if these authors necessarily had to borrow these terms from each other, or any other literary document! Living, as Asaph probably did, in Babylonia, where Syriac-Aramaic was the living language of nearly the entire population, he could readily mention names of drugs and plants current among the local doctors and druggists. Certainly, if he had written in the tenth century, as Löw claims, he could not possibly have so totally escaped the impact of the great ninth- and tenth-century works in Arabic. See also Muntner's "Sobre las fuentes de Asaf," *Sefarad*, VII, 261–69. Moreover, even before the seventh century Asaph may have consulted many Syriac medical treatises. See, e.g., E. A. W. Budge's edition of the *Syrian Anatomy, Pathology and Therapeutics or "The Book of Medicines"*; and the detailed comments thereon in J. Schleifer's "Zum syrischen Medizinbuch," published in instalments in the *Zeitschrift für Semitistik*, IV, 70–122; and *RSO*, XVIII, 341–72; XX, 1–32, 163–210, 383–98; XXI, 157–82 (especially showing the author's deep indebtedness to Galen). There also doubtless existed many other Syriac scientific writings which left no trace in the subsequent literature. On the other hand, Simon's somewhat far-fetched interpretations of a few equivocal passages in Asaph's works as adumbrations of modern theories have found little acceptance among specialists.

28. See Steinschneider's *Arabische Literatur*, pp. 13 ff., 32 ff., 36 ff.; 'Ali ben Sahl Rabban aṭ-Ṭabari's *K. Firdausu'l-Ḥikmat* (Paradise of Wisdom), ed. by M. Z. Siddiqi; the analysis thereof by M. Meyerhof in his " 'Ali at-Tabari's 'Paradise of Wisdom,' One of the Oldest Arabic Compendiums of Medicine," *Isis*, XVI, 6–54; and his observations on "Mediaeval Jewish Physicians from Arabic Sources," *ibid.*, XXVIII, 435 ff. Meyerhof here expresses doubts concerning the authenticity of Masarjawaih's *K. fi Abdal al adwiyya* (Book on the Substitutes for Remedies) which he had examined in an Istanbul MS. On Raqqa, the birthplace of Al-Muqammiṣ and other Jewish scholars, see *supra*, Chap. XXXIV, n. 4. Even if it be proved that the Christian presbyter Aaron of Alexandria had written his work in Greek (see A. Baumstark's *Geschichte der syrischen Literatur*, p. 189), a Syriac version was certainly available to Masarjawaih. The latter name is spelled differently in different MSS of the *Liber Continens*, and has given rise to extended discussions. But it is almost certainly Persian. The fact that a Persian Jew living in the early period

after the Muslim conquest should still bear a Persian name is by no means surprising. We have encountered many such names in the contemporary magic bowls and among such later authors as Ḥivi (Ḥaivaihi) of Balkh. See *supra,* Chap. XXXIII, n. 5. See also I. Holmgren's "Studies in the Ancient History of Smallpox" (Hebrew), *Harefuah,* XXXVI, 117–19.

29. See the latest summary by S. Muntner in his "Isaac Israeli (850–953). Le premier médiateur de la Médecine entre l'Orient et l'Occident," *RHMH,* VI, No. 17, pp. 85–90. See also Steinschneider's *Arabische Literatur,* pp. 38 ff.; J. Llamas's introduction to his edition of an old Castilian translation of Israeli's *Tratado de las Fiebres;* H. Friedenwald's "Manuscript Copies of the Medical Works of Isaac Israeli," reprinted in *The Jews and Medicine,* I, 185–92 (especially describing three Latin Manuscripts in the author's possession); and Ben Milad's aforementioned study of *L'Ecole médicale de Kairouan.* Israeli's medical works in the order of their appearance in the main Latin edition of his *Opera omnia,* published in Lyons, 1515, are as follows:

(1) *Kitab al-Adwiyat* (in Latin divided into two parts, entitled *Liber Dietarum universalium,* cum commento Petri Hispani; and *Liber Dietarum particularium,* cum commento ejusdem). The Arabic original is lost, while the Hebrew translations (the second part was probably rendered from Constantine's Latin version), though available in a number of MSS, have never been published. The commentator (also of the next item) was not, as is often assumed, the renowned twelfth-century Jewish convert, Petrus Alphonsi, but the later Pope John XXI (1276–77).

(2) *Kitab al-Baul* (Liber de Urinis), or, under the apparently more descriptive title, "A Collection of Sayings by the Ancients on Urine and its Varieties." Neither the Arabic original nor the Hebrew versions, extant in various manuscripts, have thus far been published. But the Latin translation was republished and analyzed in J. Peine's dissertation, *Die Harnschrift des Isaac Judaeus.*

(3) *Kitab al-Ḥumayyat* (Liber de Febribus), or "A Collection of Sayings by the Ancients on Fever." Here, too, neither the Arabic original nor the two different Hebrew versions have appeared in print. But Llamas's edition of the medieval Castilian version has made available a nummber of important variants of this work which C. Singer described as "the best account of the subject available in Europe during the entire Middle Ages." See *A Short History of Medicine,* p. 67.

(4) *Pantechni decem libri theorices et decem practices.* This volume has been attributed by many modern scholars to 'Ali Abbas, rather than Israeli, but it seems to be cited by Israeli himself as his own in his "Book on Fevers." See Llamas's quotation, p. xviii.

(5) The aforementioned introductory study, *Musar* [or *Minhag*] *ha-rofe'im,* edited in Hebrew and translated into German by Kaufmann in *MWJ,* XI, 93–112, and its Hebrew section (*Oṣar tob*), pp. 11–16. Israeli's authorship, doubted by Kaufmann, was staunchly denied by Jacob Guttmann in his "Ueber die Unechtheit der dem Isaak ben Salomo Israeli beigelegten Schrift 'Sitte der Aerzte,'" *MGWJ,* LXIII, 156–64, but was effectively defended by Steinschneider in his *Arabische Literatur,* p. 43. On the other hand, the *Viaticum,* ascribed to Israeli by two medieval Hebrew translators, was very likely written by his Arab pupil Isḥaq abu Jafar ibn al-Jazzar. On section v.5 of that work bearing the independent title *Ma'amar ha-shiqqui* (Book of Ascites, a Disease of the Liver), see the Hebrew text, ed. with an intro. by S. Muntner in *Harofé Haivri,* 1950, Part 1, pp. 62–75. Similarly wrong is the attribution to

Israeli of a treatise on melancholia, which was probably likewise written by Ibn al-Jazzar or possibly by Israeli's teacher, Ishaq ibn 'Imran (d. 900). See S. Muntner's edition of the Hebrew translation (probably by Jacob ha-Qaṭan) of this "Medieval Treatise on 'Melancholy'" (Hebrew), *ibid.*, 1953, Part 1, pp. 62–80 (Hebrew), 163–65 (English summary). Other spurious writings attributed to Israeli are listed by Muntner in *RHMH,* VI, 90. It is, indeed, high time that a critical edition of Israeli's works in their original Arabic and early Hebrew translations, wherever extant, be placed at the disposal of scholars.

30. Maimonides' aforementioned letter to Ibn Tibbon in *Qobeṣ,* II, 28d; his *Guide,* III.12 beg. (Friedländer, p. 267); S. Muntner's ed., with a Hebrew trans. and notes of Saadiah's "Commentary on *Had al-insan* [The Anatomy of Man]" in *Qorot,* I, 38–45, 99–107 (Hebrew), x–xi (English summary); and M. Plessner's additional comments thereon, *ibid.*, pp. 110–15 (Hebrew), viii–ix (English summary). Apart from reverting to the previously accepted title of "The Definition of Man," showing that the commentary was more philosophic than medical in nature, Plessner agrees with Muntner that Saadiah's authorship is uncertain, but renews D. Kaufmann's suggestion that this tract may have been written by Abraham bar Ḥiyya. On the Hebrew versions of Israeli's works, see esp. Steinschneider's *Arabische Literatur,* pp. 38 ff.; and *Die hebräischen Uebersetzungen des Mittelalters,* pp. 755 ff. Of course, some data of scientific and particularly medical interest are scattered also in Israeli's philosophic works, on which see *supra,* Chap. XXXIV, n. 5. As a matter of fact not only Razi but many later Arabic-writing physicians exerted considerable influence on the development of philosophic thought as well. See esp. M. Meyerhof, "The Philosophy of the Physician, Ar-Rāzī," *IC,* XV, 45–58 (with reference to P. Kraus's publication of Razi's texts); and A. Birkenmajer, "Du rôle des médecins et des naturalistes dans la réception d'Aristote aux XIIe et XIIIe siècles," *VI International Congress of Historical Sciences* (Oslo, 1928).

31. See Muntner's latest and most complete edition of Donnolo's *Kitbe ha-refu'ah* (Medical Works, the First Such Hebrew Writings in Europe), together with his extensive biographical and analytical comments. The incident with Abbot Nilus is told with much relish by the latter's biographer, Bartholomaios, in his "Vita S. Nili Junioris," *PG,* CXX, 91 ff., 99 f.; and excerpted in English, with brief comments, by J. Starr in *The Jews in the Byzantine Empire,* pp. 161 ff. On the somewhat remote connection between Jews, including Donnolo, and the famous school of Salerno, see S. Muntner, "Donnolo et la contribution des Juifs aux premiers oeuvres de la médecine salernitaine," *RHMH,* IX, No. 32, pp. 155–61; and, more generally, J. Askenasi, *Contribution des Juifs à la fondation des écoles de médecine en France au moyen-âge*; S. de Renzi, *Storia documentata della Scuola Medica di Salerno,* 2d ed., pp. 156 ff. (on Judah, see pp. 162 f., in connection with a grant of land to him and its withdrawal); C. and D. W. Singer, "The Origin of the Medical School of Salerno," *Essays in the History of Medicine, Presented to Karl Sudhoff,* pp. 121–38; P. Kristeller's comprehensive investigation of "The School of Salerno: Its Development and Its Contribution to the History of Learning," *Bulletin of the History of Medicine,* X, 138–94; and other studies listed by H. P. Bayon in "The Masters of Salerno and the Origins of Professional Medical Practices," in Underwood's ed. of *Science, Medicine and History,* pp. 203–19.

Nor can one offer a definite answer to the intriguing question about the continuity of Jewish medical learning in its progression from Kairuwan to Italy. S. Fried's attempt to prove that Donnolo had borrowed certain terms from Israeli's medical works led him to postulate that the Italian scholar had visited Kairuwan where he became acquainted with Israeli's school, including Israeli's Arab pupil, Abu Jafar ibn al-Jazzar. See Fried's introduction to his edition of Israeli's *Sefer ha-Yesodot,* p. 56 n. 5. But there is evidence neither for Donnolo's visit to North Africa, nor for the identification of the Babylonian Gentile scholar, *BGDS* (Bagodes?) mentioned by Donnolo in the introduction to his *Sefer Ḥakmoni* (Commentary on Yeṣirah, ed. by Castelli, pp. 4 f.) with Ibn al-Jazzar. In his edition of Donnolo's works, II, 18, Muntner has made a far better case for that author's familiarity with the writings of Asaph. See also Steinschneider's older but not superseded studies, *Donnolo: Pharmakologische Fragmente aus dem X. Jahrhundert, nebst Beiträgen zur Literatur der Salernitaner* (reprinted from the *Archiv für pathologische Anatomie,* ed. by R. Virchow, Vols. XXXVIII–XL, XLII; see the comments on the document relating to Judah, XXXVIII, 89 n. 16); and "Constantinus Africanus und seine arabischen Quellen," *ibid.,* XXXVII, 351–410; XXXIX, 333–36; also D. L. O'Leary's recent biographical sketch of "Constantine the African," *Islamic Literature,* VIII, 29–35, 395–400 (almost wholly repetitious and popularizing).

32. See esp. C. E. Dubler's careful analysis of the medieval transmission of *La 'Materia Médica' de Dioscorides,* Vol. I (see esp. pp. 50 ff., 70 f.); as well as M. Meyerhof's earlier observations on "Die Materia medica des Dioskurides bei den Arabern," *Quellen und Studien zur Geschichte der Naturwissenschaften,* III, Part 4, pp. 72–84 (mainly summarizing Ibn abi Uṣaibi'a's and Ibn Juljul's accounts); and, with further reference to Ḥisdai's and his associates' translation, in his "Esquisse d'histoire de la pharmacologie et botanique chez les musulmans d'Espagne," *Al-Andalus,* III, 8 ff. On Ḥisdai's relationships with the Byzantine court, see *supra,* Chaps. XVIII, n. 40; XIX, n. 13. Meyerhof's studies attest to the general popularity of Dioscorides' work in the early Arab world, but shed little light on the vexed question of whether Asaph had used that work in its Syriac translation. See *supra,* n. 27.

33. Ibn al-Qifṭi's *K. Tariḥ al-ḥukama,* in M. Meyerhof's English translation in *Medical Leaves,* III, 133; and Steinschneider's *Arabische Literatur,* pp. 95 ff. See *supra,* Chap. XXIV, *passim.* None of these works seem to be extant. They are known to us mainly from the biographical records by Ibn al-Qifṭi and Ibn abi Uṣaibi'a, which for the most part offer only titles, together with a few biographical data and anecdotes about their authors.

34. Qirqisani's *K. al-Anwar,* VI.12; XII.30; ed. by L. Nemoy, pp. 593 ff., 1234 ff. The latter passages are translated into Hebrew and English, respectively, in Nemoy's "Al-Qirqisani's Criticism of 'Anan's Prohibition of the Practice of Medicine," *Harofé Haivri,* 1938, Part 2, pp. 73–83 (Hebrew), 205–7 (English); and his "From the 'Kitab al-Anwar' of Ya'qub al-Qirqisani," *Medical Leaves,* IV, 96–102. See also other excerpts from Qirqisani's work in Nemoy's Hebrew articles, "Contribution to Gynaecology and Embryology," *Harofé Haivri,* 1939, Part 2, pp. 35–41 (Hebrew), 167–71 (English); and "Al-Qirqisani's Essay on the Psychophysiology of Sleep and Dreams," *ibid.,* 1949, Part 2, pp. 88–95 (Hebrew), 158–65 (English), as well as in his aforementioned essays in *JBL,* Vols. LVII, LIX (reproducing Qirqisani's views

on suicide and the transmigration of souls). On these studies as well as on the general Karaite aversion to reliance on medical treatment, see *supra,* Chap. XXVI, nn. 7, 60–61.

35. See M. Meyerhof's quotation from "'Ali al-Bayhaqi's Tatimmat Siwan al-Hikma: a Biographical Work on Learned Men of the Islam," *Osiris,* VIII, 191 f. No. 93; and M. Steinschneider's notes (largely based on Ibn abi Uṣaibi'a) on "Samaritanische Aerzte," *Hebräische Bibliographie,* XV, 84–86. David ben Solomon's *K. al-Dustur al-bimaristani* was published from a fifteenth-century MS by P. Sbath under the title *Le Formulaire des hôpitaux d'Ibn Abil Bayan médecin du Bimaristan Annacery au Caire au XIIIe siècle.* On the Samaritan physicians see, e.g., P. R. Weis's analysis of "Abu'l-Ḥasan al-Ṣuri's Discourse on the Rules of Leprosy in the Kitāb al-Ṭabbākh," *BJRL,* XXXIII, 131–37 (supplementing the essay cited *supra,* Chap. XXV, n. 34); and, more generally, Meyerhof's concise data in his "Mediaeval Jewish Physicians in the Near East," *Isis,* XXVIII, 454 f. It may also be noted that in his aforementioned supplementary list of physicians (*supra,* n. 20) Poznanski, a leading student of Karaism, was able to list but few Karaites. These names, distinguished by asterisks, belong for the most part to more recent periods. And Poznanski had made a special effort to identify the Karaite doctors!

36. Ibn Buklarish (Beklaresh), *K. Musta'ini fi aṭ-ṭibb,* analyzed by H. P. J. Renaud in his "Trois études d'histoire de la médecine arabe en Occident, I," *Hespéris,* X, 135–50; J. Leibowitz's more recent analysis of "The Book of Medical Experiences Ascribed to R. Abraham ibn Ezra (1089–1164)," *Harofé Haivri,* 1954, Part 1, pp. 127–35 (Hebrew), 155–57 (English summary); Steinschneider's *Arabische Literatur,* pp. 124 f., 148 f., 156 f.; D. Margalith, "R. Yehudah Halevi as Physician," *Qorot,* I, 94–97 (Hebrew), iv–v (English summary); and *supra,* n. 22. Ibn Buklarish's work is often cited in Renaud and Colin's ed. of *Taḥfat al-aḥbab* (Glossaire de la matière médicale marocaine) by an unknown author. Joseph ibn Ḥisdai seems to have converted himself to Islam as a grown man, and his father's preceding conversion appears rather dubious. The latter's name Aḥmad may have been used by the son only after his conversion, so as to secure a less revealing patronymic.

37. Ibn abi Uṣaibi'a's *K. 'Uyun al-Anba',* analyzed by Meyerhof in *Medical Leaves,* III, 136 f. Meyerhof denies here, without cogent arguments, the old identification of Ibn Jumay' with the Rabbi Nathaniel whom, on his visit to Cairo, Benjamin of Tudela found officiating as the chief of all Jewish communities in Egypt. See Benjamin's *Massa'ot,* ed. by Adler, pp. 63 (Hebrew), 70 f. (English). Of interest also are other names of physicians and medical matters including a few of clearly folkloristic nature mentioned in Benjamin's travelogue. See J. Seide's "On Medicine and Natural History in the Book of Travels of Rabbi Benjamin of Tudela" *Harofé Haivri,* 1953, Part 2, pp. 137–47 (Hebrew), 166–68 (English); also *supra,* Chaps. XXVIII, n. 88, and XXXII, nn. 4 ff. See also D. Margalith, "Hai Gaon as Physician," *Harofé Haivri,* 1955, Part 1, pp. 84–88 (Hebrew), 163–65 (English); L. Nemoy's Hebrew studies of "The Arabic Pharmacopoeia of Abu al-Mina al-Kuhin al-'Attar (13th Century)," *ibid.,* 1941, Part 2, pp. 68–76 (Hebrew), 156–66 (English); 1942, Part 2, pp. 88–93 (Hebrew), 144–48 (English); 1943, Part 2, pp. 77–85 (Hebrew), 144–50 (English); and "A Forgotten Thirteenth Century Jewish Physician—Ibn Kammuna," *ibid.,* 1947, Part 2, pp. 123–24 (Hebrew), 157–59 (English). The former com-

pilation has been one of the most popular medical reference works throughout the Arabian world down to the twentieth century. The works of these writers, as well as Ibn Kammuna's significant contributions to philosophy and comparative religion (see *supra,* Chap. XXIV, n. 28), will be more fully analyzed in connection with the later medieval developments. All these and many other physicians known from contemporary sources are listed by Friedenwald in *The Jews and Medicine,* I, 172 ff.; and are more fully discussed in M. Meyerhof's aforementioned essays in *Isis,* XII, 113 ff.; XXVIII, 432 ff.

On the numerous Jewish physicians practicing in early medieval Christian countries, see the index to F. Baer's documents in *Die Juden im christlichen Spanien,* I, Parts 1–2, *s.v.* Ärzte and Alfaquin. Of considerable interest also is the much-debated question of the Jewish share in the rise and evolution of the great medical school of Montpellier. To be sure, in "La Question de judéo-arabisme à Montpellier," *Janus,* XXXI, 465–73, E. Wickersheimer reported that in all the extant documents of the University of Montpellier from its foundation in 1220 there is no mention of Jewish or Arab names. Nevertheless, here as in Salerno, the presence of a vigorous and intellectually alert Jewish community which may actually have contributed to the adoption by the city of its unusual name (see *supra,* Chap. XX, n. 77) and which included a considerable number of medical practitioners, authors, and translators, doubtless contributed much to making Montpellier a major center of medical research already in the eleventh and twefth centuries. Such intensive cultivation of medical studies naturally facilitated the later establishment of a formal school. See H. Harant and Y. Vidal, "Les Influences de la médecine arabe sur l'Ecole de Montpellier," *Cahiers de Tunisie,* III, 60–85 (includes extensive bibliography); L. Dulien, "L'Arabisme médical à Montpellier du XII au XIV siècle," *ibid.,* pp. 86–95; and, particularly, R. Kohn's interesting data, though in part vitiated by somewhat daring conjectures and his failure to mention Wickersheimer's negative findings, on "L'Influence des Juifs à l'origine de la Faculté de Médecine de Montpellier," *RHMH,* I, No. 4, pp. 14–34. On the other hand, Friedenwald's "Jews and the University of Montpellier" (reprinted in *The Jews and Medicine,* I, 241–52) deals almost exclusively with modern times. One also ought to bear in mind the various medical fragments extant in the Genizah, only few of which have thus far been published, and still fewer adequately analyzed. See, e.g., R. J. H. Gottheil's text and translation, without detailed explanation, of "A Further Fragment on Medicine from the Genizah in Cairo," *Mélanges Maspéro,* III, 173–76.

38. Sa'id al-Mulk's aforementioned poem (also cited in R. V. Feldman's translation communicated by W. M. Feldman in *Moses Maimonides,* ed. by I. Epstein, pp. 121 f.); Maimonides' letter to Ibn 'Aqnin (Ibn Shime'on) in *Qobeṣ,* II, fol. 31d (in *Iggerot,* ed. by Baneth, pp. 69 f.); and *supra,* n. 14; and Chaps. XVIII, nn. 7, 32; XXI, nn. 32, 35. We need not be surprised by the invitation extended to Maimonides to come to the assistance of a Crusader prince at Acco. The superiority of Muslim over Frankish physicians was generally accepted in the Near East. See the amazing stories told by the contemporary Muslim emir Usama ibn Munqidh (d. 1188) and summarized from his autobiography (ed. with a French translation by H. Derenbourg) by E. G. Browne in his *Arabian Medicine,* pp. 68 ff. See also the extensive literature on Maimonides' life and works, listed *supra,* Chap. XXVII, nn. 65, 114; and the numerous articles on his medical work published especially in connection with the Octocentennial celebration in 1935, many of which, as far as they relate

to Maimonides the physician and scientist, are listed in Marx's essay in *Miller Mem. Vol.*, p. 141 n. 88. To these one may profitably add H. Kroner's "Maimonides als Hygieniker" in *Die Hygiene der Juden,* ed. by M. Grunwald, pp. 243–61 (with additions by the editor); J. Millaud's more recent "À travers l'oeuvre médicale de Maïmonide," *Revue de la Pensée juive,* VII, 39–49; and especially M. Meyerhof's comprehensive review of "The Medical Work of Maimonides," in my *Essays on Maimonides,* pp. 265–99, which includes a selected, but valuable, bibliography and a number of excerpts in English translation. See also L. Nemoy's Hebrew reproduction of "The Sketches of Maimonides and His Son Abraham in Ibn abi Uṣaibi'a's Dictionary of Arab Physicians" in *Harofé Haivri,* 1940, Part 2, pp. 78–81 (Hebrew), 171–73 (English); D. Margalith's analysis of "The Impact of Maimonides upon Medieval Writers in the Field of Medicine," *ibid.*, 1954, Part 2, pp. 134–43 (Hebrew), 159–60 (English, referring to Al-Ḥarizi and other Hebrew writers); and, on the modern debates concerning Maimonides' contributions to medical science, A. Levinson's citations in his "Maimonides the Physician," *Medical Leaves,* III, 96–105; and S. Muntner's "Maimonides' Greatness and Innovations in the Medical Field" (Hebrew), *Sinai,* XVIII, No. 217 (750th Anniversary Issue), pp. 420–23, somewhat overstressing the sage's role as forerunner of Bacon through his insistence on observation, unless it was more fully developed in the thus far unpublished sections of his "Medical Aphorisms." See also the various essays included in the 750th Anniversary Issue of *Qorot,* Vol. I.

Not all Maimonidean works in medicine have as yet been published. The most important single work undoubtedly was the *K. al-Fuṣul fi'ṭ-ṭibb* (The Medical Aphorisms of Moses; in Hebrew *Pirqe Mosheh*). Although several MSS of the original Arabic text are extant, including one copied from a text prepared by Maimonides' nephew under the author's supervision (Chapter xxv, the last and longest in the book, had remained unfinished at the time of Maimonides' death), only the introduction has thus far been published in the Arabic original from Gotha and Leiden MSS by P. Kahle in Appendix II to H. O. Schröder's *Galeni in Platonis Timaeum commentarii fragmenta,* pp. 89 ff. (Kahle also briefly analyzed the two MSS); and by J. Schacht and M. Meyerhof in their "Maimonides against Galen on Philosophy and Cosmogony," *Bulletin* of the Faculty of Arts of the Egyptian University, V, 53–88. See also *supra,* n. 21. The Hebrew version by Nathan ha-Me'ati, was published in Lwow, 1835 (not 1804!). Despite the additional text published by S. Sachs in *Ha-Techijjah,* 1850, pp. 35–38, this edition and those dependent on it are quite inadequate. Another translation by Zeraḥiah ben Isaac ben Shealtiel Ḥen (Gracian) still is unpublished. On the other hand, the thirteenth-century Latin translations, first published in Bologna, 1489, were republished several times with considerable variations during the following century. See Steinschneider's *Hebräische Uebersetzungen,* pp. 765 ff.

Connected with this work is Maimonides' *K. Sharḥ Fuṣul Abuqrat* (Commentary on Hippocrates' Aphorisms), available only in Moses ibn Tibbon's Hebrew translation, edited and mimeographed from a Jerusalem MS with variants from a Munich MS by M. Z. Ḥasidah (Bocian) in *Hassegulah,* Nos. 1–30 (on the Intro. in Arabic see *infra,* n. 39); and his *K. Mukhtasarat* (Extracts) from Galen's works, of which neither the incomplete Arabic MSS nor the Hebrew translation has ever been published. Since all these three works lean so heavily on the Arabic translations from Galen's voluminous works, both authentic and spurious, the task of editing them in an up-to-date fashion will be greatly facilitated when more of

Galen's Arabic texts become available in critical editions of the type prepared by P. Kraus and R. Walzer for Galen's *Compendium* on Plato's *Timaeus.*

The following medical monographs by Maimonides have appeared in print:

(1) *K. Fi'l Bawasir* (On Hemorrhoids), ed. in Arabic with a German trans. by H. Kroner in "Die Haemorrhoiden in der Medicin des XII. und XIII. Jahrhunderts," *Janus,* XVI, 441–56, 645–718. A facsimile of a characteristic excerpt with an English trans. appeared in H. Wellcome's *Spanish Influence on the Progress of Medical Science,* pp. 26 f. See also pp. 18 ff.

(2) *K. Fi'l Jima'a* (On Sexual Intercourse), edited twice by Kroner from different MSS and provided with a German translation in *Ein Beitrag zur Geschichte der Medizin des XII. Jahrhunderts;* and in "Eine medicinische Maimonides-Handschrift aus Granada," *Janus,* XXI, 203–47.

(3) *K. Fi'r Rabw* (On Asthma). Published only in the Hebrew trans. by Samuel Benveniste (about 1320) from the Latin version by Armengaud de Blaise in S. Muntner's edition of Maimonides' *Ketabim refui'im,* Vol. I.

(4) *K. as-Sumum* (On Poisons and Their Antidotes), available likewise only in the Hebrew trans. (by Moses ibn Tibbon), except that here Armangaud de Blaise's *Tractatus de Venenis* is a translation from the Hebrew. This Hebrew text was published by S. Muntner in Maimonides' *Ketabim refui'im,* Vol. II. Previously I. M. Rabbinowicz had published a French version under the title *Traité de poisons de Maïmonide.* It is also available in the English translation by L. J. Bragman in his "Maimonides' Treatise on Poisons," *Medical Journal and Record,* CXXIV, 103–7, 169–71.

(5) *K. Fi tadbir aṣ-ṣiḥḥat* (Regimen Sanitatis), ed. by Kroner with a German trans. under the title *Gesundheitsanleitung des Maimonides* in *Janus,* XXVII–IX (also reprint). Kroner had previously published a lengthy excerpt from the third chapter of this work, with the old Hebrew and a new German translation under the telling title *Die Seelenhygiene des Maimonides.* The full Hebrew and Latin versions by the famous translators Moses ibn Tibbon, Armangaud de Blaise, and John of Capua (a converted Jew), respectively, have also appeared; see Steinschneider's *Hebräische Uebersetzungen,* pp. 771 f. See also S. Muntner's "Review of 'Regimen Sanitatis' of Maimonides," *Dappim refuiim,* XIII, 69–76 (Hebrew), vii (English summary).

(6) *K. Fi Bayan al-a'radh* (Explanation of Fits), ed. by Kroner, with a fragment of the Hebrew version and a German translation in "Der medicinische Schwanengesang des Maimonides," *Janus,* XXXII, 12–116.

(7) *K. Sharḥ asmā' al-'uqqar* (Glossary of Drug Names), ed. from a unique Istanbul MS by M. Meyerhof.

(8) Of a more general character is Maimonides' brief tract *Omanut ha-rippui* (The Art of Cure), recently published in Hebrew and English translations from Arabic MSS in Paris and Madrid by U. Barzel in "The Art of Cure: an Unpublished Medical Book by Maimonides," *Harofé Haivri,* 1955, Part 2, pp. 82–93 (Hebrew), 165–77 (English). In the editor's words (p. 175), this review is organized "around a series of discourses on various types of diseases. . . . 1. Wounds, both internal and external (Chapters 3–6); 2. Fever and especially malaria (Chapters 8–12); 3. Tumors (Chapters 13–14)."

(9) On the borderline between medicine and ethics is a tract attributed to Maimonides ever since its publication in Salonica, 1596, and entitled *Sefer ha-Nimṣa* (Book of Existent Things). It was republished by J. L. Maimon in *Sinai,* XVIII, No.

217, pp. 201–11. But this attribution is rather dubious. On medical works wrongly ascribed to Maimonides, see the general data supplied by M. Steinschneider in his *Hebräische Uebersetzungen,* p. 774.

Needless to say, Maimonides never drew a sharp line of demarcation between his medical and his philosophic or juristic works. Hence many interesting medical observations are scattered in his other writings as well. For example, among his *Responsa,* one addressed to Joseph ibn 'Aqnin deals with the problem of human longevity as it affects the foreknowledge of God. See his *Über die Lebensdauer,* ed. by G. Weil from a Bodleian MS of a commentary on his *M.T.* Yesode ha-Torah x; *infra,* n. 47; and, more generally, J. Rabin, "The Influence of Religion and Philosophy upon Maimonides as Physician," *Harofé Haivri,* 1954, Part 2, pp. 110–19 (Hebrew), 161–63 (English summary). See also R. Edelmann, "Maimonides on Medicine," *Acta Medica Scandinavica,* Supplement 266, pp. 49–52.

Curiously, despite the great interest in Maimonides' contributions to medicine, evidenced by the unceasing flow of secondary publications, often extremely repetitious, modern scholars have not yet succeeded in publishing definitive editions of the available texts. Even the Arabic texts of the discourses on Asthma and on Poisons (3 and 4 above), which Kroner had prepared for publication before his demise, have remained unpublished. Even more imperative is a complete critical edition of the Arabic text of Maimonides' *Aphorisms,* which work undoubtedly represents the fruits of his medical thinking and experience over two or three decades, as seen from the vantage point of a great philosopher and jurist as well as physician. It was evidently considered by the author himself as his main medical work. The effort, so promisingly begun a decade and a half ago, by S. Muntner, to publish all of the Fusṭaṭ sage's medical works in Hebrew translation, likewise ought to be seen through to successful completion.

39. Although a great admirer of the Greek physician, Maimonides stated in his "Commentary on Hippocrates' Aphorisms" that some of the latter "are self-evident, some repetitious, some useless for medical science, and some express a simple thought without careful deliberation." He intended generally to follow Galen's interpretation; yet, as he declared in his introduction, he interpreted many of the "Hippocratic" sayings "as I understand them and in my own name." See the text of his Hebrew translation, ed. by Ḥasidah in *Hassegullah,* No. 3, p. 3, or in Steinschneider's earlier publication, "Die Vorrede des Maimonides zu seinem Commentar über die Aphorismen des Hippocrates," *ZDMG,* XLVIII, 228 f. (Hebrew), 233 (German). On the popularity of the "Hippocratic Writings in the Middle Ages," especially in the West, see P. Kibre's analytical survey in the *Bulletin of the History of Medicine,* XVIII, 371–412. See also M. Meyerhof's and J. Schacht's studies mentioned *supra,* nn. 17, 38. Maimonides' own aphorisms contain many quotations from Galen. In fact, probably taught by the criticism leveled at the major shortcoming of his *Code* which he allegedly promised, but never managed, to remedy in a revised edition (see *supra,* Chap. XXVII, n. 122), he provided every paragraph with a reference to the pertinent Galenic source. See S. Muntner, "Re-Examination of Galenus' Books Listed by Maimonides in *Pirqe Mosheh,*" *Harofé Haivri,* 1954, Part 2, pp. 120–33 (Hebrew), 159–60 (English summary), also in *Homenaje a Millás Vallicrosa,* II, 119–30 (the promised fuller list is yet to be published).

Among the medieval writers Maimonides esteemed especially Avicenna and the Spaniard, Avenzoar, with whose son he had associated in Morocco. There is a curious dichotomy in this respect between the longer Arabic and the shorter Hebrew versions of his "Discourse on Sexual Intercourse." Although the latter omits many significant medical details, it quotes the two Arabian physicians far more frequently. One wonders whether some of these references had not been inserted by the translator, Zeraḥiah ben Isaac, a Barcelonian scholar living in Rome at the end of the thirteenth century. However, there still remains a question as to whether the existing Hebrew versions stem from two translators or whether they are based on two separate treatises by Maimonides himself dealing with the same subject. Cf. Kroner's intro. to his edition in *Ein Beitrag,* pp. 19 ff., 22 f.; his observations on the shorter Arabic version, ed. by him in *Janus,* XXI, 203 ff., 216 f.; and Steinschneider's earlier remarks in *Hebräische Uebersetzungen,* pp. 763 f. On Avicenna's generally great influence on medieval Jewish students of medicine, see S. Muntner's observations on "La Médecine persane, en particulier celle d'Avicenne, et ses rapports avec la culture hébraïque," *RHMH,* [IV], No. 11, pp. 23–38; [V], No. 12, pp. 21–33; as well as his and J. Leibowitz's related Hebrew essays on the occasion of "The Thousandth Anniversary of Ibn Sina" in *Orlogin,* VII, 200–210 (on "Avicenna's Influence on Jewish Culture" and on "Hebrew Translations of Avicenna"). See also C. Rabin's survey of "The History of the Translation into Hebrew of the Canon [of Avicenna]" (Hebrew), *Melilah,* III–IV, 132–47. This highly interesting evolution will be discussed more fully in its later medieval context.

40. Maimonides' *Regimen Sanitatis,* III end, ed. by Kroner in his *Gesundheitsanleitung;* his "Discourse on Sexual Intercourse," Intro., ed. by Kroner in *Ein Beitrag,* pp. 3 (Arabic), 17 (Hebrew), 25, 50 (German; here cited from Meyerhof's English trans. in my *Essays on Maimonides,* pp. 290 f.). On the Muslim attitude to wine and song see *supra,* Chaps. XXII, n. 16; XXXII, n. 93. See also A. Machabey's "Notes sur les rapports de la musique et de la médecine dans l'antiquité hébraïque," *RHMH,* V, No. 14, pp. 117–35 (with few references to medieval sources).

41. Maimonides' intro. to his *K. Sharḥ asma' al-'uqqar* (Glossary of Drug Names), ed. by Meyerhof, pp. 3 f. (Arabic), 3 f. (French); Meyerhof's intro. to that edition, esp. pp. lxii ff.; and Renaud and Colin's ed. of *Taḥfat al-aḥbab,* p. xii. See also Meyerhof's earlier comments, "Sur un glossaire de matière médicale composé par Maïmonide," *Bulletin de l'Institut d'Egypte,* XVII, 223–35; and "Sur un ouvrage médical inconnu de Maïmonide," *Mélanges Maspéro,* III, 1–7.

42. Donnolo's intro. to his *Ḥakmoni,* ed. by Castelli, p. 4; his "Book of Drugs," ed. by Muntner, p. 12. Löw found in Asaph's works no less than 125 Hebrew plant names, side by side with some 75 Aramaic, 30 Greek, 44 Arabo-Persian, and 11 terms translated from the Greek. Donnolo, on the other hand, although familiar with Asaph's writings, preferred to use Greek and Latin designations, together with several in the local Italian dialect, wherever he was not completely certain about their Hebrew equivalents. See Löw's *Flora,* IV, 169 ff., 176 f.; and *supra,* n. 27. Since he was evidently addressing himself to doctors and druggists, Donnolo rightly considered it the better part of wisdom not to use equivocal Hebrew terms, which different scholars might render differently in their daily parlance. Maimonides was even less concerned with Hebrew names. Preparing his "Glossary" primarily for those physicians who were puzzled by various Arabic and Greek synonyms for the same or related drugs, he only had to elucidate the meaning of such terms current

in the Arab world. Nor was his treatise addressed especially to Jews. Although we possess no autographs of Maimonides' medical works, it is probable that, unlike his philosophic treatises, he published them in the Arabic script for use by Gentiles and Jews alike. We owe the very preservation of the "Glossary," as we recall, to Ibn al-Bayṭar's interest in it, which would hardly have been aroused if the work had circulated in Egypt only in the Hebrew alphabet.

43. See Meyerhof's English quotations from 'Ali al-Bayhaqi's "Biographical Work" in *Osiris,* VIII, 186 f.; and from Ibn abi Uṣaibi'a in *Medical Leaves,* III, 138. On the economic opportunities open to Jews in the medical profession as compared with public service, and on Ibn 'Abdun's anti-*dhimmi* views, see *supra,* Chaps. XVIII, nn. 31–32; XXII, n. 86. See also H. A. Savitz's concise observations on "The Role of the Jewish Physician in the Progress of His People," *Annals of Medical History,* n.s. X, 107–16.

44. On Donnolo's travels, see *supra,* n. 31. See also Steinschneider's *Hebräische Uebersetzungen,* pp. 650 ff.; C. and D. W. Singer's fine survey, "The Jewish Factor in Medieval Thought," in *The Legacy of Israel,* ed. by E. R. Bevan and C. Singer, pp. 173–282; H. Friedenwald's "Use of the Hebrew Language in Medical Literature," reprinted in *The Jews and Medicine,* pp. 146–80; and S. Muntner's "On the History of Hebrew as Language of Instruction in Medicine" (Hebrew), *Leshonenu,* X, 135–49, 300–317; XI, 59–62 (includes an extensive bibliography of medical works in the Hebrew language, with supplements by D. Neumann and A. Marx). See also *supra,* Chaps. XXXIV, n. 19; XXXV, n. 35. The large Jewish share in the translation of Arabic works into Latin, whether or not through the mediation of Hebrew, came to full fruition in the thirteenth century. It will therefore more profitably be discussed in its later medieval context. However, the more elusive problem of oral transmission, or of the lessons given by way of example, has never yet received the attention it undoubtedly merits.

45. Maimonides' *Pirqe Mosheh,* xxv (in Friedenwald's English quotation in *The Jews and Medicine,* I, 121); his book "On Poisons," Intro., ed. by Muntner, pp. 93 ff.; Meyerhof in *The Legacy of Islam,* p. 339; his remarks in *Isis,* XII, 130 f.; and L. Nemoy's study of Abu'l Mina's pharmacopoeia cited *supra,* n. 37. In his edition of Donnolo's medical writings, II, 59 ff., S. Muntner discusses at length the trade in drugs in the ancient and medieval worlds. Although unable to quote specific data, he rightly assumes that Jews, who had played an increasing role in the international trade of the Mediterranean world from the ninth century on, also significantly participated in this branch of commerce. See *supra,* Chap. XXII. The importance of the drug trade is also attested by such negative advice as was given by Israeli. He not only warned the general practitioner against administering drugs designed mainly for their effect on magic healing, "for most of them are nonsense and superstition," but also counseled him, "Do not rely on the traders and manufacturers of composite drugs. For sometimes these will be sold underweight because of their high cost, or else they will be furnished to you old and in a weakened state, and thereby destroy the efficacy of your work." See his "Guide for the Physician," xxv, xxxii, ed. by Kaufmann, pp. 14 (Hebrew), 106 f. (German). See also L. Gleisinger, "Les Juifs et la pharmacie," *RHMH,* VIII, No. 25, pp. 11–27 (also referring to his earlier German essays on this subject in *MGWJ,* LXXII); A. Dietrich, *Zum*

Drogenhandel im islamischen Aegypten (based on a Heidelberg papyrus of Egyptian-Jewish provenance); B. Ben Yahia, "Falsification et contrôle des médicaments pendant la période islamique," *Actes* of the Seventh International Congress for the History of Science (Jerusalem, 1953), pp. 210–15; and, more generally, his dissertation, *Recherches historiques sur la pharmacologie arabe au moyen âge.*

46. See Israeli's "Guide," XXXIX–XLI, XLVI, pp. 15 (Hebrew), 108 ff. (German); Ibn Tibbon's "Will" in Abrahams's *Hebrew Ethical Wills,* I, 67 f.; *Sefer Ḥasidim,* in Friedenwald's English trans. in *The Jews and Medicine,* I, 18; and Asaph's work mentioned *supra,* n. 22. On similar Arabic works devoted to the "medicine of the poor," see Steinschneider's *Hebräische Uebersetzungen,* pp. 705 f. Comparable discussions among medieval Christians are briefly analyzed by P. Diepgen in his "Zur Frage nach der unentgeltlichen Behandlung des armen Kranken durch den mittelalterlichen Arzt," *Historisches Jahrbuch,* LXXII, 171–75. As a matter of fact, care for the sick, particularly if they were poor, was not merely incumbent upon the physician, but upon every individual, and the community at large considered it a supreme religious obligation. Ever since talmudic times, communities had strained their resources to alleviate the twofold human misery of illness aggravated by poverty. See the data assembled in my *Jewish Community,* I, 360 ff.; II, 327 ff.; III, 93 nn. 16–17, 210 f. nn. 43–44. Although medieval communities rarely could afford to place regular doctors on the communal payroll, as many did in modern times, the communal authorities and Jewish public opinion doubtless exerted tremendous pressures on recalcitrant physicians to extend care to impecunious patients. See also *supra,* nn. 14 and 22.

47. Saadiah's *Beliefs and Opinions,* IV.5, pp. 156 f. (Arabic), 80 (Hebrew), 192 ff. (English); Hai's responsum cited in Yehudah ibn Bal'am's commentary, ed. by J. Derenbourg in *REJ,* XXII, 202 ff. (with D. Kaufmann's comments thereon in "Ein Responsum des Gaons R. Hâja über Gottes Vorherwissen und die Dauer des menschlichen Lebens (Aǵal)," *ZDMG,* XLIX, 73–84); and reedited with many important variants in S. A. Wertheimer's *Qehillat Shelomoh,* pp. 2 ff. (Hebrew), 74 ff. (Arabic); G. Weil's more recent combination of both texts and their reinterpretation in *Sefer Assaf,* pp. 269–79; and his ed. of the Maimonidean responsum *Über die Lebensdauer,* especially pp. 12 (Arabic), 16 (German). Here, too, the sage of Fusṭaṭ laid great emphasis upon psychological factors, which by themselves may have the effect of drying up that vital organic warmth and causing death. To bring his point home to his readers, Maimonides mentions having heard of persons who had lost their lives because of a sudden excess of joy (pp. 13 [Arabic], 18 [German]). See also Weil's note thereon, p. 50 n. 19.

48. Israeli's "Guide," XI, pp. 12 (Hebrew), 103 (German); and Maimonides' statements quoted in Friedenwald's English translation or summaries, in *The Jews and Medicine,* I, 24 ff., 211 ff.; and *supra,* n. 22. None of these teachings were strikingly novel, or in any way limited to physicians of the Jewish faith. But that unceasing refrain on behavior, with no discordant note, cannot be ascribed to mere chance.

49. Maimonides' *Regimen Sanitatis,* III, ed. by Kroner in *Janus,* XXVIII, 69 f. (Arabic), 418 f. (German; in Meyerhof's English translation in the *Essays on Maimonides,* p. 291); Israeli's "Guide," 15, pp. 13 (Hebrew), 104 (German); *Sefer Ḥasidim,* ed. by Wistinetzki, p. 22 No. 17. Characteristically, Maimonides used the

term "Mental Therapy," which was fairly common in Arabic letters (see, e.g., Al-Jauhar's works under this title) as the equivalent of ethics. See his *Eight Chapters,* III–IV, ed. by Gorfinkle, pp. 17 ff. (Hebrew), 51 ff. (English); and other passages listed by C. Neuburger in *Das Wesen des Gesetzes in der Philosophie des Maimonides,* pp. 42, 114 f. Maimonides' Aristotelian predecessor, Abraham ibn Daud, had already given the title "Mental Therapy" to the third chapter of his *Emunah ramah.* See my remarks in *Essays on Maimonides,* p. 119 n. 6; and, more generally, J. Leibowitz, "The Influence of Mental Factors on Physical Processes according to Maimonides" (Hebrew), *Dappim refuiim,* X, 150–52. One may mention in this connection also Shem Tob ibn Falaquera's didactic poem devoted to the twin subjects of physical and mental health and entitled *Bate hanhagat guf ha-bari* and *Bate hanhagat ha-nefesh.* First ed. by I. Chodos in "Falaquera's Manuscript 'A Versified Vademecum on the Care of Body and Soul'" (Hebrew), *Harofé Haivri,* 1937, Part 2, pp. 150–70; 1938, Part 1, pp. 113–25 (Hebrew), 189–95 (English; with additional notes by I. Davidson and L. M. Herbert), it was reedited with an introduction by S. Muntner. Wholly under Maimonidean influence, the author declared in his second introduction (ed. by Muntner, p. 57), that, although care of bodily wants must needs precede in time that of the soul, mental hygiene is superior in quality, though it in turn is overshadowed in significance by the cultivation of intellectual attributes.

50. Maimonides' *Pirqe Mosheh,* especially fol. 25a. See M. B. Asbell's "Vignettes in Dental History: Moses Maimonides (1135–1204)," *The Alpha Omegan,* V (Oct. 1946; also reprint); and, on the earlier background, his "Practice of Dentistry among the Ancient Hebrews," *Journal of the American Dental Association,* XXVIII, 1098–1107; also with some variations in Hebrew in *Harofé Haivri,* 1942, Part 1, pp. 91–99 (Hebrew), 142–48 (English summary). In contrast to its relative scarcity in antiquity and the Middle Ages, diabetes became in modern times both a frequent and a severe ailment among Jews. See G. Ginzburg's "Frequency of Diabetes among Jews, Pathogenesis and Prevention" (Hebrew), *ibid.,* 1941, Part 1, pp. 64–67 (Hebrew), 191–93 (English), part of an extensive "Symposium on Diabetes among Jews" by E. P. Joslyn and ten other doctors, *ibid.,* pp. 35–87 (Hebrew), 171–222 (English). Curiously, no medieval Jewish physician (except perhaps Masarjawaih, whose pertinent monograph is lost) seems ever to have written a comprehensive treatise on ophthalmology, although many of them, including Israeli, had started their careers as oculists, and although eye diseases have always been fairly prevalent in the Near East among Jews and Gentiles alike. On Palestine, see, e.g., N. I. Shimkin's "Blindness: Eye Diseases and Their Causes in the Land of Canaan," *British Journal of Ophthalmology,* XIX, 548–76. However, references to maladies of the eye are scattered through many medieval tracts. See H. Friedenwald's "Ophthalmological Notes of Jewish Interest," reprinted in *The Jews and Medicine,* II, 533–50.

51. Yedaiah Bedershi's well-known "Epistle" in Friedenwald's English translation in *The Jews and Medicine,* I, 16.

52. *Sefer ha-Yosher* (Book of Justice) in the excerpt cited, from a Vienna MS, by M. Güdemann in his *Geschichte des Erziehungswesen und der Cultur der abendländischen Juden während des Mittelalters,* II, 337. An English translation of that passage from an Oxford MS is offered by J. O. Leibowitz in "A Passage from 'Sefer ha-Yosher' (13th Century)," *Qorot,* I, 108–9 (Hebrew), v–vii (English).